WHO KILLED BOBBY?

WHO KILLED BOBBY?

The Unsolved Murder of Robert F. Kennedy

SHANE O'SULLIVAN

Skyhorse Publishing

Photo Credits

Pages 9, 12, 13, 14, 25, 36, 38, 46, 50, 60, 61, 65, 79, 81, 82, 85, 109, 114, 123,
    139, 140, 149, 150, 151, 152, 169, 171, 175, 195, 197, 218, 234, 238, 398:
    California State Archives, Sacramento, CA

Page 51: Robert Joling

Page 63: Vincent Di Pierro

Page 76: Rose Lynn Mangan

Page 411: Thomas Polgar and Jefferson Morley

Page 416: top left: Gaeton Fonzi; top right: Morales family

Skyhorse Publishing books may be purchased in bulk at special discounts for sales
promotion, corporate gifts, fund-raising, or educational purposes. Special editions can
also be created to specifications. For details, contact the Special Sales Department,
Skyhorse Publishing, 307 West 36th Street, 11th Floor, New York, NY 10018 or
info@skyhorsepublishing.com.

Skyhorse® and Skyhorse Publishing® are registered trademarks of Skyhorse Publishing,
Inc.®, a Delaware corporation.

Visit our website at www.skyhorsepublishing.com.

10 9 8 7 6 5 4 3 2

Library of Congress Cataloging-in-Publication Data is available on file.

Cover design by Rain Saukas
Cover photo credit: AP Images

Print ISBN: 978-1-5107-2960-5

Printed in the United States of America

To Kanako and my parents

In memory of Larry Teeter and Philip Melanson

CONTENTS

INTRODUCTION
TO THE 2008 EDITION

Four years ago, I knew nothing about Robert Kennedy. My wife, Kanako, was researching a Kennedy conspiracy program for Japanese television, and I was looking for ideas for a new screenplay. I listened to an interview with author William Klaber in which he summarized the controversies surrounding Bobby's death and described how convicted assassin Sirhan Sirhan has never been able to remember the shooting.

The strange tale of second guns, a programmed assassin, and a mysterious female accomplice in a polka-dot dress offered a fascinating seam of late-sixties political paranoia, capturing a defining moment in contemporary American history that marked the death of sixties idealism.

I was struck by the playful, eloquent charisma of Bobby Kennedy, taking to the streets to lead a generation disgusted with the political establishment, and to heal a nation broken after the traumas of the murder of Martin Luther King, Jr., rioting in the cities, and heavy losses in Vietnam. On June 5, 1968, an assassin's bullet killed hope and ushered in the Nixon years.

I didn't believe that Sirhan acted alone, so I went in search of an ending for my story and soon found new evidence suggesting that three CIA senior operatives may have been at the Ambassador Hotel the night Bobby died. The facts of the case seemed more compelling than any attempt to dramatize them, so I began work on an investigative documentary, turning rookie detective.

Of course, a mild paranoia attends investigating this type of material. Former CIA operatives I interviewed suggested that my phone would be monitored and that I think about my family's safety.

A few weeks after my initial discovery of apparent CIA operatives at the hotel, I had an odd visit from two undercover detectives from the Greater London Metropolitan Police. They buzzed the entry door asking to read the electricity meter. When I opened my front door, they produced credentials and asked if they could use a spare room for a surveillance operation on a flat across the street. They'd visit two or three times a week until the operation was completed.

Did this have anything to do with my recent discovery? I wondered. Was their visit a pretext to drop a listening device in the carpet? I decided it wasn't a good idea to host a police stakeout while investigating CIA involvement in a political assassination.

In November 2006, *BBC Newsnight* commissioned a twelve-minute segment on this new evidence of possible CIA involvement, and a feature story detailing my investigation appeared in the *Guardian* newspaper the same day. I secured funding to complete my feature documentary on the case, *RFK Must Die: The Assassination of Bobby Kennedy*, and the resulting DVD contains many of the interviews cited in this book, as well as the video evidence of the alleged CIA operatives at the hotel discussed in Chapters 17 and 18.

After completing the film, I began writing up my investigation for this book and reexamining the evidence in the case from the ground up, exploring more than 70,000 pages of police and FBI files and the transcript of the Sirhan trial.

For me, this case is about much more than conspiracy. It explores the workings of memory and the manipulation of the human mind: Sirhan's memory block and the psychiatrists' attempts to overcome it, as vividly captured in Robert Blair Kaiser's pioneering early work, *"R.F.K. Must Die!"*, which is being reissued in this anniversary year.

While the bizarre writing in Sirhan's notebooks played a key part in securing his conviction, today this writing is a strong indication that others were involved. We now know that the CIA had spent twenty years researching the concept of programmed assassins, and leading psychiatrists see the symptoms of such programming in Sirhan's notebooks and in his mental state on the night of the shooting.

This is also a story about the courage of young witnesses like Sandra Serrano to do "what Robert Kennedy would have wanted me to do [and] say what I saw" in the face of police bullying and attempts to change her story. While the voluminous police and FBI investigation files provide a wealth of detail, it's also clear that on issues concerning possible conspiracy, many key decisions were based not on the evidence, but on an institutional bias to cover up, shut down, or destroy problematic material.

At the same time, for any investigator, there are definite limits to how completely you can recreate a crime scene, given the vagaries of witness recall and photo identification. Multiple accounts of the same incident often defy attempts to condense witness statements into a single narrative. I present my best interpretation here.

One of the most interesting aspects of the investigation has been talking to the families of those alleged to have been involved in the assassination. I found the sons and daughters of these men refreshingly open to my questions. They were often working on their own historical research projects in search of their fathers, and the information they shared has been invaluable in seeking the truth about the Kennedy assassinations.

Why is the case still important after forty years? Because it goes to the very heart of failings in the American criminal justice system. How can an assassination that radically altered the course of contemporary American history be followed by such a hapless and willfully negligent police investigation and such a farcical trial? Why was it left to "citizen researchers" such as Ted Charach to go where the LAPD feared to tread? Was the catalog of police blunders the product of incompetence or something more sinister?

Author David Talbot notes that Bobby Kennedy became "America's first JFK assassination-conspiracy theorist" after his brother's death. In turn, the friends of Robert Kennedy have become some of the most vocal RFK assassination-conspiracy theorists. UAW official Paul Schrade, shot in the head while standing behind Kennedy in the pantry, has for nearly forty years led the campaign to get this case reopened. Attorney Frank Burns, off Kennedy's right shoulder, still insists that Sirhan could not have fired the fatal shot described in the autopsy report.

Sirhan is still in prison, convicted as the lone assassin and repeatedly denied parole. In a normal murder case, he would have been released in 1985, but this is not a normal case. Is Sirhan's conviction just? Were others involved? I hope by the end of this book, you'll have answered those questions and have made up your own mind on the guilt and criminal intent of Sirhan.

You will get a far more balanced view of the case here than the jurors did during the original trial, in large part due to the groundbreaking work of the authors before me in uncovering new evidence. I salute Robert Blair Kaiser, Bill Turner, Jonn Christian, Philip Melanson, Dan Moldea, and William Klaber, and hope my work here builds on their legacy.

What seemed, at first, an open-and-shut case, is, in truth, beguilingly complex. This book does not solve the case, but it does, I hope, provide a comprehensive and disturbing reminder of why it must be urgently reopened. As civil rights–era murders are being reinvestigated and new convictions obtained, on the fortieth anniversary of Robert Kennedy's death, surely this case deserves the same attention?

This has been a huge undertaking. In cross-referencing more than 70,000 pages of documents, I have made my best judgment, in good faith, on the evidence and witness statements. There was no room for a number of colorful characters who ultimately don't convince as possible accomplices. These include the late Jerry Owen, a preacher who told police he'd arranged to sell Sirhan a horse at the back of the Ambassador on the night of the shooting, providing a novel means of escape.

I have focused instead on issues that I feel still have relevance if the case were to be reopened today. I hope this book will play a part in making that happen. As the remaining witnesses begin to pass away, it's now or never.

If you feel moved by the injustices outlined here, please get involved at the project Web site, www.rfkmustdie.com, suggesting corrections or leads for a future edition. Until the public and media understanding of this case changes, nothing will be done in Sacramento to move things forward.

I'll close with the words of Robert Kennedy, quoting his favorite poet Aeschylus, on hearing of the death of Martin Luther King, Jr., on April 4, 1968: "Let us dedicate ourselves to what the Greeks wrote so many years ago: to tame the savageness of man and make gentle the life of this world."

ONE

THE ASSASSINATION

In a dark, candlelit room in Pasadena, California, a small, swarthy hand slowly, methodically inscribed words in a notebook in a spidery scrawl:

May 18 9.45 AM–68
My determination to eliminate R.F.K. is becoming more the more of an unshakable obsession . . . R.F.K. must die–RFK must be killed Robert F. Kennedy must be assassinated R.F.K. must be assassinated . . . R.F.K. must be assassinated assassinated . . . Robert F. Kennedy must be assassinated before 5 June 68 Robert F. Kennedy must be assassinated I have never heard please pay to the order of of of of of [1]

The hand stopped, and enormously peaceful eyes contemplated themselves in the mirror for a moment—the boyishly handsome face of twenty-four-year-old Palestinian Sirhan Sirhan.

* * *

June 4, 1968, Election Day in California
Robert Kennedy faced Eugene McCarthy in the all-important Democratic primary to determine who would challenge Vice President Hubert Humphrey for the Democratic nomination at the Chicago convention and go on to face Richard Nixon in the race for the White House.[2]

One week earlier, McCarthy had defeated Kennedy in Oregon, the first time a Kennedy had ever lost an election, so a strong performance here was critical, or the dream of a second Kennedy presidency was over.

California was "the ultimate test" of Kennedy's grassroots support. He stressed that the country wanted change and that if Humphrey were nominated, "there will be no candidate opposed to continuous escalation of the war in Vietnam and committed to remedying the conditions which have transformed our cities into armed camps. If I died in Oregon, I hope Los Angeles is Resurrection City."[3]

On election eve, Kennedy collapsed from exhaustion in the middle of his final campaign speech in San Diego, so today he slept late at film director John

Frankenheimer's beach home in Santa Monica. Taken with Kennedy's idealism, Frankenheimer had jumped on board the campaign, filming speeches and campaign spots, his handheld cameras capturing the exuberant crowds and renewed hope that greeted the senator from New York.[4]

The country was in turmoil. Eight weeks before, Martin Luther King, Jr., had been assassinated, sparking waves of rioting in American cities. The Vietnam War had polarized the country, and the burgeoning antiwar movement and Black Panther Party had become lightning rods for student revolt, racial unrest, and disenchantment with society. Now California would decide which of the antiwar candidates would carry this popular dissent forward and bring change.

Two Sundays before the primary, Pierre Salinger had organized a "fun lunch" for Kennedy at Frankenheimer's home on a rare day off. Shirley MacLaine was there with her brother, Warren Beatty. So, too, were crooner Andy Williams, composer Burt Bacharach, actress Angie Dickinson, astronaut John Glenn, and French writer Romain Gary with his wife, actress Jean Seberg, who'd earlier hosted fundraisers for the Black Panthers.

Bobby had been surfing and sat shirtless and cross-legged on the floor, holding a glass of orange juice. "You know, don't you, that somebody's going to try to kill you?" Gary asked.

Kennedy looked up slowly. "That's the chance I have to take. You've just got to give yourself to the people and trust them. From then on, either luck is with you or it isn't. I'm pretty sure there'll be an attempt on my life sooner or later. Not so much for political reasons. . . . Plain nuttiness, that's all."[5]

* * *

On June 4, at his modest family bungalow in Pasadena, Sirhan Sirhan woke just before eight and drove off to buy a newspaper in his two-door pink-and-white 1956 DeSoto. He was a wiry five foot two, 115 pounds, with bushy, black curly hair, and wore a light blue shirt, blue velour pullover, tight-fitting light blue denims, and gray suede loafers. He was home by nine thirty, and checked the racing pages. He didn't like the day's horses, so he decided to go target shooting. Around eleven thirty, he arrived at the San Gabriel Valley Gun Range, grabbed his Iver Johnson .22 from the backseat, and headed for the pistol range.[6]

* * *

Robert Kennedy rose shortly before eleven and called his traveling aide-de-camp, Fred Dutton, to set up a meeting at the house in the afternoon. He had lunch with his wife, Ethel, pregnant, again, with their eleventh child, and went to the beach with six of their kids and the family dog, Freckles. It was chilly and overcast, but he plunged into the surf. When he saw twelve-year-old David pulled down by an undertow, he dove in and pulled him up, picking up a red bruise on his forehead for his troubles.[7]

Back at the house, brother Ted and aides Dick Goodwin and Fred Dutton arrived with good news—early CBS precinct samples gave him 49 percent of the California primary vote. A win looked to be in the cards.[8]

* * *

Sirhan stayed on the firing range until it closed at five. Around six thirty, he bumped into a friend, Gaymoard Mistri, at a Bob's Big Boy restaurant in Pasadena. Fifteen minutes later, they walked across the street to Pasadena City College and joined some Arab friends in the cafeteria. Sirhan asked Mistri to go shoot pool, but Mistri had other plans. By seven fifteen, Sirhan was back at his car.[9]

* * *

At the house in Malibu, John Frankenheimer pulled out in his Rolls-Royce Silver Cloud and drove the senator to the Ambassador Hotel in downtown Los Angeles. They arrived at eight fifteen and went directly to the Kennedy suite on the fifth floor, their base for the last six weeks of the campaign. As family and aides settled in to watch the returns on TV, the word was already good from the day's other primary in South Dakota. Although Vice President Humphrey stayed out of the primaries, his supporters mounted a favorite-son write-in campaign in the state where he was born. Yet now Kennedy was winning big there, setting up a chance for two major victories in one evening, in the most rural and most urban states in the Union.[10]

The polls closed at eight o'clock in California, and the first returns gave McCarthy an early lead. "Why's he got forty-nine and I've got thirty-eight?" a startled Kennedy asked. Fred Dutton reassured him; these votes were all from outside Los Angeles County, an expected Kennedy stronghold. The LA vote count wouldn't start until ten. It was going to be a long night.[11]

Kennedy aides relaxed, confident of a comfortable victory, and the senator called close aide Kenny O'Donnell back East to discuss a major strategy meeting in Los Angeles the next morning.

"It looks like you'll be nominated," O'Donnell told him.

"I think I may," said Kennedy.

"He had arrived," O'Donnell said later. "He had won the biggest state in the Union—not as Jack Kennedy's brother, not as Bobby Kennedy, but as Robert Kennedy."[12]

* * *

Downstairs, the crowd was already building in the Embassy Ballroom for the senator's victory speech. Kennedy girls in straw hats, white blouses, blue skirts, and red sashes chanted, "Sock it to 'em, Bobby," as farmworkers' union leader Cesar Chavez arrived with a mariachi band, to exuberant shouts of *"Viva* Kennedy!"

Three parties were in full swing at the hotel. Kennedy supporters gathered in the two main ballrooms as Democrat Alan Cranston and Republican Max Rafferty celebrated respective party nominations for their upcoming Senate race.[13]

According to the LAPD, Sirhan was first sighted at the Rafferty party just before nine, wandering into an electrician's booth adjacent to the Venetian Room. By nine thirty, fire marshals had decided the Embassy Ballroom was full to capacity, and no more guests were admitted without press or staff credentials. Kennedy supporters soon started sneaking in the back way, through the kitchen pantry.[14]

Sometime between nine thirty and eleven, operator Mary Grohs was sitting at a Western Union Teletype machine in the Colonial Room—the "working press room" for the night—tabulating returns from all over the state. She turned to see a young man staring, transfixed, over her shoulder at the Teletype, "with the strangest eyes she'd ever seen."

"May I help you?" she asked.

No response from Sirhan. He just kept staring, hypnotized by the machine.[15]

* * *

Up on the fifth floor, Robert Kennedy relaxed with his entourage as the votes came in. He'd won big in South Dakota, with more votes than McCarthy and Humphrey combined. But in California, the new IBM computers weren't scanning the punch cards correctly, so he had to wait—for the votes that promised California's 174 delegates, and perhaps the Democratic nomination, and the presidency of the United States.[16]

At this point, Kennedy was confident enough of victory to give a round of TV interviews. He was gracious about his opponent, keen to counter his "ruthless" image as interviewers talked up the fight ahead for the nomination. As they waited to go live on NBC, reporter Sander Vanocur, a family friend, asked if he could relax the senator a little.

"The other night, Edith is trying to explain to Chrissy, our eight-year-old, about mythology—the man who was a horse from here down and a man from there down. It's a different kind of human being. She said, 'You know what they called him, Chris?' She said, 'Yeah. Clumsy.'"

Kennedy smiled, his mind clearly elsewhere as Vanocur and the rest of the room cracked up.[17]

* * *

Just after eleven o'clock, as the networks were about to lose their audience for the night, they made their projections. CBS predicted a Kennedy victory by as much as twelve percentage points (the final result was much tighter—46 to 42). Down in the Embassy Ballroom, a jubilant crowd of fifteen hundred campaign workers awaited Kennedy's arrival. Red, white, and blue balloons were popping, and

Kennedy girls formed an honor guard. An overflow crowd filled the Ambassador Ballroom directly below. After his first speech, the senator would go downstairs and speak again.[18]

Up in the Kennedy suite, aides took to the phones to canvass delegates around the country. As sitting vice president, Hubert Humphrey still held a big lead in promised delegates, but the support coming back from California suggested that enough of these could be turned to win the nomination. In the bathroom, next to the sink, speechwriter Adam Walinsky had his secretary type out a victory statement on an electric typewriter plugged into the shaving socket.[19]

* * *

Around eleven thirty, young Mexican American campaign worker Sandra Serrano went to sit outside on a fire escape to escape the heat of the lower ballroom. While she was out there, a man resembling Sirhan climbed the stairs past her with a pretty girl in a polka-dot dress and a Mexican American man in a gold sweater. "Excuse us," the girl said, and Sandra made way as the three went up the stairs to the Embassy Ballroom.[20]

A short time later, around a quarter to twelve, Sirhan wandered into a narrow serving pantry at the back of the ballroom reserved for Kennedy staff and the press. Kennedy press aide Judy Royer had already chased him out once that evening, but now the security guard on duty was busy chatting with Milton Berle, and Sirhan slipped through.

He approached a group of kitchen workers chatting by some stainless-steel steam tables and tapped banquet waiter Martin Patrusky on the shoulder.

"Is Kennedy coming back through here later?"

"How the hell do I know? I'm not the head waiter," replied Patrusky in a heavy Bronx accent. Sirhan tried his luck with kitchen porter Jesus Perez.

"Mr. Kennedy going to pass through here?" he asked.

"I don't know. I hope so," replied Perez.

Sirhan asked three or four times, but Perez repeated he didn't know. Perez watched Sirhan twist and fold some papers in his hand, then wander over to a tray stacker by the ice machines.[21]

* * *

As LAPD morning watch officers came on shift at midnight at Rampart Station, Lieutenant Commander Robert Sillings told them the department was not providing security for Senator Kennedy at the Ambassador Hotel that night. Twenty-year Rampart veteran Sergeant Paul Sharaga looked a little surprised.

Sillings caught up with Sharaga as he prepared to go out on his regular beat as senior patrol sergeant.

"Paul, I want you to stay here and take over on watch tonight. Sergeant Rolon and I are going out in the field."

Unusual, thought Sharaga. Before he settled in, Sillings let him make a cigarette run to a liquor store a block from the Ambassador.[22]

* * *

Close to midnight, there were fifteen hundred people in each of the ballrooms, chanting for Bobby and growing increasingly restless under the stifling heat of the television lights. It was time for the senator to come down and address the crowd.

Kennedy was summoned from his fifth-floor suite and led toward an elevator at the end of the hall, to descend to the lobby and wade onstage through his jubilant supporters. But it was late, he was tired, and he didn't want to fight the crowds. He asked whether there was another route, and Uno Timanson, the hotel's VP of banquet and sales, led him to a service elevator, so he could take the back way down through the kitchen.[23]

A live ABC video feed picked up his loose entourage as they stepped out of the elevator and paused in a hallway, waiting for their cue as Kennedy's brother-in-law Steve Smith wrapped up his introductions. Ethel adjusted the white handkerchief in Kennedy's breast pocket, flanked by former Los Angeles Rams football tackle Rosey Grier and Olympic decathlon champion Rafer Johnson, friends of the family helping out with crowd control on the campaign.

Former FBI agent Bill Barry, Kennedy's unarmed bodyguard, made a final route check, then gave the senator his cue, and the party moved forward through the kitchen. Timanson and Barry led the way, clearing a path with Kennedy advance man Jack Gallivan and hotel assistant maître d' Eddie Minasian.

The senator signed a poster for memorabilia collector Michael Wayne, shook hands with kitchen workers, and held up his left hand to block the lights of the television cameras. As he passed through a narrow serving pantry, he shook the outstretched hand of a tall young busboy, Juan Romero. Ten feet behind the line of waiters, Sirhan waited, balanced on a tray stacker.[24]

The senator turned right through swinging double doors into a hallway at the back of the Embassy Ballroom. To the cheers of the waiting crowd, who had been chanting his name for hours in sweltering heat, Kennedy emerged from a door to the right of the stage, then moved through the crowd and up three creaky wooden steps to the speaker's platform. It was 12:02 a.m. Pacific daylight time.

The temporary stage groaned with Kennedy staff and photographers, all high on the crowd's hysteria and sweating profusely. Kennedy waited for chants of "We want Bobby! We want Kennedy!" to subside, with Ethel to his right and hotel assistant maître d' Karl Uecker and California Speaker Jesse Unruh behind him.

Kennedy jokingly thanked his brother-in-law Steve Smith for a "ruthless but effective" campaign; his dog, Freckles, "who's been maligned . . . and I'm not doing this in the order of importance, but I also want to thank my wife, Ethel." Laughter all round. "Who's been . . ."

"Fantastic," someone said.

"Fantastic," agreed the senator.

He saluted Cesar Chavez and Dolores Huerta for the support of the Mexican American community, loyal to Kennedy for his support during the grape pickers' strike in Delano. He also thanked his friends in the black community, whose action programs in Watts echoed his own regeneration programs in Bedford-Stuyvesant in New York. He saluted Rafer Johnson and gentle giant Rosey Grier, "who said he'd take care of anybody who didn't vote for me"; and Paul Schrade of the United Auto Workers "for the effort he's made on behalf of the working man here in the state of California."[25]

* * *

In the northwest corner of the pantry, just inside the swinging doors, kitchen staff crowded around a TV monitor to listen to the speech. There were about twenty people in the narrow passageway, half hotel staff and half press and "outsiders." Sirhan balanced precariously on the outside edge of a tray stacker, over by the ice machines. He held on to the side of the stacker with his left hand and stood there waiting, raised four inches off the ground, looking west toward the swinging doors that led to the Embassy Ballroom.[26]

* * *

Back on stage, the senator pledged to end the divisions within the United States. "What I think is quite clear is that we can work together . . . we are a great country, an unselfish country and a compassionate country. And I intend to make that my basis for running over the period of the next few months." Huge cheers.

Kennedy hoped the Chicago delegates would sit up and take note of the national mood reflected in these primaries. "The country wants to move in a different direction. We want to deal with our own problems in our own country and we want peace in Vietnam."

* * *

At 12:14 a.m., a smiling Robert Kennedy concluded his victory speech with a sideswipe at a local nemesis. "Mayor Yorty has just sent me a message that we've been here too long already." He gave a waspish grin, and the crowd screamed its approval. Yorty was a Democrat but had supported Nixon against JFK in 1960 and had no love for the Kennedys.

"So, ah . . . my thanks to all of you, and now it's on to Chicago, and let's win there!"

He gave a thumbs-up as chants of "We want Bobby!" started up again and he turned to leave the stage.[27]

For a few fateful moments, Kennedy seemed uncertain where he was going next. Shouts came at him from three directions, but the waving arm of hotel assistant maître d' Karl Uecker caught his eye. Uecker took the senator's right hand, parted a gold curtain behind the rostrum, and led him off the rear of the platform into a small backstage anteroom. As Bill Barry helped the pregnant Ethel Kennedy down from the podium, she told him, "I'm all right. Stay with the senator."[28]

Barry and the rest of the Kennedy entourage rushed to catch up, and emerged into a backstage hallway as Karl Uecker led Kennedy toward the double swinging doors of the pantry, en route to a press conference in the Colonial Room.

"Slow down! You're getting ahead of everyone," shouted Frank Burns, a lawyer and aide to Jesse Unruh. Ace security guard Thane Eugene Cesar took hold of Kennedy around the right elbow with his left hand and Uecker and Cesar led the senator into the pantry and began to push their way through the crowd.[29]

The senator smiled and shook hands with waiters Martin Patrusky to his left, Vincent Di Pierro to his right, and student Robin Casden as she tried to get out of his way. He took another step or two, then stopped by the edge of the first steam table and broke free of Uecker and Cesar momentarily to turn to his left and shake hands with kitchen porter Jesus Perez and busboy Juan Romero.[30]

"Mucho gusto!" said Perez, framed in an alcove leading into the main kitchen. Romero was still in eleventh grade. He'd agreed to work overtime for another waiter, so he could bring meals up to Kennedy's suite. Now he was shaking hands with the soon-to-be *presidente*.[31]

Uno Timanson, afraid the crowd would surge in from the ballroom at any moment, beckoned Uecker from the door to the Colonial Room. "Let's go, Senator," urged Uecker, starting to pull Kennedy away by the right hand.[32]

San Diego high school student Lisa Urso stood by the tray stacker, watching the senator shake hands. She felt a shove from behind as a slight young man stepped in front of her, reached across his body with his right hand, took a slight step forward, reached around Uecker's left shoulder, and smiled as if he was offering the senator his hand.[33]

Instead, he pointed a small, snub-nosed .22 revolver at the senator's head. His eyes were narrowed in concentration, and he seemed to have "a sick smile on his face."[34]

"Kennedy, you son of a bitch!"

Two shots rang out in rapid succession, like firecrackers or "a starter pistol at a track meet." Urso didn't see a gun—just "flames coming from the tip of his hand."[35]

Some thought they heard a kitchen tray crash to the floor . . . the pop of paper cups when someone stands on them . . . a crackling sound, like an electrical discharge. But no, these were definitely gunshots.[36]

Uecker lost his grip on Kennedy's hand, and the senator gave a slight jump; his hands went up to the side of his face as if to push something away, and he staggered backward and fell to the floor as the shots continued. The first two were followed by a slight pause, then a staccato burst, like "a string of firecrackers."[37]

Six to eight feet behind Kennedy, UAW official Paul Schrade saw flashes and thought he was being electrocuted by wet television cables. He fell backward, colliding with student Robin Casden and waiter Vincent Di Pierro on his way to the floor. Martin Patrusky looked over to see his friend Vincent's glasses covered with blood.[38]

Just behind Kennedy and slightly to his right, security guard Thane Cesar ducked, lost his balance, and fell back against the ice machines. He looked up to see the senator lying on his back right in front of him, blood oozing from his right ear to form a crimson pool on the dirty concrete floor.[39]

The pantry, seen from the west swinging doors through which Kennedy approached. The steam table is on the left, the tray stacker on the right. The Xs on the floor mark where Kennedy and Schrade fell.

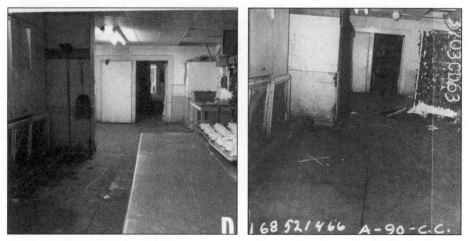

The view from the pantry, looking west toward the swinging doors. Ice machines line the wall on the left; Xs mark where Kennedy and Schrade fell; and the lighted doorway in the distance leads to the backstage area.

Karl Uecker leaped onto the man with the gun after the second shot—or possibly the third. He grabbed Sirhan around the neck in a headlock with his right arm and seized the wrist of his gun hand with the other. Uecker slammed the gun hand down on the steam table and tried to divert it away from the crowd. He dwarfed Sirhan, but the gunman's grip was strong—Uecker could still feel him pumping the trigger as Eddie Minasian and Frank Burns grabbed Sirhan around the waist from behind and tried to push him up onto the steam table.[40]

As bullets sprayed around the pantry, Burns and Romero felt powder burns on their cheeks, and Jesus Perez heard a bullet fly past his ear.[41]

Continental News reporter Ira Goldstein felt a sharp pain in his hip and threw himself against a wall. Student Irwin Stroll screamed, "My leg!" and hopped from the pantry with a wound to the shin. As ABC associate news director William Weisel was coming through the swinging doors, he saw bodies falling in front of him, and then felt "three thumps" in his side and fell to the floor. Behind him, Elizabeth Evans's shoe came off as what sounded like a string of firecrackers exploded. She leaned down to retrieve it, and when she straightened up, blood was flowing down her face from a wound to her forehead.[42]

The crowded room parted down the middle as people ducked for cover. Just outside the swinging doors, Rosey Grier pushed Ethel Kennedy to the floor and covered her body with his. Bill Barry charged through the crowd, struck Sirhan twice in the face with his fist as writer George Plimpton and advance man Jack Gallivan tried to pry the gun from his hand.

"Get a rope so we can tie him up!" yelled Barry. Frank Burns took off his belt and grabbed Sirhan's legs, and they wrestled him up onto the steam table. Plimpton was transfixed by Sirhan's eyes—"dark brown and enormously peaceful."

Thane Cesar scrambled to his feet, pulled his gun, and moved to Kennedy's side "to protect him from further attack."

"Put that gun away," shouted Barry, and Cesar put it back in his holster.

Paul Schrade lay on the floor, his feet by Kennedy's head. Political aide "Cap" Hardy, thinking Schrade was dead, put a straw hat over his face, then found a pulse and straddled him to protect him from the stampede.[43]

Burly CBS cameraman James Wilson and his crew, caught in the doorway as the shots began, shoved their way through to the senator, filming.

"Oh, my Jesus Christ!" cried Wilson as he saw Kennedy on the floor. He turned his camera away in revulsion, and his soundman, John Lewis, yelled in his ear.

"You've got to shoot, Jimmy; you've got to shoot!"

"Christ, no!"

A hysterical Wilson pointed his camera back toward the fallen senator but couldn't bear to look through the viewfinder. Lewis grabbed the lens and aimed as best he could. When the film ran out, Wilson threw down the camera and pounded the concrete floor.

"Fuck America; it's not worth it!" he cried, and vented his fury by jumping up and ferociously pushing back the crowd. "Get the hell outta here, will ya!"[44]

At the edge of the crowd, out-of-breath radio reporter Andrew West flipped on his tape recorder.

"Senator Kennedy has been shot! Senator Kennedy has been shot! Is that possible? Is that possible? Is it possible, ladies and gentlemen? It is possible; he has. Not only Senator Kennedy. Oh, my God, Senator Kennedy has been shot and another man, a Kennedy campaign manager, and possibly shot in the head. I am right here."

West's audiotape and Wilson's film caught the chaos of the moment: a low-ceilinged passageway, dimly lit by three strip lights; a swirling kaleidoscope of crazed voices, juddering cameras, and television lights flashing on and off; screams of "Close the doors! The senator's been shot! Oh, my God! Jesus Christ! Get a doctor! Get the bastard! Kill him! Kill him!"

Kennedy aides and security guards linked arms to push the crowd back as photographers crouched on steam tables, heads dislodging ceiling panels, to catch a glimpse of Kennedy, prostrate on the floor. By now, the room was thick with two clusters of activity: one around the fallen senator, the other assailing the man with the gun.[45]

In the eye of the storm, busboy Juan Romero was the first to the senator's side. He got down on his knees, cradling Kennedy's head with his right hand.

"I'm home in bed. I'm dreaming," he told himself, as he felt blood on his fingers, oozing from the back of Kennedy's right ear.

"Come on, Mr. Kennedy; you can make it!" he urged.

Kennedy's lips moved, barely perceptible, and Romero leaned in closer. "Is everybody all right?" the senator asked.

"Yes, everything will be okay," said Romero.

A voice shouted, "Throw that gum away, Mr. Kennedy."

Romero, crying, started to reach for a wad of chewing gum in Kennedy's mouth, but couldn't bring himself to do it. Kennedy's right eye was open, and his left eyelid moved up and down erratically.

Romero pulled out a crucifix his father had given him for his Catholic confirmation and pressed it into Kennedy's left hand, closing his fingers over it. Kennedy moved the crucifix to his chest.

As Romero looked up, *Life* photographer Bill Eppridge captured the most famous image of the assassination—the anguished busboy comforting a peaceful-looking Kennedy, in mortal repose.[46]

As Romero shouted for a doctor, student Paul Grieco took Kennedy's head in his left hand and lifted it gently, trying to stop the flow of blood from his ear.

Kennedy looked up and asked, "Is Paul all right? Is everybody all right?"

"Don't worry, Robert; you'll be all right," assured Grieco.[47]

Assistant Press Secretary Hugh McDonald took off his coat and propped it under the senator as Fred Dutton arrived, opened the senator's collar and belt, and took off his cuff links and shoes. McDonald was seen clutching the shoes for the rest of the night, refusing to yield them to the police.[48]

* * *

The crowd around the gunman was increasingly agitated, with people yelling hysterically, "Kill him! Kill him!" as blows rained down hard on Sirhan. Barry lunged for the gun, and it fell on the table as Rosey Grier and Rafer Johnson charged across the room.[49]

"Take care of the senator; I have him," shouted Jack Gallivan as Barry went to Kennedy's side. In the switchover, Sirhan grabbed the gun again from the table, but Gallivan got the web of his left hand between the hammer and the frame of the gun before it could be fired again. Electrician Earl Williman jumped on the table and tried to kick the gun from Sirhan's hand as a crazed tableau of limbs and bodies flailed with the assassin. Williman later told the police of Sirhan's "superhuman strength."[50]

Karl Uecker holds Sirhan in a headlock as Rosey Grier tries to twist the gun from his hand.

George Plimpton and Jack Gallivan struggle with Sirhan as (left to right) Uno Timanson, Richard Aubry, Karl Uecker, and Frank Burns look on. Rosey Grier is fast approaching, right of frame.

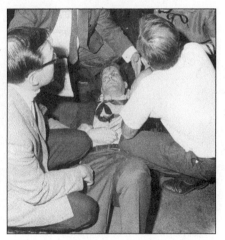

Paul Schrade lies wounded in the pantry.

Elizabeth Evans is treated for a head wound on a table in the Embassy Ballroom as a Kennedy girl and security guard Thomas Perez look on;

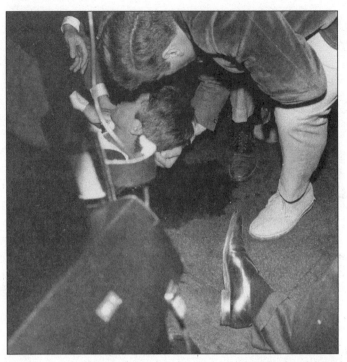

A pool of blood forms under Kennedy's head, next to Paul Schrade's right leg.

Busboy Juan Romero holds up his bloodied right hand.

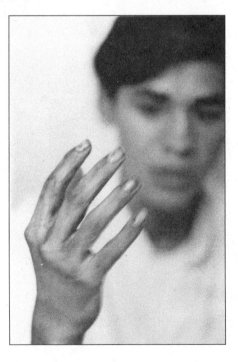

Teenage reporter Ira Goldstein, hit in the left buttock, made it to a chair, and Ethel heard him ask after Kennedy in a vulgar manner as she made her way through the crowd.

"How dare you talk about my husband that way!"

She stopped to scold Goldstein and slapped him across the face.

"Listen, lady. I've been shot, too!" protested Goldstein.

"Oh, I'm sorry, honey," said Ethel, bending down to kiss him on the cheek.[51]

Finally, Mrs. Kennedy reached her husband's side, pushed Romero away, and started talking to him in a low, soothing voice. Then she left for a moment, filled a towel with ice from the nearby ice machines, and came back with it just as Dr. Stanley Abo arrived, the first doctor on the scene.

Abo examined Paul Schrade briefly, then pressed his ear to the senator's chest. Kennedy's breathing was shallow, his pulse slow. His left eye was closed but his heartbeat was strong. The small entry wound behind his right ear was clotting, so Dr. Abo probed it with his finger to keep it bleeding and prevent pressure building up in the brain that could lead to internal hemorrhaging.

Kennedy moaned, "Oh, Ethel, Ethel . . . ," and she patted his hands.

"It's okay," she said.

"Am I all right?"

"You're doing good," soothed Dr. Abo; "the ambulance is on its way."

"The ambulance is coming," repeated Ethel.

Kennedy took her right hand in his and brought it up to the crucifix on his chest.[52]

* * *

"Take him, Rosey; take him!" shouted Bill Barry.

All 287 pounds of Roosevelt Grier slammed into Sirhan, and he grabbed the butt of the gun as Rafer Johnson lunged in and got hold of the barrel. Somehow, the diminutive Sirhan still had his finger in the trigger housing.

Radio reporter Andrew West was right there:

"Rafer Johnson has a hold of the man who apparently has fired the shot. He still has the gun. The gun is pointed at me right at this moment. I hope they can get the gun out of his hand. Be very careful! Get the gun! Get the gun! Get the gun! Stay away from the gun!"

Rosey had Sirhan around the waist, Plimpton had his right side, Uecker had him around the neck, and Joe LaHive and *Look* magazine correspondent Warren Rogers held his legs.

"His hand is frozen. Get his thumb; get his thumb," urged West. "Take ahold of his thumb and break it if you have to; get his thumb! Get away from the barrel, man!"

Rafer held Sirhan tight as Rosey twisted the gun from his hand and pointed it toward the ceiling. Veteran hotel guard Fred Murphy identified himself as a former lieutenant of the police department.

"Let me have the gun," he demanded. "Let go, Rosey; let go, Rafer."

"Shut up!" shouted Johnson, then looked across at Rosey.

"Rosey, let me have the gun," said Rafer.

Rosey passed the gun to Rafer, who put it in the left pocket of his coat and released his grip on Sirhan. Murphy ran to the bell captain's desk to call the police and an ambulance.

"All right, that's it, Rafer!" shouted Andrew West, for listeners at home. "Ladies and gentlemen, they have the gun away from the man."[53]

From beneath the pile of bodies, Sirhan cried, "Stop, you're hurting my leg!" "Like a kid," according to Plimpton. Columnist Jimmy Breslin, face-to-face with Sirhan, shouted, "Why did you have to do it?" But Sirhan's eyes were rolling and he didn't answer. His legs thrashed around, but his body was held secure.[54]

Sirhan was now on his back, his head and shoulders hanging precariously off the edge of the steam table. Hungarian salesman Gabor Kadar jumped up on the table and hit him in the chest and knee. As Watts organizer Booker Griffin aimed a punch, Rosey shouted, "Don't do that, baby! Let's take him alive; don't kill him."[55]

California Speaker Jesse Unruh, alert to the danger, jumped up on the steam table. "We don't want another Oswald! If the system works at all, we are going to try this one!"[56]

Rafer Johnson pressed his face against Sirhan's and looked straight in his eyes. "Why did you do it?" he demanded. The gunman said nothing. Johnson placed a clenched fist on Sirhan's forehead. "Why did you do it?"

"I'll explain it," said Sirhan.

"Shut up!" someone cried, and that was the end of it.[57]

* * *

As chaos swirled around the pantry, wild-eyed memorabilia collector Michael Wayne ran out through the Colonial Room and into the lobby with a rolled poster in his hand. A voice called out:

"Stop him! He's getting away!"

Several bystanders chased Wayne into a cul-de-sac, and Ace guard Augustus Mallard handcuffed him. Wayne pleaded innocence—he was just running for a phone. Several witnesses later claimed they saw a black metal object hidden inside the poster, but no gun was ever found.[58]

* * *

Campaign worker Sandra Serrano was still sitting on the fire escape below the southwest corner of the Embassy Ballroom. She heard what she thought was a car backfire six times; then the girl in the polka-dot dress and the Mexican American man in the gold sweater burst out onto the hotel fire escape and ran down the stairs, almost stepping on her.

"We've shot him! We've shot him!" the girl exclaimed.

"Who did you shoot?" asked Sandra.

"We've shot Senator Kennedy!"

The girl seemed so excited about shooting Kennedy, Sandra went back inside in a state of shock. She spotted a guard in a gray uniform just inside the door, one floor below the pantry.

"Is it true they shot him?" she asked.

"Shot who?" asked the guard.

"Senator Kennedy!"

The guard looked at her like she was crazy, then spotted a glass in her hand. "I think you've had a little too much to drink, honey."

But Serrano couldn't be shaken from what she'd heard. She ran to a public phone booth and dialed her parents in Ohio, collect, long-distance. Crying and near complete hysteria, she launched into a garbled account as a girl she recognized approached the glass.

"Has Kennedy been shot?" Serrano asked. Yes, Kennedy had been shot.[59]

12:17 a.m.

At Rampart Station, desk officer Schiller received a call from an unknown male, wanting to talk to the watch commander. Sergeant Rolon accepted the call for Lieutenant Commander Sillings.

"Kennedy has just been shot."[60]

Rolon and Sillings left to investigate the call as a very nonchalant switchboard operator at the Ambassador dialed 911:

"This is the Ambassador Hotel. . . . They have an emergency. They want the police to the kitchen right away."

"What kind of an emergency?" asked Officer Hathaway in the LAPD Communications Division.

"I don't know, honey. They hung up."

"Well, find out. . . . We have to know what we're sending on."

"Well, honey, I don't know. . . . I'll ring back; hold on. . . . That's all he said and hung up. . . . You know we have Mr. Kennedy here tonight."

"Big deal!" snorted Officer Hathaway.

"I don't know what happened, but it's something. You want me to find out what it is?"

"Yes, please!"

"Hold on. . . . I think somebody was shot."

"Oh, great."

"Great. Do you want me to still try to . . . ?"

"Yes, ma'am."

"Oh, God. I can't get the party back on here."

The switchboard operator left Hathaway holding for thirty-five seconds; then Night Supervisor Ruby Ford came on the line.

"This is the Ambassador Hotel. . . . Ahhh . . . my banquet maître d' reported that Senator Kennedy had been shot."

"He's been shot?" repeated Officer Hathaway. Now she had his attention.

"That's right, and I think you better send somebody over here."[61]

* * *

The emergency call took two and a half minutes. Moments later, Sergeant Paul Sharaga heard an all-unit call on his car radio: "All units in the vicinity . . . an ambulance shooting at thirty-four hundred Wilshire Boulevard . . . "

Sharaga looked across the street at the rear entrance of the Ambassador and gunned his car toward the rear parking lot. He jumped out to find mass confusion, hundreds of people running in all directions. As the first officer to arrive, he started setting up a command post in the parking lot.[62]

12:22 a.m.

An ambulance pulled up at the front entrance, and Uno Timanson escorted the attendants up to the pantry in a state of panic. They sauntered along behind, refusing to walk up a flight of stairs with the stretcher and insisting on taking the elevator.

More police arrived, and hotel staff took Officers Travis White and Arthur Placencia upstairs, where Rosey and Rafer were still fighting off the crowd "milling around the suspect and punching and kicking him."[63]

As White entered, the suspect was being held down on his stomach by eight or ten people on top of the third steam table at the east end of the pantry. Uecker had him in a headlock, Rosey lay across his legs, and Jesse Unruh was on the table with his knee in Sirhan's back.

"Quick, they're trying to kill him!" a man yelled to the officers.

"This is the bastard that shot Kennedy!" shouted Unruh.

White, Placencia, and three other officers pushed their way toward Sirhan and forcibly peeled people off him. Rosey wouldn't let go of his legs.

"We are police officers; step aside!" shouted White.

"This one's going to stand trial! No one's going to kill him!" cried Unruh from on top of the steam table. "I want him alive! I hold you responsible for him being alive!"

White and Officer Nunley freed Sirhan's arms, handcuffed them behind his back, and pulled him off the table.

"Let's get him out of here!" shouted White as the angry crowd screamed for the suspect's head and Unruh grabbed White by the shoulder.

"You're not taking him anyplace."

White pushed Unruh away, but he lunged again at the officers and grabbed Sirhan by the scruff of the neck.

"Okay, you can take him, but I'm going with you," said the Speaker of the California State Assembly.

"Let's get him out of here!" repeated White, and they made for the east exit.

"We don't want another Oswald! We don't want another Oswald!" hollered Unruh as Frank Burns led the group out through the Colonial Room into the carpeted lobby and down the twisting stairs to the ground floor. People tried to strike out at Sirhan and tear his clothes as the group moved quickly to the front entrance.[64]

* * *

Back in the pantry, the uniformed ambulance attendants finally reached the senator. Ethel Kennedy was applying an ice pack to his head.

"What happened?" asked medical attendant Max Behrman.

"It's none of your business," she said, not realizing who he was.

The attendants tried to lift Kennedy onto a stretcher.

"No, please don't . . . don't lift me up," said the senator.

Kennedy aide Dick Tuck helped them put him on the stretcher, and they took him out by the freight elevator, en route to Central Receiving Hospital.[65]

* * *

Out in the rear parking lot, a couple in their late fifties ran up to Sergeant Paul Sharaga, hysterical.

"Slow down, slow down," Sharaga said. "What happened?"

The lady did most of the talking. "We were coming out through the Embassy Room and a young couple ran past, maybe late teens or early twenties, well dressed and really happy . . . shouting 'We shot him! We shot him!' And I said, 'Who did you shoot?' and she said, 'Kennedy; we shot him! We killed him!'"

The woman was becoming hysterical.

"Okay, okay . . . what are your names?"

Sharaga noted down the suspect descriptions and the couple's names and contact details—he later recalled them as "the Bernsteins." He tore out a sheet from his notebook and handed it to a field courier for the Rampart chief of detectives.

"Get this to Bill Jordan."

He went over to his patrol car and put out an APB on the male suspect: "Description suspect, the shooting at thirty-four hundred Wilshire Boulevard, male Caucasian, twenty to twenty-two, six foot to six foot two, very thin build, blond curly hair, wearing brown pants, light tan shirt, direction taken unknown."[66]

* * *

12:28 a.m.

A large, hostile crowd surged forward as Sirhan was frog-marched out of the hotel under the canopied front entrance. Officer Placencia pushed the suspect into the backseat of a patrol car, locked the door, went around to the other side, and climbed in beside him.

Officer White jumped behind the wheel, and Jesse Unruh slid in beside him. Others tried to crawl over Unruh to get to the prisoner, but Burns and Uecker pulled them away and slammed the car door shut. The officers had no idea who Unruh was but didn't have time to ask. As they pulled away, Unruh heard Sirhan mumble, "I did it for my country."

As White sped out the drive, red lights flashing, Placencia turned on his flashlight and saw a strange smile on the suspect's face. He flashed the light into the young man's pupils. They were dilated and didn't respond—a sign he was either drunk or drugged.

"You'd better give him his rights, partner," suggested White.

Placencia took out his field notebook and read Sirhan his rights off the inside cover.

"Do you understand your rights?" he asked the suspect.

No reply. Placencia read them again and repeated the question.

"Yes," replied Sirhan.

"Do you wish to remain silent?"

"Yes."

"Do you wish an attorney present?"

"Yes."

Placencia gave up and glanced at Unruh in the front seat.

"By the way, who did he shoot?"

"Bob Kennedy."

"Oh," said Placencia.

Unruh turned to Sirhan. "Why him? Why him? He was trying to do something." "It's too late; it's too late," muttered Sirhan.[67]

* * *

Fred Dutton, Ethel Kennedy, and her sister Jean jumped in the back of the ambulance with the senator. Bill Barry and *Look* magazine reporter Warren Rogers were in the front seat with the driver. When attendant Max Behrman asked Mrs. Kennedy more questions, she grabbed his call record book and threw it out into the hotel parking lot.

En route to Central Receiving, as Behrman applied a bandage to the senator's head wound, a traumatized Mrs. Kennedy shouted, "Keep your dirty, filthy hands off my husband!" and slapped him across the cheek.

She shouted to Bill Barry in the front seat. "Come back here, Bill, and throw this guy out the back door!"

As the ambulance sped up Wilshire at seventy-five miles an hour, Barry tried to crawl back through the cab window as driver Robert Hulsman steered with one hand and pulled him back with the other. The senator began gasping, and Behrman administered oxygen. At 12:30, they arrived at Central Receiving.[68]

* * *

Back at the hotel, Kennedy supporters wandered around aimlessly, clutching PRAY FOR BOBBY signs, some cursing, some weeping. In the kitchen, Rosey Grier and CBS cameraman James Wilson sat side by side, heads in hands, sobbing. The Plimptons brought Rosey a glass of water, took him upstairs to the Kennedy suite, and put him to bed.[69]

In the pantry, Andrew West was signing off:

"Repetition in my speech. I have no alternative. The shock is so great. . . . At this moment we are stunned. We are shaking, as is everyone else in this kitchen corridor at the Ambassador Hotel, in Los Angeles. . . . I do not know if the senator is dead or if he is alive. We do not know the name of the other gentleman concerned. This is Andrew West, Mutual News, Los Angeles."[70]

TWO

THE AFTERMATH

And so the round of eyewitness interviews began. KNXT film runner Don Schulman was grabbed by Jeff Brent of Continental News Service in a hotel corridor.

"I'm talking to Don Schulman. Don, can you give us a halfway-decent report of what happened within all this chaos?"

"Okay. I was . . . ah . . . standing behind Kennedy as he was taking his assigned route into the kitchen. A Caucasian gentleman stepped out and fired three times . . . the security guard . . . hit Kennedy all three times. Mr. Kennedy slumped to the floor . . . they carried him away . . . the security guards fired back. . . . As I saw . . . they shot the . . . ah . . . man who shot Kennedy in the leg. . . . He . . . ah . . . before they could get him, he shot a . . . it looked like to me . . . he shot a woman . . . and he shot two other men. They then proceeded to carry Kennedy in the kitchen and . . . I don't know how his condition is now."

"Was he grazed or did it appear to be a direct hit? Was it very serious from what you saw?"

"Well . . . from what I saw . . . it looked . . . fairly serious. He had . . . he was definitely hit three times."

"I was about six people behind the senator, I heard six or seven shots in succession. . . . Now . . . is this the security guard firing back?"

"Yes . . . the man who stepped out fired three times at Kennedy . . . hit him all three times . . . and the security guard then fired back."[1]

* * *

Within minutes, reports of a security guard firing back hit the UPI newswires. Leading French newspaper *France Soir* reported a man firing "and then the Kennedy bodyguard pulls his gun out of his holster and fires from the hip like in a Western movie." But Don Schulman was the only witness who saw a security guard fire.[2]

* * *

In another part of the Ambassador, radio reporter John Marshall cornered security guard Thane Eugene Cesar for local station KFWB.

"Officer, can you confirm the fact that the senator has been shot?"

"Yes. I was there holding his arm when they shot him."

"What happened?"

"I don't know. . . . As he walked up, the guy pulled a gun and shot at him."

"Was it just one man?"

"No. Yeah, one man."

"And what sort of wound did the senator receive?"

"Well, from where I could see, it looked like he was shot in the head and the chest and the shoulder. . . ." [3]

Minutes after the shooting, Cesar gave the most accurate witness description of the senator's wounds but was never called to testify at the trial. In addition to Don Schulman's "Caucasian gentleman," witnesses variously described the swarthy gunman as Filipino, Mexican American, Puerto Rican, Armenian, and Italian.

* * *

When they arrived at Rampart Station, White and Placencia placed the prisoner in the "Breathalyzer room." Although Sirhan sat next to equipment for testing drunks, no blood-alcohol test was given. The LAPD later admitted this was a big mistake.

Minutes later, they moved him next door to Interrogation Room B, a bare room with a metal table, metal chairs, and a microphone hidden in the walls, taping everything. They assured Jesse Unruh that Sirhan was handcuffed and could do himself no harm. There wouldn't be another Oswald. White searched the suspect and laid out his possessions on the metal table. A short time later, Sergeant Bill Jordan, head of Rampart detectives, came in and took over.[4]

The audiotapes of Sirhan's time in custody are still preserved at the California State Archives, and as the late author Philip Melanson noted, throughout this first session "Sirhan sounds very scared and intimidated; he speaks in a soft, almost inaudible tone that is very different from the tone and manner in later tapes. At times, he sounds very tired and breathy. . . . He can sometimes be heard in the background gasping for air."[5]

12:45 a.m.

Jordan sized up the guy who had just tried to kill Kennedy. He was dark skinned, with black, bushy hair, intense brown eyes, a bruise on his forehead, and a cut near his left eye.

"My name is Sergeant Jordan. This is Rampart Detectives. What is your name, sir?"

Silence.

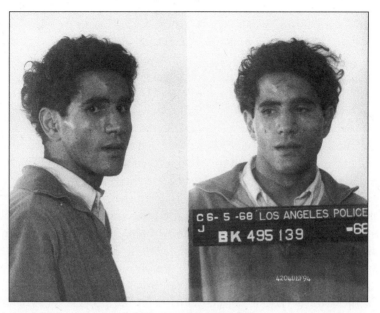

LAPD mugshots of Sirhan

"No comment?" Jordan heaved a big sigh and read the prisoner his rights. "Do you understand your rights?"

"Is this what the officers told me in the car?" asked Sirhan.

"I have no idea at this point, sir, what you were told."

"Could you please repeat it?"

Jordan repeated Sirhan's rights. "These are your rights. Do you have any questions regarding these rights?"

Sirhan shook his head.

"Now you're shaking your head. You do understand me?"

"Your name again, sir?" asked Sirhan.

"My name is Sergeant Jordan, *J-o-r-d-a-n*. I'm night watch commander at Rampart Detectives, which is where you are at the present time. Now, would you tell me what your name is?"

"I want to abide by the first admonishment, sir, to the right of keeping silence."

"All right, sir, that is your privilege." Jordan gestured to some dollar bills laid out on the table with the rest of Sirhan's property.

"I want to count this in front of you, so that you're satisfied that this is the right amount. Is that all right with you?"

"Are you saying this, sir, under the authority of the first admonishment that you gave me, of keeping silence? Is keeping silence, sir, involved in this process here?

Sirhan sounded in shock, as if he was finding it hard to breathe. Jordan paused, bewildered by the prisoner's mannered responses.

"I cannot see how that possibly could be incriminating to you. . . ." Sirhan shook his head. "You don't wish to do that, either? All right."

Jordan read the items on the metal table "into the record" anyway.

"Let's see, one-hundred-dollar bills. We have one, two, three, four one-hundred-dollar bills. We have one five-dollar bill. We have one, two, three, four one-dollar bills. We have one dollar . . . and sixty-six cents in silver. . . . We also have a comb, a key, David Lawrence's column from the *Independent Star-News*. . . ."

The column was titled "Paradoxical Bob" and began, "Presidential candidates are out to get votes and some of them do not realize their own inconsistencies." Lawrence asked why Kennedy was a dove in opposing the war in Vietnam while a hawk in advocating military assistance for Israel in the Middle East.[6]

"And a clipping here . . ." Jordan picked up the clipping and read aloud.

"'You and your friends are cordially invited to come and see and hear Robert Kennedy on Sunday, June second, 1968, at eight p.m. at the Cocoanut Grove, the Ambassador.'"

Jordan stopped to check the poker face of the prisoner. No reaction. He continued with his inventory of objects taken from the pockets of Sirhan's denim trousers.

"We have two unexpended cartridges, which appear to be twenty-two caliber, and we have one copper-jacketed slug, which appears to be expended, no casing involved, also which appears to be twenty-two caliber. And we have a white piece of paper with writing on it which has to do with 'This man is your man. This man is my man,' and apparently refers to Senator Kennedy."

It was a sing-along sheet for his campaign song. Jordan pondered the suspect for a moment. He got Sirhan to stand, so he could pat him down for weapons. Sirhan gave a quick, anxious breath.

"Sorry, what happened?" asked Jordan.

"I mentioned it to officer number 3909. . . . I mentioned to him my ankle, my knee hurt me."[7]

"Okay, I'm very sorry. . . . I'll be as gentle as possible, okay?"

"Okay."

"You're clean," said Jordan. "Sorry, I know you're clean, but I'll be as gentle as possible. . . . What happened to your leg?"

Again, silence. Jordan gathered up Sirhan's property and left, asking Officers Willoughby and Austin to keep a close eye on the prisoner. The two men lit up cigarettes.

"How long have you been in here?" asked Austin. "You don't want to say?"

"You speak English?" asked Willoughby.

Sirhan said nothing. Jordan briefly returned with a hot chocolate for Willoughby, after which further attempts to engage the prisoner in conversation were met with long silences, punctuated by Officer Willoughby slurping his drink.

"I'm thirsty," said Sirhan.

"Well, I'm not going to give you any of this," said Willoughby.

"It's hot, really?" asked Sirhan.

"It's hot."

Sirhan kicked out with his right foot, spilling hot chocolate all over himself and Willoughby.

"I'll give you some in a minute!" shouted Willoughby.

"That's enough, pal," said Austin, trying to calm the situation.

"Yeah!" screamed Willoughby, practically strangling with rage.

There's an obvious splice on the tape here, editing out some of Willoughby's rage. The transcript later presented in court reads, "They'll give you some in a minute."

As Willoughby left to get a rag to wipe the hot chocolate off the floor, Austin tried to reason with the prisoner.

"You're not gonna prove nothin' that way."

"Later, please apologize for me to him," the prisoner replied softly. "I trust you."[8]

* * *

Over at Central Receiving, an officious policeman wouldn't let a priest in to administer the last rites to Senator Kennedy. Mrs. Kennedy identified herself and pleaded with him to let Father Mundell in.

"No, I can't," replied Officer Ambrecht.

"But I'm Mrs. Kennedy!" she said.

"I'm a policeman."

At that, she hit him. He hit her, and Kennedy's press secretary, Frank Mankiewicz, and somebody else hit the cop. It almost descended into a brawl.[9] Inside, Dr. Victor Bazilauskas gave the senator closed cardiac massage, placed him on a heart-lung machine, administered oxygen, and injected him with adrenaline.

Kennedy was breathless, pulseless, and lifeless, dying right there on the table. The doctor started to rough him up a little, slapping his cheeks.

"Be gentle," pleaded Mrs. Kennedy.

"Bob! Bob! Wake up!" urged the doctor.

No response. Ten minutes later, as all seemed lost, there was a feeble breath, the senator's pulse picked up, and, finally, came the sound of a heart-beat. Dr. Bazilauskas handed Ethel the earpiece of his stethoscope. As she heard her husband's heartbeat, her distraught face lit up.

"Will he live? Will he live?" she asked.

"Right now, he's doing all right. Let's hope; let's hope."[10]

* * *

Back at the hotel, a police bus was waiting as officers tried to round up witnesses to the shooting and take them down to Rampart for statements.

Sandra Serrano was waiting in the witness room when somebody asked her what she had seen. Next thing she knew, she was being interviewed live by Sander Vanocur on NBC television. It was one thirty in the morning and she was slightly hysterical, but she had a clear picture in her mind of what she'd seen.

"Miss Serrano . . . ," said Vanocur. "Just take your time. . . . What happened?"

It was too hot in the main room before the speech, she explained, so she had gone outside for some air.

"And I was out on the terrace . . . standing there, just thinking about how many people there were and how wonderful it was. Then this girl came running down the stairs in the back . . . and said, 'We've shot him! We've shot him!' And I said, 'Who did you shoot?' And she said, 'We've shot Senator Kennedy.' . . . I can remember what she had on and everything, and after that, a boy came down with her. He was about twenty-three years old and he was Mexican American. . . . I can remember that because I'm Mexican American."

Vanocur couldn't believe what he was getting here. She seemed vivid and composed, but he knew she could also be a "ding-a-ling."

"Wait a minute, did this young lady say 'we'?" he asked.

"'We,' she said," replied Serrano.

"Meaning, we, the Mexican Americans?"

"No, she was not of Mexican American descent. . . . She was Caucasian. She had on a white dress with black polka dots. She was light skinned, dark hair. She had black shoes on and she had a funny nose. It was, it was—I thought it was real funny. All my friends tell me I'm so observant."

"Did you work for Senator Kennedy?"

"I'm co-chairman of Youth for Kennedy in the Pasadena-Altadena area. . . . In 1965, I met him in Washington, DC, in an elevator. He stepped on my foot and I shoved him, and it's an unforgettable experience."

"Thank you, Miss Serrano."

Vanocur shook his head in slight bewilderment, and so began the tale of the girl in the polka-dot dress.[11]

* * *

At 1:43, Inspector John Powers radioed Paul Sharaga in the rear parking lot to find out where his second suspect had come from.

"From a witness who was pushed over by this suspect. Witness and his wife, we have name and address . . ."

"What proximity to the shooting were these people?"

"They were adjacent to the room."

"Disregard that broadcast," said Powers. "We got Rafer Johnson and Jesse Unruh, who were right next to him, and they only have one man, and don't want them to get anything started on a big conspiracy. This could be somebody that was getting out of the way so they wouldn't get shot. But the people that were right next to Kennedy say there was just one man."

"2L30 to control," Sharaga radioed back, "disregard my broadcast. A description, male Caucasian, twenty to twenty-two, six foot to six foot two, this is apparently not a correct description. Disregard and cancel." [12]

*   *   *

Back at Rampart, the interrogation room door opened and an officer asked for a description of the suspect.

"How much do you weigh?" asked Austin. "How tall are you?" Sirhan didn't respond. "Makes no difference to me; I'm only a peon here."

"I like your humor, sir," said Sirhan, resisting further attempts at conversation.

"Just say yes or no if you understand," said Austin. "We're not recipients of voodoo, 'cause we can't outstare each other."

Jordan came back in with Sergeant Melendres. It was time to go downstairs.

"Will you please get my pants fastened for me?" asked the handcuffed Sirhan.

"Take a breath," said Jordan as he hitched up the suspect's pants.

"Jack 'em up. Jack 'em up," said Sirhan. [13]

Pants fastened, the suspect was hustled down a back stairway to the garage and lay on the floor of an unmarked Ford as Jordan, Willoughby, Sergeant Frank Patchett, and Sergeant Adolph Melendres drove him the short journey to police headquarters at Parker Center. On arrival, the suspect asked for a drink of water and got Jordan to taste it first.

At a minute past two, Sirhan was examined by Central Jail physician Dr. Elwin Lanz. His left ankle was sprained and swollen and he had a bruised left index finger and a bruised forehead. The doctor saw no indication he was under the influence of drugs or alcohol, but again he was not tested. [14]

The prisoner was placed in Interrogation Room 318 next door. Once again, the room was bugged. Bill Jordan was now joined by Deputy District Attorney John Howard; his chief investigator, George Murphy; and Sergeant Melendres. During this and subsequent sessions, Sirhan sounded a lot more alert than during his first session with Jordan. His speech was quick and intense, with a slight accent, an odd turn of phrase, and an eclectic vocabulary.

Howard started by once more reading the prisoner his rights.

"Now, understanding those rights, do you think that you want to make a statement now?"

"Sir, I said I shall remain incognito," said the prisoner.

"Would you tell me your name? Can we go that far?"

"That's it, sir. I said I wish to remain incommunicado."

"Okay, fine. Let's go," said Howard. "Thank you very much." As he got up to leave, he printed the names and numbers of the investigators on a card and put it in Sirhan's shirt pocket.

"Now, do you have anything you want to ask us?" "When will I have a chance to clean up?" asked Sirhan.

"As soon as you go through the booking process," said Murphy. Anything else?

"Not at present, sir."

"Okay, I expect to hear from you, okay?" said Howard. "Am I wrong?"

Sirhan just looked at him.[15]

*   *   *

Sirhan was taken downstairs for booking and strip-searched. At 2:20, he was booked as "John Doe" and charged with "assault with intent to commit murder." The custodial officer noted he was very composed and at ease. Mug shots were taken, but Sirhan refused to give a sample of his handwriting.[16]

As an officer took a full set of fingerprints in the Homicide squad room, Sergeant Patchett tried again for a name.

"Who are you?" No answer. "If you'd give us your name, you'd save us an awful lot of work. . . . What's the matter? Ashamed of your name?"

"Hell, no!" said Sirhan. [17]

As Patchett sent the prints off to the FBI lab in Washington, Sirhan was allowed to wash and change clothes. He took a "slow, deliberate and thorough" shower and came back in a prison uniform far too big for him.[18]

He was then brought to cell J-1 of the Central Jail and chatted with Officer Frank Foster through the steel-cage door. Foster's brief was to make sure Sirhan didn't harm himself and to keep him talking before the next interrogation. They were the same age and instantly hit it off.[19]

They chatted for some time before Howard reappeared with Jordan and Melendres. "Did you get cleaned up?" Howard asked.

"Well, I don't look very presentable," complained Sirhan, looking down at his baggy new clothes. "I wish you could accommodate me more."

They took the prisoner into an interrogation room and sat around a wooden table as their superiors watched from the darkened corridor on the other side of one-way glass.

After another rambling conversation, Howard grew a little impatient.

"You know where we are now?" he asked.

"I don't know," said Sirhan.

"You are in custody. You've been booked."

"I have been before a magistrate, have I or have I not?"

The investigators were a little confused. Was he putting them on?

"No, you have not," said Howard. "You will be taken before a magistrate as soon as possible. Possibly will be tried."

"Are you going to take me up there like this?" asked Sirhan, looking down at his pants.

"You'll be properly attired," Howard assured him. "We're not communicating very well up to now, but you are in downtown Los Angeles, okay?"

Howard tried again for a name. "If I were going to call you something, what would I call you, George or Pete or what?"

Sirhan said the officer in the jail introduced himself as Frank and "I introduced myself as John Doe."

"Did you?" replied Howard.

"I think I gave him a clue to that." Jordan laughed. "You like the name 'John Doe'?"

"Oh, it's nice for a last name."

Howard was called out of the room for a moment. When he came back in, Melendres made a last attempt to talk to Sirhan. "Young man, let's be friendly and manly here for a second, will you?"

"Yes, sir."

"We have a job to do. . . . Now, do you want to talk to us about the incident at the Ambassador or don't you? Were you at the Ambassador tonight?"

"Well, look, Mr. Jordan . . . I must act right for a minute and say that when he informed me of my constitutional rights, the first thing he said, that I have the right to remain silent."

"This is correct," said Melendres.

"This is basic American jurisprudence, no?"

"Right," seconded Howard.

"No argument," Jordan agreed.

"Now, you have the right to give up these rights if you want to talk to us—this is your privilege," said Melendres. "Now, do you want to talk to us about the incident tonight? You want to at least give us your name?"

"I thought that you had mine."

"John Doe," said Howard.

"John Doe," said Sirhan.

The interrogators gave up, and Howard asked Sirhan to call him if he changed his mind.[20]

* * *

Left alone with Murphy for a while, Sirhan debated the meaning of "justice."

"Fair play . . . that you don't take advantage of anybody," offered Murphy.

"Right," said Sirhan. "Treat others as you would want them to treat you; that's what Christ said. Beautiful thing."

"Do you go along with that?" asked Murphy.

"Very much so, sir. Very much so."

"Do you have any religious convictions?"

"My conscience," replied Sirhan.

"Is that all?"

"What more do you want, sir? If you can't live with it . . ."

"That's right," said Murphy.

* * *

Jordan soon returned with more coffee and tried another tack.

"Do you have any objections to telling us what you've done in your illustrious past here?"

"Beautiful. Beautiful," said Sirhan, as Jordan mimicked his wordplay. "I love the implication there."

"I mean, what type of work you've indulged in?"

"Oh, whatever you want me to do," said Sirhan. "Really, everything fascinates me in life, you know."

"When you go in front of the magistrate, and you're going to be asked your true name, what kind of an answer are you going to give the judge?" asked Murphy.

"Well, John or Jesse Doe, or Incommunicado."

"Jesse Incommunicado," said Jordan.

"Yeah, that's beautiful."[21]

* * *

Throughout these sessions, it's clear Sirhan was very aware that anything he said could be used against him and didn't answer specific questions about the case, citing the First Amendment. But, while the investigators mentioned the Ambassador Hotel, they never mentioned Robert Kennedy himself. Sirhan played games with them and seemed completely detached from what had happened earlier in the night, reveling in the legal jargon and being "most wonderfully entertained" by the chitchat with the investigators. Later, these tapes would be played in full to the jury by the defense to try to prove Sirhan was in an altered state at the time of the shooting.[22]

* * *

Jordan was called outside again and came back in with new information. Officers searching for the suspect's car in the vicinity of the hotel had matched his key to a vehicle parked just off Wilshire Boulevard. For a time they tried to get Sirhan to admit it was his, but he played with them teasingly.[23]

* * *

As the session came to an end, Sirhan reminded his captors to work on some new clothes before his arraignment—he couldn't wear his own clothes because they'd been booked.

"Can you buy me some? I would like this all fixed up if at all possible."

Jordan assured him he'd try to find better pants.

"You look very presentable compared to when I first saw you. You're clean, you're neat, your eyes are clear, and if we can get you something that fits you a little better . . ."[24]

* * *

Jordan later summarized his opinion of the interview: "Sirhan was in good spirits and quite stimulated. He acted like he was playing a game and enjoying it. He appeared anxious to match wits with Murphy and myself. . . . He was happy to talk about anything other than the Kennedy case. . . . I was impressed by Sirhan's composure and relaxation. He appeared less upset to me than individuals arrested for a traffic violation. I thought that his mind was keen and that he fancied himself somewhat of an intellectual."[25]

* * *

Officers were dispatched to Briar Knoll Drive, the address for the driver of the car they suspected was Sirhan's, and found nobody home. It turned out the owner, Robert Jean Gindroz, was the executive chef at the Ambassador. He never locked his car door, and any key turned the ignition switch, hence the mix-up.[26]

* * *

By six a.m., Sirhan was back in his cell, chatting quietly with Officer Foster. He sounded tired, and his voice was very soft.

"Your leg hurt you?" asked Foster. "Kind of."

"How did you hurt it?"

"I don't know."

"Did you fall down or something? When did it happen?"

"I don't remember."

"You don't remember?"

Foster was confused. Either the prisoner was very cagey or he had a very poor memory. There was a long pause. Sirhan stretched out and seemed tired for the first time. He asked Foster about life as a policeman.

"It's like any profession," said Foster. "There are cases where there's injustice. . . . Maybe you're just the victim of circumstances."

"Beautiful."

"Maybe if circumstances were different, it would be vice versa: I'd be on the bench and you'd be over here, you never know."

Sirhan told Foster he was the "complete opposite" of his stereotype of a policeman.

"Well, in some respects, I hope you think of me as just another human being," said Foster.

"We're all puppets," said Sirhan.[27]

* * *

Police chief Thomas Reddin called a news conference at seven a.m. in Parker Center, and as the press pack gathered upstairs, Officer Donald Day backed his camper truck up to the elevator exit of the police garage, so the prisoner could be discreetly transferred three blocks to the Halls of Justice without a Jack Ruby getting in the way.[28]

Reddin related a brief conversation with the prisoner. "He was very cool, very calm, very stable, and quite lucid. He almost appeared to be the calmest man in the room. He sounds well educated. Speaks good English with a slight Jamaican or Cuban accent and is a good conversationalist. . . . He was very relaxed and wanted to talk about just about everything except the events last night. If I were to judge him strictly on the basis of our conversation . . . I would say he was a gentleman."

* * *

As Reddin spoke, Sirhan was arraigned in the LA County Municipal Court by Judge Joan Dempsey Klein and advised of the charges against him.

"Do you have a name?" asked Judge Klein.

"John Doe," replied the prisoner, in white hospital pants, a blue denim shirt, and black slippers.

Judge Klein appointed public defender Richard Buckley to represent Mr. Doe and set bail at $250,000. Mr. Doe asked Buckley if he could speak to someone from the American Civil Liberties Union (ACLU), and then a team of sheriff's deputies escorted him to a waiting station wagon in the basement and put him on the floor in the back as they sped the short distance to the county jail.[29]

The prisoner was booked, weighed, and measured, and brought to the jail hospital on the second floor. X-rays were taken and revealed a fractured left finger and a sprained and swollen ankle. Around eight thirty, jail medics took a blood sample. Though there was no analysis for the influence of drugs or liquor, they performed a routine test for syphilis.[30]

* * *

Across town, Sergeant William Brandt visited the home of Gaymoard Mistri. Mistri had had dinner with the suspect the previous evening and immediately recognized his picture on TV, but now he couldn't remember his name. He called some friends who also knew the suspect, but they couldn't remember his name, either. Then Brandt got a call to go to Nash's Department Store in Pasadena. The weapon had been traced to a guy called "Joe" who worked there.[31]

* * *

Twenty-one-year-old Munir "Joe" Sirhan arrived at work at Nash's Department Store and saw news of the shooting on TV. His still unidentified brother's face flashed up on the screen, and he did a double take, then ran to his supervisor's office and asked if he could borrow his car.

"My brother just shot Kennedy."

Munir pulled up outside a modest, cream-colored clapboard cottage at 696 East Howard in Pasadena, darted inside, and woke his twenty-nine-year-old brother, Adel.

"Sirhan didn't come home last night, did he?" asked Munir.

"I don't know. Did he?" replied Adel, who worked nights as an oud player at the Fez nightclub.

Sirhan was not in his room.[32]

* * *

As Sergeant Brandt showed up at Nash's looking for "Joe," the Sirhan brothers were on their way to Pasadena Police Station. Fifteen minutes later, they walked into the station and up to the desk sergeant.

"Have you got a morning paper?" Adel asked.

"No," barked the desk sergeant, turning away. The brothers ran outside, and Adel spotted a newsstand up the street.

"I have to take my boss's car back," said Munir. As he sped away, Adel returned to the desk sergeant alone with a copy of the *Pasadena Independent*.

"I think this is my brother," he said, pointing to the picture of Sirhan on the front page. Now he had the sergeant's attention.

* * *

Munir returned to his supervisor's office to find a gentleman in a suit waiting for him. Special Agent Sullivan of the FBI's Pasadena office flashed his credentials.

"You better come with me," he told Munir.

"What for?"

"You bought a gun from George Erhard?" "No, my brother did."

Sullivan brought Erhard into the office.

"Is this the fellow who bought the gun?"

"Yes, it is," said Erhard.

"No, sir, you're mistaken. It was my brother Sirhan. We just saw his picture in the paper; my brother Adel's over at Pasadena Police Station."

They went there next.

* * *

Dr. Phillip Attalla visited Sirhan's cell in the county jail at 9:32 a.m. and applied a splint to his finger. Attalla saw no indications of narcotic withdrawal.

Sirhan was then examined by the jail's medical director, Dr. Marcus Crahan. He sat in bed as Crahan asked his personal history. Conscious of the stenographer in the room, Sirhan replied, "No comment," to questions about his age, nationality,

Sirhan's brothers Adel and Munir were the first to identify him as the suspect police had in custody.

family background, education, occupation, and medical history. Otherwise, he was chatty and curious, at one point making a face and hunching his shoulders.

"What's the matter?" asked Dr. Crahan. "It's chilly."

"Are you cold?"

"Not cold."

"What do you mean?"

"No comment."

"You mean you're having a chill?"

"I have a very mild one."

It was June, but Sirhan was shivering, as he would later, every time the psychiatrists brought him out of a hypnotic trance. He asked who had put the bandage on his finger.

"Doctor Attalla . . . one of your countrymen," ventured Crahan, on a hunch the suspect was Jordanian as well.

"No comment," said Sirhan, loudly snapping his fingers and smiling at a jail deputy.

"I might sound overbearing. I haven't brushed my teeth in two days."

"We will see that you get a toothbrush," assured Crahan.

"What's the latest on it?" he asked the doctor.

"The discoveries of the mind, being a psychiatrist?"

"Well, there's something happening every day."

"Amplify. Elucidate," said Sirhan, sitting up and adjusting his pillow.[33]

* * *

In Dr. Crahan's report on the session, he described the suspect as "an alert, wary, composed and unconcerned well-oriented male of short, slight stature, whose gestures and facial expressions indicated him to be highly pleased with himself. There was no evidence of fear, apprehension, remorse or regret in his attitude. He spoke evenly, responding quickly and calmly, even when his reply was 'no comment.' His fingernails were closely bitten [but he had] a light, happy manner."[34]

Soon after Sirhan got back to his cell, he received a visit from A.L. ("Al") Wirin, chief counsel in Los Angeles for the ACLU. The suspect immediately asked the sheriff if his cell was bugged. Sheriff Pitchess assured him it wasn't, and once alone with the lawyer, the prisoner whispered his name into Wirin's ear. Sirhan asked Wirin to represent him, but Wirin explained that the ACLU took cases only on constitutional matters. There was no constitutional right to assassinate.

"And besides, I'm Jewish," he added.

"Oh, I'm dead already," groaned Sirhan.

But Wirin agreed to help Sirhan find an attorney, to ensure he got a fair trial.[35]

* * *

At ten fifteen, Sirhan's older brother Adel was interviewed by Sergeant Brandt, Officer Evans from Homicide, and FBI agent Sullivan. Adel confirmed that he lived at the house with his mother, Mary, and brothers Sirhan and Munir. The family were Jordanian and had arrived in the United States in 1957 via Christian sponsorship. Their father never settled and returned to Jordan a few months later.

Mary Sirhan was the head of the house and the owner of the property, but she was at work at the Westminster Presbyterian Nursery School. Adel didn't want to disturb her, so he gave Sergeant Brandt permission to search the home.[36]

As the brothers were being interviewed, Mayor Yorty held a news conference across town to announce the assailant's identity.

"His name appears to be . . . Sirhan . . . *S-I-R-H-A-N* . . . Sirhan, both names. He was born in the Arab part of Jerusalem and we believe he is Jordanian. His listed address is 696 East Howard in Pasadena."[37]

* * *

The brothers drove home with the investigators, arriving around eleven fifteen. They were met by LAPD Lieutenant King, three more officers, and a crowd of several hundred who had already gathered in front of the house after the mayor's broadcast.[38]

The three-bedroom clapboard cottage dated from the twenties, with a large, blooming magnolia tree in the front yard. A rusty lawn mower sat next to the garage, by a pile of empty Pepsi bottles. There was a lucky horseshoe on the front door, and an FBI agent dispersed reporters picking through a trash can at the side of the house.

Adel Sirhan unlocked the door and led the investigators to Sirhan's bedroom. Officer Evans and Sergeant Brandt searched it in the presence of Special Agent

The Sirhan house, 696 East Howard, Pasadena.

Mary Sirhan.

Sullivan and Adel while Lieutenant King and his men checked the rest of the house and the garage.

The search of Sirhan's room revealed a large green spiral notebook on the floor next to his bed and another spiral notebook on Sirhan's desk, next to some candles and a mirror. The second notebook contained writings pertaining to the shooting of Senator Kennedy.

> *May 18 9.45 AM—68*
> *My determination to eliminate R.F.K. is becoming more the more of an unshakable obsession . . . R.F.K. must die–RFK must be killed . . .*
> *Robert F. Kennedy must be assassinated before 5 June 68*

They also found a good deal of literature from the mystical order of the Rosicrucians; other readings on the occult; a brochure by Anthony Norvill entitled *Mental Projection—You Can Project Things Metaphysically Right into Being*; and a large white envelope, with the return address of the U.S. Treasury Department, Los Angeles, across the face of which was written in pencil, *RFK must be disposed of like his brother was.*[39]

These items were taken into custody to be booked as evidence, and the search concluded around noon. The group went back to Rampart Station, where Adel was reinterviewed and Mayor Yorty started poring over the notebooks. Reporters coming out of a police briefing at one fifteen bumped into Yorty on the stairs.

"What can you tell us about Sirhan Sirhan?" asked a reporter.

"Well, he was a member of numerous communist organizations, including the Rosicrucians."

"The Rosicrucians aren't a communist organization."

"Well . . ."

The reporter smiled disdainfully, and Yorty gave an impromptu press conference in the basement on what he'd seen in the notebooks.

"It appears that Sirhan Sirhan was a sort of loner who favored Communism of all types. He said the U.S. must fall . . . He does a lot of writing, pro-communist and anti-capitalist, anti–United States . . . When he was arrested, he had a column by David Lawrence about Robert Kennedy wanting the United States to supply arms to Israel . . . There's much scribbling, repeated phrases, many references to Senator Kennedy . . . They're not very clear, but there's a direct reference to the necessity to assassinate Senator Kennedy before June 5, 1968. I don't know why."[40]

June 5, 1968, was the first anniversary of the start of the Six-Day War, when Israeli forces quickly routed several Arab states and seized Jerusalem. Arab commentators were already suggesting Kennedy had become the personification of Sirhan's anti-Zionist hatred because of his recent pro-Israeli statements to woo the Jewish vote.[41]

The next day, Yorty blamed an "evil Communist organization" for inflaming the assassin. He was soon politely told to shut up by California Attorney General Thomas Lynch for fear the notebooks might be inadmissible as evidence—no search warrant had been obtained, and Yorty's disclosures might prejudice a fair trial.[42]

* * *

Back at the Sirhan house, a young student was charging onlookers a dollar each to take pictures in front of the house of the assassin. The police had cordoned off the street to traffic and formed a guard around the house.

Reporters canvassed Sirhan's neighbors for comments:

"He hated people with money."

"He was just a normal kid. He took cars and bikes apart and put them back together again."

"He was nice," said a black girl.

"Was he an angry fellow?" asked a reporter.

She shook her head. "He didn't show it."[43]

A twenty-eight-year-old Syrian friend admitted Sirhan was violently anti-Zionist and pro-Palestine, especially since the Arab-Israeli War. "But we all were. We all had strong feelings about it. He was no more active than anybody else and he's never made any threatening remarks about anybody."[44]

* * *

When Mrs. Sirhan heard of the shooting, she collapsed. "No. No. It can't be true. My son is a good boy. He has caused no trouble," she said. The next day, she sent a telegram to the Kennedys: "It hurts us very bad what has happened and we express our feelings with them and especially with the children and Mrs. Kennedy and with the mother and the father. I want them to know that I am really crying for them and we pray that God will make peace—really peace—in the heart of the people."[45]

* * *

At four that afternoon, the FBI finally located Sirhan's two-door, pink-and-white 1956 DeSoto on New Hampshire Avenue, a couple of blocks from the Ambassador. They found a parking ticket under the windshield, issued by the LAPD at 9:35 that morning.

The police obtained a search warrant and unlocked the car door with Sirhan's key at eleven thirty that evening. They found two expended .22-caliber slugs on the front passenger seat under a copy of the *Los Angeles Times*; an empty box of CCI Mini-Mag Hollow Point .22-caliber bullets in the glove compartment, along with a wallet containing Sirhan's identification and PCC library card; an unused Super-X long rifle bullet and a sales receipt showing a purchase on June 1 of four boxes of .22-caliber bullets for $3.99 at the Lock, Stock 'n Barrel gun and fishing equipment store in San Gabriel. A Lock, Stock 'n Barrel business card lay on the floor behind the passenger seat, and a book entitled *Healing—The Divine Art* sat on the backseat. Fingerprints were obtained from the steering wheel and glove compartment.[46]

* * *

Just before two the next morning, Frank Mankiewicz walked slowly down the street in front of Good Samaritan to a gymnasium strewn with cigarette butts and empty coffee cups to meet the press. Shoulders slumped, he faltered once or twice as he spoke:

"I have a short announcement to read, which I will read at this time. Senator Robert Francis Kennedy died at 1:44 a.m. today, June sixth, 1968. He was forty-two years old."[47]

* * *

The next morning, Soviet government newspaper *Izvestia* carried reports of Kennedy's death under the headline "Such Are the Jungles of America." Back home, the hopes of young students for a "new politics" were in tatters. "'Everything we tried to do now seems so futile. All the work intended to change the country is gone, snap, with one man with a gun. All of us are left asking, "Is politics really worth it?"'

"'Such a good man to have around,' a negro supporter said, 'and someone had to go and blow his head off.'"[48]

* * *

Sirhan woke the next morning in a windowless twelve-foot-square cell in an isolated wing of the county jail hospital ward. One officer stayed in his cell while another watched through a peephole in the door. He was very quiet and spent most of his time on his bunk because of his injuries.

Sirhan didn't ask to see his family but requested and was given copies of the *Los Angeles Times* and the *Herald Examiner* and two books on theosophy—*The Secret Doctrine,* by Madame Blavatsky, and *Talks on "At the Feet of the Master,"* by C.W. Leadbeater, based on the work of spiritual writer Krishnamurti.[49]

* * *

Dr. Crahan returned to see Sirhan later that morning. Sirhan was sticking to Wirin's instructions to remain silent but thanked Crahan for getting him a can of tuna—he didn't care much for meat.

"That's the best thing I have eaten in a long time," he said. "I appreciate it very much, sir. Make sure you put that down."

"You have quite a bad nail-biting habit, don't you?" said Dr. Crahan.

"That's a presumption there only. Now, sir, are you trying to judge me here? How shall I put it? Psychically, with psychiatry in mind or medicine in mind, internally?"

"Both. Do you have trouble with your eyes?"

"No comment."

"Are you studying spiritualism?"

"I am interested in it."

"Have you ever practiced it?"

"No comment."

After a long pause, the suspect complimented Dr. Crahan.

"I like your smile, Dr. Crahan. It seems very sincere."

"I try to be."

The stenographer continued to note Sirhan's behavior during lulls in the conversation.

"Does he practice spiritualism, sir?" Sirhan asked. "He was writing something there was nothing said about . . ."

"Have you ever used narcotics?" Crahan continued.

"No, sir."

"Do you drink?"

"Occasionally."

"Ever get drunk? What do you prefer to drink?"

"No comment."[50]

Then, A.L. Wirin arrived and interrupted the session, carrying a bundle of newspapers under his arm.

"Kennedy's dead," he said.

Sirhan hung his head, then looked up at Wirin with tears in his eyes. "Mr. Wirin, I'm a failure," he said. "I believe in love, and instead of showing love . . ." He didn't finish his sentence.[51]

* * *

When Dr. Crahan continued the interview after Wirin left, Sirhan's light, happy manner had changed considerably. He appeared exhausted and complained he hadn't been able to sleep. He asked the doctor for a sleeping pill and Crahan prescribed a half grain of phenobarbital.

Sirhan continued to complain of stomach cramps over the next few days. He was allowed to purchase candy bars and ate six or eight a day, neglecting his regular meals, so he was rationed to one bar daily.

From his observations of Sirhan and the writing in his notebooks, Dr. Crahan noted the following characteristics: "Emotional immaturity. Better than average intelligence. Idealistic. Impressionable. Easily led. Zealous. Inflammatory. Dogmatic. Stubborn. Self-sacrificial. Visionary. Worshipping. Fierce hatred and animosity. Detailed planning habits. Studious. Frugal. Hunger for Knowledge. Money hungry. Power proud. Opinionated. Arrogant. Self-assured. Patriotic. Egocentric."

"It is also noted in his writings," continued Dr. Crahan, "that he has had great mood swings from elation to moody depression and self-pity."

To Crahan, it was an open-and-shut case. Sirhan had repeatedly asked kitchen porter Jesus Perez what route Kennedy would take; practiced shooting hundreds of rounds beforehand; tried to shoot his way out of the crowd after shooting Kennedy, injuring five persons; and said, "I did it for my country," at the scene, indicating that his motivation was patriotic.

"There was no evidence that he had been drinking or was drunk when examined at the Central Jail at the time of his booking. He was in complete control of his faculties, was alert and even gleeful over his accomplishment."

Crahan thus concluded that Sirhan was legally sane at the time of the shooting and had the mental capacity to form the specific intent to commit the crime of murder.[52]

* * *

But strangely enough, in all the tapes and transcripts of these sessions after Sirhan's arrest, the name "Kennedy" was never mentioned. And, for the last forty years, Sirhan has insisted he has never been able to remember the shooting. He still insists he had no idea why he'd been arrested until he saw A.L. Wirin of the ACLU the following morning.

* * *

On the plane back to New York, as Ethel slept against her husband's coffin in the cabin, Ted Kennedy talked to family friend Sander Vanocur of the "faceless men" who had killed Jack, Medgar Evers, Martin Luther King, Jr., and now Bobby.

Ted was now effectively the father of sixteen children—his own, Jack's, and Bobby's.

Also onboard were Jackie Kennedy and Coretta King, who had flown to Los Angeles on hearing of the shooting. They joined Ethel midflight to mourn another loss—widows of the three great political assassinations of the sixties.[53]

* * *

The body lay in state in New York's St. Patrick's Cathedral all day Friday, as hundreds of thousands of mourners filed past. On Saturday, June 8, Ted Kennedy delivered a moving eulogy during the funeral mass:

> *My brother need not be idealized or enlarged in death beyond what he was in life. Let him be remembered simply as a good and decent man who saw wrong and tried to right it; who saw suffering and tried to heal it; who saw war and tried to stop it. As he said many times in many parts of this nation; to those he touched and those who sought to touch him; some men see things as they are and say "why?"; I dream things that never were and say "why not?"*[54]

The remains of Robert Francis Kennedy were then transported southbound on a slow-moving funeral train from New York to Washington, DC. The railway system stopped all northbound traffic, and thousands gathered along the route to pay tribute to Senator Kennedy as news came through from London that a man named James Earl Ray had been arrested for the murder of Martin Luther King, Jr.

At ten thirty that night, floodlights illuminated an open grave at Arlington National Cemetery, and fifteen hundred candles were distributed to mourners as the casket was borne from the train by thirteen pallbearers, including former astronaut John Glenn; former secretary of defense Robert McNamara; Senator Edward Kennedy; and Robert Kennedy's personal bodyguard, Bill Barry, wrongfooted by a last-minute route change that propelled Robert Kennedy into the pantry to a rendezvous with death.

THREE

AUTOPSY AND BALLISTICS

June 5, 12:45 a.m.

"Mr. Johnson, do you have the gun?" asked a police officer in the hallway of Central Receiving Hospital.

"No, I don't," replied Rafer as he waited anxiously with the deputy mayor and last rites were administered to the ailing senator.

Two plainclothes detectives from the LAPD's Intelligence Division, James Horrall and Jean Scherrer, rolled up in a patrol car. Rafer knew Jean—he was the head of VIP security with the department. Rafer now admitted he had the gun but would surrender it only at police headquarters. In the spirit of the times, he didn't trust the cops. Horrall and Scherrer played along and escorted Rafer to Good Samaritan Hospital, so he could check on the senator's condition after his transfer before going to the station.[1]

* * *

Thirty years later, Jean Scherrer recalled the night with author C. David Heymann. He claimed he was the LAPD official assigned to work with Kennedy when he came to Los Angeles. "RFK was very concerned about his image. He didn't want his followers—the poor, the blacks, the ethnic groups, the liberals—to see him surrounded by police types. I argued with him about it on the last day, but he told me not to come to the Ambassador that night."

While there was no official police presence at the hotel on election night, Scherrer went along anyway. "I had a premonition," he told Heymann. "I don't know why; I just did."

Scherrer's presence at the hotel was never disclosed by the LAPD. "Because I wasn't supposed to be there that evening," he recalled, "the *Los Angeles Times* referred to me as the man who wasn't there."[2]

* * *

The LAPD Intelligence Division log shows the "man who wasn't there" driving around in patrol car 3Y65 with his partner, James Horrall, that evening. Horrall was presumably at the hotel with Scherrer, but their presence there has not been explained to this day.

Perhaps they were there to keep an eye on things. Perhaps they made the anonymous call to Rampart to advise the watch commander of the shooting. Either way, Scherrer later told Heymann that for five thousand dollars, he could go into more detail about the assassination.[3]

* * *

At 12:25, car 3Y65 was notified of the shooting, and ten minutes later, Scherrer and Horrall were logged as en route to Central Receiving. The close timing suggests they may well have been the police escort for the ambulance carrying Robert Kennedy.

At 12:46, Scherrer and Horrall reported from Central Receiving that Kennedy had been shot once in the shoulder and once in the head. When Rafer Johnson showed up with Deputy Mayor Quinn, they confirmed he had the gun and left with Johnson for Good Samaritan. Twenty minutes later, Rafer showed them the gun and they called in a description of an Iver Johnson Cadet .22-caliber revolver.

By 1:20, car 3Y65 was en route to Rampart, and at 1:45, Rafer was deposited in an interrogation room with Sergeant McGann and Sergeant Calkins from Homicide. Rafer began to relate the events of the evening.

"Now, how many shots did you hear?" asked McGann.

"I don't really know," said Rafer. "I really stopped counting them. Once I saw—I thought it was a balloon, the first shot, because I didn't see anything. I

Sergeants J.M. Scherrer (left) and J. Horrall (right) outside Good Samaritan Hospital with Rafer Johnson, who has Sirhan's gun in his coat pocket.

looked, and then the second shot, I saw smoke and I saw something like . . . uh . . . the residue from a bullet or cap . . . a cap gun throwing off residue.

"And when I saw that, I fought my way through, and by the time I got there . . . the fellow had—I don't know how many shots. I couldn't count them, to tell you the truth, but I know it was like four or five. By the time I got there, Roosevelt Grier had him, and I jumped on him, grabbed the gun with Rosey, and someone else grabbed a leg, and you know, everybody just had him at that point."

"Was there anybody else that appeared to be with him?"

"No."

"Did he say anything?"

"No, nothing more than, 'Don't hurt me.' Everybody was trying to beat his brains out."

"Now, I understand you have possession of the gun."

"Yeah."

Johnson took the revolver out of his pocket.

"Well, we'll take possession of it here, and then we'll take it into evidence."

McGann's partner, Sergeant Calkins, took the small weapon in his palm and handled it gingerly, so it could be dusted for prints later on. It was a snub-nosed .22-caliber Iver Johnson Cadet revolver with a double-action, eight-bullet cylinder and a two-and-a-half-inch barrel, serial number H-53725, a gun so small, some witnesses had thought it was a toy.[4]

* * *

June 5, 1 a.m.

DeWayne Wolfer got a call at home, summoning him to the Ambassador. Wolfer was the chief criminalist at the LAPD's Scientific Investigation Division, charged with investigating the firearms evidence in the shooting—what weapons were used, tracing the flight paths of the bullets, and so on.

He arrived at the hotel at two a.m. with Officer William Lee and civilian police photographer Charles Collier. Wolfer asked Collier to take orientation photos of the pantry as Wolfer and Lee searched the crime scene for physical evidence. Collier was instructed to "photograph everything," so he set about documenting the numerous holes in doorframes, door hinges, and ceiling tiles that could possibly be bullet holes. The public wouldn't see these photographs for another twenty years.

The ballistics team continued to search the crime scene until early afternoon, sweeping the entire floor of the pantry and backstage anteroom for evidence. They left with two ceiling panels and two boards from a doorframe, which were booked into evidence, so they could be checked for possible bullet holes.[5]

* * *

At this point, Wolfer knew that six people had been shot:

Reports from the hospital suggested that Kennedy had been hit twice—once behind the right ear and once in the right shoulder. One bullet had fragmented in Kennedy's brain; the other was still lodged in his neck.

Paul Schrade had a superficial wound in his forehead, just above the hairline. Two bullet fragments were found in his scalp, the rest of the bullet seemingly exiting through a hole several centimeters behind the entry point.

Further bullets were recovered from Ira Goldstein's left buttock; Irwin Stroll's left shin; William Weisel's left abdomen; and the center of Elizabeth Evans's forehead, one inch below the hairline.

Two bullet fragments were recovered from Evans during surgery. Their combined weight indicated that a quarter of the bullet was missing. There was no exit wound in her scalp, suggesting that the bullet may have struck something before it hit her.

All wounds were superficial, with the exception of the bullet fragments lodged in the senator's brain. In total, there were six victims and seven wounds. Sirhan's gun held eight bullets, so allowing for one stray shot, the balance sheet seemed pretty straightforward.[6]

* * *

After lunch, Wolfer went over to Central Property at Parker Center and retrieved the Stroll and Goldstein bullets and Sirhan's gun. Back in his crime lab, Wolfer rotated the chamber of the gun to see all eight empty shell casings still inside, indicating that all eight bullets had been fired.

Each shell casing was stamped as CCI brand Mini-Mag, hollow-nosed ammunition, used mainly for hunting. These hollow points were high-velocity bullets, which mushroomed on impact, expanding to cause maximum damage, explaining the devastation in the senator's brain.

After examining the gun, Wolfer conducted chemical and microscopic tests on a ceiling panel to check for bullet holes. When he X-rayed the panel early the next morning, he found two more bullet holes.[7]

June 6, 3 a.m.

Dr. Thomas Noguchi, LA County coroner and chief medical examiner, hurried into Good Samaritan's basement autopsy room, ready to go to work. For more than six hours, Noguchi and his two assistants labored under the gaze of three top military pathologists and sundry representatives of the LAPD, FBI, Secret Service, and sheriff's office.

Noguchi concluded that the cause of death was a gunshot wound to the right mastoid bone, one inch behind the right ear, penetrating the brain. He described three separate bullet wounds and numbered them for ease of identification—the numbers didn't designate the sequence of shots:

Bullet number 1 penetrated the right mastoid bone and traveled upward to sever the branches of the superior cerebral artery. The bullet exploded and fragmented on impact. The largest fragment lodged to the right of the brain stem, causing extensive damage on the right side of the brain, marked swelling of the brain, and flattening of the brain stem due to pressure buildup.

Bullet number 2 entered the back of the right armpit in a right-to-left direction and exited clean through the front of the right shoulder.

Bullet number 3 entered the right armpit one inch below bullet number two and traveled in an almost parallel pathway, burrowing through the muscle structure in the back of the neck and lodging just short of the sixth cervical vertebra, where the neck meets the back.

At 8:40 a.m., Noguchi retrieved this bullet by making a small incision in the back of the neck and pulling it out gently with his right index finger. Noguchi scratched his initials on the base of the bullet along with the last two digits of the case autopsy number, 68–5731: TN 31. He handed it to Bill Jordan, who nodded grimly, surprised to see the bullet still in "near-perfect" condition.[8]

* * *

Dr. Noguchi's autopsy findings give us the clearest indication of the firing position of Kennedy's assassin. All three shots that hit the senator were fired right-to-left and upward, from a shooting position slightly behind and to the right of Kennedy.

The fatal shot was fired at an angle of fifteen degrees upward, from thirty degrees behind; the bullet that exited clean through the shoulder flew fifty-nine degrees upward, from twenty-five degrees behind; and the bullet removed from Kennedy's neck traveled sixty-seven degrees upward, from five and a half degrees in front. The rotation of Kennedy's body as he spun left and raised his arm to avoid the shots would explain the variations.

So Wolfer now had three Kennedy wounds instead of two, and similar upward trajectories, suggesting that all three bullets were fired from one gun, behind and to the right of the senator. The bullet that had exited Kennedy's right shoulder was missing, and with the five other victim wounds and the two holes in the ceiling panels, Wolfer's bullet count was near the limit of what could reasonably have been achieved with one gun.

As Dr. Noguchi examined the brain, Wolfer spent most of the day examining the victim bullets.

The standard procedure in matching evidence bullets to a gun is to test-fire the same brand—and preferably the same batch—of ammunition into a water recovery tank, so the test bullet can be recovered with no impact damage.

There are imperfections in the barrel, or the "rifling," of a gun that are unique to that weapon. These imperfections scratch the bullet as it passes through the barrel, producing on the bullet a series of valleys and ridges called "striation marks."

By placing a test bullet and an evidence bullet on two stages of a comparison microscope, the criminalist can look through the common eyepiece at both bullets, line them up, and compare the striations to see whether they match.

According to Wolfer, some time after he retrieved the gun, he test-fired eight bullets into a water recovery tank. One jumped out of the tank and was lost, so he had seven test bullets to compare to the victim bullets.[9]

On the morning of June 6, Wolfer examined the Goldstein and Stroll bullets under a comparison microscope and concluded they were both CCI Mini-Mag ammunition, with the same rifling specifications as the Sirhan weapon.

The bullet fragments retrieved from the brain at autopsy were sent to the FBI lab in Washington, DC, for analysis, but Wolfer received the Kennedy neck bullet from Rampart detectives at three fifteen p.m. and the Weisel bullet and the Schrade and Evans fragments by early evening. He could now try to match six of the victim bullets to Sirhan's gun by comparing them to the test bullets.

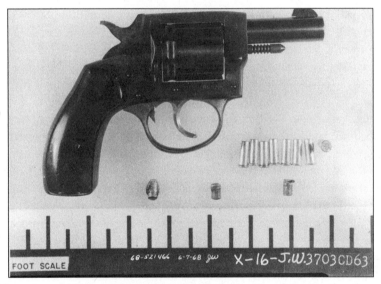

The Sirhan gun, with the eight expended shell casings found in the chamber, and the Weisel, Goldstein, and Kennedy bullets Wolfer examined.

Three of the bullets were too badly damaged for comparison purposes, but the Kennedy neck bullet, the Weisel bullet, and the Goldstein bullet could be compared to the best of the test bullets to determine if they were, in fact, fired from Sirhan's gun. Wolfer worked until one in the morning, trying to find a match.[10]

* * *

Trajectory studies by Robert Joling, based on Dr. Noguchi's autopsy findings.

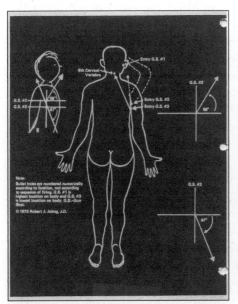

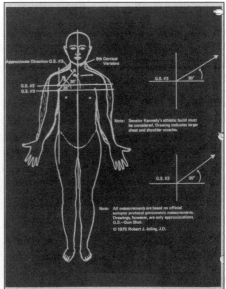

The trajectories of the gunshots that hit Robert Kennedy, as seen from behind. Autopsy measurements indicated that the armpit shots (G.S. #2 and #3) were fired at upward angles of 59 and 67 degrees, respectively, as viewed from behind and to the right.

The trajectories of the gunshots that hit Robert Kennedy, as seen from the front. Autopsy measurements indicated that the armpit shots (G.S. #2 and #3) were fired at upward angles of 35 and 30 degrees, respectively, as viewed frontally.

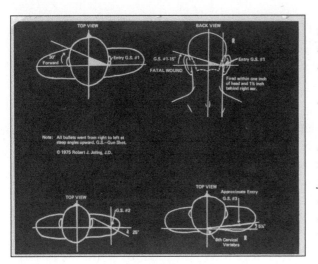

(Top) Top and back views of the fatal gunshot, fired at an angle of 15 degrees upward and 30 degrees forward. (Bottom) Top views of the armpit shots.

G.S. #2 was fired from 25 degrees behind and exited through the chest. G.S. #3 was fired from five-and-a-half degrees in front of Kennedy and lodged in the senator's neck.

The next day, Wolfer was called to present his findings before the grand jury and outlined his credentials to the court. He had a bachelor's degree from the University of Southern California, "where I was a pre-med student, [with] a background in the field of chemistry, physics, and all types of laboratory technique courses." (In fact, Wolfer had been a zoology major, with mostly C and D grades.) He subsequently worked for seventeen years at the LAPD's Crime Laboratory.

"Is it possible to read markings on a bullet that is fired from a gun and determine what gun that bullet was fired from?" he was asked.

"Yes, it is." Wolfer described the standard procedure to the jury and concluded, "If we can line up a majority of the lines, we can say it was fired from this revolver and no other."

Wolfer confirmed he had examined Grand Jury Exhibits 5-A (the Kennedy neck bullet) and 7 (the Sirhan gun). He then introduced an evidence envelope for Exhibit 5-B, containing four of the spent slugs he had fired into the water tank from the Sirhan gun. He had kept the three better test bullets for further use.

"Did you compare the markings on the test slugs in 5-B with the questioned bullet, 5-A [the Kennedy neck bullet]?"

"I did."

"And from your comparison of the two bullets, were you able to form any opinion as to the bullet 5-A?"

"I was."

"What is that opinion?"

"That the bullet in People's 5-A here marked as the bullet from Robert Kennedy was fired in the exhibit, the revolver here, People's Exhibit Number 7 at some time. Yes, it was fired in the weapon."

"Any question about that?"

"No."

The proceedings of the grand jury were then concluded, and Sirhan's gun and the victim bullets were sealed by court order until the trial.[11]

* * *

Wolfer's subsequent LAPD report confirmed that all three victim bullets came from Sirhan's gun "and no other"—that, in effect, he had successfully matched the Kennedy neck bullet, the Weisel bullet, and the Goldstein bullet to the test bullets.

He determined that all bullets recovered, including the fatal fragments found in Kennedy's brain, were the same CCI Mini-Mag ammunition, matching the shell casings found in Sirhan's revolver. So, allowing for the missing bullet that exited Kennedy's right shoulder, the bullet fragments in his brain, the bullet recovered from his neck, and Evans, Schrade, Stroll, Weisel, and Goldstein, this accounted for all eight shots.[12]

* * *

But seven years later, when Sirhan's gun was again refired after huge controversy over botched ballistics in this case, Wolfer's testimony was found to be false. Seven independent firearms examiners found that the three best victim bullets (Kennedy neck, Weisel, and Goldstein) could be matched to each other but *not* to Sirhan's gun. The examiners tried to retrace Wolfer's steps and match these three victim bullets to the test bullets Wolfer fired into the water tank, but they found that the barrel of Sirhan's gun had not left strong enough impressions on the test bullets to create striations that could be positively matched to the markings on the victim bullets.[13]

A letter buried in LAPD files seems to indicate Police Chief Reddin and Chief Houghton of Special Unit Senator (SUS, the LAPD unit set up to conduct the investigation) were aware of this from the beginning. In a reply dated July 1, 1968, to Lieutenant Hewitt in Salem, Oregon, they wrote, "In regard to your Teletype of 6-5-68, we are unable to fulfill your request for test shot from Iver Johnson Cadet .22 Revolver. This revolver and test bullet were received by the Grand Jury as evidence on 6-7-68. Micro photos of test bullet too poor for comparison."

Photomicrographs are photographic enlargements of bullet striations taken to show a match. As the striations on the test bullets were too poor for comparison, Sirhan's gun has never been positively matched to the victim bullets in this case.

The letter concludes, "We will be happy to accommodate you when the weapon becomes available to us for further testing." Why further testing was necessary is not explained. As far as we know, no further testing took place until the grand jury ordered the retesting of the firearms evidence in 1975.[14]

The work of this panel is discussed further in chapter 14.

* * *

The first witness called before the grand jury on June 7 was Dr. Noguchi. He pronounced the cause of death as a "gunshot wound of the right mastoid, penetrating the brain."

Noguchi noted a gunpowder tattoo one inch long around the fatal entry wound on the edge of Kennedy's right ear. He didn't want to preempt firearm tests, but "the position of the tattooing and the powder on the edge of the right ear indicate that . . . the muzzle distance was very, very close."

"What is the maximum distance the gun could have been from the senator and still have left these powder burns?" asked Deputy DA John Miner.

"Allowing a variation, I don't think it will be more than two or three inches from the edge of the right ear," replied Dr. Noguchi.

The armpit shots would not have been fatal, he said, but to trace their trajectories, he had to place the senator's right arm forward almost ninety degrees, suggesting Kennedy's arm was raised to defend himself at the time of these shots.

The fatal bullet was so fragmented, Dr. Noguchi could not even confirm its caliber, so the only Kennedy bullet suitable for comparison with Sirhan's gun was the bullet retrieved from the base of the senator's neck.

Miner asked Noguchi to identify this bullet, Grand Jury Exhibit 5-A, in an evidence envelope.

"How do you know that is the bullet you retrieved?" asked Miner.

"Well, I placed my identifying mark, TN, my initials, and last number of Medical Examiner Coroner's Case Number 68–5731; so I placed '31'—it is very clearly visible on the base of this bullet," said Dr. Noguchi.

This identifying mark was crucial to ensure the continuity of the physical evidence. This was the only bullet that could directly link Sirhan's gun to the shooting of Robert Kennedy. This was the last record of this identifying mark the public would ever see.[15]

* * *

After his grand jury testimony, one of the deputy district attorneys, surprised at the muzzle distance, approached Noguchi.

"Tom, are you sure three inches?" he asked. "Do you mean three inches or three feet?" If Noguchi had made a mistake, he said, now was the time to correct it.

"It was inches, not feet," Noguchi said in disbelief.[16]

* * *

This prosecutor immediately realized they had a problem—none of the eyewitnesses in the pantry placed Sirhan's gun that close to Bobby Kennedy. Five witnesses were called before the grand jury that day—hotel assistant maître d's Karl Uecker and Eddie Minasian, kitchen porter Jesus Perez, waiter Vincent Di Pierro, and shooting victim Irwin Stroll.

Uecker said he grabbed Sirhan and diverted his gun hand after the first two shots. Uecker's body was between Kennedy and Sirhan, so Sirhan had to shoot around him for the first two shots. He wasn't asked about muzzle distance.

Minasian saw the suspect holding the gun at shoulder height and pointing it at the senator.

"Could you tell how close to the senator the barrel of that gun would be?"

"Approximately three feet," said Minasian.

Vincent Di Pierro was five feet away from the senator when the shooting started.

"How close did the suspect get to the senator?"

"It couldn't have been more than six feet . . . because Mr. Uecker was almost right next to him. He was pushing the crowd back."

"How close to the senator was the suspect when this gun started firing?"

"Four feet—four to six feet."

"What did he do?"

"He kind of went around Mr. Uecker and he looked like he pulled his hand out from here and came around. And when he stuck the gun, he looked like he was on tiptoes because he wasn't that tall. Mr. Uecker is quite huge, and he tried to get Mr. Uecker out of the way, and he shot him."[17]

* * *

So, within two days of the shooting, on the first morning of testimony, there seemed to be an immediate discrepancy between the muzzle distance of two to three inches described by Noguchi and of at least three feet observed by Minasian and Di Pierro. But, strangely, apart from the deputy DA, nobody seemed to pick up on it.

* * *

Four days later, on June 11, Wolfer picked up some hogs' ears from butchers at Farmer John's market and spent the day with Dr. Noguchi.

First, they studied X-rays and autopsy photos of Kennedy's wounds. They then went over to the police academy to conduct muzzle-distance tests to determine more precisely how close the gun was to Kennedy at the time of the fatal shot.

They tried to re-create the density of the very distinctive powder tattoo found around Kennedy's right mastoid and on the edge of his right ear at autopsy by firing at various muzzle distances into pig ears, used to simulate human flesh. The ear was nailed to a board covered in a single layer of white muslin, and later, shots were fired into the muslin itself in search of a powder density that matched the powder patterns around Kennedy's right mastoid in the autopsy photographs.[18]

* * *

Because the Sirhan gun had been taken into evidence by the grand jury, Wolfer supplied a test gun "of nearly identical manufacture." Wolfer also went back to the Lock, Stock 'n Barrel gun shop in San Gabriel and bought the same brand of CCI Mini-Mag ammunition Sirhan had bought there ten days before.

At the end of the session, they concluded that "with the test weapon at an angle of fifteen degrees upward and thirty degrees forward (to correspond with the trajectory of the fatal bullet), the test pattern is most similar . . . at a distance of one inch."

Yet not one credible witness has ever placed the Sirhan gun an inch from Kennedy's head. Let's look at what witnesses have said over the years about the muzzle distance.

* * *

At the end of their investigation, the LAPD drew up a list of their "five best witnesses" for the prosecution—those closest to the senator at the time of the shooting who could best describe what happened: assistant maître d' Karl Uecker, Unruh aide Frank Burns, waiter Martin Patrusky, busboy Juan Romero, and kitchen porter Jesus Perez. But during their police interviews and during the trial, none of these men were asked how close the gun was to Kennedy's head.[19]

Juan Romero told the FBI he had just finishing shaking hands with the senator and looked up to see the gun "approximately one yard from the senator's head."[20]

Karl Uecker later told Congressman Allard Lowenstein, a close friend of Robert Kennedy's, "The gun was one and a half to two feet away. There is no way the shots described in the autopsy could have come from Sirhan's gun. . . . Sirhan never got close enough for a point blank shot. Never!"[21]

Frank Burns was interviewed by Dan Rather for the 1976 documentary *The American Assassins*. Asked if the gun was ever close enough to inflict the wounds described in the autopsy, Burns replied, "No, never closer than a foot and a half to two feet."

"You know, the theory is that the gun was held about this close?" said Rather, indicating an inch.

"Well, it wasn't that gun," replied Burns.

"No way?"

"No way."[22]

Martin Patrusky told attorney Vincent Bugliosi, "I would estimate the closest the muzzle of Sirhan's gun got to Kennedy was approximately three feet."[23]

Jesus Perez, who used a magnifying glass to read because of poor vision, has never been asked about the muzzle distance. When the police asked him about the size of the gun, he said, "It was big like this," gesturing.

"It looked awful big to you, huh? You thought it was about a foot long?"

"Yeah."[24]

* * *

But a number of other witnesses had a clear enough view to express an opinion on the muzzle distance. Ace guard Thane Cesar was right behind Kennedy and estimated "two feet."

Writer Pete Hamill told the police that "Sirhan was four to six feet away and the gun was about two feet from" Kennedy.

At trial, Valerie Schulte testified that Sirhan was "three yards" away.[25]

Richard Lubic was at Kennedy's right side when Sirhan appeared: "The muzzle of the gun was two to three feet away from Senator Kennedy's head. It is nonsense to say that he fired bullets into Kennedy from a distance of one to two inches, since his gun was never anywhere that near to Senator Kennedy."

When I recently interviewed another witness, photographer Evan Freed, his estimate of the muzzle distance was "five feet."[26]

Finally, there's San Diego high school student Lisa Urso. The summary of her initial police interview states, "From what she observed, she thought the shot was fired from 'point-blank' range."

In 1977, after years besieged by second-gun theories, the LA district attorney's office decided to fly Urso back from Hawaii to settle the distance issue once and for all. Under heavy security, Urso was wined and dined and asked to participate in a videotaped reconstruction. A VHS tape of the reenactment was discovered by researcher Greg Stone in 1985.

When she saw the first flash, Urso said she was standing close enough to touch Sirhan.

"How far was this man from the senator?" she was asked.

"Well, from where I was standing, it looked, maybe, between three and five feet." She said the first shot was closer to her head than to Kennedy's.[27]

Only one witness put the muzzle distance inside a foot and a half during the original investigation. Bill Barry put the distance at twelve inches, but he also told the LAPD that he was six to nine feet behind the senator, moving up on him when the firing started, and that he didn't even see the first shot.[28]

* * *

When the second-gun controversy began in the early seventies, *LA Times* photographer Boris Yaro claimed the distance was "within a foot or less." But Yaro was looking through the distorting viewfinder of his camera lens. He told the FBI two days after the shooting that "the senator and the assailant were little more than silhouettes."[29]

Several years after the shooting, Vincent Di Pierro also claimed Sirhan's gun came within inches of Kennedy's head, but his earlier grand jury testimony placed Sirhan "four to six feet" from the senator.[30]

Muzzle distance became such a hot issue, Sirhan's researcher Lynn Mangan actually sent him a tape measure and asked him to extend his arm and measure his reach. With a clenched fist (as if holding a gun), Sirhan's reach was two feet, so Di Pierro's estimate of the muzzle distance was effectively "two to four feet."

The LAPD measured Sirhan as five-two, and he measured himself as five-four. As Robert Kennedy stood five-ten, their height difference might account for the upward trajectory of the shots, but, according to the witnesses, Sirhan never got that close to the senator.[31]

* * *

After the grand jury hearing, there should have been questions about the muzzle distance, but nobody blinked. The grand jury took Wolfer's word that the bullets matched the Sirhan gun, but Wolfer still had a problem accounting for where all the bullets went.

Up to now, the balance sheet looked healthy: eight shots, six victims, eight wounds. But when Wolfer examined Kennedy's suit coat the morning before testifying in front of the grand jury, he found two more holes in it.

As expected, there were two holes of entry made by the shots under the armpit and an exit hole where the bullet passed clean out through the right shoulder. A Walker's H-acid test conducted on the area of the two entry wounds indicated that the muzzle of the gun was held at a distance of between one and six inches from the coat at the time the senator was shot.

But Wolfer also found two more holes in the right shoulder just below the seam, indicating that the senator had been hit a fourth time. This time, the bullet had entered his coat just below the armpit, missed his body, went through his raised shoulder pad, and exited just below the coat seam.

This shot had the steepest trajectory of all—eighty degrees from behind—so, again, it's likely the senator's arm was raised to ward off attack at the time, accounting for the bunching of his shoulder pad.[32]

This gave Wolfer a lot to think about. On Tuesday, June 11, after the tests with the pig ears, he went back to the Ambassador pantry with Dr. Noguchi and Officer Lee and spent the afternoon "doing ballistic studies and reconstructing the crime scene."

The photographs of this session—released twenty years later—are intriguing. Dr. Noguchi assists Wolfer as they take turns trying on a suit coat through which two metal rods are threaded to simulate the sharp upward angles of the shots. The two rods clearly represent the bullet that exited Kennedy's right front shoulder and the bullet that went through the shoulder pad of his coat. Both bullets were missing, leaving only six bullets for the other seven wounds.

It's clear from the photographs that Wolfer believed the only possible trajectory for these bullets was that they flew up and hit the ceiling. Some of the photographs are taken from the floor, illustrating the point of view of a gunman firing from such a steep angle.

Ceiling panels had been removed and a lot of time seems to have been spent looking for ricochet marks in the plastered ceiling. In later photos, two rods run from the steam table to holes in the ceiling.

There are also photographs of Dr. Noguchi holding an LAPD ruler to four holes in the pantry doorframes and Wolfer and Lee holding rods to two possible ricochet marks high above each of the swinging doors and running rods from Sirhan's firing position up to these ricochets.

It was an extraordinary dilemma for Wolfer. He had testified, incorrectly, that all the victim bullets matched the Sirhan gun. Now he was walking a ballistic tightrope, trying to keep to a lone assassin while new bullet holes were being discovered almost daily, and the trajectories just did not add up to one gun.[33]

* * *

The other key factor to remember here is Kennedy's body position at the time of the first shot. Wolfer and Noguchi had him facing north, still shaking hands with the busboys. In photographs from the same session, Dr. Noguchi has drawn a pair of chalk shoes on the floor, with chalk arrows pointing backward to indicate where the senator fell. He then plays the part of Sirhan, cheating himself out a little from the steam table, just enough to fire at the requisite thirty-degree angle into the mastoid behind Kennedy's right ear. If you accept that Kennedy was turned to his left and you ignore the witness testimony about the muzzle distance, you can line up the trajectory for Sirhan to fire the fatal shot.

But, even if we accept this scenario, how do we explain the other three shots into Kennedy's suit coat from much steeper upward angles?

Virtually all the witnesses describe Sirhan's gun arm as fully extended and parallel to the floor. Not one witness describes the gun pointing upward. Frank Burns has it pointing slightly downward as the senator falls to the floor, and Boris Yaro has Sirhan jabbing violently downward, firing the gun as if he's stabbing Kennedy with a knife. None of these descriptions come close to the photographs of Noguchi and Wolfer, where metal rods run at very steep angles through the coat into the ceiling.[34]

And what of the other holes? Wolfer inexplicably didn't find time to X-ray the doorjamb from the pantry until the following Friday afternoon, June 14. Four days later, he returned to the Ambassador for more ballistic tests, and then received more bad news when he examined Ira Goldstein's pants. There were entry and exit holes in the left pant leg where a bullet passed clean through.[35]

Wolfer spent the next three weeks trying to figure out what happened. His log for the case finishes on June 20, but he didn't report his findings until July 8. A recurring question was asked at the weekly interagency meetings of the LAPD, FBI and district attorney's office—"Is Wolfer finished yet?"[36]

He was now under tremendous pressure. He'd already told the grand jury that the bullets matched Sirhan's gun. What was he going to do if he found that more than eight bullets had been fired? Would the public believe that Sirhan shot Kennedy and a second gunman missed?

On July 8, Wolfer presented his analysis of the bullet trajectories to SUS. Wolfer concluded the following:

Bullet one entered Kennedy's head behind the right ear, and fragments were recovered from his head and booked as evidence.[37]

Bullet two passed through the right shoulder pad of Kennedy's suit coat without entering his body and traveled upward at an eighty-degree angle, striking victim Schrade in the center of his forehead. "The bullet was recovered from Schrade's head and booked as evidence."

Bullet three entered Kennedy's right rear shoulder, seven inches below the top of the shoulder. The bullet was recovered from the sixth cervical vertebrae and booked as evidence.

Bullet four entered Kennedy's right rear back, one inch to the right of bullet three. The bullet traveled upward and forward and exited the victim's body through the right front chest. The bullet passed through the ceiling tile, striking the second plastered ceiling, and was lost somewhere in the ceiling interspace.

Wolfer and Noguchi work on bullet trajectories while an officer wears Kennedy's coat.

Wolfer wears Kennedy's coat as Noguchi runs white rods through the bullet holes to simulate the steep trajectories.

Dr. Noguchi points to apparent bullet holes in the center divider between the swinging doors.

Bullet five struck victim Goldstein in the left rear buttock. This bullet was recovered from the victim and booked as evidence.

Bullet six passed through victim Goldstein's left pant leg without entering his body, struck the cement floor, and entered victim Stroll's leg. The bullet was later recovered and booked as evidence.

Bullet seven struck victim Weisel in the left abdomen and was recovered and booked.

Bullet eight pierced a one-inch-thick plaster ceiling tile, ricocheted off the inner ceiling, reentered through the tile, and struck victim Evans in the head, fifteen feet from the point of reentry from the ceiling. "The bullet was recovered from the victim's head and booked as evidence."

What had Wolfer done here to resolve his dilemma? His investigation revealed three holes in the ceiling but none in the door frames.

Bullet two went through Kennedy's shoulder pad at an eighty-degree angle, but instead of hitting the ceiling, Wolfer had it hitting Paul Schrade in the head. But Schrade told the FBI he was standing six to eight feet behind Kennedy.

Schrade told author Dan Moldea that the only way a bullet could pass through the shoulder pad of Kennedy's coat, travel upward at an eighty-degree angle, and strike him in the forehead would be "if I was nine feet tall or had my head on Kennedy's shoulder." It's impossible.[38]

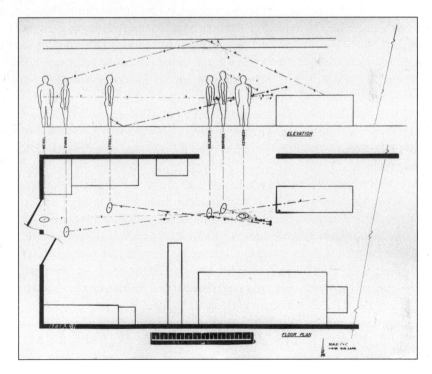

LAPD bullet trajectory diagram.

Wolfer didn't explain how bullet four, fired at a fifty-nine-degree angle, could have hit the ceiling, while bullet two, fired at a steeper trajectory, hit Paul Schrade. Both were fired back-to-front, from behind and to the right of the senator. How could one of these hit Schrade if he was "six to eight feet" behind Kennedy? It's also troubling that one of the key Kennedy bullets could get "lost somewhere in the ceiling interspace."

Bullet six, clean through Goldstein's pants into Stroll's shin, seems possible, but bullet eight, ricocheting downward from the ceiling to hit Elizabeth Evans, makes no sense at all.

Bullet eight pierced a one-inch-thick plaster ceiling tile, ricocheted off the inner ceiling, reentered through the tile, and struck victim Evans in the head, fifteen feet from the point of reentry from the ceiling. Two bullet fragments were recovered from the victim's head and booked as evidence.

The medical report described the Evans bullet entering "just below the hairline" and traveling "upward," not downward. Evans reported she was bending down to retrieve her shoe when she was hit. The bullet fragments recovered from her head retained three-quarters of the bullet's original weight despite piercing a one-inch-thick plaster ceiling tile, ricocheting off the inner ceiling, reentering through the tile, and striking Evans in the head.[39]

Three of these four "difficult" bullet trajectories are just not credible.

There is also evidence of another bullet hole. When author Philip Melanson interviewed Vincent Di Pierro in 1987, Di Pierro pulled out the orange turtleneck he was wearing that night. When Di Pierro washed the blood-splattered shirt, he discovered "two small, well-defined holes in the upper left sleeve" that weren't there previously. "Their size, shape and alignment appear consistent with a .22-caliber slug having passed clean through."

Di Pierro confirmed this to me in a later interview. When he showed the turtleneck to Detective John Howard before the trial, Howard said it was a bullet hole, and told Di Pierro to "keep it; we might need it." Howard never asked him about the shirt again.[40]

While it's impossible to be certain about the sequence of shots, the key question is: when was Paul Schrade hit in relation to Robert Kennedy? If Karl Uecker grabbed Sirhan's gun arm after the second shot and one of the first two bullets hit Paul Schrade, how could Sirhan have hit Kennedy four times at close range?

According to Wolfer, the fatal shot came first, then the shoulder-pad shot that hit Paul Schrade in the forehead, then the two shots to Kennedy's armpit as he fell.

As Kennedy lay on the floor and Paul Grieco tried to staunch the blood behind his right ear, the senator looked up and asked, "Is Paul all right?"

Grieco was almost certainly referring to Paul Schrade, walking right behind him. Eddie Minasian told the police he saw Schrade fall first, then Kennedy. Schrade remembered seeing more than one flash and "a crackling sound like electricity."[41]

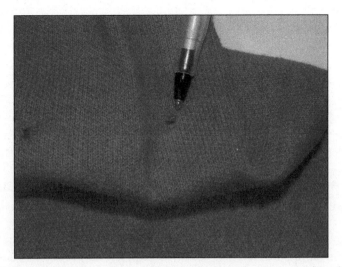

Bullet entry and exit holes in Vincent Di Pierro's orange turtleneck.

This suggests that as Kennedy turned his head and raised his arm to defend himself, he saw that Schrade had been hit behind him. It seems logical to deduce that as Kennedy tried to duck the bullets and was hit in the armpit and through the shoulder pad, a bullet hit Paul Schrade in the head. He went down; then the fatal shot hit Kennedy and he also slumped to the floor. But by then, Karl Uecker had already diverted Sirhan's gun.

* * *

So the muzzle distance, bullet trajectories, number of bullet holes, and sequence of shots all seem to indicate a second gun. The last key issue to examine is Kennedy's body position at the time of the first shot.

Wolfer had him turned all the way to his left, still shaking hands with busboy Juan Romero, facing north. This presents the right side of Kennedy's face to Sirhan, who was facing west toward the swinging doors. The upward angle of thirty degrees can be explained by the difference in height. Some witnesses even describe Sirhan standing on tiptoe to gain elevation—Richard Lubic thought he placed his right knee on the steam table to raise himself.[42]

In this position, could Sirhan have shot Kennedy from fifteen degrees behind? Well, yes, he could have. Frank Burns said the senator was turned more than ninety degrees to his left, slightly west of north. As Sirhan was facing directly west, this gives the shallow angle from behind described in the autopsy.

So the position of Kennedy's body at the time of the first shot is critically important. If he had turned away from the busboys to walk east again or even started to turn, it seems impossible for Sirhan to have fired the fatal shot from fifteen degrees behind.

The problem for Wolfer is that, according to Juan Romero, Kennedy *was* already moving away from him, turning east toward the Colonial Room.

Right after the shooting, Romero told the *Los Angeles Herald Examiner*, "He was shaking my hand and had just turned away when this guy came out and started shooting."

The next day, he told the FBI, "He held out his hand and I shook it. Senator Kennedy kept walking for approximately one or two steps"; then Romero saw a man to his left "who was smiling and who appeared to be reaching over someone in an effort to shake Senator Kennedy's hand." Then Romero heard gunfire and saw the gun in Sirhan's hand "approximately one yard" from Kennedy's head. Kennedy "placed his hands to his face and staggered backwards a few steps and slumped to the floor."

Romero told the LAPD that after they shook hands, "he turned around—no, he hadn't finished turning around, he just kept on walking, you know, sort of looking this way. He took two steps and all of a sudden I just seen somebody . . . reaching over." Romero also felt powder burns on his cheek.[43]

* * *

As Romero finished shaking hands with Kennedy, assistant maître d' Karl Uecker said he took hold of Kennedy's right hand and was pulling him forward again at the time of the first shot. Here are his three earliest accounts of what happened:

To the LAPD: "I saw him shaking hands with one of the dishwashers, and then he came back and I grabbed his hand again, and then at that time it happened." Sirhan suddenly appeared right in front of Uecker, pressed against the steam table, and reached around him and shot with his right hand. "I didn't even realize at the first shot that it was a gun, but by the second shot, I turned around and saw Kennedy falling down out of my hand. . . . I realized it must have been a gun; then I grabbed him, you know. . . . He was right in front of me. He was trying to get away from me and I was afraid if I let him loose, he's going to shoot me in the stomach, you know."

To the FBI: "While Kennedy was still observing [Romero], I took his hand to lead him along, somebody reached around me and before I knew what happened two shots were fired and the senator fell to the ground. I immediately grabbed the gun hand of the assailant and pushed him onto the steam table. During this time, he continued to fire the gun."

To the grand jury: "He shook hands again with one of the dishwashers. And while I was holding his hand, I was turning to my right towards the Colonial Room. At the same time, something rushed on my right side. At that time I didn't recognize what it was, and I saw some paper flying . . . paper or white pieces of things. Then I heard the first shot and the second shot right after that, and Mr. Kennedy fall out of my hand. I lost his hand. I looked for him, and I saw him falling down. And I turned around again, and I saw the man—right standing next to me [and] pushed the arm down against the steam table."

After the second shot, Uecker grabbed Sirhan's gun hand, got him in a head-lock, and tried to push the gun arm away from the crowd as Sirhan kept firing. He pushed Sirhan down to the middle of the steam tables and kept him in a headlock until the police arrived. He heard six or seven shots.[44]

In an interview with the DA's office three years later, Uecker said that when the shooting started, Kennedy was facing him and he had grasped the senator's right hand around the wrist to lead him from the pantry. "I took Senator Kennedy's hand again and said, 'Senator, we have to go.' . . . He was still talking towards the busboy and he starts looking at me and we start going."

Dr. Noguchi simulates Sirhan's firing position in relation to Kennedy. Note the many ceiling panels removed overhead.

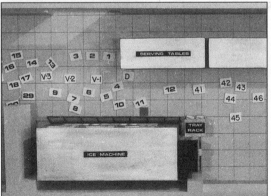

LAPD diagram of victim and witness positions in the pantry at the time of the shooting. D, Sirhan; V-1, Kennedy; V-2, Schrade; V-3, Goldstein; 1, Perez; 2, Romero; 3, Patrusky; 4, Uecker; 5, Burns; 6, Lubic; 7, Schulte; 8, Cesar; 9, Yaro; 10, Freed; 11, Minasian; 12, Aubry; 13, Drew; 14, Unruh; 17, Casden; 29, Di Pierro; 41, Freddy Plimpton; 42, Guy; 43, George Plimpton; 44, Kawalec; 45, Urso; 46, Royer.

After fifteen years in Los Angeles, Uecker returned to Dusseldorf in his native Germany, from where he provided this summary in 1975: "I have told the police and testified during the trial that there was a distance of at least one and a half feet between the muzzle of Sirhan's gun and [Senator Kennedy's] head. The revolver was directly in front of my nose. After Sirhan's second shot, I pushed his hand that held the revolver down and pushed him onto the steam table. There is no way the shots described in the autopsy could have come from Sirhan's gun. When I told this to the authorities, they told me that I was wrong. But I repeat now what I told them then: Sirhan never got close enough for a point-blank shot, never."[45]

* * *

Uecker's partner, Eddie Minasian, corroborated his story. He told the FBI he was three to four feet ahead of Uecker when he turned around, sensing the senator had fallen behind: "My partner, Karl, was on the senator's left, one or two steps in front of him. While the senator was shaking hands, I saw out of the right corner of my eyes someone darted behind my partner and reached around him, with a gun in his right hand. Before I could react, he fired two shots. My partner grabbed the gunman in a headlock, and I grabbed him around the waist, and forced him up against a steam table. We could not control his gun hand until after he fired a number of shots in rapid succession."

Minasian's statement to the LAPD is also very interesting: "All of a sudden, I looked up and someone reached around from the front—to the senator's left as he was facing him—I guess Karl was blocking my view because all I saw was the arm extended with the gun and I personally saw two shots fired. Then I saw Karl grab him and I jumped across and we grabbed him. Just before I grabbed him, I glanced to the left and I saw [Paul Schrade] go down first and then I saw the senator fall."

Minasian had Sirhan firing from the front left of Kennedy, not the back right, and indicated that Schrade fell first, then the senator.[46]

* * *

Waiter Martin Patrusky was standing to the right of Juan Romero, three or four feet from Kennedy, when the shooting started. Sirhan "came out from behind the tray rack, crossed in front of Uecker, and was standing against the steam table to Uecker's left." Patrusky thought he was going to shake hands with the senator; then he leaned around the left side of Uecker's body and pointed his gun over Uecker's left shoulder toward Kennedy. "The guy looked like he was smiling.

"At the time, Kennedy was leaning slightly to the left and shaking somebody's hand or reaching to shake someone's hand. . . . Kennedy's back was not facing Sirhan. Sirhan was slightly to the right front of Kennedy. I would estimate the closest the muzzle of Sirhan's gun got to Kennedy was approximately three feet. After Sirhan fired the first shot, Uecker grabbed Sirhan around the neck with one hand

and with his other hand he grabbed Sirhan's right wrist." As Sirhan continued to fire, Patrusky heard "a ping noise" come off the ceiling.[47]

* * *

Freelance writer Pete Hamill told the FBI he was walking along in front of Kennedy, looking back. "Kennedy turned to his left to shake hands with someone . . . and then turned to continue walking straight ahead" when what Hamill thought were five shots were fired "in very rapid succession." Hamill saw Sirhan standing "in front of and to Senator Kennedy's left about seven or eight feet with his arm fully extended and his face in tremendous concentration shooting a gun at Senator Kennedy. Senator Kennedy was falling to the floor and someone caught Senator Kennedy."[48]

Paul Schrade was walking directly behind Kennedy at the time of the first shot, six to eight feet back. He insisted that Kennedy had just finished shaking hands with the busboys and had turned to walk forward again when the shooting began.[49]

* * *

Vincent Di Pierro was five feet behind Kennedy, by the ice machines, at the time of the first shot. Within hours of the shooting, he told the police he saw Sirhan get down from the tray stacker and appear behind Karl Uecker at the steam table, with one hand covering the other "like if he had a sore hand or something. . . . I thought he was going to go and shake his hand . . . and then he kind of swung around and he went up on his . . . tiptoes and he stuck over with the gun and he shot, you know, and the first shot I don't know where it went, but I know it was either his second or third one that hit Mr. Kennedy and after that I had blood all over my face from where it hit his head."

What stuck in his mind about Sirhan was "the stupid smile he had on his face . . . kind of like an envious smile . . . villainous—I don't know how to describe it."

Two days later, Di Pierro told the FBI, "I saw this individual reach his right arm around Mr. Uecker and in his hand he had a revolver which was pointed directly at Senator Kennedy's head. The revolver was about 3–5 feet from Senator Kennedy's head. This individual then shot Senator Kennedy in the head. Senator Kennedy at this time threw his hands and arms up, reeled backwards and fell to the floor. . . . After the first shot was fired, I heard 3 more rapidly fired shots. At this time the individual standing next to me on my left [Paul Schrade] fell into my arms and I saw that he had been shot in the forehead." Then, Ira Goldstein fell on top of Di Pierro, pushing him to the floor. His glasses were covered in blood, and he thought it was Kennedy's.[50]

* * *

Other witnesses also saw Sirhan reach around Uecker. Guard Thane Cesar was behind Kennedy as he turned to shake hands with some busboys. He remembered the gun being two feet from Kennedy and said, "It looked like [Sirhan] was arching his arm a little bit like he was getting over the group of men in front of him."[51]

Kennedy aide Frank Burns, in a written statement to the LAPD on June 12, gave a slightly different picture. When Kennedy stopped to shake hands with the two busboys "I would judge that he turned slightly more than ninety degrees from his original direction of travel." Burns now caught up with him "and got perhaps half a step in front of him. I also turned to my left and was facing in the same direction as the senator. It was at this moment that I heard a noise like a string of firecrackers going off."

Burns felt a burning sensation on his cheek, turned his head to the right, and saw an arm extended, holding a gun, "about even with the front edge of the serving table. The arm did not appear to belong to anyone. I immediately glanced to my left toward the senator, and he was falling backward. He had thrown his hands up and his body appeared to be spinning to the left. I looked back toward the gun, and by then the person holding the gun had stepped forward past the edge of the serving table so that he was directly in front of me. He was aiming the gun down toward Senator Kennedy's falling body, and appeared to be shooting at him. My impression is the noise of the gunfire had ceased by then."

Burns had Kennedy turned slightly more than ninety degrees away from Sirhan at the time of the first shot and did not appear to see Uecker tackle Sirhan after the second shot. But he had Sirhan firing downward at Kennedy as Kennedy spun to the left and fell backward, totally inconsistent with the upward trajectory from behind described in the autopsy.

* * *

Valerie Schulte was about four to five feet behind Kennedy, to his right, when he turned to greet a group of kitchen workers lined up against the wall.

She was pushed sideways and forward by the crowd, "and then I saw this gun. It was a small gun. It looked like a cap gun"—at first, she thought it was a toy. "The suspect raised up, pushing it forward and started shooting. He kept shooting rapidly, more than four times. The gun seemed parallel to his head, aimed at the side or back of his head." "He appeared to be reaching over someone to point the gun."

She later testified at trial that she could see Sirhan "from his shoulders up" and that the gun arm "was pointed at the Senator's head . . . approximately five yards from me, approximately three yards from the Senator."[52]

* * *

But some witness testimony did suggest Sirhan might have acted alone. Freddy Plimpton was interviewed by the LAPD within hours of the shooting and told essentially the same story to the FBI three weeks later:

"As she was walking along, she was looking back at Senator Kennedy and saw him turn to his left to shake hands with a male kitchen employee. At this moment, Senator Kennedy gave a slight jump and his hands went up to the side of his face as if to push something away. She then saw an arm go up towards Senator Kennedy's head, but did not see a gun, heard shots and it was obvious to her that the Senator had been shot. All of this happened very quickly and some of it almost simultaneously.

"She saw Sirhan very clearly. She saw his arm go up towards Senator Kennedy's head but did not see the gun. She saw Sirhan's arm working and his eyes were narrow, the lines on his face were heavy and set and he was completely concentrated on what he was doing."

She was barely five feet tall but could see Sirhan very clearly and so thought "he was raised in some way. . . . He may have been sitting on a table or the [dense] crowd may have pushed him onto or against a table . . . before the shooting."

She thought that "Senator Kennedy, in turning to his left to shake hands, put himself in close range of Sirhan . . . and that when Senator Kennedy gave a slight jump, he was being shot in the arm. . . . There were about five shots in very rapid succession and two or three scattered shots after that."[53]

* * *

High school student Lisa Urso told the LAPD she was standing in the middle of the pantry, between the first and second steam tables, watching Kennedy shaking hands. A hotel employee was between her and the senator. "A male entered her field of vision three or four feet in front of her, to her left. She observed [him] take his right hand, move it across his body in the area of his waist and then move his hand back across his body, extend his arm in an upward position and at this time, she observed the gun and the flash of the first shot. She heard three shots. After the first shot, she recalled the Senator move his right hand in the vicinity of his right ear and possibly stagger forward slightly or backward. She was not sure."

Urso told author Philip Melanson that, at the time of the first shots, Kennedy was turned to his left, shaking hands with a busboy.[54]

* * *

TV producer Richard Lubic told the LAPD that when Kennedy "stopped to shake hands with part of the help, I was only an arm's length away from him and was reaching over to try and shake hands with him when I observed an arm with a gun come up and point at the Senator's head. I did not see the flash of the gun, but I heard one shot, short pause, five more shots. . . . I turned to my right and ducked down near the ice machine. When I looked up, the Senator's head was lying right next to my leg." Lubic got Kennedy's blood on his pants.

Lubic told the FBI he heard a voice say, "Kennedy, you son of a bitch," and heard two shots that sounded like a starter pistol at a track meet. He looked up to see a man with a gun on the left side of the pantry, with "his knee on a small table or air-conditioning unit [who] had lifted himself up on this knee to obtain elevation while shooting." He did not see the suspect's face but saw the gun and the arm of the assailant and noted the jerk of the gun and the arm caused by the recoil action.[55]

* * *

As is often the case with eyewitness testimony, it is hard to distill these statements into a definitive picture of what happened, but what can be said is that not one witness placed Sirhan's gun close enough to Kennedy and in the correct firing position to inflict the wounds observed in the autopsy.

* * *

Photographer Boris Yaro was the only witness who placed Sirhan's gun "less than a foot" from Kennedy.

The day after the shooting, he told the FBI, "I was about three feet behind and to the right of him and was trying to find [Kennedy's] head in my camera viewfinder when I heard what I thought were two explosions [like firecrackers]. . . . All of a sudden, the two people that had been blocking my view of the senator disappeared, leaving me with a clear view of what was happening.

"The senator and the assailant were little more than silhouettes, but the senator was backing up and putting his hands up in front of him in a protective effort. The suspect appeared to be lunging at the senator; I don't know which hand the gun was in—I didn't realize it was a gun until he started firing again—this time I could see flashes from the short-barreled muzzle. . . . I felt powder from the weapon strike my face. I thought I heard three shots; in retrospect I know it's more."

In a later LAPD interview, Yaro placed himself four to five feet from Kennedy. He put his camera up and heard two shots like firecrackers, and then three more. Two men standing next to the senator moved off to the right when the shooting started. He saw Kennedy backing away with his arms raised toward his head as Sirhan, "with a snub-nosed gun held extended and high," lunged toward the senator and fired several times. He then saw Kennedy slump to the floor.

In an article in the *LA Times* on June 6, Yaro said he was "getting ready to take a picture when the gunman started firing at point-blank range. Senator Kennedy didn't have a chance. Kennedy backed up against the kitchen freezers as the gunman fired. He cringed and threw his hands up over his face. The gunman moved closer toward the senator, holding a short-barreled revolver. Three or four people grabbed him but by then it was too late."

In the mid-seventies, Yaro emphasized the lunging at Kennedy: "'Boom! Boom! Boom! It was like he was stabbing at Kennedy each time he pulled the trigger. The Senator was backing up. He cringed. He turned. He put his hands over his face. As he backed up, he twisted and he turned, both ways. Later on, when you hear people say, 'Well, the angle of the bullet was this . . .' Well, for crying out loud, if anybody had seen how the Senator was backing up, they'd understand how there could be a bullet in the right side or a bullet in the left side just because of the way in which he was turned."

But shots from above, stabbing down at Kennedy, make no sense at all, and I don't find Yaro a very credible witness. As he was taking his famous pictures of Kennedy on the floor, a distraught woman kept telling him, "Don't take pictures."

"Lady, this is history," he told her. When she kept pulling his arm, he shoved her into the wall and kept shooting.[56]

* * *

In preparing for court, the LAPD final report noted that "because the statements of various witnesses essentially duplicated one another, it was decided that only certain witnesses would be necessary."

The five "best witnesses" the prosecution picked were Burns, Uecker, Patrusky, Romero, and Perez. Burns and Uecker disagreed on Kennedy's body position but vigorously stated that Sirhan's gun never got close enough to fire the fatal shot. Patrusky and Romero also placed the gun a yard away.

The five witnesses chosen "to establish Sirhan's approach from the ice machine to the Senator and the capture of Sirhan" included Urso, Di Pierro, and Minasian, all of whom placed the gun at least three feet away.

Boris Yaro, looking through his camera lens, didn't make the cut.[57]

* * *

On November 12 and 13, the DA's office and the LAPD set up camp at the Ambassador Hotel as key witnesses were called back to the pantry to reenact the shooting. Eddie Minasian was the only key witness missing from the group discussed above.

"It was critical that the statements of witnesses be as accurate as possible," so the DA's office shot film, video, and photographs.

These films and videos make for awkward viewing. No attempt is made to reenact the sharp upward angle of the armpit shots, and Karl Uecker pulls the "senator" forward before "Sirhan" can get close enough to fire the fatal shot. The report notes that "such inconsistencies which might arise from seeing the shooting at different angles had to be resolved to prevent the prosecutor's case from appearing to conflict on its own witnesses accounts."[58]

In practice, this meant cheating Sirhan closer with a stand-in, after Uecker had left.

* * *

On November 14, Wolfer returned to the pantry as Schrade, Goldstein, Stroll, and Evans came in to place themselves where they stood as the first shot was fired. Wolfer checked these positions, "verifying his findings as to the flight and direction of the bullets." Oh, to have been a fly on the wall as he watched Elizabeth Evans bend down to pick up her shoe and tried to explain to Paul Schrade how the bullet that flew up eighty degrees through Kennedy's coat hit him in the head.

* * *

As the case was prepared for trial, Sirhan's defense team didn't pick up on any of the inconsistencies between the evidence and Wolfer's findings, as we'll see in later chapters, but for Dr. Noguchi, doubts remained.

Two days after the shooting, he consulted Dr. Vincent Guinn, an expert in neutron-activation analysis (NAA), regarding possible testing of all bullets and bullet fragments recovered from the scene. NAA uses a tiny scraping from a bullet to analyze its chemical composition and determine whether bullets tested come from the same lead batch of the manufacturer and, hence, from the same gun. Dr. Guinn thought this would be extremely helpful in determining how many guns were used.

Wolfer later testified that he discussed such tests with Dr. Noguchi, "the District Attorney, the Attorney General, the FBI, our chief . . . the whole works."[59]

In early October, Dr. Noguchi met President Johnson at the White House for a conference on the case. The president asked Noguchi to get a federal laboratory to do the tests.

Deputy Medical Examiner Dr. Holloway then submitted a request to the FBI asking their laboratory to examine a specimen bullet and metallic deposits the bullet had left on bone and brain matter in Kennedy's head to determine if the lead deposits "originated from a bullet of the same lot" as used by Sirhan.

But as the LAPD was already handling the ballistics in the case, the FBI policy was not to get involved, and Dr. Guinn heard nothing more on the matter. The tests were never done.[60]

* * *

As the New Year began, the LAPD was still concerned about its ballistics work. On January 7, as jury selection began for Sirhan's trial, Chief Reddin and Robert Houghton, head of SUS, wrote to the FBI to thank them for their part in a "painstakingly thorough and accurate parallel investigation, commensurate with the historical significance of the incident":

> *Desiring to maintain the highest level of integrity in every phase of the investigation, the Chief of Police and District Attorney agree that a back-up analysis by personnel of your agency would obviously strengthen this phase of the investigation. A separate and independent analysis would be of value in later refuting any claims attacking the validity of the examination by a single department and should preclude disputes or frivolous complaints.*
>
> *If such an analysis can be made by your agency, the District Attorney recommends that in the interest of preserving the control and continuity of*

evidence that it be done at the [LAPD], using our laboratory facilities and equipment as required.

The letter was forwarded to J. Edgar Hoover from the FBI's LA office with a confidential briefing that is still redacted and a recommendation that, as the trial was under way, "there is little or nothing to be gained for the FBI in conducting these examinations." A week later, Hoover duly confirmed "that the Bureau will not re-examine the Kensalt firearms evidence."[61]

LA County sheriff Peter Pitchess stood ready to do an independent analysis of the evidence, but after the trial, DA Evelle Younger judged this "an unnecessary precaution. . . . At the trial, no issue was raised with respect to the [LAPD analysis] and there appears little likelihood that any questions will be raised in the future."[62]

This soon proved to be a major miscalculation.

* * *

Dr. Noguchi remained skeptical, later noting in his autobiography, "Eyewitnesses are notoriously unreliable but this time sheer unanimity was too phenomenal to dismiss. Not a single witness in that crowded kitchen had seen him fire behind Kennedy's ear at point-blank range. There are lessons to be learned from this case: Do not take for granted that the one who is in custody is the one who committed the crime. Until more is positively known of what happened that night, the existence of a second gunman remains a possibility. Thus I have never said that Sirhan Sirhan killed Robert Kennedy."[63]

FOUR

SIRHAN B. SIRHAN

Sirhan Bishara Sirhan was born in Jerusalem on March 19, 1944. His father, Bishara, worked in the city's sanitation department. The family of his mother, Mary, had lived in Jerusalem for generations. Sirhan was the name of an ancient tribe that roamed the Syrian Desert and means "wolf " in Arabic. Bishara means "good news."

When Sirhan was born, the city of Jerusalem was a part of Palestine. After the British withdrew in 1948, Sirhan lived in the Old City, ruled by Jordan until June 5, 1967, when Israel launched a preemptive attack on Arab forces, routing them in what came to be known as the Six-Day War. Israel then took full control of Jerusalem.

On May 18, 1968, Sirhan wrote that Robert Kennedy must be assassinated by June 5, 1968, and he rationalized the shooting as a channeling of his anger at American support for the Israelis and Kennedy's campaign promise to send fifty jet bombers to Israel.[1]

The Jewish claim to Palestine was rooted in Zionism, a movement founded by Jewish leaders in Europe based on biblical prophesies of a return to Zion by the Jewish people.

The dissolution of the Ottoman Empire after World War One led to a carve-up of territory by the Allied Powers in the Middle East. In 1917, British foreign minister Arthur Balfour published the Balfour Declaration, establishing long-term plans for a Jewish homeland in Palestine, and in 1922, with Zionist support, the League of Nations approved the British mandate of Palestine.

Over the next twenty years, the Jewish population in Palestine rose from 11 to 30 percent, accelerated by the oppression of the Jews by the Nazis in Germany. In 1939, under pressure from the Arab states and facing another war, a British white paper severely limited further Jewish immigration and aimed to establish Palestine as an independent state to be governed by both Arabs and Jews. Zionist terrorist groups resisted this move and assassinated Lord Moyne, the British minister in the Middle East, in 1944.[2]

* * *

Sirhan family photo, c. 1945. Sirhan as a baby in the arms of his mother, Mary (bottom left); father, Bishara (bottom right).

In March of that year, Sirhan was born in the feuding city of Jerusalem, the sixth child of the Sirhans. Two years later, his oldest brother, Munir, was run over and killed by a British army truck in the city. A seventh Sirhan child was born in 1947 and also called Munir, in his memory.[3]

Heavy fighting, destruction, sporadic sniping, and terrorist activity were a constant presence in Sirhan's early childhood. By 1947, the violence had brought Palestine close to a state of anarchy, and Britain announced plans to terminate its mandate. Arab leaders rejected a United Nations plan to partition the territory into separate Jewish and Arab states, and the fighting continued.[4]

On December 12, the Zionist terrorist group the Irgun, led by future Israeli prime minister Menachem Begin, bombed the Damascus Gate, killing twenty passersby. Five thousand casualties were reported over the next few months as armed skirmishes between Arab and Jewish paramilitary forces continued. The following April, the Irgun carried out the massacre of 120 Palestinian men, women, and children in the village of Deir Yassin. Palestinian survivors were driven like ancient slaves through the streets of Jerusalem by the celebrating terrorists.[5]

With the British mandate set to end on May 15, 1948, British forces began their withdrawal, and the Sirhan family left their home in the New City to seek refuge near the Jewish quarter of the Old City. They lived with friends or in church buildings with other refugees. Food and water were rationed in the fifteen refugee villages, and housing consisted of tents, bombed-out buildings, and caves.

On May 14, the last of the British withdrew and the Zionists proclaimed the establishment of the state of Israel. Neighboring Arab states immediately attacked Israel following its declaration of independence, and the 1948 Arab-Israeli War ensued.

On July 11, Arab forces subjected the Israeli sector of Jerusalem to its first air bombardment. The Jews retaliated by bombing the Arab sector, and Sirhan witnessed an Israeli soldier killing an Arab in front of his home.

Following the 1948 Arab-Israeli War, the 1949 Armistice Agreements between Israel and neighboring Arab states eliminated Palestine as a distinct territory. With the establishment of Israel, Jerusalem was divided, with Jordan taking the eastern parts, including the Old City, and Israel taking the western parts. But Jerusalem continued to be home to intense fighting and artillery bombardment between the Arab and Israeli sectors of the city from 1948 until the Sirhans left in 1957. Mary Sirhan advised investigators that Sirhan witnessed much shooting and bombing by Israeli planes during this time.[6]

* * *

In 1955, Mr. and Mrs. Haldor Lillenas were visiting Jordan when they were contacted by Sirhan's father, Bishara, about the possibility of coming to the United States. Mr. Lillenas, an ordained minister of the Church of the Nazarene, found the Sirhans to be "a worthy Christian family" and decided to sponsor them through the Church World Service and the Quakers. The family qualified for visas as Palestinian refugees and made plans to move to the United States in late 1956. But Sirhan "wanted to stay with his people" and briefly fled to a relative's house in Ramallah ten or fifteen miles away.

Sirhan traveled by ship to New York and arrived on January 12, 1957, with his father, Bishara; mother, Mary; brothers Adel and Munir; and sister Ayda. Lillenas refused to sponsor his other brothers, Sharif and Saidallah, as they were of legal age. Twelve-year-old Sirhan asked his mother if, by coming to the United States, he would get blond hair and blue eyes. From an early age, he would always refer to himself as a "Palestinian Arab" even though, technically, he was a Jordanian citizen.

The family traveled by train to Pasadena, California, where they were greeted three days later by Reverend Lillenas and his wife, with whom they stayed for the next three months.

With the help of the church, Mrs. Sirhan found a job as a housekeeper at the Westminster Presbyterian Nursery School in Pasadena. Ayda enrolled at Pasadena City College, and Sirhan and Munir were enrolled in the Pasadena City school system to continue their education.

Reverend Lillenas rented and furnished a house for the Sirhans, and they moved into their first home at 1321 North Mentor, Pasadena, later that spring.[7]

* * *

By the time Sirhan completed sixth grade, his father had become unsettled in his new life. At the end of July, he flew back to Jordan without telling the family, and they never saw him again.[8]

Contrary to some reports, the family was never Muslim. They belonged to the Greek Orthodox Church prior to leaving Jordan and began attending the First Baptist Church on arrival in Pasadena.[9]

Sirhan maintained a consistent C-plus average through high school. His teachers described him as quiet, well-mannered, reserved, and sensitive. One thought he had gone to a British school because all his responses were either "Yes, sir" or "No, sir." He was very proud of the fact that he was an Arab and had strong nationalistic feelings but expressed no strong political views. Teachers often remembered him only for his unique name.[10]

When Munir, the youngest Sirhan boy, got into fights with students who teased him about his name, fourteen-year-old Sirhan visited the school principal, Mr. Hornbeck. He said his mother spoke very little English, so he had taken it upon himself to visit Hornbeck to discuss Munir's difficulties. Munir's misconduct was a threat to the family honor, he said. It was important to preserve their good reputation. Hornbeck remembered Sirhan as a very intense boy who would visit him from time to time just to chat.[11]

Sirhan stood out among the predominantly white student body and was teased about his strange name and nationality. He was very obedient and well behaved but didn't mix or take part in school activities, appearing to be something of a loner.[12]

Carol Neal took classes with Sirhan in tenth grade and regarded him as an odd person since he didn't really mix with other students, go out with girls, or attend school dances or games. He frequently argued with the social studies teacher and, if not called upon during discussions, waved his hand and snapped his fingers to get the teacher's attention. But Sirhan's term paper on his country was held up by the teacher as an example of good work.[13]

Sirhan's eldest brothers, Sharif and Saidallah, were granted refugee status with the help of the Church World Service and joined the family in Pasadena in the summer of 1960. That September, Sirhan entered John Muir High School, graduating in June 1963. As he started his final year, Sharif and Saidallah moved out and Mary Sirhan bought the house at 696 East Howard. Sirhan's classes included two years of Russian and three years of German and California Cadet Corps—a military science course covering military history, drill, rifle range practice, and firearm safety.[14]

His eleventh-grade history teacher said he fell under the influence of fellow student Tom Good, who was very antigovernment and "the closest to being an anarchist of any boy that age." Good wasn't into rules and possibly influenced Sirhan's political development.[15]

* * *

Sirhan's first contact with the police came on August 4, 1963, when he approached Officer Cannow at an intersection near the Sirhan house and said he'd had an argument with his mother and was afraid to go home. Cannow brought him home and was told by Mrs. Sirhan that Sirhan was at an age where he would not listen to the advice of his elders. Mother and son started to argue again, so Cannow advised Sirhan to leave the house until he "cooled off."[16]

Sirhan had been working for gardener William Beveridge during his last year of school and now moved into a camper truck in Beveridge's garden for seven months before making up with his mother and returning to the family home.

Ron Sibbrel
Anna Silvera
Bonny Simmons
Marie Sims
Sirhan Sirhan
Elenore Skarsten
Beuna Smith

Sirhan's high school yearbook.

In September 1963, Sirhan entered Pasadena City College (PCC) and juggled part-time jobs as he worked his way through college. He continued to work as a gardener but by the following summer, was also working the night shift at a gas station while pulling shifts as a short-order cook at Peak's Hamburger House. He saved up some money and bought his first car for four hundred dollars—a pink-and-white 1956 DeSoto.

At the end of August 1964, he was caught napping in the car twice as the water from the sprinkler system he had going was running off the lawn onto the street. He got his marching orders, but despite this setback, his employers consistently described him as an excellent worker who got along well with his coworkers.

As he went back to college for his second year, he kept up the night shift at the service station. He didn't appear to have many friends, but he loved to talk about horses and his desire to become a jockey. His boss at the gas station thought he spent most of his money gambling at Santa Anita. One friend said he sometimes bet sixty to eighty dollars on one race.[17]

Another friend reported that Sirhan asked a few girls for dates but none accepted. The typical reaction was, "He's a nice guy, but I'd feel funny if I went out with him." Gwendalee Gum remembered one time, when she was a contestant for Carnival Queen at PCC, she was sitting in a booth collecting donations—a penny donation counted as one vote. Sirhan approached the booth and dropped in a ten-dollar bill. He later asked her for dates, but she declined.[18]

* * *

Sirhan wasn't politically active at college, but he held strong views on the Middle East, as did most of the Arab students. He wanted to be a diplomat and had a keen interest in languages, but in most courses, he got barely passing grades. When his beloved sister Ayda was diagnosed with leukemia in February 1965, Sirhan stayed home to care for her until her death on March 20 that year.

Two months later, he was dismissed from PCC for poor grades and poor attendance, with no leniency for his sister's illness. The pressure was building, and

Sirhan snapped. On June 7, he had an argument with his manager at work about cleaning duties and was fired from Richfield Gas Station.[19]

* * *

Where next for Sirhan? He had developed a love of horses and, with his five-foot-two-inch, 115-pound frame, dreamed of becoming a jockey. He went down to Santa Anita Race Track in August and asked English horse trainer Gordon Bowsher for a job. Sirhan offered to work for free initially, cleaning out stalls and walking horses, and finally landed a job on October 15 as a stable hand.

While working for Bowsher, Sirhan was introduced to theosophy and the occult by thirty-eight-year-old groom Thomas Rathke. He gave Sirhan a half dozen pages on meditation by a group called the Rosicrucians. Later, when Rathke moved north to Pleasanton, they kept in touch.

On December 16, 1965, Sirhan applied to the State Horse Racing Board for a Hot Walker's license and had his photo and fingerprints taken—records that would help identify him after the shooting.

On New Year's Day, he was issued his license and Bowsher let him start riding horses. But foreman John Shear said Sirhan was a poor rider, constantly being thrown. He allowed Sirhan to practice on nonthoroughbred ponies, but Sirhan quit at the end of March.[20]

* * *

On June 2, Sirhan was hired by Burt Altfillisch to work as an exercise boy at Granja Vista Del Rio Ranch in Corona for $375 a month. He left home and shared a motel room in Norco with an alcoholic named Edward Van Antwerp. He spent weeknights in his room, drinking large quantities of tea, and on weekends went home to Pasadena.[21]

A few weeks later, inspired by Tom Rathke, Sirhan applied for membership in the Ancient Mystical Order of the Rosy Cross (AMORC)—the Rosicrucians, a worldwide fraternal organization operating on a lodge system, exploring mysticism and the occult.

On his application, he indicated he'd been a student of metaphysics, psychology, and philosophy for three years and "by reading your book 'Mastery of Life,' I have discovered much I do not know about myself despite all the philosophical works that I have been reading. I sincerely want to better myself, and on that basis I submit my application."

Sirhan became a "corresponding member" of the Supreme Grand Lodge in San Jose—"he received correspondence and instructions by mail and in turn submitted his lessons."[22]

* * *

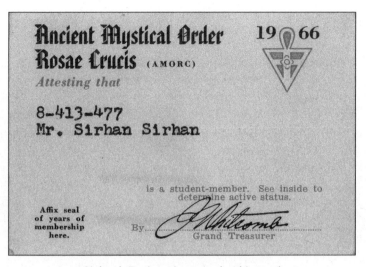

Ancient Mystical Order Rosae Crucis (AMORC)

19 66

Attesting that

8-413-477
Mr. Sirhan Sirhan

is a student-member. See inside to determine active status.

Affix seal
of years of
membership
here.

By................................
Grand Treasurer

Sirhan's Rosicrucian membership card.

Sirhan settled quickly in Corona. He didn't drink, but he'd go to bars with coworkers from the ranch and buy everyone a round. Everyone knew him as "Sol," and he soon became good friends with Terry Welch, a fellow exercise boy. Sol was an avid reader of law, and they often discussed cases he'd read about. Welch considered Sirhan his best friend and described him as "neat, clean, intelligent, and a gentleman in every way." He was easy to get along with, generous with friends, and always curious and trying to improve himself. He would visit dairy and poultry farms in his spare time and could talk intelligently on almost any subject, though he didn't seem particularly interested in politics.

Sirhan told Welch he'd been expelled from school after an affair with a math teacher, but Welch never saw Sirhan dating and thought he'd made up the story to answer ribbing about his lack of girlfriends.[23]

Sirhan later wrote obsessively in his diary about another employee at the ranch, Peggy Osterkamp. "She looked beautiful on a horse," he said later. Peggy had a few short conversations with him about horses, but they never dated. One time, when she was having lunch at a restaurant in Corona with a friend, Sirhan walked past her table, said "Hello," picked up her check, paid it at the register, and left.[24]

* * *

Just as Sirhan was settling into his new life, disaster struck. Early one morning, on September 25, several trainers set up a race and asked the exercise boys to ride. The morning fog was so thick, some owners withdrew, but three horses set off, including "Hy-Vera," ridden by Sirhan.

As they thundered around the track at full speed, the fog suddenly closed in, causing the horses to bump one another. Sirhan fell between his horse and the fence, hitting his head. As he lay crumpled up, cut and bleeding on the ground, he screamed in pain.

"I was supposed to work the horse for three hundred yards," he said later. "Fifty yards after I started, sir, I don't remember anything. . . . I fell from that horse and was knocked unconscious."[25]

He was taken to Corona Community Hospital, where Dr. Richard Nelson reported a two-inch cut on his chin, a cut on the upper lid of his left eye requiring stitches, and bruises and abrasions.

Sirhan complained he "hurt all over" and "was a very nervous patient, afraid of needles." He was hospitalized overnight but discharged himself the next day and was back at work a week later with a pay raise for his troubles. The following week, he fell again, reopening the cut over his left eye and sending him back to the hospital for more treatment.

At first, Dr. Nelson referred him to two eye specialists working out of the same office in Corona, Dr. Paul Nilsson and Dr. Milton Miller. Sirhan complained he suffered pain, blurring, and "extreme motion" in his eyes, but they found no evidence of an eye injury, and Miller thought Sirhan was exaggerating.

Sirhan continued to seek treatment for his eye injury and was examined by nine doctors in at least fifteen different visits over the next fifteen months.[26]

* * *

On November 13, 1966, Sirhan quit. He didn't give a reason, but the writing was on the wall. Sirhan wanted to be a full-time jockey, but Altfillisch didn't think he

Sirhan on a horse at the Altfillisch ranch, July 1966.

was up to it. One of the trainers, Robert Wheeler, got Sirhan a job with his father as an exercise boy at Del Mar Race Track. But two weeks later, supervisor Larry Peters saw Sirhan fall from a horse, and a few days later, he almost fell again. At the end of the month, Peters told Sirhan he'd never make it as a jockey and dismissed him.

Wheeler remembered Sirhan as intelligent and well mannered, but once, he lost his temper and kicked a horse. When Wheeler asked why, Sirhan replied, "He provoked me."

On December 2, Sirhan returned to the Granja Vista Del Rio Ranch, and Burt Altfillisch gave him his old job back. He exercised horses at the ranch for ten days, then quit for good and moved back to Pasadena.[27]

* * *

Sirhan telephoned Dr. Miller after his second visit on December 20 to request a letter verifying his injuries for a disability claim. When Miller declined, "Sirhan said I'd better do what he told me to, or he was 'gonna git me' and I 'would be sorry,' or words to that effect. I didn't know what to think. Before I could answer him, he just hung up."[28]

Sirhan was unemployed for the next nine months. Details about his life during this period are sketchy. He started work at a health food store in Pasadena on September 24, 1967, but there are only four entries in his FBI chronology for earlier in the year—three medical exams related to the fall—on February 21, April 6, and September 6—and a job consultation at PCC in July.

In April 1967, he filed a disability complaint for workmen's compensation. He visited eye doctor Albert Tashma and complained he couldn't rotate his left eye or "look in both directions like I used to," but Dr. Tashma reported "normal binocular function" and "no permanent disability." Sirhan also saw neurologist Forrest Johnson and complained of back pain, but the radiology report was normal. Undeterred, Sirhan continued to seek medical documentation of his eye and back ailments until the end of the year, but the doctors he saw didn't find much wrong with him.[29]

* * *

Though there seemed to be no lasting physical damage, those around Sirhan noticed a marked personality change after the falls. He became more withdrawn and irritable. His mother felt "he wasn't himself. I can't talk to him." Terry Welch said Sirhan "underwent a complete personality change." He became a loner—quiet and aloof, unpredictable and resentful toward anyone with money.[30]

Tom Rathke visited Sirhan in Pasadena that year: "Something happened to him after he got hurt. He just wasn't the same kid. . . . You really couldn't even talk to him. . . . He had his mind made up and that was the end of it. . . . There was no more laughing. . . . [He was] just rigid."[31]

Sirhan's older brother Sharif also lamented the change: "He was so nice before the fall . . . everybody liked him. But he changed suddenly—snap—and became reclusive and irritable. . . . He'd disappear for four or five hours at a time. . . . He no longer listened when family members tried to talk to him. The way he acted was abnormal. I discussed it with our mother and she agreed something was wrong but said Sirhan was already seeing a doctor."[32]

* * *

Now that Sirhan wasn't working, he read more than ever. Anything he could find on the Arab-Israeli situation, even the Jewish newspaper the *B'nai B'rith Messenger*. He figured "the best way to know what the Zionists are up to is to read what they say." He developed an intense interest in mysticism, self-hypnosis, and improving his mind.[33]

John Strathman was a good friend of Sirhan's at PCC, and they shared a love of languages. John helped Sirhan with his Russian, and Sirhan taught him Arabic. "He was a very intense person . . . extremely considerate . . . and very eager to learn. . . . I taught our oldest child a couple of Arabic words, and that seemed to just thrill him."[34]

Strathman lost touch with Sirhan while he was away working on the ranch but after that, he saw him two or three times before the shooting. Sirhan told him the accident meant he couldn't be a jockey, "and that seemed to embitter him considerably." He seemed increasingly restless, lonely, and depressed. He said "school wasn't quick enough"; he wanted a more direct route to success and talked of his interest in mystical powers and the occult.

One night, in a restaurant, he claimed he could conjure up a vision of his "guardian angel" for Strathman and his wife to see. When the couple confessed they couldn't see anything, Sirhan admitted his powers weren't fully developed yet.

The last time Strathman and Sirhan saw each other was in front of Sirhan's house in April. He seemed extremely impatient and depressed. "He didn't invite me into the house, which was strange for Sirhan." Strathman couldn't figure out what he'd done wrong, "so I didn't invite him to my home, either, and I stopped calling."

* * *

That April, Sirhan's membership in the Rosicrucians lapsed when he failed to pay his four-dollar monthly dues, but he kept up his mystical studies. Whatever books he couldn't afford to buy, he'd read at Bryton's used bookstore in Pasadena.

He tried out experiments from a book called *Cyclomancy* after ordering it through an astrological magazine. He explained in court that it was about white magic: "You can do anything with your mind if you know how . . . how you can install a thought in your mind and have it become a reality if you want it to . . . the book gave some elementary exercises. One of them, sir, was to put your hand in a very hot pail of water and think cool. I know this sounds queer but, sir, the boiling water on my hand was cool when I put it in. I thought it was cool and I felt that it

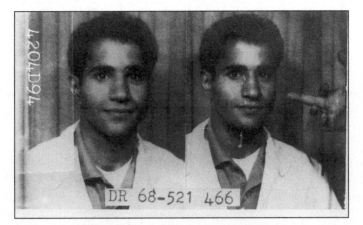

Undated photos of Sirhan from police files.

was cool. And I did it the other way around, with ice cold water, and thought hot; and I believe, sir, it was hot."

He practiced other experiments at the desk in his room, using a mirror and some candles to improve his powers of concentration. He placed a candle between himself and the mirror and if he concentrated on the yellow flame for five or ten minutes, he could change the color of the flame to whatever color he wanted.

He also played with thought transference a bit: "I was in my room, late at night, and my mother was in bed, and just for the hell of it, I thought I would try it. I sent this thought message . . . for my mother to get up and go to the toilet. I waited about ten minutes and it didn't work. Nothing happened. I said, 'This is not going to work,' then I got into bed and started to doze. I kept that thought of my mother going to the toilet and the minute I got into bed, the radio switched on and all the lights in the house turned on and about five minutes later, I heard the toilet flushing."

He was impressed with his new powers. "Whenever I heard about it before, I thought it was a lot of baloney but I said, 'I'll take you up on it, I'll try what you say' . . . and it worked."

"Where did you feel it would lead you eventually?" he was asked later.

"I didn't really know, except it would lead me to being a better human being, a better mind."[35]

* * *

Sirhan had kept two spiral notebooks since his days at PCC, with pages full of Russian and Chinese lessons and random scribbling. But during this period, his jottings seemed to take a markedly political turn. The notebooks will be discussed fully in Chapter 10 but three pages in particular are dated and can be slotted into a chronology.

The first two are dated June 2, 1967, three days before the onset of the Arab-Israeli War. A series of border incidents between Israel and its Arab neighbors had escalated to the point where Egypt closed the Straits of Tiran to Israeli ships and amassed a thousand tanks and a hundred thousand troops on the border. As tension rose in the Middle East, Sirhan wrote, *"Editorial by Geo. Putnam June 2 10.30 P.M,"* on top of page twenty—Putnam was the top-rated local newscaster in Los Angeles at the time. Sirhan continued:

> *An individual's freedom of speech is guaranteed as long as he remains aligned and in accord with what his decadent leaders want him to be. . . . We the leaders want to be in power and decree as we please and as to what ever is materially expedient to us and our families—at your cost. Should you dissent, we will find some means to kill you (economically—socially—politically—etc). We will use some of the loopholes that we have constructed in our legislation (which by the way we established with or without your concent—even tho we tell you that we live in a democracy where the people decide on all important matters that concern them, not their appointees in Congress (the No. 1 clique in degeneration and stagnation and decadense which incidentally we are proud of) American Capitalism will fall an give way to the worker's dictatorship.*[36]

While capturing Sirhan's alienation, it's an odd, Communist-inspired rant for a person who had shown no prior interest in "the worker's dictatorship." Two of Sirhan's friends espoused these views. Walter Crowe was a member of the Communist Party and Tom Good was an anarchist, but neither saw Sirhan very often, and he never expressed much interest in their politics.[37]

Page twenty-one is written in pencil, apparently two hours later:

> *2 June 67, 12.30 p.m.*
>
> *A Declaration of War Against America*
>
> *When in the course of human events it has become necessary for me to equalize and seek revenge for all the inhuman treatments committed against me by the American people.*
>
> *The manifestation of this Declaration will be executed by its purporter(s) as soon as he is able to command a sum of money ($2000) and to acquire some firearms—the specifications of which have not been established yet.*
>
> *The victims of the party in favor of this declaration will be or are now— the President, vice, etc.—down the ladder.*
>
> *The time will be chosen by the author at the convenience of the accused.*
>
> *The method of assault is immaterial—however the type of weapon used should influence it somehow.*
>
> *The author believes that many in fact multitudes of people are in harmony with his thoughts and feelings.*

The conflict and violence in the world subsequent to the enforcement of this decree, shall not be considered lightly by the author of this memoranda, rather he hopes that they be the initiatory military steps to WWIII—the author expresses his wishes very bluntly that he wants to be recorded by historians as the man who triggered off the last war.

Life is ambivalence

Life is a struggle

Life is wicked

If life is in any way otherwise, I have honestly never seen it. I always seem to be on the loosing end. Always the one exploited to the fullest.[38]

Sirhan was later asked about this passage in court.

"What was in your mind when you wrote that?"

"I must have been a maniac at the time. I don't remember what was on my mind."

"Did you have in mind on the 2nd of June, 1967, at some time killing the President and Vice-President of the United States of America?"

"Sir, if that is what I wrote and that is how I felt at the time, I must have been provoked to the point, sir, where I would have blasted anybody."

"Is it your recollection now that you had in mind acquiring a weapon of some kind for the purpose of killing the President, the Vice-President and so on down the ladder?"

"No, sir, I don't know what I had in mind."

"That is what you said, isn't it."

"That is what I said, but it's not me, sir. It's not Sirhan sitting right here who wrote that."

"Did you feel you had been exploited?"

"That's the problem, sir. I don't think I have ever been. I could have been provoked, sir, by that editorial by George Putnam. . . . Something must have moved me to write this. . . . I don't remember what my exact frame of mind was at the time."[39]

* * *

The "$2000" reference was odd because it matched the disability award Sirhan got for his injuries the following April. After lawyers' fees, Sirhan pocketed $1,705. Sirhan was disappointed he got so little, so how could he have predicted the size of his award nine months before? Were these statements really written on June 2, 1967, or postdated to look that way?

It should be noted the dates on both pages and "the America must fall" reference are written in slightly different writing and different pen than the main body of text on each page, suggesting they may have been added later.[40]

* * *

On June 5, 1967, a surprise preemptive strike by the Israeli air force destroyed more than 300 of the 450 planes in the Egyptian Air Force before they could even get off the ground. Six days later, the war was over. Jerusalem was under full Israeli control, and Sirhan was "burned up."

*　*　*

Sirhan was still out of work come September. His mother was a long-standing customer at John Weidner's health food store, Organic Pasadena, and asked Weidner if he could give Sirhan a job. Weidner needed help on Sundays, so on September 24, Sirhan was taken on as a part-time store clerk and deliveryman for two dollars an hour. Two months later, Sirhan became a full-time employee.[41]

"He was a good worker," Weidner said later, "an honest man, with principles. He didn't smoke or drink, but he was emotional. He would resent authority. He didn't like taking orders."

He was neat, courteous to customers, and he got along well with the rest of the staff. Weidner trusted him to take money to the bank but felt he had an inferiority complex because of his height. "He had a lot of complexes," he said, "mainly related to Israel. He claimed when he was young, he had seen some relatives, I think, killed by Israelis."

Weidner told Sirhan he was a member of the Dutch resistance in World War II, helping Jews escape Nazi-occupied Holland. "I spoke with him about the Jewish people who suffered so, and told him how my own sister was killed by the Germans, my best friends tortured and arrested. I told him I had forgiven the Germans. He said: 'I would like to be like you—but I cannot forgive.'"[42]

*　*　*

Mrs. Donald Boyko first met Sirhan when she started work as a saleslady at Weidner's store shortly after Christmas, 1967. Everybody called him "Sol," and he drove around making deliveries in Weidner's station wagon. He was polite and respectful and carried customers' groceries to waiting cars.

Over the next few months, Boyko gained a close insight into Sirhan's life at the time. He went to Santa Anita on Saturdays but kept losing on the horses. This frustrated him because he was very interested in money and "harbored a great envy for the good fortunes of others," criticizing rich Jews and Nelson Rockefeller, but never mentioning Robert Kennedy.

"He was very conscious of his size," she said. "Being a little person, he felt disadvantaged and had a defensive complex about it."

No one ever came to visit him at the store and he showed no interest in girls, saying dating was a waste of time. Instead, he was making "a comparative study of religion."

Boyko and Weidner were Seventh-day Adventists, and Sirhan asked Weidner's nephew, Henry Peters, a minister visiting from Wisconsin, to come to the house and give him Bible lessons. On Tuesday nights, they sat with Mrs. Sirhan in the dining room and covered topics like "God's Forgotten Riches" and "The Problems of Sin."

Boyko said Weidner was a domineering taskmaster, harsh and rude to his employees, particularly Sirhan. At first, Sol would try to stand his ground: "You just don't talk to me like that. You have to treat me like a man," he'd say, then walk away in desperation and frustration.

Boyko tried to mediate, but after a while, there were arguments almost every day. "Sirhan wanted Weidner to fire him so he could get some severance pay, but Weidner sensed this and would not fire him."

Despite his heated exchanges with Weidner, Sirhan never expressed any strong hatred toward him, and when Sirhan's picture appeared in the paper after the assassination, nobody at the store could believe it.

"Mr. Weidner's reaction was electric," recalled Boyko. "He walked around the store beating his fists to his head, saying 'It's him, it's him—it's got to be him,' and then to a customer who had been friendly to Sirhan in the past, he said, 'You see—I was right about him. I don't know why he didn't kill me—he hated me so.'"[43]

* * *

In late January, while still working at Weidner's store, Sirhan asked his brother Munir if he knew anyone who had a gun to sell. Munir knew a guy at work who had one—George Erhard. After work one day in the middle of February, Munir chatted with George about the gun in the parking lot of Nash's Department Store. Erhard went home to get the gun, and they agreed to meet later on a street corner near the Sirhan home.

Sirhan's car was broken at the time, so when he walked home that evening, Munir approached him and told him these friends at work had a gun they wanted to sell and were waiting on the corner.

"Let's go down and see what they have," said Sirhan.

Sirhan had looked at guns before in a couple of gun stores and had experience handling them, taking them apart, and even shooting .22s and .45s in the Cadet Corps. The brothers didn't realize at the time that it was illegal for an alien to have a gun.

Erhard brought along his friend William Price, and Sirhan approached Price and asked to see the gun. The brothers examined the gun and spoke in Arabic. Sirhan thought it was a pretty good gun. Erhard asked for thirty dollars but settled for twenty-five. Munir was six dollars short, so Sirhan gave him the balance, and Price handed Sirhan the gun.

It was an eight-shot, Iver Johnson, double-action, .22-caliber revolver. Later, in court, perhaps to protect his brother, Sirhan said he bought the gun and paid for it himself.

"Your brother paid most of the cash?"

"No, sir. I am the one that paid for the gun. It was my money that paid for the gun."[44]

Munir was the wild one in the family. While he was still at school, his list of "police contacts" was impressive—malicious mischief; reported missing and later found sleeping in a neighbor's garage; chased by California Highway Patrol in a high-speed pursuit through Pasadena, which resulted in Munir crashing Saidallah's car into a tree and being knocked unconscious; subject of a juvenile investigation prompted by lewd photographs found in his car, later involving an alleged sex and homosexual party—all before he was seventeen.

In 1966, he was arrested for vagrancy and possession of and selling marijuana to a state narcotics agent. He was convicted on the drug charge that October and sentenced to a year in jail and five years' probation. His attorney later persuaded the court to vacate the sentence and transfer it to juvenile court, but Munir was ordered deported by the INS the following July as a result of his felony conviction.

Now he was on probation, appealing deportation. If there was evidence he bought a gun, he'd be kicked out of the country.[45]

* * *

"What did you want a gun for?" Sirhan was later asked by prosecutors.

"I don't know, sir. . . . It could have been from watching the westerns on television."

"You don't know whether it was for hunting or target shooting?" "Probably both."

"Have you ever been hunting?"

"No, sir, I never have."[46]

"Why did you want to buy one?" asked Cooper.

"I liked guns, sir. . . . It was cheap. . . . It was a fairly good gun, almost a new one. It appealed to me."

"Well, what did you intend to do with it after you bought it?"

"Shoot it, I guess."

"Shoot what?"

"Shoot at the shooting ranges."

How did he explain the writing dated June 2, 1967—his talk about revolution and the weapon being undecided—and his purchase of a gun six months later?

"I can't, but that writing, sir, as I said, was good as long as the pen was in my hand writing that and, after that, I had no recollection of it."

"You mean it was just like turning off a water spigot?"

"That is my nature, sir."[47]

* * *

The brothers bought the gun, Sirhan put it in his room, and Munir "just forgot about it." In February and March, Sirhan sent off two money orders to reactivate his Rosicrucian membership and soon started receiving the *Rosicrucian Digest* again.[48]

* * *

On March 7, Weidner and Sirhan had their final argument at work. Weidner rebuked Sirhan for failing to cover a vegetable stand before closing, and Sirhan became extremely angry and defensive. When store manager Retta Drake tried to calm Sirhan down, Weidner ordered her not to talk to him, and she immediately quit in disgust.

Weidner ordered Sirhan out of the store, but he sat down and refused to leave until he was given two weeks' pay he believed he was owed and $180 severance pay. Weidner called the police, and when the officers arrived, Sirhan left without further incident.[49]

Later in the day, Sirhan filed a labor claim against Weidner, and at a subsequent hearing, Weidner claimed he fired Sirhan because his work was unsatisfactory. The labor commissioner found insufficient evidence in favor of Sirhan and dismissed the case without prejudice.[50]

Sirhan interviewed for other jobs but was turned down due to his lack of educational background.[51]

* * *

Contrary to previous claims, Sirhan did not mysteriously disappear for three months in the period leading up to the Kennedy assassination. His family confirmed to the FBI that "Sirhan never stayed away from home one night in the past year until he was arrested for the shooting of Senator Kennedy."[52]

Out of work again, Sirhan spent more time at the racetrack while continuing his Rosicrucian experiments. He tried out an experiment at Santa Anita on his birthday, March 19. He bet the daily double on horses one and nine but then found out horse one was Press Agent, a long shot owned by his old boss Burt Altfillisch.

"I didn't want that horse to win, sir," he later told his trial attorney Grant Cooper. "I don't know why. And I kept saying in my mind, 'you son-of-a-bitch, you are not going to win, period.' When I watched him in the parade . . . 'He's not going to win, he's not going to win, he's not going to win.' Well, when that horse got in the gate, sir, and the horses started to run, three paces out of the gate, sir, and that horse wheels and broke through the temporary rail, dropped his jockey and was disqualified."

"And I take it you felt that was your power of concentration?"

"I can't prove it, sir, but it worked."[53]

* * *

Sirhan also had time to try out his gun. He went to the San Gabriel Valley Gun Range on weekends and stayed around two hours, long enough to acquaint himself with the gun and how to shoot it. He fired two or three boxes of ammunition, then put the empty gun on the backseat of his car. He went shooting in San Gabriel or at the Corona Police Range about six times before the assassination.

"Why did you practice with the gun?" asked his attorney Cooper. "I liked to. I didn't have any work at the time."

"Well, did you want to become proficient in this revolution you were about to create?"

"Sir, that was completely out of my mind at the time. I was interested, sir, in practicing, target practicing, perfection."[54]

* * *

On April 12, 1968, the Argonaut Insurance Company sent Sirhan a check for $1,705 to settle his compensation claim. Sirhan didn't have a bank account, so he cashed the check, fixed up his car, and gave the rest to his mother for safekeeping. He had no regular friends but would chat with garbage collector Alvin Clark when he stopped on Howard Street for his noontime break on Wednesdays. Sirhan would bring out lemonade and sandwiches, and they'd shoot the breeze.[55]

On May 2, Sirhan met high school friend Walter Crowe at Bob's Big Boy. Crowe hadn't seen Sirhan since PCC, back when Crowe was trying to organize a campus chapter of Students for a Democratic Society; Sirhan hadn't shown much interest. Crowe became a member of the Communist Party and later worried that he might have inspired some of the Communist writing in Sirhan's notebook. He was treated as a "hot potato" for a while by the feds.

But that night, they went out on the town. They met two friends, drank four pitchers of beer, and cruised topless bars like the Cat Patch in Pasadena. They discussed Crowe's involvement with the Communist Party, and Sirhan talked about the Arab terrorist group Al Fatah. But Crowe's attempts to interest Sirhan in communism seemed to "turn him off."[56]

* * *

In early May, Sirhan received the new issue of the *Rosicrucian Digest*. An article on page 191 caught his eye—"Put It in Writing," by Arthur Fettig:

* * *

"Plan to Dare something different—something exciting! Plan to become a success in some endeavor and be ready to jump barefoot into the excitement of living. But here's a word of advice: put it in writing! Put your plan, your goal, your idea in writing, and see how it suddenly catches fire. See how it gains momentum by the simple process of writing it down!

"Try it. Pick a goal. Set a target date.

"I Dare you to write it down!"

On May 18, Sirhan dared to write it down.

> *May 18 9.45 AM—68*
>
> *My determination to eliminate R.F.K. is becoming more the more of an unshakable obsession . . . R.F.K. must die–RFK must be killed Robert F. Kennedy must be assassinated R.F.K. must be assassinated . . . R.F.K. must be assassinated assassinated . . . Robert F. Kennedy must be assassinated before 5 June 68 Robert F. Kennedy must be assassinated I have never heard please pay to the order of of of of of of*[57]

"Do you recall what your feelings were about Robert Kennedy on or about May 18?" he was later asked.

"It could have been the time, sir, when he came out and said he would send fifty planes to Israel," said Sirhan.

Sirhan recalled one evening when he brewed himself some tea and sat down to watch TV. "Well, as I flipped the channel, sir, this mention of Robert Kennedy came over and there was a biography of Robert Kennedy and I sat there and started to watch it. . . . The last part of this program, sir, he spoke of Robert Kennedy as being for the underdog, the disadvantaged and the scum of society, that he wanted to help the poorest people and the most prejudiced against and the weakest.

"And at that moment, sir, they showed on the television where Robert Kennedy in 1948 was in Israel helping to, so I thought, celebrate the Israelites, sir, and the establishment of the state of Israel. And the way that he spoke, well, it just bugged me, sir, it burned me up.

"Up until that time, I had loved Robert Kennedy, I cared for him very much and I hoped he would win the Presidency until that moment, sir. But when I saw, heard, he was supporting Israel, sir, not in 1968, but he was supporting it from all the way back from its inception in 1948, sir. And he was doing a lot of things behind my back that I didn't know about . . . it burned me up, sir. And that is most likely, sir, when I had written this."[58]

* * *

The documentary in question was *The Story of Robert Kennedy*, a thirty-minute campaign film directed by John Frankenheimer. Kennedy didn't talk of sending bombers to Israel or even state his present support for Israel, but one sequence spoke of his reports from Israel as a young journalist in 1948. "He wrote his dispatches and came to a decision," intoned the narrator, as an Israeli flag fluttered for thirty seconds on the breeze. "Bobby Kennedy decided his future lay in the affairs of men and nations."

According to Sirhan, this none-too-subtle play for the Jewish vote—Kennedy juxtaposed with an Israeli flag—led to an instant decision to assassinate him. To me, this just doesn't make sense.[59]

* * *

Author Robert Blair Kaiser pointed out another problem with this story. The notebook was written on the morning of May 18. The documentary was first shown in the Los Angeles area on Channel 2 (KNXT) at nine p.m. on May 20. It was repeated on Channel 7 five days later, billed as "an intimate and surprising account of the candidate through his years as Attorney General and a member of the National Security Council."

Kennedy didn't advocate sending fifty jet bombers to Israel until a speech on May 26 at Temple Neveh Shalom in Portland, Oregon. How could Sirhan write of his increasingly "unshakable obsession" to kill Kennedy on May 18 when he wasn't even aware of Kennedy's support for Israel until two days later and the bombers weren't mentioned until six days after that?[60]

* * *

To complicate matters, Sirhan claimed he couldn't remember writing in the notebooks.

"You don't remember writing it?"

"I don't remember writing it."

Cooper got Sirhan to read a couple of lines.

"Robert F. Kennedy must be assassinated, Robert F. Kennedy must be assassinated by 5 June 68."

"Now, what is the significance of 5 June 68?"

"5 June means the beginning of the Israeli assault, the Israeli aggression against the Arab people in 1967 . . . it invoked in me something that I can't describe . . . the Zionists to me is just like the Communists to you."

"And did you feel Robert F. Kennedy must die?"

"At that time, sir, that was the way I felt about it, and if he were right in front of me, so help me God, he would have died right then and there."

But Sirhan didn't remember writing it.

"I must have been burned up. . . . That writing was good just for that period of time that it was written there, sir."

"Well, how do you know how you felt at the time when you don't remember writing it?"

"As I say, I was provoked. I was just pissed off."

"You try to watch your language, Sirhan, please. Do you remember writing 'Please pay to the order of of of of of of of of of of of this or that?'"

"No, sir, I don't remember that. . . . I don't have a bank account. I don't understand it."

"But you don't deny writing it?"

"No, I don't deny it. It is my writing."[61]

* * *

Kennedy made three public pledges of military support for Israel during his primary campaigns in Oregon and California. The first was at Temple Isaiah in Los Angeles on May 20. Kennedy spoke in the sanctuary, wearing a Jewish skullcap, or yarmulke, and columnist David Lawrence noted some hypocrisy in what he said. In an article titled "Paradoxical Bob," he wrote:

> *Presidential candidates are out to get votes and some of them do not realize their own inconsistencies. Just the other day, Sen. Robert F. Kennedy of New York made a speech in Los Angeles which certainly was received with favor by Protestant, Catholic and Jewish groups which have been staunchly supporting the cause of Israel against Egypt and the Arab countries.*
>
> *Kennedy said: "We cannot—and will not—permit the Soviet Union to achieve an imbalance in the Middle East. We can and will fully assist Israel—with arms if necessary—to meet the threat of massive Soviet military build-ups. We cannot—and will not—render Israel defenseless in the face of aggression.*

Yet, Lawrence went on to say, the Soviet Union had been supplying North Vietnam with a billion dollars' worth of weapons a year for the last three years and Kennedy was now advocating U.S. withdrawal. Kennedy said the United States should use its power "only as a strategic reserve against the most serious of threats." Why then the double standard, sending military support to Israel when many saw it just as necessary to protect the countries of Southeast Asia from aggression? Why were liberal-minded politicians "doves" on Vietnam and "hawks" on the Middle East? The fear of the draft taking young Americans to Vietnam on the one hand, concluded Lawrence, and the Jewish vote on the other.

Sirhan clipped Lawrence's column from the May 26 edition of the *Pasadena Independent Star-News,* and the clipping was found in his shirt pocket after his arrest at the Ambassador.[62]

* * *

On the night of May 26, Kennedy spoke at Temple Neveh Shalom in Portland and outlined a more detailed program of aid for Israel. He said the United States must defend Israel "from whatever source" and drew a sharp distinction between Israel and Vietnam: "Our obligations to Israel, unlike our obligations to other countries, are clear and imperative. . . . Israel is the very opposite of Vietnam. Israel's government is democratic, effective, free of corruption, its people united in its support. The Soviets have sent supersonic fighters to the Arabs. Soviet planes and pilots they have trained are on Arab soil. Forty Soviet warships are in the Mediterranean, and their advisers are in Arab nations."

He said that the United States could not permit such an imbalance and "the United States should without delay sell Israel the 50 Phantom jets she has so long been promised."[63]

* * *

The next day, the *Pasadena Independent Star-News* carried a photograph of a skull-capped Kennedy speaking to the congregation across two columns at the top of page three. The caption read, "Bobby Says 'Shalom'—Senator Robert F. Kennedy, wearing a traditional Jewish yarmulke, addresses the Neveh Shalom congregation in Portland on his campaign tour of Oregon. He told the congregation the U.S. must support Israel against outside aggression."[64]

Sirhan had read David Lawrence's article in the same paper the day before, so it's quite likely Sirhan saw this photograph. While the text of the speech was not reported in the Los Angeles papers, it was carried by the Associated Press in a late-night wire and may have been picked up by some of the local radio stations. Sirhan remembered hearing news of it on KFWB all-news radio, his mother's favorite station, playing in her room next to his.

"It was the hot news . . . the announcer said that Robert Kennedy was at some Jewish Club in Beverly Hills . . . and that is where he had committed himself to formally sending 50 jet bombers to Israel."

"What did that make you think?"

"I thought Robert Kennedy was not all the good guy he claimed to be. . . . It boiled me up again."

Sirhan was still practicing his Rosicrucian studies in the mirror.

"He bugged me to the point, sir, where as I was concentrating in the mirror, sir, instead of seeing my own face, I actually saw his face, sir. I was that burned up about him."

"You actually saw his face."

"Again, sir, this is an illusion. I can't prove it but I saw it in that mirror. His face."[65]

* * *

While this political rage was churning in Sirhan, to the outside world, he was the same mild-mannered young man as before. Ten days before the shooting, Sirhan stopped by to play Chinese checkers with two elderly neighbors he visited occasionally. On the day of his arrest, one of the neighbors, Mrs. Blakeslee, called him "a wonderful boy, an example of a good boy."[66]

On Tuesday, May 28, a week before the assassination, Sirhan attended his first Rosicrucian meeting at the lodge in Pasadena. He volunteered for an experiment on touch sensations and was blindfolded. As the master, Ted Stevens, touched his skin with different objects, Sirhan had to guess how many there were. After the meeting, he browsed the literature briefly, then left as if he was in a hurry.[67]

* * *

On June 1, Sirhan asked his mother for three hundred dollars of the insurance money, saying he needed it to get a job. There was only four hundred dollars left, so she threw it at him angrily, saying he wanted it only to bet on horses. He picked the money up, put three hundred in his pocket, and gave her the rest.

"This is for you, Mother."

Sirhan's worldly possessions at this point ran to four hundred sixty-odd dollars in his pocket, a patched-up pink-and-white DeSoto, a gun, two spiral notebooks full of strange, repetitive writing, and an impressive library on Rosicrucianism.[68]

* * *

At 12:50 that afternoon, Sirhan paid a dollar and signed in at the Corona Police Pistol Range and practiced for a couple of hours. Prosecution handwriting expert Lawrence Sloan later confirmed that the signature in the log book was in Sirhan's handwriting, and according to the rosters, no one else was shooting on the range at that time.

But was it really Sirhan? The only people who saw him at the range that day were the range master, William Marks, and his deputy, Harry Starr, both regular Corona policemen.

Marks identified Sirhan from a police mug shot but described him as twenty to thirty years old, six foot to six foot two, and 215 to 225 pounds, with brown hair. This was at least eight inches too tall, double Sirhan's weight, and the wrong hair color. Marks said "Sirhan" was accompanied by a man of about the same age, five-five to five-seven and 130 to 145 pounds, with brown hair, a pencil moustache, and horn-rim glasses. The second man spoke with an unknown foreign accent and questioned Marks about aliens using the range, but did not shoot. "Sirhan" fired a .22-caliber gun, which he carried in a zippered carrying case (something the real Sirhan did not own).

Officer Harry Starr provided the same description.

By late December, Marks was "still positive that the person who signed Sirhan Sirhan on the roster is over six feet and over two hundred pounds with a face similar to Sirhan's."

Although no witnesses placed Sirhan on the gun range and the range masters described an apparent imposter signing his name, "investigators felt that Marks and Starr were confusing Sirhan with some other shooter."[69]

During the trial, the prosecution called Marks to testify to Sirhan's handwriting on the sign-in sheet, in an attempt to show the premeditation of an assassin getting in some practice at a police range, of all places. Marks's mother had died back in Tennessee, so Harry Starr took his place on the stand.

Starr said Marks was in the office and he was out on the range when "Sirhan" signed in but Starr talked to him on the range later. Deputy DA John Howard asked Starr if he could identify the defendant as the same man.

"Do you want a stipulation?" asked defense counsel Grant Cooper, somewhat bizarrely.

"No, I don't think so," said Howard. "Thinking back to that Saturday, June 1st . . . did you see the defendant?"

"I can't truthfully say that that is the man," said Starr. "I picked out a picture that resembled the man but to be truthful about it, I cannot say that he is the man."

"I will offer a stipulation, having first talked to counsel," said Cooper.

"We will accept the stipulation," said a grateful Howard.

Cooper, shamefully unaware of the range master's statements, stipulated that Sirhan was on the range.[70]

* * *

Sirhan left the range at three and stopped off at the Lock, Stock 'n Barrel gun shop in San Gabriel on his way home. Retired fireman Larry Arnot was the clerk who served him.

Sirhan said he asked for Federal long rifle .22s, his favorite brand, but Arnot didn't have any.

"Well, give me your best," said Sirhan.

Arnot pulled out some CCI Mini-Mags and a cheaper brand of Super-X. Sirhan hadn't tried these brands before, so he bought two boxes of each. The receipt was later found in the glove compartment of his car.

But according to Arnot, Sirhan entered the store with two other men. The group looked very serious and didn't talk among themselves.

"I want two boxes of Mini-Mags," said Sirhan.

"Standard or hollow points?" asked Arnot.

"Hollow points," came the reply.

"Going rabbit hunting?"

"That's the plan," said Sirhan.

"And give me two boxes of Super-X Westerns," chimed in one of the others. Arnot put the four boxes on the same sales slip; the men paid him and left. Later, the FBI showed Arnot photographs of the five Sirhan brothers—the eldest Saidallah, Sharif, Adel, Sirhan, and Munir. Arnot identified Sirhan as "identical" to the guy who asked for the Mini-Mags and Sharif as strongly resembling the guy who asked for the Super-X. Arnot described the second man as the same age as Sirhan but a couple of inches taller, with a darker complexion, a broad, flattened nose, short, black, kinky hair, and somehow looking Mexican or American Indian. But Sharif was ten years older than Sirhan and hadn't spoken to him for three years, so it's highly unlikely it was him.[71]

* * *

One of the owners of the shop, Donna Herrick, was not there that day, but she told the FBI that back on April 3, Sirhan had come into the shop with two other foreign males and asked for .357 tank-piercing ammo. Her husband, Ben, said they didn't have any, and the three left. She was positive the man who spoke was Sirhan. She couldn't understand his accent and asked Ben to help. The other men bore a strong resemblance to Adel and Sharif Sirhan.

Adel denied ever going to a gun shop with Sirhan.

Arnot and Donna Herrick later failed polygraphs conducted by LAPD sergeant Enrique Hernandez on August 6. Hernandez concluded that Donna Herrick had never seen Sirhan, and "Arnot subsequently admitted that he did not remember seeing Sirhan in the store."[72]

* * *

If Sirhan missed the May 26 reference to the bombers, they came up again during Kennedy's televised debate with Senator McCarthy on Saturday night. Kennedy stressed the U.S. commitment to Israel and renewed his promise to send fifty Phantom jets.

On June 4, the Israeli Air Force bombed the Jordanian town of Irbin, twenty miles inside the border, killing seventy civilians. The news reached Los Angeles on the afternoon of June 4, and the next day's *Los Angeles Times* carried the headline "Israel Jets Rip Jordan as New Fighting Erupts" on its front page, alongside news of the Kennedy assassination.[73]

* * *

On Sunday, June 2, Sirhan got up early and drove his mother to church. In the early afternoon, he went back to the Corona Police Range but was turned away—only large-bore guns were allowed on Sundays. On the way home, he bought a copy of the *Los Angeles Times* and saw a big advertisement inviting the public to come down to see and hear Robert Kennedy at the Ambassador Hotel.

"It said, 'You and your friends are invited to come down.' I thought I was as eligible as anybody else," he recalled later in court.

"On May 18th, you had written that Senator Robert F. Kennedy must die and that he must die by June 5, 1968."

"Yes, sir."

"When you read this on Sunday, the 2nd of June, did you have in mind going to the Ambassador Hotel for the purpose of killing Robert F. Kennedy?"

"No, sir, I did not. . . . That was completely forgotten from my mind." "Completely forgotten?"

"Like I said, sir . . . the feelings that I had when I wrote it were good as long as I was writing it—for that period of time only, sir."

"In May, you had heard Senator Kennedy advocate sending bombers to Israel. Did you forget that?"

"No. Every time I was provoked, I would have written it that way. My feeling about Robert Kennedy was only good as long as I was writing that stuff."[74]

* * *

Sirhan stopped off at Stan's Drive-In in Hollywood for some coffee and some of their home-made cherry pie. He got directions to the Ambassador and arrived at the hotel between six and seven thirty. He walked up a circular stairway to the main lobby on the second floor and saw a policeman and a guard. He showed them the ad and was directed to where the rally was going to be.

"Were there many people in that room?"

"Hundreds and hundreds."

"And did you talk to anybody that you recall?'

"I talked to whoever wanted to talk to me, sir."

"Did you have the gun with you?"

"No, sir, I did not."

"What did you do with it?"

"I left it at home, sir."

After a while, he left the room where the reception was being held.

"It became too hot for me, too many bright lights."

At the other end of the lobby, he found an urn with some coffee and Chinese fortune cookies. By the time he went back, Kennedy was addressing the crowd, and it was so packed, he and many others couldn't get in. The Kennedy staff said the senator would come out later to address the overflow crowd by a fountain outside, so Sirhan waited around, figuring "I came down to see him; I might as well see him."

* * *

Sirhan couldn't remember how long he waited.

"With all the excitement, sir, I couldn't keep track of the time."

"Did you listen to the speech?"

"Yes. . . . He encouraged all his supporters to go out for the last drive . . . and he sang with a movie star, I think." Actually, it was the crooner Andy Williams.

"Did you enjoy yourself?"

"I was really thrilled, sir."

"Was it the first time you had seen Robert Kennedy?"

"The first time, sir, yes, sir. And my whole attitude towards him changed. Because every time before, I associated him with the Phantom jet bombers that he was going to send to Israel and I pictured him as a villain . . . but when I saw him that night, he looked like a saint to me."

"You honestly mean that?"

"I honestly mean that, sir. . . . He looked like a saint to me. I liked him."

Two prosecution witnesses testified that they got lost in the hotel corridors and ran across Sirhan in the pantry area that night.

"Did you go browsing around looking for the kitchen and the pantry and other places where you might be able to shoot?"

"No, sir. I did not. I might add, sir, those ladies who said I was going around, in my own words, sir, were complete liars."

"Well, now, pardon me, Sirhan. Maybe they were mistaken."

"Well, they swore to tell the truth, sir, and they didn't."[75]

* * *

In a later interview, NBC's Jack Perkins returned to this point: "Sirhan, the obvious question is, of course: did you go to the Ambassador Hotel that Sunday to case the place, to plan, to plot, to wait, to stake it out, to find out where you could shoot him?"

"Sir, I know this sounds unbelievable but I went there just to see Senator Kennedy."[76]

* * *

Sirhan couldn't explain to his attorney Grant Cooper why his view of Kennedy changed so drastically over the next few days. On June 2, he saw him as a saint, "but his willingness, his commitment to send those 50 Phantom jet bombers to Israel was still solidified in my mind. . . . I didn't like that at all."

After seeing Kennedy at the hotel, Sirhan went home and went to bed. He didn't do any writing that night.[77]

FIVE

THE GIRL IN THE POLKA-DOT DRESS

The last thing Sirhan remembered before the shooting was pouring coffee for a beautiful girl. Probed by defense psychiatrist Dr. Diamond, he tunneled back into his memory, struggling to recall the sequence of events that led him into the pantry.

Sirhan wasn't normally a drinker, but when he got to the Ambassador Hotel that night, it was hot and he wanted to fit in, so he drank four Tom Collins cocktails as he wandered around the campaign parties. This made him very sleepy, so he decided to walk back to his car to drive home. He then realized he was too drunk to drive, so he went back to the hotel in search of coffee. And he found some. There was a girl there, next to a big, shiny coffee urn. She was tired and wanted coffee, too. She was dark skinned and appeared to be Armenian, Spanish, or Mexican. He couldn't remember what she was wearing or where exactly they were, but there were a lot of bright lights, "a helluva lot of lights."

"So I gave her a cup; then I made some for me and we sat there. Then she moved and I followed her. She led me into a dark place."

The next thing he knew, he was being choked on the steam table.

"I only remember the girl and the coffee. That's it. It's a blank. . . . When people talked about the girl in the polka-dot dress," he told his defense team, "maybe they were thinking of the girl I was having coffee with."[1]

A mysterious girl was first spotted with Sirhan at a series of Kennedy campaign rallies in the weeks leading up to the assassination. The LAPD rejected these sightings—the stalker pattern fit their "lone gunman" profile, but a female accomplice didn't. While Sirhan has always denied being at any rallies, the witnesses in each case are fairly convincing.

On May 20, two days after Sirhan's infamous notebook entry, there was a luncheon for Senator Kennedy and four hundred guests at Robbie's Restaurant in Pomona. Pomona police officer William Schneid spotted an attractive young woman in a satin blouse standing by the door to the restaurant kitchen, looking as if she was trying to get inside.

Schneid described her as Caucasian, five-six, twenty-five to thirty, with medium-blond, shoulder-length hair and a nice figure. He intercepted her.

"I'm sorry, you can't go in there."

"Which way will Kennedy go in to lunch?" the girl asked.

"He'll probably go up the stairs to the second floor."

As Kennedy made his entrance and climbed the stairs to the second-floor banquet room, Schneid watched the girl bolt to the foot of the stairs.[2]

As a line formed at the bottom of the stairway and Albert LeBeau, a brawny thirty-five-year-old blond bartender, started taking tickets, Schneid saw the young woman climb over a brick flower holder and jump onto the stairs behind LeBeau. Then a man climbed over the rail and dropped onto the stairs behind her. LeBeau later said the man resembled Sirhan. The bartender then grabbed the woman to stop her from crashing the luncheon.

"Do you have tickets?"

"We're with the senator's party," the girl replied.

"Then, where are your tickets?"

"We're part of the senator's party. He just waved us to come upstairs."

The young man LeBeau thought was Sirhan said nothing but held his hands against the woman's back, as if pushing her forward. It was an unusually hot day, but "Sirhan" had a heavy jacket draped over his right arm.

The couple returned to the bottom of the stairs, and LeBeau proceeded to admit those with tickets. The would-be crashers seemed to give up trying to get in, and LeBeau lost sight of them.

A few minutes later, LeBeau went upstairs to find a "runner" for one of the newsmen present and found the pair standing against the back wall of the dining room as Kennedy gave a speech to a hundred people. As LeBeau moved through the crowd, he bumped against "Sirhan."

"Pardon me," said LeBeau.

"Why should I?" replied the man. He stood in a suspicious crouch, the coat still over his arm. LeBeau challenged the couple.

"If you're with the Kennedy party, what are you doing in the back of the room?"

"What the hell is it to you?" said "Sirhan."

* * *

LeBeau was later interviewed by the FBI: "The way his coat was draped over his right elbow, you couldn't see his right hand . . . he could have hid a gun under there very nicely."

He picked out Sirhan's mug shot from twenty-five photos of male, Latin types between twenty and twenty-five years old—"I'm pretty sure this is the man I saw."

Police investigators pulled no punches. "Could you under oath swear that Sirhan is the man involved in the incident on May 20th?"

LeBeau hung his head and stared at the floor.

"No."

And that was the end of their investigation. The final LAPD summary report said LeBeau "initially stated the man was Sirhan, but later admitted he lied." But there were more sightings.[3]

* * *

Dr. Joseph Sheehan, a professor of psychology at UCLA, and his wife, Margaret, were also positive they saw Sirhan after a Kennedy rally at the LA Sports Arena on May 24, as a good-natured crowd waited to see Kennedy leave. Dr. Sheehan recalled that Sirhan stood in front of him for two or three minutes. He seemed to be alone and "appeared very intense and sinister" and "completely out of character in the crowd." The Sheehans remarked on how suspicious he was and immediately recognized his picture in the paper after the shooting. There was no girl this time, so the LAPD included the Sheehan sighting in their log of Sirhan.[4]

* * *

On May 30, volunteer Laverne Botting saw two men and a woman come into Kennedy Campaign Headquarters in Azusa. One of the men very closely resembled Sirhan and walked up to her desk while the other two stayed in the background.

"I'm from the Pasadena (campaign) office," "Sirhan" said. "Is Kennedy going to come into your office?"

"No," replied Botting.

The man thanked her, then turned around, and all three of them left.

Botting described the woman as twenty-two to twenty-five years old, five-seven, slim, with an excellent figure and dishwater blond hair; and "Sirhan" as five-four, twenty to twenty-five years old, with dark eyes, black kinky hair, and a broad nose and shoulders.

She picked out Sirhan's mug shot for Patrolman Thompson of the LAPD but could be sure of her identification only if she saw Sirhan in person. The LAPD never gave her the opportunity. Officer Thompson rejected her description of the broad nose and shoulders, concluding, "Witness has obviously made an honest mistake."[5]

* * *

But Ethel Crehan was also a witness to what Laverne Botting saw. She told the FBI she overheard Ms. Botting talking to the man, and she was "fairly certain" it was Sirhan.

In her first LAPD interview on June 7, Crehan estimated his height as five-five, but when reinterviewed two months later, she remembered it as five-eight. This alone led Officer Thompson to disregard her statement. He concluded, "The person described by Mrs. Crehan as possibly being Sirhan is 4" taller than Sirhan. It is doubtful if the person she observed was Sirhan."

Crehan described the female in the party as five-eight, thin, "nineteen, but made-up to look 23 to 25 years old," with brown or blond shoulder-length, bouffant-styled hair and a "prominent nose."[6]

Botting and Crehan both agreed to take a polygraph test, but none was given. Later, Ms. Botting received an anonymous telephone call.

"I hear you think you saw Sirhan," said a male voice. "You had better be sure of what you're saying."[7]

* * *

Early Saturday morning, June 1, insurance executive Dean Pack was hiking in the Santa Ana Mountains south of Corona with his teenage son when they came across two men and a woman shooting at cans set up on a hillside.

One of the men strongly resembled Sirhan and was shooting with a pistol. When he saw Pack, he just glared at him. The other two were equally unfriendly. Pack said the second man was six foot tall and ruddy-complexioned, with sandy hair, and the girl was in her early twenties, with long brown hair.

Pack later told author Jonn Christian he was relieved to get out of there before they put a bullet in his back. Pack offered to take the FBI up to the spot to recover bullets, shell casings, and fingerprints, but they weren't interested. Pack's five-line LAPD summary states, "Mr. Pack viewed a photograph of Sirhan [but] could not be positive of his identification." In fact, the LAPD interviewed Pack by telephone and never showed him a photograph.[8]

June 4, 9:15 a.m.

Forty-year-old chemical salesman John Henry Fahey entered the back of the Ambassador Hotel, forty-five minutes late for a meeting with a sales colleague. He couldn't find him in the hotel coffee shop and as he stepped out into the hallway, he spotted a pretty young woman in her late twenties and made a flirtatious comment.

"Do you know where the post office is?" she asked.

Fahey said he didn't realize there was a post office in the hotel.

The young woman left and Fahey went into the coffee shop and sat at the counter. Ten minutes later, she returned and sat down beside him. She had a slight accent he couldn't place and was dressed well and spoke very good English. She was five-eight, with a light Arabic complexion and dirty blond hair, pulled down in a ponytail on one side. He described her nose as "prominent" and "of the hooked fashion . . . from the Arabic world," and her clothes, shoes, and purse were all tan.

She'd been in Los Angeles only three days and had just come back from a trip to Eilat, Beirut, Aqaba, and Cairo. At first, she said her name was Alice; then she changed it to Jean.

"I can't go by my real name," she said. When Fahey asked why, she said, "I don't want to get you involved. . . . I think we're being watched."

Fahey discreetly followed her gaze to a man near the door of the coffee shop, with a dark Mediterranean complexion and sideburns.

Alice or Jean seemed shook up and in trouble—very nervous, with clammy hands. She asked Fahey if he could help her get a new passport. She wanted to go to Australia to "get away from these people." She said Kennedy was "no good" and asked Fahey to come to "Kennedy's winning reception" that night and "watch them get Mr. Kennedy."

"What d'you mean?" asked Fahey.

"I don't want to get you involved," she said.

"Well, you can trust me, I'm for McCarthy."

"Well, they're going to take care of Mr. Kennedy tonight."

"Who?" asked Fahey.

"I don't know if I can trust you to tell you the whole thing."

At first, Fahey "figured the lady was either nuts, sick or drunk or something, but she wasn't." She seemed genuinely troubled and in need of help. He told her he had a couple of business calls to make in Oxnard and Ventura, and she invited herself along. When she opened her purse to pay the check, Fahey saw a fistful of money inside—"big stuff—fifty dollar bills—hundred dollar bills." But as a gentleman, he insisted on paying for breakfast.

* * *

As they drove up the Pacific Coast Highway through Malibu, Fahey noticed they were being tailed by a thin, gray-haired man in a blue Ford. When Fahey sped up, the Ford sped up. When he slowed down, it slowed down. When he eventually lost the Ford, it was soon replaced by a dark blue VW.

He pulled off the highway above Malibu onto a sightseeing promontory with two large boulders on the left-hand side. The VW pulled in and parked thirty to forty feet behind him.

A stocky man with dark gray hair got out and stretched and stared at Fahey, then backed his VW behind one of the rocks. Fahey pulled out and sped north toward Oxnard. The VW didn't follow.

By the time Fahey got up to Oxnard, his new acquaintance had changed her name to Betty, and they had picked up the blue Ford again.

"They're really after us," she said.

"They use radios to communicate with each other."

"Would you like to go to the police?" he asked.

"No, no, no. Just take me back to Los Angeles."

Fahey decided not to call on his accounts after all and lost the Ford coming back down through Ventura. They drove back down the coast, stopping for a bite to eat, and the young woman finally admitted her real name was Gilda Dean (or Gilderdine) Oppenheimer.

She was staying near the Ambassador—"on Kenmore but near Olympic"—and Fahey dropped her off at the front entrance to the hotel around seven thirty.

She asked him to come to the "winning reception" that night and meet her in the Ambassador lobby at eight thirty. When Fahey refused, she got angry and jumped out of the car and slammed the door. Fahey watched her walk up the canopied sidewalk from Wilshire Boulevard toward the Ambassador.[9]

* * *

More than a dozen witnesses saw "the girl in the polka-dot dress" at the Ambassador Hotel that night. Key witnesses consistently described a girl in a white dress with black polka dots either with Sirhan, or making statements while fleeing the scene that implicated her in the shooting.

Chief among these was Sandra Serrano, whose interview with NBC still stands up today as an extraordinarily vivid and credible account of a very traumatic incident. It was to be the first of many interviews: Serrano was quizzed by the LAPD at 2:35 a.m. and again at four o'clock, while the FBI interviewed her the following day. Her story was remarkably detailed and consistent all four times.

Serrano arrived at the hotel with friends around nine fifteen p.m. and spent most of the evening in the Ambassador Ballroom downstairs, thinking this was where Kennedy would speak later. But the room grew hot and claustrophobic—she'd seen Kennedy speak several times and knew he'd win, so she walked outside onto a fire escape for some air.

She sat down on the fifth or sixth step of a metal stairway that led up to fire doors in the southwest corner of the Embassy Ballroom, where Kennedy would eventually appear. She was sitting there, savoring the occasion and the cool night air, when two or three minutes later, three people came up the stairs—a girl and two guys. They didn't talk but they seemed to be together. As the woman approached, she said, "Excuse us," and Serrano moved to one side.

Sandra described the girl as a light-skinned Caucasian (Anglo, not Latino), five-six, between twenty-three and twenty-seven years old, with brown eyes and nicely combed, dark brown hair, curled bouffant style to just above the shoulder. She had a nice figure and wore black shoes and a white, voile, knee-length dress with black, quarter-inch polka dots, three-quarter-length sleeves, and a bib collar with a small black bow. She had a "funny nose," a little bit turned up, like "a pixie nose maybe . . . a Bob Hope type."

Both men were short, needed a haircut, and looked Mexican American. One was twenty to twenty-five and a bit shorter than the girl—about five-five—and overweight, maybe 160 pounds. He had black, greasy hair, long on top and combed straight, but he was "clean shaven and cute." He wore dark trousers, a light sports shirt, and an "autumn gold" cardigan sweater.

The other guy "looked like what we call a 'borracho,' somebody who, you know, just doesn't look right. . . . He didn't look drunk but sort of messy . . .

seedy-looking . . . like he didn't belong there . . . he just didn't fit in with the rest of the crowd." He was "a little man," even shorter than the other two, about five-three, 130 pounds, slim, between twenty-two and twenty-five years old, with black, bushy, curly hair. He wore light, wrinkled clothes—a light sports shirt and possibly beige pants.

Soon after these three went up, Serrano heard noise from inside, suggesting Kennedy was speaking. No one else came past. Then, fifteen to twenty minutes after seeing the three go up, Serrano heard what sounded like six backfires from a car.

Thirty seconds later, the same girl came running down the stairs, closely followed by the guy in the gold sweater. "She practically stepped on me and she said, 'We've shot him! We've shot him!' Then I said, 'Who did you shoot?' And she said, 'We've shot Senator Kennedy.'" The girl looked pleased, "like 'We finally did it,' like, you know . . . 'Good going.'"

Serrano wasn't sure whether to believe her, "so I walked down the stairs. I went to the first floor and everybody was still partying and everything, and I stopped an officer [a hotel security guard] and I says, 'Is it true?—did they shoot him?' And he said, 'Shoot who?' And I said, 'Senator Kennedy.' And he looked at me and goes, 'No, no.'" She had a glass in her hand and he said she'd had too much to drink.

"And by this time people were starting to form around me and they said, 'What happened?' And I says, 'Well, somebody got shot up there on the second level. . . . They said Senator Kennedy got shot.' And everybody was saying, 'Oh, you're nuts,' you know. And some other girls came down and they were crying and crying. And I said, 'What's wrong?' They said, 'They've shot him,' but still nobody would believe anybody. So I walked directly to a telephone and called my parents long-distance."

Above, Left: Sandra Serrano reenacts where she sat on the fire escape for the police. Above, Right: Wider view of the same stairway leading up to a fire door in the southwest corner of the Embassy Ballroom.

Sandra was crying hysterically on the phone, trying to explain to her mother what had happened, when a girl she recognized came down the hall. She told her mother to wait, then opened the door, and her friend confirmed that Kennedy had been shot.

A distraught Serrano kept repeating to her mother, "Why would they do anything like this? He was such a good man!"

When the FBI asked Serrano why she would call her parents long-distance in Ohio before she was sure Kennedy had been shot, she said, "If you could have seen the expression on [the girl's] face and heard the way she said, 'We shot him,' you would have believed her, too."

After calling her parents, Serrano was still crying and near hysterical. "I was crying and crying and crying and people were fainting all over the place; it was quite a turmoil." She sat in front of a television set and said aloud, "I saw these people come down the stairs; what should I do?" Somebody said she should find a police officer, so she walked out of the ballroom and about five minutes after the shooting met her housemate Irene Chavez.

She described what she'd seen and heard, and Chavez tried to calm her down. Then they walked out to the car but the police weren't letting anybody leave. Serrano felt she had to tell someone, so as they came back to the main entrance, she walked up to a man, very excited, and said, "'I don't know what to do; I'm not crazy and I'm not drunk. I seen two people running down the stairway . . . who should I tell?' And he said, 'You just happened to stop the right person, I'm a deputy district attorney.'"[10]

The man was John Ambrose, a Los Angeles County deputy DA just arriving at the hotel after hearing news of the shooting on his car radio. Serrano proceeded to tell Ambrose the same story she later told the police and FBI. Ambrose recalled the key phrases as "We just shot him . . . we just shot Senator Kennedy." He asked if the girl could possibly have said "they just shot him," but Serrano distinctly remembered her using the pronoun "we."

Ambrose told investigators Serrano impressed him as "a very sincere person and although she was alarmed and excited over what was told her by the couple, she remained insistent in the wording of the girl's statements."

The only major difference in Ambrose's account was the girl saying "We just shot him" while passing Serrano in a hallway rather than on the fire escape. The LAPD later used this detail to discredit Serrano, but moments before meeting Ambrose, Serrano told Chavez she heard the statement on the outside stairway, and in all subsequent interviews, she always referred to the stairway. Ambrose probably confused Serrano running into the hallway to see what had happened with the girl running past her on the fire escape.

* * *

It was now fifteen minutes after the shooting. Ambrose took Serrano up to the crime scene and turned her over to a police officer, and she was led into a witness area to await questioning. The next thing Ambrose knew, Serrano was live on national television with Sander Vanocur.

He asked one of the officers if it was a good idea to have Serrano interviewed on TV before the police had gotten her story.

"I guess there's nothing we can do about that now," came the reply. When Serrano came back, Ambrose shook his head.

"Oh, God, you were on TV."[11]

* * *

Just before Serrano appeared on television, another witness, Vincent Di Pierro, overheard her talking about what she'd seen and said he'd seen a similar girl in the pantry just before the shooting. Di Pierro later told the FBI, "they did not describe the dress to each other, except to mention . . . that it was a white dress with black polka dots." Before they could discuss the girl, a police officer saw them talking and warned them not to discuss the case. From this point on, Serrano's fate as a witness was intertwined with Di Pierro.[12]

* * *

Vince was a college student. His father, Angelo, was the maître d' of the hotel, and had gotten him a part-time waiting job working nights for Uno Timanson. June 4 was Vince's day off, and he was studying for his finals, but as Kennedy was winning, his father called to say, "Come down and see the victory speech."

He arrived at eleven thirty and was in the pantry talking to his waiter friend Martin Patrusky when Kennedy passed through on his way to the ballroom. Di Pierro shook the senator's hand but didn't get to say congratulations, so he thought he'd catch him again on the way out. After the speech, he followed Kennedy into the pantry, about three feet behind. Kennedy walked though the swinging door on the left side, and Vincent took the door on the right.

Kennedy stopped, shook hands with Martin and Vince, then turned to his left to shake hands with Perez and Romero. Di Pierro was standing level with the ice machines, five feet to the right of Kennedy. He noticed Sirhan in a powder blue jacket, white shirt, and light blue pants at the opposite end of the ice machine, twelve to fifteen feet away. He was standing up on a tray stacker "in a kind of funny position . . . like in a crouch—like if he were trying to protect himself from something. . . . I thought he was sick."

The tray stacker was raised four inches off the ground and had trays piled up on it. Sirhan was holding onto the stacker with his left hand and seemed to be cramped and "clutching his stomach, as though somebody had elbowed him." His right hand was down by his stomach and obscured "like he had it inside his shirt or something. . . . When I first saw him there was a girl behind him, too; I don't know if you need that. There were two people that I saw."

In fact, the only reason Di Pierro noticed Sirhan in the first place "was because there was this good-looking girl in the crowd there."

"All right, was the girl with him?" asked the police.

"It looked as though, yes."

The girl was up on the tray stacker behind Sirhan, and "she was holding on to the other end of the tray table and . . . it looked as if she was almost holding him." Just before he got down, Sirhan turned and smiled and seemed to say something to her or flirt with her. She just smiled. When Sirhan got off the tray stacker, she stayed where she was. But "when she first entered, she looked as though she was sick also. . . . She was good-looking, so I glanced over once in a while."

Di Pierro described the girl as Caucasian, between twenty and twenty-four years old, at approximately the same eye level as Sirhan on the tray stacker, with dark brown hair to just above the shoulders, a little puffed up on one side, and a short, "pug" nose.

"How about her build; could you see that?" "Oh, yeah," said Vincent.

"'Oh, yeah,' what does that mean?"

"Very shapely."

She wore a white dress with black or dark violet polka dots on it and a bib collar made of the same material as the dress. Her face wasn't that pretty, "but I would never forget what she looked like because she had a very good-looking figure—and the dress was kind of lousy."

He didn't see her after the shooting.[13]

* * *

Worse followed for investigators anxious to avoid another Dallas. When Serrano saw Sirhan's picture in the *Los Angeles Times* later that day, she told the FBI "she felt certain this was the same person she saw go up the stairs with this woman."

Early descriptions of Sirhan ranged all over the map—Spanish, Mexican, Filipino. Serrano had grown up in Ohio, where there weren't that many Mexican Americans. She'd been only a year in Los Angeles, and these swarthy guys "all looked the same" to her.[14]

At 11:50 a.m. on June 5, the LAPD finally put out an APB on the girl in the polka-dot dress: "Prior to shooting, suspect observed with a female cauc, 23/27, 5–6, wearing a white viole dress, ? inch sleeves, with small black polka dots, dark shoes, bouffant type hair. This female not identified or in custody."[15]

* * *

As Di Pierro was testifying about the girl before the grand jury on June 7, Serrano was taken back to the Ambassador Hotel for more interviews and asked to reenact her story for a gaggle of investigators from the LAPD, FBI, and Secret Service. No summaries exist for Serrano-related interviews, just the notations "polka-dot story phoney" and "girl in kitchen I.D. settled . . . witt. can offer nothing of further value" scrawled across blank report sheets by lead supervisor Manuel Pena.[16]

* * *

Di Pierro's grand jury testimony only added to the intrigue about the girl in the polka-dot dress, and new sightings soon came flooding in. One report told of a white female matching the description, boarding a 10:30 a.m. flight in Atlanta on June 4. She was overheard telling another woman she was going to Los Angeles "to be there when the bullets fly about Kennedy."[17]

The LAPD advised the FBI that "several women classified by this department as 'psychos' (had called up) and were so obviously not connected, their names were not even taken."[18]

Late that Friday afternoon, nineteen-year-old Kennedy volunteer and belly dancer Cathy Sue Fulmer called Sheriff Peter Pitchess's office to say she thought she might be the girl in the polka-dot dress. At a hastily-arranged press conference with Pitchess, Fulmer told reporters she was at the door to the pantry when she heard the shots and ran into the ballroom, yelling "They shot him!" not "We shot him!" Pitchess thought she matched the description in the APB: "She was young, attractive and wearing a blond, bouffant wig . . . she seemed sincere in wanting to eliminate herself [from the inquiry]."[19]

Sandra Serrano viewed Fulmer at police headquarters and rejected her as "definitely not" the girl she saw. "She didn't even fit the description," Serrano told the *Los Angeles Times*. Not only was she not on the stairs where Serrano claimed to have seen the fleeing woman, but she was wearing a green dress with no polka dots and an orange polka-dot scarf—"You've got to be color-blind to think that's the girl." Serrano was upset that some were already calling her a nut. "I did what Robert Kennedy would have wanted me to do—say what I saw."[20]

* * *

On June 7, Serrano was taken to NBC studios in Burbank but didn't recognize any of the three people she'd seen on the fire escape in TV footage of the crowd. The police interviewed the friends Serrano had been with that night. Irene Chavez "never knew her to imagine incidents or make up stories," and David Haines called her "reliable, level-headed and responsible." The cops couldn't shake Serrano's story.[21]

On June 10, Serrano and Di Pierro were each shown eight assorted dress styles in an effort to find a match for the polka-dot dress the girl was wearing. Serrano stated dress number six looked the same except for the sleeve length. Di Pierro picked out dress number four.[22]

Serrano was then brought back to the Ambassador for another reconstruction with an LAPD detective, FBI agent Richard Burris, and four men from the DA's office.

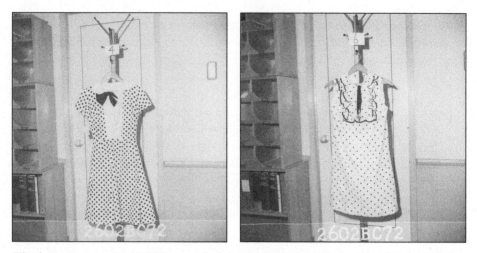

The dresses Serrano and Di Pierro picked out as the closest to the one the girl was wearing.

They zeroed in on a slip of the tongue in Serrano's two LAPD interviews on the night of the shooting. In the first one, Serrano was asked if she heard gunfire.

"Yes."

"When did you hear this sound, approximately?"

"Well, I didn't know it was a gun. I thought it was the backfire of a car."

In the second interview, she said, "I was sitting there for a while and then I heard, I thought it was the backfire of a car. And I thought, to me, I thought I heard six shots, six backfires."

"What did you do when you heard this noise?"

"I just looked around for a car . . . and then about half a minute later, this girl comes tearing down the stairs saying . . . 'We shot him, we shot him.'"

The audiotapes of these interviews make it very clear that Serrano heard backfires from a car, which she later logically associated with shots because of the girl's statement. But the investigators seized their chance—if they could prove it was impossible to hear gunshots from the stairway, by a certain twisted logic, they could say Serrano was lying. [23]

They proceeded to lead Serrano from the pantry, across the Embassy Ballroom to the doors leading out onto the fire escape "she claimed to be sitting on at the time Senator Kennedy was shot." It was impossible, they said, for the girl and her accomplice to run 170 feet across a crowded ballroom within thirty seconds of the shooting. Did she still feel she heard shots?

"I've never heard a gunshot in my life," Serrano said. "I never said I heard shots. I heard six backfires of a car and four or five of them were close together." She then interpreted them as shots, but the investigators weren't listening.

As Serrano again stuck to her remarkably consistent story, Special Agent Burris began to pick holes where he could.

"Why did you not say anything about the woman and the two men going up the stairs in your television interview?" he asked. "The fact you claimed one of the men was Sirhan Sirhan was the most significant part of your story."

"I don't know why," said Serrano. "She then accused those present of lying to her and trying to trick her," reads the FBI report.

She was right. It was a trick question. Serrano appeared on television before any pictures of Sirhan were released. The second man, who didn't come down, was the least significant part of the story when she was interviewed by NBC. Although Sirhan's mug shot was shown on television within hours of the shooting, the police didn't show it to her in her initial interviews, so the connection with Sirhan wasn't made until her June 6 interview with the FBI.[24]

Burris must have known this, and it merely fueled Serrano's rightful paranoia that she was being bullied into retracting her story.

Deputy DA John Howard then asked Serrano if he could videotape the reenactment on the stairs to avoid future misunderstandings. Serrano agreed, but only if two of the hotel kitchen staff would act as witnesses. She didn't trust the "damn cops."[25]

* * *

By now, the investigation was clearly taking its toll on Sandra. A surviving audiotape of the interview on the stairway, clearly indicates she has been crying, and the FBI report concludes, "Following the video tape interview, Serrano stated she was very upset, could not continue, and requested to be taken home."[26]

Later that day, Sandra told her supervisor at the United Insurance Company of America that she had become so nervous, she would have to quit her job as a keypunch operator and return to her parents in Ohio. Her aunt Celilia, who was taking care of her throughout the ordeal, was admitted to a hospital with "a nervous condition."[27]

Late the following afternoon, Serrano called the FBI to say she now had two attorneys who were to be contacted before she would talk any further. She had just changed her phone number after several crank calls, and somebody had tried to break into her house. The LAPD decided to ease off. They advised the FBI that "no effort was being made by the D.A.'s office" to give Serrano a polygraph test "for at least three or four days."[28]

The LAPD used this time to work on more ways of shooting Serrano down.

On June 19, they interviewed Captain Cecil Lynch of the Los Angeles Fire Department, who had been assigned to enforce fire regulations at the Ambassador that night. During Kennedy's speech, Lynch began checking various stairways and exits for possible violations and "checked the stairs Serrano was alleged to have been seated on moments before Senator Kennedy was shot. . . . No one was seated on the stairs."

But Captain Lynch had a vested interest in saying the stairs were clear—he was to blame if they weren't—and Serrano had already talked about a guard chasing people off the fire escape who hadn't seen her sit down. The fact that the police kept digging up such weak counterclaims shows how desperate they were to make Serrano's story disappear.[29]

On the morning of June 20, the LAPD took the "shots-backfires" nonsense to its inevitable conclusion by bringing in prize troubleshooter DeWayne Wolfer to conduct sound-level tests in the pantry. These proved, as if it had any relevance, that "it would have been impossible for Serrano to have heard the shots" from the outside stairway. And, if we believe Captain Lynch, she wasn't even on the fire escape.[30]

These were the only flaws the police could find in Serrano's story. After two weeks of aggressive questioning, this was the best they could come up with. Unfortunately for Serrano, things would get even worse.

* * *

Serrano's story bears uncanny similarities to that of the elderly Jewish couple who ran up to Sergeant Paul Sharaga in the rear parking lot within minutes of the shooting.

The couple were in their late fifties or early sixties and clearly distraught. Sharaga thought they were Jewish and vaguely recalled their name as "the Bernsteins."

The woman did most of the talking and said she and her husband were "just outside the Embassy Room, on the balcony" when a young couple in their early twenties ran by them from the direction of the Embassy Ballroom shouting, "We shot him! We shot him!" in a state of glee.

"Shot who?" Mrs. Bernstein asked.

"Kennedy; we shot him! We killed him!" replied the young woman.

The Bernsteins were too excited to give detailed descriptions, but said the young couple were in their late teens or early twenties, Caucasian, and the girl had blond or light hair and was wearing a polka-dot dress. To Sharaga, "they were excited but their statements were rational . . . not hysterical. They just didn't have time to dream up a story. . . . It was too spontaneous."

Sharaga took the information down in his notepad, tore out the page, and gave it to a field courier to give to Bill Jordan at Rampart Detectives.

As Sharaga set up a command post in the rear parking lot, he recalled radioing the suspects' descriptions to Communications, asking them to broadcast them every fifteen minutes.

At 12:28 a.m., twelve minutes after the shooting, the tape of police transmissions recorded an out-of-breath Sharaga broadcasting the following:

"2L30, roger—Description suspect, the shooting at thirty-four hundred Wilshire Boulevard, male Caucasian, twenty to twenty-two, six foot to six foot two, very thin build, blond curly hair, wearing brown pants, light tan shirt, direction taken unknown."

There was no mention of a girl. At this point, Sharaga didn't know Sirhan was in custody. Presumably, he gave the male suspect priority because the crowd was talking about "the guy who shot Kennedy," and this might have been the guy.

* * *

So, an hour before Serrano appeared on television, this couple provided a second independent sighting of a girl in a polka-dot dress fleeing the scene, shouting "We shot him! We killed him!" The parking lot where Sharaga met the Bernsteins was directly below the stairway Sandra Serrano was sitting on, and the girl and her companion ran past the Bernsteins "just outside the Embassy Room, on the balcony."

It's not clear whether this was a balcony inside the hotel or the small terrace directly above Sandra Serrano, but either way, the Bernsteins may have seen this girl just before Serrano did. Radio cross-talk indicates that confusion swirled about possible suspects in the wake of Sharaga's report:

"Is the suspect in custody or what's the story?"

"He left there approximately five minutes ago . . . in a police car, and there was another suspect being held within the building."

"2A68, regarding the shooting at the Ambassador, witness stated the suspect is a male Latin, twenty-five to twenty-six, five-five, light build, dark bushy hair and dark eyes. Wearing blue Levis, blue jacket, blue tennis shoes. It is unknown whether this suspect is in custody."

Sirhan, the man described by Officer Blishak (unit 2A68) here, was the man in custody. The suspect being held in the building was memorabilia collector Michael Wayne. But stuck out in the parking lot at his command post, Sharaga was out of the loop. At 1:13, he was contacted by Communications: "2L30, the description we have is a male Latin, twenty-five to twenty-six, five-five, bush hair, dark eyes, light build, wearing a blue jacket and blue Levis and blue tennis shoes. Do you have anything to add?"

"2L30, that's not the description that I put out."

Sharaga repeated his description, and the dispatcher contacted Rampart Detectives to check if the second suspect was in custody. As Bill Jordan was preparing to transfer John Doe to Parker Center, he was handed Sharaga's description. This didn't sound like the man he'd been questioning.

When Inspector John Powers arrived on the scene at 1:44 a.m., he radioed Sharaga, asking where he got this second suspect.

"2L30, the second suspect came from a witness who was pushed over by this suspect. Witness and wife, we have name and address. The juvenile officers who were collecting witnesses initially have a sheet of paper with the name and address and phone number of this witness."

"What proximity to the shooting were these people?"

"2L30, they were adjacent to the room."

"2L30, disregard that broadcast. We got Rafer Johnson and Jesse Unruh, who were right next to him, and they have only one man, and don't want them to get anything started on a big conspiracy. This could be somebody that was getting out of the way so they wouldn't get shot. But the people that were right next to Kennedy say there was just one man."

"2L30 to control, disregard my broadcast. A description M/C twenty to twenty-two, six foot to six foot two, this is apparently not a correct description. Disregard and cancel."

* * *

Powers canceled the APB after satisfying himself it was a false lead—a surprising move, only an hour and a half after the shooting.

After closing down his command post, Sharaga went back to Rampart station and spent nine hours dictating his initial report to Captain Floyd Phillips' secretary, then took a copy home.

Although the story of the girl in the polka-dot dress was all over the papers, Sharaga was working nights and didn't take much notice. He'd passed the lead on to the detectives and left them to follow up on it. He was a patrol sergeant, not an investigator. He didn't notice any irregularities until further down the line.[31]

* * *

Irene Gizzi was chairman of Youth for Kennedy in Panorama City and arrived at the hotel with six other girls. Around nine o'clock that night, Gizzi noticed a group of three people talking in the lobby "who did not seem to fit with the exuberant crowd. Observed the female to be wearing a white dress with black polka dots; the girl was standing with a male, possibly Latin, dark sun-bleached hair, gold-colored shirt, and light-colored pants, possibly jeans. Possibly with the suspect [Sirhan] was a third party, a male with a funny nose and black greasy hair."[32]

Two fourteen-year-old high school volunteers with Gizzi also saw this group during the evening. Jeanette Prudhomme was listening to the mariachi band downstairs in the Ambassador Ballroom just after eleven o'clock when she thought she saw Sirhan with a dark-skinned man in a gold-colored shirt and light (possibly blue) pants and a girl in a white dress with black polka dots one inch in size. The man was five-eight, twenty-six or twenty-seven years old, of medium build, with light brown hair. The woman was between twenty-eight and thirty, five-six, with brown, shoulder-length hair.[33]

Katie Keir gave a very similar description of this group—a man in a "gold-colored sport shirt" and blue jeans, another man of medium build with a T-shirt and jeans, both with dark brown hair, and a girl in a white dress with black polka dots. The girl was about twenty-three, five-eight and slightly heavy-set, with dark brown hair fixed in "love-locks." Immediately after the shooting, Keir was standing on the "platform" of a stairway when the girl in the polka-dot dress ran out of the Sunset Room and down the stairway, yelling "We shot Kennedy."[34]

Sandra Serrano was sitting on an outside stairway and ran into the Sunset Room after she saw the girl, so Keir may very well be describing the same couple. All three witnesses were interviewed within days of the shooting.

Washington Post reporter Mary Ann Wiegers may have been describing Keir when she told the FBI she was in the Kennedys' fifth-floor suite after the shooting when a young girl, about fifteen years of age, was brought in by two policemen and a young woman. She saw a girl in a black dress with white polka dots rush by yelling, "We killed him; we killed him." Wiegers said this teenage girl was hysterical at the time she saw her.[35]

* * *

Twenty-one-year-old college student Richard Houston was a few feet away from the double doors leading into the pantry when he heard the shots. Elizabeth Evans came running out, followed by another woman wearing a black-and-white polka-dot dress with "ruffles around the neck and front." As she fled, she said, "'We killed him'; . . . then [she] ran out onto a terrace area outside."

Houston described her as twenty-two to twenty-four years old, five-six, 120 pounds, with long blond hair, brown eyes, and a thin face. His story appeared in the *Alhambra Post Advocate* on June 7, but he wasn't interviewed by the police until September 22 and then never contacted again.[36]

* * *

So, in four separate instances, witnesses saw a girl in a white dress with black polka dots fleeing, saying "We shot him," or "We killed him." Numerous witnesses also saw a girl in a polka-dot dress leaving the pantry right after the shooting.

Jack Merritt, a uniformed security guard working for Ace Guard Service, gave this account: "Just after the shooting, in the confusion of the struggle to disarm Sirhan, I noticed two men and a woman leaving the kitchen through the back exit. I didn't get a good look at the woman's face but she was about five-five, had light-colored hair, and wore a polka-dot dress. One of the men was about six-two . . . with dark hair and a dark suit; the other was five-five or five-six and also wearing a suit. They seemed to be smiling."[37]

Thirty-three-year-old Watts organizer George Green told the FBI that at about eleven fifteen to eleven thirty, he was in the pantry area, watching Kennedy's press secretary, Frank Mankiewicz, being interviewed. At the edge of the crowd, Green noticed a man he would later positively identify as Sirhan, standing near a tall, thin man with black hair—about five-eleven and twenty-two years old—and a girl in her early twenties with "long, blond, free-flowing hair." She wore a white dress with black polka dots and had a "good figure." Green accurately described Sirhan's attire but put his height at five foot eight.

Green was just outside the pantry when he heard the shots. Once inside the pantry door, he noticed the same man and woman "running with their backs toward him . . . attempting to get out of the kitchen area. They seemed to be the only ones who were trying to get out of the kitchen. . . . Everyone else was trying to get in." Green then jumped onto the steam table to help subdue Sirhan.[38]

* * *

More and more stories started appearing in the papers about the mysterious girl in the polka-dot dress. Still shaken by his experience, John Fahey read an article by Fernando Faura in the *San Fernando Valley Times*. He thought twice, then gave the reporter a call.

Faura took Fahey's detailed description of the girl to a police artist in Long Beach. Fahey tweaked the image with the artist until he saw a match, and they had the sketch photographed in color. Faura then showed the picture to Vincent Di Pierro.

"That's her; she's the girl in the polka-dot dress. The girl's face is a little fuller than this sketch has it, but this is the girl."

Faura, convinced he was onto something, brought Fahey before top polygraph operator Chris Gugas, and Fahey passed the lie detector test "like a champion." By now, Faura had *Life* magazine bureau chief Jordan Bonfante interested in running the story. Faura took Fahey to a doctor who specialized in hypnosis, hoping to improve his recall of the girl.

Fahey was skeptical and worried about side effects, but two positives emerged from the session—his jaw no longer ached after recent oral surgery and he remembered another detail about the girl.

"She told me she was leaving LA for San Jose to visit the headquarters of some organization called the Rosalyns, or something like that."

"San Jose? The Rosicrucians?" asked Faura.

"Yeah, that's it. The Rosicrucians."[39]

SIX

THE POLYGRAPH TEST

On June 20, SUS lead supervisor, Lieutenant Manny Pena, suggested that Sergeant Enrique "Hank" Hernandez take Ms. Serrano out for a steak and talk her into taking a polygraph test to determine whether she was telling the truth about the girl in the polka-dot dress.[1]

In 1992, Pena reflected on his dilemma, with attorney Marilyn Barrett: "We got to a point in the thing, where we had to establish something on an investigative basis, that she was mistaken. So I suggested to him that why don't you take her out to dinner and talk nice to her and see if she will take a polygraph. It was a necessary move on my part. I wasn't about to leave the case hanging there. You know very well if we didn't dispel that, we'd still be looking for the girl in the polka-dot dress, you know, and never found her."[2]

Pena's antipathy to Serrano was founded on bad information: "These stories about hearing shots and what have you, it's impossible! Impossible. . . . I requested the reconstruction of the shots. The ballrooms had veloured drapes that thick, all drawn. They had three orchestras going with music on three floors, balloons popping everywhere, and I had a decibel-graph placed at strategic locations to see if you could pick up any sound of the actual reconstruction of the shooting and they couldn't hear a damn thing!"[3]

* * *

In his widely used textbook on criminal investigation, Pena defined the polygraph as a scientific instrument to diagnose truth or deception based on the emotion of fear. Typically, an arm cuff is strapped to the subject's forearm, and changes in breathing, blood pressure, pulse rate, and the electrical resistance of the skin are charted as the subject is asked a series of yes-or-no questions. "Fear of detection by an untruthful subject will cause physiological changes to occur in the subject's body at the point of deception," noted Pena. These changes can be diagnosed only by a "trained, competent examiner."[4]

The accuracy of the polygraph has been contested since its invention by Dr. William Marston in 1915. Marston later created the comic book superhero Wonder

Woman, who carried a golden lariat in her belt that compelled enemies to tell the truth.[5]

Polygraphs are inadmissible as evidence in federal and most state courts. One Supreme Court judgment states that "there is simply no consensus that polygraph evidence is reliable."[6]

A 1997 survey of 421 psychologists estimated the test's average validity at about 61 percent, a little better than chance. "A big problem is that it's not really a test of anything," explained psychophysiologist William Iacono of the University of Minnesota. Nobody knows how the nervous system acts when a person is lying, he said, and people who don't believe in the polygraph may be more likely to fail tests, as their disbelief and nonresponsiveness may look like deception.[7]

* * *

Bearing this in mind, we examine Sergeant Enrique "Hank" Hernandez, the "Terminator" of all conspiracy allegations in this case. Hernandez was the sole polygraph operator for SUS, assigned to "background investigation and conspiracy aspects of the case." He was thirty-seven years old at the time, with fifteen years of police work behind him and, like Pena, had served in the Korean War.[8]

Hernandez would conduct examinations alone with the subject and discuss his findings with Pena. The tapes of his sessions with Serrano could be listened to only with Pena's approval, so a jury of two would decide her fate.

Pena told Barrett that the polygraph is only "as good as the objectivity of the operator." In his book, he advised that "extensive interrogation of the subject within four hours prior to the examination should be avoided. . . . Prolonged interrogation produces an exhausted or antagonistic subject who may not be a fit subject for the examination."[9]

In fact, Hernandez spent at least an hour interrogating Serrano and Di Pierro before their tests, leaving them highly emotional and anxious prior to the examination. By then, they knew Hernandez didn't believe their answers to key questions, so their physical responses were likely to spike on the "pressure" questions.[10]

Serrano's interrogation also took place at night, between nine and ten, after intense questioning that clearly upset her and left her exhausted before the test. But Pena "had every confidence in the guy. He's a very skilled operator . . . very intelligent, very charming and I knew he wouldn't spook her, you know."[11]

* * *

The evening started well. Hernandez took Sandra and her aunt out to dinner and even bought Sandra two drinks—though she was underage—plying the subject with alcohol before the polygraph.[12]

"I'm the last person that you will talk to about the tragedy from an investigative standpoint," Hernandez assured her. "You're a very intelligent girl . . . I'll believe everything that you tell me."

SPECIAL UNIT SENATOR (S.U.S.)

NAME PENA, Manuel S.

RANK LT. SERIAL # 3226 AGE 49

APPOINTED P.D. (Date)10-18-48 TOTAL TIME DEPT. 22 yrs.

PROMOTED LT. 1-2-62 TIME IN PRESENT RANK 6 yrs.
(Rank & Date)   7 mo.

EDUCATION (College, Special courses, Major)
96 Units Police Adm. (Major Police Science)
U.S.C. - Graduate CID School, US Army
E.L.A.C. - Japanese Course Univ. of Hawaii

FOREIGN LANGUAGE (Speak, Write, Proficiency)
Spanish: Read, write, speak, translate fluently
French: Speak, read, write limitedly

MILITARY EXPERIENCE (Rank, Specialty, Etc.)
U.S. Navy, WWII-Chief Petty Officer(Air Corps)
U.S. Army, Korean War-Warrant Officer-Agent in charge 35th C.I.D., France

SPECIAL TALENTS & ABILITIES
Member of Police Science Teaching Staff ELAC 10 yrs. Wrote text "Criminal
Investigation" Published by Calif. Dept. Educ. Used at ELAC & Valley College

SPECIFIC ASSIGNMENT IN S.U.S.
Supervisor, Preparation of Case for trial and Day Watch investigators.

PREVIOUS ASSIGNMENTS (Most recent first)
(Dates)   (Division)   (Total time)   (Assignment)

1. 6-13-68 to pres. S.U.S   2 mo. 7 days   Supv., Case Prep
2. 4-68/6-68   HiPk Det. Div. 2 mo.   Div. Commander
3. 1-68/4-68   Robb. Div.   3 mo.   Supv. Bank Robb. Team
4. 6-64/1-68   Fthl Det. Div. 3½ yrs.   Div. Commander
5. 6-46/6-64   Robb. Div.   18 yrs.
6.
7.
8.

TOTAL INVESTIGATIVE EXPERIENCE (Years) 22 (Months) 1

SPECIAL COMMENDATIONS RECEIVED (Medal of Valor, Military decorations, Etc.)
U.S. Navy Commendation Medal WWII
Class "A" Commendation for Bravery LAPD

SPECIAL UNIT SENATOR (S.U.S.)

NAME HERNANDEZ, Enrique

RANK LT. SERIAL # 7101 AGE 37

APPOINTED P.D. (Date)10-3-53 TOTAL TIME DEPT. 15 yrs

PROMOTED LT. 7-68 TIME IN PRESENT RANK 2 mo.
(Rank & Date)

EDUCATION (College, Special courses, Major)
A.A. EAST LOS ANGELES COLLEGE
Police Admin./L.A.P.D. Polygraph Exam School

FOREIGN LANGUAGE (Speak, Write, Proficiency)
Spanish

MILITARY EXPERIENCE (Rank, Specialty, Etc.)
Sgt./Forward Observer Field Artillery/Korean Conflict

SPECIAL TALENTS & ABILITIES
Dept. Polygraph Examiner/Teach Interrogation Techniques at Police Academy.

SPECIFIC ASSIGNMENT IN S.U.S.
Investigator, Assigned to the Background Invest. and Conspiracy aspects of
case/ Administer poly exams as required.

PREVIOUS ASSIGNMENTS (Most recent first)
(Dates)   (Division)   (Total time)   (Assignment)

1. 1966-68   S.I.D.   Approx. 2 yrs.   Polygraph Examiner
2. 64-66   B.A.D.   " 2 yrs.   Burglary Invest.
3. 63-64   Univ. Dets.   " 1½ yrs.   Robb. Invest.
4. 61-63   Homicide Div. " 2 yrs.   P.M. Homicide Invest.
5. 59-61   Cent. Vice   " 2 yrs.   Gang Squad, Vice Squad
6.
7.
8.

TOTAL INVESTIGATIVE EXPERIENCE (Years) 10 (Months)

SPECIAL COMMENDATIONS RECEIVED (Medal of Valor, Military decorations, Etc.)

Lieutenant Manuel Pena,
lead supervisor, Special Unit Senato

Sergeant Enrique Hernandez,
LAPD polygraph operator.

They then adjourned to Parker Center, and an enthusiastic Serrano told her story over again, the same as before.

Hernandez explained the workings of the polygraph, but Serrano was still unsure. Her lawyers had advised her not to take one, and from what she'd read, she didn't trust the polygraph.

"I don't want it to put me in a bad way," she said. "We went on a field trip one time to Cleveland and they asked the teacher her name and the polygraph machine showed she was lying."

Hernandez said the success of the test was down to the skill of the operator. He talked up his credentials, but Serrano wasn't convinced: "The thing that I don't understand is why a polygraph is administered, if it will not even stand up in court?"

"Somebody has given you wrong information on that," said Hernandez, deliberately misleading her. "If that was the case, we wouldn't have polygraphs . . . but we're not going to court with this thing." He'd make sure of that.

"I will give you a fair, honest and objective test," he said. "I like you as a person. . . . You see, Sandy, this is a great tragedy, probably the second greatest tragedy we've had in this country."

"I know!"

"We don't want to give anyone an opportunity of saying this was not the truth . . . to make sure that this report is not incomplete [like] the Warren Report that was written in Dallas, Texas."

Sandy was hooked up to the polygraph, and Hernandez performed a "control test," to gauge her normal physiological response. He asked Sandy to stop nervously tapping her fingers and to answer questions with one-word answers—yes or no. He then asked her aunt to leave and began the test proper.

"Is your true first name Sandra?" he asked.

"No." Sandra laughed nervously, trying to test him.

"Do you believe I will be completely fair with you throughout this examination?" "No."

"Between the ages of eighteen and nineteen, do you remember lying to the police about something very serious?"

"No."

"When you told the police that a girl with a polka-dot dress told you she had shot Kennedy, were you telling the truth?"

"She didn't say, 'We had shot Kennedy.' She said, 'We shot him.'"

"Did a girl in a polka-dot dress tell you that 'We have shot Kennedy'?"

"It was a white dress with black polka dots."

"Did a girl in a white dress with black polka dots tell you 'We have shot Kennedy'?"

"Yes."

"You can relax now," said Hernandez. "Remember I asked you to answer all my questions with one word—yes or no."

"Yeah, but they can't be answered like that."

"Well, we'll review them, okay? I'll word them any way that you want me to, so you can answer them with one word, yes or no. Are you afraid right now, Sandra?

"I don't like this. It's not that I'm afraid; I just don't like it."

"I know you don't."

"May I ask you something? When you asked me what my name was, what'd it turn out?

"Sandra?"

"Yeah," she said.

"That you said no. It was meaningful to you. I think you have a different name . . . you use a different name. I'm not concerned with it, though."

Sandra snorted in derision. "See . . . this is what I mean!"

"Do you believe me, what I'm telling you?"

"No." She laughed. "Because I think it was rotten in the beginning that you never mentioned it to my aunt that I was going to take a polygraph."

"Oh, yes, I did. I told her this morning."

"She said you just wanted to talk to me, 'cause I asked her. And I think that's rotten . . . but anyways, go ahead. We're here; we can't do anything about it. Let's go and get it done with."

Hernandez reminded Sandy that they needed to do this so the family of Senator Kennedy could rest—"Ethel wants to find out what happened to her husband. This isn't a silly thing."

"I know it's not a silly thing, but don't come with this sentiment business. Let's just get this job done."

He asked another question. "What state is it now that we're in?"

"Ohio," said Sandra, doing everything in her power to mess up the machine.

"Sandy, I want to talk to you like a brother," ventured Hernandez. "You're an intelligent young girl. You know that for some reason this was made up. . . .

"You owe it to Senator Kennedy, the late Senator Kennedy, to come forth and be a woman about this. You don't know and I don't know if he's our witness right now in this room, watching what we're doing here. Don't shame his death by keeping this thing up! I have compassion for you. I want to know why you did what you did. This is a very serious thing."

"I seen those people!"

"No. No. No. No, Sandy. Remember what I told you about that? You can't say you saw something that you didn't see. I can explain this to the investigators so you won't even have to talk to them. What you say you saw is not true. Tell me why you made up the story and no one else will talk to you. You can't live a life of shame knowing what you're doing right now is wrong. . . . Please, in the name of Kennedy!"

"Don't say 'in the name of Kennedy.'"

"You know that this is wrong."

"I remember seeing a girl!"

"No . . . no . . . I'm talking about what you have told me here about seeing a person tell you, 'We shot Kennedy,' and that's wrong!"

"That's what she said!"

"No, it isn't. Sandy, please . . . I loved this man!"

"So did I! Don't shout at me."

"Well, I'm trying not to shout, but this is such an emotional thing with me, you see. If you loved the man, the least you owe him is the courtesy of letting him rest in peace."

* * *

Hernandez told Sandy she could either confide in him or he could tell the press she was a liar—"but this is the wrong way because I have to look at myself when I shave in the morning. You're a young lady and I wanna try to do whatever I believe is best for you. I have the authority to cancel the report that you've made but the only way I can do it is by you telling me the truth."

"But there's nothing more to tell!" Sandra insisted.

"It's like a disease that is gonna grow with you and make an old woman out of you before your time. I'm asking you to redeem something that's a deep wound that will grow with you—like cancer."

He asked her to go back over her story.

"Well . . . there was this girl coming down the stairs and she said, 'We shot him, we shot him.'"

"No, Sandy."

"This girl in a polka-dot dress, a white dress with polka-dots." Hernandez shook his head as they stared down at the charts drawn by the polygraph needles.

"Sandy, it's like a disease."

"It says I never even seen a girl with a polka-dot dress?"

"No, it's saying that nobody told you 'We have shot Kennedy.'"

"Somebody told me that they have shot Kennedy. I'm sorry, but that's true! That is true. I'm not gonna say, 'No, they didn't tell me,' just to satisfy anybody else. . . . I remember seeing the girl!"

"You mark my words that one of these days, if you're woman enough, you will get a letter from Ethel Kennedy, personal, thanking you for at least letting her rest on this aspect of this investigation. And I'm not going to put words in your mouth but I want you to tell me the truth about the staircase. Nobody on that staircase told you that 'We have shot Kennedy.'"

"Somebody told me that. Honest!"

"Right now, I have my deepest compassion for you because . . . you're an intelligent girl . . . you have a nice future ahead of you, but . . . you're growing real fast in this room right now because you know that you have to make a decision to tell what's truthful, what's honest, what's right."

"I've already told you that."

"No, you can't say that."

"I can so!"

"With your lips you can say it. But with your feeling, your heart, your soul . . . You know you feel like crying right now."

"Who, me? No, I don't."

"Yes, you do."

"I'm not crying!"

"Well, you feel like crying. . . . How come you're making yourself suffer like this?"

"I'm not making myself suffer! I'm not suffering."

Hernandez changed tack. "Do you want me to try and take care of this thing as easily and as sensibly as we can for you?"

"Yeah."

"Okay, let me tell you this. After some time, I will have to make a report. . . . I can make the report myself if you take me into your confidence, but there's people out here waiting, and if you don't tell me the truth, Sandy, they're gonna want to talk to you again. And the way it was mishandled last time, what if it's mishandled again?"

"I'll tell them they can go to hell."

Hernandez could see Sandra's resolve beginning to crumble. He started up the machine again and began to chip away at her story by insisting the machine said she was lying. First, he removed the polka dots from the dress. Now, it was a white dress. Next, he tried to change "we shot him" to "they shot him" and suggested she only saw the girl, and no one else.

"Somebody was with her . . . somebody else was there." "Somebody else was where?"

"On that stair. Coming down."

"Below?"

"Above!"

* * *

Hernandez was obviously trying to confuse her—it's quite disgusting to listen to. Finally, exhausted and distraught, Sandra recanted. She started crying and blamed the whole thing on "the damn cops" who first interviewed her.

"They messed me all up and I knew all along they were messing me up. That's when we first hired the lawyer, 'cause they'd been messing me up. They'd keep asking me over and over, 'What did you see that night?' . . . All I know is that it was one big mess."

"Well, we're gonna stop it right now, aren't we, Sandy?" soothed Hernandez. "And I'm gonna go see if we can get a stenographer to come up and take a statement and stop it right now. Okay?"

Sandy let out a big sigh, and Hernandez put his polygraph machine back in his briefcase, mission accomplished.[13]

* * *

When Hernandez came back with a stenographer and a tape recorder, he offered Sandra a chance to "rectify her misquoted statements."

"When was the first time you knew that this was a pack of mistruths somebody else had misquoted or printed?" he asked.

Serrano admitted, under guided questioning, that "the whole thing was a lie." She got the polka dots from Vincent Di Pierro, when they met in the witness room before her TV interview and talked about the girl.

"So that's where this thing about the polka-dot dress, that's where it started," he suggested.

"I guess, I don't know," said Serrano.[14]

This was obviously not true. Vincent Di Pierro said he didn't share any details of the mystery girl with Serrano because an officer saw them talking and warned them not to discuss the case. Now, Sandra herself remembered talking to Deputy DA Ambrose about a polka-dot dress out in the parking lot before she met Di Pierro.[15]

"Well, regardless of what was said before," said Hernandez, swatting away the facts, "now we know it was a girl in a white dress that you saw?"

"Right," said Sandra, anxious to play along.

But even at this point, there was something halfhearted about her responses, and she didn't suffer Hernandez's fabrications easily.

"The facts that you saw were mistelevised," he said at one point.

"Well, they can't have been mistelevised, because I said that; I actually said that!"

"Also, before, you said that you had heard some shots?"

"No, I never said I heard shots."

"Well, now, somebody quoted you as saying you heard shots?"

"I heard backfires of a car. . . . I know they weren't gunshots."

* * *

Sergeant Hernandez's report of the interview states that while Serrano "was sitting on the stairway, approximately four or five people came running down the stairway screaming that Kennedy had been shot. . . . Miss Serrano was interrogated extensively and ultimately she admitted that the story about Sirhan Sirhan, the girl in the polka dot dress and the gunshots was not true. She stated that she had been sitting on the stairway at the time that she had mentioned and that she did in fact hear a car backfire a couple of times, but knew that the sounds did come from a car, and were not gunshots." The later LAPD summary characterized Serrano as the young woman who admitted she concocted her story after failing a polygraph.[16]

* * *

The day after the Serrano polygraph, the APB on the girl in the polka-dot dress was canceled and the LAPD announced to the press that they were calling off their hunt for the mystery girl. Inspector John Powers told reporters "they had established that no such person ever existed but was the product of a young Kennedy worker's hysteria after the assassination." Once Serrano had retracted her story, the LAPD was off the hook.[17]

Sandy Serrano quit her job as a keypunch operator and fled back to her parents' home in Ohio to escape further harassment. In mid-July, the LAPD interviewed her friend, Greg Abbott. Sandy told him she had cooperated with investigators but had been unfairly treated. She still stuck to her story about seeing the girl in the polka-dot dress. A month later, Sergeant Hernandez was promoted to lieutenant.[18]

* * *

Three days after the LAPD investigation files were finally released to the public, on April 22, 1988, Serrano surfaced to tell radio interviewer Jack Thomas, "There was a lot of badgering that was going on. I was just twenty years old and I became unglued. . . . I said what they wanted me to say."[19]

* * *

In 1992, Marilyn Barrett read some of the more objectionable passages of Serrano's polygraph test back to Manny Pena:

> *Using good emotional techniques to bring somebody around to admitting something, that's just interrogating technique.... I don't see anything wrong with the use of those words, trying to draw out compassion ... there's all kinds of ways to draw somebody into a crying jag for the purpose of getting to the truth.... I don't see anything harmful in the way Hank handled this ... He was a fine polygraph operator ... and he came back with a positive on it, that she admitted she was probably mistaken and that she didn't hear them say "we shot him" and quite frankly, I welcomed it because we tried every way in the world to find the gal in the polka-dot dress and see if we could substantiate her story and we couldn't do it.*
>
> *I'm a professional—I've never faked a piece of evidence in my life. I sincerely believe that she was just honestly mistaken. Because everything else in the case points to Sirhan working alone.*
>
> *She was a young kid and she was projected into the national limelight. She was on every television set in the country overnight. There were interviews on top of interviews and she was a real celebrity. She was the hottest thing on TV, nationwide. And for a young kid like that to be projected into this kind of limelight—it might be a little difficult to give it up. I felt at the time that it was very difficult for her to say, "Yeah well, I was mistaken." She'd be losing a lot of celebrity status.[20]*

This is nonsense. Serrano gave only one television interview, to Sander Vanocur, and it was the press and police attention that made her life difficult. Pena's attitude amply illustrates the pigheaded thinking within LAPD at the time.

* * *

In December 2006, Sandra Serrano granted me the first full interview she has given since the polygraph test with Enrique Hernandez. She was a California delegate to the Democratic National Convention in 2004 and still lives in Los Angeles, where she runs a children's center.

Sandra still clearly describes what happened that night:

> *It was very claustrophobic in the ballroom; you could barely move ... so I just stepped out onto the fire escape and a little balcony attached.... While I was sitting there, three people passed by—a woman and two men. The woman, I remember, was definitely an Anglo and, at the time, I thought both men were Latinos. And it struck me that an Anglo woman was with two Latinos. One*

of the guys looked like service help, and she was dressed better, so I thought, "Oh, that's strange."

And they went in, said, "Excuse me," very polite. Then, a little later, two of them came out and, like, tripping over each other and tripping over me. And I said, "What happened?" They said, "We shot him, we shot him." I said, "You shot who?" And they said, "The senator."

And I said, "What?" And I remember going into the ballroom, and everything was chaotic, absolutely chaotic. People were crying and screaming. . . . I remember having to ask somebody what happened. And they said the senator had been shot."

Sandra recalls that the girl did the talking. She was a light-skinned brunette with "a Bob Hope, Richard Nixon kind of nose . . . a little bit ski [turned up]. . . . I remember very distinctively [*sic*] that she was wearing a white dress with black polka dots. With a round collar and a little ruffle around the collar, like a bib top, sort of."

Were the three who went up, together? "Yes. Oh, they definitely were together." The guy in service clothes resembled Sirhan—when she saw the photo in the *LA Times* the next day, "I said, 'Wow, it really does look like that guy.' I remember being frightened because he lived about a mile and a half from my house."

The attitude of the two on the way down was "'Get out of my way, I'm leaving,' 'cause I distinctly remember them tripping, like ready to fall on me, they were moving so quickly."

Sandra remembers meeting Vincent Di Pierro amid all the confusion. "He said, 'Why are you here?' and I told him what happened, and I remember him saying, 'Oh, I saw that woman, too,' and I said, 'You did?' and he said, 'Yeah,' and I said, 'Wow.' And I don't remember anything more. If we were together five minutes, that was a long time, 'cause it was just like somebody that was sitting next to you and the next moment they were gone, you know? Things were moving so quickly."

Watching the Sander Vanocur interview again, Sandra says, "I seem very controlled—you're gonna break down at any moment but you're controlling it—but at the same time, very sure of what I'm saying."

After the Vanocur interview, she was turned over to the LAPD. "The interviews after were just horrible. I felt like I was a criminal. That's my best description. I felt like I was a criminal and I had done something wrong. I didn't make the connections that other people were trying to make. I just simply reported what I seen."

She was fearful for her safety, after the wave of political assassinations, "and the LAPD interviews played very heavily into that. They made me feel unsafe. They made me feel like if I made a spectacle of myself . . . I could be next. Which is simply ridiculous now that I think of it—as an adult, I've thought of it many times—but when you're eighteen and you have people in power telling you things, you sort of fall into the trap. So I thought the police were mean; I thought they were really, really mean."

First came the polka-dot dresses. "I distinctly remember feeling like they were trying to drive me crazy, to say that I was mentally unstable, because they had hung probably ten to twelve polka-dot dresses in a room and left me there with all these polka-dot dresses all hanging around. And then coming in and asking me, 'What dress most looks like the dress that the girl wore? Were the polka dots the size of a nickel, were they the size of a dime, were they the size of a quarter?' You know . . . you're trying to confuse a person, trying to make them feel like 'Oh I don't know. . . . I don't know what it was.'"

Then came the sessions with Hernandez:

He was a very frightening person, a very frightening person. He was like some Dr. Jekyll–Mr. Hyde type, you know. One minute, he was just really nice and soft-spoken, like a wonderful big brother. Then, the next minute, he was like, "You're an awful person and you're hurting the Kennedys and Mrs. Kennedy asked me personally to tell you," and I'm like, "Oh, my God," you know.

I think a lot of it was classic "good cop, bad cop" kind of stuff. . . . I had a vague feeling it was his job to make me sound like a crazy person . . . to discredit me . . . and all through the interview he kept turning on and turning off the tape recorder. And I remember saying, "Why do you keep turning that off and turning that on; you're only recording some of what I'm saying. Why aren't you recording it all?" And him convincing me that I was being hysterical, so I needed composure time. . . .

In retrospect, I think he was using a form of editing. I might have said some things that they didn't want to hear . . . and I remember thinking that he was lying and then thinking, "No, he can't lie, he's the police, the police don't lie, the police stand for good and honor and all that stuff you're raised with in the Midwest in the fifties.

She laughs.

"When I was asked to go through my time on the fire escape, I said 'I heard backfires of a car.' 'Oh, are you saying you heard gunshots?' 'No, I heard back-fires of a car.' And before you knew it, backfires became gunshots. But again that was all in the questioning."

Gradually, Hernandez wore her down. "I felt like I was going crazy. I just wanted to be done with it . . . so I remember saying to him, 'Whatever you want me to say, I'll say, okay. I'm not here to hurt anybody, I don't want to do anything bad, so whatever you want me to say, I'll say.' I mean they were the cops, they were the good guys."

* * *

Today, Sandra still stands by her original story. "I saw the two people come down and saw three people go up. They made those statements to me and that's what I saw, that's what I experienced. . . . There's certain things about what happened that day that I will never forget and the statement 'We shot him, we shot him,' I'll never forget that. So I'm very clear in my mind that that's what was said."

She's also suspicious of Hernandez's motives: "'You didn't do that, you didn't see that, you weren't there . . . you're making all of this up.' Just a lot of browbeating. So, you know, during later years, it crosses your mind—'if there was nothing there, why did they beat you up so much?'"

* * *

In the early seventies, Serrano became heavily involved in Latino politics, and the same guy would always be at the fund-raisers, staring at her across the room. Years later, she asked a politician friend who he was.

"'Oh, that's Hank Hernandez,' and I said, 'Oh . . . who's he?' and he said, 'Oh, he used to work for LAPD but he's really with the CIA.' I said, 'The CIA?' and he said, 'Yeah, he's got something going on the side with security.' So, like a week later, my friend calls me, 'You know who that guy is? The guy that's staring at you. He's the guy who interviewed you during the Kennedy stuff.' I said, 'What?' And he said, 'Don't mess with him. Don't talk to him, just stay away from him.' And I remember getting scared again.

"And I remember at one event, years later, he was staring at me and I just stared at him and made a face at him and him just sort of like chuckling and walking off . . . like he was saying, 'Oh, she finally figured out who I was,' you know. . . . I just blocked him out. Bad man. Put him aside."

I asked Sandra if she thought there had been a conspiracy. "If you think about it unemotionally . . . common sense tells you, yes, more than one person had to be involved. It's just too big of a deal. I think, like the guy in Dallas . . . certain people are just fall guys. So, yeah, I think there was something bigger behind the whole thing. But time does not necessarily tell all. Some things, for whatever reason, are left to be a mystery."[21]

* * *

On July 1, Vincent Di Pierro was given a polygraph examination by Sergeant Hernandez. Audiotapes of these sessions still exist, but the first hour of tape, before the test began, is inaudible. The next audiotape begins with Hernandez selling the virtues of the polygraph to Di Pierro.

"It's a piece of machinery; that's what it is," said Hernandez.

"I guess it can make mistakes, too," said Vince.

"No, no. That's the funny thing about it. It has no feelings. . . . The thing is this, Vince, that there are people who are capable of taking a lie detector test, lying and not being found out. . . . But the last national survey found only thirty-three people out of a thousand could beat the system."

"I'm curious; has it ever been wrong?" Vince asked. "No. In fact, you know Sandra Serrano?"

"Yeah."

"I gave her a test the other day," teased Hernandez. "Yeah? What happened?"

"Well . . . it wasn't wrong."

"It wasn't wrong?" Vince suddenly sounded worried.

"It wasn't wrong."

Vincent sat in silence for a moment. "Did she make it up or what?"

"Well . . . I think in all fairness to you," said Hernandez, "I'll discuss this with you later."

Vince apologized for being so nervous, saying he was keen to testify but wanted to know "what you advise on what I should testify to."

Hernandez then played magician as he ran Di Pierro through a control test by asking him to pick one of five numbered cards and place it facedown on the table. He then asked Vince to answer no as he ran through each of the five numbers, expecting Vincent's nervous response to reveal which card he was holding.

Hernandez started asking for numbers: one, two, three, four. When he got to five, Vince swallowed his answer and comically mumbled no, making it obvious that was the card he was holding. Hernandez guessed correctly and Vince was impressed.

"So I'm not one of the thirty-three!" said Vince. "It's amazing. There's absolutely no way you can fool it. That's good."

When the test started, Vince answered yes, he believed Hernandez would be completely fair with him, but seemed to choke with nerves on the key questions. "Is there anything about the story that you have told me that is not really true?" asked Hernandez.

Vincent's "no" is almost inaudible. He sounds petrified.

But he did stick to his story. Yes, he was telling the truth when he said he saw a girl standing next to Sirhan right before Kennedy was shot. No, there wasn't any question he was afraid to be asked.

Hernandez stopped the test after the first few questions, clearly unhappy, saying they needed time to talk away from the machine.

"Because I think if we go through with this . . . you know that you're gonna flunk the test. . . . I think that you want to square off whatever you want to square off in your mind before we continue here. . . . You don't want a piece of machinery to find out for you what you know."

Vince was impatient. "I'm sorry. When you mentioned about the girl, did it say I was lying or what?"

"Well, no . . . I'm not going to put it that way. . . . I want you to tell me and correct what you should correct at this point. Okay?"

"Okay. Fine. You asked about the girl and I say that there is a girl. I saw a girl there. Now, whether the machine said yes or no, I don't know. . . . I won't change it because that's what I remember seeing."

Hernandez pointed to the spike on his charts and coaxed Vince to a point where he was no longer convinced that he saw the girl.

"And we can't go ahead and say that you did see a girl when you're not convinced that you did see a girl," reasoned Hernandez.

"All right. Okay. That's fair."

"I want you to be clear with yourself. . . . Did you first get the idea about a girl being next to Sirhan when you talked to Sandra Serrano?"

"Maybe I did. . . . I don't know," said Vince. "Like I say, there was so much confusion that night."

"You know, it could be a very easy question for me to ask you, 'Did you make up the story about the girl in the polka-dot dress?' And you can't say maybe."

"Can you ask that? I'd feel better. . . . Seriously, I want to find out myself."

When Hernandez started up his questions again, Vincent insisted he saw a girl with a polka-dot dress looking at Sirhan and that he didn't make the story up.

"What does it say? Did I or didn't I?"

"You know what it says. . . . You made the story up. You didn't see a girl with a polka-dot dress."

"I didn't?"

Hernandez showed him the charts, allegedly spiking at the key questions. "Let's do this, I'm gonna go back here, get a stenographer to clarify the statement, and we'll get it squared off and nobody's gonna talk to you anymore as far as I'm concerned."

"Okay . . . and you want me just to leave the girl or what?"

"I want you to tell the truth about the girl."

"According to that, I'm lying. I don't see how."

"Well . . . like I said to you before, I think you made it up after you heard Sandra talking about it . . . and, for your own information, she was lying about it, too."

Hernandez praised Vince for being a man about this—"maybe you saw her in the ballroom somewhere."

"She was in the same room, though. . . . I swear it looked as though she was with him."

The session ends with Vince apologizing if the machine says he wasn't truthful. "I don't know, maybe it was because I was nervous, I'm sorry. . . . Could it possibly be, though, that I heard it from Serrano and then kept it in my mind?"

"You know, Vince, the human mind is a funny piece of machinery."

"'Cause I'm confused myself now, you see. . . . I don't know."[22]

They moved to another room and a stenographer joined them. Now that Vince had his story straight, it would go on the record. What went before was only on tape, and that would be locked away for twenty years.

We hear an off-the-record comment by Hernandez before the reinterview begins. "I'm gonna try and keep it from being an outright lie, you see, so we'll try and approach it that way".

"Uh-huh," agreed Vincent. He then takes a backseat as Hernandez guides him through a stage-managed charade.

"Okay, Vincent, there are many statements in that previous conversation that we know are false, right?"

"Yes, sir."

"As a matter of fact, you have now told me that there was no lady standing next to Sirhan."

"That's correct."

"I think what you have told me is that you probably got this idea about a girl in a black-and-white polka-dot dress after you talked to Miss Sandra Serrano."

"Yes, sir, I did."

"What did she tell you that prompted you to dream up . . . a woman behind Sirhan?"

"She stated that there was this girl that was wearing a polka-dot dress came running down, I guess it was this hallway, saying that 'we shot him' and then we started asking each other questions about the girl, and evidently, I went along with what she said as being a person that I imagined I saw."

"Is there anything else that you have told me previously . . . that you know now is not the truth?"

"No. Nothing. Only about the girl," says Vincent. "That good enough?" "I think this is about all we need."[23]

* * *

I met Vincent in Los Angeles a couple of hours after I interviewed Sandra Serrano. He followed his father into the catering business and is now retired, with a love of old sports cars. Unfortunately, there are major problems with Vincent as a witness. Today, he insists he saw Sirhan's gun a couple of inches from Kennedy's head, but he told the grand jury it was two to four feet away.

He also has his own take on his encounter with Hernandez:

He was trying to say that there was no girl. And I said, "No, there was a girl. . . . I'm not going to say I didn't see a girl. I'd be lying." He says, "You're lying now."

I say, "Really? The polygraph doesn't say that."

"Well, you can't read a polygraph."

I wouldn't change my story and he finally had to give in because [Deputy DA] John Howard said, "Stop, he's testifying, period,". . . and I was on the stand for three days in the trial with Grant Cooper. . . . I was scared out of my mind.[24]

While Vincent strongly resisted Hernandez at first, his memory of this encounter was highly selective. He forgot that he finally crumbled under pressure with Hernandez and that he was on the stand for twenty minutes with Grant Cooper, not three days. His testimony was a shambles for the prosecution, as will be shown in Chapter 11, as Vincent contradicted both his grand jury testimony and his "corrected statements" to Hernandez.[25]

* * *

On July 19, Lieutenant Manuel Pena forwarded his second progress report to Captain Hugh Brown, commander of the LAPD Homicide Division. Of the 1,485 interviews that had been assigned, 838 had been completed. "To date, no factual information has been developed that would in any way substantiate a conspiracy."[26]

* * *

What happened to fourteen-year-old Katie Keir, who saw a girl in a white dress with black polka dots run out of the Sunset Room and down a stairway, yelling, "We shot Kennedy"?

A later progress report on Keir and her friends, Irene Gizzi and Jeanette Prud-homme, carried the instruction "Re-interview all persons named in this interview. Inform that Serrano story [false]. Offer tactful opportunity to correct statements."[27]

Two months later, each girl was reinterviewed in the presence of her parents, and the police persuaded Keir that she had heard the girl say, "Someone shot Kennedy" or "They shot Kennedy." The other girls "who initially thought they saw Sirhan . . . retracted much of their earlier observations," which the police blamed on "the publicity concerning the woman in the polka-dot dress."

By the end of August, a progress report concerning witnesses claiming to see Sirhan with coconspirators at the hotel concluded that "each individual was re-interviewed in depth and has either retracted . . . statements after they have been proven false or . . . voluntarily modified . . . previous statements. To date, there has been no evidence located or truthful witnesses contacted that indicate a conspiracy existed to assassinate Robert F. Kennedy."[28]

* * *

The last man standing was John Fahey. Hank Hernandez stepped up to the plate with his foolproof polygraph, and Fahey was summoned to Parker Center and wired up to the machine.

Fahey gamely stuck to his story, but Hernandez concluded that most of his answers were lies—he had never seen Sirhan and the girl had never told him of a plan to assassinate Kennedy.

"These answers will have to be changed," Hernandez informed him. "Either you change them, or I'll change them in my report."

"Can I come back later and make my own corrections?" asked Fahey.

"Of course you can," said Hank.

On September 9, Fahey returned to Parker Center to see Hernandez and Sergeant Phil Alexander "in order to clarify the situation." A stenographer recorded the proceedings.

"Now, what we're trying to do here, John," began Hernandez, "is to determine the truth. . . . Was there anything during your association with that woman that led you to believe that she was in any way connected with the assassination of Senator Kennedy?"

"No, sir."

Fahey said he had been overexcited and the lady's "bad taste toward Mr. Kennedy led me to believe that possibly she had something to do with it."

"Okay, as a matter of fact, John, now you know that in your mind all along there was nothing that happened that would lead any reasonable person to form a belief that she was connected with the assassination of Senator Kennedy, was there?"

"Now that I have sat down and thought it all through, yes, you're right, sir."

Hernandez suggested to Fahey that "the man following you and the girl to Oxnard might have been a jealous boyfriend or husband . . . have you ever thought about that?"

"No, sir," said Fahey.

"Will you think about it now?"

"Yes, sir. That could be true."

Hank blamed the newspaper reporter for the confusion. "I think Faura romanticized you."

"He put words in your mouth, so to speak," chipped in Sergeant Alexander, "led you to believe certain things that you consequently found out not to be true and so forth. He created some of these beliefs in your mind."

"Yes, sir . . . he romanced me," agreed Fahey.

"As a matter of fact, John," said Hernandez, "this girl that you're referring to from the IdentaKit, you knew all along that this girl didn't exist, didn't you?"

"The girl exists," insisted Fahey. "The girl was with me that day. That's who the girl is, the picture is of." It was a "pretty close" likeness to the girl, as later verified by Vincent Di Pierro.

Faced with an awkward fact, Hernandez changed the subject.

"In my mind, though, John, as I understand you, you had no sound basis for . . . any connection with this woman and the assassination of Kennedy."

"No, sir, only that someone was after me for my car possibly, or I was getting hijacked or something."

"Right. . . . Maybe you concocted this whole story to cover up your secret meeting with this girl, Gilderdine?"

"No, I didn't state all this to cover up anything," insisted Fahey, "but I would appreciate if you didn't bother my wife about this . . . because I love my wife, and, gentlemen, I want to keep her."

"No problem," replied Hernandez.

"Could you also help me get rid of Faura?"

"If he bothers you any more, you refer him to us," said Alexander. "If he refuses to go, he can be put in jail for disturbing the peace or trespassing."

"Sure. This is your inherent right," confirmed Hernandez. "Nobody can go around bothering you, John."[29]

* * *

The final report stripped Fahey's story to the bone: "Fahey stated he had actually picked up a woman at the Ambassador Hotel on June 4th and spent the day with her. The rest of the story had been a figment of his imagination."[30]

* * *

After dismissing or discrediting every witness to a sinister girl in a polka-dot dress, the LAPD decided to produce its own polka-dot girl. Their summary report offers a section titled "Actual Girl in the Polka-Dot Dress." Valerie Schulte, an attractive blond Kennedy girl, models a green dress with large yellow polka dots and is photographed in front and profile shots.[31]

But there are a couple of obvious problems: Schulte was a blonde, not a dark brunette; she wore a green dress, not a white one; her dress had large yellow polka dots instead of small black ones; and on the night of the assassination, her leg was in a cast from hip to ankle and she walked with a crutch—a detail every witness to the girl in the polka-dot dress seems to have missed.[32]

Vincent Di Pierro said the girl caught his attention as he walked through the swinging doors into the pantry with the senator. Schulte was walking right behind Di Pierro at the time. She was later pushed forward into his line of vision, but at no point was she standing anywhere near Sirhan.[33]

As with the polygraph examinations, such subtle nuances weren't allowed to get in the way of what the LAPD decided had happened. Vincent Di Pierro was later called to testify at Sirhan's trial and readily identified Valerie Schulte as the girl he had seen. The defense attorneys then read his craven responses to Hernandez into the record, destroying his testimony.[34]

The crux of the problem was that Vincent had insisted there was a girl by Sirhan wearing a white dress with black polka dots, yet he identified the girl as Valerie Schulte. As Grant Cooper demonstrated, this didn't make any sense, but Vincent still sticks to this story today:

> *I was sure it was Valerie. . . . John Howard made me look at a whole bunch of pictures and I picked Valerie out sixteen times. . . . I actually had the ability to talk with her prior to the trial and I apologized for putting her in a bad position because . . . I think she had a broken foot at the time, so I don't think she was the one running through the hallway, screaming anything, so*

I'm sorry that people have made a big thing of that. I really never should have even mentioned her because I really don't think she had anything to do with it.

He glanced at her as though a guy was checking out a girl. Whether they were together I doubt it. . . . I don't think that she would have wanted to go out with someone like him, but . . . he was standing on the stacker and she was behind that . . . to his left. . . . It looked like he turned to her [and] said something; he may have been just checking her out.

Vincent can no longer remember what Valerie looked like—"all the years of questioning . . . I've literally put it out of my mind." He looked unsure when I reminded him of the discrepancies in hair and dress color between Schulte and the girl: "I remember her face . . . and it was the same girl I identified in court. . . . Do I think it was her? I think it was Valerie that I saw. That's the way I remember it. . . . Whether she had brown hair at that time or not, I don't remember, but I remember seeing what I thought was brown hair. . . . All I remember was she was very pretty. And she looked just like Valerie, unless she has a twin that had dark brown hair."[35]

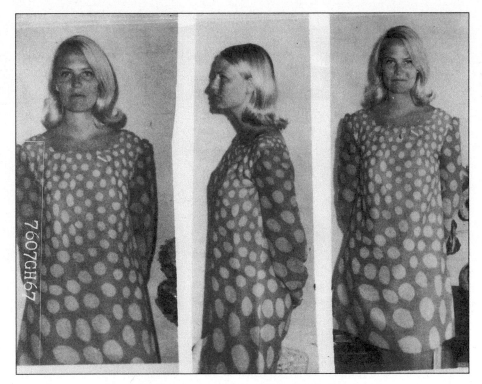

Police photos of a blond Valerie Schulte.

Valerie Schulte as she appeared in the pantry—wearing a green dress with yellow polka dots and carrying a crutch.

* * *

In late September, Sergeant Paul Sharaga was instructed to prepare a follow-up report by SUS, which he based, almost verbatim, on a copy of his first report. He personally delivered a copy of the new report to SUS Headquarters, but nobody there expressed any interest in interviewing him.

Several weeks later, Sharaga needed to refer to his report but found that the copies he had placed in his personal box in the Sergeants' Office, the watch commander's desk, and the Records section were all gone. His fellow officers seemed to know nothing about the missing reports, but Day Watch Sergeant Cravens told him two plainclothes SUS investigators had been there earlier in the day and had taken all the reports, including his initial one. "I called SUS and was told, in no uncertain terms, 'Nobody from SUS has been to Rampart, much less removed any of those reports.'" His superiors at Rampart were also uncooperative, and his inquiries began to irritate them.

By the end of the summer, Bill Jordan was made lieutenant and became Sharaga's immediate superior. Suddenly, Sharaga's usually high proficiency ratings began to plummet. Sharaga took premature retirement in July 1969 on service pension— pushed out, he felt, by his refusal to go along with the official story.

In December 1974, Sharaga phoned in to Art Kevin's radio show on KMPC in Los Angeles after he heard news reports that the "girl in a polka-dot dress and male companion" fleeing the crime scene was "a made-up story" by a witness. Kevin interviewed him, and Sharaga stuck to his story—he still felt this couple was involved in the killing with Sirhan. Sandra Serrano's story "was incredibly similar to what my two independent witnesses had told me, relating to near-identical time frames and location."

Sharaga first felt there was something odd about the police investigation when there was no mention of the Bernsteins in Chief Houghton's book on the case, *Special Unit Senator*. Sharaga wrote off the omission as the product of an "inadequate investigation" and found it hard to believe that anyone in the LAPD "would have deliberately done anything wrong." After the radio interview, Inspector Powers phoned Kevin and called Sharaga "a liar."

* * *

In 1988, author Jonn Christian contacted Sharaga after the long-awaited release of the LAPD investigative files. Christian showed Sharaga the summary of an alleged LAPD interview with him dated September 26. The summary recounts the older couple telling Sharaga their story and states that their "names and addresses [were] given to Rampart detectives." Yet there is no mention of this information in the LAPD files or a record of any attempt to contact the Bernsteins. The interview summary also states that Sharaga "believes that due to the noise and confusion at the time . . . what was probably said was 'they shot him,'" and that Sharaga gave Communications "a description of the suspect as given to him by additional witnesses."

An angry Sharaga told Christian, "Nobody from LAPD ever interviewed me, at any time. That interview is a phony, and many of the statements in it are just plain lies, containing false and deliberately misleading statements."

The summary reads as a fraudulent redrafting of Sharaga's detailed report, censoring any hint of conspiracy. It falsely implies that Sharaga rejected the Bernsteins' story and that the couple mistakenly heard "We shot him," a tactic the police also applied to the other witnesses. Sharaga called altering his report in this way a criminal act.[36]

Sharaga told me he now strongly believes the LAPD covered up the true circumstances surrounding the assassination of Robert Kennedy and that Jordan, Sillings, Powers, Hernandez, and Pena were all involved. Sharaga's morning watch commander at Rampart, Lieutenant Sillings, died of a brain tumor a couple of years after he left the force in the early seventies.[37]

* * *

When Marilyn Barrett showed the doctored interview summary and Sharaga's later affidavit to Manuel Pena, he sounded genuinely taken aback: "That's an interesting statement by Sharaga. . . . I personally have never talked to this Sharaga, and I don't recall ever reading his report, quite frankly. . . . I can't imagine why anyone would want to change anything."

Pena said he never knew about the Bernsteins. "The statements of this couple never figured into my decision to ask Hank to put Sandy on the polygraph. I had no knowledge of this." Barrett told him Sharaga's report had seemingly disap-peared. "Well, that's possible, but I certainly haven't seen it. It would've been interesting if, at that time, I knew of these Bernstein people, I'd put them on the polygraph, too . . . but I've never seen that report."[38]

SEVEN

SECURITY ON THE NIGHT

Witnesses in the pantry described Secret Service agents jumping Sirhan when they heard the shots, but there was actually no Secret Service protection for presidential candidates until President Johnson ordered it in the early hours of June 5, after the shooting. During the 1968 campaign, Kennedy's security rested with one man alone—his personal bodyguard, William Barry, charged with getting him through thick crowds and running interference. It was an impossible job.

Look magazine reporter Warren Rogers traveled with Kennedy on the campaign and neatly summed up the senator's attitude to security: "Bob despised the very thought of bodyguards. Even when he hit the campaign trail, he only had one security man, William Barry, and he tolerated Bill because he liked him. . . . Once, when I expressed concern about how he waded into churning crowds without protection, he told me: 'Oh, hell! You can't worry about that. Look at their faces. Those people don't want to hurt me. They just want to see me and touch me. And, if there's somebody out there who wants to get me, well, doing anything in public life today is Russian roulette.'"[1]

Barry had first met Kennedy when the senator was attorney general in the early sixties. Barry was the FBI agent assigned to be Kennedy's driver when he was in New York. They grew so close that when Kennedy ran for the Senate from New York in 1964, Barry spent his vacation traveling with the candidate through the last few weeks of the campaign. When J. Edgar Hoover got wind of this, he transferred Barry to Mobile, Alabama, so Barry resigned. When Barry congratulated Kennedy on election night, the new junior senator from New York replied, "Well, if my brother was alive, I wouldn't be here. I'd rather have it that way."[2]

On March 23, 1968, they teamed up once more. "When I got off a plane at San Francisco and saw that first [crowd], the shock sobered me on what the job was," Barry later recalled. "People hit me, tried to pull me away. At the end of the day, [Kennedy's] hands and mine would be bleeding. Once, at the beginning, I told the senator, 'I wish these people would be more courteous.' He answered, 'They're here because they care for us and want to show us.' After that, I never had any trouble adjusting to crowds."

As they traveled through thick crowds in open convertibles, Barry would kneel next to Kennedy, locking his left arm around the senator's waist to keep him from being pulled out of the vehicle. After one nine-hour motorcade, Barry's knees were rubbed raw and bleeding. "Ethel Kennedy got him a rubber kneeling pad," Jules Witcover wrote, "but still it was sheer physical punishment. Yet Barry, perhaps more devoted to the candidate than any other member of the party, maintained his consistent cheerfulness and gentleness."

For Barry, it was a labor of love: "I loved him intensely as a human being. . . . I wanted him to be President of the United States for the sake of my children and generations to come. It was not just a professional job with me. It was something my life qualified me for."[3]

Once, as a group of kids pedaled their bikes alongside Kennedy's car, Barry noticed a ten-year-old boy with one arm in a cast, tugging his younger sister along behind him as he ran beside the car. The girl stumbled; the boy swept her up on his shoulders and never broke stride. Barry pointed them out to Kennedy, who asked the driver to stop. Barry lifted the brother and sister into the convertible and sat one on either side of the senator. They stayed with the motorcade all day, and later, Kennedy had his car pulled out of the motorcade to drive them home. The children's mother served iced tea as Kennedy sat on the steps of their small frame house and chatted while the motorcade waited.[4]

Kennedy didn't want Barry to carry a gun, so he resorted to less conventional methods of protection. At a school rally in Oregon, a young man went berserk and charged after Kennedy as he left. Dick Harwood of the *Washington Post* tried to wrestle him to the ground, but he slipped through and an alert Barry intercepted him. He pushed the man to the ground and got Kennedy supporters to sit on him until the police arrived.[5]

Fred Dutton, Kennedy's campaign manager, was a veteran of the JFK administration and a constant presence alongside Barry and the senator. He skillfully balanced the egos of the older Kennedy aides from Jack Kennedy's 1960 campaign— who worked as volunteers—and the young, salaried speechwriters, who were in tune with the new generation of voters.[6]

At night, Kennedy would skip the late-night drinking sessions with staff and press and go back to his hotel room with Barry or Dutton, make a few phone calls, relax with a bottle or two of Heineken or a scotch, take a long, hot bath, and retire. Barry tried hiring off-duty policemen to stay in the hotel lobby, but when Kennedy found out, he got rid of them.[7]

* * *

In this campaign year of unprecedented violence and discord across the country, Kennedy often returned to a quote from his favorite poet, Aeschylus: "To tame the savageness of man and make gentle the life of the world." This optimistic, perhaps overly romantic vision seemed to permeate the campaign, but there were also real threats along the way.[8]

On April 11, at the Jack Tar Hotel in Lansing, Michigan, Barry told Dutton the police had spotted a man with a rifle on a rooftop across the street. Dutton went into Kennedy's bedroom and discreetly shut the blinds. Kennedy, slipping on a clean shirt, looked up at once and said, "Don't close them. If they're going to shoot, they'll shoot."

When it was time to leave, Dutton led the senator into the hotel elevator and down past the first floor into the basement, where the car was waiting. "What's the car doing down here?" Kennedy wanted to know. "Well, we have a report—maybe serious," Dutton said. Kennedy was furious. "Don't ever do anything like that again!" he told Barry. "If somebody's going to shoot me, they'll shoot me. But I'm not sneaking around like a thief in the night." "When we got out in front of the hotel," Dutton recalled, "Bob said, 'Stop the car.' And he got out and shook hands [with the crowd]." The gunman on the roof turned out to be an insurance company employee preparing to leave on a hunting trip after work.[9]

* * *

Barry and aide Walter Sheridan continually discussed the security problem. "And we knew," said Sheridan, "that, really, there wasn't anything you could do about it because he was uncontrollable, and if you tried to protect him, he'd get mad as hell." Someone later asked Barry whether Kennedy was foolhardy. "I don't know whether that's the correct word. . . . He just didn't want to live in fear. So I think he was making a personal judgement of his own, based on his own life force."[10]

The traveling press pack could sense what was coming. Columnist Jimmy Breslin asked John Lindsay of *Newsweek* if Kennedy had the stuff to go all the way. "And I said, 'Yes, of course, he has the stuff to go all the way, but he's not going to go all the way . . . somebody is going to shoot him. I know it and you know it, just as sure as we are sitting here. . . . He's out there now waiting for him.' There was a sort of stunned silence around the table, and then, one by one, each of us agreed."[11]

Kennedy told NBC reporter Charles Quinn he thought about the danger a lot but he wasn't going to change his style. He wanted to get as close to the people as possible. He got pulled out of a car and chipped a tooth and had his shoes and cuff links stolen, "and he knew that he got a lot of publicity by having all this wild hysteria swirling around him to the point of physical danger . . . [but] the touching of Kennedy and the pulling and the pushing and the screaming and all that frenzy and turmoil and turbulence that used to surround him . . . had a great symbolic meaning. He was not only there, saying 'I'm here because I want to help you.' But he was also there to let them touch him . . . so that they really could feel physically—not just emotionally—that here was a guy who was interested in them. . . . 'You know, if I'm ever elected President,' he said, 'I'm never going to ride in one of those bubble-top cars.'"[12]

* * *

The irresistible passion and excitement of the Kennedy motorcades hit an immovable object when they came to Los Angeles—the LAPD. The city saw two sides of Fred Dutton and the tensions between law, order, and bureaucracy, and Kennedy's freewheeling campaign.

First, on May 20, came a three-hour motorcade through raucous Mexican American crowds in East LA. At one point, Kennedy looked down to see a young teenager removing his shoes. He carried on shaking hands, regardless, in his stocking feet, until the motorcade reached Temple Isaiah, a synagogue in Los Angeles, well after dark. As he was about to go in to make a speech, Kennedy looked down. "My shoes," he said, turning to Dutton. "I'll have to borrow yours." His faithful lieutenant took off his shoes and waited in the car.

Kennedy donned a yarmulke and spoke to the assembled Jewish voters in Dutton's shoes, pledging support for Israel with remarks Sirhan may have later heard on all-news station KFWB. When the speech was over, the party went for dinner to a fancy restaurant. Kennedy walked in and Dutton, shoeless, followed. The Mexican boy wore Kennedy's shoes to school the next day.[13]

* * *

But tensions with the LAPD and Mayor Yorty undercut the spontaneous outpourings of hysteria in Los Angeles. Police files report that when officers responded to telephoned death threats against RFK during his speech at Valley College on May 15, campaign workers yelled, "We don't want you fascist police here. We didn't call for the Gestapo." The department had been widely criticized for abuses against antiwar and black activists, which included beatings and false arrests on made-up charges.[14]

On May 29, the day after the loss in Oregon, the LAPD saw another side to Dutton during a thirteen-vehicle Kennedy motorcade through downtown Los Angeles. The head of the Traffic Bureau played hardball, instructing his commanders that "this man is on his own. No service will be given other than that which would be given any other citizen." Officers were assigned to accompany the motorcade only; they were not to act as escorts, and no traffic violations were to be allowed.

The *Los Angeles Times* reported the incident the following day in a story titled "Police Charge 100 Traffic Violations to Kennedy Caravan." The Kennedy campaign had contracted Riggs Funeral Home to provide seven motorcycle escort riders for the motorcade. As thousands lined the streets to see the senator, the civilian escorts started running red lights and blocking intersections, and the police stepped in with verbal warnings.

"We've been booby-trapped by Mayor Yorty," a Kennedy aide grumbled later. When a colleague sought permission for the motorcade to disregard traffic signals that morning, "he was told police did not have the authority to grant such immunity."

At one point in the motorcade, at Ninth and Santee, Kennedy was tugged from his car by a large, enthusiastic crowd. Sergeant Paul Duncan, a motorcycle cop, feared for Kennedy's safety. When he plunged into the crowd to help, Kennedy berated him: "I don't need your help. We did not ask for you. We don't want you." "I'm sorry," said Duncan, and withdrew.

Dutton grabbed Duncan by the arm and said, "I'm the chief security officer here. We didn't ask for you, and we don't want you here. So leave. . . . I know what you guys on motorcycles will do. You have a reputation. You will gun your motorcycles into the crowd and run over the people to keep them back so that our man cannot talk to them. We have been in Los Angeles twice, and it happened the same way the last time. . . . I'm going to report you."

As the motorcade continued, police telling the crowd to keep back were drowning out the senator. Dutton ran up to two motorcycle officers: "Why don't you bastard cops get out of the way? All you bastards want to do is push people around and fuck over them. They're going right back into the street to shake hands with him anyway, you stupid ass."

The officers considered arresting Dutton for breach of the peace and filed a complaint about his vulgar language, but after the assassination, all charges were "withdrawn in the interest of justice."[15]

It was an extraordinary performance from the mild-mannered Dutton but captured the deep unease about authoritarian tactics in the face of popular expression at the time. As a regent on the board of the University of California, Dutton championed student protesters at Berkeley's People's Park and anti–Vietnam War demonstrations, often clashing with Governor Ronald Reagan.[16]

* * *

The LAPD final report on the assassination acknowledges hostile relations with the Kennedy camp: "During the primary campaign . . . Department security policies and the attitude of Senator Kennedy came into conflict . . . immeasurably affecting the conditions which existed just prior to the assassination." But the report is evasive in explaining why there was no police protection at the Ambassador hotel that night, turning strangely philosophical: "The ultimate question which will be asked is whether law enforcement in a free society can provide the necessary security for its leaders and political candidates [given] the right of individuals to come and go freely whenever they wish and . . . to be free from the unsolicited concern of others."

Barry told the LAPD he was responsible for the liaison between Kennedy staff and law enforcement agencies. A contact in the Department of Justice kept him apprised of any threats against the senator and the identification of possible suspects in cities on their schedule during the campaign. When additional protection was considered necessary, Barry would contact the Kennedy advance man in that city, who would make arrangements with the local police. He said motorcade escorts were hired for crowd control, not protection, and he had not contacted the LAPD with a request for security for the Ambassador Hotel. Barry admitted that Kennedy was extremely difficult to protect. In fact, he had intended to discuss security with the senator when they got back to New York.[17]

Los Angeles Police Department policy was that they did not provide security for visiting VIPs, unless specifically asked. The day after the shooting, LAPD spokesman Inspector Peter Hagan told the *LA Times*, "We were not there because we were not wanted. These candidates never want us around. They want to get with the people. They think we get in the way. This was true of President John Kennedy . . . and especially true with Robert Kennedy. He has told us on several occasions that he didn't want us around. In any case, we would never attend a private party unless we were asked, and we definitely were not asked."[18]

Chief Reddin and Mayor Yorty also said they were never asked to provide security. Interviewed in 1976, Reddin said, "Robert Kennedy very definitely wanted no part of us from the beginning of the trip, despite implicit hazards. . . . He blocked us out of the Ambassador, where we were allowed only outside plainclothes and traffic details. Had we been able to control security from the start, certainly the attack on him quite possibly could have been averted." In a further interview, Reddin was more blunt: "The indisputable fact is that he told us to get lost—and he paid for that order with his life."[19]

Kennedy's press secretary, Frank Mankiewicz, and Pierre Salinger refute this—Salinger said they asked for protection, and the LAPD refused. No paperwork has been produced by either side, so it's hard to know how much of this is face-saving.[20]

* * *

In the days before the California primary, strange things were afoot at the hotel. Busboy Juan Romero told the FBI that two days before the shooting, he was approached at work by two white men wearing Kennedy pendants on chains around their necks. One was "very stout, about six feet tall and 45 years old" and asked Romero where he could get a hotel jacket like the one Romero was wearing. He said they were police officers, but Romero did not ask for or see any identification. Romero reluctantly took the men down to the supply room, but it was closed. He never saw the men again.

Later the same day, two Caucasian males returned to the Uniform Room and asked Frances Bailey for two waiters' jackets, so they could get in to see the senator while he was at the hotel. She refused. While she could not provide a description, she felt neither of the men was Sirhan.[21]

Sometime during the evening of June 4, student Mark Armbruster tried to enter the Embassy Ballroom by going through the kitchen. Two men stopped him—one a security guard in uniform, the other in a suit. The man in the suit stated, "I'm a sergeant, Los Angeles Police Department; you can't come in here." He produced some sort of badge, and then withdrew it. Armbruster then left the kitchen and went back out into the lobby as the same man positioned the uniformed guard outside the kitchen doors.

Armbruster didn't think anything of the incident until he heard there were no LAPD officers present at the hotel prior to the shooting. He described the man as a male Caucasian in his thirties, six foot one, 170 pounds, dark hair with a slight touch of gray. This was too young to be William Gardner or Fred Murphy, both retired LAPD lieutenants and the only plainclothes hotel security officers. Who was this man, quite possibly positioning Thane Cesar? Could it have been Gene Scherrer? The LAPD never followed up.[22]

* * *

And so, on the night of June 4, Kennedy's security was in the hands of Bill Barry alone. He was not armed—primarily because he worked in crowds, "where a gun would be impractical." If Barry lost the senator, there was no protection.[23]

One of the most elusive aspects of the assassination is the last-minute route switch that propelled the senator headlong into the pantry toward a waiting gunman. How did Sirhan know that Kennedy would be coming through the pantry after the speech, when the decision was made only five minutes before? And if there was a conspiracy, how was the senator manipulated into the "killing zone," a narrow, dimly lit, and poorly guarded corridor where press came looking for sandwiches, and waiters and an off-guard Kennedy entourage mingled in a euphoric mood?

* * *

Kennedy snapped by a supporter as he arrives on stage. To his left, California Speaker Jesse Unruh; to his right, his wife, Ethel, and hotel captain Karl Uecker.

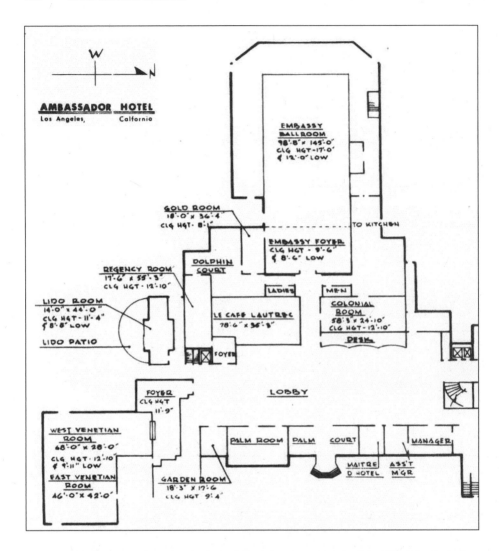

LAPD diagram showing the second-floor layout of the Ambassador Hotel. At bottom left, the West Venetian Room, where Sirhan visited the Rafferty party. At bottom right, the Palm Court, from where he went outside to a patio area and met Rabago and Cordero. They went inside to the lobby, and at one point Sirhan was seen staring at the Teletype machines in the Colonial Room, center right. Senator Kennedy spoke from the podium on the north wall of the Embassy Ballroom, then went backstage. Instead of turning left and going downstairs to the Ambassador Ballroom, he turned right and went through the kitchen en route to the Colonial Room. The fire doors in the southwest corner of the Embassy Ballroom can be seen in the top left corner of the Embassy Ballroom. Sandra Serrano sat on a fire escape below these doors.

After the polls closed at eight o'clock, huge crowds began building in the hotel's two main ballrooms for Kennedy's anticipated victory speech. According to Richard Kline, PR director for Kennedy's California campaign, the original plan was for the senator to speak first to seven hundred Kennedy staff and news media in the Embassy Ballroom on the second floor. He would then go downstairs to address the overflow crowd of supporters in the Ambassador Room directly below before meeting twenty selected newsmen in his fifth-floor suite and going on to a private victory party at the Factory, a Hollywood club part-owned by Pierre Salinger.

Kline expected a press briefing around nine thirty but the vote count dragged on much longer, so he moved it to the Colonial Room, a space assigned to the "writing press," a short walk from the Embassy Ballroom through the pantry.[24]

Fred Dutton and Bill Barry were in charge of the senator's movements, with Rosey Grier and Rafer Johnson helping out on crowd control. Barry didn't ask for help from hotel security and worked with Uno Timanson, VP of banquet and sales, to move the senator around the building. Out front clearing a path for the senator were advance man Jack Gallivan and assistant maître d' Eddie Minasian. As Ethel was pregnant, Rosey was assigned to her that night.[25]

Three FBI photos reconstruct Kennedy's route from the stage.

The podium where Kennedy spoke, with curtain drawn back to reveal the door to the back hallway. The stage was raised and extended out on a temporary platform for Kennedy's speech, so he jumped down onto the permanent stage as he left after his speech.

Light spills from the stage through the door to the back hallway. In the distance are the swinging doors to the pantry.

The swinging doors to the pantry, viewed from the backstage hallway. Kennedy walked through these on his way to the stage, and then back through them on his way to the Colonial Room.

Close to midnight, the networks were projecting a comfortable victory, so Kennedy went down to address the crowds. To huge cheers, he emerged through a door to the right of the stage (stage left) and walked up some wooden steps to the speaker's platform.

As Kennedy spoke, the temporary stage was jammed with so many people, Timanson feared it might collapse. It had been raised and extended out eight feet for the night. Behind the gold curtain was a two-foot drop into darkness onto the regular stage. From there, a door led out to a dim backstage hallway. To the left was a staircase leading down to the Ambassador Ballroom. To the right lay the pantry and the Colonial Room.[26]

Behind Kennedy stood smiling German assistant maître d' Karl Uecker, in a black tuxedo. Tonight, Karl was in charge of the Embassy Ballroom. His boss, maître d' Angelo Di Pierro, had briefed him, and now he stood poised behind Kennedy, ready to help him leave: "I was going to take him behind the stage, and we were supposed to go downstairs to the Ambassador Ballroom where he had more guests, and he was going to make another speech there."

Di Pierro watched from the wings, waiting for the senator to come back out the same door he entered.

But after the speech, to almost everyone's surprise, Kennedy didn't go downstairs to the Ambassador Room. Amid confusion onstage, he was ushered through the gold curtain at the back of the platform by Uecker and led through the backstage area to the door into the backstage hallway. Instead of turning left and walking down a back staircase to speak to the crowd downstairs, he was led to his right through double swinging doors into the pantry, en route to an impromptu press conference in the Colonial Room. Within seconds, he was shot.[27]

One of the first things the LAPD wanted to know in the early phase of their investigation was: Who changed the plans? When and why?[28]

* * *

Detectives got to work immediately and interviewed Dutton and Barry at five o'clock that morning, while the senator was still in surgery. Both interviews were audiotaped, and this is what Dutton said:

"While the senator was speaking, Barry and I went to look to see what would be the route to take him from the stage to where he went next. There was one possibility of his going off to the right of the stage and down a flight of stairs to an overflow crowd in a room on the next lower floor.

"However, in order to avoid further crowd scenes which we had in the Embassy Room . . . and because we had a number of reporters waiting to talk to him, we decided to take him . . . to a press room adjoining the Embassy Room. Barry and I saw the senator was speaking, walked that route, through the hallway where the shooting finally occurred. Walked over, walked back very quickly. As far as we know, nobody knew what we were doing or why we were there. We came back and went up on the stage."

In a telephone interview with the LAPD three months later, Dutton told a similar story. "It was a last-minute decision I would say made within five minutes before the shooting occurred . . . and only Barry and I really knew about it."

During the speech, Dutton said he and Barry left stage right, "circled around in back of the stage, and went straight down through the narrow hallway [the pantry] to the press room." They stayed there "for less than thirty seconds, standing just inside the door there, and then walked back until the senator was finished speaking."

Dutton didn't notice Sirhan in the pantry during this trial run and didn't tell anyone else about the change—"Barry and I were really the only ones [who knew]. . . . We didn't stand around discussing it. We just walked through. There is no reason, unless Sirhan knew our movements, which I doubt that he did, to let him know why we were walking it." Either Sirhan was "entirely fortuitous" or somehow, he knew about the change. Dutton and Barry then returned to their positions at stage left, expecting the senator to leave the same way he had entered.[29]

* * *

But between the Dutton interviews that bookended their investigation, the LAPD struggled to confirm this was the case. A Colonial Room Progress Report dated July 30 states, seven weeks after the shooting, "'When was the decision made?' and 'Why?' cannot be answered at this time."[30]

Part of the problem was that key individuals were not asked the right questions by investigators. Bill Barry was interviewed right after Dutton at Good Samaritan at 5:05 in the morning but never mentioned the walk-through to investigators and was never asked about it in subsequent interviews.[31]

To further muddy the waters, three other versions of this walk-through were described to investigators, causing some confusion about who did this last-minute route scout. Thirty-year-old Kennedy volunteer Thadis Heath told the LAPD he did it with Dutton:

"During [Kennedy's] speech, Fred Dutton came to me and asked me to go with him as he wanted to check a rear hallway." They passed hotel staff in the pantry, "stayed about four or five minutes in the press room, then returned . . . through the rear door to the stage."[32]

Hotel liaison Uno Timanson told the FBI he also scouted the route. The first he knew of a route change was just before the end of the speech, when Dutton asked him if there were television sets in the Ambassador Room downstairs. Timanson said there were, and Dutton decided that as the crowd downstairs was already watching the speech on TV, the senator would go straight to the Colonial Room.

Timanson then left the podium to check out the Colonial Room and returned to tell Dutton there were only four or five people there. Dutton wasn't bothered. Kennedy had gone to the press room right after his victories in Indiana and Nebraska, so Dutton knew the press would go there after the speech.[33]

Advance man Jack Gallivan told the FBI he accompanied Timanson on this route scout. They then returned to the stage and advised that the most convenient way for the senator to leave was the same way he had entered—through the door at stage left.

Timanson and Gallivan then left the platform and began clearing the way through the pantry. Gallivan said there was no question in his mind as to the safety of the senator—"instead of a spirit of tight security, there was a spirit of relaxation and celebration."[34]

Word filtered through to the security guards, and just before the end of the speech, Ace guard Stanley Kawalec was instructed by hotel guard Tom Perez to clear the crowd in the kitchen area, as the senator would be coming through.[35]

* * *

The LAPD never made any attempt to clarify these conflicting accounts. NBC Unit Manager James Marooney later confirmed to the FBI that he had accompanied Dutton and Barry off the stage to check out the Colonial Room, so the net result seems to be this: Dutton, hearing that the impatient and unruly crowd below was watching the senator's speech on television, decided on the route switch. He then walked the route himself with Barry and, possibly, Heath. Timanson and Gallivan did a second check after this.[36]

But what's puzzling is that even during the trial, Bill Barry never mentioned this. If Barry did check the kitchen, why didn't he notice Sirhan standing on a tray stacker as he walked past?

* * *

If this had been the only change made during the speech, Kennedy might have survived. Yes, he would now enter the "killing zone," but his bodyguard, Bill Barry, customarily led the way, with CBS cameraman James Wilson and his team providing a security wedge in front of the senator—a wedge a gun would need to penetrate to get within an inch of the senator's head.

But amid the confusion of the route change, a second change concerning how the senator would leave the stage proved catastrophic, catching Kennedy's security team out of position and sending the senator into the pantry fatally exposed.[37]

* * *

As Kennedy finished his speech, Barry, Dutton, and Rafer Johnson started to clear a pathway for him through the crowd at the bottom of the stairs, expecting him to leave stage left, the same way he had entered. Dutton was ready to brief him on the change of plan, and Barry would lead the way back through the kitchen to the Colonial Room.

But Kennedy aides on the other side of the podium had also cleared a path stage right—Pierre Salinger wanted the senator to come off that side and greet campaign workers at the "anchor desk," busy working the phones all night to canvass returns from colleagues across the state.

According to Kennedy fund-raiser Nina Rhodes, Salinger explained this to a tall blond man at the anchor desk during Kennedy's speech, but this man said it would take too long—the senator would be better going off the back of the stage through the curtain. The tall blond man sounds like Uno Timanson.

The smiling man in the tuxedo standing behind Kennedy during the speech had the same idea. Karl Uecker quite logically felt that the quickest way off the stage was out through the back curtain. But none of Kennedy's party knew who Uecker was or expected the senator to leave this way, setting the scene for tragedy.[38]

* * *

Standing onstage and filming these key moments was CBS cameraman James Wilson, caught as flat-footed as everyone else by what happened next. It's very poignant reviewing Wilson's footage today. Watching these images in slow motion, you realize that these thirteen seconds on a packed and noisy stage played a fateful part in the assassination. A look here, a glance there, made all the difference.

As Kennedy concluded his speech, he answered a question from newsman Andrew West, who was to the right of the podium. His pregnant wife, Ethel, and Karl Uecker waited behind him, shadowed by Rosey Grier. On a concurrent audio track, Fred Dutton is heard telling someone, "Yes, we're gonna go for a press conference."

As Kennedy turned away from the crowd, he moved stage right, and Karl Uecker tapped him on the right shoulder. Kennedy turned around to see Uecker and Ethel at midstage. His eye was caught by Uecker's right hand, beckoning him toward the curtain. Another hand beckoned to Uecker's right and a voice shouted, "Senator! Senator, this way!" The voice may be Uecker's colleague Eddie Minasian, waving from beside the curtain.

Bill Barry was caught out of position on the left side of the stage. As Kennedy was distracted, Ethel and Rosey Grier spotted Barry shaking his head and pointing frantically back the way they had come. We hear, "No, Rosey, no, no!"—possibly Barry shouting to Grier that they're going the wrong way.[39]

But in the maelstrom, Kennedy didn't see Barry. He pointed stage right and seemed to ask Uecker, "Aren't we going this way?" Uecker shook his head, parted the gold curtain, and ushered him off the back. Kennedy turned and followed Uecker and Minasian through the gold curtain, jumped down two feet onto the regular stage and moved quickly through the anteroom to a doorway leading into the back hallway.[40]

At this point, nobody had told Kennedy, Minasian, or Uecker about the route change. They still thought the plan was to go downstairs to the Ambassador Ballroom.

* * *

Five hours later, on the ninth floor of Good Samaritan Hospital, a stunned Bill Barry remembered the scene: 'Well, the senator finished his speech and turned to leave the platform and turned the wrong way. . . . I called him to come back toward the kitchen . . . and I wanted to lead him down the steps and someone parted the curtains in back of the platform and motioned him to jump off the platform that way and he did."

Later, at trial, Barry testified that Kennedy "was called by someone at the mid-rear of the stage, and he turned that way. The curtains were parted and he jumped down . . . about three feet, I guess [into the backstage area], and of course, I was committed on the other side of the stage." Barry didn't recognize the man who beckoned Kennedy but noted he was wearing a black tuxedo.[41]

Fred Dutton was also caught out of position: "Instead of coming off where we were, he stepped off that back side . . . and because that little stage was so crowded . . . we got a few feet behind him rather than being right with him like we should have been. And from then on it was—we were rushing to catch up. . . . I was still not quite in the hallway when I heard the damn gun go."[42]

* * *

As Grier, Dutton, and Barry helped the pregnant Ethel negotiate the two-foot drop from the stage down into the backstage area, Mrs. Kennedy told Barry to "stay with the senator," and he raced to catch up.[43]

Uecker and Minasian emerged from the doorway at the back of the stage and turned toward the stairway to their left, leading downstairs to the Ambassador Room. Then somebody told Uecker, "No, we're not going to go there; we're going to the press room." Uecker couldn't recall who it was, "but somebody was talking to the senator and to Uno Timanson, and Uno told me, 'This way; we will go to the press room.'" Uecker took Kennedy's right hand in his left and started down the ramp toward the pantry.[44]

The only Kennedy staff with the senator at this point were advance men Jack Gallivan and Rick Rosen and press aide Judy Royer, all of whom walked ahead of the senator through the pantry. Gallivan had done the route scout with Timanson and was probably the one who redirected the senator. Gallivan, Rosen, and Timanson then led the way into the pantry, with Royer alongside.

At the time of the first shot, Gallivan and Rosen were ten or fifteen feet ahead of the senator, looking toward the Colonial Room. Timanson was six feet ahead of the senator, looking back at him and indicating which way to go, and Bill Barry had just caught up and was abreast of the senator on the outside of the crowd.[45]

The CBS crew who normally acted as a security wedge were just entering the doors when soundman Bob Funk heard "what sounded like paper cups popping when someone stamps on them."

"Oh, my Jesus Christ!" shouted cameraman James Wilson, pounding the concrete floor. (Wilson never recovered from the shooting. He had a nervous breakdown soon after and died six months later.)[46]

Grier, Johnson, Dutton, and Mrs. Kennedy were all just outside the double doors when they heard the shots. As Rosey shielded Mrs. Kennedy, Dutton rushed up to the senator, unbuttoned his shirt, took off his shoes, and loosened his belt. Bill Eppridge took Dutton's photograph as he stood, horrified, over Kennedy, hands to his face in anguish.[47]

* * *

The LAPD ran a background check on Dutton, but it seems clear the last-minute change was a terrible accident. Dutton and Uecker have since died. Timanson still works in the hotel industry in Los Angeles but declined to discuss the case with me. Bill Barry remains close to the Kennedy family and also politely declined. "I don't answer questions; I never have. It's hard stuff and it just rakes it all up again. But, good luck."[48]

* * *

The LAPD final report skirts all of these issues, stating that the reason for the press conference "was not determined" and that "as Kennedy finished his speech, one of his aides said 'This way, Senator' and he turned and exited through the rear of the stage." There's no mention of the aborted plan to go to the Ambassador Ballroom or of the unexpected way the senator left the stage, wrongfooting Barry.[49]

* * *

One key question remains: How did Sirhan know Kennedy would be coming through the pantry? Perhaps he had seen Kennedy come down through the kitchen on his way to the Embassy Ballroom and assumed he would leave the same way.

Perhaps he was one of several gunmen, positioned at various exits, ready to fire. Perhaps he just got lucky. But Sirhan wasn't the only one with apparent foreknowledge that Kennedy would be coming through the pantry.

* * *

Although the group escorting the senator down from his suite expected to go downstairs after the speech, Kennedy's press people had other plans. An hour before the speech, Pierre Salinger told assistant press secretary Dick Drayne the senator would go straight to the Colonial Room. Salinger and Drayne told reporters, and Richard Kline asked twenty-year-old press aide Judy Royer to go tell the press in the Colonial Room.[50]

One AP reporter described a young Kennedy aide (probably Royer) coming into the busy Colonial Room between eleven fifteen and eleven thirty and briefing each member of the press individually about the press conference.[51]

About forty-five minutes before the speech, Kline or Royer also told Captain Kenneth Held of the Los Angeles Fire Department that Kennedy would go to the press room after the speech. Held then assigned two of his men to the Colonial Room to cover crowd control for the press conference and requested a security guard to keep the public out.[52]

So, while the group with Kennedy thought he was going downstairs, his press aides, the press themselves, and the hotel guards all thought he was going to the Colonial Room. Though not all reporters knew about the press conference, most of the heavyweights assumed the senator would visit the press room. As columnist Jimmy Breslin told the police, he "always did."[53]

* * *

Whether Sirhan picked up on any of this, we don't know. As we've seen, around 11:45, a group of waiters were talking in the kitchen when Sirhan approached Martin Patrusky and asked, "Is Mr. Kennedy coming through here?" He then asked Jesus Perez the same question three or four times. Patrusky and Perez didn't know. Sirhan had already seen the teletype machines in the Colonial Room and may have assumed Kennedy would go to the press room after the speech.[54]

* * *

When I've discussed the possibility of a planned assassination with covert operatives, one key question is always asked—how was the senator manipulated into the "killing zone?" Was there someone inside the Kennedy party or among the hotel staff wittingly or unwittingly feeding information to the assassins about the senator's plans? The chaos outlined above seems to preclude this, but it's equally possible a well-planned assassination conspiracy would position shooters both in the pantry and downstairs in the Ambassador Room.[55]

It's difficult, though, to point a finger of suspicion at any of the characters mentioned here. Ironically, Karl Uecker, the man who led Kennedy to his death, went on to become the strongest advocate of the second-gun theory.[56]

Remember that Uecker was set to lead Kennedy away from the kitchen when Timanson and Gallivan, on orders from Dutton, redirected him into the pantry.

All roads lead back to Fred Dutton and his tragic and fateful decision to protect his exhausted candidate from more rowdy and boisterous crowds.

The senator himself seems to have ignored Barry in his desire to avoid the crowd massing in the doorway, opting for the cleaner exit through the back curtain, which stripped him of protection. Kennedy and Barry had been inseparable throughout the campaign, and Barry, with his law enforcement background, would have had a far better chance of intercepting Sirhan than Uecker.

If there was a plan to this assassination, it's hard to discern it in this tragedy of errors.

* * *

The hotel security force that evening consisted of eleven hotel guards, supplemented by six men from Ace Guard Service. The Ace guards carried .38-caliber guns and nightsticks, while the hotel guards were unarmed. The force was headed by two former LAPD lieutenants—the hotel's head of security, William F. Gardner, a retired homicide detective, and his elderly assistant, Fred "Pat" Murphy, who'd retired from the department in 1944. All guards wore gray uniforms, of either the hotel or Ace design, except Gardner and Murphy, who patrolled in plainclothes, and Ace guard Willie Bell, who turned up in a black sweater and a white helmet and "looked ridiculous."[57]

The Kennedy campaign had used the hotel as their base in California for six weeks prior to the shooting, reserving the Royal Suite on the fifth floor for the senator. Gardner discussed security with Kennedy's staff, who "did not want anything to interfere with the Senator mingling with the people." They also made it clear the senator did not want uniformed guards with him, so Gardner saw his men's primary role as crowd control, assisted by six safety officials from the fire department.

Gardner initially placed five guards on the ground-floor Casino Level and four on the upper Lobby Level, home to the Embassy Ballroom. Five more were at regular posts around the hotel, and one on the fifth floor restricted traffic to the Kennedy suite. Gardner did not receive an itinerary for the senator, so he tried to move his guards around during the evening as conditions changed, or at the request of fire inspectors or Kennedy aides. Ace supervisor Jack Merritt checked on his men every thirty minutes.[58]

As the Embassy Ballroom quickly filled with supporters, Kennedy press aide Hugh McDonald stood at the doors with Ace guards Jack Merritt and Albert Stowers, supervising the admission of Kennedy campaign workers and press with the correct badges.[59]

Two guards were screening the inside stairs from the Ambassador Ballroom foyer up to the Embassy Ballroom, but it was easy to avoid the guards by going around the back way—through the Colonial Room and serving pantry.[60]

Fire inspectors closed the Embassy Ballroom doors at nine thirty, but Kennedy supporters continued to sneak in through the pantry, so Gardner posted Ace guard Thane Eugene Cesar there an hour later. Cesar wasn't doing a very good job, as witnesses Marcus McBroom and Valerie Schulte described freely walking though the kitchen into the ballroom. Judy Royer chased Sirhan out of the pantry, and other Kennedy staff tried to police the area. When one staff member berated Cesar for leaving the doors unattended, he shrugged and said they didn't have enough manpower.[61]

Cesar later admitted to the police that he'd been having problems—"Everybody imaginable was trying to sneak into the Embassy Room to see Kennedy when he come down. And the only ones that I was actually letting through the kitchen area was the working press. Also the staff that had staff cards that was working for Kennedy."

At nine thirty, Cesar was told that Kennedy would walk through the Embassy Ballroom to the stage. "I asked if we were to be out there to assist him through the crowd and I was told 'no.'"

Around eleven fifteen, Fred Murphy moved Cesar from the east doors of the pantry to the west swinging doors, through which Kennedy would eventually enter the pantry after the speech. Cesar was told Kennedy was coming downstairs through the kitchen area, up on the stage and then back from the stage through the pantry to the Colonial Room for a press conference. Soon after, Bill Gardner instructed Cesar to accompany Kennedy through the pantry to the Colonial Room. "He just said, 'Keep the aisle clear. Make sure that everybody's out of the way, so that Kennedy's group can walk through freely.'"[62]

Fred Murphy could see that unauthorized people were getting into the ballroom through the kitchen, so at 11:50, he stationed himself just outside the double service doors leading into the southeast corner of the pantry from the Embassy foyer. As the crowd left after the speech, he could stop them from coming through these doors and impeding the senator's short walk to the Colonial Room.[63]

* * *

When Kennedy entered the Embassy Ballroom from the back hallway, Gardner was at the doorway with hotel guard Thomas Perez. At this point, four hotel guards and three Ace guards were in the vicinity of the pantry. Perez stood by the door to the Embassy Ballroom, Kawalec by the door to the rear of the stage, and Cesar by the west swinging doors into the pantry. Ace guards Jack Merritt and Albert Stowers were on the main doors to the Embassy Ballroom, Arthur Maddox was at the main entrance to the Colonial Room, and Fred Murphy was outside the service doors leading from the Embassy foyer into the southwest corner of the pantry. None of these guards reported seeing Sirhan before the shooting.

Perez was told to keep his doorway clear, as Kennedy would leave the same way he came in. "They told us he was supposed to come through this door and leave down these steps, that's the route we had, but the crowd he had went that way through the kitchen."

Near the end of the speech, Gardner was in the rear hallway behind the stage and told Kawalec to clear the crowd in the kitchen area, as the senator would be coming through. As Karl Uecker led Kennedy toward the swinging doors leading into the pantry, Thane Cesar grabbed the senator by the right elbow. They walked toward the steam tables and the senator stopped to shake hands.

When Cesar looked up, he saw a hand with a gun, the shots went off, and he fell back against the ice machines. Stanley Kawalec was up ahead, still pushing the crowd back, when he heard four shots. Tom Perez was being pushed toward the swinging doors and heard seven shots, one after the other. Then everyone went wild, yelling, "Close the doors! Call the police! Call an ambulance!" Elizabeth Evans emerged from the pantry with blood streaming from her head, and Perez helped her onto a table in the ballroom as Kawalec joined hands with two firemen to hold the crowd back in the pantry.

Fred Murphy was blocking the service doors leading into the southwest corner of the pantry: "I was standing with my back to the door, facing where these people would endeavor to come in and I heard a series of what appeared to be shots"— three at first, then a series. "I immediately jumped through the door in the direction of where I heard the shots. . . . I observed several men screaming, 'Kill him! Kill him!' and women who appeared to be hysterical, yelling." No one obstructed his entry or walked past him toward the exit. Rosey Grier and Rafer Johnson were struggling with the suspect, and Karl Uecker had his arm around the suspect's neck. Murphy identified himself as a former police lieutenant and tried to get the gun from Sirhan but was pushed away. Then Rosey got the gun and passed it to Rafer, who put it in his pocket. Murphy then ran for a telephone and called the police and ambulance from the bell captain's desk.[64]

* * *

Over the years, Thane Eugene Cesar has emerged as the lead suspect in the search for a second gunman, and his story is explored in depth in Chapter 13 But much can be gained from the interviews with other security guards that night. Among the most puzzling are the interviews with the hotel's head of security, William F. Gardner. He gave conflicting accounts of his actions before the shooting, and his immediate response was frankly bizarre.

Three days after the shooting, in the first of five FBI interviews, Gardner said that shortly after midnight, he was at the bottom of the inside staircase leading down from the backstage area of the Embassy Ballroom, with Ace guard Willie Bell and hotel guard Lloyd Curtis. He was there at the request of a Kennedy aide who said the senator would come down those stairs to go to the Ambassador Room for another speech. Gardner understood that the senator would then go down the fire escape to his car and leave the hotel. The next part of the report is very strange: "At approximately 12:20 a.m., a female aide of Senator Kennedy came to where he was located and advised him that there had been a terrible accident. She did not tell him anything about a shooting at that time." Gardner didn't hear any gunshots and estimated it "was probably fifteen minutes after the actual shooting . . . that he heard Senator Kennedy had been shot." Gardner told the FBI that he didn't walk up the stairs to "the level where the shooting took place until sometime after Senator Kennedy and the other wounded individuals had been taken from that location."

Gardner's statements are simply not credible. What was the terrible accident the Kennedy aide described? If she didn't tell him about a shooting, what did she tell him and what did he do to respond? All he had to do was climb the stairs; the pantry would have been right in front of him. He would be able to command the scene of the "terrible accident" until the police arrived.

Instead, as hysteria spread through the hotel in reaction to the shooting, the head of security would have us believe he heard nothing about it for fifteen minutes and didn't check the crime scene until the senator had been evacuated from the building. None of these statements were challenged at any point by the investigators. Police interviews with Curtis and Bell, who were with Gardner at the time, render his statements completely untenable.[65]

At 11:25, Gardner let Curtis take a break and told him to report back to the Ambassador Ballroom, "where Mr. Kennedy was supposed to speak later." When Curtis came back at midnight, Gardner told him to clear the way to the lower ballroom.

Curtis said Gardner then "went upstairs to see how the situation was and when he came back down, he just shook his head and said 'forget about it.' And then a girl came down, crying, screaming and hollering. She sat about halfway down the stairway and started crying. . . . 'It couldn't be true, it couldn't be true,' she just kept repeating. . . . So then, another girl came down beside her, she was also in hysterics. . . . This was the stairway leading right in the corridor where he was shot."

"And Mr. Gardner was with you?"

"Yes . . . and a gentleman came down right after her and ordered myself and another guard, an Ace guard, to 'lock the doors,' 'lock the doors.' Kept on screaming, 'lock the doors.' . . . Well, anyway, me and Mr. Gardner, we shut the doors."

Curtis was with Willie Bell, an Ace guard who hadn't brought the right uniform—in his black sweater and white helmet, Curtis thought he "looked ridiculous." Both men were standing at the bottom of the stairs, by the fire doors, at the time of the shooting.[66]

Willie Bell confirmed Curtis's story. He was at the bottom of the stairs when two women came and sat on the steps, saying Mr. Kennedy had been shot. Both men agreed the first girl had a pink dress and the second girl wore blue. Bell chained the doors and stopped people going up the stairs to the kitchen. Neither man heard shots, but Bell heard shouts of "Kill him, Rosey!" and "Take the gun, even if you have to break his fingers" (reporter Andrew West).[67]

Clearly, from Curtis's account, Gardner lied to the FBI and was in the vicinity of the pantry at the time of the shooting. He knew what happened, walked away shaking his head, and by his account, didn't return until Kennedy had left the building.

* * *

Gardner's accounts of where Kennedy was going after the speech also seemed to fluctuate every time he was asked. At 11:25, he gave Curtis instructions to clear a path to the Ambassador Ballroom, yet Gardner later told the FBI he understood Kennedy would proceed to the Colonial Room for a press conference after the speech.

Kawalec told the FBI that while he was standing in the rear hallway behind the stage as Kennedy was completing his speech, Gardner moved him into the pantry to clear a path for the senator. Gardner told the FBI and LAPD that near the end of the speech in this same rear hallway, a female Kennedy aide in her mid-thirties, in a green dress, advised him the senator was not going to return via the kitchen, but was going to go directly downstairs and out the fire exit to his waiting car. She asked him to clear a pathway for the senator's exit, so Gardner telephoned his gate man and verified that the car was in front of the hotel. He then added two guards and went to the bottom of the stairs himself, to clear the area for the Kennedy party.

But the two guards, Curtis and Bell, were already at the bottom of the stairs expecting Kennedy to go to the Ambassador Room. Gardner said he assumed Kennedy would no longer go to the Colonial Room but did not remove any of the guards from the kitchen area. In fact, he had just moved Kawalec into the pantry.

Why, in the space of six days, Gardner gave such conflicting accounts of where the senator would go next is a mystery. As with his disappearance after the shooting, he was never challenged on these inconsistencies.[68]

In a later FBI interview, Gardner stated that he "selected two waiter captains to lead the Kennedy procession to and from the Embassy Room where Senator Kennedy was to speak." As we know, Uecker and Minasian expected to go downstairs to the Ambassador Room but were diverted by somebody at the rear doorway, instructing them to turn right into the kitchen. Gardner was at this doorway as Kennedy was completing his speech. Did Gardner give the order to Uecker and Minasian to change direction? This question was never asked by investigators.

Within two months of the shooting, Gardner left the Ambassador to go to law school. Frank Hendrix, the owner of Ace Guard Service, later told researcher Betsy Langman that Gardner committed suicide on Christmas Eve 1969. When Hendrix asked about Gardner down at the hotel, nobody would talk. I have been unable to confirm Gardner's death through a public record search, but his accounts of what he did that night remain highly suspicious.[69]

* * *

There are only two pages in the investigation files for Ace supervisor Jack Merritt—summaries of interviews with the LAPD and FBI. He gets a ten-line summary in the LAPD final report, part of which reads, "Merritt drew his gun and ran into the pantry in time to see two men struggling with Sirhan. . . . He observed two men and a woman walking away from him and out of the kitchen. They seemed to be smiling. He added that the woman was wearing a polka-dot dress."[70]

The guns of Merritt and Thane Cesar were never checked by the police on the night of the shooting, and neither man was reinterviewed until 1971, when controversy about Wolfer's ballistics work accompanied allegations that Cesar had fired his gun in the pantry.[71]

Twelve days after interviewing Cesar, Sergeants Patchett and Sartuche traveled to Las Vegas to interview Merritt on July 26, 1971. He had moved to Vegas in August 1968 and was now the manager of the Blue Skies trailer park off the Strip. The surviving audiotape of the thirty-minute interview makes one wonder how on earth Merritt's story was ignored for so long. He gives measured answers throughout, reflecting his experience in law enforcement, and seems to speak through an artificial voicebox—he would die of throat cancer in 1975.

On the night of the shooting, Merritt was forty-four years old and the supervisor for the other five Ace guards at the hotel. He was carrying a two-inch .38 revolver and stationed at the main entrance to the Embassy Ballroom with young Ace guard Albert Stowers. Every half hour, he and Stowers took turns to go check on the other men, and every so often, they went to the kitchen for a cup of coffee.

Merritt thought that after his speech in the Embassy Ballroom, Kennedy would go backstage, turn left, and go downstairs to the Ambassador Ballroom, to address the overflow crowd. A short time after Kennedy left the stage, a woman came running out of service doors in the southeast corner of the pantry into the hall outside the main doors of the Embassy Ballroom where Merritt was standing, yelling, "My God we need a doctor, Kennedy's been killed."

Merritt ran into the pantry through the same service doors and drew his gun. He saw Karl Uecker, Rosey Grier, and Rafer Johnson wrestling with the suspect on the steam table and went over and asked Karl what had happened. Uecker said the senator had been shot, and Merritt looked to his left and saw the senator on the floor, with Mrs. Kennedy kneeling by his side. As it took Mrs. Kennedy a minute or two to reach her husband, this must have been two or three minutes after the shooting.

Merritt stood over Kennedy for about a minute with his gun arm high and his .38 pointed toward the ceiling. There was pandemonium to the west end of the pantry by the fallen bodies of Schrade and Weisel, and to the east, as several men struggled with Sirhan. But where Merritt was, for a moment, it was calm. He looked up and saw a girl and two men standing a few feet north of him, by an opening into the main kitchen. They were all smiling, looking down at Kennedy. The girl especially had a big smile on her face and held both hands over her head in a V-for-victory sign and "yelled either, 'We shot him,' or 'He shot him,' perhaps meaning Sirhan. Twice. One of the men then took her arm and pulled her away and they all turned and left through the kitchen."

Merritt didn't get a good look at their faces, but he originally told the FBI the woman was about five-five, with light-colored hair, and wore a white dress with dark polka-dots. One of the men was six-two with dark hair and a dark suit. The other was thin, five-five or five-six, with dark hair, and was also wearing a suit.[72]

As they left, an Ace guard walked up to him and asked, "What happened?" Merritt said Kennedy had been shot and put his gun back in his holster. He told the guard to stand there and went back through the west doors into the Embassy Ballroom to find a telephone. The other guard did not have his gun out, and the interviewers didn't even ask Merritt for a description. They knew that the only other Ace guard in the pantry was Thane Eugene Cesar. Cesar told police he ran out of the pantry to alert Merritt, but in Merritt's account, he seems to disappear from the pantry after the shooting and come back minutes later, asking, "What happened?"

As the interviewers go back over Merritt's story about the girl saying "We shot him" or "He shot him," they sound increasingly troubled by what Merritt is saying, as if it's suddenly dawning on them that there may be something to this story about the girl after all. They then ask a question I have never heard on any other audiotaped police interview—"Is it your opinion that there's a conspiracy involved here?" Merritt contemplates this for a few seconds and replies, "I would say yes." He also expresses regret that he did not pay that much attention to these three people in all the confusion.

"Did you at the time think that you should have apprehended them or attempted to?"

"Not at the time. But as the excitement wore off a little bit . . . I should have tried maybe to ask what they were talking about or why they were going out through the kitchen area."[73]

While Merritt's account has the girl and her companions fleeing on the opposite side of the hotel from where Sandra Serrano was sitting, the dress description, smile, and comments clearly echo both Serrano and Di Pierro's descriptions. But by 1971, the girl and her companions were long gone.[74]

* * *

Merritt's statements deepen the cloud over Thane Eugene Cesar's movements after the shooting. Cesar claimed he ran out of the pantry to the main doors of the Embassy Ballroom and summoned Merritt into the pantry, but Merritt makes no mention of Cesar until he turns up a few minutes later as Kennedy lies on the floor.

Albert Stowers, the guard stationed with Merritt, was alerted by a Kennedy aide and also doesn't mention Cesar. Stowers did not enter the pantry but stood outside the service doors with Merritt until one a.m. to block the crowd from entering—again, he doesn't mention Cesar, who claims he did the same thing.

Where did Cesar disappear to in those few minutes after the shooting? Why did he ask Merritt what happened when he returned? Nobody can account for his movements. If he needed to get a gun out of the pantry during this time, no one was any the wiser.[75]

In the Vegas interview, Merritt could not remember the name of the Ace guard in the pantry and the interviewers never mentioned Cesar by name, which, given the notoriety of Cesar at that point, is astonishing.[76]

* * *

Merritt was a fascinating and highly credible witness. Nobody had contacted him about the case since 1968, until two days before the visit of Sartuche and Patchett. At nine on that Saturday morning, a man approached him at the trailer park and asked, "Are you Jack J. Merritt?" Merritt said he was, and the man introduced himself as a police officer from Los Angeles. When Merritt asked for ID, the man checked both sides of his jacket, said, "By golly, I think I left it at home," and without missing a beat, turned and walked all the way back down the drive out of the trailer park and onto the Strip.

Merritt thought it odd because the man didn't carry a briefcase or papers and didn't seem to have a car. He described the man as white, in his early fifties, about six-two and 220 pounds, clean cut, with "a dangling gut" and light blond hair, and dressed in a light gray suit and tie. "He was not a native of this part of the country," Merritt said.

Merritt died in West Virginia in 1975. His death certificate lists his occupation as "Retired—Security officer" and names two companies he worked for, Hughes Corporation and Allied Security. (By then, Thane Cesar also worked for the Hughes Corporation at Hughes Aircraft, a company with known ties to the CIA.)[77]

Thirty minutes before the shooting, as Sirhan asked the waiters which way Kennedy would come, Cesar knew the route and was ready to take the senator by the right elbow as soon as he left the stage, to lead him into the "killing zone."

EIGHT

SIRHAN'S DEFENSE TEAM

At 7:25 a.m. on June 5, seven hours after the shooting, John Doe was arraigned by Judge Joan Dempsey Klein in Division 40 of the Los Angeles County Municipal Court. The prisoner was represented by LA County Public Defender Richard Buckley, and Deputy District Attorney John Howard appeared for the prosecution. The complaint alleged a violation of six counts of Penal Code 217, Assault with Intent to Commit Murder, and bail was set at $250,000.[1]

* * *

Later, during the trial, Sirhan told his chief defense attorney, Grant Cooper, he recalled very little of his time in custody. He chatted freely with the detectives and Dr. Crahan, who examined him, but he didn't discuss the case because "they never brought it up, sir."

He knew Kennedy was involved because he heard his name mentioned by the "lady judge" during the arraignment, but he didn't actually realize he was charged with shooting Kennedy until A.L. Wirin of the ACLU came to see him later that morning. He told defense psychiatrist Dr. Diamond he didn't give his name because he was "still dazed . . . why not keep my mouth shut until I could see what the hell's going on?"

"You joked," said Diamond.

"I didn't give a shit."

"You think you were out of contact with reality?"

"I think I was high, sir."

"You were very talkative. You were willing to talk about anything except yourself."

"Hell, that's what I don't understand!" said Sirhan.[2]

* * *

In the audiotapes of these sessions, Sirhan's explanation rings true. After the trial, NBC's Jack Perkins again challenged him on this point.

"You didn't know while you were being held at the police station what had happened?"

167

"No, sir."

"Why did you think you were there?"

"It all seemed like a nightmare to me, sir. It seemed unreal. . . . Nothing ever dawned on me to ask."

"But you were being held in the middle of the night in a police station, with officers all around you, and you were handcuffed. It must have occurred to you to ask, 'Why am I here?'"

"I wish I could have, sir. I wish I could have."

"Which, of course, makes it look like you knew why you were there."

"I honestly did not, sir."

"And then when the attorney Al Wirin for the Civil Liberties Union came and visited you, he told you what had happened, did he?"

"Yes, sir . . . [later] he told me . . . that Mr. Kennedy had ten children . . . and I couldn't believe it, sir."

"That bothered you?"

"It bothered me. . . . The whole thing was so unreal, sir. I couldn't believe the whole thing has happened yet!"[3]

* * *

Wirin later told author Robert Blair Kaiser that during his first visit with Sirhan, the young suspect whispered a confession: "You know, I did it. I shot him." "He pulled an imaginary trigger on an imaginary gun," wrote Kaiser in his book.[4]

Wirin may have had an agenda here. He had earlier publicly defended the Warren Commission Report, which ruled out conspiracy in the JFK assassination. In a debate with assassination researcher and author Mark Lane shortly after its release, Wirin said, "I say thank God for Earl Warren. He saved us from a pogrom. He saved our nation. God bless him for what he has done in establishing that Oswald was the lone assassin." When Lane asked Wirin if he would feel the same way if Oswald were innocent, he thought for a moment and replied, "Yes, I still would say so."[5]

* * *

On Friday, June 7, twenty-three witnesses were called to testify before Superior Court judge Arthur L. Alarcon and the Los Angeles County Grand Jury. A murder indictment was returned against Sirhan and in late afternoon, the court reconvened in the Chapel facility of the Los Angeles County Jail, and Sirhan was informed of the indictment. Sirhan was again represented by Public Defender Richard Buckley, who now assigned Sirhan's case to his colleague Wilbur Littlefield. Wirin was present as a "friend of the court" to ensure that Sirhan's constitutional rights were preserved.

Littlefield requested that two psychiatrists be appointed to ascertain Sirhan's mental state at the time of shooting. Dr. Eric Marcus and Dr. Edward Stainbrook were so appointed. Judge Alarcon also issued an order limiting publicity on and discussion of the case to ensure that the defendant received a fair trial. Witnesses could no longer talk to the press, by court order.[6]

Robert Kaiser had been among a group of thirty reporters in the front yard of the Sirhan bungalow at 696 East Howard the morning after the shooting. Kaiser had just retired as a writer for Time & Life but was now pressed back into action. He watched Al Wirin pull up and go in to meet the family; two days later, after the grand jury, Kaiser gave Wirin a call.

"Mr.Wirin, I'd like an interview with the assassin," he said.

"You and all these other guys, right?" Wirin replied.

"Well, he hasn't lost his right to free speech."

"Who told you that?" asked the expert on constitutional rights.

"Well, Grant Cooper, a friend of mine."

"Wirin flashed on the name Grant Cooper," Kaiser told me, "because he was one of the most, if not the most, prominent criminal attorneys in Los Angeles at the time.

"He said, 'Do you know Grant Cooper?'

"I said, 'Yeah.'

"He asked, 'Could you persuade him to take the case?'"[7]

Cooper was a friend of Kaiser's—he had represented him in his divorce. On Sunday, Kaiser went over to Cooper's house and found him in an office overlooking the pool, poring over evidence for a case involving card cheating at the Friars Club, which was to start the next day.[8]

Sirhan in custody.

Cooper was sixty-five years old and one of the leading criminal defense attorneys in the country. He had recently served as president of the LA County Bar Association and the American College of Trial Lawyers. After passing the bar exam in 1927, he earned a reputation as a tough prosecutor during six years at the LA County district attorney's office. As chief deputy DA in the early forties, he successfully fought the powerful crime and gambling interests that had corrupted the mayor's office and the police force.[9]

Cooper subsequently built up a thriving practice as a defense attorney and, in June 1967, flew halfway around the world into a war zone to win acquittal for a Marine sergeant charged with murdering a Vietnamese civilian. When asked why, Cooper replied, "I've never defended a man in a military court before."[10]

Back by the pool, Kaiser told Cooper that Wirin was having trouble finding a private attorney for Sirhan. It wouldn't look good if Sirhan had to rely on the public defender. Cooper agreed the boy had a right to a fair trial, and agreed to take the case pro bono on one condition—that the Sirhan case would be postponed until after the Friars Club case, which Cooper estimated would be "sometime in September."[11]

* * *

The Friars Club case bears some background discussion here, as it would get Cooper into hot water later and present major conflicts of interest to his defense of Sirhan.

Cooper was defending Maurice Friedman, an obese Las Vegas hotel and casino developer, who, along with four others, had been charged in federal court with a five-year conspiracy to cheat wealthy members of the exclusive Friars Club in Beverly Hills. They had rigged gin rummy games by sending electronic signals to certain players from peepholes in the ceiling. The highly publicized scam had cheated celebrities including Phil Silvers and Zeppo Marx out of substantial sums.

One of the codefendants was the notorious mobster Johnny Rosselli, a close associate of Friedman's who spent a lot of time at the Friars Club. The word was that Rosselli was the Chicago Mob's man on the West Coast. When he got wind of the scheme, he demanded a cut. Rosselli described himself as "an investor," and two alleged peephole operators were too scared to testify.[12]

These were troubling bedfellows for an attorney representing Sirhan. Beside his Mob ties, Rosselli also had a strong Kennedy connection. In January 1967, Rosselli had gone public with allegations that Bobby Kennedy had gotten his brother killed by supervising assassination plots on Castro.

Rosselli's attorney Ed Morgan leaked the story to syndicated columnist Jack Anderson and New Orleans DA Jim Garrison. When Lyndon Johnson finally learned of the plots from Anderson's boss, Drew Pearson, he called the attorney general, Ramsey Clark:

"It's incredible! . . . They have a man that was . . . instructed by the CIA and attorney general [Bobby Kennedy] to assassinate Castro after the Bay of Pigs. . . .

So he [Castro] tortured [the would-be assassins] and they told him all about it. [Castro] called Oswald and a group in and told them . . . go . . . get the job done."[13]

Fifteen minutes after the shooting at the Ambassador, foreign policy adviser Walt Rostow called Johnson with the news that Robert Kennedy had been shot. Twelve minutes later, Johnson called Rostow back with questions. Johnson's handwritten notes of the conversation contain the following: "Guard him. Local FBI. Keep away from Press. Way interrogated—not to do things that will create error. Movie made." The notes also show Johnson was still consumed with the Castro plots and seemed to connect them to RFK's shooting: "Burke Marshall [the Kennedys' lawyer] . . . Ed Morgan [Rosselli's lawyer] . . . Cosa Nostra [Mafia] . . . Send in to get Castro . . . Planning."[14]

Years later, Rosselli testified that he had been contracted by the CIA to oversee an assassination attempt on Castro. One account has Rosselli working with CIA operatives in Miami on the project under military cover as Colonel Rosselli. Cooper's proximity to Rosselli in this context is troubling.[15]

* * *

So Cooper agreed to take the case, but only if another attorney could be found to file motions and handle the initial phases, so his future participation could be kept secret and not prejudice the jury in the Friars Club case.[16]

Sirhan as he later appeared with attorneys Russell Parsons (left) and Grant Cooper (right).

Wirin went up to see Sirhan and showed him a list of five prospective attorneys. Sirhan loved reading about famous legal cases and recognized Cooper's name right away. On Tuesday, June 11, Sirhan signed retainers for Cooper and two other lawyers Cooper wanted to bring into the case—Herman Selvin and Joseph Ball, who had served on the Warren Commission. When both turned Cooper down, the attorney asked Kaiser about the other two names on the list.

"Russell Parsons and Luke McKissack."

"Let's have Parsons take over," said Cooper. "I don't know McKissack and I've worked with Russ before."[17]

Russell Parsons was seventy-three years old and had been practicing law for more than fifty years. Like Cooper, he had worked for the LA County DA's office as a prosecutor in the late thirties and, before that, had gained some notoriety defending a murderer called "Rattlesnake" James, who tried to kill his wife by forcing her foot into a box of rattlesnakes. When that didn't work, he drowned her. By filing numerous appeals, Parsons managed to keep James from the gallows for seven years, at a time when appeals were rarely successful.

On June 19, over breakfast, Al Wirin offered Parsons the chance to handle the Sirhan case while Cooper was busy with the Friars Club trial. Parsons immediately accepted and, by noon, was on his way to visit Sirhan in his cell. Sirhan seemed delighted to finally have an attorney of his own, and Parson's feisty, talkative style seemed to put the young prisoner at ease.

Parsons returned to his office to find fifty reporters waiting for him and his phones ringing off the hook. He told the collected newsmen that he would represent Sirhan without a fee as a public service—"there's a poor devil in trouble and that's enough for me." Asked his age, Parsons replied, "In the late sixties, that good enough? Who are you going to tell? Some girl?"

Parsons said he'd be joined later by another attorney, but newspaper speculation that this might be Cooper was met with a flat denial from Cooper himself—"Definitely, positively, unequivocally, no."[18]

* * *

Parsons also brought some odd baggage to the case. As Kaiser notes, in the forties, when he was defending some well-known members of the Mob, a deputy DA named Grant Cooper tried to run them out of town. The LAPD substantiated claims that Parsons had represented mobster Mickey Cohen's henchmen, the Sica brothers, dating back to the mid-fifties.[19]

Parsons also held a grudge against Bob Kennedy. When Kennedy was an investigator for the Senate Rackets Committee, he once paid a call on Parsons's banker in LA, wanting to know "if Parsons was holding any funds for Murray Chotiner." Chotiner once shared an office with Parsons and had raised funds for Richard Nixon through Mickey Cohen. Parsons couldn't get a loan from his bank as a result—"Kennedy hurt me with my banker. He was a dirty son of a bitch and I never forgave him for that."[20]

* * *

Also waiting with the press in Parsons's office that first day was his routine investigator and process-server, Michael McCowan, and his partner, Ron Allen. When the press left, McCowan told Parsons, "I know you need help. I'll drop everything I'm doing." "And so they went right to work with me," recalled Parsons, again without a fee.[21]

McCowan was a thirty-four-year-old former Marine who had served ten years in the LAPD while putting himself through law school. Kaiser later described him as "a natty Irishman with clear, blue eyes and a roguish smile" who drove around town in an air-conditioned Cadillac.[22]

After graduating from law school, his ambition to be an attorney was set back when he resigned from the LAPD in 1965 "in lieu of disciplinary action after being arrested for theft and tampering" with U.S. mail. According to police reports, McCowan got involved with a pretty blond housewife named Jean Ortiz. McCowan helped send her husband to prison on a burglary charge, then started sharing the Ortiz bedroom, leading to a divorce suit from McCowan's wife. One LAPD report continues: "Ms Ortiz' charms weren't the only thing that interested officer McCowan . . . the woman's husband had gathered a small arsenal of weapons in the home and McCowan . . . took possession of them. Then, too, Mrs. Ortiz had three diamond rings valued at about $4500. She decided she wanted to send the rings to her sister in the East to get money that would help pay her husband's legal bills. Wearing civvies, McCowan went to the post office and mailed the rings. A short time later he returned in police uniform, persuaded postal officials to hand over the rings, then took them and sold them."[23]

* * *

Parsons defended McCowan during his legal difficulties—"The trial of McCowan itself would make a book! He was a detective, worked on a case and got involved with two women, which of course is the kiss of death! They claimed that he stole their jewelry. They were angry with him . . . he had intercourse with them!"

Parsons helped McCowan appeal a five-year sentence, and on January 29, 1968, McCowan was given three years' probation. Parsons was a client of Ron Allen Associates, a successful attorney service run by McCowan and Allen. They had six or seven men serving papers for law firms, and McCowan did a lot of the routine investigation. When Parsons became Sirhan's attorney, they came with him. Allen later rued ever getting involved:

"Our firm handled the investigation for Parsons. . . . The Sirhan case is the reason Mike and I aren't in business anymore. . . . We lost our shirt. . . . We put in eight or nine months on that case. . . . We had a good investigation business going.

. . . It all went right down the tubes because of the Sirhan case. . . . It's a very touchy subject. I lost a lot of friends on the Sirhan thing. . . . I was threatened with bombs. . . . I was spit on."[24]

* * *

Today, Mike McCowan lives in a beautiful house, full of Chinese antiquities, in California wine country. I visited one Sunday in late 2006 and found him a real gentleman as we chatted for four hours about the case while his charming wife painted in her studio out back. When I first made contact with him, McCowan had just taken his files out of storage and was planning to give them to the Secret Service Museum. His only previous interview about the Sirhan case was given to researcher Betsy Langman in 1973.

He showed me his archive—a sketch of Sirhan by courtroom artist Howard Brodie signed by Sirhan: "Mike, you're a hell of an investigator, Sirhan Sirhan"; and a telegram for Mary Sirhan: "Please accept my sincerest and deepest sympathy, Marguerite C. Oswald." Mrs. Sirhan gave it to him as a memento.

When we sat down for the interview, my cameraman and I couldn't help feeling Michael seemed quite nervous. He was hard to maintain eye contact with and his voice quavered a little—we weren't sure why. Perhaps he was feeling defensive, worried that we were going to rub his nose in all the bad press he'd had over the years. He's been accused of being a plant on the defense team for the FBI or the CIA, or both.

"When I got asked to come into the case," he explained, "I knew there wasn't a lot of monetary remuneration, but it was an exciting thing to do and I was doing quite fine financially, so I could afford to do it. And I like to investigate things; I really wanted to find out really what happened. And I really tried to find out to the best of my ability if there was a conspiracy. If Sirhan acted alone or if he didn't."

When I asked Michael about the mail fraud conviction, he rubbed his eye uncomfortably. "I think several people thought I got a really bad deal. A really bad deal. Because the two officers that were supposed to testify for me didn't testify or were scared to testify . . . they were worried about their job. And so they left me sitting out on a branch. And I've talked to both of them people and they know how I feel."[25]

* * *

On July 3, 1968, Jacquelyn Caporozzo notified detectives that six months earlier—around the time his probation started—McCowan had asked her to keep a collection of guns in her house for safekeeping: "He told her that he had confiscated them from Jean Ortiz who had been involved in a burglary with her husband and that the guns were possibly stolen. Los Angeles Police detectives took four rifles, two shotguns, eight pistols and one automatic .25 caliber pistol into custody."

Even though McCowan had successfully appealed his conviction, it seems he was still hiding a cache of possibly stolen guns from Jean Ortiz. This was a clear violation of his probation, so before the case had even started, the LAPD had the goods on McCowan, though he was never prosecuted or suffered any probation-related consequences.[26]

* * *

Two weeks into the Friars Club trial, Grant Cooper also found himself in trouble for the first time in his career. On July 23, Assistant U.S. Attorney David Nissen spotted a transcript of comedian Phil Silvers's grand jury testimony lying on Cooper's counsel table—in federal cases, such transcripts are sealed by court order. Cooper was called into chambers by U.S. District Judge William P. Gray and asked for an explanation the following day.

He pleaded innocent—"I found it on the table in the courtroom. I have no knowledge how it got there." That night, he reportedly went home and burned three other transcripts before further questioning in chambers two days later. It soon emerged that Cooper had been trying to obtain the transcripts for six months, finally receiving the stolen transcripts from a cocounsel two weeks before the trial began. The truth would out, however, and soon Cooper had an indictment hanging over him.[27]

* * *

So with Cooper obtaining stolen grand jury transcripts for a Mob front man in federal court and a chief defense investigator with a probation violation hanging over him, the defense team set to work.

Robert Kaiser shakes hands with Sirhan as the rest of the defense team looks on: (left to right) McCowan, Parsons, Cooper.

As the forty-member SUS team and the FBI conducted well-resourced investigations, McCowan was, in his own words, a "lonesome cowboy" following up leads on witnesses by reading the grand jury transcript and press reports. He would not see any police or FBI files until the first motion for discovery was granted by the court in mid-October.

"Russell, I think, was like late seventies," McCowan told me, "and he didn't have a lot of energy, so I basically tried to hold the thing together until Grant Cooper could get there. . . . I'd go over to the federal courthouse and speak with him from time to time." But Cooper didn't really want to think about the Sirhan case until the Friars Club trial was over, and, in the meantime, the prosecution wasn't making life any easier.[28]

"The police were not cooperative with us," recalled Parsons. "Did Mike tell you how the police refused to let us look at their reports? The FBI denied to Mc-Cowan they were even investigating the case and told witnesses not to speak to us. The D.A. and the Sheriff and the FBI stopped the people at the little hospital in Corona from giving us any information about Sirhan getting his head injury after he was thrown off a race-horse. Whatever I got from the police, I had to wring out of them." According to McCowan's partner, Ron Allen, the defense team was also put under surveillance by the LAPD, and the FBI had their phones tapped.[29]

* * *

On August 2, Sirhan pleaded not guilty to murder and intent to commit murder, and Parsons strongly hinted that the defense strategy would be based on the California legal definition of "diminished capacity"—that Sirhan did not have the emotional or mental capacity to meaningfully and maturely reflect on the gravity of his contemplated act.[30]

Parsons's main worry at this point was money for the defense. Nobody was getting paid, but there were expenses to cover, and writer Bob Kaiser told Cooper he had a possible solution: "I said, 'Look, Grant . . . I know there's no money here, the family is poor but I can do some journalism and sell some stories to *Life* magazine and maybe some European magazines like *Paris-Match* and I can generate some funds, so you don't have to go into this thing out of your own pocket.' And he flashed on that, he kind of liked that idea and that's what I did. So, once I got Cooper in the case, he got me in the case. He made me an investigator for the defense."[31]

Parsons met Kaiser and agreed to bring him on board, and a deal was struck whereby Kaiser would contribute half of his earnings from magazine articles and a book on the case to the defense in return for access. But Parsons wouldn't let Kaiser anywhere near Sirhan until he came through with some money. In the meantime, Kaiser worked with McCowan on the investigation. They prepared discovery motions to find out what the prosecution knew about Sirhan and interviewed witnesses.[32]

Kaiser eventually contributed $32,000 to the defense team, a figure dwarfed by the $203,656 spent by the prosecution, but much needed at the time.[33]

So now there were four on the defense team, split into two camps—McCowan and Parsons on one side; Kaiser and Cooper on the other. Kaiser knew that Cooper had control of the case and that Parsons needed Kaiser for the money. But Parsons remained skeptical: "Kaiser did little for us. I never trusted Kaiser! I trusted McCowan. McCowan didn't like Kaiser and vice versa. He called him 'a failed priest' [he had spent some time in the seminary], digging up sensational facts about the Kennedy case to sell his book, digging up as many conspiracies as he could find." McCowan told Betsy Langman, "I did the defense investigation alone. . . . Sirhan hated Kaiser's guts. . . . He liked me because I had a law degree."[34]

In his book, Kaiser later described Parsons as "garrulous, funny, senile and a fool. . . . Cooper wanted an attorney who wasn't going to take over the case, somebody who would do what he was told, and not be a problem later on. So he got harmless old Russell Parsons . . . and Parsons enjoyed his few months basking in the publicity and seeing his face on television . . . until Cooper came into the case and then he was decidedly a fifth wheel."[35]

When I interviewed McCowan and Kaiser for this book, they were notably diplomatic. "Our personalities clashed," admitted McCowan, "but I have to say he was very helpful. He was basically interested in writing a story about it, and I was basically trying to find the facts about it, and he didn't have access to Sirhan, which I did, so that led to a little bit of inconsistency in our relationship, but he did come up with some good stuff. He was a good reporter."

According to Kaiser, "McCowan didn't tell me everything because he was trying to sell his own book. It created a certain amount of tension between us during the trial." They both continually described themselves as "lone investigators," overwhelmed by their workload, pursuing their own separate investigations, and keeping certain information from each other—hardly ideal circumstances for a successful defense.[36]

The key for both men was gaining Sirhan's trust, so they could get as much information from him as possible. McCowan built up the initial relationship: "My job was to learn everything I could about Sirhan that would be profitable for the defense to know. He confided in me, I believe, and I took my leads from there and checked the witnesses, talked with law enforcement people."

McCowan showed me yellow legal pads where he got Sirhan to write down what he could remember about the night of the shooting and asked him to draw a detailed floor plan of the Lobby Level of the Ambassador. The sketches show the Embassy Ballroom and Colonial Room but no pantry—illustrating a good memory of the hotel layout up to a certain point in the evening.

McCowan put the apparent memory block down to the Tom Collins cocktails: "He's not a drinker, really, and apparently he was drinking that night, maybe to get some false courage or whatever. And maybe that's what caused him to black out or to have some fade in his memory."

McCowan would see Sirhan during the day, and at night, pore over the pile of books Adel Sirhan had given him from his brother's room. Some were obviously stolen from John Muir High School or the Pasadena Public Library, but two in particular caught McCowan's attention.[37]

The first was *History of the American People*, by David Saville Muzzey. The following paragraph on President McKinley was underlined: "It was his last public utterance. The next day, as he was holding a reception in the Temple of Music, he was shot by a young Polish anarchist named Czolgosz, whose brain had been inflamed reading the tirades of the yellow press against 'Czar McKinley.' After a week of patient suffering the President died,—the third victim of an assassin's bullet since the Civil War." After that was written in pencil, "many more will come."[38]

Another book, *The Transformation of Modern Europe*, from the John Muir High School Library, summed up the assassination of Archduke Ferdinand, and someone—McCowan assumed Sirhan—had underlined parts of the following paragraph, as indicated: "It is conceivable that if the chauffeur of the archduke's car, having taken the wrong road on the way back from the official reception at the town hall, had not backed up to correct his error, the assassin would not have been successful. On the other hand, another assassin might have been because the plot to kill the archduke had been carefully laid under the direction of the colonel in charge of the intelligence division of the Serbian general staff, and more than one assassin was lying in wait that day."[39]

This second passage is an alarming echo of the route switch discussed in Chapter 7. Both passages clearly show that whoever underlined them had assassination on the brain when they marked them. But were the notations Sirhan's? Russell Parsons didn't try to find out. As Kaiser notes, he ordered McCowan to make no mention of them in his report and hid the books in his office. To Parsons, these passages proved one thing: premeditation.

But the writings made a huge impression on McCowan, who somehow extrapolated that Sirhan had been thinking of assassinating someone since high school.[40]

Grant Cooper later overruled Parsons and proceeded to introduce these passages and notations into evidence at trial, stipulating that the writing was Sirhan's without even subjecting it to handwriting analysis. Cooper elicited from defense psychiatrist Dr. Diamond an image of a Sirhan "obsessed with the idea of assassinations . . . even in high school," and court-appointed psychiatrist Dr. Marcus noted "a paranoid schizophrenic . . . who commits a murder . . . takes about ten years to develop, and this is quite consistent with these ideas beginning to be formed back in high school."

Yet, there was really no basis for this suggested dating. If the underlining and notations were, indeed, Sirhan's, it's far more likely he did them during the period he was writing of assassination in his notebooks: from the days before the Six-Day

War in early June 1967 up to the shooting of Kennedy. There is nothing to indicate that Sirhan had any thoughts of assassination before this time.[41]

In the nineties, Sirhan's then attorney, Larry Teeter, noticed something odd about the "many more will come" notation. In a pretrial memorandum to the defense team, McCowan explained that "Sirhan underlines, italicizes and writes in the margins of almost all his books." But when McCowan attached a list of such passages—including four from the Muzzey book—the "many more will come" reference was missing. Teeter and Sirhan's family accused McCowan of fabricating it.[42]

* * *

But at the time, the notations left their mark on McCowan. He began to research previous assassination attempts in the Secret Service archives to study the behavioral patterns of assassins.

"With Sirhan, I felt pretty certain that there wasn't a conspiracy—reading those passages and the underlining things led me to believe that this guy was thinking about assassinating somebody all along. Now, in that vein, it's my understanding that the FBI had followed him [Sirhan] down to San Diego. A couple of weeks before Robert Kennedy's assassination, he was trailing Hubert Humphrey."

McCowan pinned Sirhan's rage not on the promise to send jet bombers to Israel but on his upbringing: "His mother was always telling all of her children all about the massacres at Deir Yassin, how they were put out of their own homes, and I'm sure she really believed all of that, but I think when it was imparted to you when you're very young and it continues on and on and on and on, I think that was a large basis for him to commit this assassination of Robert Kennedy.

"I see a kid that wanted to be a hero to the Palestinian people and promote that cause. His mother had harangued him over all those years about the way they were left without their home and all that. I think he would have shot any high-ranking political official, and the Secret Service told me that, two weeks [before], they were trailing him, following Hubert Humphrey, and . . . I think they had some film on it."

This was the first I had ever heard of this story. It does not appear in any of the investigation files, and Kaiser wasn't aware of it, so it must be treated with caution. McCowan's confusion as to whether the FBI or the Secret Service told him this does not breed confidence. When challenged, he said it was the Secret Service, and clearly this information had a huge influence on the way McCowan approached his investigation.[43]

* * *

As Sirhan sat in jail with no memory of the shooting, his head was turned by letters of support from the Middle East. He was hailed as a hero, and the Palestinians made a poster of him with the strapline "I did it for my country." He began to rationalize the shooting as a political act and to dream up ways he could use international diplomacy and political blackmail to get out of his nightmarish predicament.[44] McCowan read me a note Sirhan wrote from jail at the time:

> *"This deal will be a secret between the President, Mr. Parsons, Michael McCowan, the Judge and myself and permanently binding. We will agree to sign an agreement, second degree or manslaughter. Doctor from San Diego. The D.A. must be unaware of our deal. Remember D.A. Garrison. The Judge is to guarantee me parole at first request, my safety in jail and a private cell. . . . What can the President do if he rejects our proposition?*
>
> *Definitely I will not accept life imprisonment. The President can contact the Judge through the Attorney General. One hundred years ago, they tried to impeach a President Johnson. How about it nowadays? Another Johnson to be impeached. Well, try to caution the President not to be patriotic by refusing to cooperate because he will not enjoy his over-patriotism too long. It is better for him and HHH [Hubert Humphrey] to swallow their pride than be impeached and be subjected to public shame. I may be a son of a bitch, Truman called me so. They may tell us to go to hell, we'll go but we will take them with us.*

Page two consists of random jottings:

> *Will tell about election. Other gents hired me. Arab countries helping me. LBJ's own prestige is at stake. This is a small price. . . . We will play legitimate trial. Tell the President we have a ready market to sell our story if he doesn't comply in a foreign country. Show letter of support from Arab countries. Ask $750,000 because they might Jew us down to $500,000. Minimum that we'll accept. Money to be in used unmarked cash. Will put it in a safe deposit box. Penalty assessment: imprisonment in Chino only.*
>
> *Nasser. New Middle East War. Challenge him to dare us. . . . Arab oil countries pressure H.L. Hunt to pressure LBJ. Tell LBJ that we will tell Nixon that LBJ wanted to knock off Kennedy so that Nixon uses this against the Democratic party.*

McCowan still rolls his eyes at Sirhan's "grandiose ideas" of a deal with the president in exchange for his freedom. Sirhan's offer seems to be this: Guarantee him a conviction of manslaughter or second-degree murder based on "diminished capacity." Get the doctor from San Diego, Dr. Schorr, to verify it. Put Sirhan in Chino for a few years, then give him half a million dollars to go into exile in Jordan. If not, Sirhan will tell Nixon that LBJ wanted to knock off Bobby, Nixon will win the election, and, with pressure from the Arab states, Sirhan may touch off a new Middle East War.

I read these notes myself, written on sheets from a yellow legal pad. McCowan didn't feel it was appropriate to give me copies, so I didn't have the handwriting analyzed, but they seem legitimate and do make Sirhan look bad. While Sirhan was heading for death row for a crime he couldn't remember, his desperation tactics here seem pretty inexcusable. I can understand McCowan seeing these notes, at the time, as further confirmation of Sirhan's guilt.[45]

The notes seem to be a precursor to a plea Sirhan made to Russell Parsons on September 24 to negotiate with the State Department for his extradition to Jordan or he'd "blow the top off this thing." Parsons let it blow over.[46]

* * *

When Robert Blair Kaiser came into the case in August as a defense investigator, he was charged with developing "all the background material he could obtain for the purpose of establishing Sirhan's mental state at the time of the shooting for the benefit of the psychologists and psychiatrists working on the case." Again, the most direct route to this was Sirhan himself—to try to get Sirhan's story as completely as he could.

After a couple of initial meetings, on August 27, Kaiser, Sirhan, and the defense team signed a contract giving Kaiser exclusive access to Sirhan's story and splitting all proceeds three ways—Kaiser would be paid to write magazine articles and a book on the case; the rest would go to the defense team and the Sirhan family, to cover defense expenses and basic living costs.

As a result, "I interviewed the assassin almost every day for six months before, during, and after the trial, much more than the attorneys did," Kaiser recalled. "A good interviewer tries to be open, friendly, elicit stories by telling stories, like a couple of guys having a beer at a bar and gradually, Sirhan loosened up with me, telling me all about his life and his aspirations, his hopes and despair.

"Sirhan was a highly suggestible young man. He was not an idiot. He was quite intelligent; he was well-read. I would use big words on him on a Monday, and on Tuesday, he would use them back to me, sometimes correctly even, so he was a sponge, he was soaking in information all the time. We had some fascinating conversations, political conversations and so forth. But he stuck to the story that he didn't remember killing Robert Kennedy."

Kaiser felt and still feels that there were others involved with Sirhan. "One of the reasons I think Sirhan didn't act alone is that he was such an unlikely assassin. He was a kind of a chickenshit, to use an American expression. Example—he worked as a grocery boy in a store in Pasadena, and he got very angry with the owner one day, and then he said, 'And then I called him a goddamn son of a bitch.' And I said, 'Oh, did you call him a goddamn son of a bitch right to his face?' And he said, 'No, I said it under my breath so he couldn't hear me.' Well, that kind of a guy, it's very unlikely that he's gonna be a macho assassin. How does he make that transformation?"

Kaiser also makes it clear that he didn't believe everything Sirhan was telling him and that there were certain subjects Sirhan wanted to avoid. "Sirhan usually got evasive with me when I got into the involvement of others, and I think he was lying much of that time. And I found a little tic in his conversation. He used the word 'sir' as a kind of filler. Whenever he was lying, he sprinkled this word 'sir' throughout his conversation. It was like a tell a poker player will find to figure out when his opponent is bluffing."[47]

Sirhan also withheld certain information from Kaiser. At first, he told him he wasn't at the Ambassador on the Sunday before the shooting. He later confessed to Parsons and McCowan that he was, "but I didn't want to tell Kaiser." Why not? "Well, because Kaiser's only interested in writing a book. I'm worried about the trial."[48]

* * *

By mid-September, SUS was winding down. Investigators returned to their normal divisions, and only fourteen men stayed on to tidy up conspiracy allegations, prepare the case for trial, and write the final report. Manny Pena worked only mornings, and the job was almost done. Mike McCowan had still found no trace of conspiracy or any witnesses who might challenge the idea that Sirhan was the lone assassin.[49]

* * *

On October 12, Parsons arranged an EEG for Sirhan to discover whether the fall from the horse in 1966 had resulted in any brain damage. Sirhan was hoping the test would show some abnormality and make the "diminished capacity" defense more credible to a jury. Sirhan didn't like being called crazy, but brain damage was outside his control. He reputedly asked McCowan whether he should bang his head against his cell wall to prepare for the test.

Electrodes were fitted to Sirhan's head by brain specialist Dr. Edward Davis, and electrical activity in the brain was found to be normal. Dr. Davis then prepared the equivalent of four Tom Collins cocktails according to the Ambassador Hotel recipe, using six ounces of Gordon's gin. Sirhan drank the mixture down in eight minutes, but again, over the next seventy-eight minutes, no unusual brain activity was noted.

Sirhan did put on an interesting show while drunk, however. For ten minutes, he shivered violently as Dr. Marcus, the court-appointed psychiatrist, looked on. Sirhan had always been friendly and polite to Dr. Marcus, who happened to be Jewish. But now, when someone told him Dr. Marcus was present, he shouted, "Get that bastard out of here!"

Dr. Marcus recalled the test at the trial:

"He kept grabbing for his throat, and he said, 'What the hell is going on here?' And you would have thought we were choking him."

"I hate his guts," shouted Sirhan; then, later on, he kept repeating, "I will get even with those Jews, goddamn it."

Twice, Sirhan asked a young female technician in uniform for a glass of water. She declined, as it would interfere with the test.

"You're a hell of a waitress!" said Sirhan.

"He thought, apparently, that he was back at the Ambassador," recalled Dr. Marcus, "when, I believe, a waitress refused him a drink, as he looked a little too erratic."

Sirhan was in a kind of "hostile delirium," throwing out phrases:

"Twenty years is long enough for the Jews . . . We have got to have justice . . . Didn't have to help them by sending planes . . . That bastard just can't, he can't help those bastards! One year and those goddamn Jews are still left!"

Sirhan mistook Dr. Marcus for his brother Adel and kept telling him to speak Arabic. "He thought he was back at the Ambassador Hotel and he had had too much to drink and he wanted me to drive him home."

When Dr. Marcus corrected him, Sirhan muttered darkly, "You're one of them." He looked around at the four or five deputy sheriffs guarding him and thought they were Israeli soldiers.

"During this entire time, he was trembling and he got irritated and very depressed. I asked him repeatedly to describe killing Kennedy and he never said that he did. He kept talking about Kennedy as if Kennedy was alive. He kept saying, 'That bastard isn't worth the bullets,' and I constantly tried to get him to admit what happened, and he never said that he committed the act."

When Marcus tried to goad Sirhan about the power of the Jews over the Arabs, Sirhan replied, "They'll have to drink every drop of my blood."

"My interpretation," Marcus concluded, "is that although he had more to drink than he undoubtedly had at the Ambassador, the alcohol triggered off the same sort of delusional type of personality, and he became sort of a wild beast."

When Sirhan got the results of the EEG, he was dismayed to hear there was no brain damage, fearing the death penalty was now a step closer. "Well, if it's going to cost me my life," he said, pledging his future course, "I want to help the Arabs."[50]

* * *

While Sirhan rationalized the shooting as a political act, he still insisted he couldn't remember the shooting or the writing in his notebooks. He struggled to make sense of the weird chain of events on June 4: "Why did I not go to the races that day? Why did I not like the horses? Why did I go to that range? Why did I save those Mini-Mags? Why did I not expend those bullets? Why did I go to Bob's? Why did Mistri give me that newspaper? Why did I drink that night?" He clenched his fists as he spoke. "It was like some inner force."

"But you wrote in your notebook 'R.F.K. must die,'" said Kaiser.

"After that, I forgot it all," said Sirhan. "The idea of killing Kennedy never entered my mind, sir. I just wanted, sir, to stop him from sending planes to Israel."[51]

* * *

On October 14, Judge Herbert V. Walker put the trial date back to December 9—due to Cooper's involvement in the Friars Club case—and granted the defense their first motion for discovery. McCowan and Kaiser had drawn up a list of files held by the prosecution that the defense team wanted to see. Deputy DA David Fitts duly surrendered 111 witness statements, six transcripts of interviews with Sirhan, and a seven-page report covering the activities of Los Angeles police officers on June 5, 1968.[52]

Chief Deputy DA Lynn Compton told the court the surrendered witness interviews showed no evidence of a possible conspiracy but stressed that the prosecution had nothing to hide or withhold from the defense, turning over all statements that "could possibly be of any value at this time."

But seven months later, in a posttrial meeting with Judge Walker to discuss where the investigation files and evidence should be housed, David Fitts and SUS chief Robert Houghton indicated otherwise. Fitts admitted that the discovery material had been "scaled"—interview summaries were left in, interview transcripts were left out, and investigators' assessments and conclusions were "abstracted from the file."

Parsons would never pick up on this. When he spoke to reporters after receiving the discovery material, he parroted Compton's statement. Before he could even review the files, he boomed, "We have seen no evidence of conspiracy." The following morning, the *LA Times* ran a front-page story under the banner "Both Sides Agree Sirhan Was Alone."

Only the two defense investigators, Mike McCowan and Bob Kaiser, reviewed the witness statements in any detail. To uncover any conspiracy, they would have to have been extraordinarily resourceful. Up to now, they had to rely on press reports, the 273-page grand jury transcript, and their own witness interviews. Now, here they were, four months after the shooting, wading through thousands of pages of LAPD and FBI files for the first time, playing catch-up with police and FBI investigations that were almost complete. And they weren't reading raw files but summaries that were often sanitized, with any hint of conspiracy written out of the report or debunked, often with the help of the Hernandez polygraph test.[53]

"We had so much eyewitness evidence that Sirhan was, indeed, the shooter," remembered Kaiser; "we weren't looking to exculpate him for not being the guy who shot Kennedy. We kind of took the LAPD's word for it and, in the trial, that's what Cooper did. He didn't challenge them."[54]

Cooper never questioned the muzzle distance or the ballistics, and it seems the possibility of a second gun never occurred to the defense team, despite clues in the grand jury testimony they'd had a copy of for months. Vincent Di Pierro placed

Sirhan four to six feet away from Kennedy, while Dr. Noguchi set the muzzle distance at an inch. A deputy DA asked Noguchi about the discrepancy, but the defense investigators never did.[55]

McCowan and Kaiser overlooked the discrepancies regarding muzzle distance and bullet trajectories, and still dismiss them today. "Kennedy was not a statue standing there, looking at Sirhan," says Kaiser. "The fact that Sirhan was only three feet away . . . Well, if you're only three feet away and you reach out your arm and your gun is extended, you've narrowed the gap, so that isn't persuasive to me."

McCowan makes a similar point, recalling the muzzle distance as "two feet, approximately." He's casting his mind back forty years, but his loose grasp of the muzzle distance seems to confirm it was never a big issue for him.[56]

* * *

McCowan wrote up a thousand-page briefing book to get Cooper up and running quickly when he started on the case. The book included brief summaries on key witnesses, which often seemed like distillations of LAPD or FBI reports, with rough edges explained away and, often, no analysis or indication that McCowan had interviewed these people himself. Here's what he wrote about Vincent Di Pierro: "This is the young man who stated that he saw Sirhan with a girl in a polka dot dress standing with him by some stairs prior to the shooting. He later admitted that he had made up the story and that it was Sandy Serrano who had told him that she saw a girl in a polka dot dress running out of the kitchen yelling, 'We shot him! We shot him!' Miss Serrano's testimony was also proven false."

This shows a mangled understanding of events (here, Di Pierro sees the girl out on the stairs and Serrano sees her running out of the kitchen) and a conclusion that toes the police line. It's clear from this report that McCowan could not have interviewed either witness.

On Thane Cesar: "This man was holding on to Kennedy's arm when he was shot. He was on Kennedy's right side and places the arm and gun two feet from the senator's head and four feet from him. He claims he heard five shots and that all he saw was an arm and a gun arched over people, and then it fired. He never had a chance to stop it, and he was knocked down in the ensuing confusion."[57]

This seems to be a condensed version of Cesar's FBI interview, leaving out the most important detail—that Cesar had a gun and that he pulled it. When Betsy Langman later asked Parsons if he ever suspected the security guard, Parsons said he was never told about a guard with a gun close to Kennedy. "They never pressed me enough to subpoena such a person. . . . I asked them for a complete investigation of everything." Cooper and Parsons did not recall being told about Thane Cesar or Don Schulman, who saw a security guard fire—they found out about them only after the trial.[58]

Kaiser and McCowan both told me they interviewed Cesar but they never examined his weapon.

"I could never go along with the theory that there was a second gun in the pantry," said Kaiser. "Teddy Charach did a whole documentary on the second gun and he found a security guard named Thane Eugene Cesar who had voted for George Wallace, a conservative Democrat in the primary. And, to him, that was prima facie evidence that he must have shot Robert Kennedy, which is absurd. I interviewed Thane Cesar; he was innocent; there was no doubt in my mind."

Kaiser also told me he spent a lot of time with Sandra Serrano and listened to tapes of her sessions with Hernandez. But it's clear from his book that Kaiser never connected Sirhan with the third man going up the stairs before the shooting who never came back down. Kaiser ultimately dismissed Serrano as a "red herring"—"I was a lone investigator. I relied so heavily on the FBI and the police reports."

The result of all this was that Cooper and Parsons were never properly informed of the key witnesses to conspiracy in the case and didn't call them to the stand.[59]

* * *

Various LAPD documents also suggest that McCowan was open to helping out the other side. SUS Chief Houghton's stated position was that he would release LAPD files to the defense team only on court order through the discovery motions initiated by McCowan and Kaiser.

The SUS Daily Summary of Activities (DSA) shows McCowan, overstretched and underresourced, cozying up to the LAPD, attempting to trade information. On November 1, he met with SUS lieutenant Enrique Hernandez:

"McCowan was in, saw Hernandez. Michael professed cooperation and indicated he'd obtain needed background information from family. He wants photos or maps showing kitchen and location of witnesses."

Three days later, the DSA reads: "Made decision to decline McCowan's offer of help in obtaining miscellaneous information from family; information is not worth what he would want in exchange. It also raises the specter of 'dealing with the enemy,' which could embarrass the investigation at a later date."

Secretly working for the prosecution to elicit information from the Sirhan family was a dangerous game, even allowing for the LAPD's hardball tactics in releasing routine information to the defense camp. It's also curious that McCowan's contact would have been Hernandez, of all people, the polygraph operator.[60]

* * *

On November 5, 1968, Richard Nixon edged Hubert Humphrey to take the presidency. Kaiser asked Sirhan what he thought of the result. "Nixon! He's worse than Kennedy. To get the Jewish vote, he said he'd help the Israelis. But what good did it do him? Hell, he only got 4 per cent of the Jewish vote. Humphrey got most of it, the son of a bitch. Nixon! Hell, I gave him the election, I gave it to him!"

Sirhan reasoned that in return for giving him the election, Nixon should arrange his freedom, a passport to Jordan, and a million dollars. He printed out his demand on a legal pad, underlining the phrase "We are desperate!!!" three times.[61]

* * *

On November 26, Dr. Martin Schorr visited Sirhan and gave him a battery of psychological tests in search of a psychosis that would support a defense of "diminished capacity." Schorr believed that men killed to avenge the wrongs of their dominant mothers or fathers. He was planning a book on this psycho-dynamic pattern, called *Murder Is a Family Affair.*

At the end of the interview, Schorr asked Sirhan, "If you had three wishes, what would they be?"

"One—a pardon from President Nixon," said Sirhan. "Two—two million dollars. Three—the freedom to spend it."

The next day, Sirhan was freaked out by Schorr's visit. "I want to plead guilty," he told Parsons. "I don't want a trial. I don't want the doctors proving I'm insane." He wrote an angry note to Judge Walker, protesting his decision to allow the notebooks into evidence. "You're a bloodthirsty bastard," it read, "so take a good deep drink of my blood because justice will not be served." Between the judge and the Kennedys, Sirhan felt he had no hope of a fair trial. "I want to plead nolo contendere," he said.

McCowan said that's funny, they'd been thinking of pleading guilty for weeks, but if they did, they wouldn't be able to introduce the material about the Arab-Israeli War and promote the Palestinian cause.

"Oh, yeah," said Sirhan.[62]

* * *

On December 2, the Friars Club case finally ended—the five defendants were found guilty on all counts after a six-month trial. Cooper now formally announced he was to lead the Sirhan defense. He was granted a continuance until January 7 to completely familiarize himself with the case.

The next day, the papers also ran stories about Cooper's trouble with the grand jury transcripts, but Cooper told Parsons he wasn't worried. A lawyer's first duty was to his client, and his conscience was clean.

Aside from a few brief meetings with Parsons and the briefing book from McCowan, all that Cooper knew of the Sirhan case he'd read in the newspapers. A month's preparation would never be enough.[63]

"Cooper was kind of a Johnny Appleseed," recalled Kaiser, "a warm, friendly human being who didn't think along the lines of conspiracies. He didn't have a suspicious mind at all. He pretty much took people at their face value." Al Wirin told Cooper that Sirhan admitted he did it and everyone else assumed he did it, so it was case closed regarding conspiracy. Cooper would never ask the prosecution to prove Sirhan killed Kennedy. Instead, he would stipulate to the killing and try to find a way to save the boy's life.[64]

From reading McCowan's summary of the state's evidence, it seemed to Cooper a clear case of first-degree murder. "Would we be derelict in our duty," asked Cooper, "if we pleaded guilty in return for a sentence of life, rather than death in the gas chamber?"

Parsons argued that the psychologists' testimony and the influence of alcohol provided a good chance of second-degree murder, based on "diminished capacity." Cooper agreed on this direction.

From this point on, the defense focus narrowed to psychological rather than witness testimony, exploring Sirhan's mental and emotional state before, during, and after the shooting. But McCowan was still not ruling out conspiracy: "I got a feeling in the back of my mind that somebody put him up to this." He noted Sirhan was reluctant to talk about the influence of the occult on his life and was insistent that McCowan and Kaiser stay away from the Rosicrucians.[65]

* * *

Cooper visited an excited Sirhan for the first time on December 3. "We're looking into the possibility of pleading guilty and arguing to the penalty," said Cooper. "The main thing we're trying to do is save your life." A prisoner trade in the future with the Russians might be a possibility—like the Russian spy Abel traded for U-2 pilot Gary Powers—but Cooper ruled out a deal with the State Department until after the trial.

"My life is in your hands," Sirhan told him.[66]

* * *

On his next visit, Cooper asked Sirhan to level with him, forget what he'd told Parsons, and just tell him the truth about the notebooks and the day of the shooting—the whole story. Sirhan repeated the account he gave to Parsons, Kaiser, and McCowan, and would later give in court. These statements are remarkably detailed and consistent and have a strong ring of truth.

Sirhan admitted that the writing in his notebook promised to kill Kennedy. "But, honestly, sir, I had no intention of carrying it forward."

"But, nevertheless, you still wrote it down."

"I still wrote it down."

"Where was it, though, that you very definitely decided to do it?"

"I honestly did not decide to do it, sir—very definitely. Objectively, I had no awareness of what I was doing that night. I will swear to anything on that point. . . . I never believed that I would do it."

"Well, who do you think killed him?"

"Obviously I must have—but I have no exact—no objective of what I was doing."

Cooper shook his head. He didn't get it. He got Sirhan to go back over the writing in the notebook again. Sirhan said seeing that TV program "was the last straw."

"You felt he should be dead?"

"I didn't like him at all. So whatever in hell happened to him, I didn't give a damn."

"Well, obviously you felt that you were the one to stop him."

"Yes, I did."

Why, then, Cooper asked, was Sirhan so admiring of Kennedy when he saw him at the Ambassador on the Sunday before the shooting?

"You have to hit me at the time. At the time I heard these things I was mad, but again, sir, the madness, this feeling or emotion or whatever, had subsided. . . . I had to do it but I didn't, or I couldn't or shouldn't—this double feeling here, and that's why, I thought I decided to like him again when I went down there to see him."

"Why did you cool off, though, if you had this inborn hatred and he was going to give aid to the enemy?"

"He could have just said that story for the votes, and then maybe he could have decided not to send those arms after those Jews voted for him." Sirhan's anger at Kennedy was only "good for while it lasted, you might say."

* * *

Cooper wasn't happy with Sirhan's memory lapse. It was too convenient, and the jury wouldn't like it, but "since that's the situation, I am going to prepare, based on what you have told me. . . . If this doesn't work, don't blame me."

"This is the truth—as far as I can objectively be, sir. That's the truth."

Cooper felt that Sirhan was sane enough to know the difference between right and wrong. "One of the psychologists has indicated that you are psychotic, but talking to you, you seem as normal as apple pie."

It would be an uphill battle to avoid the death penalty, so Cooper saw no harm in letting the prosecution psychiatrist Dr. Pollack in to see Sirhan. If Pollack found mental illness, it might help the defense strike a deal with the DA.

"There's no question about the facts: He killed Kennedy, and he planned it in advance," said Cooper when he got back to the office, so "diminished capacity" seemed the best strategy. But the jury wouldn't like Sirhan's story, particularly the memory lapse.

"It would be better for Sirhan if he could remember, if he could say, 'Yes, I got mad at Kennedy and set out to kill him and I did!'"

"But he doesn't remember," said McCowan.

"Yes, I know," said Cooper. "What the hell you gonna do? You gotta go with what you've got. That's why I lean to a plea."[67]

* * *

On December 10, Cooper met the prosecutors. Deputy DA David Fitts, according to his own memo of the meeting, asked Cooper if Sirhan would submit to a lie detector test "performed by an acknowledged and totally impartial expert with a view to determining whether Sirhan acted alone or in concert with others. . . . The results of such test would be for their ultimate historical significance and would not be available to the parties."

Later the same day, Fitts told the FBI that Cooper had suggested the polygraph, restricting it to questions concerning a possible conspiracy, on the understanding that nothing obtained could be used against Sirhan in the trial but anything of benefit to Cooper could be used in any subsequent executive clemency hearing.

Why would the defense and prosecution in such a high-profile case collude to conduct a polygraph for the historical record? Fortunately, this polygraph never happened.

In the same meeting, Cooper also floated the possibility of pleading "no contest" or "a possible guilty plea on behalf of Sirhan after the jury is selected and sworn in, obviating the necessity of a trial to determine guilt. The jury would then merely hear evidence to determine the degree of penalty following the guilty plea."

Thus, a week into the case, Cooper was already colluding with the prosecution and floating plea bargains. He seems to have been more interested in striking a deal than going beyond Sirhan's hazy memory to examine the evidence.[68]

* * *

In the week before Christmas, New York attorney Emile Zola Berman was added to the defense team and the court granted the defense a second motion for discovery. At last they could see Sirhan's notebooks.[69]

* * *

Bob Kaiser visited Sirhan in late December, for a background piece that would appear in *Life* magazine at the start of the trial. Sirhan's thirteenth-floor cell in the Halls of Justice was six feet wide by eight feet long, with a sink, a lidless toilet, and a steel bunk. He wore prison slippers and faded bell-bottom prison jeans and had stopped ordering the *Los Angeles Times*, depressed by world events. "It's all violence, chaos, unrest. Whatever happened to the old days, peace and quiet?"

Sirhan was now smoking ten Muriel perfecto cigars and six packs of cigarettes a day—"three different brands"—and reading books on logic and Indian philosophy. He felt like "a man without a country," seen as a foreigner by Americans and in his native land. He enjoyed discussing trial strategy with his three attorneys, each of whom was old enough to be his grandfather—paternal figures perhaps standing in for the father he hadn't seen since his early teens.

Sirhan's mother Mary stayed home, read her Bible, and prayed for a miracle at the trial. She kept the June 14 issue of *Time* and the June 17 issue of *Newsweek* on a table in the dining room. Every so often, she would pick up the *Time* cover and talk to the face of Robert Kennedy. She'd tell him how sorry she was, and he'd say, "It's O.K., Mary, I forgive you."[70]

NINE

SIRHAN'S MEMORY

A s Sirhan's defense team prepared for trial, Sirhan still could not remember shooting Robert Kennedy. Over and over, he was asked to re-create the night of the shooting, and his story came out the same every time. It's also never been clear where Sirhan was on Monday, June 3, the day before the shooting.

Sirhan got up early that morning and drove his mother to work. At around ten thirty, he put gas in his car at Richfield Service Station, where he used to work. waved to his former boss, Jack Davies, and drove off.[1]

According to one FBI report, sometime during the day a man from the telephone company was doing service work at a house across the street from the Sirhan home when he saw Sirhan being dropped off in a green or metallic-colored Mercedes. The car was driven by a male, and a female was riding in the front seat.[2]

Mary Sirhan was at work in the morning but said Sirhan was home the rest of the day; Sirhan himself has contradicted this statement, and has always been vague about his movements that day.[3]

According to Robert Kaiser, he changed his story three times. "First, he said he was home all day. Then he admitted to me he'd gone to Corona. Later still, he told me it wasn't Corona at all, but 'someplace in that direction.' And still later, he told defense investigator Michael McCowan with some satisfaction that he'd put 350 miles on his car June 3 and no one knew where he'd gone . . . [he said] 'the FBI doesn't know everything.'"

McCowan speculated that Sirhan may have gone to the El Cortez Hotel in San Diego to see Kennedy speak there that night. The senator started his speech, then collapsed with exhaustion. After going backstage and vomiting, he returned to the stage and finished his comments. But there were no sightings of Sirhan, and his old DeSoto probably wasn't up to such a lengthy trip.[4]

Grant Cooper skipped over June 3 in his questioning of Sirhan.[5]

* * *

June 3 was a busy day for Sirhan's twenty-one-year-old brother, Munir. He was on probation after an earlier narcotics charge and appealing deportation.[6]

Vernon Most, Munir's supervisor in the houseware section at Nash's Department Store, said that "Joe, on the first of every month, is supposed to report to someone, I assume his probation officer, since he returned to work here last November. . . . Last Monday [June 3], Munir left to report, but never returned that day as he had in the past. The excuse he gave me for not returning was that he lost a certain piece of paper, at the office of the probation officer, which allows him to leave and return to work."[7]

Elizabeth Raaegep, working security at Nash's, told a different story. On Saturday, June 1, Munir had asked her for the numbers for the Department of Immigration, but they were closed and he became very upset. That Monday, June 3, he called from Immigration and said they had lost his papers and he couldn't come to work. The next day, Raaegep was in Most's car and was discussing handgun laws with Most and Munir. Munir said, "Boy, I shouldn't have bought that gun."[8]

On June 5, when Munir told Most his brother had shot Kennedy, Most asked if the gun his brother used was Munir's. "He told me, 'I can't say.'"[9]

Munir later denied to police and his probation officer, Darrel K. Gumm, that he bought the gun, and Sergeant Hernandez later claimed the polygraph showed he was lying.[10]

While the timing of Munir's conversation with Most about guns is extremely odd, the fact remains that Munir hadn't spoken to Sirhan for three months. They'd had a fistfight when Munir asked Sirhan to drive him to El Sereno in a borrowed car, but Sirhan refused because it had no insurance.[11]

While some researchers claim that one or more of Sirhan's brothers were also involved, I can find no credible evidence to support this. Munir's deportation appeal was eventually delayed until June 23, 1969, after his brother's trial. Today, he is still living in the family house in Pasadena.[12]

* * *

On June 4, Sirhan woke up just before eight, and Munir saw him on his way to work, buying a newspaper on a street corner in Pasadena. Sirhan had been going to the races, betting, nearly every day for two weeks, and today he planned to go again to Hollywood Park. But he'd been losing money and he didn't like the horses that were running that day, so he decided to go shooting instead.[13]

He counted what ammunition he had—a box of Mini-Mags, a box of Federal long rifle .22s (his favorite), and a box of Super-X—then drove off to pick up another six or seven boxes of Federal long rifles at the East Pasadena Firearms Co. He was in luck. They were on sale at seventy-five cents a box. He stopped off for a quick coffee at a Denny's and arrived at the San Gabriel Valley Gun Range on Fish Canyon Road in Duarte around eleven thirty.

He signed in, paid the range master, Everett Buckner, the two-dollar admission fee, set up his target at the west end of the pistol range, and stayed until Buckner came around at five and announced that the range was closed for the day.[14]

"What kind of a shot are you?" Grant Cooper asked him later.

"With a good gun, sir, I consider myself to be a pretty good shot."

Sirhan's gun had a fixed sight, which he had to adjust himself to hit the bull's-eye. Several witnesses described him aggressively shooting rapid-fire, against range rules, but Sirhan denied it—they were mistaking him for an elderly NRA member in a military jacket and earmuffs, who was shooting a .38 rapid-fire next to Sirhan for about an hour.[15]

Every so often during the day, Buckner would call a break, and Sirhan would go over and buy a Coca-Cola and talk to him about the operation of the range. He fired all the Federals he had and bought three or four more boxes of Federals from Buckner later on.[16]

Just before three, Sirhan struck up a conversation with college student Michael Saccoman, who was firing beside him on the range with a brand-new gun.

"That's a pretty nice gun you have there. Sort of heavy. Can I see it?"

The two swapped guns and Sirhan fired Saccoman's gun a couple of times. "His were the best two shots in my target," Saccoman said later. He then fired Sirhan's gun. "I put it down because I didn't want it to blow up in my hand. He was firing hollow points, and the gun looked like a piece of junk."

It was a cheap .22 with black plastic grips and a short barrel. Sirhan said he had bought it for forty bucks from a friend. Saccoman asked Sirhan why he was firing high-velocity Mini-Mags for target shooting.

Sirhan's signature on the gun range sign-in sheet. By odd coincidence, LAPD officer Harry Lee had signed in seven names above him.

Sirhan shrugged. "They're supposed to be the best brand."

"They're for hunting," Saccoman corrected him. "They're way too strong for this gun. They're what you use to kill rabbits."

"Well, this can kill a dog," said Sirhan.

"How did you learn to shoot so well?"

"I learned up north. I've only been shooting for a couple of months." Saccoman left at three fifteen, and Sirhan took his advice and stopped using the Mini-Mags. He would shoot and throw his empty shell casings on the range.[17]

"Did you have in mind shooting Kennedy at that time?" Cooper asked. "No, I did not. He was totally off my mind, sir."[18]

* * *

Later on, Sirhan struck up a conversation with Claudia Williams, a pretty blond (five-two, twenty-six years old), trying out a new .22-caliber revolver she'd received as a Christmas present.[19]

On June 6, Williams called police to say that Sirhan was shooting next to her on the pistol range—"He asked her if she wanted to try his gun and she shot several rounds. This is the gun that killed the Senator?"[20]

Williams and her husband, Ronald, arrived at the range at around 3:50, to find the place deserted except for the range master and Sirhan. Mr. Buckner set up Claudia's target while her husband went over to the rifle range.

She found it hard to pull the trigger on her double-action revolver and called down the range to Sirhan to ask for help. He came over and showed her how to properly "sight" and fire the gun and demonstrated by firing off about eighteen rounds of his high-powered Mini-Mags from her revolver, She then fired about sixteen rounds from his.

"He was very polite," she recalled. "Didn't make any advances or anything like that, even though it was only him and I out there." They chatted for about twenty minutes; then her husband, Ronald, returned from the rifle range. They chatted briefly about guns, and then, around five o'clock, Buckner said the range was closing and they left.

"Mr. Buckner just came over and . . . told us that the range was closing . . . ," recalled Sirhan. "I think I had . . . about eight or nine Mini-Mags left . . . and I loaded my gun. . . . And at that moment, sir, Mr. Buckner came by and he said that the range was closed. I didn't expend the bullets from that gun."

"Why didn't you take the bullets out?" asked Cooper.

"I had quite a difficult time, sir, with the ejection system in my gun."

In fact, Sirhan was forced to use a screwdriver to pry empty shell casings from his barrel. When time was called, he picked up his screwdriver and empty boxes and went home. He had two bullets in his pocket and the remaining eight in his gun. As Sirhan told it, another minute firing on the range and he would have been out of ammunition.

"And you weren't saving these bullets to shoot Robert Kennedy?"

"No, sir, I was not," said Sirhan.

"Weren't you practicing that afternoon so you would be able to hit accurately?"

"I was so thrilled with my performance on that target sheet. That was my main interest at that time."[21]

* * *

The prosecution would later argue that the firing on the gun range showed premeditation of the first magnitude: the assassin spent hours perfecting his shooting skills, and even signed the register. But, curiously, when DeWayne Wolfer examined 489 expended shell casings collected by Michael Saccoman and another 37,815 collected by FBI agents from firing positions adjacent to where Sirhan was on the range, they found not one that was fired from Sirhan's gun.[22]

Sirhan's pink-and-white 1956 DeSoto.

Sirhan climbed into his beat-up, pink-and-white 1956 DeSoto and threw his loaded gun on the backseat. On the way home, around six thirty, he dropped by Bob's Big Boy in Pasadena, next to his old college, for a hamburger and some coffee. He spotted a college acquaintance sitting at the counter—an East Indian, by the name of Mystery.

"*M-y-s-t-e-r-y?*" asked a bemused Cooper.

"Yes," replied Sirhan. In fact, it was Gaymoard Mistri. Sirhan joined him and treated him to a burger. After a few minutes of chitchat, Mistri began reading a newspaper with a caption concerning the Israeli-Jordan situation. "Things are wrong there," said Sirhan, but Mistri didn't take him up on it and they chatted about horses for the rest of the meal.

They were there about fifteen minutes. As they left, Sirhan asked Mistri where he was going.

"Back to PCC."

"I think I'll come with you," said Sirhan.

Mistri bought a preview edition of the *Los Angeles Times* from a newspaper rack and they talked horses again as they walked over to the cafeteria in the PCC Student Center. Sirhan spotted a friend in a group of four Arab students and chatted with them in Arabic. When the group left for a seven o'clock class, Sirhan and Mistri moved to another table, and as they talked, Mistri remembered Sirhan "toying with a small metal object . . . in his hands"—what seemed to be a spent .22 caliber bullet.

"Are you a hunter?" asked Mistri.

"Sometimes," said Sirhan, "but I'm still learning." From the ensuing conversation, Mistri thought Sirhan actually knew very little about hunting or firearms.

As they walked back to their cars, Sirhan challenged Mistri to a couple of games of pool, but Mistri begged off—he had to go check the classifieds in the paper for a summer job. Sirhan was going to buy a paper to check the racing results, but Mistri took just the classified section and gave him the rest of his.

Sirhan lingered a few minutes more, asking after some former students, how many children they had now. To Mistri, he seemed to have nothing to do and just wanted his company. There was no mention of Kennedy or the primary and "no indication of emotional instability or any type of contemplated violent act." When Mistri left, it was about seven fifteen.[23]

* * *

Sirhan got in his car and was leafing through the Sports section when an advertisement caught his eye—"Join in the Miracle March for Israel on the Miracle Mile tomorrow, Wednesday, June 5, at 6 p.m. on Wilshire Boulevard."

That jolted Sirhan back to the Six-Day War the previous year—"I was completely pissed off at American justice at the time." Now these emotions started up again. "The fire started burning inside of me, sir. These Zionists, these Jews, these Israelis . . . and the fact that they had beat hell out of the Arabs one year before."

Sirhan had nothing to do until the Tuesday night Rosicrucian meeting at eight, and his friend had turned him down for pool, so he decided to go down "to see what those God damned sons-of-bitches were up to."

In his rage, Sirhan had mistaken the date—"I was that burned up, sir. I thought it was for that evening, sir. . . . I was driving like a maniac and I missed the turnoff." He couldn't remember where Wilshire was and got lost and asked for directions. He kept driving down Wilshire, looking for the parade.

"Where was your gun?" asked Cooper.

"My gun was completely out of my mind," said Sirhan.

"Where was it, though?"

"Where I left it, sir—the backseat of my car."

He was ready to give up, then spotted a well-lit building hosting an election-night party for former senator Thomas Kuchel. He parked the car a few blocks away, left his wallet in the glove compartment, and locked up, as usual. He carried his money loose in his pocket—about $440.

"Did you put your revolver in your pocket?"

"No, sir. My revolver was still in the backseat of my car."

Dressed in blue denim pants, a blue long-sleeved shirt, and blue sweater, he went in and had a look around. It was dull. "I heard these two kids say there was a bigger party down at the Ambassador, so I said, 'Well, I'm on Wilshire Boulevard. I couldn't see the parade, so I might as well go down there and see what was going on.'"[24]

Sirhan later struggled to make sense of the day with prosecution psychiatrist Dr. Pollack.

"What I did that whole day, what happened before the shooting at the Ambassador, it just all didn't fit in when I look at it. There are so many points that are unexplainable . . . my whole going to the range that day. I decided not to go to the races. I didn't want to lose any more money . . . at the very last, when I had these few [bullets] left and I put them into my gun . . . the range master comes and announces that the range is closed."

"So why didn't you empty it?" asked Pollack.

"That's what pisses me off, sir. I've told this to Kaiser a thousand times. Why did I do that? Why didn't I fire 'em, despite the range master's orders? This is what I can't explain to myself. . . . Why didn't I take 'em out, throw them away instead of firing 'em? I didn't. I don't know. It was loaded. I was just ready to pop it, the range was closed, so I said, 'Fuck you, you son of a bitch,' and I started walking to my car and put the gun on the backseat and kept going to Pasadena."

"It's almost as if you yourself, maybe without being aware of it, were always planning this," suggested Pollack. Sirhan didn't take the bait.

"I challenged Mistri to a game of pool. Had he just taken me up on that, this whole mess wouldn't have happened, you see. . . . Why couldn't I have fired the first time at the range? Why did I keep my gun loaded? Why didn't I go to a game of pool with Mistri? I was planning to go to that Rosicrucian meeting on Tuesday night and I had some tires in my trunk that I was gonna replace for my car."

"And you didn't know that Kennedy would be down there?"

"He was off my mind that night. He was off my mind, sir. It's just that ad that took me down there."[25]

* * *

Sirhan walked down to the Ambassador, and on the way, he saw a big sign for a Jewish organization in a shop window, and that boiled him up again. He arrived at the hotel about eight. The crowd was very mixed, and everybody was "all dressed up. . . . The whole place was milling with people, sir. There were many TV cameras, a lot of bright lights, sir."

He walked up the circular stairway to the lobby and saw a big sign for Republican Senate candidate Max Rafferty, and the name rang a bell. Rafferty's daughter Kathleen had been in Sirhan's Russian class at high school. He dropped into the Rafferty reception in the Venetian Room, thinking he might see her. The room was filled with "brilliant lights," but Kathleen wasn't there.

He was still mad about the parade, but there was a pleasant mood throughout the hotel, so he went to the bar and bought a Tom Collins cocktail. He didn't normally drink, but "it was a hot night. There was a big party, and I wanted to fit in. . . ." He liked the Tom Collins; it tasted like lemonade.

He stayed at Rafferty headquarters for about an hour, then bought another Tom Collins and went outside to a lawn area where Kennedy had addressed the overflow crowd on Sunday.[26]

* * *

Around nine thirty, auto mechanic and Kennedy supporter Enrique Rabago got separated from a friend in the hotel lobby and walked out onto the front porch to look for him. He spotted Sirhan sipping a drink alone and started chatting with him about the election.

"Are we going to win?" asked Rabago.

"I think we're going to win," Sirhan replied.

"I don't know; McCarthy is ahead now."

"Don't worry about Kennedy if he doesn't win. That son of a bitch is a millionaire. He just wants to go to the White House. Even if he wins, he's not going to win it for you or me or any of the poor people. He's just going to buy the presidency."

Rabago was a little disgusted by Sirhan's anti-Kennedy comments and was about to walk away when his friend Humphrey Cordero found them and suggested they go back inside the lobby. Rabago was worried he was too casually dressed, and Cordero turned to Sirhan, also in working clothes.

"Look at my friend; he doesn't want to go in because of his clothes. What do you think of that?"

"I'm dressed the same way. Why shouldn't we go in there? We're voters. We're putting them in office."

"Where did you get your drink?" asked Cordero.[27]

"I just came from the Rafferty party. As I walked in, the hostess looked down at me because they were dressed like millionaires and I was dressed like this. I took out a twenty-dollar bill, bought a drink, and left her the change. Then she was all smiles. It goes to show you, it's not how you look; it's the money you got that counts."

Sirhan seemed extremely aggrieved that these "rich people looked at me as if I was dirt." Cordero described him as intelligent and a gentleman, but he had a chip on his shoulder about people with money.

Cordero said he "didn't sound like he was on drugs or dope or drink or anything. . . . He didn't appear to be in any other state of mind. . . . He was just a little disgusted with the party." Rabago agreed that Sirhan didn't seem drunk or belligerent. He described him as "educated but arrogant." A few minutes later, Cordero and Rabago wandered inside to watch the returns on a television in the lobby, and they didn't see Sirhan again.[28]

Around ten o'clock, waiter Gonzalo Cetina-Carrillo saw Sirhan standing outside the restrooms behind the Venetian Room. Sirhan had a Tom Collins glass in his right hand and rolled newspapers under his left arm. Sirhan said he was tired, and Cetina pointed to a stack of chairs. Cetina took his glass while Sirhan unstacked a chair and sat down. Cetina gave Sirhan back his drink and went back to work.[29]

Around the same time, Lonny Worthey accidentally bumped into Sirhan while ordering a drink at a bar in the Ambassador Room. He apologized, but Sirhan didn't respond. A few minutes later, Worthey saw a female standing alongside Sirhan. He didn't see them speak and, with the large number of people in the room, he couldn't tell if they were together.

It's hard to trace Sirhan's movements from this point on, because of different timings given by or assigned to witnesses in various reports.[30]

Sirhan does remember standing in front of a Teletype machine in the Colonial Room, staring at it over the shoulder of Western Union Teletype operator Mary Grohs, as the keys tapped out their messages. "I was mesmerized," he said. "I had never seen anything like that before. . . . The keys were going all by themselves."[31]

Grohs told the LAPD that sometime between nine thirty and eleven, she saw a young man with "intense eyes" staring at the Teletype machine. He was "dressed like a poor Mexican," and she told him the Teletype tapping out Kennedy election returns was farther down the line. He looked at her "with that intense look," then walked away without saying anything.

Later, when Sirhan was brought out of the pantry through the Colonial Room, Grohs jumped up and screamed, "That's the man I talked to!" and Sirhan gave her "the same intense look."[32]

When Bob Kaiser learned about Grohs after the trial, he called her up, and after some hesitation, she recounted the episode: "Well, he came over to my machine and started staring at it. Just staring. I'll never forget his eyes. I asked him what he wanted. He didn't answer. He just kept staring. I asked him again. No answer. I said that if he wanted the latest figures on Senator Kennedy, he'd have to check the other machine. He still didn't answer. He just kept staring."

"In retrospect," Kaiser asked, "do you think he might have been in some kind of trance?"

"Oh no!" she said. "He wasn't under hypnosis. . . . I just assumed he couldn't speak English." When Kaiser tried to pursue the matter, Grohs asked for his name. "I want to talk to the police about you. They told me not to say anything about this."[33]

Was Sirhan's staring a form of hypnosis, or was he just intently curious? In Sirhan's own words, "I was shit-faced drunk."[34]

* * *

At one point, Sirhan appeared at the door to the electrician's booth in the Venetian Room and started chatting with the hotel's Danish electrician, Hans Peter Bidstrup. While the LAPD final report times this as eight forty-five, in his first FBI and police interviews, Bidstrup timed it as around eleven o'clock.

Sirhan was holding a half-empty Tom Collins glass and asked Bidstrup if he was a Democrat. Bidstrup said he was. "Shake hands with another Democrat," said Sirhan. He then sat down on an empty cable spool and they talked for ten or fifteen minutes. Bidstrup thought Sirhan was "half drunk" and chatty, but not slurring or staggering. Sirhan remembered asking Bidstrup about his job "and all the switches and communications and what have you" and offered to buy Bidstrup a drink.

Bidstrup said Sirhan asked if Kennedy was going to be at the hotel that night, what floor he was staying on, and what time he would arrive. He also asked about Kennedy's security, whether or not he had bodyguards. As they were talking, a Los Angeles fireman came into the booth, startling Sirhan, and chatted with them for a short while.[35]

But Bidstrup later told McCowan and Cooper that Sirhan showed no more interest in Kennedy than any other Democrat.[36]

By this time, Sirhan had drunk four Tom Collins cocktails. "It was like drinking lemonade. I was guzzling them. My body is small. It was hot in there, and I wasn't used to it. I was feeling it, and I got sleepy. So I wanted to go home." During the trial, Sirhan added, "I was quite high and I was alone. If I got any more drunk, there was nobody with me to take care of me . . . so I decided to go home, sir."

He went out the same way he came in and walked uphill and back to his car. When he got in, he realized he was in no condition to drive. He had no insurance and was afraid he'd get a ticket or get into an accident.

"What did you do, then?" asked Cooper.

"I decided, sir, to go back down to the party and sober up, drink some coffee."

"Did you pick up your gun?"

"I don't remember, sir. . . . I must have, but I don't remember."

"And where did you go when you got back to the Ambassador?"

"In search of coffee. . . . I don't know where I found it, but eventually I found some."

Sirhan found a big, shiny coffee urn, surrounded by "piles and piles of cups and saucers."

"Did this place look like a kitchen?"

"I don't know, sir."

"Were there bright lights there?"

"No, sir, there weren't. There weren't any mirrors, either."

Sirhan seemed to take pleasure in debunking Dr. Diamond's theory that it was confusion caused by the bright lights and mirrors near the Embassy Ballroom that triggered his trance state.

"Did you see any people there?"

"I don't remember, sir. I was so glad to have found the coffee; that was the only thing on my mind, sir. . . . As I was pouring my coffee, some girl came up and said she wanted some, too. I like my coffee with cream and sugar, lots of cream, and that's exactly the way she liked it . . . so I gave her my cup and poured myself another."

"Do you remember what this girl looked like?" "She had some dark hair . . . about my age."

"A good-looking girl?"

"Beautiful."

"Did you engage her in conversation?"

"As long as the coffee was being served, I told her how I would like to drink some coffee, too."

"What was the next thing you did?"

"The next thing I remember, sir, I was being choked."

"Do you remember anything in between?"

"No, sir."

"That you were standing in the pantry?"

"That is what I later learned in this court, sir."

"That you walked up to Senator Kennedy and put a gun toward his head, possibly within an inch or two, and you pulled the trigger and he eventually died."

"Yes, I was told this."

"Now, you believe it is true?"

"Obviously, sir."

"And after that you were choked?"

"I was choked, yes, quite severely. . . . I don't know who was doing the choking, but he was doing a good job at it."[37]

Sirhan couldn't remember anything between drinking coffee with the girl and being choked, but several witnesses filled in the blanks. An hour or two before the speech, Kennedy press aide Judy Royer was trying to keep the backstage and pantry areas clear after a fire marshal complained of overcrowding in an area reserved for press and Kennedy staff. She saw Sirhan by the double doors at the west end of the pantry leading into the backstage area. He wasn't wearing a press or staff badge, so she asked him who he was. Without a word, Sirhan turned and walked back out into the ballroom. She watched him walk away and didn't notice anything unusual about his behavior and didn't see anything in his hands.[38]

Shortly after eleven, Royer's friend Robert Klase was standing backstage by some ABC television cameras, awaiting Kennedy's arrival. Klase was asked to watch the door to the ballroom Kennedy would later come through, for a few minutes. While doing so, Klase saw Sirhan trying to pass through. He tapped him on the shoulder and said only ABC staff were allowed in the area. Sirhan turned around and went back into the central area of the Embassy Ballroom. Klase accurately described Sirhan's clothing and reasoned that "since the shirt and trousers were tight fitting, it was unlikely that Sirhan had a gun in his possession at that time."[39]

Half an hour before the shooting, kitchen staff Jesus Perez and Martin Patrusky remembered Sirhan asking if Kennedy was coming through the pantry. Cooper asked Sirhan if they were lying.[40]

"Sir, I don't know whether they were telling the truth or not; I cannot contest it; because I don't know myself, sir."[41]

Barbara Rubin arrived at the hotel with her husband at 11:55 p.m. Rather than go into the Embassy Ballroom through the main doors and fight the crowd, they entered through the pantry and came out right next to the stage. On the way through, Rubin noticed Sirhan on her left, leaning against a table by the ice machines. He stood out because "he wasn't dressed like the rest of the workers and he was standing still whereas everyone else was moving around."[42]

Cooper asked Sirhan what he remembered next after the choking.

"I remember getting to the police car and one of the policemen pulling my hair and jerking my head backwards and putting a light for a long time in my eyes."

He was told that Jesse Unruh said he heard him say, "I did it for my country."

"Sir, Jesse Unruh must have been correct in saying that, but I myself don't remember saying that to him or to anybody."

"Do you remember eventually getting someplace that looked like a police station?"

"I didn't know what it was at the time, sir."

The only officer Sirhan remembered at the police station was Bill Jordan— "because of his name, Jordan." The police were very friendly, and Jordan "was a very nice man."

"You refused to give the officers your name, didn't you?"

"Yes."

"You wouldn't discuss anything about the case?"

"They never brought it up, sir."

"Well, what did you think you were there for?"

"We were so engrossed in the discussion of what, I don't remember exactly, sir, and it was so friendly, the discussions were so interesting to me."

"Did you know in the early morning hours . . . that you had shot Senator Robert Kennedy?"

"No, sir, I did not."

"When was the first time you remember that you were accused of shooting Senator Robert Kennedy?"

"When this Mr. Jordan took me to this courtroom and I was in front of a lady judge. I couldn't believe it, sir. That is the first lady judge I had ever seen in my whole life, and she started reading these names and Kennedy was on that list of names."[43]

Sirhan was arraigned before Judge Joan Dempsey Klein at 7:25 that morning. He asked to see a representative of the ACLU so he could "find out what was going on."

Cooper led him through his blackout in custody right up to the visit from Al Wirin the next morning, when he finally realized what had happened. Summing up, Sirhan admitted to Cooper that he had bought the gun and wrote the notebooks, but he did not remember the shooting.

"You have told the jury that when you came to the Ambassador Hotel that night you didn't come there with any intention of shooting Kennedy, is that right?" asked Cooper.

"That is correct, sir."

"And you did kill him?"

"Yes, sir."

"How do you account for all the circumstances?"

"Sir, I don't know," said Sirhan.

"You don't remember shooting him?"

"I don't remember shooting him."[44]

TEN

INSIDE SIRHAN'S MIND

From the outset, defense attorneys Cooper and Parsons believed the best way for Sirhan to escape the death penalty would be with a defense of diminished capacity. Through psychiatric testimony, they hoped to prove that Sirhan's mental condition at the time of the shooting prevented him from forming criminal intent to kill Robert Kennedy. They would show he acted without malice or premeditation—that, as defined by California law, he was unable to "maturely and meaningfully reflect on the gravity of his contemplated act." If their strategy worked, Sirhan would still bear partial responsibility for the crime but would be spared the death sentence and might expect a lesser charge of second-degree murder or manslaughter.

Cooper appointed an old friend, Dr. Bernard Diamond of UC Berkeley, as the defense psychiatrist. As associate dean and professor of the School of Criminology and a full professor in the Schools of Law and Psychiatry, Diamond seemed an ideal choice.[1]

Cooper first brought Diamond to see Sirhan on December 23, the first of eight visits, during which Diamond spent almost twenty-five hours with Sirhan, often in the company of Bob Kaiser and prosecution psychiatrist Dr. Pollack. Diamond also interviewed Sirhan's mother and brother Munir, visited their house, saw Sirhan's room, and read all the defense and police reports and the various psychological tests conducted on the prisoner.[2]

Diamond found Sirhan "superficially cooperative" during their first meeting. He had picked up colloquial language from his six children and his students at Berkeley, and this helped put Sirhan at ease, allowing him to open up about his memory of the Ambassador Hotel.

To Sirhan, that night was like a dream, but Diamond encouraged him to remember details from the dream. Sirhan remembered someone in the kitchen wearing a uniform—a policeman or a fireman. He was leaning on a table, and then he was being choked. He didn't remember much about the police station, but he did recall kicking the hot chocolate out of the officer's hand. He was thirsty, but they wouldn't give him a drink.

"When I'm mad, sir, I don't give a damn what happens."

"Why didn't you talk about the killing with the police?" asked Diamond.

"They kept telling me about my constitutional rights."

"You wouldn't even give them your name?"

"Why should I?" protested Sirhan.

"What do you think the truth about the shooting is?" asked Diamond.

"I don't really know, sir."

"You sure of that? How do you know this wasn't a put-up job? How do you know it wasn't some kind of fix?"

"Well, it could have been. I don't know." Sirhan shrugged.

"Do you believe deep down inside that you shot him?"

Sirhan paused and thought for a moment. "I hated him, sir. I loved him before. He would finish what President Kennedy started. President Kennedy tried to help the Arab refugees. But then, when I watched him on the television, how he was trying to get all that Jewish vote behind him and how he was always for the persecuted people—meaning the Jews, sir!—my whole . . . feelings toward him suddenly changed, and sharply. I hated his guts, sir."

"Did the thought that you wanted to kill him occur to you then?"

"Never. Never. Never," insisted Sirhan.

"Do you think what you did sort of helped things?" asked Diamond. "I'm not proud of what I did."

"What do you mean you're not proud of it? You believe in your cause, don't you?"

"I have no exact knowledge, sir, that this happened yet. . . . It's all in my mind, but goddamn it, when my body played with it, I couldn't understand it. I still don't believe it. My body outsmarted my brain, I guess."

"What did your body do?"

"Pull that trigger."

"Does your body remember it, even if your mind doesn't?"

"I don't give a damn, sir, in a way. Now I don't even care."

"Did you feel Robert Kennedy betrayed you?" asked Diamond.

"Yes."

"What sticks in your mind about him?"

"Saying he would send fifty jet bombers to Israel."

"When did you decide to do something?"

"I don't think I ever decided. I'm mad, and it's good as long as it lasted, for the duration of the aggravation."

"So you don't think you carefully planned this, then?"

"Oh, hell, I never planned it. Sir, I wake up every morning and I say, 'Oh, hell, what's this all about?' My dreams are more pleasant than this predicament."

"Do you think you're crazy, Sirhan? Do you think you are a queer fish?" asked Diamond.

"I think I am just as normal as anybody else. Although I am a fanatic about the Arab-Israeli . . ."

Sirhan didn't put much stock in the psychologists' opinions. He'd gotten off track for one night, but that didn't make him mentally ill. Diamond asked if he'd be willing to take truth serum or a lie detector test to help find out what had happened. He said he would. "All right," said Diamond. "I'm going to try to help you remember."[3]

In this first interview, Diamond detected little sign of the paranoid schizophrenia suggested by the psychological tests performed on Sirhan. He felt that Sirhan was telling him a mix of truth, evasions, and lies, but he couldn't figure out which was which. He later noted that paranoid schizophrenics "simply do not trust any other person. They are abnormally suspicious; they believe that no one will believe them; other people are trying to harm them, persecute them [and] they are extremely reluctant to admit the existence of any signs or symptoms of mental illness." So, before he could get to the truth, he would have to gain Sirhan's trust.

Sirhan also fit into a pattern Diamond had once described in a 1956 paper for *The Journal of Social Therapy*, entitled "The Simulation of Sanity." Diamond wrote that faking sanity was much more common than faking insanity, particularly in the case of paranoid schizophrenia:

> *The paranoid schizophrenic is especially averse to admitting that his actions are due to mental disease, and will insist, even in the face of the threat of the death punishment, that his criminal actions were intentional. . . . Such schizophrenics pretend to be mentally healthy, because to admit mental illness would destroy their self-esteem and break down the remnants of their contact with reality. . . . So they would rather go to prison or even to the gas chamber than to violate the dictates of their delusional system.*

"I had this very much in mind when I interviewed Sirhan for the first time," said Diamond. What was the truth, what were the evasions, and what were the lies and the reasons for the lies?[4]

* * *

On January 2, Diamond paid a second visit to Sirhan and asked him about going to see Kennedy on June 2. Sirhan said he had seen an ad in the paper inviting people to come and meet Senator Kennedy at the "Cocoanut Grove."

"A guy like me! A nobody getting a personal invitation to go down to the Ambassador! Too much out of my class!" He took the clipping down with him, so "they couldn't throw me out of the place."

"How close to Kennedy were you?" asked Diamond.

"Oh shit, I was very far. I was in the crowd watching. Kennedy told the people to get started on the last drive."

"Did he talk about the Jews, Israel?"

"No, he was very quiet that day."

"Was that the first time you actually ever saw Kennedy?"

"It was, sir—in reality. . . . It was a thrill to see him."

"It was a thrill to see him?"

"Shit, yes, really. Hell, you know, a presidential candidate, my first time. And especially the advertisement, the public is invited. Really, I enjoyed it."

Diamond was incredulous. "You had no idea that three days later you were going to kill him."

"Goddamn it, no, hell no, I didn't. I don't know what the hell made me, sir. I seem to have just been railroaded into this thing. But, hell, would I have left so much evidence behind me? I'm not that stupid!"

Sometimes, people who don't care about being caught don't bother to cover up things like the notebooks, said Diamond.

Sirhan did not buy this theory. "No, sir. I care what happens to me."

"You care?"

"You're goddamn right, I care, sir! That bastard is not worth my life, sir. He isn't worth a minute of all the agony I've had up here."[5]

* * *

Diamond had three "shortcuts" to choose from in trying to recover Sirhan's memory of the shooting in the time available—a polygraph, truth serum, or hypnosis. "I didn't use the lie detector because I have little or no faith in its accuracy and little faith in its ability to provide the information I wanted," he said at trial. The intravenous injection of sodium amytal, a very powerful sedative, carried a slight risk of causing respiratory paralysis, so that was also ruled out. Diamond settled on hypnosis "as a means of gaining access to the patient's mind."[6]

Hypnosis was not a lie detector, Diamond later told the court, but it was a valuable tool in overcoming unconscious resistance and evasions. While a person could lie under hypnosis, overcoming memory loss through hypnotic techniques provided "considerable evidence that the amnesia was genuine."[7]

After establishing a good rapport with Sirhan, Diamond broached the subject in this second meeting. "Sirhan, you know what hypnosis is?"

"Isn't it the domination of the weaker will by the stronger?"

"No, it isn't that at all," said Diamond. "It's simply a way of demonstrating one's own ability to concentrate . . . and the hypnotist is not dominating over the will of the other. No one can be hypnotized against his own will, and the hypnotist really just gives suggestions and encouragement to a person so that he can use his own willpower to strengthen his own abilities."

Sirhan hadn't studied it much but agreed to be hypnotized. Diamond had him lie down and asked him to concentrate on a quarter held eight inches from his eyes.[8]

"Somewhat to my surprise, he went to sleep fairly promptly," Diamond later told the Court, "It took less than ten minutes."

"I think you've always underestimated yourself, Sirhan," Diamond intoned. "Did you ever hope you could do that? Are you aware that you could have helped your people?"

Suddenly, Sirhan began to cry, and a startled Diamond moved quickly to encourage him. "Let your feelings out, Sirhan. Don't be afraid," he said as Sirhan's sobbing intensified.

"I don't know any people!" cried Sirhan.

"Go on, tell me about it, Sirhan. What about your people? Say what you feel, Sirhan. Say what you feel." Sirhan, still sobbing, cried, "What the hell did they do?"[9]

"Sirhan went into a sort of convulsive rage response in which his fists clenched, arms tightened up, and he got a most dramatic contorted rage expression on his face and sobbed," Diamond recalled later. "The tears poured down his face. For the first time, I had a glimpse of a completely different Sirhan. Never before had Sirhan shown any signs of what I would consider real emotional depth. Everything was a certain superciliousness, a certain superficiality; every other word was a "fuck" or a "shit" and it was a very coarse kind of clever, supercilious, smart-alecky type of approach without any kind of depth to it. Here was a different picture."

After a while, the sobbing gradually subsided, and Sirhan slipped too deep into trance to say anything more.

In further sessions, Diamond found that the merest hint about the Arabs and their unfortunate plight, and any talk about the Jews, the bombs, and what had happened to Jerusalem were enough to trigger more sobbing.

"I was immediately struck by the close similarity of this kind of emotional convulsive state under hypnosis with his reaction to the television broadcasts and to the early childhood bombing experiences in Palestine," Diamond later testified. "And I believe that these are one and the same condition, which have varied in intensity."[10]

As Sirhan's sobbing abated, Diamond woke him up. "Wake up, Sirhan. Wake up. Sirhan! Open your eyes."

Every time Sirhan emerged from a trance, he followed the same pattern. He would wake up "kind of startled; he looks around and is quite bewildered, obviously quite confused. It takes him a portion of a minute almost to reorient himself. His paranoia comes to the surface right away, immediately suspicious that somebody has done something to him, but he doesn't know what."

"Do you know what happened, Sirhan?"

"I don't know what the hell you're doing, doc," he said, wheezing. "Is this a game, doc?"

Diamond assured him it wasn't. "Are you afraid?"

"I don't have any fear."

"Oh, yes, you do. You are full of fear back there."

"It's cold, doc, cold."[11]

Sirhan's coldness was reminiscent of the shivering Dr. Crahan had observed in him on the day of the assassination.[12]

Sirhan could never remember the hypnosis—last thing he knew, he was staring at the quarter—but he always denied he'd been hypnotized, implying he had tricked Diamond.

Diamond put Sirhan under a couple of times more, but Sirhan simply started snoring. Diamond gave Sirhan a posthypnotic suggestion to follow. When Diamond counted to five, Sirhan would go to sleep. At the count of three, he would wake up.

Diamond was surprised that Sirhan took to his instructions so quickly. "He learned this very well, which made me suspicious because usually in my experience it is the exception rather than the rule that people pick this up so readily. It requires a certain kind of training period." It was as if Sirhan had been hypnotized before.[13]

* * *

On January 11, Dr. Diamond hypnotized Sirhan and asked him a series of questions drawn up by Cooper. He stuck a sterilized safety pin into his hand to make sure the hypnotic state was authentic. Sirhan didn't flinch at all, and they continued.

Although Sirhan went under very easily, it was difficult to get him to talk. "He would mumble in a very soft tone and talk like someone who is profoundly asleep," recalled Dr. Diamond. "Whenever you put pressure on him or tried to push him where he was showing some initial resistance, he would go off into a real deep sleep in which you couldn't get anything out of him at all. This is a kind of emotional resistance, but it also indicated something peculiar about his hypnotic experience."

"Talk loudly and clearly and don't mumble," ordered Diamond, and they began. "Sirhan, did anyone pay you to shoot Kennedy? Yes or no."

Sirhan was silent for a few moments. "No."

"No? No one paid you to shoot Kennedy. Did anybody know ahead of time that you were going to do it, Sirhan?"

"No."

"Did anybody from the Arabs tell you to shoot Kennedy? Any of your Arab friends?"

"No."

"Did you think this up all by yourself?"

After stopping to think, Sirhan replied, "Yes."

"Are you the only person involved in the Kennedy shooting?"

Again, "Yes."[14]

Here, Sirhan seemed to momentarily "block" a spontaneous response on two key questions, but Diamond let it pass. [15]

"Why did you shoot Kennedy?" Sirhan did not respond.

"Why did you shoot him, Sirhan?"

"The bombers."

"You mean the bombers to Israel?"

"Yes."

"Why did you decide to shoot Kennedy?" No answer. Diamond repeated the question several times, and Sirhan finally said, "I don't know."

Diamond tried to get Sirhan to remember the shooting, and Sirhan finally remembered when Kennedy came into the pantry, but nothing else. After again suggesting that Sirhan remember more about that night at the Ambassador, Diamond woke him up.

Sirhan went through his usual reorientation ritual, then looked down at his hand, aghast. "Jesus Christ! What's that?" He pulled at the pin, and blood trickled down his hand. "You've got a lot of guts, doc."

"You're the one who's got the guts," said Diamond. "You're the one who controlled the pain."

"You put the son-of-a-bitchin' pin right in there."

The suggestion worked. Gradually, more details came back to Sirhan. He recalled seeing a man in uniform. Sirhan was leaning on a table.

"What kind of table?" asked Diamond.

"I'm not sure, but I recollect giving a girl a cup of coffee. I served myself. I didn't remember paying for it. . . ." He remembered the mirrors—they were bothering him, and it was too bright. He looked for coffee and met a girl. She looked Spanish or Armenian.

"I might have tried to hang around with her," he said. "She could have been a fast one."

"Did you talk about Kennedy with her?"

"Kennedy was out of my mind then."

He had remembered Kennedy under hypnosis, but he couldn't remember him now.

"Wait a minute," said Sirhan. "This is the press room? There was a lady there. A Teletype machine. Western Union. I was there."

Sirhan asked if he could go down to the Ambassador to help him remember where he went next. Diamond didn't think there was much chance of that.

"Hell," said Sirhan. "This girl kept talking about coffee. She wanted cream. Spanish, Mexican, dark skinned. When people talked about the girl in the polka-dot dress, maybe they were thinking of the girl I was having coffee with."

Diamond put Sirhan back in a light trance and asked him to think about the bombers over Jerusalem. Like clockwork, Sirhan started sobbing.

"He can't. He can't."

"What's happening to you, Sirhan? Don't run away from your feelings, Sirhan. Think of the bombers, Sirhan. Did Kennedy send the bombers?"

"He was going to."

"Were you going to stop him?"

"I don't know."

Mention of the bombers triggered tears, while mention of Kennedy had very little effect. Diamond visited Mary Sirhan and asked her about the bombings in Jerusalem during Sirhan's childhood.

The bombings were the reason the Sirhans came to the United States, she told him. The sounds of gunfire and explosions in the streets would make the children "cry and scream and shake all over." It seemed to affect Sirhan more than the other children. A soldier was blown to bits, and Sirhan saw his foot hanging from a church steeple. Afterward, Sirhan was pale and paralyzed with fear, then fainted. A bomb blasted a storekeeper across the street, and Sirhan blacked out in shock, as if he'd been hit, too.

When Sirhan was seven, he saw a nine-year-old girl hit in the knee by a piece of shrapnel with blood gushing down her leg. "What did she do? What did she do?" he cried; then he fainted.

There were other times when Sirhan fainted on the street, sometimes twice in one day. Why? Mary didn't know. "From fear. A bombing. . . . If Sirhan would see blood on the ground, he used to faint."

Mary Sirhan knew nothing about Sirhan's experiments with the occult, but his brother Munir remembered Sirhan staring into a mirror at the desk in his room and looking into candle flames. A lead fishing weight hung on a string from the ceiling. "Sirhan said he could make this move back and forth just by concentrating on it real hard. I'd come into the room and he'd be staring at it real hard and it would be swinging back and forth."[16]

Later in court, Diamond described "the profound shock state" in Sirhan after the bombings—"he would just stand motionless, trembling with fear, his fists clenched . . . [an] agonized expression on his face. . . [with] no response to questioning at all; and on at least one occasion this may have lasted several days." These "shock responses" were Sirhan's first "trances" or "dissociated" states. Such states are often out of an individual's conscious control and followed by amnesia, like an unremembered dream.

Diamond traced "Sirhan's illness, his pathologically sick mental and emotional condition," back to these "shock responses" in very early childhood. They started in 1948 at the time of the first Arab-Israeli War, when Sirhan was four years old, "a very critical period in the development of the emotional life of a child."

He pinpointed another incident in the summer of 1957 of considerable psychological significance. Sirhan's father, Bishara, and brothers Adel and Munir were digging an irrigation ditch around a tree in their backyard. Sirhan was running around, being a nuisance, trampling mud onto the cement of the driveway. He ignored warnings to stop, and eventually, when his father tried to beat him, Adel stepped in to stop him.

Bishara was incensed and demanded of Mary Sirhan that she choose between him and the children—he was the head of the family, and either he maintained the discipline or not. Mary Sirhan defended the children, so he told her he was going back to Palestine and took the family savings and left. "I think this episode had a considerable psychological effect not only on Sirhan but on the whole relationship of all the members of the family," said Diamond.

After dropping out of college in the mid-sixties, Sirhan saw himself "largely as a failure, as a nothing; yet he was full of daydreams of leadership, of sometimes becoming a very great man, a great hero; he thought oftentimes of his experiences in Jerusalem and the war and of the tensions in the Middle East; at the same time he was very lonely" and what Diamond "would consider an isolated, alienated person."

Diamond thought Sirhan's mental illness predated the fall from the horse but the "personality change" the family observed afterward helped them become aware of it. Munir had been away from home for more than nine months and returned in September of 1967, very shocked and alarmed to find that Sirhan had changed so dramatically—from a "kind, gentle, sweet, loving personality to an angry, irritable, explosive kind of a person; very suspicious and distrustful."

Diamond later described in court how Sirhan's illness grew progressively worse and culminated in "various alarming responses" to radio and television broadcasts concerning the Arab-Israeli War in the year leading up to the shooting. He would go into "dissociated states," recalling the terrified child of the Jerusalem bombings—"his fists were clenched and there would be a frozen expression of rage on his face." His family would try to calm him down, but "he didn't hear anything. . . . These broadcasts were quite sufficient to trigger off at least a partial loss of contact with reality," concluded Diamond.[17]

On the afternoon of January 18, Cooper, Berman, and Kaiser visited Sirhan and showed him a copy of his notebook for the first time since his arrest. Sirhan seemed more concerned with Kaiser's impending book on the case. Kaiser suggested he write his own book. Berman rolled his eyes. "Judging from some of your writings, Sirhan, your book would be somewhat incomprehensible."

Cooper started to read from the notebook. "Lookit here. '*Long live Communism. Long live Communism. Long live Communism. Long live Nasser. Nasser. Nasser. Nasser. Nasser.*'"

"Nasser was no Communist," said Berman.

"Yeah . . . ," said Sirhan, struggling to understand his writing. "All this repetition!"

"'*Peggy Osterkamp, I love you. I love you. Osterkamp. Miss Peggy. Peggy. P. P. P.*' What is—who is this?" asked Cooper.

"This must have been a long time ago!" said Sirhan. He hadn't seen Peggy since he worked at the ranch in Corona in 1966.

At Cooper's request, Sirhan translated a page of Arabic. It was a letter to his mother, asking her to forward his mail. Toward the end it read, "*I especially beg of you in a special way to discuss the matter of my location with no one at all at all.*" If Sirhan wrote this from the ranch, why did he want to keep his location so secret?

"*'Tonight. Tonight. Tonight. We. I must buy a new Mustang tonight. Tonight. Tonight. Tonight. Tonight. Meet me tonight,*'" read Cooper.

"I must be psychotic," he said.

"*'Let us do it. Let us do it. Let us do it do it it it. Let us do it. Please pay to the order of. 50. 50. 50. 50,000. 5. 50,000. Very good. Very good. One hundred thousand dollars.*'"

"Whew!" said Sirhan.

"How much did you say you made a week?" asked Berman.

"Seventy dollars a week," said Sirhan.

"*'Please pay to the order of Sirhan Sirhan the the the the amount of 15 15 15 15 death life 15. $15,000. Must die. Die. Die. Die. Dollar sign. Life and death.*'" "For Christ's sake," said Berman.

"Were you smoking hashish?" Sirhan denied that he smoked anything.

"Is it possible you wrote in your notebook when you were in a trancelike state?" asked Kaiser.

"I don't know," said Sirhan.

"Here, right here," said Cooper, clutching a page in Arabic and its translation, "you've written in Arabic, right between '*one hundred thousand dollars*' and '*one hundred thousand dollars*': '*he should be killed.*' What about that?"

No comment from Sirhan.

"That could be interpreted that you were getting $100,000 to kill Kennedy," said Kaiser.

"Where is that money?" asked Cooper. "You holding on to it?" Cooper said Sirhan didn't have to answer that.

"*'Workers of the world, unite. You have nothing to lose but your chains.*'"

"He didn't write that," said Berman. "Give Mr. Marx some credit."

Cooper had had enough. He explained to Sirhan that the prosecution would enter the notebooks as evidence.

Sirhan was outraged. "What? It's unconstitutional!"

Maybe it was, said his lawyers, but they might also help establish diminished capacity.

"What kind of writing involves this kind of repetition of a word?" asked Berman.

"Yeah, that's what I've been wondering," said Sirhan. "Are they gonna say I'm psychotic? Crazy or something?" He would do anything to avoid the stigma of mental illness, though it was probably the only thing that could save him from a death sentence.

On the way out of the building, according to Kaiser, Cooper said, "I can't figure this kid out." Cooper knew Sirhan was sick, but the jury wouldn't like his memory lapses when it came to the notebooks and the shooting. They'd say he was lying. As Kaiser notes, "either Dr. Diamond had to help Sirhan remember or find out why he couldn't."[18]

Diamond and Kaiser visited Sirhan again on January 25, to unravel the mystery of the notebooks, despite Sirhan's insistence they would never be used as evidence. Diamond turned to another page. "What about this '*$15,000*'? Does that amount ring any bells?"

"No," said Sirhan. "The only amount that rings any bells is $1,705. The money I got from the Industrial Accident Commission."

"'*Please pay to the order of.*' What's that?" Sirhan didn't know. "That's what you see on a check, isn't it?" Sirhan didn't even have a bank account. "'*Kennedy must fall Kennedy must fall.*' What do you think of that?"

"He fell," said Sirhan.

"Do you remember writing that?" No. "It's going to be very hard to convince a jury you could forget something like this, Sirhan. It's not gonna make much sense to them. They're going to think you're lying to protect yourself."

"Sir. Look, they can throw me in that gas chamber anytime they want, sir, and I wouldn't give a damn."

"Can I hypnotize you again, Sirhan?"

Diamond put Sirhan into a light trance and stuck a safety pin into his hand. As before, Sirhan didn't flinch.

"Sirhan, did you tell anybody you were going to shoot the senator?"

"No," said Sirhan.

"Did you tell that girl you had coffee with at the Ambassador?"

"No."

"Sirhan, when did you get the gun?"

"When I was working."

"Why did you buy a gun?"

"I liked guns."

Diamond got Sirhan to open his eyes while still under hypnosis. He admitted the writing was his but said he couldn't remember writing it. Diamond turned to the most incriminating page and read, "'*My determination to eliminate RFK is becoming more the more of an unshakable obsession.*'"

"You're back in your room. You're thinking of killing the senator. You're writing in your notebook. Are you watching TV? Huh? Remember the jets to Israel. Remember the jet planes, Sirhan? Remember the bombs and the Jews, Sirhan?" Mention of the bombs and jets triggered another flood of moaning and sobbing. Diamond gave Sirhan a posthypnotic suggestion that his traumatic feelings about the bombs would come out while he was awake. Then he woke him up and asked about the bombs.

"What bombs?" asked Sirhan. It hadn't worked. "Under hypnosis, the merest mention of bombs triggered a real hysteria in Sirhan," wrote Kaiser. "Awake, he intellectualized about the injustice of the bombs he had seen explode back in Jerusalem."

"I asked how you *felt*," said Diamond, his frustration showing. "Oh, shit, doc. I don't know. It helps not to remember."

The most incriminating page of Sirhan's notebook.

* * *

Diamond put Sirhan under again but had him keep his eyes open. He handed him the notebook and pointed to the top of the page. "Read what it says, Sirhan."

"'*RFK must dee.*'"

"No," said Diamond. "It doesn't say 'dee.'"

"Die," said Sirhan. Kaiser watched Sirhan read "very poorly, like a second or third grader, his voice . . . a barely audible whisper." Then he got stuck on a long word.

"Spell it out, Sirhan."

"*A-S-S-*," spelled Sirhan.

"What does that word spell, Sirhan?" No answer. "Sirhan, read like a grown-up. '*Robert F. Kennedy must be*'—what's the next word?"

"Killed."

"No, that isn't what it says. Open your eyes and look. '*A-S-S-*'—what does that say?"

"Assassinated."

"Right. Read on."

"'*RFK must be assassinated. RFK must be assassinated.*'"

"When did you write that, Sirhan?"

"'*RFK must be assassinated. RFK must be assassinated.*'" Sirhan repeated the sentence over and over again.

"What happened to Kennedy? Who killed Kennedy, Sirhan?"

"I don't know."

* * *

Diamond put Sirhan under again, gave him another suggestion to remember the notebooks, then woke him up and had him read some more.

"'*Kennedy must fall. Kennedy must fall. Please pay to the order of Sirhan Sirhan. We believe that Robert F. Kennedy must be sacrificed for the cause of the poor exploited people.*'"

Could he remember what he was thinking when he wrote this? No.

"Was it in your room at home?"

"It had to be at home."

"Think very hard. An image should come to you."

Sirhan remembered reading at his desk when he heard a radio news report about Kennedy speaking at a temple or a Jewish club somewhere. Maybe he wrote the page after that.

He recognized some of the pages as schoolwork. "Did the DA write the dates in?" he asked. No, said Diamond, the writing was his. Did he ever practice writing for his Rosicrucian exercises?

"I've read about—I don't know, there's a special name for it."

"Automatic writing," offered Diamond.

"Yeah, where you have a blank sheet of paper and you can transfer it telepathically or somehow."

Diamond had Sirhan read out another page. "'*A declaration of war against American humanity. When in the course of human events, it has become necessary for me to equalize and seek revenge for all the inhuman treatments committed against me by the American people.*'" Sirhan stopped midway. "This sounds . . . big. But shit, this is not like my handwriting. There's a difference in style in my handwriting."

"It looks a little sprawly," conceded Kaiser, "like you're a little out of control when you wrote this. Although it's your writing, it's bad writing. Like maybe you were tired."

Sirhan read on. "'*The author . . . expresses his wishes very . . . bluntly that . . . he wants to be . . . recorded by . . . historians as the man . . .*'" Sirhan stopped and whistled again, as if reading this for the first time.

"Go on," said Diamond.

"'*The man who triggered, triggered*'—what's this?"

"'*Triggered off.*'"

"Whew! . . . '*The last war.*'"

"What do you think of that, Sirhan?"

"I don't."

"Well, think, Sirhan! When did you write that?"

"I can't, doc. My mind's a blank. I don't remember this."

The jury wouldn't like his memory lapses. "They'll really think you're a mental case then," said Diamond.

"I'm not mental, sir . . . [but] that's the problem. If I say I'm mental, this whole defense of diminished responsibility, they're gonna say, hell, he's begging for his life. . . . I don't wanta beg for it, sir. If you don't have fucking justice in America, piss on you. And if America's the best country in the world and I cannot have what it gives, I don't wanta live at all."

"Well, that's big talk, Sirhan."

"Like I say, doc, take me up on it."

"Are you afraid that if they saw this notebook they'd think you're crazy? It's a crazy notebook, isn't it?"

"It's just none of their business."

"But it became their business when you shot Kennedy. . . . You can't get away from that. But it is a crazy kind of notebook."

"Hell, I know it, doc. I laughed at it as if I had listened to it or saw it for the first time."

Kaiser pointed out to Sirhan that the writing seemed to be inspired by the article in the *Rosicrucian Digest* called "Write It Down." "So, in a very remote way, at least, the Rosicrucians are involved, aren't they?"

"Yeah, but I don't want—oh, shit—I don't want to put any blame on them in that way. Oh, hell no. No, shit, no. Hell. No."[19]

* * *

Dr. Seymour Pollack had been hired as the psychiatrist for the prosecution. He was a distinguished forensic psychiatrist from the University of Southern California, where he headed a special Institute on Psychiatry and the Law. Talking to Sirhan, Grant Cooper thought Sirhan seemed "as normal as apple pie," but they needed to show diminished capacity to counter the apparent premeditation shown in the notebooks to escape the death penalty. He had nothing to lose by letting Pollack see Sirhan—if Pollack found him mentally ill, Cooper might be able to strike a bargain with the DA.[20]

Pollack was introduced to Sirhan on January 18 and went up to see him again with Diamond and Kaiser eight days later. Sirhan told Dr. Diamond and Dr. Pollack that "he was through," recalled Kaiser. "He didn't want any more doctors bugging him. . . . He was going to plead guilty as charged. He'd rather go to the gas chamber than have anybody 'fuck around' with his mind."

"You guys are goofing up my mind; I don't understand it," he said. They were going to call him "a fanatic or some stupid person or something like that. I'd rather die and say I killed that son of a bitch for my country, period."

"You don't really trust the psychiatrists, do you, Sirhan?" asked Diamond.

"You know more about me than I know about myself," said Sirhan.

"Would it help," asked Pollack, "if, after Dr. Diamond hypnotizes you today, you listen to the tape yourself?"

"You don't understand, doc. I don't wish to cooperate any longer."

Diamond explained to Sirhan how important it was to recover his memory. He wanted Dr. Pollack to see "another Sirhan" under hypnosis—"a part of you you don't seem to know anything about. I think you, too, should know about these feelings, Sirhan. . . . They're deep down inside you and they may be the real key to what's causing everything. . . . You don't remember yesterday, Sirhan? You sobbed and sobbed and sobbed?"

"Goddamn. That's not me, doc."

"That *is* you, Sirhan." Sirhan didn't get it.

"I'd like to put you to sleep one more time," cajoled Diamond. "Let me show this to Dr. Pollack. Let me show it to you. And I'll play the tape for you."

"Okay," said Sirhan.

Diamond put him back into a trance and tried to bring back his memories of the bombs.

"Remember the bombs, Sirhan? Remember the bombs?"

Once more, the sobbing fit from Sirhan. This time, Diamond woke him halfway through. Sirhan came to. It frightened him.

"What happened, Sirhan? What happened?"

"I saw that poor man. . . . They killed him." Sirhan had seen the grocer across the street in Jerusalem, blown to bits by a bomb outside his shop.

"Can you see him now, Sirhan? Close your eyes and look at him right now."

Sirhan closed his eyes and started sobbing again. "It's too bloody. Get me out of this, doc, get me out of this."

But there was nothing to get Sirhan "out of"—he was awake.

"Sirhan, these are your feelings," said Diamond. "These are your feelings you've been running away from. Don't be afraid to cry, Sirhan. Real tears, Sirhan. Let it all come out, Sirhan." Sirhan broke down, his body shaking, in floods of tears—at last his emotions bleeding into real life.

"The whole world has to know the truth, Sirhan. No lies, no cover-ups. Only you can let them know what the truth is, Sirhan. You mustn't be afraid of your feelings. You're awake now. You're not hypnotized, Sirhan. These are your feelings and you can't hide them."[21]

Diamond put Sirhan under hypnosis again, but he went in too deep and mumbled incoherently. Diamond tried to pull him out into a light trance. "Sirhan, open your eyes and wake up," ordered Diamond. "One, two, wake up." Sirhan moaned and his eyelids fluttered.

"Now, Sirhan, we were talking about on Tuesday night, you'd gone back to your car. You're tired. You had four Collins to drink and you're too drunk to drive and you go back to the car and you see the gun on the back seat. Do you remember?"

"They can't steal it, they can't steal it," said Sirhan in a sing-song voice.

"You were afraid they were going to steal your gun," said Diamond.

"So what did you do with it? Did you put it in the band of your pants?"

Sirhan continued his sing-song mumbling, so Diamond gave Sirhan a suggestion to remember everything discussed so far and woke him up. '1-2-3,' wake up, Sirhan, wake up."

Sirhan slowly woke up, shivering as usual.

"Are you cold again?" asked Pollack.

"How in the hell did you get here?" asked Sirhan, coming to, as if clocking Pollack for the first time.

"You don't remember my coming in?"

"Think, Sirhan, remember," said Dr. Diamond. "Dr. Pollack's been here all this afternoon."

"You're trying to frighten me," said Sirhan softly, like a little kid.

Diamond tried to pick up from where they stopped off a few minutes earlier under hypnosis.

"You had four Tom Collins to drink, remember that? When you were asleep, you told us that you counted them on your fingers, 1-2-3-4. Does that sound right?"

"I guzzled that stuff like lemonade, doc," said Sirhan.

"And then you got real tired, and you decided to go home and you went out to the car and you were too drunk to drive, you remember that?"

Sirhan remembered walking up a slant, he must have gotten into his car but "I was hazy, doc . . . I wanted to sleep. Coffee was on my mind again."

Under hypnosis, he spoke of picking up the gun but, awake, he couldn't remember.

"You said the Jews were going to steal your gun," Pollack reminded him.

"I don't remember that, sir." He didn't remember where he put the gun either. "Those pants were pretty tight."

Pollack asked Sirhan to remember what happened when he got back to the Ambassador.

"I remember I got coffee. She wanted cream . . . and there was a policeman there."

"Then what? Did you talk to the policeman?"

"It was dark. Oh hell, it was dark."

"It was dark? I thought there were a lot of lights there," said Pollack.

"How can you drink coffee in the dark?"

"I don't know. It was dark. . . . A lot of lights, too. There was a hell of a lot of lights."

"This was consistent with what he said before, too," said Diamond. There were a lot of lights there, but he was in the dark."

"And there was a lot of silver around. . . . " Possibly the steam tables in the pantry. "She was tired, too. She wanted coffee just as much as I did."

"Did she tell you her name?"

"Coffee was all our discussion."

Earlier, under hypnosis, Sirhan told Diamond about getting coffee and going into a room with a Teletype machine. "Do you remember the Teletype machine? Concentrate, Sirhan. . . . Where is the Teletype machine?"

"Tap, tap, tap, tap," said Sirhan, mimicking the Teletype machine. "It was one of those Western Union jobs. . . . I was looking at the lady that was operating it. . . . It was a funny machine, doc. A funny machine."

"Sirhan, right next to the Teletype machine is a door, a swinging door. Do you remember a door?" The door led into the pantry.

"I don't remember any door," said Sirhan.

"When you were asleep, you said you went through the door next to the Teletype machine."

"That girl. I followed her."

"The girl with the coffee?"

"The coffee . . . She led me into a dark place."

"Led you into a dark place. Was this where the Teletype machine was?"

"I don't know."

"What did she have in mind? What did you have in mind?" asked Pollack.

"I was just trailing her, that's all."

"He told me before what was on his mind is he hoped to be able to screw her afterwards, was that right, Sirhan?" asked Diamond.

"I guess I was. . . . Lot of empty rooms down there."

"You were thinking of taking her into one of the empty rooms?"

"Why not?"

"Why not? Sure. It makes sense," said Diamond, sounding more confused than ever.

"Is she the one who gave you the coffee?" asked Pollack.

"She's the one that asked for it . . . and that's what I wanted . . . and I gave her a cup and I made some for me and we sat there. Then she moved and I followed her."

"And then what?"

"There was a policeman. . . . He had a funny uniform."

Diamond explained to Pollack that this was probably a fireman but Sirhan couldn't say for sure.

"And then what happened?"

"Damn . . . I was tired."

"Alright, you were tired," said Pollack. "Still drinking coffee or did you put the coffee down?"

"I remember lying on the table, together with the coffee, I had my elbows on there and I was just resting. And all of a sudden I was choked."

"Oh wait!" said Diamond. "You skipped something. You skipped a lot, Sirhan."

"You were choked because something happened, Sirhan," said Pollack.

"Now, lookit," said Diamond sternly. "You're back at the press room. You had your coffee already. You followed this girl around. Did you lose her?"

"I don't know. . . . A lot of darkness there."

"Do you remember the mirrors, Sirhan? Remember the mirror that you looked into when you saw Kennedy's face?"

"Oh yeah . . . that fucker."

"That fucker, yeah . . . Now, remember the mirror when you saw it at home. Now, do you remember the mirrors in the Ambassador Hotel?"

The only mirrors Sirhan could remember were in the Venetian Room.

"There are two entrances to the kitchen very close together," Diamond explained to Pollack. "One is from the press room; the other one is a little alcove that is totally mirrored. Doors mirrored, walls mirrored, everything is mirrored, so that you see a great many multiple reflections."

Diamond thought these may well have triggered the trance.

"Are there mirrors also in the other rooms?" asked Pollack.

"A lot of lights, a hell of a lot of fuckin' lights."

Kaiser suggested the coffee urn might have been in the pantry itself. Sirhan remembered a lot of cups stacked up by the coffee. He was lying on the table but he couldn't remember what kind of table it was.

"Were you looking for more coffee?"

"I was resting."

Sirhan seems to have been "resting" on the steam table after the shooting as Kennedy aides struggled to pin him down. The "enormously peaceful eyes" George Plimpton described fit this state of mind.

"I was leaning on the table and I was looking at that policeman."

"What did you say to yourself when you saw the policeman?" asked Kaiser.

"I don't know."

"Were you afraid of the policeman? Did you think he was going to arrest you?" asked Diamond.

"I was drunk."

"You told me, that when you were asleep, that you could see Kennedy walking towards you. And you told me you wanted to shake hands with him."

Sirhan smiled ruefully. "I wish to hell I did. Ohhh, goddamn!"

"Well, try to remember," said Diamond. "Put your head back and concentrate. You see Kennedy coming towards you and you wanted to shake hands with him, Sirhan."

Pollack provocatively challenged Sirhan: "Why would you shake hands with that son of a bitch? That I don't get. Why would you shake hands with that son of a bitch?"

"I don't know," said Sirhan.

"Sirhan, you know that you told me once that you loved the Kennedys," said Diamond.

"I liked him. I liked him."

"He was gonna be the hope for the Arab people?"

"I thought so."

Pollack found this incredible. "Bobby was gonna be the hope of the Arab people? Huh?"

"He was for the underdog," explained Sirhan. Diamond tried to refocus.

"Why not hypnotize me again, doc? On that part alone?" At the start of the session, Sirhan had said he didn't want any more hypnosis; now he was once again a willing volunteer.

"One-two-three-four-five . . . now, try to go into a fairly light sleep, that's it," said Diamond. "Now, try to picture in your mind the scene. You're in the kitchen there, you're standing in the corner, there's lots of people around, lot of noise. And you see Kennedy coming. Now what do you see, Sirhan? You're back in the kitchen there. What do you see?"

Sirhan remained motionless, eyes closed.

"Sirhan, open your eyes! You're back in the kitchen. Kennedy is coming toward you. Look at his face." No response from Sirhan. "Sirhan, you asked me to hypnotize you and I did. And you said you would talk; now, you keep your word and I'll keep mine. Sirhan, open your eyes and talk. What do you see?"

"He's running at me."

"Who's running at you?"

"People." Perhaps the rush of Kennedy and his party walking swiftly through the pantry toward the Colonial Room.

"Why are they running at you? Concentrate, Sirhan. Concentrate. Why are they running at you?" No response. "Remember, Sirhan. Why are they running at you? Sirhan, think back. You see Kennedy. What did he look like? Look in his face, Sirhan. Open your eyes. Look at Kennedy."

Sirhan groaned and grew increasingly disturbed.

"Open your eyes, Sirhan, and look at Kennedy. Sirhan, don't shake your head. Look at him. You must remember! I order you to open your eyes and look at Kennedy. Look at him. There he is. Don't shake your head. He's coming toward you, Sirhan. What do you see?"

"Bobby . . . You—son—of—a—bitch."

"'You son of a bitch.' Were you mad, Sirhan? That son of a bitch is coming. What do you see?"

"What's *he* doing here?"

"'What's he doing here?'" Diamond repeated. "Go on."

Sirhan started to breathe hard. "You—son—of—a—bitch."

"'You son of a bitch,'" repeated Diamond. "You're talking to Kennedy. . . . Sirhan! Open your eyes and look at Kennedy."

"'You son of a bitch' has been verified by a witness," Diamond whispered to Pollack. "That's the first time he's talked about that. . . . Open your eyes, Sirhan! Open your eyes and look at Kennedy. There he is right there."

Sirhan gave a quick jump and suddenly started choking in his chair.

"Are they choking you, Sirhan?" asked Diamond.

Sirhan's face turned a little blue as the pronounced sound of choking was accompanied by anguished gasps for air.

"All right, Sirhan. They're not really choking you. It's all right. Sirhan, they're not really choking you. Sirhan, open your eyes. You haven't shot him yet, Sirhan, he's still there. Sirhan, there is Kennedy, open your eyes. Open your eyes, Sirhan. 'You son of a bitch,' you said, Sirhan."

"He can't. He can't."

"'He can't?' He can't do what?"

"Can't send those bombers."

"He can't send the bombers. You're not gonna let him, are you, Sirhan? Hmmm?"

"He can't. He can't. He can't. He can't," repeated Sirhan, in a fast, excited, breathy rhythm.

"Sirhan! Did you know Kennedy was coming this way?"

"No."

"Did you expect him?"

"No."

"Sirhan, were you waiting for him?"

"Uhhhh."

"Yes or no, Sirhan?"

"No."

"No. Are you sure you weren't waiting for him?"

"No."

"But you see him now. He's coming, Sirhan. He's coming down the hall." Sirhan let out an anguished groan.

"Look at him, Sirhan. Open your eyes."

"He's running, he's moving at me," said Sirhan, by now very disturbed. "C'mon, look at him."

"You cocksucker," spat Sirhan.

"'You cocksucker,' yeah, go on."

Sirhan was trembling violently, still panting, his breath quickening as he approached the climax. "You can't. You can't. You can't," he repeated, over and over. "You can't. You can't. You can't. You can't. You can't."

"Are you reaching for your gun, Sirhan?" With his right hand, Sirhan grabbed an imaginary gun crudely from his left hip bone.

"You can't. You can't. You can't. You can't."

"Are you reaching for your gun, Sirhan?" asked Diamond again.

Sirhan's panting became faster. "You can't. You can't. You can't. You can't. You can't."

"You can't do that. You can't send the bombers," intoned Diamond. "Are you gonna stop him, Sirhan?"

Sirhan grabbed for the gun again, not from his left hip bone this time, but from his crotch.

"He can't. He can't. He can't."

"All right, he can't. Are you gonna stop him? How are you gonna stop him, Sirhan?"

"He can't, he can't," sighed Sirhan. He was still grabbing for his crotch; then he became quiet for a moment.

"Sirhan, open your eyes and look at Kennedy!" barked Diamond.

"Tell him to reach for his gun," whispered Kaiser.

"Sirhan, open your eyes. Look at Kennedy. He's coming. Reach for your gun, Sirhan. It's your last chance, Sirhan. Reach for your gun!

Sirhan's quick breathing started up again. "He can't. He can't. He can't."

"For the record," Diamond noted for the tape, "he is reaching spasmodically into the waistband of his pants on his left side in a crude kind of grabbing or gesture reaching for the gun."

"He can't. He can't."

"All right, what happened, Sirhan? Take the gun out of your pants. You've got the gun in your hand now. Let me see you shoot the gun, Sirhan. Shoot the gun. Shoot the gun."

Sirhan's panting intensified.

"Sirhan, take the gun out and shoot it. Who are you shooting, Sirhan? Who are you shooting? His fingers are going through repetitive spasmodic movements like pulling a trigger on a double-action revolver. . . . Sirhan! You're shooting Kennedy now, huh? The double-action gun. It's hard to pull the trigger."

According to Kaiser, "Sirhan's right hand pounded climactically on his right thigh—five times. His right forefinger squeezed and twisted three more times in a weakening spasm. Then he was still."

"Sirhan, you have wanted to remember the shooting of Kennedy," said Pollack as he gave him a posthypnotic suggestion to remember everything he had just experienced in trance when he woke up.

Diamond started to bring Sirhan out, suggesting he remember everything but feel warm and relaxed when he woke up. "You won't be worried," said Diamond reassuringly. "And you won't be frightened. You got a lot of bad feelings out of you and you'll feel clean inside, Sirhan. You'll feel clean and you'll trust us. . . . We're doctors, Sirhan, and we want to help you. We're Jews, Sirhan, but we want to help you because we hate war, too, Sirhan. We hate war, Sirhan, just like you hate war."

Sirhan woke up, relaxed and smiling. "I don't see you smile very often," said Diamond.

"I can't afford to," said Sirhan, and the doctors laughed.

But he couldn't remember seeing Kennedy, saying "you son of a bitch," pulling a gun, or anything else from his trance state five minutes before.

"I must have been crazy."

"No, you weren't crazy, Sirhan," Diamond reassured him. "You were blind with anger. You're not a crazy person. . . . Do you remember where you told us where the gun was? Point to me where the gun was."

"I don't remember."

"Five minutes ago, Sirhan, you showed me where the gun was. . . . The gun was right there on your belt. You showed us, Sirhan, how you reached for the gun. Go ahead and reach for it."

"I never reached for my gun," said Sirhan, genuinely mystified.

"You reached and you showed us how you pulled the trigger."

Sirhan was nonplussed.

"All right, Sirhan. You had a long day and you did very well, and you got us a lot of information. We'll help you remember all this, Sirhan."

"What I said at the beginning, sir, still stands," said Sirhan, "that I don't want you to call me crazy."

"That we promise you," said Diamond. "You're not crazy, Sirhan. You've been very badly mixed up. Sometimes, you can't remember things, but no one's going to call you crazy; nobody's going to put you in a crazy house."

Sirhan was also determined to plead guilty because he didn't think he could get a fair trial. "Why go to court, sir, and have you convict me and then turn around and have the State Department tell the world and the Arab people, especially after you gas me—"Well, he's dead but we gave him a fair trial!"

"In other words, it would be better for the Arab world if you didn't have a trial," said Diamond.

"I think it would."

"It would be better for the Arab world if you weren't crazy."

"Yes, sir."[22]

* * *

Over the next several days, Sirhan had three sessions alone with Dr. Pollack. "You've convinced me that you do have trouble remembering what took place," said Pollack. "But your trouble remembering doesn't mean to me that you didn't intend to kill him; do you see my point?"

Pollack didn't really think Sirhan had a chance but agreed with Cooper and Diamond that the clearer Sirhan was about all of this, the better chance he had—because the jury wouldn't believe him if he said he didn't remember, and the diaries showed premeditation.

"Those writings, you'll admit, don't look good, do they?"

"No, sir, they don't."

"You realize that they definitely indicate that you wanted to kill Kennedy before he was killed; you realize that, don't you?"

"Yes, sir."

But Pollack still couldn't fit the notebooks to the person sitting next to him. "You hypnotize very easily, you know that? You're very suggestible. . . . I look at you as a very emotionally filled, intense kid. . . . But I can't conceive of you doing this. It doesn't jibe."

Sirhan called the angry part of him "the little punk" but insisted he didn't know what he was doing when he killed Kennedy.

"What you're doing is discounting the real Sirhan," said Pollack, "the intense—what shall I say?—freedom fighter? You didn't want the Arabs to be hurt more. . . . You felt it necessary to bring this to the attention of the world."

"Oh, shit, sir. I could have slapped him in the face; I could have broken his nose. I could have thrown my cup of coffee at him. . . . Why? Why not? Why the hell didn't I do that?"

"Because that wouldn't stop the jet bombers," replied Pollack, searching for an explanation. "I don't really think you thought the whole thing out. You certainly didn't work out a good way of killing him."

"That's what I don't understand," said Sirhan. "If I'd wanted to kill a man, why would I have shot him right there where they could have choked the shit out of me? Would I, sir, be so stupid as to leave that notebook there, waiting for those cops to pick up?"

"It might be that you wanted to be caught, if you wanted the world to know it was an Arab who did it." Sirhan made a face. "You don't think so."

"I may have done more damage to the Arab cause," said Sirhan ruefully. "I'm not a killer; I'm not a killer," he repeated.

He wasn't a killer in the cold-blooded sense, argued Pollack, but a political assassin, to whom such details weren't important. "It's almost as if you're being a martyr. . . . To have the world see that, through your death, the U.S. is really pro-Israel?"

"No, I said this, sir, a thousand times; I'm not proud of this. . . . You could shoot me right here for what I did, sir. . . . My own conscience doesn't agree with me."

"Your own conscience?" said Pollack, a little incredulous.

"My own conscience. . . . It's against my upbringing, my very nature, sir," said Sirhan, sounding anguished. "My childhood, family, church, prayers . . . the Bible and all this, sir. 'Thou shalt not kill.' Life is the thing, you know. Where would you be if you didn't live, sir? And here I go and splatter this guy's brains. It's just not me."

Pollack looked at his watch. It was close to six thirty p.m. He had to be going. Before he did, he again told Sirhan where he stood.

"As a psychiatrist representing society, I have to be able to put my feelings aside and offer an opinion, whether I like you or not. . . . When I look at the material . . . so far, Sirhan, the evidence appears to indicate that you carried your gun down there to shoot him; you see . . . people don't carry loaded guns unless they intend to use them."

"Well, a layman could come up with the same conclusion. . . . They saw me shoot him, so kill that son of a bitch. . . . I only wish that I could agree with you. I only wish that I knew what I really carried a gun down there for."

"You told me that you were down at the Ambassador and Kennedy wasn't on your mind, you said, so why would you shoot him if he wasn't on your mind? Why would you bring the gun back if he wasn't on your mind?

"It's possible that your drinking gave you enough release so that you went ahead and did this," conceded Pollack.

"I need to be more mad to do something like that, then be released," said Sirhan.[23]

* * *

Diamond met Sirhan again on February 1 and tried to solve the riddle of the notebooks one last time. Sirhan was still insisting he would ask for the gas chamber if his notebooks were introduced in court, and for an hour, Diamond's probing went nowhere. Then Diamond acted on a hunch that Sirhan wrote some of his notebooks in an altered state and made a breakthrough. He hypnotized Sirhan with a quarter and asked him to go into a very light sleep, "so light a sleep that you'll be able to remember everything."

He propped a yellow legal pad in Sirhan's lap, gave him a ballpoint pen, and asked him to write his name. Sirhan began to write, "*Sirhan B Sirhan Sirhan B Sirhan Sirhan B Sirhan*" over and over again, thirty seconds to a line.

For fifteen minutes, Diamond, Pollack, and Kaiser sat watching him fill the page with his name in a slow, robotic scrawl—"automatic writing" triggered by the simple instruction to write his name. When Sirhan couldn't finish his name on one line in English, he started writing, right to left, in Arabic for a line and a half before correcting himself and switching back into English, "*Sirhan Sirhan Sirhan Sirhan Sirhan Sirhan*" to the bottom of the page.

"Write about Kennedy, Sirhan," prompted Diamond.

He wrote, "*RFK RFK RFK RFK RFK.*"

"Write it all out, not just the initials."

"*Robert F. Kennedy Robert F. Kennedy.*"

"Tell us more than his name, Sirhan. Write more than the name."

"*RFK RFK RFK RFK.*"

"More than the initials. What's going to happen to Kennedy, Sirhan? What's going to happen to Kennedy?"

Sirhan wrote, "*RFK must die RFK must die RFK must die*" nine times, until Diamond stopped him. It looked very similar to what Sirhan had written in his notebook.

"When must Kennedy die? When is Robert Kennedy going to die?" asked Diamond.

"*Robert Kennedy is going to die Robert is going to die Robert is going to die.*"

"Don't write what I tell you, Sirhan. Answer my questions. . . . Start a new line over here. Who killed Kennedy?"

"*Who killed Kennedy?*" wrote Sirhan.

"You're writing the question; now write me the answer." Diamond couldn't help laughing.

"*I don't know I don't know.*"

Diamond concluded that for Sirhan, emotionally, Kennedy was still alive. Diamond kept his questions going: Did Kennedy talk to Sirhan? Did anyone tell him to shoot Kennedy? Did anyone give him money to shoot Kennedy? Did anyone help him? Was anybody with him? Sirhan wrote, "*No no no . . .*"

"What's the name of the person who was with you when you shot Kennedy, Sirhan? Who was with you? Write it down."

"*Girl the girl the girl.*"

"Do you know the girl's name?" Sirhan groaned. "Write out the name of the girl."

"*No No No.*"

"Start a new line, Sirhan. Is this the way you wrote the notebook at home? Write the answer, not the question. Is this the way you wrote the notebook at home?"

"*Yes yes yes.*"

Diamond's hunch was right—much of the notebook was written under hypnosis.

"Is this crazy writing, Sirhan?"

"*Yes yes yes yes yes yes yes yes yes.*"

"That's enough 'yeses,' Sirhan. Go to another line. You're like the sorcerer's apprentice here. Are you crazy, Sirhan. Are you crazy?"

"*No no no. N—*"

"If you are not crazy, why are you writing crazy?"

"*Practice practice practice practice practice.*"

"Practice for what, Sirhan?"

"*Mind control mind control mind control mind—*"

"Mind control for what? What are you going to do with your mind control, Sirhan?"

"*Self improvement self improvement.*" Sirhan was tiring and began to drop off, his writing looser, more of a scrawl.

"Are you asleep now? Are you hypnotized?"

"*I am sleepy.*"

"Are you hypnotized?"

"*Yes yes yes.*"

"Were you hypnotized when you wrote the notebook?"

"*Yes yes yes.*"

"Who hypnotized you when you wrote the notebook? Write his name down."

"*Mirror mirror my mirror,*" wrote Sirhan, "*my my mirror.*"

It was now clear to Diamond that Sirhan's previous sessions of self-hypnosis in his bedroom mirror produced much of the writing in the notebook. This helped explain why Sirhan was so readily hypnotizable and also why he responded better in written rather than spoken form. He didn't speak to himself in the mirror; he wrote out his thoughts, so writing answers naturally came easier to him in the sessions with Diamond than speaking them.

"Who taught you how to do this?" asked Diamond.

"*AMORC,*" wrote Sirhan. "*AMORC AMORC.*"

AMORC stood for the Ancient Mystical Order of the Rosy Cross. "That's the Rosicrucians, isn't it? Did they show you how to do that?" asked Diamond.

"*No.*"

"Sirhan, did you read it in a book?"

"*Yes yes yes.*"

"Who gave you the books, Sirhan?"

"*I bought the books I b.*"

Dr. Pollack asked Diamond to take Sirhan back to the Ambassador on the night of the shooting. "Write down how many drinks you had, Sirhan," demanded Diamond. "Don't go to sleep. Write the number. Write it down."

"*1234 1234 1234.*"

"What kind of drinks were they, Sirhan?"

"*Give me a Tom Collins Collins.*"

"Were you drunk, Sirhan?"

"*Were you drunk*" wrote Sirhan.

"That's my question, Sirhan. Write the answer. Were you drunk?"

"*Yes Yes Yes.*"

"Where is the gun?"

"*I don't know.*"

"Did you take the gun out of the car?"

"*Go home, go home, home go*," wrote Sirhan, while mumbling "Go home, go home, go home."

Prompted by Pollack, Diamond asked Sirhan if he was thinking of shooting Kennedy.

"*No no*," wrote Sirhan, sliding off the legal pad and writing in the air. "Were you hating Kennedy then?"

"*No No*," wrote Sirhan. Then he groaned and stopped writing. He'd come to the end of the page.

Sirhan's writing was getting more and more incoherent as he sank deeper into sleep. As Diamond took the pen and pad away, Sirhan kept writing on his trouser leg with an imaginary pencil. Diamond thought it best to start afresh another time and woke him up, suggesting that he remember everything that had happened in this session.

"I don't want you to run away from your thoughts; I want you to remember . . . and feel warm and relaxed after a good sleep . . . one-two-three, wake up, Sirhan."

Sirhan woke up slowly and yawned, in a smiling, relaxed mood.

"What's this, Sirhan, on your lap? Do you recognize that?"

Sirhan couldn't remember writing on the pad and didn't recognize the writing as his. It was too "scribblish . . . like chicken scratches." He didn't even remember using the pen before. He was troubled.

"Sirhan, do you feel okay?" asked Diamond.

"I'm puzzled with all this. I don't understand it, sir, period."[24]

"Do you think it's possible, Sirhan, that you were asleep when you wrote part of the notebooks?"

"Sir, honestly, I don't remember much of the notebooks. Those writings, they're not Sirhan. That's what bugs me, sir . . . it's not the real me."

"That's another side of you, Sirhan. Did you ever hear of a double personality . . . do you think you have a split personality, Sirhan?

"If I have a split, the other split of my half is not good," said Sirhan, and the doctors laughed. "Some mutation . . . Those guys on the jury, sir, they go for computers and all that shit, they don't go for this stuff, so I don't want [the notebooks] presented in court. . . . What does it show?"

"What do you think it shows, Sirhan?"

"That I'm crazy, but I don't feel it, sir."

"No, it shows that you told us the truth, Sirhan."

If Sirhan wrote the notebooks in a trance, how could he remember writing them?[25]

* * *

Diamond later noted that the notebooks contained three types of writing: Schoolwork and language studies; political manifesto, which Diamond ascribed to paranoid schizophrenic psychosis; and a third type to do with Kennedy's assassination.

Sirhan answers Diamond and Pollack's questions through automatic writing on a yellow legal pad.

"It is my opinion that these were written in a self-induced trance, a dissociated state similar to that in which I believe he committed this killing itself."[26]

* * *

Sirhan repeatedly told Mike McCowan he was fooling Diamond during the hypnotic sessions—that he wasn't really asleep, he was just pretending. No doctor was going to "bug him" by hypnotizing him. McCowan wanted to see for himself, so on February 8, he came in to watch the session and they devised a secret finger signal—Sirhan would lift his middle finger off his lap "in trance" and wave it to show he was faking.

As Diamond put Sirhan under, McCowan waited for the signal. "It was very curious," recalled Diamond. "In the state of hypnosis, you could see him trying to lift his finger, and he couldn't budge it."

To prove his point, Diamond suggested that when Sirhan came out of the trance and Diamond blew his nose, Sirhan would climb the bars of his cell like a monkey. Sirhan woke up, Diamond blew his nose, and up the bars Sirhan climbed, swinging upside down like a monkey.

"Why are you climbing the bars, Sirhan?" asked Diamond.

"For exercise," said Sirhan, matter-of-fact.

Diamond then played back the tape of the session to show how Sirhan had been programmed. "It wasn't your idea at all, Sirhan. You were just following my instructions."

Sirhan was quiet for a moment, then shivered. "Oh, it frightens me, doc."

"Now, get this straight, Sirhan. I do not believe that anybody hypnotized you and told you to kill Kennedy. I think you did it to yourself. You get the distinction?"

"Yes, sir. I understand."

Diamond told Sirhan he believed he had programmed himself like a computer.

"It frightens me," said Sirhan. "It frightens me."[27]

But Diamond branded Sirhan's belief that mind power could influence real world events delusional. "I asked him once if he could make the president's airplane crash by just concentrating on it and his answer was no, because he, Sirhan, is too weak and doesn't possess the power; but that if about fifty people all concentrated together, they could make it happen."

In the same vein, Sirhan admitted consciously and under hypnosis that he thought of the death of Kennedy—"that he willed him to die so that the bombers would not go to Israel." But while part of him "believes in this magical power, another part of his more rational mind . . . quickly dismisses it and says, 'this is ridiculous, this can't happen.' Sirhan did this frequently, I think, in a waking state, specifically sort of thinking of the death of Senator Kennedy."[28]

Diamond concluded that when Sirhan was practicing in front of the mirror, he went into a hypnotic trance without realizing it, and when he came out, he found this material in the notebook, which he had no memory of writing. "To him," said

Diamond, "the notebook is written proof positive of the 'crazy writing' which he knows he wrote and which was a product of this mirror-gazing, the self-hypnotic trances . . . [but] he would prefer to go to the gas chamber than have it made public and be seen as crazy."[29]

At trial, Diamond concluded that "Sirhan was suffering from a chronic paranoid schizophrenia, a major psychosis at the time of the shooting. He was in a highly abnormal dissociated state of restrictive consciousness as a direct consequence of his psychotic condition."[30]

Diamond's opinion on "diminished capacity" was clear: "The defendant was unable because of mental disease to maturely and meaningfully reflect on the gravity of his contemplated act and . . . comprehend his duties to govern his actions in accordance with the duties imposed by law."[31]

ELEVEN

THE TRIAL

In early January, as Cooper was preparing for jury selection, he got a warning call from the respected criminalist William Harper, a consultant in more than three hundred cases in his thirty-five-year career. "Beware of Wolfer," he said. "He gives [the prosecution] what they want." Harper had come up against Wolfer's work before and had accused him of manipulating evidence to order. "He will do what's expected of him."

Cooper was unconcerned—there was no question in his mind that Sirhan had shot Kennedy—so Harper let the matter drop, but Russell Parsons was also wary of Wolfer from past experience—"I had him in a murder case against me, and he was a smart alec, catered to juries, did everything but kiss their butt." But Parsons never expressed these misgivings to Cooper, and Wolfer got a free ride.[1]

* * *

Coming late into the case, Cooper had a very poor grasp of the physical evidence. He was going to stipulate that Sirhan had killed Kennedy, so the less time spent discussing bullets and gunshot wounds in front of the jury, the better. The defense was chock-full of psychiatrists and psychologists but had no forensic expertise. Cooper stipulated to the bullets presented by Wolfer and asked Dr. Noguchi to spare the court "the gory details" of the autopsy. At no point in the trial were the issues of extra bullets or extra guns mentioned, and there was no meaningful examination of the ballistics.[2]

The defense focused not on possible coconspirators but on Sirhan's mental and emotional state at the time of the shooting. "Cooper wanted to look good in front of the jury," recalled Bob Kaiser. "His idea was not to make the LAPD look bad; it was to try to convince the jury that Sirhan did not have the emotional capacity and the mental capacity to meaningfully and maturely reflect on the gravity of his contemplated act. That's the law of diminished capacity in California."[3]

* * *

But, as the New Year began, Cooper's participation in the trial was in doubt. On Friday, January 3, he admitted to a federal grand jury that he had lied in court about the source of the unauthorized transcript found on his counsel table during the Friars Club trial.

Cooper said he had nothing to do with acquiring the transcripts—he was on a fishing trip to the South Seas at the time. He cited attorney-client privilege in refusing to answer forty-six questions about how they were obtained and said he would risk contempt and jail before revealing anything that would damage his client.[4]

An urgent three-page FBI Teletype, titled "Re Illegal Possession and Use FCG Transcripts," to J. Edgar Hoover later that day is still heavily redacted. Two pages are blacked out; then the last eight lines read, "USDJ set hearing for such argument at two PM Monday next. USA W. Matthew Byrne, Jr. today advised that if government obtained facts suitable to indict [Grant Cooper] and others while Sirhan case in progress, such indictment would be returned secretly and not released until Sirhan case concluded." The threat of an indictment weighed heavily on Cooper throughout the Sirhan trial. In fact, hearings on the stolen transcripts would resume the day after Sirhan was sentenced.[5]

So, U.S. Attorney Matt Byrne was prosecuting Sirhan and pursuing a possible indictment of Sirhan's attorney at the same time. If an indictment was returned before the trial, it would be hushed up but still secretly hanging over Cooper while he defended Sirhan.

Three days later, Cooper played down the possibility of an indictment to Judge Herbert Walker, who would preside over the Sirhan trial. Al Wirin appeared in chambers to advise Sirhan that he should continue to be represented by Cooper, despite the conflict of interest posed by Cooper's possible indictment by an agency participating in the prosecution. Sirhan consented, and Cooper stayed.[6]

But, according to Mike McCowan, "he was under stress all during the Sirhan case because he had never done the slightest thing wrong during all his years of trials. It was very disturbing to him and to his wife, Phyllis, who was an attorney also. And it wasn't resolved until after the case."[7]

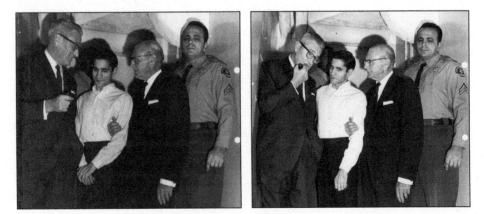

Sirhan had a tempestous relationship with Cooper and Parsons.

On January 7, the trial commenced in Department 107 of the Superior Court on the eighth floor of the Los Angeles County Halls of Justice. With breathtaking arrogance, Cooper tried and failed in chambers to get a further thirty-day continuance from Judge Walker, arguing that the reports in the papers about his difficulties with the transcripts would prejudice the jury. It was a clear admission he wasn't ready, but Walker denied the motion—there had been quite enough delays.

The attorneys for the prosecution were Chief Deputy DA Lynn "Buck" Compton and Deputy DAs John Howard and David Fitts. Cooper, Parsons, and Berman acted for the defense, and two SUS investigators, Sergeants Collins and Patchett, advised the prosecution on evidence, exhibits, and witnesses.

Eighty-nine witnesses would testify over the next three months and seven days, but the initial jury selection would go on for weeks, allowing the defense psychiatrists crucial time to explore Sirhan's memory of the shooting.[8]

* * *

On the morning of February 10, three days before the start of the witness phase of the trial, DA Evelle Younger went up to see Judge Walker in his chambers. Cooper, without consulting the Sirhan family, had gotten together with the prosecution and worked out a plea of guilty to all counts, submitting only the issue of the penalty to the jury, with a recommendation from the DA of life imprisonment, not the death penalty.

"I understand that the defendant is prepared to plead guilty and accept a life sentence—is that right, Mr. Cooper?" asked Younger.

"Yes," replied Sirhan's counsel.

"We favor it, Judge," said the DA, explaining that he had finally gotten a psychiatrist's report from Pollack. "Our psychiatrist," he said, "a man we have great confidence in . . . says that the defendant is psychotic and his report would support the position of the defense because of diminished capacity."

On that basis, the result of the trial was "a foregone conclusion."

"We can't conscientiously urge the death penalty [and] we don't think under any circumstances we would get the death penalty even if we urged it. . . . Are we justified in going through the motions of a very traumatic and expensive trial, when we say we can't conscientiously ask for the death penalty anyway? We don't think we are."

Cooper said Dr. Diamond felt that Sirhan had diminished capacity and was entitled to a charge of second-degree murder, but the likelihood of obtaining such a verdict from the jury in such a high-profile case had to be weighed against the possibility of the jury ignoring the psychiatrists and returning a death sentence. Cooper concluded, "The odds were not in our favor, so the wise thing to do would be to enter a plea of guilty to first degree murder with life imprisonment."

If such a plea were accepted, to ensure the public didn't think "there was any hanky-panky going on," Younger promised to work with the LAPD to "put into the record all pertinent materials including statements of witnesses and that sort of thing and the psychiatrists' reports, so that the second-guessers, and they will be legion . . . will have all the evidence upon which we base our recommendations." In fact, these files would not be released for another twenty years.

Judge Walker was having none of it, however. "I think you have got a very much interested public . . . and they continually point to the Oswald matter, and they wonder what is going on because the fellow wasn't tried."

Cooper suggested putting on "a very skeleton outline of the case at the time of plea instead of submitting reports."

"Well, then they would say that it was all fixed, it was greased," said the judge, "so we will just go [on with] the trial."

Lynn Compton wasn't giving up. "If defendant were to plead guilty to first degree murder, there wouldn't be any evidence put on; we simply would offer no evidence on the penalty and there would be no trial."

"What I am trying to tell you," scolded the judge, "[is that] the jury ought to determine that and what they come out with . . . is the jury's business. . . . Let's go on with the trial. . . . I don't think psychiatrists should determine the outcome."[9]

* * *

Judge Walker gave them two days to decide what to do. "If we start dragging our feet, it would damage the case tremendously. . . . We are in a very precarious position. We've got a lot of smart people out there."[10]

The press could sniff what was going on. On February 12, on the eve of opening statements, the *Los Angeles Times* ran a story that a plea of guilty to first-degree murder had been offered by the defense. The next day, Cooper moved for a mistrial on the grounds that the article would prejudice the jury. After questioning each of the jurors in chambers, Judge Walker was assured they could set aside this publicity and decide the case only on the evidence to be presented in court.

Walker denied the motion, and David Fitts made his opening statement for the prosecution before the jury was sequestered at the Biltmore Hotel.[11]

During the trial, Mike McCowan would sit at the counsel table with the volatile Sirhan, trying to keep him under control. He'd also review the daily trial transcripts overnight and correct them in the morning with the judge and the prosecution, to make sure the court reporter's shorthand was accurate.[12]

By now, Sirhan had grown distant with Kaiser. "We had a pretty good relationship for the first few months and then, the trial came and he began to cool toward me," Kaiser recalled. "I'd go to see him and he'd be pretty close to the vest. He didn't want to tell me things as he was telling me before. I found out later that Russell Parsons, one of the other attorneys in the case, told Sirhan's mother, Mary Sirhan, not to trust Kaiser because he was telling the DA's office everything he knew, which is not true.

"But there was a struggle for power inside the defense team, and that was one of the results of it. Parsons was not in the loop, and I think he resented my having more information than he did . . . and so, maybe Sirhan got the word, you know, that I couldn't be trusted."[13]

* * *

On February 14, Emile Zola Berman delivered a short opening statement for the defense. "The evidence in this case will disclose that Sirhan is an immature, emotionally disturbed and mentally ill youth," he began.

He told the story of Sirhan's traumatic childhood in Palestine, that he was three years old when the war broke out and his street became the dividing line between the Jews and Arabs. "One night, the building he lived in became a machine-gun nest and another night, his very home was bombed.

"They lived with a great many uprooted, evicted Palestinian Arabs in a hungry, war-torn, violent existence. . . . He saw a little girl's leg blown off by a bomb . . . blood spurting from below her knee as though from a faucet. He went into a spell. He stiffened. His face became contorted. He lost all sense of where he was or what was happening to him. These severe reaction spells from the horrors of war occurred again and again.

"A bomb exploded when he was playing near the Damascus Gate. Sirhan went into a spell. Someone called his mother, who took him home, where he remained in a trance for four days. A bomb exploded outside the window of the Sirhan flat and tore apart the body of a man and again the spell—the boy stiffened, his fists clenched, his mouth contorted. He lost all sense of what was happening around him."

As Berman recalled the traumatic moments in Sirhan's childhood that prompted his disturbed mental condition, Sirhan became agitated. Beating on the defense table with his hands, he repeated over and over, "No, no, no," shaking his head and attempting to rise from his chair. Judge Walker asked McCowan to "calm him down," and McCowan pushed Sirhan back down again and they had a whispered squabble.

"Jesus Christ," whispered Russell Parsons, "calm down, for my sake. We gotta have some defense."

Berman described Sirhan's early life in America—his father abandoning the family within months and his failure to fit in at school, become a diplomat, make money at the races, or become a jockey. He told how Sirhan changed after the fall from the horse—"he became more and more irritable, brooding, quick to anger and preoccupied with fanatical obsessions of hatred, suspicion and distrust. He took to long hours of reading works on the power of the mind."

Berman introduced the notebooks, quoting Sirhan's "Declaration of War Against American Humanity" on June 2, 1967, as "clear evidence of diminished capacity." He said the outbreak of the Arab-Israeli War three days later again "triggered his spells."

"In his fantasies, he was often a hero and savior of his people. In the realities of life, he was small, helpless, isolated, confused and bewildered by emotions over which he had no control. He was unable to plan or think clearly, to maintain any meaningful direction in life.

"He became concerned with mystical thoughts and searched for supernatural powers of the mind over matter. He started mystical experiments in his room. He would concentrate on a hanging lead fishing sinker and make it swing back and forth by the power of his mind. He would concentrate on a candle flame and make it dance, first to the right and then to the left.

"But the mystical experiments gave him no peace of mind, only further bewilderment and confusion. Then came another heavy shock. . . . Senator Kennedy, whom he admired and loved, said that if he were President he would send fifty Phantom jets to Israel. That did it. Israel. Back to mysticism. He concentrated in front of a mirror in his room and thought about Senator Kennedy until at last, he saw his own face no longer, but that of Senator Kennedy himself in the mirror.

"Sirhan never thought he would ever kill Kennedy, but through his mystic mind power he could fantasize about it and relieve that feeling of emptiness inside him."

Then, "while in a disturbed mental state, intoxicated and confused, he had the same spells that he had in Palestine. There is no doubt, and we have told you this from the beginning, that he did in fact fire the shot that killed Senator Kennedy. The killing was unplanned and undeliberate, impulsive and without premeditation or malice, totally the product of a sick, obsessed mind and personality. At the actual moment of the shooting, he was out of contact with reality, in a trance in which he had no voluntary control over his will, his judgment, his feelings or his actions."

Berman promised that "the tests of great men in the fields of psychiatry and psychology conclusively show that because of mental illness and emotional disorder, Sirhan did not have the mental capacity to have the mental states that are the essential elements of murder: namely, maturely and meaningfully premeditate, deliberate or reflect upon the gravity of his act, nor form an intent to kill, nor to harbor malice aforethought, as these are defined by the laws of California."

Berman's speech got a good reception in the press. "It promises to be a bizarre trial," wrote George Lardner in the *Washington Post*. "Only the hashish seems to be missing."[14]

* * *

Over the next seven days of testimony, the prosecution put fifty-six witnesses on the stand. First, the LAPD's chief surveyor oriented the jury with a three-dimensional scale model of the first and second floors of the hotel. The pantry model featured miniature steam tables and an ice machine, but the nearby mirrors, which would become a key motif for the defense, were missing.

"When you get to the entrance to the Embassy Room, aren't there four floor-to-ceiling mirrors at these corners, so wherever you stand you can see yourself reflected in the mirrors?" asked Berman.

"I'm not sure, sir," replied Sergeant La Vallee, bemused by the line of questioning.

"Do you suggest that there are no mirrors?"

"They are not there on my drawing."

"But you don't suggest that those mirrors were not there on the day of this occurrence?"

"No, I don't say that," said the sergeant.[15]

* * *

The first fifteen witnesses described the shooting and the capture and arrest of Sirhan. First on the stand was Karl Uecker, closely followed by Eddie Minasian. On cross-examination by Cooper, Uecker was first asked to point out where the mirrors should be on the scale model—full-length mirrors along the east wall of the ballroom and mirrors on both sides of a foyer leading to the lobby. Besides mirrors, the defense also collected data on the height and weight of the men who tried to wrest the gun from Sirhan. Uecker was thirty-six, five-ten-and-a-half, and 190 pounds.

"Did he seem to be strong?" asked Cooper.

"He had very strong muscles because I was hitting the gun on top of the steam table very hard and I couldn't get rid of the gun," replied Uecker.

Later, Uecker discussed the sequence of shots.

"There were two or three shots fired before you grabbed his wrist, is that right, sir?" inquired Cooper.

"Yes, sir. Before I got hold of his wrist."

Cooper didn't ask about muzzle distance or bullet trajectories or even wonder aloud how Sirhan could fire four shots at Kennedy if Uecker grabbed him after two or three.[16]

* * *

The afternoon session got off to a shaky start when busboy Juan Romero was called to the stand. Howard asked him if anyone in the courtroom resembled the gunman. Romero looked around.

"I don't think so," he said.

"Stand up please, Mr. Sirhan," said Cooper. Sirhan rose.

"I don't believe that's him," said Romero.

Unperturbed, Parsons established that Romero was three feet from Kennedy when the shots began and that he heard four shots. Parsons also didn't ask about the muzzle distance or how Kennedy's body was positioned at the time of the first shot.[17]

* * *

And on it went. A procession of witnesses and an absurdly narrow focus for the defense—mirrors, Sirhan's abnormal strength, and impatience to get the witnesses out of the way, so Cooper could get on with the psychiatric testimony.

En route, there were exceptions. Cooper took Vincent Di Pierro to the cleaners, reading his postpolygraph surrender to Hernandez into the record and pointing up numerous contradictions in his testimony.

John Howard led off by asking Di Pierro to recount seeing Sirhan on the tray stand, while carefully avoiding any mention of a girl. Di Pierro placed himself less than a foot from Paul Schrade and five feet from Kennedy when "I saw the gun aimed toward the Senator and I saw the flash."

"How many shots did you hear?" asked Howard.

"After the first shot was fired it was a pause, then two rapidly fired, and that's . . . all I really heard, because then people started screaming and people started falling and Mr. Schrade fell into my arms."

Di Pierro said Sirhan had a "smirk or semi-smile" on his face and was "kind of crouching along," trying to push his way through to Kennedy. He pulled out the gun from his left side and fired.

"How close to the Senator was Mr. Sirhan when he produced the gun?"

"I would say within two feet to eight foot."

That was quite a range. Karl Uecker had ahold of the senator and was pulling him along. Sirhan then pushed Uecker with his left hand, "went around" him, came up with the gun, and fired.

"After the first shot was fired, [Kennedy's] head reared back and the blood from [his] head sprinkled on my face. . . . After the second shot . . . he made a sudden jerking motion and he let go of Karl's hand . . . and his hands started to go up as if to grab his head. . . . He started falling and then the third shot was fired and he hit the ground just prior to the third shot."

Uecker grabbed Sirhan around the neck and by the wrist "after the second or third shot." As Uecker threw him onto the steam table, the gun was still firing. Vincent heard another "seven . . . possibly eight" shots. "Everyone was trying to get him away from Karl and . . . really trying to kill him. It was just complete pandemonium."

Vincent thought Kennedy fell first, then "Mr. Schrade fell and I looked down at him, [then] Ira Goldstein fell on top of me."

This should have been a gold mine for a defense team with their wits about them. Di Pierro heard ten shots, but the murder weapon only held eight bullets. Kennedy hit the floor before the third, and Uecker grabbed Sirhan after the second or third, yet four shots hit the senator. Cooper told the judge that cross-examination would be somewhat lengthy, so court was adjourned until Monday.

When Cooper began his questioning, he didn't go near the ballistics but asked what caused Di Pierro to notice Sirhan on the tray stacker.

"At the time, there was, I believe, a girl standing within the area of Sirhan," said Vince. "It could have been at that time or possibly immediately after the shooting."

He first noticed the girl as he walked into the pantry because she was pretty. Then he wondered why the "dishwasher" (meaning Sirhan) was standing on the tray stand. The girl was wearing a polka-dot dress. He looked at her for "a matter of seconds," then shook hands with the senator and kept his eyes on the senator's head from then on.

"Did you see the girl talk to Mr. Sirhan at all?"

"Whether he conversed with her or whether he just looked at her, I could not say." It was a natural impulse to look at a pretty girl.

"In other words, he looked toward her?"

"For a split second."

"Did she look toward him?"

"I believe she did."

"Then what happened?"

"Then the Senator turned to me and I shook hands with him and I lost sight of her."

Cooper then skillfully questioned Vince based on what he said in his first police statement, taken in the chef's office less than an hour after the shooting. Forced to walk a fine line between contradicting his initial statement and sticking to his "corrected" story, Vince started to falter.

"Was she holding on to the trays?"

"No."

"Was she holding on to Sirhan?"

"No."

"Did she have a smile on her face?"

"Yes, I believe she did."

"She smiled at Sirhan?"

"Well, whether it was at him . . . I do not recall."

"Did he return the smile?"

"I believe he did."

She was in her early twenties, wore a dress with black polka dots, and had dark brown hair. Cooper then turned to the statement Vince gave Hernandez on July 1.

"Now, let me show me your statement because I want to clear that up and, frankly, I have no desire to embarrass you. . . ."

"I am going to make an objection as improper impeachment," cried Howard. The prosecution was worried, but the objection was overruled. Where was Cooper going with the girl in the polka-dot dress?

Cooper then read virtually the entire transcript of Hernandez's corrected interview with Di Pierro, then asked Vincent to explain it.

"As I said, she could have been standing in the area at the time, I do not recall. There was an enormous amount of confusion at the time, and by speaking to Miss Serrano I could possibly have interjected the fact that she was standing next to him, whether it was next to him or beside him, I do not really remember."

On redirect, a surprised Fitts asked, "Are you telling us in substance there was a girl standing next to Sirhan at or near the time of the shooting, sir?"

"Yes, sir."

"With a polka-dot dress?"

"Yes."

The girl Hernandez had claimed didn't exist was back in the pantry. Fitts took out some photos of Valerie Schulte and asked Di Pierro if he recognized her.

"Yes, I believe I saw her that night."

"Are you telling us this appears to be a picture of the girl you saw in the pantry at or near the time of the shooting?"

"Yes, but I believe she had darker hair than that."

"In any event, she seems to be pretty blond in the pictures, doesn't she?" said Fitts witheringly.

"Yes, she does."

"Other than the difference in the color of the hair that you noticed, does she seem to be the girl?"

"Yes, I would think she would be."

Cooper took the photos on recross-examination.

"Is that the dress she was wearing at the time?"

"As to the dress, I do not recall. I can say it was, but I'm not sure."

"You have described a dress with black polka dots, is that correct?"

"Yes."

He pointed to the color photos of Schulte's dress. "What color would you say that is?"

"They are yellow polka dots on a green background."

Cooper showed the photos to the jury, also pointing out that while now Di Pierro said he heard seven or eight shots, in his original police interview he said he heard "four distinct shots." "Isn't that true?"

"Yes."

"I have no further questions."

"Anything further, Mr. Fitts?"

"Nothing further of Mr. Di Pierro."[18]

* * *

So Cooper shredded Di Pierro, but to what purpose? Perhaps he was waiting for Valerie Schulte herself to testify the following morning. Schulte told Fitts she had walked into the pantry two people behind Kennedy, which would put her just behind Di Pierro. As the senator was shaking hands, she was pushed forward toward the ice machine by people coming in behind her.

"I noticed an arm extended with a gun and heard and observed the shots," she said.

"Was your attention on the Senator where he was shaking hands?"

"I turned and I spotted the Senator and immediately switched to the arm again."

"Where did you see the arm of the gun, please?"

"Approximately five yards from me, approximately three yards, something like that, from the Senator. . . . It was pointed at the Senator's head."

"What did you see then?" asked Fitts.

"I observed the shots and I either fell or was pushed . . . to the floor."

She heard two shots, then fell to the floor, pointed back toward the Embassy Ballroom. Head down and crutch in hand, she crawled back the way she had come as the shots continued, past Paul Schrade, and behind a partition.

She stayed on the floor for a while; then a friend picked her up and stayed with her right in front of the dish rack.

She did not see Sirhan before the shooting, but as he fired, she could see him "from his shoulders up." She showed the jury the green dress with yellow polka dots she was wearing that night.

* * *

Cooper began his cross-examination by asking, "Obviously, Miss Schulte, you never knew Mr. Sirhan before that evening?"

"No, sir."

"I have no further questions. Thank you very much."

* * *

That was it—astonishing. Cooper obviously didn't want to find a girl with Sirhan and was happy to allow the obvious police fudge to stand. But Schulte said Sirhan was three yards—*nine feet*—from Kennedy when she saw him. She was closer to Kennedy than Sirhan was, and Cooper didn't question it. What was more extraordinary, none of the press did either, missing out on the muzzle distance and the absurd concoction regarding the girl. The reaction to Schulte's testimony perfectly illustrates what a shambles this trial was.[19]

* * *

After this debacle, the prosecution shifted swiftly through the gears in presenting a fairly straightforward case. Thirteen witnesses established premeditation—the purchase of ammunition, Sirhan's firing at the ranges, and his presence in the pantry area prior to the shooting.[20]

Judy Royer told of chasing Sirhan out of the kitchen, and Jesus Perez and Martin Patrusky both said Sirhan asked them half an hour before the shooting if Kennedy would be coming that way. As Kaiser recalls, Sirhan was upset. He leaned over to McCowan and whispered that he hadn't said any such thing. McCowan reminded him that he couldn't remember what he'd done in those moments before the shooting. Sirhan nodded and gulped.[21]

* * *

Alvin Clark was less convincing as a witness. Clark said he had worked for ten years for the City of Pasadena Sanitation Department. He had collected trash in Sirhan's neighborhood every Wednesday for the last three years and had become friends with "Sol," as he called him.

Shortly after Martin Luther King, Jr., was assassinated, Sirhan asked Clark how Negro people felt about it and what they were going to do about it. Then talk turned to the upcoming California primary, and Clark said he was going to vote for Kennedy.

"What do you want to vote for that son-of-a-b for? Because I'm planning on shooting him," Sirhan allegedly said.

"Well, you'll be killing one of the best men in the country," replied Clark.

On cross-examination, Berman established that Sirhan used to come out and bring Clark coffee, soft drinks, and sometimes sandwiches when he came by on Wednesdays. Clark said he thought "very much of him."

"Now, do you remember being examined by the FBI in September, 1968?" asked Berman.

"I do, sir."

"Weren't you asked whether you'd be willing to testify?"

"Well, I didn't want to testify."

Clark actually called the police to complain he was being harassed.

"And did you [say] you would not want to take the oath because you hated Sirhan so much that you would do anything to see him convicted?"

"Yes, I did."

"I have nothing else," said Berman.

Berman could also have cited Clark's prior arrests for burglary and child molesting, information the prosecution had but chose to suppress.

* * *

Sirhan later remembered many conversations with Alvin Clark but no specific details—"mostly that was just plain, if I may use the word, B.S." He was absolutely sure he had never told Clark he was going to kill Kennedy.[22]

* * *

Officer Arthur Placencia then recounted the trip to Rampart with Sirhan: He asked Sirhan his name several times but got no reply. He read him his rights, then asked Jesse Unruh, "Who did he shoot?"

"Bob Kennedy," replied Unruh.

This was the only time Kennedy's name was mentioned in Sirhan's presence from the time of his arrest until the arraignment. Sirhan later said he remembered Placencia grabbing him by the hair and shining a flashlight in his eyes. Did he hear Unruh say "Bob Kennedy"? He didn't remember.

Placencia had been with the force a year and two months and had graduated from the police academy three weeks before the shooting. On cross-examination, Cooper asked him, "Why should you examine a defendant's eyes?"

"To check for pupil reaction," said Placencia. "Pupil reaction [to light] usually can give you an idea to see if anybody that you have in custody might be under the influence of a drug or alcohol."

Placencia had arrested six or seven people who were under the influence of alcohol and performed the same test on Sirhan. He shone his flashlight in his face to examine his eyes.

"And how did his pupils react to the light?" asked Cooper.

"I can't recall," said Placencia.

Cooper read back a statement Placencia gave Mike McCowan on September 13:

"How did you check his pupils?" asked McCowan.

"With the flashlight. Put it up to his face and sort of looked to see if his pupils react," said Placencia.

"How did they react?" asked McCowan.

"They didn't."

"They didn't react to the light at all?"

"No. His pupils were real wide."

This helped refresh Placencia's recollection.

"In other words, his pupils did not react to the light, did they?" asked Cooper.

"No, sir," replied Placencia.

"Now, what did that mean to you as an officer?"

"That he was under the influence of something."[23]

* * *

John Howard argued that Placencia wasn't qualified to give the test, and two days later, Placencia's more experienced partner, Travis White, testified that Sirhan's eyes were normal when he checked them later at the station. But once again, the defense noted discrepancies between White's testimony in court and what he'd told McCowan back in September. The fact remains: Sirhan was never properly tested for drugs or alcohol.[24]

* * *

The chain of possession for the gun was established from clerk James Pineda, who first sold it to George Erhard, through to Sergeant Robert Calkins, who received it from Rafer Johnson. The victims of the shooting were called to describe their injuries, and doctors described how they had treated the senator.[25]

Then, on February 24, DeWayne A. Wolfer was called to the stand. He gave substantially the same testimony as he had to the grand jury but could now add his conclusions on muzzle distance after examining Kennedy's suit coat and test-firing into the hogs' ears.

In the absence of Sirhan and without his knowledge or consent, Grant Cooper had agreed to stipulate to the ballistics evidence during a meeting in Judge Walker's chambers before Wolfer even took the stand. The defense didn't bother to hire a ballistics expert, so Wolfer's at times garbled responses were outgarbled by Cooper's often pointless questioning.[26]

Cooper began by objecting to a photograph of the fatal bullet fragment and two photographs of the powder burns on Kennedy's ear as "highly inflammatory."

"We will stipulate that there was powder tattooing on the ear," he said, "[and] that the gun was held as close as the witness wants to testify it was held. I realize the prosecution has a right to prove its case; at the same time . . . with respect to this bullet fragment, it looks like a bullet from an exceptionally large revolver."

It was an enlarged photograph, explained Fitts, witheringly.

"We will stipulate that these fragments did come from Senator Kennedy," continued Cooper. "We will further stipulate that they came from the gun."

Wolfer was given carte blanche. All Cooper wanted to do was exclude the photographs from evidence, "having in mind the Kennedy family."

* * *

Fitts argued that "your Honor has heard Karl Uecker and any number of witnesses who attempted to describe what happened. One witness has put the muzzle of the revolver some three or four feet from the Senator's head, others have had it at varying ranges. The only way we can clear up whatever ambiguity there may be there and to show the truth is by the testimony of this witness who, on the basis of the powder tattooing and the experiments he performed with respect thereto, will testify that the muzzle range with respect to the Senator's head was approximately one inch."

This assumed there was only one gun and that all the witnesses had somehow seen it much farther away than it actually was.

"We don't quarrel that it was held within one inch," piped Cooper. "But I don't feel it's necessary to illustrate it."

Keeping the photos from the jury was more important to Cooper than witness discrepancies. The court overruled him anyway, and the photos were introduced.

Cooper then stipulated to the rest of the bullets and bullet fragments.

"Your Honor, I think this stipulation will save a couple days' testimony," said Fitts.

"Undoubtedly," said the judge, making serious presumptions about the integrity of the evidence bullets. These would be the subject of much controversy later on.

Wolfer then described firing the murder weapon into a water tank, to generate test bullets for comparison with the victim bullets, and Fitts presented an evidence envelope.

"If the Court please, I have an envelope which contains, and I can't read the writing and it is about time I got glasses, but I have not done it yet."

"Do you want to borrow mine?" asked Cooper.

"I would rather use the eyes of Mr. Wolfer," said Fitts, marking People's 55, an envelope containing three test shots from People's 6 (the "Sirhan gun"), which Wolfer had used "for comparison purposes."

The envelope was dated June 6 and bore the serial number of a different gun, H-18602—the test gun Wolfer had used for the powder-pattern tests on the hogs' ears. The serial number of the Sirhan gun, H-53725, was not read into the record at either the grand jury hearing or the trial, but nobody noticed the error. Having introduced test bullets from the wrong gun into evidence, "the eyes of Mr. Wolfer" proceeded to match them to Sirhan's gun, testifying that the three victim bullets suitable for comparison—Kennedy, Goldstein, and Weisel—could all be matched to the Sirhan gun, to the exclusion of every other gun. But again, no one was paying attention.[27]

* * *

Kennedy's suit coat was then introduced into evidence. Bullet holes had been found in the right sleeve but the entire left sleeve was missing. Fitts explained that during the senator's treatment at Central Receiving Hospital, parts of the coat had been removed with scissors.

"And it accounts for the absence of one sleeve?" asked the judge.

"I should certainly suppose so," guessed Fitts. "I would have thought it would have had a sleeve at the time it was worn."

"The only point is that, obviously, it wasn't done by the defendant," said Cooper.

"I will stipulate he didn't cut up the coat," replied Fitts, turning back to Wolfer. "Did you find bullet holes in the coat?"

Amid this nonsensical repartee, nobody stopped to ask if the missing left sleeve might have contained more bullet holes. It was cut off at Central Receiving and never subsequently recovered by the police.[28]

* * *

Cooper began his cross-examination by deferring to Wolfer's schedule.

"Officer Wolfer, let me ask what time you are leaving?"

"When we get through. Then I will go over and make my reservations for the first flight I can get on."

He was dashing off to a firearms convention.

"We won't keep you," said Cooper, as if Wolfer's travel plans were more important than his questioning.

Cooper started brightly by giving Wolfer a hard time for using a different gun—not the murder weapon—for the test-firing into the hogs' ears. Wolfer, defying industry practice, said it was not necessary to use the same gun for powder-pattern tests. Would he have preferred to use the Sirhan gun?

"No, I don't believe I would . . . we did not make that exacting of a determination." He was allowing for an inch variation here or there; it wasn't that important. Wolfer estimated the muzzle distance at one inch.

"Now, also, sir," said Cooper, "there has been testimony by eyewitnesses of varying distances from the Senator's person, who actually say they saw it. This is your opinion, is that right?"

"It is my opinion based upon the scientific evidence, which we have to base it upon."

This tortured question was Cooper's only comment in the whole trial on the discrepancies between the muzzle distance described by Wolfer and Dr. Noguchi and the muzzle distance described by witnesses.

Cooper proceeded to go over and over the tests with the hogs' ears and whether the muzzle was three-quarters of an inch or an inch away but never related the findings back to what the witnesses testified they saw. He finally alighted on the test gun used for the powder-pattern tests.

"You say it wasn't possible to use the revolver that was in evidence?"

The DA's office had told Wolfer the Sirhan gun "wasn't available. "I was told that the gun would not be released for any further tests until they had a Court order approved by different counsel as such and there was never any time that they could get it approved. That was my understanding."

Is the test gun still available? asked Cooper.

"Yes, the revolver is still available."

Wolfer could easily have obtained a court order to use the Sirhan gun for the powder-pattern tests, preventing any possible inaccuracies. This test gun would become a hot item when the ballistics in the case were reexamined.

Cooper finished with the following bewildering exchange.

"Let me ask you this . . . a weapon like this can cause death, and it did cause death, is that true?"

"That is correct."

"And it can cause death from one inch, two inches . . . three feet, five feet, six feet and what are the outermost limits?"

"[With Mini-Mags], I would estimate about half a mile would be the maximum," replied Wolfer.

What on earth was Cooper blathering on about? He had established, for reasons best known to himself, that the murder weapon could kill from a distance of one inch to half a mile, but steadfastly ignored witnesses who could testify that Sirhan never got close enough to fire at the muzzle distance scientifically determined by Noguchi and Wolfer. It was a truly dreadful performance.[29]

* * *

Later in the afternoon, Sergeant William Brandt took the stand and admitted he had searched the Sirhan house and confiscated the notebooks without a warrant.

Brandt said Adel Sirhan had consented to the search. The judge overruled defense objections and was about to admit the notebooks into evidence when Sirhan blew up in court and a recess was called. Defendant and judge adjourned to chambers.

"Mr. Sirhan, will you put out your cigarette, please? Court is in session," chided Cooper.

"Your Honor, if these notebooks are allowed into evidence," said Sirhan, "I will change my plea to guilty as charged. I will do so, sir, not so much that I want to be railroaded into that gas chamber, sir, but to deny you the pleasure, sir, of after convicting me turning around and telling the world: 'Well, I put that fellow in the gas chamber, but I first gave him a fair trial,' when you in fact, sir, will not have done so.

"The evidence, sir, that was taken from my home was illegally obtained, was stolen by the District Attorney's people. They had no search warrant. I did not give them any permission, sir, to do what they did to my home. My brother Adel had no permission to give them permission to enter my own room and take what they took from my home. . . . I am adamant on this point."[30]

Cooper took Sirhan away for a few minutes to calm him down. When he came back into chambers, Judge Walker assured Sirhan that while he had admitted the notebooks into evidence, "if there is an error, the upper court can reverse this case. You have got three counsel and . . . they are running the lawsuit to your very best interest and there is no question in the Court's mind about that. . . . You are not going to go to the gas chamber unless that is the determination of the jury and I have an opportunity to set it aside if it is warranted. . . . Guide yourself by your attorneys. They are excellent, conscientious attorneys. They are doing an excellent job."

"I understand that," said Sirhan.

"Let's go to work."

* * *

After the pep talk, Officer Young of the Pasadena Police Department described how he found an Argonaut Insurance envelope in the trash while guarding the Sirhan house the day after the shooting. On the back of the envelope was more repetitive doodling in pencil:

> *"RFK must be be be disposed of d d d disposed disposed d of disposed disposed of properly Robert Fitzgerald Kennedy must soon die die die die die die die die die die."*[31]

Prosecution handwriting expert Laurence Sloan testified that most of the pages in the notebooks were written by Sirhan, but after lunch, as Fitts began reading the notebooks to the jury, Sirhan flipped out again and another recess was called.

"We are having a repetition of what we had this morning," Cooper told the judge. "He is insisting on pleading guilty, which would be against the advice of all counsel." Sirhan was demanding the gas chamber rather than sit there and hear his notebooks read to the jury. His mother was dispatched to the holding tank to try to calm him down, and they both emerged in tears ten minutes later. "They are throwing even the trash at him," she said.[32]

* * *

The next morning, Parsons showed Sirhan the proposed witness list for the defense, and he was incensed, scratching off a dozen names he didn't want called. Cooper and McCowan went up to see him at lunchtime to try to explain why they wanted to call certain witnesses, but Sirhan wouldn't budge.

"If we can't call the witnesses we want, we'll have to withdraw from the case," warned Cooper.

"If that's the way it is, that's the way it is," said Sirhan.

He told McCowan he wouldn't testify if these witnesses were called.

Cooper told the judge that he would normally ask to be relieved from the case, but "believing as I do that he has diminished capacity—not that he's insane—I don't think he's in a position to exercise judgment and therefore I owe him a duty . . . but I have got to have some control over him. I don't want him blowing up in courtroom and ruining my case."[33]

* * *

On February 26, after nine days of testimony, the prosecution wrapped up its case with Dr. Noguchi. As he began his explanation of the autopsy, Cooper interrupted.

"Pardon me, your Honor. Is all of this detail really necessary? I think the witness can express an opinion that death was due to a gunshot wound but these details . . ."

"Counsel doesn't suggest we are limited to asking one question?" asked "Buck" Compton.

"Maybe you can omit some of these details without damaging the value of the doctor's testimony?" suggested the judge.

In Dr. Noguchi's opinion, the cause of death was a gunshot wound to the right mastoid, penetrating the brain, and the gun was "one inch to one and a half inches from the edge [of the right ear]; and this takes it about two inches away from the skin of the right mastoid, sir."

Noguchi found unburned gunpowder embedded deep in the subcutaneous tissue of both entry wounds under the armpit, suggesting that these shots were fired "at very close range . . . we are talking about either contact or a half-inch or one inch in distance."

"Did you measure the height of Senator Kennedy?" asked Compton.

"Yes, sir."

"How tall is he?"

"Your Honor please, how tall he was, I object to it as I don't think it is material," said Cooper.

"I believe it is in view of certain angles and things," said Compton.

Cooper was quick to overlook such details as bullet trajectories.

"Well, I will withdraw the objection," he said sheepishly.

"Kennedy was five foot, ten and a half," replied Dr. Noguchi.[34]

* * *

Probing the wounds and assuming the senator was in an upright position, Dr. Noguchi found the direction of the fatal shot (wound 1) and the through-and-through wound (wound 2) to be back to front and upward at angles of fifteen and thirty-five degrees, respectively. The "slightly deformed" Kennedy "neck bullet" entered one inch below wound 2 and traveled slightly backward and up at an angle of thirty degrees.

Kennedy's arm was raised nearly ninety degrees for the armpit shots. Noguchi raised his right arm to demonstrate wound 2, holding his hand "about the level of his shoulder and extended forward from his body." For wound 3, the shoulder was raised a little higher and the elbow was drawn back to a point even with his shoulder.

"If it were a watch, it would be a quarter to twelve," said Cooper.

From Noguchi's examination of the wounds and clothing, "although there were different directions of the gunshot-wounds," the overall pattern was right to left and upward, consistent with a rapid succession of shots.

As before, the issue of muzzle distance went unchallenged by the defense. The prosecution then rested its case and, despite Sirhan's vehement objections, the jury was given copies of his notebooks.[35]

* * *

The next day, LAPD investigators met with Fitts and Howard to review a job well done: "Prosecution witnesses testified as expected. Each witness was briefed as to what would take place in court. Each familiarized himself with his original statement made during the investigation. As a result, the witnesses listened, kept their answers short and did not volunteer information to questions."[36]

For the defense, however, Cooper's muddled, bungling performance was merely a taste of things to come.

TWELVE

THE CASE FOR THE DEFENSE

The defense began its case on February 28 and called two witnesses to testify to the bombings, shootings, and killings Sirhan had experienced in the war-torn Jerusalem of his childhood—experiences, the defense contended, that created a twisted mind, diminishing Sirhan's capacity to premeditate murder.

Sirhan was still edgy about the witness list. At first he agreed to cooperate, but as court resumed after lunch, he again forbade his attorneys from calling a dozen different witnesses.

During the afternoon session, John Harris of the Pasadena School District testified about Sirhan's grades at high school. They were slightly above average, but according to one test, Sirhan's IQ was a slightly below-average 89, and at age seventeen, he had had a mental age of fifteen and two months. After a few minutes more of this testimony, Sirhan flipped out again.

He stood up and asked to be allowed to address the court. Judge Walker dismissed the jury and Sirhan came right out with it.

"I, at this time, sir, withdraw my original plea of not guilty and submit the plea of guilty as charged on all counts. I also request that my counsel dissociate themselves from this case completely."

He was boiling.

"Do I understand that you want to plead guilty to murder in the first degree?" asked the court.

"Yes, sir, I do. I will offer no defense whatsoever."

"All right, and what do you want to do about the penalty?"

"I will ask to be executed, sir," replied Sirhan.

"Now, I know nothing in the law that permits a defendant under any circumstances to enter a plea of guilty to murder in the first degree and ask for execution," said the judge.

"Well, I have, sir."

"Well, now, just a minute. Why do you want to do this?"

"I believe, sir, that is my business, isn't it?"

"No, it isn't. When we come to accepting a plea, you have to give me a reason."

"I killed Robert Kennedy willfully, premeditatively, with twenty years of malice aforethought. That is why," said Sirhan.

Judge Walker called him on his statement. "Well, the evidence has to be produced here in court."

"I withdraw all evidence, sir."

"There is no such procedure."

"To hell with it."

"Well, the Court will not accept the plea. Proceed with the trial."

Walker had had enough of Sirhan's tantrums and told him to sit down and follow the advice of his counsel.

"Any further interruptions will result in you being restrained . . . you will have a face mask put on you which will prohibit you from talking and your arms will be strapped to your chair and the trial will proceed."

"I understand," said Sirhan. "However, sir, I intend to defend myself pro per"—by himself.

"You have retained counsel. Counsel is staying in the trial."

"You are not going to shove a trial down my throat, sir, in any way you want."

"You say you want to go pro per?"

"Yes, I will."

"What are the defenses to murder in the first degree?" asked the judge.

"Sir, I don't know. I don't understand all of this legality."

"I find you are incapable of representing yourself. Sit down and keep quiet, and, if not, I intend to keep you quiet."

* * *

Judge Walker called afternoon recess, and Sirhan went into the holding tank, dragging furiously on a cigarette. The testimony about his IQ of 89 wasn't what prompted his outburst.

"I told you not to bring those two girls in here," he screamed.

Bob Kaiser didn't know what he was talking about. Which girls?

"Those two girls sitting next to you. As if you didn't know! One of them is Gwen Gumm and the other is Peggy Osterkamp."

These were the girls Sirhan had had a crush on and whom he wrote about in his notebook. But the girls in court were Sharon, an LAPD typist, and Karen, a beautician from Ohio. Sirhan shook his head—his lawyers were trying to trick him. Adel and Mary Sirhan tried to talk to him in the tank, but he wouldn't back down, so Cooper made a motion to withdraw from the case, citing, with a poor choice of words, "a very violent difference of opinion as to how the defense should be conducted."

Judge Walker denied the motion and ordered the trial to proceed.

"I don't want it misunderstood that we are deserting him, your Honor," said Cooper. "I just wanted to make our position clear to him."

"Well, I appreciate your position," said the judge. "I think you have prepared a good defense, if not the only logical defense that could be presented."[1]

* * *

That Sunday, Ambassador Issa Nahkleh of the Palestinian Arab delegation to the UN visited Sirhan in jail and brokered a compromise with the defense team. If the two girls he objected to weren't called, Sirhan would agree to the other witnesses. Before Nahkleh left, Dr. Diamond did a little hypnotic demonstration for the ambassador. He put Sirhan under and soon had him wailing and groaning about the war in the Middle East. This upset Nahkleh so much, he asked Diamond to bring Sirhan out of the hypnotic state immediately. Before he did, Diamond suggested to Sirhan that when he woke up, he sing an Arab song when Diamond took a handkerchief out of his pocket.

The sound of Sirhan's favorite Egyptian singer, Umm Kulthum, was soon filling the room. Diamond was still convinced that Sirhan had been in a trance when he shot Bobby Kennedy, but Cooper wasn't interested in fantastic theories. Mental illness and political paranoia were enough.[2]

* * *

Mary and Adel Sirhan testified on Monday morning, and after the recess on Monday afternoon, Sirhan began just over three days of testimony. Cooper led him through the charges.

"Did you on or about that date of June 5, 1968, shoot Senator Kennedy?"

"Yes, sir."

"Did you shoot Paul Schrade?"

"That is what the indictment reads. I must have."

"Were you aware of the fact that you shot Mr. Schrade?"

"I was not aware of anything."

And so it went with the rest of the victims. If the indictment said he shot them, he must have shot them, but he bore them no ill will and had never heard of them. Sirhan admitted to Cooper that the writing in the notebooks was his even if he couldn't remember writing it.

Cooper led him, step by step, through the traumas of his childhood in Palestine, coming to America, his upbringing in Pasadena, his failure as a jockey, and the months and days leading up to the shooting at the Ambassador.

Sirhan shared his earliest childhood memories: a "dismembered soldier with his body exploded"; walking around the casket of his dead brother, Munir; the panicked move, naked, to the Old City when war broke out; a local grocer blown to bits; bringing a bucket to the well and drawing up water to find a dismembered hand in the bucket, cut off at the wrist; hiding in the basement during bombings; and his mother stuffing cotton in his ears.

When he was eleven, Sirhan and some other kids were invited up to a military outpost where Arab soldiers overlooked the Jewish section with binoculars. "I could see, sir, the emotions . . . of the soldiers. [One] was looking out there and he said, 'This is our land out there, that is our country, our property,' sir. I couldn't really understand but now I do."

Sirhan then gave a very scholarly dissertation on the origin of the Palestine problem, from the birth of Zionism up through the first Arab-Israeli War. His erudition startled the press and belied his supposed IQ of 89.

* * *

"What were your feelings toward John Kennedy?" asked Cooper.

"I loved him, sir," said Sirhan, "because just weeks before his assassination he was working, sir, with the leaders of the Arab countries to bring a solution, sir, to the Palestine refugee problem, and he promised these Arab leaders that he would do his utmost to force or to put some pressure on Israel, sir, to comply with the 1948 United Nations Resolution, sir; to either repatriate those Arab refugees or . . . give them the right to return to their homes. And when he was killed, sir, that never happened."

* * *

After Cooper's questioning of Sirhan on the notebooks and the days leading up to the shooting, Sirhan was cross-examined by chief prosecutor Lynn Compton.

"Mr. Sirhan, are you nervous now, as you sit there on the witness stand?" began Compton.

"A little bit, yes."

"I notice you drink considerable water. Are you thirsty as a result of this nervousness?"

"No, sir, not really. It's something to do."

Compton proceeded to zero in on some of the key issues at hand. Sirhan told him he could clearly remember the bombing in his former homeland.

"You don't have any recollection of any incident where you blacked out, so to speak?" asked Compton.

"No, sir, I don't remember any actual blacking out, sir," said Sirhan. "I remember being nervous, being sick about it, yes. Being afraid, frightened—I was. Very much so."

"As a matter of fact, except for this night at the Ambassador Hotel, you have never had any experience where you couldn't remember the things that you have done?"

"No, sir. There are some things I couldn't remember. I don't remember those notebooks, sir . . . when I fell from that horse, sir, the same thing, sir."

Sirhan said he naturally had a great interest as an Arab in solving the problems of the Middle East. He wanted to be a diplomat to find a peaceful solution but admitted "a very intense hatred for the Zionists."

"And I assume this hatred would apply to anybody who appeared to be aiding the cause of the Zionists?"

"Yes, sir. I hold to the Arab proverb, 'The friend of my enemy is my enemy.'"

* * *

Compton turned to Sirhan's notebook and his "Declaration of War against America," dated June 2, 1967. "When did you develop that hatred of the United States as a country?"

"I never did have any hatred, as such, for the United States. I am most grateful, sir, to the United States for having lived here for the second half of my life. Although, from June, 1967 on, sir, I was very resentful towards the United States for their foreign policy, sir, in the Middle East; for their one-sided support, sir, for Israel against the Arab people."

"So you are telling us that never in your whole lifetime up to now that you had any hate for the United States Government or its policies?"

"No, sir, because government in school, sir, was my favorite subject. I had A's in some of those subjects. I loved the United States Government, the elections, checks and balances, Congress."

"Yet you don't deny that at some point in your career you felt very strongly about the overthrow of the United States Government?"

"As I said . . . when I wrote it down and only at that time, sir. I don't remember entertaining it after or before. I don't remember that itself right then." Sirhan talked of "dirty politics" in American elections, how when Harry Truman ran against Dewey in 1948, he asked, "Do the Arabs have any votes in the American Presidential elections?" implying that only the Jews could vote, so he would support Israel in the Middle East.[3]

Compton asked about his fondness for Senator Kennedy.

"I had always associated him with President Kennedy," said Sirhan, "and I was hoping he would become President and continue what his brother started, sir. . . . I was for him, very much so. . . . I still loved him but when he came out with this support for the State of Israel and when he said he would give fifty Phantom Jet bombers . . . that is enough cause for me, sir, to hate him."

"Enough to kill him?" asked Compton.

"I don't know about that, sir," said Sirhan.

"Well, didn't you tell us that if you had him right there you would have blasted him?"

"At the time he came out and said he would send those fifty jet bombers I would have done that. . . . I am a very impulsive person." He snapped his fingers. "Whatever my objective would be, it is just good for that time only." He snapped them again.

* * *

Compton moved on to May 18. Sirhan was sure he wrote "RFK must die" in his notebook when "extremely provoked." Was it after the TV show?

"Sir, again, I don't remember what the exact provocation was. I have heard so many instances where Robert Kennedy was going to give those Phantom Jets to Israel. When he was in Oregon, sir, he came out again and spoke of sending those jet bombers to Israel."

"Well, you followed him pretty closely, didn't you in his campaign as to where he went and what he said?" suggested Compton.

"No, sir, I didn't. I was always certain that the stuff would come to me. I didn't go to it, sir."

Compton argued that the words "becoming more of an unshakeable obsession" indicated that he had been thinking of eliminating Kennedy for some time. "You wrote that the minute that you saw that television show?"

"Yes. I'm a very impulsive person. I thought to fight the minute when I saw that television program at home. I felt he had betrayed me and he was for Israel in 1948. . . . I was mad. I was burned up."

"As a matter of fact, you told us that if he had been right there you would have blasted him?"

"Yes. . . . Whatever I had written in there was good as long as it was being written . . . as long as my emotions were charged up."

"But the minute you finished writing, you forgot about it?"

"As long as the provocation is withdrawn, sir, I don't respond to it."

* * *

Sirhan explained that his hatred for Kennedy wasn't continuous from May 18 to June 2—"I would have had to have been provoked to sustain this feeling." But his hatred for Zionists was there all the time. "Sir, I have a built-in bug in this brain of mine against the Jews and the Zionists, sir, and Israel; anything, sir, involving them turns me on." He gave another snap of his fingers.[4]

* * *

Compton turned to Sirhan's interest in mysticism.

"When you read these books about how to improve your mind . . . you didn't really expect to acquire some supernatural power, did you?"

"You're wrong, sir. I did. . . . The Bible says if you have as much faith as a drop of mustard, you can move mountains, sir. I believe that, sir. It has been proven to me, sir."

"So when you wrote down in your notebook 'Kennedy must die . . .' you were following the Rosicrucian idea that if you write things down and think about them hard enough they will happen, right?"

"Yes, sir. I was thinking about that exactly at the time I was writing it."

"Did you think that they would occur by some other force or that it would help you accomplish the goal?"

"That you would be helped by some force," replied Sirhan.

"Without you having to actually do it yourself?"

"I don't know, sir. I'm not that well versed in it. . . . I only read what they tell me and I do the exercises as told, sir."

"Was it going to happen by somebody else or was it going to help you do it?" asked Compton, probing possible conspiracy.

"I don't know, sir . . . the way I felt at the time, sir, it might as well have been me."

* * *

Compton said the notebook contained many things Sirhan was interested in—names of race horses, girls, little songs, poems, jockey's names, racing terms like "tell them to put blinkers on the son-of-a-bitch."

Sirhan admitted they were his notebooks, in his handwriting, bought when he was at Pasadena City College (PCC). But he couldn't remember the last time he saw them in his room or wrote in them.

"Well, do you ever remember looking in the notebook at things you had previously written out?" asked Compton.

"Again, sir, I don't remember."

"You don't remember ever going through that and saying, 'Here is something I wrote down, that Kennedy has got to be assassinated, and I don't know why I wrote that?'"

"No, sir, I never have."[5]

* * *

Compton asked Sirhan if he remembered actually signing his name at the Corona gun range on June 1.

"You're asking me to remember when I wrote my name, sir, is the same as asking me to remember every bullet that I put in that chamber. That's stupid."

"I confess at times I do ask stupid questions." "Yes, sir, you do," said Sirhan.

* * *

Sirhan denied he was shooting rapid-fire in San Gabriel on Election Day, contrary to what the other witnesses said. He must have fired six or seven hundred rounds that day—"I fired a hell of a lot of holes." He normally used up all his ammunition, and he stayed later than usual that day; even so, time was called before he could fire the last few bullets.

Sirhan didn't normally drink, so Compton asked him about going back to his car after drinking at the Ambassador. "When you began to feel high . . . what sort of symptoms did you experience?"

"I wasn't myself, sir. I wasn't the same Sirhan that came into the Ambassador that night."

"Did you feel dizzy?"

"I was like this, sir." He made a weaving motion with his hands. He didn't have trouble standing, but "I was so glad to have gotten that coffee, that was the only thing on my mind, sir."

Compton asked about the girl. "She was a pretty girl?"

"Sir, you could have had the ugliest gal in the place there and the way I was drunk or my mind wasn't with me, sir, you could have said she was the most beautiful, and I would have no way of disputing it."

"The last thing you remember is standing by this coffee urn talking to this girl?"

"Yes, sir. I gave her my cup and I was telling her how happy I was to get this coffee . . . she wanted the coffee as badly as I did."

"The next thing you know you are being choked?"

"Yes, sir."

"And you told us this morning that you remember an officer grabbing you by the hair and pulling your head back."

"I didn't know it was an officer, sir, but when I was in that car this guy yanked my head back and had some light in my eyes."

"You told us about kicking a cup out of the hands of an officer there."

"I didn't know he was an officer, sir."

"Do you remember Officer Jordan going through your property with you?"

"The only thing that I remember about Jordan, sir, is when I was with him in that little room and we were talking about the coffee and when Mr. Howard was there. . . . He looked monstrous to me at the time."

"Were you still feeling kind of woozy?"

"I was tired, sir. I wasn't myself."

"You didn't think you had done anything at that time, did you?"

"No, sir, I didn't," said Sirhan.

"Everybody was very friendly?"

"They were extremely friendly . . . so friendly, sir, that I didn't know what was going on."

"But you never were curious about why you were handcuffed or why you were in the police station?"

"No, sir, I wasn't myself, sir. I didn't know what was going on."

"Because you were still suffering from the effects of liquor?"

"I don't know from the effects of what, sir. I was not myself, sir, as I am now."[6]

* * *

On Thursday afternoon, Compton completed his cross-examination.

"You told us earlier this morning that you were willing to fight for the Arab cause, right?"

"Yes, sir. The Palestinian Arab cause."

"And do you think that the killing of Senator Robert Kennedy helped the Arab cause?"

"Sir. I'm not even aware that I killed Mr. Kennedy. . . . I'm in no position to explain that."

"There's no question in your mind that you did it?"

"All this evidence has proved it. Your evidence," said Sirhan.

"Are you glad he is dead?"

"No, sir, I'm not glad."

"Are you sorry?"

"I'm not sorry, but I'm not proud of it, either."

"But you are not sorry?" asked Compton.

"No, sir, because I have no exact knowledge, sir, of having shot him."

"Well, the other day right here in this courtroom did you not say: 'I killed Robert Kennedy willfully, premeditatively, with twenty years of malice afore-thought'—did you say that?"

"Yes, I did, sir."

"Are you willing to fight for the Arab cause?" "I'm willing to fight for it."

"Are you willing to die for it?"

"I'm willing to die for it."

* * *

This "twenty years of malice aforethought" was a low blow, and came to be used often over the years by those who wanted to reduce the complexities of the case to a sound bite damning the lone Arab madman. On redirect, Cooper asked Sirhan if he remembered making this statement the previous Friday, in the absence of the jury.

"Yes," said Sirhan.

"And twenty years ago, how old were you?"

"Four years old."

"And at that time did you entertain any malice against Senator Kennedy?"

"I didn't even know what malice was, sir."

* * *

Cooper read Friday's lengthy exchange into the record, and described the circum-stances in which Sirhan made his absurd statement in midtantrum, after he was asked to give a reason for his sudden guilty plea.

"Did you have counsel's permission to do that?"

"You were fired as far as I was concerned," replied Sirhan.

* * *

"Are you mad at your lawyers today?"

"No, sir, I am not."

"Are you satisfied with your lawyers?"

"Very much so."

"After that flare-up . . . did Mr. Parsons take your mother upstairs?" "No, in the tank."

"And she told you to behave yourself."

"You all did, sir."

Sirhan was excused as a witness.[7]

* * *

On, Friday, March 7, thirteen witnesses testified for the defense on Sirhan's background, the fall from the horse, and events at the Ambassador Hotel. Later in the trial, Murphy, Patchett, and Melendres were asked to describe Sirhan's condition in custody. Apart from them, all the other testimony came from psychiatrists and psychologists of one stripe or another. The leadoff, Dr. Martin Schorr, was on the stand for *four days*.

So the thirteen witnesses crammed into one day's testimony on March 7 were the only chance the jury had to hear an alternative take on the case from those who knew Sirhan before the shooting or who encountered him at the hotel.

By day's end, the press wondered what Cooper was up to. These witnesses seemed to help the prosecution. The DA was thrilled. The LAPD final report later gloated that "three witnesses [at the hotel] established that Sirhan had a drink in his hand but that he was not drunk. . . . Enrique Rabago testified that Sirhan referred to Senator Kennedy as a 'son of a bitch who was a millionaire and wouldn't help the poor' [while] Humphrey Cordero . . . recalled that Sirhan was sober. Sirhan's former boss John Weidner said he was a good worker but displayed flashes of anger."[8]

* * *

The last witness called was Richard Lubic, the only defense witness who was actually in the pantry at the time of the shooting. He was on the stand for literally two minutes. Cooper established that he was in the pantry and there were a lot of people around.

"Do you recall—you heard a shot fired or something that sounded like a shot or a popping of a balloon?"

"It sounded like a track meet starter," said Lubic.

"Like a starter's gun?"

"Yes."

"Alright, where were you standing?" Cooper asked. By the ice machine, said Lubic. He dropped down behind it when he heard the shots.

"Now, at the time you heard the first shot, did you hear someone say something?" "Yes."

"What did you hear?"

"I heard a voice say, "Kennedy, you son-of-a-bitch.""

"Was that simultaneously with the shot?"

"No, not simultaneously. I'd say the 'Kennedy, you son-of-a-bitch,' then the shot."

"Thank you."

And that was it.[9]

* * *

In later interviews, Lubic placed the gun at least two feet from the senator's head, right next to security guard Thane Eugene Cesar, whose gun he saw pointing to the floor, by Kennedy. But during the trial, no one asked Lubic about Cesar or the muzzle distance. Instead, Cooper used Lubic to establish that Sirhan said, "Kennedy, you son-of-a-bitch."

The LAPD later smugly noted that "the prosecution anticipated the introduction of defense evidence without problems and no surprise evidence was introduced by the defense."[10]

* * *

Central to the psychiatric testimony that followed were two sets of psychological tests given to Sirhan—the first, in July, by Dr. Orville Richardson at the request of Dr. Eric Marcus, the court-appointed psychiatrist; the second, in November, by Dr. Schorr. The results were then reviewed by five clinical psychologists and four psychiatrists, including Marcus, Pollack, and Diamond.

Sirhan was described as a paranoid schizophrenic by all except Dr. Pollack and Dr. Olinger, on the prosecution side. Pollack said Sirhan was a paranoid personality but not as severely ill as a schizophrenic. Dr. Olinger said Sirhan was suffering from pseudo-neurotic schizophrenia.[11]

The prosecution psychiatrists also questioned the validity of the Rorschach inkblot test. According to Kaiser, "one of them said, remarkably, 'Everyone in the Middle East can take the Rorschach and they all come out as paranoid schizophrenics, so what does that prove?'"[12]

* * *

The psychiatrists' testimony was punctuated by recordings of Sirhan's time in custody being played into the court record. Bizarrely, Cooper entered these recordings into evidence but did not play the tape of Sirhan reenacting the shooting for Diamond under hypnosis—to my mind, the strongest indication that he had been programmed.

"During the trial, I wanted Grant Cooper to at least tell the jury this was a possibility," recalls Kaiser, "and show various clues that Sirhan was, in fact, not himself that night, that he might have been acting under some other influences, even programmed under hypnosis. Dr. Diamond had put Sirhan under hypnosis at least a dozen times and we had tape-recorded all of those hypnotic sessions, so those could well have been shown to the jury and let the jury make up its own mind. Cooper decided, 'Hey, they're never going to believe that and I'll look like a laughingstock, it's an incredible theory, let's drop it.' So that was a huge disappointment for me during the trial."

Even Dr. Diamond was loath to attribute Sirhan's programming to another. "Dr. Diamond shied away from that theory, that Sirhan was a 'Manchurian Candidate,'" said Kaiser. "And I'm not sure why—I think because he didn't want to look silly."

Instead, Dr. Diamond took the testimony of the psychologists to conclude that Sirhan was, in fact, a paranoid schizophrenic. After describing in great detail his six sessions with Sirhan, he summarized his conclusions in court:

> *The combination of events which led to the assassination of Robert F. Kennedy . . . I think started with Sirhan's exposure to violence and death in Jerusalem in 1948, and it continues with his immigration to the United States, the development of his mental illness in which his whole personality altered and he became preoccupied with revolution, violence, destruction, paranoid fantasies of glory, power and becoming the savior of his people.*
>
> *As his delusional fantasies grew bolder, and his fanatical hatred and fear of the Jews increased with each radio and television broadcast concerning the tension in the Middle East . . . Sirhan was withdrawing into a ruminative, brooding, isolated sense of failure and insignificance. To improve his mind and to gain control, he hoped, over his personal destiny, he read mystical books and subscribed to . . . Rosicrucian correspondence courses in self-hypnosis and mind power.*
>
> *He practiced his lessons diligently to the point where he became frightened by his own magical, supernatural powers of concentration. He actually believed that he could stop the bombers from reaching Israel and thereby save the Arabs, simply by willing the death of all who would help the Jews. His experiments in inducing the magical trances worked better than he realized— they worked so well that they frightened Sirhan and convinced him that he was losing his mind. . . .*
>
> *He sought the remedy in his books on mysticism and the occult, and he daydreamed of the power of his gun, taking every opportunity on many different days to shoot it, firing hundreds and hundreds of shots as if each shot would somehow make up for his ever growing sense of helplessness, impotence and fear of loss of self-control.*
>
> *With absolutely no knowledge or awareness of what was actually happening in his Rosicrucian and occult experiments, he was gradually programming himself . . . for the coming assassination. In his unconscious mind, there existed a plan for the total fulfillment of his sick, paranoid hatred of Kennedy and all*

who might want to help the Jews. In his conscious mind, there was no awareness of such a plan or that he, Sirhan, was to be the instrument of assassination.

It is my opinion that through chance, circumstances, and a succession of unrelated events, Sirhan found himself in the physical situation in which the assassination occurred. I am satisfied that he had not consciously planned to be in that situation, that if he had been fully conscious and in his usual mental state, he would have been quite harmless, despite his paranoid hatreds and despite his loaded gun.

But he was confused, bewildered and partially intoxicated. The mirrors in the hotel lobby, the flashing lights, the general confusion—this was like pressing the button which starts the computer. He was back in his trances, his violent convulsive rages, the automatic writing, the pouring out of incoherent hatred, violence and assassination. Only this time, it was for real and this time, there was no pencil in his hand, this time there was only the loaded gun.

I agree that this is an absurd and preposterous story, unlikely and incredible. I doubt that Sirhan himself agrees with me as to how everything happened. . . .

Sirhan prefers to deny his mental illness, his psychological disintegration, his trances, his automatic writing and his automatic shooting. . . . Sirhan would rather believe that he is the fanatical martyr who by his noble act of self-sacrifice has saved his people and become a great hero . . . ready to die in the gas chamber for the glory of the Arab people.

However, I see Sirhan as small and helpless, pitifully ill, with a demented, psychotic rage, out of control of his own consciousness and his own actions, subject to bizarre disassociated trances in some of which he programmed himself to be the instrument of assassination. . . . Then, in an almost accidentally induced twilight state, he actually executed the crime, knowing next to nothing [of] what was happening. . . . I am satisfied that this is how Sirhan Bishara Sirhan came to kill Senator Robert F. Kennedy on June 5, 1968.[13]

* * *

Fitts's cross-examination of Diamond was spiky and filled with mutual disdain. "You go along with me so far?" asked Fitts, at one point. "Well, I hear your words," replied Dr. Diamond.

To Fitts, Sirhan was lying when he said he didn't remember the shooting or the notebooks. He suggested that Mary Sirhan had magnified the "horrors of war and the effect on her son in hopes that they will have some impact on this jury and your psychiatric opinion."

"I don't think it is possible to magnify the horrors of war on children," said Diamond; "my daughter, son and granddaughter live in Israel . . . and I am fully aware of what the conditions are. I don't feel they were exaggerated."

* * *

Fitts suggested that Sirhan had simply made up his story from newspaper reports and talking to the defense team, deciding in advance what he would remember and what he would forget.

"Well, no, that was the difficulty," responded Diamond. "He was talking in ways which to me seemed very strange. He was admitting information which certainly would not help him, and was concealing information which might help him; so there seemed to be no logical rhyme or reason to his stories.

"He was quite prepared to admit to me or anybody who would ask him that he had killed Senator Kennedy; that he hated Senator Kennedy; and that he had done this to prevent Senator Kennedy from getting elected to the Presidency and sending fifty bombers to Israel. . . . This did not impress me as a sociopath who is inclined to help himself by concealing his crime. . . . What he wouldn't talk about were all of these things which were related to his psychological state and that I regarded as mental illness."[14]

"Did Sirhan have a true amnesia at the time he shot Kennedy?" asked Fitts.

"I think this was a true amnesia *for* the time he shot Kennedy. . . . He does not remember in his conscious state the shooting of Kennedy. He does remember in hypnotic state." But hypnosis merely accessed unconscious thoughts in his mind, explained Diamond, so it was possible the memories under hypnosis were influenced by the newspaper reports he'd read or Diamond's own hypnotic suggestions.

If it was a true amnesia, "should he not have inquired of the police why he was in custody and what he had done?" asked Fitts.

"That's not how dissociative states respond to police apprehension," explained Diamond. "From my study of Sirhan's behavior following his being taken to jail, I think it is very characteristic of this type of slow emergence from a state of dissociation, psychosis and partial intoxication, which I think accounts for some of the behavior here."

* * *

Fitts asked Diamond if the mirrors at the hotel "have significance for you in terms of his going into the dissociative state?"

"Of course they do," said Diamond, as if Fitts had not been listening to a word he'd said. "When Sirhan came back to the hotel and talked to this girl . . . he was exhausted, he felt intoxicated, he felt too drunk to drive [and] he wanted the coffee to sober up. He was thinking sexy thoughts of this girl. And in his wanderings in search of more coffee, he came into this little alcove. . . .

"He was the one who mentioned the mirrors under hypnosis . . . and this of course made me . . . immediately recall these hypnotic experiments [at home]." Diamond had no way of knowing for sure if the mirrors at the hotel triggered a dissociated state in Sirhan, but he thought it quite plausible. "I would have no difficulty in triggering off such a state right now with Sirhan in front of everybody," he said. Judge Walker didn't take him up on it.[15]

* * *

Three and a half days of testimony from Dr. Diamond was closely followed by four days of testimony from Dr. Seymour Pollack. "Pollack did everything to get Sirhan nailed," recalled Kaiser, "and that's the long and the short of it. He pretended to be very sympathetic to Sirhan, but it was an act."[16]

* * *

On April 8, the defense rested its case after calling twenty-eight witnesses over nineteen days of testimony. Of the thirty-six days of trial testimony, more than half were spent examining Sirhan's mental condition.[17]

Closing arguments began the next day. David Fitts led off for the prosecution; then Russell Parsons made a short but impassioned plea for the defense:

"I would like your verdict to spell, in every hamlet, on every desert in the Arab republic and in Europe, that a man can get justice in America. And justice is not the death penalty or life imprisonment in this case because that isn't warranted for this poor, sick wretch who did not know what he did."

Sirhan sat smiling through Parson's emotional forty-five-minute speech, by one account "savoring the emotional high-points like a disinterested observer at a speech contest." Emile Zola Berman then reprised the deep psychological "traumata" suffered by Sirhan since his arrival in Pasadena.[18]

* * *

It was then left to Grant Cooper to make a final stand for Sirhan's life.

"We are not here to free a guilty man," he began. "We tell you, as we always have, that he is guilty of having killed Robert Kennedy. Under the facts of this case, Mr. Sirhan deserves to spend the rest of his life in the penitentiary," he said, immediately contradicting Parsons.

"I wouldn't want Sirhan Sirhan turned loose on society, as he is dangerous. There are two sides to Sirhan Sirhan, as has been pointed out by the psychiatrists, which I think demonstrates the type of mental illness he has.

"There is a good Sirhan and a bad Sirhan, and the bad Sirhan is a very nasty Sirhan but I have learned to love the good Sirhan."

* * *

Cooper summarized the choices available to the jury. He defined "murder in the first degree" as "willful, deliberate and premeditated murder with malice aforethought—the specific intent to kill." Second-degree murder was diminished premeditation or deliberation plus malice aforethought. Without malice aforethought, it was manslaughter.

"As I view the evidence," Cooper said, "it would be illogical to suggest this wasn't a willful, deliberate and premeditated murder. There's no suggestion in this case that it was upon a sudden heat of passion, which reduces it to manslaughter."

So everything rested on diminished capacity—"the extent and quality of the mature, meaningful reflection. . . . You must consider what effect, if any, this diminished capacity had on the defendant's ability to form any of the specific mental states that are essential elements of murder: the intent to kill, willful, deliberate and premeditated, and the reflection upon the gravity of the complicated act. If you have a reasonable doubt about this, you cannot find him guilty of murder of the first degree.

"If because of mental illness, intoxication, or any other cause, the defendant is unable to comprehend his duty [to act lawfully], he does not act with malice aforethought" and would be entitled to manslaughter. The psychiatrists, even Dr. Pollack, had testified that Sirhan had diminished capacity, so the psychiatric evidence did indeed point to manslaughter, a view shared by Russell Parsons.

"But we are not going to ask for it," said Cooper, discarding his colleagues. "In my opinion as a lawyer, the verdict should be second degree."

* * *

Cooper then proceeded to trample roughshod over the other issues in the case in a desperate plea for second-degree murder, throwing out any good work the defense had done:

"For the purpose of this argument, we can admit that he bought the gun with the intention of killing either Senator Kennedy or President Johnson or [UN] Ambassador Goldberg or any one of those people that he mentioned in his notebook. We can admit that he did it because he was angry at this country for . . . supplying arms to Israel.

"We can admit that on June 2nd, he went to the Ambassador Hotel, having in mind that he wanted to kill Senator Kennedy . . . for the purpose—as Mr. Fitts said—of casing the joint.

"We can admit that he made inquiries of the different persons, sometimes on the 2nd and sometimes on the 4th, as to the route that Senator Kennedy would take; where he was going to be; whether there were going to be bodyguards or not—all of these things go to show premeditation and deliberation. It shows some planning, some thinking.

"But we come back to the law, and whether or not that is mature and meaningful thinking. The issue in this case is diminished capacity with respect to premeditation and deliberation. It isn't what happened at the time of the firing of the shot. The deliberation took place a long time before that. I don't care if he was in a hypnotic state at the time he fired the shot, or whether he was in a trance, as Dr. Diamond said; this is beside the point."

* * *

He then bizarrely dissociated himself from Dr. Diamond: "Were you to accept the fact that he shot Senator Kennedy in a dissociated state, he would be not guilty by reason of insanity, because he didn't know what he was doing at the time."

Instead, Cooper depicted an increasingly sick Sirhan. "Twelve witnesses would testify to his change of personality after he fell from the horse. . . . Dr. Pollack said he had been going downhill for more than a couple of years. Pollack told you the thing that distinguished between a psychotic and a person who was . . . less mentally ill was the amount of glue that held them together. . . . Sirhan became unglued when he shot Senator Kennedy. His brakes wouldn't hold."

Cooper was becoming unglued himself as he accepted the discredited testimony of Alvin Clark at face value, although Sirhan denied it. "We know from the notebooks that he was thinking about doing it and he did do it." He told the trash collector, who knew where he lived, "I am going to kill Senator Kennedy." "Was this mature, meaningful thinking?"

"You remember Dr. Pollack told you that Sirhan told him he believed he had the right, the duty to kill Senator Kennedy and he didn't feel he should be punished for his act . . . if he was going to be punished at all it should be a couple of years. Weigh that. Is that mature thinking? Is that meaningful thinking?" How about the rants in Sirhan's notebook? "Why in God's name did Sirhan deny these writings?" Perhaps it was amnesia, but Cooper stressed that Sirhan didn't try to hide anything.

While Cooper couldn't prove that Sirhan was drunk, and Sirhan couldn't remember how many drinks he'd had, "under hypnosis he did say he had four drinks." Cooper couldn't explain Sirhan's behavior in custody, but "he didn't say I am an Arab and I wanted the world to know. He wouldn't even tell them he was an Arab."

What about the outbursts in court? When the notebooks were received into evidence, "he pointed his finger at the Judge and told him 'You are not going to send me to the gas chamber and then tell the world you gave me a fair trial. I will plead guilty.' Is that mature thinking?"

* * *

Cooper stressed the transparency of the defense effort: "We permitted the prosecution's psychiatrists not only to examine Sirhan but also to place him under hypnosis and ask him anything he wanted. . . . Dr. Pollack told you it wasn't heard of, never had it happened before. . . . Could anybody be more open, more aboveboard than that?"

Cooper's argument was long-winded, garbled, rambling, confused, and incomprehensible. He sounded tired, complained of the heat, misquoted prior testimony, and disavowed his colleagues. He tried to sound smooth and urbane to the jury, but he came off as a patronizing fool, merely annoying them. As Kaiser noted, it was not his finest hour.

* * *

Cooper finished by distilling the majority of the psychiatric testimony, which he said would "reduce" Sirhan's penalty "to manslaughter." He wrote the names of the seven doctors who agreed Sirhan was paranoid-schizophrenic on the board in the courtroom—Diamond, Richardson, Marcus, Schorr, Seward, De Vos, and Crane.

Cooper asked the jury not to be swayed by the fact that the victim was Robert Kennedy. "Suppose the deceased in this case had been a fellow by the name of John Smith or Jose Gonzales . . . and suppose you had the same kind of testimony by the Court-appointed psychiatrists, do you think you would hesitate two minutes in returning a verdict of second degree murder as a result of diminished capacity? You wouldn't hesitate one minute."

Cooper reminded the jury that even if they rejected the idea that Sirhan was in a trance and cited the notebooks as premeditation, they would still have to determine beyond a reasonable doubt whether Sirhan's plans were mature and meaningful.

"I am not suggesting Sirhan Sirhan should be given a medal for what he has done . . . but I feel that the evidence and the law justifies . . . a verdict of guilty of murder of the second degree, and it would certainly take care of the situation."

The *Herald Examiner* summed up Cooper's argument as "Sirhan was a killer, but a killer who doesn't think straight."[19]

* * *

In his closing argument for the prosecution, Buck Compton called the case "highly overcomplicated" by psychiatric testimony. Cooper had conceded malice and premeditation, so Compton asserted that it all came down to the quality of the premeditation.

"Did Robert F. Kennedy," he asked, "breathe his last breath on the dirty floor of the Ambassador Hotel because he favored U.S. support for the state of Israel or because he somehow became a substitute father image in some Oedipus complex in Sirhan's mind?"

Compton said the psychiatric testimony was so confusing, "as I stand here, I can't answer the question as to what Sirhan's real motive was.

"If you believe Dr. Diamond with his mirror act, and believe Sirhan was in some kind of trance, so completely out of it that he didn't know if he was on foot or on horseback, it would be inhumane to punish him for any crime. How can you take a poor guy who doesn't know anything about what he's doing and say, 'You're guilty'? It can't be done. So if you believe those so-called experts, you have to turn him loose. But if you don't buy it, there's nothing left but a plain old cold-blooded, first-degree murder."[20]

Compton's diatribe on psychiatry was plainly ignorant, skating over the facts to score cheap points. Referring to Sirhan seeing Kennedy's face in the mirror, he said "I got a picture of Munir standing there trying to get into the bathroom for hours on end while Sirhan was there practicing his mirror act." [In fact, Sirhan practiced in his room.]

Compton later said the whole reason for the psychiatric discipline "is to find something wrong with somebody and what better way to foist their theories on the whole world than in the case of People vs. Sirhan Sirhan."[21]

* * *

He dismissed the "intoxication gimmick" used by the defense, and asked the jury to look at the facts. "This guy went out to the Ambassador on the night of June 4. He parked his car three blocks away . . . he stuck a gun in his belt and he goes into the Ambassador and he gets into the kitchen area, which is unusual for [a] guest at the Ambassador. . . . Then he asks people if Kennedy is coming this way, and Kennedy does come that way.

"He pulls a gun out of his belt and goes up and at point-blank range puts a bullet right through his head . . . [says] 'Kennedy, you S.O.B' . . . then he says 'I can explain, I did it for my country.' Then he refuses to identify himself to the police. He is alert and oriented, no odor of alcohol and he refuses, when questioned, to discuss his conduct."[22]

"Anybody, using good common sense and ordinary reason, would conclude from this that the man premeditated the murder." Compton saw the world in black and white—good guys and bad guys—with no room for psychiatry or excuses in the courtroom.[23]

At three p.m. on April 14, the trial ended and the case was sent to the jury for deliberation. The options were manslaughter, carrying a penalty of one to fifteen years; second-degree murder (five years to life); or first-degree murder (life in prison or death in the gas chamber).

The jury of seven men and five women deliberated for sixteen hours and forty-four minutes. McCowan had been telling everyone that they'd come back with second-degree, and during the second full day of deliberation, the jury requested clarification of the instructions for second-degree murder.

As he awaited the verdict, Russell Parsons told the press that Sirhan expected to be traded by the government for concessions in the Middle East if convicted, and that Ambassador Nakhleh had discussed the matter with King Hussein of Jordan at the UN.[24]

* * *

At 10:47 a.m. on April 17, the jury returned a verdict of guilty of murder in the first degree against Sirhan. They also found him guilty of assault with a dangerous weapon with intent to commit murder on the five other counts in the indictment.

At 11:04 a.m. on April 23, a separate penalty trial was concluded when the jury returned the death sentence. Sirhan calmly chewed gum as the verdict was read to him. Kaiser looked on as "Parsons shook his head in disgust, and McCowan put his face in his hands. Sirhan shrugged at his brother Adel, swept the jury with a con-temptuous look, threw back his shoulders, and swaggered into the holding tank."

"It's all right," he said, comforting Cooper, Parsons, and McCowan. "Even Jesus Christ couldn't have saved me."

Cooper pledged to take the case to the Supreme Court and cried out to news-men, "Do any of you think this will act as a deterrent to the kind of crazy mind that assassinates public figures? Assassination has happened before. It will happen again . . . but only from those who have warped and diseased minds. I had hoped this circle of violence would end here. It hasn't."[25]

* * *

Two of the jurors had argued for second-degree murder and life, but the jury finally found unanimity. They considered Sirhan mentally ill but to an insufficient degree for second-degree murder. Juror George Stitzel thought Sirhan deserved death as a "cold-blooded murderer." He said the jury felt Sirhan lied about not remembering the shooting or writing in the notebooks.[26]

* * *

The verdict came as no surprise to Kaiser. "I think the defense of diminished ca-pacity was over the heads of the jury. They spent far too much time trying to prove it, and the proofs for it were in conflict and so the jury got very confused and they kind of threw up their hands.

"They knew that Sirhan did it. Cooper, in fact, admitted it to the jury and Sirhan on the stand admitted it in a way. He said 'I don't remember doing it but if you say I did it, I guess I did it.' And so the jury went simple.

"You know, juries in America are usually twelve ordinary dummies. Anybody that's got a college degree or a graduate degree is automatically excluded . . . be-cause they would be considered prejudiced, but this jury needed some people with graduate degrees to understand this defense, it was too complicated.

"So Sirhan was given the death sentence and it was only later when California changed its death penalty law that Sirhan's death penalty was commuted to life."

"I was upset," recalled Mike McCowan. "I feel he did have diminished capac-ity but . . . it was a long shot that we would be able to keep him from getting the death penalty and you maybe feel that you didn't do your job . . . but later on, I said, 'Well, I worked for nothing and I did the best I could do and I can't change the world but I think he got a good defense."[27]

* * *

On May 5, Kaiser visited Sirhan in his cell. He gave his defense team pretty good marks for their performance but thought the prosecutors were "crooked." Sirhan still couldn't understand the shooting. To satisfy himself with Kennedy, "all I would have needed to do was just to give him a good punch in the nose at that

Robert Kennedy motorcade,
California, 1968

Kennedy making a campaign speech

Figure 3-4: Kennedy with his dog Freckles

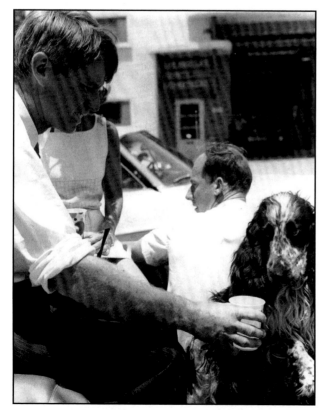

Figure 5: Kennedy among crowds on the campaign trail

Figure 6: Deserted stage after the assassination

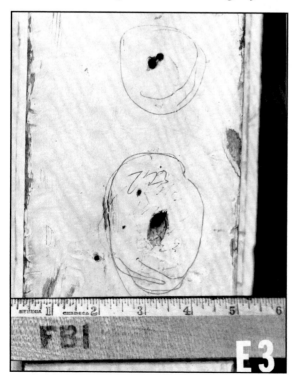

Figure 7: An FBI photo of extra bullet holes in the center divider

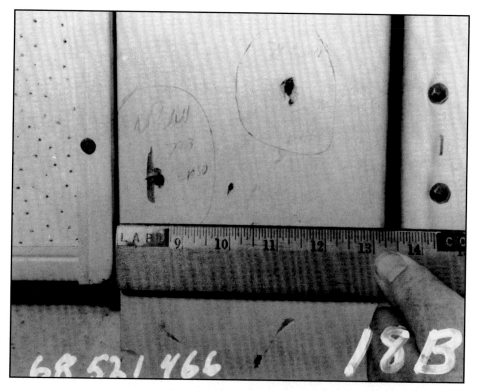

Figure 8: An LAPD photo of extra bullet holes in the pantry door frame

Figure 10: Photos of "Elaine," from 1963 and the late 1970s.

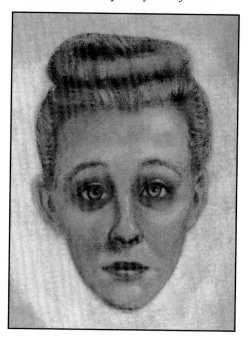

Figure 9: A police artist's sketch of the girl described by John Fahey

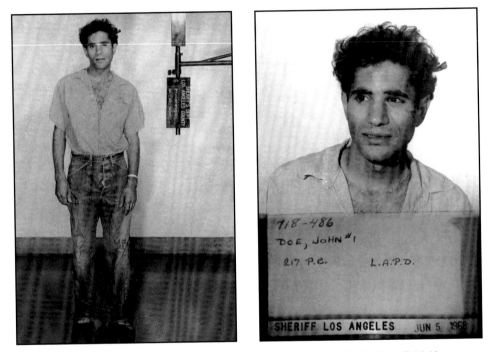

Figures 11-12: The suspected assassin is booked as "John Doe," 1968

Figure 13-14: Sirhan in his cell, August 1968

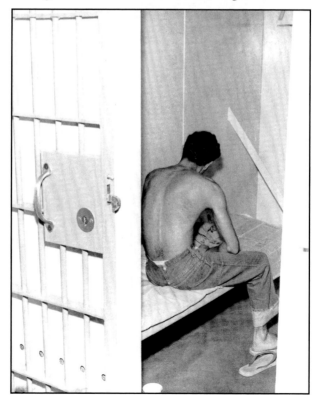

Figure 15: Sirhan mugshot 2016

Ambassador. It was a symbolic way of defeating him. It would have been enough for me—had I been conscious and awake at the time I saw him."

He thought there might be something to Diamond's theories. He compared himself to the ancient sect of the *hashshashin*, "where the assassin was drugged—dulled, mentally—at the time that he commits the crime. . . . I wasn't under the influence of marijuana, hashish or heroin or whatever. Just a few mirrors and a couple of shots of Tom Collins was enough to put me in that same mental state as the ancient assassins were."

He couldn't understand why anyone in their right mind would kill somebody. "Where's the satisfaction?" Kaiser said, suggesting that the way he shot Kennedy was less cowardly than the snipers who shot Jack Kennedy and Martin Luther King, Jr.

"There you go!" said Sirhan. "At least, Kennedy saw me. I think. I don't know . . . you see, this is what I don't understand. How did the man himself feel, you know, when he saw me pulling the trigger? I can't imagine that." Kaiser reminded Sirhan that coroner Noguchi said the first shot came from behind the right ear, so Kennedy couldn't have seen him.

"I don't know about that," said Sirhan. "I must have faced him. How the hell else would I see him from profile? Uh, uh, I don't know if I could see him or distinguish him."[28]

* * *

On May 21, Cooper's motion for a new trial, based on thirteen alleged court errors, was denied, and a letter from Senator Edward Kennedy to DA Evelle Younger was read into the record: "My brother was a man of love and sentiment and compassion. He would not have wanted his death to be a cause for the taking of another life. You may recall his pleas when he learned of the death of Martin Luther King: 'What we need in the United States is not division . . . hatred . . . violence or lawlessness, but love and wisdom and compassion towards one another.'"

But the judge had his mind made up, and Sirhan was formally sentenced to death and remanded to San Quentin, where he would await the apple-green gas chamber. Sirhan listened, with hands on hips, then turned and smiled at McCowan.

"Well, now the real battle begins."[29]

* * *

A new defense team with a background in Palestinian affairs was already in place for Sirhan's appeal—Lebanese Americans George Shibley and Abdeen Jabara would be joined by Luke McKissack, a Hollywood attorney for the Black Panthers. McCowan had worked with McKissack before and stayed on to help with the appeal. The new team was formally announced on July 2, and it would be years before all legal avenues were exhausted.[30]

* * *

The day after confirmation of his death sentence, Sirhan was interviewed by Jack Perkins of NBC on the eve of his move to San Quentin. Sirhan walked into a large room in Los Angeles County Jail, past McCowan, Parsons, and Cooper, and took a seat opposite Perkins under the television lights.

"I'm so nervous!" he kept telling Perkins as Cooper looked on, rather disconcertingly, like a proud father. NBC paid a reported $11,500 to the defense fund for the interview, and the eighteen-minute cut subsequently broadcast on June 3, 1969, is a fascinating distillation of the mysteries and conundrums of the trial. Perkins led Sirhan through the case and often seemed slightly bewildered by his responses.

Early on, he asked Sirhan what he thought about Senator Kennedy.

"I thought that he was the prince, sir. I thought he was the heir apparent to President Kennedy and I wished the hell that he could have made it."

"You admired him?"

"I loved him, sir. . . . He was the hope of all the poor people of this country, sir. And I'm with the poor people—the minorities."

"You consider yourself a poor person."

"Yes, sir, I do. . . . I'm not rich." He broke into a wide, ironic smile. "Otherwise, I wouldn't be here, sir, on this program."

* * *

Sirhan spoke of his disillusionment, while unemployed, in the aftermath of the Israeli victory the year before: "I sincerely tried to find a job, sir. After I was dismissed from school and after this Arab-Israeli War . . . I had no identity, no hope, no goal, nothing to strive for and I simply just gave up. There was no more American Dream for me."

"Well, why not?"

"Because I was a foreigner in this country, sir. An alien. A stranger. A refugee." He spat out the phrases with an anguished look on his face. "I wasn't an American. I was an Arab, sir. And that's my greatest setback I've got in this country, especially after the Arab-Israeli War. Because everybody in America loved a winner! And the Israelis won, sir, but I was a loser and I did not like it one bit."

* * *

Perkins moved on to late May, when Sirhan had first heard the reports of Kennedy's promise to send jet bombers to Israel. Sirhan became "terribly mad"—"every time I heard the reports . . . he would seem like a villain to me. Like a man who wants to kill. Like a man who wants to throw those bombs on the people and destroy . . . all of a sudden, he wants to send the very same things that we're going to withdraw from Vietnam to Israel. It seemed paradoxical to me, sir. I couldn't believe it."

"You said in court that at the time you heard that . . . you got so mad, I believe your words were, 'I could have blasted him right then.'"

"I could have. . . . I was that terribly mad, sir. I could have done anything right then and I wouldn't have known what I'd done, sir."

* * *

"All right, Sirhan, now on the night of the assassination, you said you went to the Ambassador Hotel, had a few drinks and then you said you were too drunk to drive home, didn't you?"

"Yes, sir. I did."

"And what happened?"

"I started searching for coffee. That was all that I wanted to do. And I found some."

"Out in the kitchen area?"

"But where, I don't remember, sir. I don't remember where I saw it but I remember getting the cup. It was a shining . . . urn. And there was a girl there."

"She was a pretty girl?"

"I thought she was."

"Did you think you might try to pick her up?"

"Why not?"

"Did you know Senator Kennedy was in that hotel that night at that time?"

"Sir, I did not know that." For a moment, Sirhan seemed unsure of himself. Perkins didn't catch it and moved on.

"After you poured coffee for the girl, then what happened?"

"Then, I don't remember much what happened after that."

"You don't remember much? Do you remember anything that happened after that?"

"Other than the choking and the commotion, I don't remember that."

"The last thing you have distinct recollection of, you say, is pouring coffee for a girl in the hotel. . . . You remember nothing in between?"

"If I do, sir, I don't know it. . . . It's totally out of my mind, so obviously I don't remember it."

Perkins turned to the May 18 reference in Sirhan's notebook.

"You were planning to kill Senator Kennedy."

"Only in my mind, sir."

"Well, that's the only place you can plan it."

"Not to do it physically—I never thought of doing it. . . . I don't have the guts to do anything like that."

Sirhan didn't remember writing in the notebook.

"I know, sir, that they are my writings. It's my handwriting; they are my . . . thoughts. But I don't remember them, sir."

"Well, did you only write them when you were in great fits of anger?"

"I must have been, sir. I must have been. They are the writings of a maniac, sir."

"They're the writings of Sirhan Sirhan."

"Yes, sir, but . . . they're not the writings of me now, sir."

"Well, if you were writing in your notebook now, what would you write about Robert F. Kennedy?"

There's a long pause.

"To me, sir, he is still alive."

Perkins looked dumbfounded. "How?"

"To me, my whole life stopped on June fifth. . . . Reality to me stopped right then, I guess. . . . All the time over the past year, from June fifth of sixty-eight on, is unreal to me, sir. I still don't believe what has happened. . . . I have no realization still that I have killed him, that he's in the grave and all that."

* * *

"Do you wish he were alive again?"

"Very much so, sir. Every morning when I get up, sir, I say 'I wish that son of a gun were alive, I wouldn't have to be here now.'"

"Oh! Well, that's why you wish he were alive? You wish he were alive, so that you wouldn't be in jail."

"No, I wish he were alive, sir, just . . . to be president."

* * *

Perkins asked Sirhan about the derivation of the word "assassin."

"It comes from the Arabic, doesn't it?"

"Yes, sir. *Hashashin*, I think. Which means drug takers—consumers of drugs."

"Because originally, this was a sect that took drugs to commit political murders."

"Yes, sir. Sort of to dull the senses of the killer. . . . Because I don't think a person, sir, in his right mind would have the . . . guts to do what I did."

"You have heard the psychiatrists . . . say you are a mentally ill man—emotionally disturbed. Do you believe that?

"Emotionally disturbed, yes," says Sirhan.

"Are you mentally ill?"

"I'm not mentally ill, sir, but I'm not perfect either."

* * *

"Arab people, in many Arab countries, seem to consider you something of a hero," suggested Perkins.

Sirhan looked down, embarrassed. "Yes, sir."

"A martyr. They look up to you, it seems."

"I don't feel it, sir. I don't feel myself as a hero. I said that before. Although I think that the world, sir, should know . . . that twenty years of suffering, depravation, of injustice for the Palestinian Arab people, sir, is enough."

"Do you think your case has brought this to their attention?"

"I think whatever little attention it has brought, sir, is worth it. My life and . . . regrettably, Mr. Kennedy's."

* * *

"How is your family taking this, Sirhan?"

"Well, it was hard, sir. . . . I think that they're more sorry for President Kennedy, Senator Kennedy, than they are for me, to tell you the truth. . . . I'm the only one that is responsible for what happened to Robert Kennedy, not my family. And . . . I beg society out there not to deprive them of their livelihood as they have been deprived for the past year. Just because they are my family."

"Sirhan, this is a question I think the doctors asked you several times. And I'll ask you now, just to see what your response is. If you had three wishes now, what would they be?"

Sirhan winced.

"The first wish, sir . . . I wish that Senator Kennedy were still alive. . . . I've wished that every day that I've been here. Second one . . ."

Tears came to Sirhan's eyes and he started to cover his face with his palm. There was a nineteen-second pause as he struggled to compose himself.

"That there should be peace in the Middle East. That's all."

Sirhan covered his face with his hand, overcome with emotion. That night, he was moved to death row in San Quentin.[31]

THIRTEEN

THE SECOND GUN

Thane Eugene Cesar studied police science at junior college and wanted to be a police officer but was rejected because of an ulcer he had suffered since his teens. By 1968, he was a twenty-six-year-old maintenance plumber at Lockheed in Burbank, home of the U-2 spy plane. He had a security clearance from the Department of Defense, so he could make repairs anywhere in the plant, and worked from seven a.m. to three thirty p.m.

He was six feet tall but out of shape at 210 pounds, with a pudgy, boyish face, two young kids to feed, and a marriage in trouble. He was also "in deep shit for money," so he took a part-time job as a security guard with Ace Guard Service, earning a buck fifty an hour. There was minimal training required—all you needed was a uniform and a gun. In the last week of May, he worked his first assignment.

The following Tuesday, Cesar got home from work around four thirty and received a call from Tom Spangler, his contact at Ace. Spangler wanted him to work the Ambassador that night on the regular shift from six to two in the morning. Cesar was tired after his day shift, but Spangler twisted his arm—he'd pay Cesar the full eight hours, but he could leave at midnight. Cesar agreed.[1]

Cesar arrived at the hotel at 6:05 p.m. and reported to head of security William Gardner. Gardner initially posted him at the main doors to the Embassy Ballroom. "At eight-thirty, a quarter to nine, he took me downstairs to the Ambassador Room . . . [to] mingle amongst the crowds and kind of keep an eye on things. . . . At nine o'clock . . . he took me back downstairs to the main entrance . . . to direct people to the Ambassador Room and keep them from going upstairs to the Embassy Room, which was filled up, [so] nobody could get in. I was only there about twenty minutes. At that point, he came back down and took me up to the kitchen area."

By now, because of massive overcrowding, Los Angeles fire marshals had closed the main doors to the Embassy Ballroom and were admitting people on a "one-in, one-out basis."[2]

At nine thirty, Cesar was reassigned to the east doors of the pantry, leading to the Colonial Room, and at around eleven fifteen, he was moved to the west swinging double doors of the pantry, next to the backstage area. When Cesar left the east

283

doors to the Colonial Room, nobody replaced him, so anybody could have walked in during the hour leading up to the shooting. As Cesar stood by the west swinging doors, ABC television conducted interviews in an alcove just inside the pantry. He listened to Milton Berle crack jokes and chatted to Rafer Johnson and Rosey Grier. While he was busy enjoying himself, Sirhan came into the pantry.

When Kennedy finally came down to make his speech, Cesar held the crowd back and was waiting by the swinging doors as the senator left the stage.[3]

* * *

Cesar was interviewed by the LAPD at Rampart station within hours of the shooting and again on June 24, at his home. The FBI questioned him on June 10. His account of what happened up to the shooting is pretty consistent across these interviews, but his account of his actions afterward seems to change every time he was asked.

In his first LAPD interview, Cesar described picking up Kennedy in the backstage hallway, a couple of feet from the swinging doors. Karl Uecker was leading the senator into the pantry by the right hand, and Cesar fell in behind Uecker and took ahold of the senator's right arm, just below the elbow, with his left hand, and they started pushing their way through the crowd. Kennedy never looked at him, keeping his eyes on the cameras out in front of him.

"I was right behind him all the way down to where the steam table was . . . on his right side . . . when we got to the edge of the steam table, he had reached out and sort of turned [to his left] to shake hands with some busboys . . . my hand sort of broke loose, away from his arm, and, of course, I grabbed it again because people were all over the place.

"Now, at that time, I just happened to look up and that's when I seen . . . an arm and a gun. And I reached for mine, but it was too late. He had done fired five shots and when he did, I ducked because I was as close as Kennedy was . . . I grabbed for the Senator . . . threw myself off balance and fell back [against the] iceboxes . . . and then the Senator fell right down in front of me and then I turned around [and] seen blood coming down this side of his face [the right side] . . . Murphy—I think it was Murphy, one of the security guards . . . helped me up and he says 'Let's get out in front here and stop the pandemonium.'"

Cesar did not see Sirhan's face "because he was a short man . . . standing behind the camera crews and all I could see was his hand and the gun. As soon as I looked up and spotted it, the shots went right off . . . to me it looked like he was arching his arm a little bit like he was getting over the group of men in front of him."

"Reaching around somebody or something?"

"Yeah. That's why I suspected he was short also. I didn't see his face."

"Did you get a good look at the gun?"

"I really didn't get a real good look at it. I knew it wasn't a .38 when it went off, because I've shot a .38 and a .22, and I can tell the difference."[4]

* * *

In his second LAPD interview, Cesar put it slightly differently: "We walked down through the kitchen area with the camera lights in front of us and the camera-crews. I would say five, six, seven people was in front of us. . . . As we got to the ice-box area and a row of steam-cabinets, Senator Kennedy stopped and sorta turned and broke away from me to shake hands with a couple of gentlemen at the edge of the steam table, I think they were busboys. At this time, I was up against the ice-box, approximately 12–14 inches, two feet ahead of Senator Kennedy. . . . I had my eyes on the Senator when he moved up forward a little more to shake hands with them. I happened to turn around and look up and just as I looked up, I seen a gun and when I seen it, it went off.

"At this time, the maitre d' [Karl Uecker] . . . in front of me, to my right, either ducked or jumped or something, but he knocked me down against the icebox. Then, I scrambled to my feet, pulled my gun and, meantime, several of the camera crews and whoever was standing around there had grabbed the man that had done the shooting and I wasn't able to get to him."[5]

Cesar's FBI interview summary states that "as Kennedy was shaking hands with a busboy, Cesar looked up and suddenly saw a hand sticking out of the crowd between two camera men and the hand was holding a gun. Cesar continued to be blinded by the brilliant lights and could not see the face of the individual holding the gun. Just as Cesar started to move to jump on the gun, he saw the red flash come from the muzzle [and] was shoved by an unknown individual and the next thing he remembered, he was on the floor against the ice machine.

"Cesar stated he was approximately four feet from the gun when it went off and that Senator Kennedy was approximately two feet from the gun. Cesar scrambled to his feet, drew his gun and moved to the Senator."[6]

* * *

It's interesting to compare these accounts with what Cesar told John Marshall of KFWB radio at twelve thirty a.m., fourteen minutes after the shooting:

"Officer, can you confirm the fact that the senator has been shot?"

"Yes. I was there holding his arm when they shot him."

"What happened?"

"I don't know. . . . As he walked up, the guy pulled a gun and shot at him."

"Was it just one man?"

"No. Yeah, one man."

"And what sort of wound did the senator receive?"

"Well, from where I could see, it looked like he was shot in the head and the chest and the shoulder. . . ."

"How many shots did you hear?"

"Four."[7]

* * *

Cesar's hesitant "No. Yeah, one man" response is interesting, as is the fact that he would be the only witness to accurately describe the location of Kennedy's three wounds. Standing behind and to the right of the senator, he had a clear view of Kennedy's right ear and right shoulder and was blocking the view of many of the other witnesses.

Right after the shooting, Paul Hope of the *Washington Evening Star* also quoted Cesar as saying "I fell back and pulled the Senator with me. He slumped to the floor on his back. I was off balance and fell down and when I looked up, about ten people already had grabbed the assailant." Cesar would never again state that he pulled the senator back with him as he fell.[8]

* * *

Putting all of Cesar's statements together, we can infer that he either fell back and pulled the Senator with him or was knocked to the ground by Uecker. He then either scrambled to his feet or was helped up by Fred Murphy and drew his gun. Murphy then told him to go out the service doors in the southeast corner of the pantry to the outer doors of the Embassy Ballroom "to get the other security guard to keep the crowd out."

One famous photograph by Boris Yaro shows Kennedy spread-eagled on the floor, as waiter Juan Romero tries to cradle his head. Kennedy's right arm is outstretched, and a few feet beneath it lies Cesar's clip-on tie, evidently knocked off when Cesar fell back against the ice machines. Kennedy had just fallen and Romero was first to reach him, but Cesar is nowhere to be seen.[9]

The Ace guard that Cesar supposedly went in search of, Jack Merritt, did not mention and was never asked about Cesar in his police statement. Cesar claimed he and Merritt stood outside the southeast doors to the pantry, keeping the crowd out "for the next forty, forty-five minutes," but Merritt and Stowers told police they stood guard there, never mentioning Cesar.

The only television footage of Cesar shows him shortly after this, at 1:07 a.m., following Merritt through the lobby, walking calmly past the fountain and away from the Embassy Ballroom. His clip-on tie is missing, but we only see his left profile—his holster is on his right side, so his gun is not visible.[10]

* * *

Also troubling are Cesar's repeated references to a camera crew supposedly out in front of the senator, which blinded Cesar with their camera lights. The police were never able to find this camera crew, and no film or photographs ever emerged of the senator before he fell to the floor. During early interviews with witnesses, the final questions investigators would ask as a matter of routine were: Did you see a girl in a white dress with black polka dots? and Did you see a camera crew? Neither was ever found.

* * *

Cesar later said he was "all but ignored during the chaos following the shooting" and was getting ready to go home when he volunteered himself to police officers for questioning. On the audiotape of Cesar's subsequent interview at Rampart station, he sounded calm throughout, joking that he would be "retired after tonight. I like those quiet jobs." Cesar was asked to identify Sirhan's gun but was never asked about his own. During the second LAPD interview, in Cesar's kitchen, Sergeant Paul O'Steen asked him to describe his uniform and the equipment he was wearing. "I had a Sam Browne on with a, uh . . . [coughs] . . . with a .38 revolver with a four-inch barrel." The police asked nothing further about the gun until shamed into doing so in 1971.[11]

Cesar got one sentence in the LAPD final report: "Two other guards, Stanley Kawalec and Thane Cesar, waited for and accompanied Senator Kennedy through the pantry." There's no mention that Cesar had a gun, pulled a gun, or was in a position behind and to the right of Kennedy, which matched the bullet trajectories described in the autopsy.

When one witness said he saw a security guard pull his gun in the pantry, the police told him there were no other guns pulled in the pantry; he was wrong. The name of that witness was Don Schulman, and over the next several years, Cesar and Schulman would be intertwined in the maverick reporting of the Father of the Second Gun Theory, Theodore Charach.[12]

* * *

On June 4, Don Schulman was a nineteen-year-old film runner with KNXT, the local CBS affiliate, and a Kennedy fan. He'd been assigned to Alan Cranston's party at the Ambassador but that finished early, so he and his camera crew went over to check out the Kennedy celebrations. He hadn't eaten all day, so he went into the pantry in search of some sandwiches, as huge crowds awaited the senator's arrival. The crew were tired of humping their cameras around, so they took a break in the ballroom and asked Schulman to cue them when the senator came down to speak.

* * *

When Kennedy finally appeared, Schulman said he was standing on a ledge by the door at the east side of the stage through which the senator entered the Embassy Ballroom. In television footage of Kennedy's entrance, Schulman can clearly be seen in a blue sport coat, standing on the ledge as the senator passes by, smiling and signaling with his hand to the back of the room.

After the speech, Schulman expected Kennedy to leave by the same door he came in. Instead, Kennedy went around the back way, so Schulman jumped down from the ledge to follow, to "get a good spot for the camera crew." He was pushed through the narrow doorway by a surge of people into the wake of the senator's party, and through the swinging doors into the pantry—"he was in front of me and . . . I was just being shoved along with the crowd. I couldn't have gone back if I'd wanted to. . . ." On the way in, he spotted a college friend, Ira Goldstein, in the crush and said hello.

There were blinding lights, and the crowd was jammed in like sardines. Schulman's eyes were on the senator as somebody led Kennedy by the hand through the pantry. Then the shots rang out.

* * *

Schulman's first instinct as he saw Kennedy fall was to find his news crew and call his assignment editor at KNXT. He "high-tailed it out of there before the Senator hit the floor." As he turned to leave, he saw a woman screaming hysterically, with blood gushing from her forehead. In the chaos, unknown to Schulman, his friend Ira had been shot in the leg. He hurried out through the ballroom into the lobby, looking for a telephone.[13]

Jeff Brent, another friend of Schulman's, was just outside the pantry when the shooting happened, reporting for Continental News Service. Brent switched on his tape recorder and narrated the scene: "Ladies and gentlemen, Kennedy has been shot! . . . Robert Kennedy has been shot! . . . I was near the senator. I heard gunshots . . . coming from inside this room in here. Ladies and gentlemen, there was mass chaos, you heard it as it happened!"

Brent, Goldstein, and Schulman had all worked at a campus radio station together at Pierce Junior College. Within ten minutes of the shooting, Schulman recalled bumping into Brent on his way to the phone. Brent pushed RECORD and taped Schulman's immediate reaction:

"I'm talking to Don Schulman. Don, can you give us a halfway-detailed report on what happened within all this chaos?"

"Okay. I was, ah . . . standing behind Kennedy as he was taking his assigned route into the kitchen. A Caucasian gentleman stepped out and fired three times . . . the security guard . . . hit Kennedy all three times. Kennedy slumped to the floor. As they carried him away, the security guards fired back . . . As I saw . . . they shot the, ah . . . man who shot Kennedy, in the leg. He, ah . . . before they could get him he shot a—it looked like to me—he shot a woman . . . and he shot two other men. They then proceeded to carry, ah, Kennedy into the kitchen and . . . I don't know how his condition is now."

"From what you saw, Don . . . was he grazed or did it appear to be a direct hit? Was it very serious from what you saw?"

"Well, from what I saw, it looked . . . fairly serious . . . he was definitely hit three times. Things happened so quickly that . . . there was another eyewitness standing next to me and she is in shock now and very fuzzy, as I am, because it happened so quickly."

"Right. I was about six people behind the senator, I heard about six or seven shots in succession. Now . . . is this security guard firing back?"

"Yes, ah . . . the man who stepped out fired three times at Kennedy, hit him all three times . . . and the security guards then fired back . . . "

"Right."

"Hitting him, and he is in apprehension."

At first, Schulman seemed to say that the security guard hit Kennedy all three times, but later he stated that the Caucasian man who stepped out fired three times at Kennedy, hitting Kennedy all three times, and then the security guards fired back. From this ninety-second recording was born the "second gun" theory and its self-appointed father, Ted Charach.[14]

* * *

Schulman's description was extraordinarily accurate on several key points. He correctly stated that Kennedy was shot three times even though reports by Kennedy's press secretary and the police would mistakenly say for days that the senator was shot only twice. Schulman also saw security guards drawing their guns in the pantry. Very few witnesses saw this, but it turned out to be true. He saw an injured woman (Elizabeth Evans) and two injured men (the wounds of Weisel and Schrade were bloody and clearly visible, while Stroll and Goldstein had minor injuries.).

After speaking to Brent, Schulman called in his story to assignment editor Jack Fox at the station. Within minutes, news anchor Jerry Dunphy was relaying it on air—"Don Schulman, one of our KNXT employees, witnessed the shooting that we have been telling you about. . . . A man stepped out of a crowd and shot Kennedy. Kennedy's bodyguards fired back. A suspect now in custody . . . Don Schulman, of KNXT, tells us that Kennedy was shot three times." It seems a UPI reporter was listening in to the Brent interview, because the story immediately hit the wires and was reported by Phil Cogan of KLA radio at 12:52 a.m.[15]

Schulman was told to go speak to CBS reporter Ruth Ashton-Taylor, who was interviewing witnesses in the Venetian Room. At six minutes before one, Schulman appeared live on air and retold his story:

"Well, I was standing behind him [Kennedy], directly behind him. I saw a man pull out a gun; it looked like he pulled it out from his pocket and shot three times. I saw all three shots hit the senator, then I saw the senator fall, and he was picked up and carried away.

"I also saw the security men pull out their weapons; after then it was very, very fuzzy; next thing that I knew there were several shots fired. And I saw a woman with blood coming from her temple. Also a man was shot in the leg and I saw the security police grab someone. . . ."

"Thank you, Don."[16]

* * *

Schulman's story stayed broadly the same during this interview. He didn't explicitly state that the guards fired back, but their guns were drawn, and he heard several more shots. As he later told the DA's office, "when I got to Ruth Ashton . . . apparently, she didn't ask the same questions that [Jeff Brent] asked and even though it was a couple of minutes' difference, the response was different. Not a different story, just some left out, some more detail . . . it's a matter of semantics."[17]

Schulman was then told to go to Good Samaritan, where he reported on the senator's condition from a communications car. When he got back to the station at three in the morning, Schulman was exhausted, but KNXT news anchors Jerry Dunphy and Clete Roberts wanted to interview him live on air about what he'd seen. He breezed through it quickly, with no mention of guards with guns or conspiracy—"Clete said to me, 'Did you see a security guard pull a gun?' I think that was one of his lead questions, and at that time, I said 'No, I didn't see anything.' 'Was there a conspiracy?' 'No, I didn't see anything.'"

"I'd been up almost two days. I had my contact lenses in the whole time and I didn't take them out and my eyes were inflamed. I was tired as can be. I didn't give a goddamn." He'd had it; he just wanted to go to bed.[18]

The next day, the *Boston Herald American* carried a UPI story that quoted Schulman as saying "the gunman was shot by Kennedy's bodyguards." *France Soir*, the largest French newspaper, reported a man firing "and then the Kennedy bodyguard pulls his gun out of his holster and fires from the hip like in a Western movie."[19]

The LAPD logged Jerry Dunphy's aircheck regarding Schulman and the guard firing in its media files, and a few days later, investigators visited CBS to talk to witnesses who had been at the hotel. Schulman later recalled the interview for Deputy DA Thomas Kranz:

"I said, . . . 'The Senator was shot three times.' They said, 'No, he was shot twice.' I said, 'Well, I saw three times.' They said, 'No, he was shot twice.' I said, 'Fine, whatever, I thought I saw three times.' Then they said, 'Anything else?' I said, 'Yeah, I saw other guns pulled and possibly fired.' They said, 'Why do you say that?' I said, 'Well, because there was just like firecrackers, a whole bunch of shots.' They said, 'There was no other guns.' I said, 'I thought I saw them.' They said 'No, you didn't.' I said, 'Okay.'"[20]

In other interviews, Schulman said, "As soon as I told them [my story], they weren't interested in me . . . They filled out their reports, thanked me very much and . . . the officer who interviewed me [said] they had enough witnesses and none of them saw that, so there's no use him even writing it down."[21]

This official disinterest is reflected in the summary of Schulman's police interview in LAPD files, dated August 9, 1968: "Just prior to Kennedy coming down, [Schulman] stationed himself just inside door at east end of the stage so he could signal camera crew when Kennedy arrived. Stayed at this location until after Kennedy's speech, then went into area just inside doorway to [opposite] direction Kennedy was leaving. Witness forced by crowd following Kennedy *to go through double doors* [emphasis added] and was just outside serving kitchen when he heard noise like firecrackers. Saw woman bleeding and Kennedy on floor. Did not see actual shooting or suspect due to crowd. Saw no woman in polka dot dress. Did not take photos. Thinks he saw three gunshot wounds when he looked at Senator."

This is an amazing report. If Schulman was just inside the doorway from the Embassy Ballroom and was pushed through the double doors, as the report states, he was inside the pantry at the time of the shooting. And Schulman was positive he saw Kennedy hit three times. If he didn't enter the pantry until Kennedy was lying on the floor, how could he have possibly known this? While a pool of blood formed under the senator's right ear, the two wounds under Kennedy's right armpit were not visible as he lay on the floor.[22]

* * *

Curiously, the officer who interviewed Schulman was Sergeant Paul O'Steen, the same officer who had interviewed Thane Cesar in his kitchen on June 24. Cesar's interview was cursory, lasting fifteen minutes, and no attempt was made to check his gun. If Schulman is correct and he was interviewed prior to this, the Cesar interview is shockingly negligent. If Schulman was actually interviewed on August 9, after Cesar, why is O'Steen so keen to dismiss a second gun and why did it take over a month to contact Schulman to check out reports of a guard firing back?

O'Steen's report had the desired effect. Schulman was ignored and KNXT colleagues fell in with the police—he must have been mistaken, they said; nobody else saw what he saw. "I got to the point where everybody was telling me I'm out of my mind . . . so I just related the story. . . . If they all thought I was mistaken, that was all right with me."[23]

* * *

Grant Cooper was never told about either Cesar or Schulman. Cooper told researcher Betsy Langman he had no idea there was an armed guard on Kennedy's right side just before the shooting. "I never dreamed that anybody else fired a shot . . . that thought never entered my head."

While Cooper was tied up with the Friars Club case, he was depending on defense investigator Michael McCowan for his information. McCowan had access to all the police files and told me he did interview Cesar, but his eight-line summary on him seems to be drawn entirely from Cesar's FBI report. McCowan doesn't mention that Cesar had a gun, much less that it may have been fired.

McCowan had concluded early on that Sirhan did it alone. So, despite being the only witness to accurately describe Kennedy's wounds, Cesar was never called to testify at trial. And the eyewitness account of Don Schulman, the only witness to report seeing another gun fired, was suppressed and ignored.[24]

* * *

When Sandra Serrano completed her interview with NBC's Sander Vanocur an hour or so after the shooting, Teddy Charach took her seat. It quickly became clear Charach wasn't in the pantry, but as he rattled on with his unsolicited report, Vanocur's face betrayed the thoughts of many after him—"Who let this guy in here?"

Charach grabbed the spotlight and never really let it go, a true eccentric who has made this case his life's work. He puzzled the LAPD to the point of suspicion. When they checked gun-range rosters for Sirhan's name, Charach's name was also checked, along with more than a dozen others.

Charach was a constant thorn in the side of the LAPD and district attorney's office in the early seventies, and their intelligence files portray a Canadian newsman "of questionable prominence," with a string of traffic citations for excess smoke coming from his vehicle, prone to releasing press statements from an address at the Washington Hilton. Charach had a theatrical style of presentation that looks pretty funny now, but he did truly pioneering work at the time, conducting "audio-video interviews" with key witnesses the authorities either ignored or willfully misinterpreted.[25]

Two or three months after the assassination, Charach picked up the phone and called Don Schulman. He was doing an investigation on the Kennedy killing, Charach said, and it was most important he come talk to him. Schulman said, "Fine, come over."

"I was a little skeptical at first because he had this funny look about him," Schulman recalled. "I didn't know what his story was." Schulman made Charach a copy of the Jeff Brent recording, and about a week later, Charach returned. "He tells me that on the tape—he had listened to the tape over and over again—I said I saw a security guard pull a gun and shoot Senator Kennedy. I said, 'No, I didn't. If you listen to the tape, you can see that point where I get confused or where I was just shook-up.' 'Oh, no,' he says. 'You saw it. You saw it.' I said, 'No, I didn't.' We got into about an hour-and-a-half debate on his interpretation of what I saw."

Schulman had played the tape five or six times for friends and had never noticed anything odd about it, but now, as he played the tape back with Charach, "it shook me up . . . and it could very easily and it has been misconstrued to say that I saw the guard pull out the gun and shoot Kennedy three times."

Charach told him to stick to his story, but it wasn't his story—"I've never not stuck to my story. . . . My story is that I saw a guard pull out a gun and fire. That's what I've said, and that's what I've always said. . . . I never knew where the shots came from. . . . I didn't even see Sirhan shoot Kennedy, I have no idea who shot or not, to tell you the truth. . . . I just said I heard the shots and I saw him shot, in my mind, three times. . . . I did say I saw a guard with a gun and I really feel that it was fired. But as to whether he shot [Kennedy] . . . Jesus! You know, it's crazy; it's insane."

But Charach took Schulman's "slip of the tongue" and ran with it, using the Brent tape to promote his theory that it was the guard who shot Kennedy. At one point, Charach said to Schulman, "If you could only remember, think what you'll do. . . . What you saw is history."

"Well, it's not a question of thinking what I'll do," replied Schulman. "I just didn't see anything like that. I saw a guard pull his gun and I'm pretty sure he fired. I'm pretty cotton-pickin' sure he did."

Charach then came back and told Schulman he was making a documentary record album. Schulman said, "'Okay, fine. But I'm only gonna say what I said before. I've nothing new and startling.' He then claimed that he'd like to put me under hypnosis because he feels that I saw a lot that I didn't know I saw. I tell him that I would have no objections. He said, 'Well, what if we put you under a lie-detector test?' I said, 'That'd be all right too.'" Schulman didn't follow the trial very much and let Charach get on with it.[26]

* * *

Thane Eugene Cesar was having marital problems. By the fall of 1969, his wife, Joyce, had left him for a clarinet player. Cesar was playing cards one night when he bragged that there was "a helluva lot more to the Bobby Kennedy assassination than anyone knew about." Life was about to get a lot worse. A man named Ken Marshall was at the card table and tipped off Ted Charach, who happened to share an attorney with Cesar. Two exclusive interviews were arranged with the Ace guard that October.

Charach taped these sessions and would later use excerpts in his documentary film, *The Second Gun*. Cesar gives an extraordinarily candid account of his actions at the Ambassador Hotel, revealing a right-wing, seemingly racist worldview that would haunt him for years to come. Cesar later claimed he was candid with Charach because he had nothing to hide and that his remarks were distorted. But the audio excerpts in *"The Second Gun"* seem to be straight representations of what he said.

Cesar told Charach he wasn't a Democrat "and I definitely wouldn't have voted for Bobby Kennedy because he had the same ideas as John [Kennedy] did, and I think John sold the country down the road. . . . He literally gave it to the Commies, the minorities, the blacks." Cesar told Charach he voted for segregationist George Wallace in 1968 and passed out handbills and made donations to the Wallace campaign.

The man who'd guarded Kennedy had very strong opinions: "The black man, for the past four to eight years, has been cramming this integrated idea down our throat . . . so you've learned to hate him. And one of these days, at the rate they're going, there is going to be a civil war in this country. It's going to be white against the black . . . and the blacks ain't never gonna win!

"I'm fed up and I know a lot of people that I work with have the same feeling. . . . We had it shoved down our throat enough. But one of these days, it's going to be shoved too far, and then . . . we're going to fight back! First of all, I think the white man is going to try and do it with his voting power. And if they can't do it by getting the right person to straighten the thing out, then he's going to take it in his own hands. I can't see any other way to go!"

SUS chief Robert Houghton would later claim there was nobody "with right-wing connections inside the kitchen pantry," but Cesar's views make a mockery of this.

Cesar then took Charach through what happened that night, interspersing his comments with his trademark chuckle. "At eight thirty, quarter to nine," he said, "I can remember it as long as I live—I was standing at the main door of the ballroom. [Ace guard] Jack [Merritt] looks at me and he says, 'You know, I got a funny feeling there's gonna be big trouble here tonight,' and I looked at him and I says, 'Why?' He says, 'I just got that feeling,' and I just laughed it off as a joke. But maybe he knew something I didn't." Cesar gave a dirty laugh.

Charach, acting on Don Schulman's story, then tried to zero in on when Cesar drew his gun:

"When the shots were fired, that's when I reached for my gun, and this is when I got knocked down."

"Did you get your gun out of your holster?"

"Yeah, but it didn't do me no good, because I'm on the floor. But anyways, I got back up and I had my gun out."

"Did you see the other guys pull their guns after you pulled your gun?"

"No. After we went through the swinging doors, yeah, there were three of us who had their guns out [Cesar, Merritt and Murphy]."

"What about in the kitchen?"

"Naw, I didn't see anybody else pull their guns in the kitchen area . . . except for myself."

"And you pulled it out the instant you saw . . ."

"When I seen the flashes in the gun go off, I pulled it, but I got knocked down!"

"How far did you have it out?"

"I had it in my hand."

Asked again about when he drew his gun, Cesar answered, "When I saw the gun [Sirhan's] go off, I pulled it . . . just as soon as the shots were fired."

* * *

So now, off the official record, Cesar described pulling his gun not as he scrambled to his feet after the shooting but as soon as the shots were fired, as he was thrown off balance and fell and, by one account, pulled Kennedy with him.

Cesar also mentioned for the first time to anyone that he got powder burns in his eyes: "I got powder in my eyes from the flash. I was a little behind Bobby, so I would say I was about three feet from the flash, 'cause I looked up and seen a red gun flash and, like I say, I got a little bit of powder in my eyes." Cesar later confirmed this story to author Dan Moldea.

When Charach later checked this with ballistics expert William Harper, Harper said Cesar would not get powder in his eyes from Sirhan's gun at that range but if Cesar himself had fired, the powder could have been blowback from his own barrel.

Cesar described seeing an open wound in the back of the Senator's head "because the back of his head was blown off!" He then raced out of the pantry to hail fellow Ace guard Jack Merritt at the Embassy Ballroom outer doors, who then charged into the pantry, also brandishing his gun.

When Charach brought up the obvious discrepancies with Cesar's statements to investigators, Cesar admitted those reports were "wrong, inaccurate and misleading . . . he had fabricated his testimony." Charach then addressed the issue of Cesar's gun.

"What caliber gun did you have on you?"

"Thirty-eight."

"Is there any chance that gun could have gone off?"

"My gun?"

"Yeah."

"Ahhh . . . the only way it would have [gone] off is if I had pulled the trigger, because the hammer wasn't cocked. It would have taken more pressure. . . . I would have had to want to fire the gun. . . . It wouldn't have been something where I would have slipped on the trigger."

Cesar admitted to Charach that it was possible to build a .22-caliber gun within the frame of a .38 and said there was "something in the back of his mind" he wanted to share with him—something he would never share with investigators.

"A month after [the assassination], I had a little H&R .22, just like the one that was used on Bobby . . . and I took it out in the woods and I had three or four guys with me, and I fired it as fast as I could. . . . I asked each one of them. I said, 'How many times did I fire that gun?' And not one of 'em said over five times. So it's impossible to count how many times you fire a revolver if you pull the trigger fast enough, because you can make two shots sound like one."

"What is a H&R .22?" asked Charach.

"It's exactly the same kind of .22 like he had . . . same length barrel, same size; the only difference is his was, I think, an eight shot and mine's a nine. That's the only difference between . . . the one Sirhan used and the one I had."

Cesar said he'd sold the .22 about a year before (October 1968) to a colleague who was retiring from Lockheed and going back to Arkansas. H&R stood for Harrington & Richardson, and Charach discovered that H&R manufactured lookalike .22s and .38s.[27]

Cesar again confirmed this story during a polygraph examination arranged by Dan Moldea in 1994. He recalled firing the .22 "one time after the assassination, [and] it was unbelievable how quick you could rap off [eight] shots."[28]

* * *

Ted Charach decided to put the evidence he'd collected "on the record." He approached Dr. Noguchi's attorney, Godfrey Isaac, with his findings, but Isaac initially dismissed him as just another conspiracy nut. Charach persisted, though. He waited in reception to grab a free moment with Isaac, played him the tape of his conversation with Cesar, and finally convinced him to take the case.

On June 4, 1970, Isaac filed a complaint against the LAPD and LADA on behalf of Charach, charging them with "deliberately, intentionally and knowingly" suppressing evidence regarding the assassination. At a press conference the same day, Karl Uecker appeared with Charach as he publicly outlined his second-gun theory for the first time, relating new evidence not presented at the trial.

Schulman saw a guard fire his gun and saw Kennedy hit three times; Karl Uecker grabbed Sirhan after the second shot; anti-Kennedy right-winger Gene Cesar drew his gun from a firing position matching the rear, upward trajectory of the shots described in the autopsy; and the discrepancies between the witness statements and the muzzle distance were made public for the first time. The 4,818 interviews conducted during the RFK murder investigation and $1 million spent had somehow glossed over all these issues. The "heart-breaking conclusions" of Charach's "two-year probe" were impressive but thoroughly ignored by the mainstream press. Only the *Los Angeles Free Press* reported the story.

* * *

Witnesses generally described two shots, then a pause, then a barrage of shots. Charach suggested that Sirhan's first two shots missed or went through the shoulder pad of Kennedy's suit coat; the next three came from Cesar's gun, behind Kennedy, as Uecker jumped on Sirhan and he sprayed bullets at the other victims. Charach called Schulman "one of history's most important witnesses." The official story was a fraud. "Karl Uecker's heroic actions saved the life of Senator Kennedy before the intervention of a second weapon."

Charach insisted that Uecker grabbed Sirhan in the pause after the second shot, not the fourth, as prosecutor Fitts suggested at trial. He appealed for a reexamination of "the cancer of . . . the American political assassination syndrome. . . . We are the witnesses and we will not remain silent, less history judge us with the guilty."

Charach subsequently introduced Isaac to Mary Sirhan and, after meeting Sirhan in prison, Isaac agreed to represent him.[29]

* * *

By now, CBS had grown increasingly irritated with Charach's touting of its former employee Schulman as a prime witness. Charach had apparently threatened to sue CBS for negligence, so its Los Angeles affiliate, KNXT, aired an editorial by newsman Carl George, attempting to debunk Schulman's story: "We checked videotapes recorded the night of the assassination [the Ruth Ashton-Taylor interview]. Schulman made no reference to having seen a security guard draw and shoot his gun from a position on the floor. . . . He does not say it until two years later."

This was not true. Schulman told Jeff Brent, and the KNXT aircheck by Jerry Dunphy reported Schulman seeing the guard fire—presumably prompted by what Schulman called in to the station.

CBS cameraman John Viazenko then claimed that Schulman was in the ballroom, not in the pantry, and CBS colleagues Frank Raciti and Dick Gaither later told Robert Kaiser the same thing. Again, these claims are not credible. While there is no footage of Schulman at the time of the shooting, he was where he said he was before the speech, and seemingly alone. I don't believe that any of Schulman's colleagues were close enough to know where he was during the shooting. It sounds to me like CBS staff were ganging up on a lowly film runner to support their news agenda.

Schulman was angered by the story and made his feelings known to CBS News. They eventually apologized on air.[30]

* * *

By 1971, Schulman had quit the news business and loved his new job, fighting narcotics in the city schools. Charach had completed his investigative audio probe *Why?* and was now making his documentary film on the assassination. He told Schulman he was being supported by the Kennedy family, and Don finally consented to a short interview, filmed in his backyard: "I was in the pantry way following the senator. He stopped and shook hands with several people and started to progress again. We were packed in there like sardines. There were lights and cameras and people and a lot of excitement. The senator had just finished shaking hands with someone, and another man, I think it was the maître d', walked up and took his hand. As we were slowly pushed forward, another man stepped out and he shot. Just then, the guard who was standing behind Kennedy took out his gun and he fired also. The next thing I knew is that Kennedy was shot three times."

"Now, how far was Sirhan from Senator Kennedy at the time?"

"I would say approximately from three to six feet."

"Where was this guard who was firing his gun?"

"He was standing directly to the side and back of Kennedy."

"On what side?"

"He was standing on the right-hand side. . . . I didn't see everything that happened that night because of the blinding lights and the people screaming, but the things that I did see, I'm sure about. And that is, Kennedy being shot three times; the guard definitely pulled out his gun and fired."

At this point, Schulman didn't know what to think. "Charach may turn out to be some great investigative genius and he may turn out to be some nut you lock up."[31]

* * *

Charach screened the first fifty-minute cut of his film on May 21, 1971, to an invited audience including Jesse Unruh and Rafer Johnson. The DA's office was worried, so an informant smuggled in an undercover ballistics specialist from the DA's office as his guest. They reported back that the screening was very impressive. Jesse Unruh cried after the presentation and had to go outside. Rafer said it opened his eyes to what had really happened.

Watching the longer cut of the film today, it's easy to make fun of the action-figurine reconstructions Charach uses to illustrate the bullet paths but, the testimony of these primary witnesses still retains its power, and Charach presents a sober and compelling case for a second gunman firing the fatal shots.[32]

* * *

At this point, Charach was proving to be a real thorn in the side of LA justice. The district attorney's office, worried about Sirhan's impending appeal, sent out feelers to the FBI, seeking information about Cesar. As press coverage of Charach and his second-gun theory began to proliferate, the DA's office called Cesar in for questioning on July 14, 1971.

Three years on from the assassination, a deputy district attorney, two DA investigators, and two sergeants from LAPD would question Cesar about his gun for the first time. According to LAPD files, Cesar was scheduled for a polygraph examination at the end of the interview "as a result of a misquoted statement which appeared in the June 12, 1970 issue of the *Los Angeles Free Press.*"

Cesar admitted to the investigators that he had owned a .22 but sold it to workmate Jim Yoder just before he retired from Lockheed, "somewhere around" February 1968—four months before the assassination. The .22 had been purchased in 1961 for home protection.

Once more, Cesar had changed his story. A few minutes later, his loose tongue began to get him tangled up again. He recalled Sergeant O'Steen coming to his home and taping their interview. Cesar said after the interview was over, in a conversation not recorded, "I did mention to him—in fact, I don't remember if I showed it to him, but I mentioned I had a gun similar to the one that was used that night." Sergeant Charles Collins quickly seized on the apparent contradiction.

"Did you own that .22 on the night of the Kennedy assassination?"

"No," replied Cesar.

"Well, how did you show it to the sergeant the night he came out to interview you?"

"No, I didn't," said Cesar. "That's what I said. I just told him about it, and I wanted, you know, I was telling him what it was. I wanted to show it to him, you know, what kind of gun it was."

"But you didn't have it available that night to show it to him?"

"No, no. In fact, I don't remember whether Jim Yoder had left the state or not for Arkansas, but I had already sold it to him for $10."[33]

* * *

Cesar's shifting statements were highly suspicious. Years later, he told Dan Moldea he did, in fact, show his .22 to O'Steen that night. They talked about how easy it was to conceal such a weapon—you could hide it in the palm of your hand. Cesar brought the gun out and said, "His was just like mine, except it was a different brand."[34]

But once again, Cesar's deception was swept under the carpet. At the end of his 1971 interview, investigators decided that "a polygraph examination would not add to the investigation . . . because Mr. Cesar answered all questions put to him in a thorough, straightforward and honest manner . . . all questions were satisfactorily answered and the evidence given by Mr. Cesar coincided with other evidence received by investigators. . . . The investigators never doubted Cesar's word regarding his activities in the pantry. . . . Subsequent investigation, including comparison of his own statements, indicates that Schulman was inaccurate in his allegation that Cesar fired his weapon."[35]

District Attorney Busch subsequently told the press that Mr. Yoder, the new owner of the gun, had been contacted and Cesar's statement had been verified, but this was another lie. Nobody had bothered to call Yoder to check this out.

When Ted Charach finally located Yoder, he said he had retired from Lockheed in the fall of 1968 and returned to his native Arkansas. Before he left, Cesar sold Yoder a .22 he had decided to "get rid of." Yoder produced a receipt from Cesar dated September 6, 1968, and sent a copy to Charach—he paid fifteen dollars for a nine-shot H&R .22 pistol, serial number Y13332.

"Something came up and he said he went to the assistance of an officer," recalled Yoder. "He seemed a little worried, and he said there might be repercussions from that and that was, I would say, to the best of my knowledge, sometime in June." Yoder was sure Cesar had told him he had fired the gun while giving "emergency assistance with that unidentified officer."

Unfortunately, Yoder no longer had the gun. In October 1969, it was stolen during a burglary. Five years later, when the LAPD belatedly tried to verify the burglary, they found the local sheriff's department's files had been purged. The gun wasn't recovered until the mid-nineties, when Charach launched Operation Tinker Toy with producer Beaux Carson and had it fished out of a lake in Blue Mountain, Arkansas.[36]

* * *

Nine days after the Cesar reinterview, Don Schulman was called in by Deputy District Attorneys Richard Hecht and Sid Trapp and two others. Much of the interview is taken up with the men from the DA's office trying to get as much information as they can on Charach, and feverishly speculating whether the Brent tape has been edited to make it sound like Schulman said the security guard shot Kennedy.

The rest of the interview explores the key points with Schulman, and his story holds up well, even three years after the shooting. Schulman placed himself in the pantry, about level with the partition, twelve feet behind and to the right of Kennedy when the shooting started. His attention was focused on the senator, and he had a fairly clear view of him.

"As I recall, the man stepped out and shot Kennedy three times. The whole place broke out into a panic. There was a lot of guards around. I saw their guns and one fired back, as I recall, and that's it."

"Did you see the person who fired the three shots?"

"No, I did not."

He's referred to the Jeff Brent interview.

"This statement here—'It looked like he pulled it out of his pocket and shot three times.'"

"I think I was referring to Sirhan but . . . it all happened so quickly."

"Alright. Well, did you see Sirhan shoot the Senator?"

"I don't know. As I said, I focused my attention mostly on Senator Kennedy."

"Well, did you see somebody pull out a gun?"

"Um . . . I saw a guard pull out a gun. I saw several guns."

"Alright, now did you see someone fire a gun three times?"

"No, I did not see anyone fire three times; I saw the Senator hit three times . . . three blood splotches . . . One minute he was standing up; the next minute he was on his way down."

"Can you say with certainty in your own mind that that particular security guard fired a weapon at that time?"

"Um . . . well, as I said in the past, I could be pretty sure he pulled out the weapon and fired. I could be pretty sure somebody fired back."

"What was it that you saw to indicate to you that he fired?"

"I had thought someone had hit Sirhan, it all happened so fast, he was yelling, 'My leg! My leg!' . . . and I saw the Senator was hit and then, I saw their guns and the security guard pulled out his gun and fired."

He had a picture in his mind of a guard with a gun in his hand. He didn't see him draw or point it—"all of a sudden, he was there with the gun." The guard was wearing a dark uniform and standing—not kneeling or lying down—behind and to the right of Kennedy. He saw the guard fire once. He also saw other guns drawn just after the shots were fired but couldn't say who was holding them or whether they were guards in uniform.

He didn't remember Kennedy's hand going up to his head or his head jerking back—"I just in my mind saw the three splotches of blood. . . . At first, I heard three shots. Then I heard a whole series of shots and it happened, just, in an instant. . . . He was standing one minute and then he started to slump down . . . after that, I just wanted to get the heck out of there."

"What do you mean by hit three times?"

"Well, as I recall right now, I saw three blood splotches and heard . . . three shots. And this in my mind told me three times."

* * *

Schulman couldn't recall much beyond his key statements.

"I wish you'd come to me when it had happened," he said.

"Well, a lot of times people's memory improves as time goes on," strained his inquisitors as they aired their doubts about his statements:

"You are correct about a lady being struck in the head and bleeding and you are correct about a security guard with a gun in his hand. However, in the position that you're standing, you would have to have been almost directly behind or right next to a man, six foot three [Paul Schrade] who was struck in the forehead and fell to the ground immediately. How you missed him, I don't know."

Toward the end of the interview, Hecht set out his position: "I don't think anybody would dispute that you were there . . . we know you were there . . . [and] it's not our intention to, in any way, ask you to change your story . . .

"I don't question what you saw," he continued, "but I wonder about the sequence. . . . I think there's a very good possibility that you're right outside the room when this happens, outside these doors and there you would have seen Mrs. Evans and as you come in here, right after it, you would have seen the guard with the gun in his hand."

"Well, that's how I recall it," replied Schulman. 'I don't mean to argue with you but . . . that's not the way it happened."

Schulman was positive of the sequence of events. He had to be in the pantry before the shooting because he said hello to Ira Goldstein while he was in there. "I didn't see everything," he concludes, "and I really didn't see that much . . . but I know what I saw."

* * *

Hecht asked Schulman what he could swear to in court "if we've got somebody's life on the line."

"Okay, the thing I could swear to—that I, in my mind, saw the Senator hit three times, that I saw and heard three gunshots simultaneously and three that I assumed to be wounds because of the blood. Also, that I did see other weapons. One in particular was a guard behind the Senator and that I did see the woman shot in the forehead and that I saw Ira Goldstein . . . those are the things that I'm absolutely concretely positive about. . . . I did see a guard pull a gun and I'm pretty sure that the guard fired."

"Don, I don't want to tell you what to do but temper what you say. You say you saw a guard pull a gun but a minute ago, you said you only saw him with the gun out."

"Well, it's like here we go with the [Brent] tape. . . . I assume he pulled it because where else is he gonna get it?"

"Did you assume he fired it?"

"Uh . . . I'm pretty darn sure he fired it."

"Are you positive?"

"I'm pretty positive he fired it . . . [but] I could not in clear conscience get up and swear before God . . . when a man's life is at stake."

* * *

By the end of the interview, Schulman was sick of the whole thing: "If I could walk away from this whole thing right now and say the hell with you and Ted Charach, I really would . . . to hell with it, just there it is, forget it."

The investigators played it cool when Schulman offered to let them copy the Jeff Brent tape, but as soon as he left, the room broke out in consternation.

"Do we want his tape now?"

"You bet your life I want that tape now. What the hell are you doing? It's the only goddamn tape in the world of that original conversation."

"It's not. . . . He copied it from Brent."

"Brent's got the original. . . . [Brent] has altered that fuckin' thing with Charach. That's how it comes out. . . . Hey, Charach's right on his ass. Charach and Isaacs . . . As soon as he gets back, they're gonna be right on his ass to find out what happened and they'll . . . wanna hear the tape."

"We can delete this swearing later," said the secretary.

Moments later, the tape recorder was turned off. All these guys seemed to care about was confiscating a tape that made them look bad.[37]

* * *

In October 1971, six months after losing his job at Lockheed, Cesar filed for bankruptcy. In 1973, he was hired by Hughes Aircraft, where he would stay for the next seven years. Again, he received a special security clearance from the Department of Defense, joining a company closely tied to the CIA.[38]

* * *

It seems very strange that despite this renewed interest from the DA's office, investigators never questioned Cesar's contact at Ace Guard Service, Tom Spangler, or the company owners, Frank and Loretta Hendrix.

Once again, it was left to a "citizen researcher" to step into the breach. By 1973, Betsy Langman, a flirtatious and fast-talking New Yorker who would later marry novelist and screenwriter Budd Schulberg, was writing an article on the case for *Harper's* magazine. She visited the Ace office in Sepulveda and interviewed owner Frank Hendrix, a salty, straight-talking character who called himself a two hundred percent American. Hendrix fought the Japanese in World War II and was fiercely protective of the police—"dirty filthy rotten people call a cop a pig. Nobody dared call me a pig; I'd kill him."

On the night of the shooting, Hendrix was at the Century Plaza with six guards, and his men were also with Senator McCarthy over at the Hilton. Guards were assigned randomly, and he had a turnover of a thousand guards a year. All his guards carried .38s and worked a six-to-two shift. He didn't know if Cesar fired back, but Cesar told him the crowd was pushing in on him too much to pull his gun—he couldn't get his arms up.

Hendrix was very cooperative and pulled Cesar's work records, which showed his first assignment was the week before the shooting. Hendrix explained that Ace had the Ambassador account for a year prior to the assassination and a year afterward. He had to have a guard on the pantry door for a month after the shooting to keep tourists out.

* * *

Hendrix's own view was that "Robert Kennedy killed himself" because of his unwillingness to have uniformed security around. While Hendrix does not seem suspect, not all of his statements check out. Ace was actually incorporated on January 2, 1968, and didn't receive its license until the following March, so it couldn't have held the Ambassador account for a year before the shooting. By 1988, the company had rebranded as Ace Security Services, and former LAPD criminalist DeWayne Wolfer was listed as company president.

Mike McCowan, it turns out, was a very good friend of Hendrix's. When Langman interviewed McCowan in 1973, he was president of a rival guard service, American Protection Industries. The two companies held the accounts for a lot of the big hotels in Los Angeles. Hendrix first knew McCowan as a cop who came to his home after a burglary in the mid-sixties.[39]

* * *

Ted Charach kept refining his film, and the completed 110-minute cut was screened to critical acclaim in New York in October 1973 and nominated for a Golden Globe the following year. By this time, Congressman Allard Lowenstein, a close friend of Robert Kennedy's, was investigating the case. He got Paul Schrade involved, and in 1975 a civil suit brought by Schrade and CBS led the DA to appoint Special Counsel Thomas Kranz to reexamine the case.[40]

It was also clear that Don Schulman was not the only one who saw a guard with a gun in his hand in the pantry. Bill Barry saw a guard with a gun out and told him to put it back in his holster, and Karl Uecker told Ted Charach that "just after releasing Sirhan from the headlock," he also saw a guard with a gun in his hand: "I just couldn't believe my eyes. . . ." He confronted the guard, shouting "Are you crazy! Pulling your gun . . . you could've killed me."

Television producer Richard Lubic was three feet to the right of Kennedy at the time of the shooting: "I was at Senator Kennedy's right side when Sirhan appeared. The muzzle of the gun was 2 to 3 feet away from Senator Kennedy's head. It is nonsense to say that he fired bullets into Senator Kennedy from a distance of 1 to 2 inches, since his gun was never anywhere that near to Senator Kennedy."

"I was kneeling at Senator Kennedy's right side after he fell to the floor. I saw a man in a guard's uniform standing a couple of feet to my left behind Senator Kennedy. He had a gun in his hand and was pointing it downward." Lubic told the police about this second gun, but it was omitted from his police interview summary, and Cooper never asked him about it during the trial: "They told me what to say before I went on the stand. What questions they would ask me and what I was supposed to answer and don't change."[41]

On October 24, Don Schulman was once again summoned to the DA's office, to meet with Kranz and his fellow investigators. The tapes of these sessions suggest that Kranz hadn't done his homework or even listened to the 1971 interview. As Schulman described Kennedy walking ahead of him into the pantry, Kranz exclaimed, "Oh, he was ahead of you! I didn't know that." He mistook Kennedy bodyguard Bill Barry for TV detective Gene Barry; called reporter Andrew West, Adam West, star of *Batman*; and renamed the Colonial Room the Empire Room.

Rather than let Schulman tell his story, Kranz continually interrupted and made elementary blunders that reveal the depth of his ignorance. When Schulman claimed he was right when he said Kennedy was shot three times, Kranz corrected him:

"Well, actually, he hadn't been hit three, there was [*sic*] only two wounds."

"Oh, well, at the time I said he was shot three times."

"Well, there were three bullet holes," said Kranz, "but one didn't hit his wounds. One just went through a coat."

In fact, there were four bullet holes and three wounds—one went though Kennedy's coat. Schulman was correct and Kranz would make the same mistake in his report—astonishing ignorance, given that Schulman's accuracy in describing three hits was key to his story.

Schulman told essentially the same story he'd described in 1971. He remembered saying hello to Ira Goldstein and being pushed along with his eyes on the senator—"the next thing I knew, I saw three blood splotches."

"But you didn't actually see him shot?"

"No, I didn't see Sirhan step out and shoot. . . . I saw the blood splotches. When I said, 'The man stepped out and shot the Senator three times' [on the Brent tape] . . . that was an afterthought of people telling me, 'Hey, somebody shot him' and it was a man."

On guns, Schulman said, "I saw other guns pulled and possibly fired. . . . I thought I saw three guns. They were in front of me."

"Do you know what position they were pointed at?"

"No idea. . . . Some people can remember every detail. I'm just not that kind of person. . . . I'm very, very positive I saw other guns but were they aimed at the Senator? I don't recall."

After the shooting, he saw blinding camera lights, he noticed a big, black man pounce and wrestle with someone, and he heard someone yelling, "'My foot, my foot, my leg,' or something." Although Sirhan was not shot, other witnesses also heard him complain that someone was twisting his leg, and he was later diagnosed with a sprained ankle.

For the most part, Kranz and his fellow investigators seemed more interested in Charach's politics—who was backing him, was he tied to the Black Panthers, was there a connection to Watergate? Classic seventies paranoia. But Schulman's reply disarmed them:

"Ted? Pure money . . . He's admitted that to me several times . . . he didn't say I would lie but he said if I could jolt my memory to tell the truth, as he saw it, we could make a lot of money."

The room erupted in laughter.

* * *

At the end of the interview, Kranz praised Schulman for his consistent accounts over the years and gave him his card, in case he had any more problems from Charach. When Schulman left the room, the tape was left running. Suddenly, we hear the voice of Bill Jordan, who had been sitting in on the interview with Frank Patchett from Special Unit Senator. Jordan wasted no time in criticizing Kranz's performance—"From that . . . conversation we held here, you can't place him anywhere."

Kranz said he was more interested in how Schulman was led astray by Charach than by Schulman's story: "I had the feeling he was wearing contact lenses, he had blurred vision and that affected what he saw. . . . I never felt, particularly in light of the ballistics examinations, that his statements regarding the security guard had that much weight, but to me, it was intriguing about the way he's been used and misinterpreted over the years."

"He really doesn't change his story," admitted Jordan.

"No!" agreed Kranz.

"He's still sticking with . . . he sees guns and this kinda shit. I think if this thing is gonna go anyplace and he's gonna be a problem," said Jordan, "I'd like to call him in and we'll interrogate him. . . . But I don't think it'll go that far."

"No, I don't," agreed Kranz. "To me, he's consistent with Cesar's statement, that Cesar pulled his gun, ran out, I forget where Cesar ran out, did he run out through the revolving doors?"

"Well, he didn't really run out," said Jordan. "See, Cesar, when the shooting started, discretion is the better part of valor and he hit the deck. . . . And right after it's over, he jumps up and pulls out his gun, and I think it's Jess Unruh or somebody says, you know, 'Put it away.' . . . So he puts the gun away."

"Then, did he leave the room?" asked Kranz.

"He said he went out and got his two Ace security guards."

"His supervisors . . . restationed him to another location," added Patchett, "and he was so excited he lost his tie and didn't remember how he lost it."

As Cesar's tie lay next to the dying figure of Bobby Kennedy, Cesar disappeared from the pantry. He didn't alert Ace guards Jack Merritt and Albert Stowers, as Jordan could have seen from their police statements. But where exactly Cesar went is still a mystery.

* * *

There's a surreal moment in the Kranz interview when Schulman and Kranz one-up each other with jaw-dropping statements.

"Let me tell you the weirdest thing in the whole world that you're not gonna believe," said Schulman. "Ace Guard Service . . . while I was going through college and needed extra money, I worked for them." He'd spent three weeks at Zodi's discount store in San Pedro.

Kranz then trumped Schulman. "Well, I used to go out with Valerie Schulte, the girl in the polka-dot dress!" he said. "On the Muskie campaign [in 1972]."

So, there they were: the key witness and the key suspect to a second gun in the pantry working for the same guard service; and the man whose report would finally close the lid on the reinvestigation of the case dating the "official" girl in the polka-dot dress.[42]

* * *

A month later, in the office of Cesar's attorney, Thomas Kranz interviewed Gene Cesar and subsequently whitewashed his story in the Kranz Report, belatedly published in 1977, after delays in "proof-reading." Kranz devoted eight pages of his sixty-page opinion to Schulman, Cesar, and Charach.

His discussion of Schulman doesn't start promisingly: "There is some confusion as to Schulman's exact physical location, in or out of the pantry, at the time Sirhan started firing." Kranz proceeds to quote Sergeant O'Steen's LAPD report at face value, despite Schulman's statement that it was wrong.

Recapping Schulman's 1971 interview with Hecht and Trapp, Kranz stated that Schulman's "recollection of that evening was poor but he recalled seeing certain things." All mention of a gun firing is omitted.

The report goes on to state, "Schulman told Kranz . . . he saw a security guard with a weapon drawn, but never saw the guard fire. . . . He states that he saw the guard, presumably Thane Cesar, with his gun out and pointed toward the ground, only after Kennedy was lying on the ground injured."

The tape of the Kranz-Schulman interview clearly shows that this statement is completely false. Besides being pretty sure the guard fired, Schulman never saw Kennedy lying on the ground—he was already on his way out of the pantry. He saw the gun drawn but couldn't recall where it was pointed. But in 1977, researchers could not hear the Kranz-Schulman tape. It was discovered loose in a box in the DA's office years later.

* * *

Kranz stated that "Cesar was in full uniform of the Ace Guard Service which required .38 calibers in holsters, and Cesar had been checked out earlier in the evening by his superiors and determined to be carrying the regulation .38 caliber weapon." Even if this is true—and there is no paperwork to support it—Cesar could have swapped weapons at any time.

Cesar told Kranz he was a registered Democrat and acknowledged making a three-dollar donation to the Wallace campaign but said he never campaigned for him. At the beginning of his interview, Kranz asked, "Why didn't you fire your gun? You were there to protect Senator Kennedy."

Cesar's reply was simple and direct: "I was a coward." The moment he saw the gun fire, he hit the deck.

Kranz concluded, "In hindsight, it seems obvious that the LAPD should have seized the .38 weapon that Cesar was carrying on the night in question. Additionally, it was proved by the very determined and thorough investigative research conducted by Ted Charach that Cesar owned a .22 caliber revolver at the time of the shooting. Cesar was somewhat vague as to when he had sold the weapon, at first telling investigating officers that he remembered selling the weapon in the spring of 1968 . . . such inconsistencies in [his] statements . . . suggested that good judgment required the LAPD to at least inspect and test the weapon beyond a cursory search at Rampart Division" (which, as indicated, never took place).

Cesar told Kranz he had never fired his .38 on the evening in question and that his gun was examined at Rampart station. According to the Kranz Report, "The LAPD orally verifies, but have no documents to substantiate," that the .38 was examined by "an unnamed LAPD officer, but was not seized or subsequently test-fired."[43]

The audiotapes of Cesar's LAPD interviews, available to Kranz but released to the public only in 1988, clearly show that Cesar's gun was not examined after the shooting. This unattributed oral verification seven years after the fact is clearly fabricated, and Cesar's statement that the gun was checked is false.[44]

* * *

The Kranz Report effectively closed the lid on the official investigation of the RFK investigation. Although Kranz recommended that the LAPD open its files to the public, this didn't happen for another eleven years. When the files were finally released in 1988, twenty years after the shooting, they clearly showed up the Kranz Report for the sham it was.

Kranz went on to serve as principal deputy general counsel of the army in the Reagan administration and as a special assistant to President George H.W. Bush. In 2001, President George W. Bush appointed him as principal deputy general counsel of the navy. He is a member of the Council on Foreign Relations, and the case remains closed.[45]

* * *

After Cesar's interview with the DA's office in 1975, he disappeared from view. One Los Angeles official said he had died in Arkansas, the last home to his missing gun. Then, in 1987, author Dan Moldea found him working as a plumber in Simi Valley. He had filled out over the years and weighed well over 250 pounds and sported a neatly trimmed beard.

Cesar had learned to live with the "second gun," and blamed Charach for all the controversy. He could have sued him, but his lawyers said, "Why bother; Charach doesn't have any money."

Cesar shared his financial records with Moldea. He had never been a wealthy man. After his bankruptcy in 1971, he worked the night shift at Hughes Aircraft, remarried, and divorced. He'd visited the East Coast only once, to visit relatives, and had made only two trips abroad, to the Philippines to visit his third wife, Eleanor, before she became a U.S. citizen after their marriage in 1986.

Cesar admitted he had been burned up after the Watts riots and was now a staunch Reagan supporter. He still thought the Kennedys were "the biggest bunch of crooks that ever walked the earth" but joked that "just because I don't like Democrats doesn't mean I go around shooting them."

Cesar had no criminal record or association with extremist groups, but did have some odd connections. After his initial FBI interview, Cesar remembered calling up "a very good friend [and former neighbor] who works for the FBI . . . he went and pulled the files to see exactly what they reported on me. They gave the same conclusions the LAPD did; that I wasn't a suspect."

Cesar acted out the shooting with Moldea. He positioned himself behind and to the right of Kennedy, almost touching his back. He recalled "bright television floodlights" in front of him, an arm, and a gun. Kennedy was not face-to-face with Sirhan. He was still facing north toward the busboy, shaking hands, and the barrel of Sirhan's gun was "perpendicular" to his head, at a muzzle distance of about two feet.

Cesar didn't see any other guns, and nobody came between him and the senator before the gunfire began. At first, Cesar told Moldea he didn't see Kennedy fall or get hit because as soon as he heard the shots, he stumbled and fell to the floor "instantaneously." In later interviews, he told Moldea he did see Kennedy fall—in one account, the senator fell backward two feet to his left. In another, Kennedy fell backward right in front of him.

Cesar got up "after a five count" and pulled his gun, with his arm cocked at a forty-five-degree angle. Thirty seconds later, when he was sure Sirhan had been restrained, he put the gun back in his holster. His adrenaline was pumped up, and "I was scared . . . you know, physically shaking."

But Cesar's memory was still defective on key points. Cesar told Moldea he had worked at Ace for six months before the assassination (his first assignment was actually the week before). He also said he had worked at the Ambassador "several times before the incident," which was clearly not true. June 4 was his first time.

Cesar told Moldea his two guns were shaped about the same. His .38 was about eight inches long with a four-inch barrel, the H&R six inches long with a two-inch barrel—"you can hide a H&R in the palm of your hand." He denied carrying a .22 instead of his .38 that night—it wouldn't have fit in his holster. He also denied ever using his .22 as a backup gun.

At the end of their first interview, Moldea asked Cesar point-blank if he shot Bobby Kennedy, either intentionally or accidentally. Cesar glared back and simply replied, "No." Cesar admitted that "some of the evidence makes me look bad" but insisted "no matter what anybody says or any report they come up with, you know, I know I didn't do it."[46]

Moldea concluded, "Gene Cesar may be the classic example of a man caught at the wrong time in the wrong place with a gun in his hand and powder burns on his face—an innocent bystander caught in the crossfire of history. However, considering the current state of the evidence, a more sinister scenario cannot be dismissed."[47]

* * *

The release of the police investigation files in 1988 yielded a possible encounter between Cesar and Sirhan. "Kennedy girl" Eara Marchman was walking out toward the kitchen area and observed "a man in a blue coat, dark complexion, possibly about 5'3/6', wearing lt. colored pants, standing talking to, and possibly arguing with, a uniformed guard who was standing by swinging kitchen doors." She saw the man in profile only, but identified his mug shot as Sirhan.[48]

* * *

Author Philip Melanson also found two further witnesses to a second gun.

Lisa Urso didn't see a second gun fired but "she clearly recalled someone she assumed to be a 'security guard' drawing a gun" right after the shooting, then putting it back in his holster. But Urso's "guard" was not wearing a uniform—she described him as blond, wearing a gray suit, and standing "by Kennedy." When she told investigators about this guard, "they reacted with disinterest on one occasion; hostility, on another."

Urso was also puzzled by the senator's reaction after the first shots. She told Melanson that "Kennedy grabbed his head behind the right ear and jerked forward about six inches before moving in the opposite direction and falling backward. Why this [double] motion, she wonders, if Sirhan fired from the direction the Senator first moved toward."[49]

Melanson also located Kennedy fund-raiser Nina Rhodes, and asked her to write a statement in support of a petition to the LA County grand jury to look into LAPD misconduct during the original investigation:

"As the speech came to a close," recalled Rhodes, "I left the Press Room to wait for the Senator at the bottom of the ramp. . . . The entourage moved rather quickly. I chased after the Senator and as I did, I heard a series of popping noises which I first thought were flash bulbs but then realized were gunshots. There were 12–14 shots in all. I was 6–7 feet from the Senator when I saw him and a number of others fall. Rosie Grier and Rafer Johnson charged after someone ahead and to the left of me. This surprised me because it was my impression that some of the shots had come from ahead of me and to my right [the Senator's position] and my attention was focused there . . . in conclusion, I would like to stress . . . I heard 12–14 shots, some originating in the vicinity of the Senator, not from where I saw Sirhan."

When Melanson gave Rhodes a copy of her FBI interview summary, she identified fifteen errors. Most important, she stated, "I never said I heard eight distinct shots. From the moment the tragedy began I knew that there was at least 10–14 shots and that there had to be more than one assailant. The shots were to the left and right from where I was."

Investigators ignored Nina Rhodes. The FBI altered her troubling statements, and the LAPD omitted her from their list of witnesses in the pantry at the time of the shooting.[50]

Her statements seemed to echo what another witness, Joe LaHive, told a radio interviewer on the night of the shooting. LaHive said the shots "went off with a staccato burst and it was almost like rapid-fire. The guy must have just squeezed them off as fast as he possibly could, and if there were two people, that would account for the seeming sequence of shots."[51]

* * *

In 1992, an investigative reporter for the television series *Now It Can Be Told*, confronted Gene Cesar as he walked out of his garage to speak to his paperboy. A portly Cesar, with a beard and glasses, briefly rebuffed the reporter's questions in his doorway:

"Did you have a .22 caliber gun on you? Did you fire a shot that night?" she asked.

"Still the same answer—you'll have to go through my agent. . . . I don't want to talk to nobody," said Cesar.

* * *

Dan Moldea kept in touch with Cesar after his initial interview and spent time with him and his wife during frequent trips to Los Angeles. Once, over lunch, Cesar casually mentioned some diamond purchases he had made from a local business-man who was an associate of the Mafia in Chicago. When Moldea asked him about this again in later meetings, there were discrepancies in the date of the initial pur-chase, ranging from 1968 to 1974. This was very odd, as Cesar was "in deep shit for money" at this time, worked a second job as a security guard, and was going bankrupt in late 1971.

Moldea would not tell me the name of the Mafia associate. It was an Italian name but not Rosselli. Moldea said he could never figure out who the guy was, just a tangential associate of the Chicago Mob or something more sinister. He thinks Cesar was involved with a lot of shady people.[52]

* * *

Moldea subsequently asked Cesar to submit to a polygraph test and Cesar agreed. Dr. Edward Gelb, the former president of the American Polygraph Association, was asked to administer the test, and Cesar passed "with flying colors," convincing Moldea he was innocent.

Cesar said he agreed to the test because he had nothing to hide—"If I was guilty . . . you never would've found me. . . . You don't kill somebody, and then be open about it."

But given the misuse of the polygraph in this case, it was an odd way to reach a conclusion. Polygraph tests are not accepted in court because they can be fooled. If Cesar was part of any conspiracy, he had twenty-five years to think up a way to beat the polygraph. His belated test results had little value.

But Moldea had his ending—"To sum up, Gene Cesar proved to be an in-nocent man who since 1969 has been wrongly accused of being involved in the murder of Senator Kennedy."[53]

An article Moldea published on his Web site gives some insight into the writing of his book and illustrates the contrivance at work regarding his eventual U-turn. The final switcheroo seems to be inspired by the advice of his writing coach and the dramatic story structure of Hollywood:

"Then, in Chapters Twenty-Eight and Twenty-Nine, there is The Twist—the essential element of nearly every great story. In Chapter Twenty-Eight, Cesar takes and conclusively passes a polygraph test. Then, in the final conflict in Chapter Twenty-Nine, Sirhan and I face off in a very dramatic confrontation in a prison-visitation room at Corcoran State Penitentiary in central California over what Sirhan does and does not remember about the night of the murder."

While such a scenario is all very well as a sales pitch, in print, it simply doesn't work. It's perverse to catalog the abuse of the polygraph by the LAPD to cover up conspiracy, and then declare a prime suspect innocent when he passes a polygraph twenty-six years after the fact.[54]

As to the "chilling prison interview" with Sirhan, while Moldea strains to be cinematic, Sirhan comes across in the chapter as very thoughtful and polite, and the reader is left bemused when, in the last few pages, Moldea goads Sirhan into an angry exchange with the classic windup line—"Sirhan, when your mother dies, God forbid, are you going to remember everything and come clean?"

* * *

When I interviewed Moldea regarding Cesar in August 2005, he had spoken to him the previous Sunday. Cesar was now living in the Philippines, but they were still in regular contact, and there was a film project in the works. Moldea was now the primary contact for Cesar, effectively his agent.

Cesar was so grateful to Moldea for "getting him off," he later asked Moldea to be the godfather to his child. When I asked how I might interview Cesar for my film, Moldea told me it would cost fifty thousand dollars. Would Cesar tell me anything he hadn't already told Moldea? Probably not, said Moldea, but that was his price. A year or so later, during filming for a BBC story on my investigation, I invited Moldea to do an on-camera interview to discuss new evidence of CIA operatives at the hotel. Moldea said his fee would be twenty-five hundred dollars. My BBC colleagues rolled their eyes, but Moldea said if we didn't want to pay for his opinion, somebody else would.[55]

* * *

While I acknowledge Moldea's excellent research in this case, these experiences do make me wonder about the objectivity of his relationship with Cesar. It seems odd that the perpetually broke and publicity-shy Cesar would insist on a fifty-thousand-dollar fee for an interview, while previously volunteering to undergo a polygraph test, unpaid, with an author who, at the time, believed in conspiracy.

Moldea completed his book, *The Killing of Robert F. Kennedy,* in October 1994, but he quoted no date for the polygraph test. A public records search shows that Cesar and his wife filed for bankruptcy in June 1994. Cesar was still living in Simi Valley and owed a long list of creditors—primarily credit card companies, the IRS, and credit unions at his previous employers, Anheuser Busch and Hughes Aircraft.

Cesar unsuccessfully filed an Employment Discrimination suit against Anheuser Busch two years later and subsequently moved to the Philippines. It doesn't sound like the profile of an assassin on a CIA pension, but unanswered questions remain.[56]

* * *

The best illustration of the second-gun theory I have seen came in a Discovery Channel program first broadcast in December 2005. The producers built a reconstruction of the pantry and replayed two scenarios. In the first one, Dan Moldea illustrated his theory that the crowd pushed Kennedy toward Sirhan, helping him achieve the muzzle distance required by the autopsy. In the second reconstruction, ballistics expert Michael Yardley donned a security guard uniform and played Gene Cesar. As the crowd was distracted by Sirhan, Yardley pulled Kennedy to one side and shot him from behind, with his body masking the gun. None of the witnesses noticed.

Yardley's second-gun scenario was by far the more convincing of the two, but, strangely, it was cut from the U.S. version of the show. When I discussed the program subsequently with Yardley, he was in no doubt, having examined and acted out the evidence, that there was a second gun in the pantry. There were too many bullets for there to have been only one gun, and his reenactment showed it was very possible for a second gunman to slip in unnoticed and kill the senator.

If we put all this together, it's clear that Cesar's position behind and to the right of Kennedy matched the shooting position described in the autopsy, and if there was a second gun fired, either he fired it or he was best placed to see who did.

Could Cesar have shot Kennedy by accident? Well, if he instantaneously reached for his gun, lost his balance, and pulled Kennedy back with him, one accidental shot is very possible, but four seem highly unlikely. If Cesar did fire his gun that night, his firing position suggests he inflicted all of Kennedy's wounds and that it could not have been an accident.

Cesar's inconsistency regarding when he hit the floor is also troubling. How could Cesar so clearly describe Kennedy's wounds if he hit the deck instantaneously? Only Cesar and Schulman were accurate about the number of shots that hit Kennedy, and only Cesar was accurate about the location of the wounds. Because Kennedy landed on his back, nobody had a clear picture of these wounds until Kennedy reached the hospital. Cesar obviously saw the bullets hit Kennedy before he fell back against the ice machines.

As to what gun Cesar was carrying, as Ted Charach discovered, H&R made lookalike .22s and .38s. Who would be any the wiser if Cesar had been carrying his .22? We'll probably never know, because his gun was never checked.[57]

* * *

At first, the police insisted there were no other guns drawn in the pantry, and told Don Schulman he was mistaken. But we now know there were others guns drawn in the pantry. Barry, Lubic, Uecker, and Urso saw other guns, and Jack Merritt admitted he drew his. Just because Schulman was the only one to see a second gun fired doesn't mean he's wrong.

Cesar has repeatedly changed his story on when he drew his gun, and his movements after the shooting. He repeatedly lied to investigators about when he sold a .22 revolver very similar to Sirhan's. He was the guard William Gardner assigned to the "killing zone," with advance notice Kennedy was coming through, in position to guide Kennedy through the pantry. He was on duty when Sirhan slipped into the pantry, and was possibly seen talking to Sirhan. His hatred for Kennedy and minorities gave him ample motive for the shooting, and Cesar himself has conceded that the evidence makes him look bad. His gun was never seized, and questions remain as to who pulled his tie off. Did Kennedy grab for it as he felt the shot behind his right ear?

Balancing this evidence is the fact that Cesar had no criminal record, was only given the assignment at the last minute, volunteered himself to police officers afterward, and agreed to take a polygraph test. Also puzzling is why an assassin would sell the murder weapon and sign and date the receipt.

* * *

The jury is still out on Cesar—but there's no doubt investigators over the years have done their best to give him an easy ride.

FOURTEEN

THE REINVESTIGATION

In February 1969, Los Angeles County Coroner Dr. Thomas Noguchi met attorney Robert Joling at the Drake Hotel in Chicago. He handed him a black-and-white negative of a photomicrograph—a photographic enlargement of a bullet comparison made by DeWayne Wolfer on June 6, 1968, between the Kennedy neck bullet and, ostensibly, a test bullet.

If this was proof that the Kennedy bullet matched a test slug from Sirhan's gun, Noguchi wasn't convinced. "Hold on to this for safekeeping; we may need it someday," he told Joling.[1]

As Sirhan's trial began in earnest, Noguchi was beset by power struggles within the County Coroner's Office and a bitter feud with Lin Hollinger, the county chief administrative officer. Hollinger tried to transfer Noguchi to Rancho Los Amigos Hospital as chief pathologist. When Noguchi refused, Hollinger demanded his resignation, citing sixty-one charges he was ready to file against him. Noguchi later described this extraordinary smear campaign in his autobiography as "perhaps the most lurid ever brought against a public servant. . . . I described to associates a splendid vision I had in which a fully loaded jet liner collided with a hotel and amidst the flames, I, Thomas T. Noguchi, stood [and held a press conference]."

During subsequent hearings, Deputy LA County Counsel Martin Weekes alleged that a smiling Noguchi danced in his office while waiting for Kennedy to die and told associates: "I am going to be famous. I hope he dies, because . . . then my international reputation will be established." A secretary described Noguchi slashing a piece of paper in two with a penknife and telling her he'd like to perform a live autopsy on Lin Hollinger.

* * *

"In sum," Noguchi later wrote, "the implication was that I was mentally disturbed—crazy. I was furious but at the same time, thought it would be hopeless to fight back—suicidal. The Board would produce witnesses to 'support' the charges, and my reputation would be destroyed."[2]

Noguchi resigned on February 25, the day before he testified at the Sirhan trial, but then withdrew his resignation before supervisors could act on it. When

Hollinger finally fired him and filed charges on March 18, Noguchi enlisted attorney Godfrey Isaac to fight the case and clear his name.[3]

Hollinger cited a delay in handling the Kennedy autopsy in his complaint, so Dr. William Eckert, former chairman of the pathology section of the American Academy of Forensic Sciences, was called to testify in Noguchi's defense. "Forensic science had taken a black eye in the United States because of the Texas assassination," Eckert explained, so he flew out after the autopsy to assist Noguchi as a consultant in completing the case. Eckert called the autopsy "probably the best, most thorough and most minutely handled forensic case I've ever seen."[4]

Finally, on July 31, Noguchi was cleared of all charges and reinstated as Los Angeles County Coroner. Isaac blamed the charges on in-house grudges and a misunderstanding of Noguchi's "graveyard humor."[5]

* * *

How much of this harassment was engineered to deflect attention from the troublesome Kennedy autopsy is unclear, but the timing was problematic. There was also evidence of a provocateur within the County Coroner's Office.

Dr. Donald A. Stuart, a graying, bespectacled Englishman in his late forties, applied for the position of deputy medical examiner on June 27, 1968, just three weeks after the assassination. Stuart claimed he had both legal and medical degrees from the University of London, and Dr. Noguchi felt his dual qualifications marked him as "ideally suited" to the job. He started on July 1.

Stuart later played an important role in the hearings on Noguchi's conduct, testifying to Noguchi's alleged use of amphetamines and supposedly unstable behavior. Noguchi's attorney, Godfrey Isaac, claimed that Stuart "absolutely, unequivocally lied" about a capsule test he conducted to determine what drugs Noguchi was allegedly taking.[6]

On February 2, 1972, after three and a half years as deputy medical examiner, Stuart was arrested as an imposter who had faked his medical degree and physician's license, and practiced in Chicago, Toronto, Buffalo, the Bahamas, and the Florida Keys on false credentials. While Stuart may have been a garden- variety English con man, the timing of his appointment within weeks of the assassination is highly suspect. As deputy coroner, he was ideally placed to monitor Noguchi and the drafting of the autopsy report in the run-up to Sirhan's trial.[7]

* * *

Defense attorney Grant Cooper was also in hot water. The day after the end of the Sirhan trial, the federal investigation into his use of the stolen transcripts resumed. On August 6, after a year-long investigation by U.S. Attorney Matt Byrne, Cooper and Rosselli's attorney, James Cantillon, were charged with contempt of court and faced a fine or imprisonment, with no maximum prescribed by law. This was an ignominious end for Cooper, one of the country's most prominent criminal defense lawyers.[8]

On September 23, Cooper was fined one thousand dollars for contempt of court by Judge Stephens, who said he was treating the offense as a misdemeanor, not involving moral turpitude. But the state bar association subsequently disagreed, concluding that Cooper's crime had involved moral turpitude, and the state supreme court publicly reprimanded him on July 1, 1971. The *LA Times* noted, "It was the mildest form of discipline the court could impose. Other choices available were disbarment or suspension."[9]

It was a curious episode. Was the Los Angeles legal establishment taking care of one of its own, or was Cooper given an easy ride in return for his weak defense of Sirhan at the trial?

* * *

Away from the legal disputes of Cooper and Noguchi, DA Evelle Younger tried to wash his hands of the Sirhan case with a press conference a week after sentencing. Younger said that, after more than four thousand interviews with witnesses, there was no credible theory to support a conspiracy. Now that the court order on publicity was lifted, he promised "full disclosure of the results of the investigation . . . so any doubting members of the public can satisfy themselves . . . that Sirhan acted alone."

Duplicate copies of documentation and photographic evidence would be available for review in the county clerk's office, and the "literally tons of information" in LAPD files would be made available "to the fullest extent that security precautions and administrative resources will permit." The police investigation files would not be released for another nineteen years.[10]

* * *

On May 20, Judge Herbert Walker had restricted further access to the Sirhan exhibits to counsel of record, to ensure the preservation of evidence pending Sirhan's appeal. But County Clerk William Sharp later claimed he was never properly informed of the order, so, incredibly, over the next two years, researchers visiting the Exhibits Room in the county clerk's office gained full access not to duplicate copies of exhibits, but to much of the original evidence itself.

John Kennedy Assassination Truth Action Committee researchers Lillian Castellano and Floyd Nelson were frequent visitors, and on May 23, two days after Sirhan's formal conviction, they published the first article to suggest that a second gun had been fired in the pantry.

Their *Los Angeles Free Press* story was inspired by two photographs of apparent bullet holes at the crime scene unaccounted for during the trial. Even one extra bullet would have meant a second gun.

Amateur photographer John Clemente's picture appeared to show two bullet holes in the center divider between the swinging double doors at the west end of the pantry. John Shirley was in the kitchen with Clemente and provided an affidavit confirming what he'd seen:

"In the wooden jamb of the center divider were two bullet holes surrounded by inked circles which contained some numbers and letters. . . . It appeared that an attempt had been made to dig the bullets out from the surface. However, the center divider jamb was loose, and it appeared to have been removed from the frame work so that the bullets might be extracted from behind. It was then replaced but not firmly affixed."

The second photograph, by AP photographer Wally Fong, depicted LAPD officers Robert Rozzi and Charles Wright kneeling down with flashlights to inspect a hole in a doorjamb leading from the backstage area into the narrow corridor that led into the pantry. Under the headline "Bullet Found Near Kennedy Shooting Scene," the officers point to a hole in the doorjamb, and the AP caption reads, "A police technician inspects a bullet hole discovered in a door frame. . . . Bullet is still in the wood."[11]

* * *

According to an LAPD Property Report postdated June 28, Wolfer removed two pieces of wood from the kitchen door frame and booked them as evidence on June 5—"both contained numerous holes." Wolfer also booked "two pieces of ceiling insulation" from the pantry.[12]

According to Wolfer's log, he conducted chemical and microscopic tests on a ceiling tile that first afternoon to check for bullet holes, and X-rayed it early the next morning. On June 14, he X-rayed a "door-jam."[13]

The Analyzed Evidence Report states analysis was completed on June 28, but no analysis is given—just a reference to two "boards from door frame" and two "ceiling panels."

According to Wolfer's trajectory analysis, bullets struck two ceiling tiles, but on June 27, 1969, more than a month after the *Free Press* article appeared, both tiles were destroyed by the LAPD, along with the door-frame wood, before Sirhan could even start his appeal. This destruction was not made public until 1975.[14]

* * *

Soon, word was filtering through to Sirhan on death row about Charach's second-gun theory and all the ballistics evidence that was never presented at trial. Sirhan tried unsuccessfully to block Robert Kaiser's new book on the case, and Kaiser's subsequent radio appearances to promote *R.F.K. Must Die!* merely fuelled Sirhan's paranoia about all the horrible things the defense investigator had written about him. He started writing furious letters to Grant Cooper that really began to worry his former attorney.

Cooper met the Sirhan family in his office in downtown LA and agreed to give the letters back to the family if a meeting could be arranged with Sirhan to defuse the situation. Cooper went up to see Sirhan in San Quentin and explained that had he known about any of the ballistics issues, he would have presented them at trial. Sirhan accepted Cooper's explanation, and peace was restored.

But while the Sirhan family waited in Cooper's office for the letters, there was a slight delay—Cooper's secretary was making copies of the letters in another room. One of them later turned up as an exhibit at Sirhan's parole hearing in the early 1980s as evidence that he shouldn't be released.[15]

The undated, handwritten letter was addressed to Cooper but mainly referred to Kaiser's book, with a swipe at his earlier studies for the priesthood:

Hey Punk;

Tell your friend Robert Kaiser to keep mouthing off about me like he has been doing on radio and television. If he gets his brains splattered he will have asked for it like Bobby Kennedy did. Kennedy didn't scare me, don't think that you or Kaiser will—neither of you is beyond my reach—and if you don't believe me just tell your ex-monk to show up on the news media again—I dare him.

RBK must shut his trap, or die.

In the margin, Sirhan wrote a p.s. for Cooper: "Don't ever forget, you dirty son of a bith [sic] that you cost me my life."[16]

While author Dan Moldea cited this as proof that Sirhan can remember the killing, the target of the piece, Robert Kaiser, took it with a grain of salt. "I took it as a piece of literary criticism—he didn't like my book!" Kaiser laughed heartily. "And said so in the only way he knew how, 'RBK must die.'"

As we have seen during the trial, Sirhan was prone to the occasional outburst, and Kaiser had heard other potential incriminating statements: "After the trial, he said to me in a very braggadocio moment, 'Look, they can gas me if they want, but I achieved in one day what it took Kennedy his whole life to achieve. I'm now as famous as he is.' So that could, out of context, be taken as an admission. But I'm not so sure that it was anything other than braggadocio, because it doesn't fit with so many other things that I knew about Sirhan."

Kaiser, the butt of the "Hey Punk" note, dismissed it as a temper tantrum, and still feels it's 95 percent probable that Sirhan was hypnotically programmed to commit the assassination.[17]

* * *

Just before Kaiser's book came out, SUS chief Robert Houghton published his account of the investigation, *Special Unit Senator*. Houghton's description of the bullet fragment taken from Kennedy's brain aroused the professional curiosity of "crusty septuagenarian" William W. Harper, a consulting criminalist in more than three hundred cases over thirty-five years. The dimensions of the fatal fragment sounded larger than a .22 to Harper, so he visited the county clerk's office and began to examine the physical evidence.

Harper had been in charge of technical investigations for the Office of Naval Intelligence for three years during World War II and had spent seven years as a consulting criminalist to the Pasadena Police Department, in charge of their crime laboratory. He had a long-held distrust of DeWayne Wolfer, having tangled with him in a previous case. He had warned both Grant Cooper and District Attorney Evelle Younger about Wolfer before the Sirhan trial, but they had ignored him.

With the consent of Sirhan's appeal attorneys, Harper spent seven months carefully reviewing the ballistics evidence—the gun, the bullets, the shell casings, the autopsy report, and relevant portions of the trial testimony.

According to county clerk's office records, Harper visited nine times between August 12, 1970, and January 12, 1971, and was given free access to all of the physical evidence and the autopsy photographs.

In November and December, Harper brought along a portable Hycon Balliscan camera he had helped develop. As a bullet is rotated in phases in front of the lens, the Balliscan takes a longitudinal photograph of the entire circumference of the bullet, which can be subsequently enlarged for examination. Harper found the Weisel bullet (People's 54) to be "in near perfect condition" and selected it as his "test" bullet for photographic comparison with People's 47, the Kennedy neck bullet, to establish if both were fired from the same gun.[18]

* * *

Harper's examination of the rifling impressions on People's 47 and People's 54 disclosed no matching individual characteristics to establish they that had been fired from the same gun, so he proceeded to measure the "rifling angle"—the slant angle of the impression made on each bullet, by the spiral rifling grooves and ridges ("lands") cut into the barrel during the boring process.

Harper measured a difference in rifling angles of twenty-three minutes between the bullets—about a third of a degree. "Since the rifling angle is a basic class characteristic of a fired bullet," he wrote, "it is my contention that such a difference would rule out the possibility of those bullets having been fired in the same weapon." To Harper, this was "independent proof that two guns were being fired concurrently in the kitchen pantry of the Ambassador Hotel at the time of the shooting."[19]

On December 28, Harper published his conclusions in a seven-page sworn affidavit. His key finding was that:

Senator Kennedy was fired upon from two distinct firing positions while he was walking through the kitchen pantry at the Ambassador Hotel. Firing Position A, the position of Sirhan, was located directly in front of the Senator, with Sirhan face-to-face with the Senator. This position is well established by more than a dozen eyewitnesses. A second firing position, Firing Position B, is clearly established by the autopsy report. It was located in close proximity to the Senator, immediately to his right and rear. It was from this position that four shots were fired, three of which entered the Senator's body. One of these three shots made a fatal penetration of the Senator's brain. A fourth shot passed through the right shoulder pad of the Senator's coat. These four shots from Firing Position B all produced powder residue patterns, indicating they were fired from a distance of only a few inches. They were closely grouped within a 12-inch circle.

In marked contrast, the shots from Firing Position A produced no powder residue patterns on the bodies or clothing of any of the surviving victims, all of whom were walking behind the Senator. These shots were widely dispersed. Senator Kennedy received no frontal wounds. The three wounds suffered by him were fired from behind and he had entrance wounds in the posterior portions of his body. . . . It is self-evident that within the brief period of the shooting (roughly 15 seconds) Sirhan could not have been in both firing positions at the same time.

The second gunman could not have been firing back at Sirhan, because Gun B was fired at an almost contact distance, with two shots traveling steeply upward and one hitting the ceiling. The shoulder-pad shot was fired back-to-front from an inch away, so this must also have come from Firing Position B and could not have hit Paul Schrade, who was behind the senator and walking in the same direction. This meant a ninth shot was fired and another bullet was missing.

Harper concluded that the Weisel bullet was fired by Sirhan from Firing Position A and the Kennedy bullet was fired by a second gunman from Firing Position B. Had Sirhan escaped, the autopsy report and physical evidence would have led the police to seek two gunmen. The autopsy would have pointed to a fatal shot from an inch behind the senator. But five additional victims were shot behind the senator. "Had the gunman, after shooting the Senator, turned to his left and fired apparently indiscriminately into the crowd of his followers? If so, why?" asked Harper. There must have been two guns.

"When all recovered bullets are the same caliber, the conclusion that a single gun is involved must not be hurriedly reached," wrote Harper. "The capture of Sirhan with his gun at the scene resulted in a total mesmerization of the investigative efforts. . . . The well-established teachings of criminalistics and forensic pathology were cast aside and by-passed in favor of a more expedient solution and, unfortunately, an erroneous oversimplification."[20]

* * *

Harper also found two evidence envelopes at the county clerk's office with alarming implications for the case. The first was the envelope prepared by Dr. Noguchi after extracting the Kennedy neck bullet at autopsy. Noguchi wrote "5 grooves" on the envelope, but Wolfer and Harper agreed the bullet had six. "Maybe they didn't count right," Harper later told the DA's office, but "this is a conflict that deserves some explanation . . . bullets don't grow grooves."

Harper also discovered that the test-shot envelope containing three test bullets fired on June 6, presented as Exhibit 55 at the trial, bore the serial number of a different gun. Sirhan's gun had serial number H-53725, but the serial number H-18602 was written twice on the envelope. Why would Wolfer fire test bullets with a different gun?[21]

This second gun, H-18602, was found hidden under the dashboard of a Buick Century owned by petty criminal Jake Williams, after his arrest in a robbery case on March 18, 1967. The Williams gun was test-fired four days later. As it was the same Iver Johnson Cadet model as Sirhan's, Wolfer later used it for the muzzle-distance tests on the hog's ears.

Wolfer had custody of Sirhan's gun from 1:45 p.m. on June 5 until the morning of June 7, when it was booked as evidence before the grand jury. On June 10, Wolfer sent his partner, Officer William Lee, to the LAPD Property Division to book out the Jake Williams gun for the powder pattern tests and later sound tests in the pantry to disprove Serrano's claims that she'd heard gunshots.[22]

Wolfer later dismissed the mislabeled envelope as a "clerical error." Before testifying before the grand jury on June 7, Wolfer asked the DA if he could retain three of the seven test shots for further examination. Four were sealed by the grand jury, and he took the "three better ones'" back to his office, and locked them away in his desk drawer. He labeled the evidence envelope at a later date, and a colleague simply read him the wrong serial number. He insisted he didn't have custody of the Williams gun until June 10, so that couldn't have been the test gun he used on June 6.

But Wolfer's log shows that at eight a.m. on June 8, he performed "chronograph tests on Mini-Mag ammunition—2" Iver Johnson—California State College at Long Beach." If Sirhan's gun was with the grand jury, it's highly probable Wolfer used the Jake Williams gun for this test. If the booking date of June 10 is wrong and Wolfer had H-18602 early on the eighth, he may well have had it as early as the sixth. Later in the chapter, I'll consider why he may have needed two guns.[23]

Unfortunately, by the time Harper made this discovery, the Jake Williams gun had been destroyed. Unclaimed guns were routinely destroyed a year after they were no longer needed as evidence. The LAPD property card for the gun shows that it was "reactivated 6-10-68" and "destroyed July 1968."

It was later explained that the gun was awaiting scheduled destruction in July 1968 when booked out by Lee and Wolfer. It was then routinely destroyed a year later, in July 1969, despite its key role in the Sirhan case. (I have been told the gun was never actually destroyed and is now in the possession of a gun collector in Florida.) The test bullets fired from the Williams gun never materialized.[24]

* * *

The industrious Harper was beginning to ruffle feathers and connecting to other researchers troubled by the two-gun theory. Grant Cooper had referred Ted Charach to Harper the previous summer, and he was also consulted by a Los Angeles attorney named Barbara Blehr.

When Wolfer was recommended for promotion to chief forensic chemist at the LAPD Crime Lab, Blehr, with the support of Harper, filed a complaint with the Civil Service Commission against Wolfer, seeking to block his appointment, citing major errors in the Kennedy case and two others.

Blehr's petition, filed May 28, 1971, charged that Wolfer, in his zeal to help the prosecution, had violated four universally accepted precepts of firearms identification in the Sirhan case, centering around his "glaring error" in mislabeling Exhibit 55 with the wrong serial number. Blehr's petition was supported by declarations from Ray Pinker, who founded the LAPD crime lab in 1929; Jack Cadman, chief criminalist for the Orange County crime lab; and Dr. Lemoyne Snyder, author of the landmark textbook *Homicide Investigation*. All expressed deep unease about Wolfer.

New district attorney Joseph P. Busch promised to investigate Blehr's petition, which incorporated Charach's second-gun theory, but a "whitewash" seemed likely when Police Chief Edward Davis set up a Police Board of Inquiry to look into the charges, comprised of two deputy chiefs and a commander. Wolfer came out fighting and filed a two-million-dollar defamation suit against Blehr on July 23, as he awaited the outcome of the inquiry.[25]

* * *

The same day, Deputy DA Richard Hecht interviewed Don Schulman, nine days after interviewing Cesar and waiving his polygraph test. It was clear where the DA's investigation was going. During this time, Harper paid a visit to Dr. Noguchi with an investigator from the DA's office and asked the investigator to simulate Sirhan's firing position while shooting Kennedy.

"Using Dr. Noguchi as a model, the DA's investigator placed himself in a position almost beyond belief," Harper recalled. "The position reminded me of something between Rudolf Nureyev performing the pas de deux and the shooting stance of a left-handed detective friend of mine when shooting right-handed around the front left corner of a simulated building in the FBI Combat Course."[26]

In early August, Busch claimed his grand jury investigation found no evidence of a conspiracy but that "serious questions" had been raised about the handling of the exhibits in the county clerk's office. He suggested that the bullets Harper examined may have been "tampered with" after the trial and that the staff in the county clerk's office were negligent in allowing unauthorized access to the exhibits, resulting in "altered" or even "switched" evidence.

As Harper was the only researcher who'd accessed the firearms evidence, he was clearly the one being accused of "tampering." This was obviously a diversionary ruse to deflect Harper's testimony about a second gun. The day before Harper was due to testify before the grand jury, he was shot at in his car by two "workmen" in a blue Buick who tailed him from his Pasadena home. The next day, he stood firm before the grand jury and vehemently denied any tampering.[27]

In 1975, a panel of firearms examiners confirmed that the striations on the key evidence bullets were in the same condition then as they were in 1968, proving that the LAPD and DA's claims of tampering were a diversionary tactic to sling mud at Harper, with no factual basis whatsoever.[28]

In September, Wolfer gave a sworn deposition to the LAPD Board of Inquiry about his work on the Kennedy case and angrily refuted Blehr's allegations. "I have never in my life been approached to change opinions or go for the prosecution," he said. "I call them as I see them."

But interesting new information emerged in a deposition given by Wolfer in the case of *Blehr v. Wolfer* on September 20. In a normal case where the evidence was clear-cut, there would be no need for spectrographic or neutron-activation analysis of the bullets to ensure they all came from the same batch of lead and the same gun.

But in the Kennedy case, Wolfer said he had, in fact, made spectrographic analyses of the various bullets and bullet fragments recovered, indicating further checks were needed to establish that they'd all come from the same gun.

Wolfer never mentioned these spectrographic tests or their results at trial, but later told Blehr that all the spectrograms showed "identical" results. When asked to produce them, Wolfer said they had been either "lost" or "destroyed." Earlier in the case, Wolfer had quashed Dr. Noguchi's request for neutron-activation analysis. Presumably, Dr. Noguchi either wasn't told of, or wasn't convinced by, Wolfer's spectrographic tests.

Blehr also produced the photographs from the *Free Press* article and asked Wolfer about apparent bullet holes in the kitchen circled by investigators.

"We did open up the holes that were circled and examined all other possibilities," said Wolfer. "We took a knife and cut into the holes . . . and saw what was in it."

"You mean you probed the holes?" asked Blehr.

"We didn't probe, because if there were bullets I wouldn't want to scratch or damage the bullet to see what was in the back or what was in the hole."

"Was that photographed?"

"No, because this is a negative type. . . . If you don't find a bullet we just wouldn't photograph just any hole. I mean there were too many holes to photograph."

In 1988, when the police files were finally released, a dozen police photographs emerged of these holes.[29]

A few weeks later, the police board rejected Harper's findings, calling the one-third-of-a-degree difference in rifling angle "questionable . . . when the difficulty of exactly aligning the two bullets is realized."

The expected "whitewash" of Wolfer materialized, and he was cleared for promotion to chief of the LAPD Crime Lab. Chief Davis, a right-winger who often railed at the city's "swimming-pool Communists," dismissed Blehr's allegations as a "vendetta" and lauded Wolfer as "the top expert in the country."[30]

Despite all the controversy around Wolfer and the ballistics, Sirhan's appeal attorneys were strangely indifferent to the possibility of a second gun. Luke McKissack refused to include Harper's findings in Sirhan's appeal, and later said—rather implausibly—that if there was a second gun, it was someone unconnected to Sirhan "who seized on the impulse of the moment" to fire at the senator.[31]

In 1972, the California Supreme Court ruled the death penalty unconstitutional, and Sirhan's death sentence was commuted to life. As Ted Charach completed his film, the controversy continued to build, drawing an affidavit of support from Grant Cooper.[32]

In late 1973, Charach recruited independent criminalist Herbert MacDonell to review Harper's Balliscan photographs of the Kennedy and Weisel bullets.[33]

MacDonell had his own independent crime lab in Corning, New York, and had been a defense consultant in the murder of Black Panther leaders Mark Clark and Fred Hampton by the Chicago police in December 1969. The police claimed they shot the Panthers in self-defense, but an appeals court later found the Panthers were shot while they slept. The police fired up to ninety-nine shots while the Panthers fired once in response.

MacDonell accepted Charach's assignment, and his main contribution concerned the bullet cannelures—knurled rings running around a bullet's circumference that lessen resistance to the rifling. He concluded that the Weisel bullet had two cannelures while the Kennedy bullet had only one. The Omark-CCI shell casings found in Sirhan's revolver indicated that he fired CCI long rifle Mini-Mag ammunition, which had two cannelures. Omark confirmed to MacDonell that they had never manufactured such ammunition with fewer than two cannelures.

MacDonell concluded that if the Kennedy bullet had only one cannelure, it was a different type of ammunition. He also measured a half-degree difference in rifling angles between the Kennedy and Weisel bullets and found no matching individual characteristics between the striations on the bullets. "Overall sharpness of the Kennedy bullet suggests that it was fired from a barrel whose rifling was in far better condition than the one from which the Weisel bullet was fired."

Based on the photographs, he agreed with Harper that the bullets removed from Kennedy and Weisel "could not have been fired from the same weapon" and added that, due to the single cannelure, the Kennedy bullet was not fired from the Sirhan revolver.[34]

As a KHJ news reporter, Baxter Ward had aired a series of reports on the case in 1971. He was elected to the Los Angeles County Board of Supervisors in 1972 and when he launched a bid for governor in 1974, reopening the Sirhan case played a prominent role in his campaign.

Ward asked Dr. Noguchi to rephotograph the Kennedy and Weisel bullets with a Balliscan camera from the coroner's office, and on May 13, Ward held a special three-hour hearing on the ballistics evidence, calling for a new investigation into the "unanswered questions" in the case. "There's an angle of fire that seems haywire, a distance of firing that seems haywire, and now the bullets," he said.

Wolfer and DA Joseph Busch refused to appear, dismissing the hearing as a campaign stunt, but Herbert MacDonell and fellow criminalist Lowell Bradford testified, as did Dr. Noguchi.

MacDonell and Bradford said they were unable to match the Kennedy and Weisel bullets "based on the photographic evidence," but neither had actually examined the bullets under a comparison microscope. Why Ward brought them to Los Angeles but didn't arrange such analysis is very puzzling to me and an omission Ward would come to regret. William Harper was ill, but his sworn affidavit set out his position, and MacDonell and Bradford called for an independent panel to refire Sirhan's gun.

Dr. Noguchi reiterated his grand jury and trial testimony regarding muzzle distance, and said he regretted not pressuring Wolfer into having neutron-activation analysis done on the bullets. Wolfer had told him such analysis might change the chemical composition of the slugs. Noguchi also admitted his own error in counting five grooves on the Kennedy neck bullet, when it had six.

The *LA Times* attacked Ward's "strange and ghoulish inquiry . . . his attempt to capitalize politically on a national tragedy smacks of cheap sensationalism." DA Busch also blasted Ward's hearing as "ridiculous," saying the "two-gun" theory had been "fully investigated and rejected" in previous inquiries. The board of supervisors rejected Ward's bid to have the Sirhan gun refired by an independent firearms panel and Ward also lost his bid for governor.[35]

* * *

A month later, former congressman Allard Lowenstein officially entered the case after a year spent reviewing the evidence at the behest of researcher Jonn Christian and the actor Robert Vaughn. Vaughn and Lowenstein had been close friends of Robert Kennedy's. Lowenstein had been at the forefront of the "Dump Johnson" movement in 1968, recruiting Eugene McCarthy to run for president, and later in the year, supporting RFK.

Lowenstein's interest, in turn, brought shooting victim Paul Schrade back into the case, and on Sunday, December 15, they held a joint press conference in New

York to demand that the case be reopened, citing too many bullets, bullets from different guns, and the muzzle distance issue.

They called for an independent panel to examine the firearms evidence; retest the gun; oversee neutron-activation tests on the bullets; and conduct a new trajectory study to account for the extra bullet holes. They also demanded the release of the official LAPD ten-volume report.

Busch batted them off the next day, saying he'd already refuted their claims and declaring that the evidence that Sirhan acted alone was "absolutely overwhelming." But he said he would be open to reopening the case if Sirhan requested it. Sirhan's attorney Godfrey Isaac started work on a writ of error in the California Supreme Court, seeking a new trial based on this new evidence.[36]

The following Sunday, December 22, Paul Sharaga was interviewed by Art Kevin on radio, publicly outlining his tale of the girl in the polka-dot dress for the first time.[37]

Isaac's petitions followed in mid-January, charging that police and prosecutors deliberately suppressed evidence of conspiracy—Cesar and Schulman were never called to testify, and Cesar's gun was never checked by the police. Isaac's petition was denied without comment a month later, but the pressure on Busch continued to build.[38]

On February 19, 1975, Ted Charach's film, *The Second Gun*, was shown at the American Academy of Forensic Sciences convention in Chicago. At the invitation of President Robert Joling, William Harper also gave a presentation based on his affidavit. Harper insisted that spectrographic or neutron-activation analysis should still be done on the firearms evidence. "It will be, indeed, a very dark day in the history of criminalistics if the RFK-Sirhan case is laid to rest shrouded in the clouds of technical uncertainties, of which there are many—far too many."

* * *

At the end of May, Sirhan was given a parole date of February 23, 1986. If parole was granted, he would be released after sixteen years and nine months—"at the top range for first-degree murders," said Phillip Guthrie, assistant director of the state department of corrections. The average was eleven years. "He was extremely well behaved all the time he has been in prison—absolutely no problem," said Guthrie, acknowledging Sirhan's exemplary prison record and positive response to psychiatric evaluations. "The Adult Authority considered that while he killed a very well known figure they had to treat him as if he killed an ordinary person."[39]

State Treasurer Jesse Unruh called such reasoning "asinine" and branded Sirhan a "traitor," guilty of "treason," who deserved to stay in prison for life. Unruh argued that the parole date sent out an "open invitation" to an assassination attempt on Ted Kennedy.

But under the liberal governorship of "Jerry" Brown, the Adult Authority chairman stood firm. "This should prove we don't have any political prisoners," he said. Mary Sirhan felt her son would be safe if paroled because "when they find out my son's shot did not kill the senator, there'll be nothing to be mad about."[40]

On June 27, District Attorney Joseph Busch died suddenly of a heart attack, just as it seemed he was considering a limited reopening of the case. Sirhan prosecutor John Howard was named acting DA and started to think of a judicial framework in which to conduct a limited reinvestigation.

Howard was still unconvinced by the two-gun claims of Harper and Mac-Donell. "Their findings are based on photographs, and the only accepted method of bullet identification is under a comparison microscope," he told the *Los Angeles Times*. "God help us if all the bullet comparisons are inconclusive after refiring the gun. Then someone will probably come up with a third gun theory."[41]

* * *

On July 13, a special committee of the American Academy of Forensic Sciences recommended that the case be reopened to answer "legitimate questions . . . regarding the firearms identification." Committee chair Ralph Turner, a professor at Michigan State University, agreed with Harper's findings on the rifling-angle discrepancies, and did not think bullets showing such a variance could be fired from the same gun.[42]

On July 24, Schrade, Lowenstein, and CBS News formally asked the police commission to release all investigative files on the case. "As a victim of that assault who was nearly killed," said Schrade, "I have the legal and moral right to learn if anyone other than Sirhan Sirhan was firing a gun in there."[43]

On August 14, Thomas Kranz, a former aide to Kennedy in the 1968 campaign, was sworn in as a special counsel to probe the case after the board of supervisors authorized reopening the investigation.[44]

A week later, during police commission hearings into disclosing LAPD files, Assistant Police Chief Daryl Gates revealed that the ceiling panels, the X-rays of the ceiling panels, and the door-frame wood taken from the crime scene had been destroyed on June 27, 1969, after Sirhan's conviction. He said these items were not technically evidence, as they hadn't been introduced at the trial. "They have absolutely no value whatsoever. All of the . . . real important testing, as far as the trajectory and the line of fire and the number of bullet holes, that was done prior to their removal. . . . We made those tests and they showed absolutely nothing."

Dion Morrow, special counsel for the city attorney's office, justified the destruction to the press: "There was no place to keep them. You can't fit ceiling panels into a card file."[45]

* * *

By now, the board of supervisors, the DA, and the state attorney general had joined a separate Schrade-CBS firearms petition in the hope of ending the long-running controversy. On September 11, 1976, Superior Court Judge Robert Wenke approved their bid to reinvestigate the firearms evidence, and a panel of seven examiners was appointed: Patrick Garland, a firearms examiner with the Virginia Bureau of Forensic Sciences; independent firearms examiner Stanton Berg from Minneapolis, Minnesota; Lowell Bradford, a forensic consultant from San Jose and former head of the Santa Clara County Crime Lab; Alfred Biasotti, assistant chief of the California Department of Justice investigative services branch; Cortland Cunningham, chief of the firearms and tool-marks unit at the FBI lab in Washington, DC; Charles Morton, a criminalist with the Institute of Forensic Sciences in Oakland; and Ralph Turner, a professor at Michigan State University's school of criminal justice.

Wolfer lodged an unsuccessful objection, claiming the panel was biased in favor of conspiracy. He also argued that the condition of the gun and the bullets had changed so much since 1968 that the new tests would be meaningless. But on September 14, Wenke ordered a reexamination of the evidence, and two days later, Wolfer was subpoenaed as Wenke put his work in the Kennedy case under the microscope.[46]

Wolfer was first asked to verify that the bullets introduced as evidence were the same bullets he examined in 1968, but without proper documentation, this verification relied heavily on Wolfer's memory and integrity. He located his initials on the bullets with a magnifying glass, but the "31" marked by Dr. Noguchi on the base of the Kennedy neck bullet and the "X" marked on the base of the Goldstein bullet by his surgeon, Dr. Finkel, were not checked. When the firearms panel later made an inventory of these bullets, the markings made by the doctors on extraction were no longer present. In effect, these could have been any bullets previously marked for ID by Wolfer. It was a precarious start.[47]

The 1975 panel unexpectedly discovered two four-by-five-inch black-and-white photo negatives and four contact prints among records received from the LAPD evidence clerk. Marked Special Exhibit 10, these were copies of the photomicrograph dated June 6, 1968, that Robert Joling had previously given Dr. Noguchi a copy of in Chicago. Wolfer identified the photomicrograph under oath as a comparison between the Kennedy neck bullet and a test bullet fired from Sirhan's gun. But when the firearms panel compared the surface defects on the bullets in evidence with the photomicrograph, they determined it was actually a comparison between the Kennedy neck bullet and the Goldstein bullet. They also noted that the condition of the bullets had not changed appreciably since the original photograph was taken.

Questioned as to why he said he didn't prepare photographs and yet here was a bullet comparison identified in his printing, Wolfer thought for a moment, then remembered that a detective giving a class on evidence was in the lab on another matter and wanted to show his students a comparison photomicrograph. Wolfer took a picture of the comparison "as a favor to him, not as evidence." It was a bizarre story, but it still didn't explain how Wolfer mistook the Goldstein bullet for a test bullet.[48]

While Wolfer supplied an analyzed evidence report for the Kennedy neck bullet, there were no such reports for the other victim bullets, so Wolfer's trial testimony was based on his word alone. One of the firearms examiners later characterized Wolfer's working practices as highly contentious: "He bragged to cohorts that he did not make notes of work; take pictures of bullet comparisons or any other laboratory identifications; did not write reports, instead submitted a declaration, the general format of which was: 'If called as a witness in this case, I will testify that . . .' This meant everything rested on his word and his memory, with few if any back-up records. He could not be cross-examined on notes, reports and photographs and without these, there was no record of tests performed or a traceable chain of possession."[49]

With Wolfer's foggy memory and glaring lack of documentation, the panel examiners had to do the best they could with the exhibits in evidence. Judge Wenke issued a court order on September 18, asking them to retest the victim and test bullets to determine if they were in good enough condition to make reliable firearms identification; if such identifications confirmed Wolfer's original findings or supported the conclusion that a second gun was fired; and if all bullets had the same rifling angles and number of cannelures.[50]

At the end of the first day, the group immediately agreed that the condition of the test bullets in People's 55 (the three test bullets presented at trial) and grand jury Exhibit 5-B (the four test bullets presented to the grand jury) was not sufficient for identification.[51]

During the trial, Wolfer had testified to a match between the three least-damaged victim bullets—Kennedy, Goldstein, and Weisel—and a test bullet fired from Sirhan's gun. But when Bradford and Berg examined these test bullets in 1975, they found that the copper alloy coating had been stripped away, leaving no bore impressions for comparison. The examiners couldn't match the test bullets to each other, much less to the Sirhan gun. How could Wolfer have possibly testified to a match with these test bullets in 1968 if they had no identification markings?

Cunningham described the surfaces of the four test bullets that Wolfer submitted to the grand jury as "practically devoid of microscopic marks, which could indicate that they had been fired from a barrel in a leaded condition." This was another mystery. Lead bullets can either be left untreated or coated with a copper alloy. Firing lead bullets through a gun barrel builds up microscopic lead deposits on the barrel over time. These can cause the copper alloy coating of other bullets to be stripped away as they're fired through the barrel, leaving no bore impressions on the bullet for identification.

Conversely, firing copper-coated bullets through a barrel tends to clean out these lead deposits. So why would Sirhan's barrel be in a leaded condition if he had fired eight copper-coated bullets through it in the pantry? If Sirhan's copper-coated Mini-Mags cleared out any lead deposits in the barrel, why was the copper coating stripped from Wolfer's test bullets the next day? Were lead bullets fired through the gun in the meantime? If so, by whom?[52]

As the original test bullets were unusable for identification, a panel request to test-fire the Sirhan gun was granted on September 26. The gun was examined and, as predicted, had severe leading in the bore. A dry cloth patch was pushed through the bore and each of the cylinders. Then Garland fired two copper-coated CCI Mini-Mag .22 long rifle bullets into a water tank in the basement of the Halls of Justice, followed by two lead CCI long rifle bullets, which tend to leave stronger bore impressions for identification.

The first four test bullets didn't create sufficient striations for comparison, and lead was still obvious in the bore, so four more copper-coated bullets were fired, removing most of the remaining lead.[53]

Although the new test bullets could be identified with one another, Cunningham found "significant differences" between the individual striations on these test bullets and the marks present on the three victim bullets. The leaded barrel may have altered the character of these markings, making a conclusive match impossible.

Over the next eleven days, each examiner conducted his own individual bullet comparison using a comparison microscope and consulting the photographs previously made by Harper and Noguchi, where necessary. Each expert finished his individual report before the group assembled to complete a final joint report to present to Judge Wenke.[54]

Contrary to later spin by the LAPD, the panel's conclusions unanimously rejected Wolfer's key findings. They found that not one of Wolfer's seven copper-coated test bullets had sufficient striation marks for identification with the victim bullets, with one another, or with the Sirhan gun. "The examination results contradict the original identification made at the trial of Sirhan," noted Lowell Bradford, "in that there is no basis for an identification of any of the victim bullets . . . because of the failure of the test bullets to receive bore impressions."

The panel agreed that the Stroll bullet was a CCI Mini-Mag with the same rifling characteristics as the Sirhan weapon. But they again contradicted Wolfer in determining that the Evans, Schrade, and fatal Kennedy fragments were too badly damaged to determine class characteristics and manufacturer.

Garland later noted that "carelessness, incomplete notes [and] improperly marked evidence are unacceptable in a job in which a man's life or freedom are dependent on an examiner's competence."

Yet, with no supporting documentation or analysis for his opinion and no challenge from the defense, Wolfer's fraudulent testimony had gone undetected at trial.[55]

The examiners were equally dismissive of Harper and MacDonnell's findings. They all agreed the Kennedy neck bullet had two cannelures, not one. The quality and black-and-white nature of the Harper and Ward Balliscan photographs were blamed for obscuring the second cannelure on the Kennedy bullet. (Herbert

MacDonell later told me that Harper lit his Balliscan photo from above—cannelure photographs should be lit from the side.)

The panel concluded that the alleged "sharper rifling" of the Kennedy bullet was due to impact damage on the Weisel bullet. The examiners found no significant differences in rifling or rifling angles among victim bullets, and Harper was later criticized for failing to examine these bullets under a comparison microscope before embarking on his campaign to refire the gun. Harper claimed that such a microscope was too heavy to carry to the county clerk's office, but there were plenty of researchers who could have helped.

The gross characteristics—weight, number of grooves, land width, number of cannelures, and so forth—of Kennedy, Goldstein, Weisel, Stroll, and the test bullets all matched and were consistent with the .22-caliber CCI long rifle ammunition used by Sirhan. But the lack of sufficient matching individual striations again prevented a positive identification.

Belying the mishandling furor four years earlier, none of the bullets revealed "any unusual amount of oxidation or deterioration." The problem was that individual striations didn't reproduce very well on the copper-coated bullets Sirhan used; the leaded barrel stripped striations from the test bullets; impact damage left "very limited areas with undamaged rifling impressions" on the key victim bullets; and some fine detail may have been lost due to subsequent handling or oxidation over the intervening years.

Nonetheless, Berg, Cunningham, Bradford, and Garland identified the Kennedy, Goldstein and Weisel bullets as having been fired from the same gun, while Biasotti thought it "very probable." Berg, Cunningham, Garland, and Biasotti also strongly suggested that the Sirhan gun had fired these bullets but couldn't make a positive identification.

The fact that the victim bullets could be matched to each other but the test bullets could not was strange, though. Why would the Sirhan barrel produce clearly defined striations on the victim bullets on June 5 and poorly defined striations on Wolfer's test bullets in the next firing?[56]

* * *

The examiners' joint report concluded that, while they could not match any of the bullets to the Sirhan gun, the matching class characteristics and "gross imperfections" of the bullets examined suggested "there is no substantive or demonstrable evidence that more than one gun was used" and that no further tests were needed.[57]

"There is no substantive evidence . . . that suggests or supports a second gun theory," wrote Lowell Bradford in his report. "The question of a second gun is open, but the weight of findings is against it . . . unless it were of identical class characteristics as the Sirhan gun and using ammunition of class characteristics identical with the Sirhan ammunition."[58]

During subsequent hearings, Stanton Berg said the odds were "up around ninety-nine per cent" that the bullets came from Sirhan's gun, but conceded there was a "very slim possibility" a second gun was used.

As Special Counsel Kranz later noted, "For a second gunman to fire at Kennedy, he would have to have a gun exactly like Sirhan's. . . . What were the chances of two . . . Iver Johnson .22 caliber revolvers firing the same copper-jacketed, mini-mag, hollow-tipped ammunition at the same time? Additionally, five of the seven experts found that Kennedy, Goldstein and Weisel were fired from the same gun. All three were in Sirhan's line of fire. Goldstein was eight feet east of Kennedy. Weisel twenty-seven feet east. A second gunman would have to shoot Kennedy close-up from the right rear, then turn around, without being seen and fire at Goldstein and Weisel."

Later it was determined that Cesar's .22 had similar class characteristics to Sirhan's gun, so if he was firing Mini-Mags, the bullets in evidence could fit his gun. But to me, the idea of Cesar shooting Kennedy and then turning around to shoot Goldstein and Weisel just doesn't make any sense.[59]

After their meticulous two-week study, on October 6, the firearms panel publicly announced their findings. "No 2nd Gun, Kennedy Case Panel Reports" was the *LA Times* headline, while Sirhan's attorney Godfrey Isaac conceded the findings "have effectively laid the second-gun theory to rest."

LAPD Chief Davis completely misinterpreted the findings as a triumph for the head of his crime lab: "After years of unwarranted attack on criminalist DeWayne Wolfer, his integrity and professional excellence have been vindicated. However, this will not stop the conspiracy theory profiteers or the conspiracy theory nuts from drumming up additional allegations which will tend to undermine the police, the prosecution and the courts."[60]

In an October 8 news conference, Lowenstein, Joling, and Schrade insisted that the second-gun issue was still open and that further trajectory studies in the pantry were needed, but Schrade acknowledged that "in great part the second-gun theory has been refuted. These bullets . . . most likely came from the Sirhan gun. Doubt has been reduced by these tests, but not eliminated."

William Harper was called back for questioning on November 7 and asked if he had seen anything in the panel's report that caused him to modify or change his opinion. Harper replied, "The answer to that is 'no.' Just plain 'n-o'"—though he admitted he hadn't really digested the examiners' report yet and, five years after his original examination, he wasn't inclined to get back into it.[61]

Proconspiracy writers have tended to gloss over the panel's conclusions over the years, claiming they were inconclusive and never linked Sirhan's gun to any of the bullets in the case. But the finding that the Kennedy neck bullet and the Goldstein and Weisel bullets were fired from the same gun must be addressed in any responsible analysis of the ballistics in the case.

Assuming the bullets examined in 1975 were the same bullets Wolfer examined in 1968, it's hard to refute the panel's contention that these three key victim bullets were probably fired from Sirhan's gun. Goldstein and Weisel were in Sirhan's line of fire, but if Sirhan also hit Kennedy in the neck, it means, contrary to witness testimony, that his gun did come within an inch of Kennedy's right armpit, and that he was not in front of Kennedy, but to his right side.

If Sirhan's gun arm closed the muzzle distance to within an inch and lined up with the bullet trajectory of one armpit shot, he must also have fired the other, as the two armpit shots were only an inch apart.

From the same firing position, it's quite possible that Sirhan fired the fatal shot and the shoulder-pad shot as well, but these have different bullet trajectories that could also have been fired by a second gun. Dr. Noguchi couldn't identify the caliber of the fatal Kennedy bullet fragments, and we don't really know where the bullet that passed clean through Kennedy's suit coat went. If more than eight shots were fired in the pantry, it must be considered possible that these shots were fired by a second gun.

The Wenke hearings wound down by calling the firearms examiners back for questioning about outstanding issues that still needed clearing up. Allard Lowenstein asked Charles Manson prosecutor Vincent Bugliosi to conduct the cross-examination, and on December 16, the last of the seven experts, Patrick Garland, was called to testify.

Garland blamed heavy leading in the barrel of Sirhan's gun for wiping out the individual striations necessary to identify it as the murder weapon. Questioned by Bugliosi, he could not say on what basis Wolfer positively identified the evidence bullets as coming from Sirhan's gun. Sixteen copper-jacketed slugs were fired through the weapon, tending to clean the barrel, Bugliosi said, so how could he account for the heavy leading?

"I said before it was strange," Garland told Bugliosi, "and I can't explain that." Had someone fired the gun after Wolfer? "Yes, sir," replied Garland.[62]

Had there been an unauthorized firing of the alleged murder weapon using lead bullets after Wolfer's initial test? The truth finally came to light in 1994 when Dan Moldea interviewed Dave Butler, who worked alongside Wolfer in the LAPD's Scientific Investigation Division.

"I've still got test bullets from that gun," said Butler. "We fired some extra test shots and I saved them."

"How many?" Moldea asked.

"I don't know. We fired a bootful of test shots."

"More than twenty?"

"Yeah. What we do is submit x amount to the court as evidence . . . but extra rounds are saved, and they are maintained in our files. Well, when the [Schrade suit] came up, the gun barrel was grossly changed internally. . . . The examiners basically found out that the gun barrel had been tampered with . . . and they couldn't come back with a positive comparison."

Butler eventually took two bullets and casings home as souvenirs.

"And this is from the test firings?"

"Yeah, this is before the gun's released (to the grand jury). This is after the main test-firing."

So, according to Butler, the extra test-firings occurred on June 6, before the gun was released to the grand jury and within hours of Wolfer's initial firing. Butler doesn't seem to realize that this extra firing and the fact that the barrel was not subsequently cleaned are more likely to be the cause of the changed barrel characteristics than any alleged "tampering."

But this still doesn't explain why the copper-alloy coating was stripped from Wolfer's initial test bullets. Did Butler fire lead bullets through the barrel before Wolfer did his tests with the copper-coated Mini-Mags? We don't know.

* * *

His interest piqued by the cross-examination of the firearms panel, Vincent Bugliosi began to investigate other areas. Paul Schrade showed him the AP photo, captioned "Bullet Found Near Kennedy Shooting Scene," of Officers Rozzi and Wright kneeling down to inspect a hole in a doorjamb leading from the backstage area into the narrow corridor that led into the pantry.[63]

Attempts to identify or interview the officers over the years had been fruitless, but now Bugliosi obtained an affidavit from Rozzi confirming that "sometime during the evening when we were looking for evidence, someone discovered what appeared to be a bullet a foot and a half or so from the bottom of the floor in a door jamb on the door behind the stage. I also personally observed what I believed to be a bullet in the place just mentioned. What I observed was a hole in the door jamb, and the base of what appeared to be a small caliber bullet was lodged in the hole."[64]

Bugliosi then phoned Officer Wright: "The bullet was definitely removed from the hole, but I don't know who did it," he told the lawyer. Under pressure from the LAPD and the DA's office, Wright subsequently backtracked, refusing to confirm the telephone conversation or to provide a statement. Years later, after Wright retired, Dan Moldea asked him, on a scale of one to ten, how sure he was that the object he saw was a bullet. "You can never be 100 percent sure," said Wright, "but I would say it would be as close to a ten as I'd ever want to go without pulling it out."

Bugliosi also interviewed assistant sound man Robert Alfeld and electrician Paul Dozier, who both worked at the hotel. While walking through the pantry on the morning of June 6, the day after the shooting, they spotted some objects under the base of the last ice machine on their right and picked them up to discover three rimfire, long rifle .22-caliber expended shell casings. At first, they thought someone was playing a "morbid joke" and had thrown them there after the assassination. They couldn't believe the FBI and police had not noticed them in their extensive search of the crime scene.

They took the shells up to their office, still thinking they were a joke, put them in a desk and forgot about them. Alfeld's father died two days later, and while he was away from work for a few weeks, the FBI interviewed Dozier and he told them about the casings. Alfeld placed no value on the casings until 1975, when he read an article about the mishandling of evidence in the RFK case and called William Harper.[65]

On November 18, Bugliosi subpoenaed Rozzi, Wright, and Alfeld to appear before Judge Wenke, but Wenke was interested only in the firearms experts and refused to widen the scope of his inquiry to include the issue of how many shots had been fired in the pantry.[66]

Undeterred, Bugliosi continued to interview witnesses to the "bullet holes" in the doorframes, including Dr. Noguchi himself: "I asked Mr. Wolfer where he had found bullet holes . . . he pointed, as I recall, to one hole in a ceiling panel above and an indentation in the cement ceiling. He also pointed to several holes in the door-frames of the swinging doors leading into the pantry. I directed that photographs of me be taken pointing to these holes. . . . I got the distinct impression from him that the holes may have been caused by bullets."[67]

Hotel maître d' Angelo Di Pierro told Bugliosi he was inspecting the pantry with police in the hours after the shooting: "I observed a small caliber bullet lodged about a quarter of an inch into the wood on the center divider of the two swinging doors. Several police officers also observed the bullet." The bullet was at head height and Di Pierro remembered thinking if he'd walked through the door, it might have hit him:

> I am quite familiar with guns and bullets, having been in the infantry for three and a half years. There is no question in my mind that this was a bullet and not a nail or any other object. The base of the bullet was round and from all indications, it appeared to be a .22 caliber bullet.
>
> A day or so later, the center divider that contained the bullet was removed by the Los Angeles Police Department for examination. I don't know who removed the bullet or what happened to it. The hole that contained the bullet was the only new hole I observed after the shooting. Even prior to the shooting, there were a few holes from nails, et cetera on the two swinging doors.[68]

Waiter Martin Patrusky also gave Bugliosi an affidavit, stating that during a police witness reconstruction four or five days after the shooting, "one of the officers pointed to two circled holes on the center divider of the swinging doors and told us they had dug two bullets out of the center divider. The two circled holes are shown in [the photograph] . . . I am absolutely sure that the police told us that two bullets were dug out of these holes."[69]

On June 5, while working as a carpenter at the Ambassador, Dale Poore was asked by two police officers to "remove the wooden facing, which was less than one inch in depth, from the center post of the double door area on the pantry side of the door located at the west end of the pantry. Before removing the material [Poore] noticed two apparent bullet holes on the east portion [pantry side] of that center post. These two holes were approximately four feet from ground level, with one about four inches higher than the other." The wood was taken away for inspection and replaced with a new piece of wood.

In 1975, Poore told the DA's office: "It looked like the bullet had went in at sort of an angle as it was traveling this way. So it made a bit of an oblong hole and the fiber of the board had closed in some after it went in. And that's the only reason I thought it had been a bullet went in there because you put any kind of a metal instrument, punch nail sets, anything in the hole, it won't have a fiber around the edge."

The other carpenter employed by the hotel, Wesley Harrington, assisted Poore and was asked if he would describe the holes he saw as bullet holes: "Yes, I would. During my teenage years . . . we had use of air rifles and .22 rifles and we had fired into old buildings and trees, and this looked like a hole similar to a small caliber bullet."[70]

After gathering these affidavits, Bugliosi and Schrade presented a new petition to Wenke, which described the LAPD trajectory analysis as "shamefully superficial" and called for a new panel to conduct "photographic reconstruction of the assassination scene, a re-examination of bullet pathways and a determination of how many shots were fired." They were once again denied.[71]

* * *

If two bullets were extracted from the door frames in the pantry, where are they now? Suspicion has long fallen on People's 38, two spent bullets allegedly found on the front seat of Sirhan's car. The panel examined these slugs and confirmed that traces of wood were embedded in the base and tip of each. Were these bullets really found in Sirhan's car or dug out of the pantry door frame?

The wood facing was destroyed by the LAPD in 1969, but the wood tracings in the bullets could have been microscopically compared with the original door frame in the Ambassador pantry. They weren't.

This leaves us with two possibilities: either Sirhan fired two rounds into a tree or board, dug them out, and put them in his glove compartment before he drove to the crime scene; or the bullets dug out of the wooden door frame were planted in Sirhan's car or falsely labeled.

In May 1976, a Freedom of Information Act request by researcher Greg Stone uncovered four FBI photographs of four circled holes in the door frames, with captions describing them as "bullet holes." Two were in the center divider and two were in the left doorframe. Both sets of holes were circled, and inside one circle in each was an officer's badge number 723, the initials LASO, and the name W. Tew (Deputy Sheriff Walter Tew of the LA sheriff's office).

By November 1976, former FBI agent William Bailey had heard of Bugliosi's claims of extra bullets in the pantry and approached him after a speech in New Jersey. Bailey had resigned from the FBI in 1971 and was now an assistant professor of police science at Gloucester County College nearby. He'd been in the pantry four to six hours after the shooting, on FBI assignment to interview witnesses and carefully examine the crime scene. He wrote out an affidavit for Bugliosi on the spot, stating, "At one point during these observations, I [and several other agents] noted at least two small caliber bullet holes in the center post of the two doors leading from the preparation room [pantry]. There is no question in our mind that they were bullet holes and were not caused by food carts or other equipment in the preparation room."[72]

A few months later, Bailey received a call from DA investigator William Burnett.

"There were at least two bullets in the center post," confirmed Bailey. "Can other agents corroborate this?"

"Yes, Agent Robert Pickard can."[73]

Nobody doubts that Bailey was in the pantry. Indeed, he was also present when Sandra Serrano and Vincent Di Pierro reviewed polka-dot dresses a few days later. And in a succession of television interviews over the years, he has consistently stuck to his story:

"There were two very distinct holes in the center divider, and I looked closely at the holes—I could see that they were bullet holes. You could actually see the base of a bullet in each hole.[74]

"I've serious reservations whether or not any of Bobby's wounds were inflicted by Sirhan's gun. I, at this point, feel that there probably was a second gun there and that it was fired."[75]

* * *

When the Kranz Report finally appeared in March 1977, it was a predictable whitewash. But while Kranz said the LAPD did an "excellent job" in its conspiracy investigation, he was extremely critical of Wolfer, whose work was "sloppy" and whose lack of records was inexplicable.

Kranz was also at a loss to explain the destruction of the door frames and ceiling tiles before Sirhan's appeal: "Potential evidence should never be destroyed until the entire case has run out. What the hell were these things destroyed for? . . . They were opening up the doors to total criticism and doubt."

He also called the destruction of the Jake Williams gun "just idiotic. There's no excuse or explanation that justifies why it was done."[76]

In 1988, after twenty years, the LAPD finally released its investigation files, revealing more destruction of evidence. On August 21, 1968, LAPD Officer Roy Keene had signed an order sending 2,400 photographs to County General Hospital in Los Angeles to be burned in a medical-waste incinerator. Of the 4,818 interviews and interrogations LAPD conducted during its original investigation, tapes of only 301 survived.[77]

The release of these files inspired a new generation of investigators and provided further evidence of bullet holes in the pantry. Fifty-one photographs taken in the hours after the shooting by LAPD photographer Charles Collier showed multiple holes in the door frames and ceiling panels and, again, Wolfer and Noguchi pointing to these holes. One photo shows Wolfer pointing to a spot on the upper door frame. Another shows Dr. Noguchi measuring two holes in the left door frame and pointing to two holes in the center divider.[78]

Karl Uecker told archivist John Burns he also saw what appeared to be two bullet holes in the center divider of the pantry doorway upon returning to the crime scene after a police interview on the morning of June 5. He passed through those swinging doors dozens of times each night and was positive the holes were not there prior to the shooting.[79]

The most comprehensive study of the bullet holes in the pantry was conducted by author Dan Moldea. In the spring of 1990, he interviewed more than one hundred LAPD officers and sheriff's deputies, a dozen of whom recalled seeing bullet holes in the pantry.

Sergeant James MacArthur, senior police detective at the crime scene, said he saw "quite a few" bullet holes. Inspector Robert Rock told Moldea that a couple of bullets were dug out of a door frame. Officer Kenneth Vogel was positive he saw two bullet fragments on the pantry floor, which he brought to the attention of an LAPD official. No such fragments are recorded in police files.

Sergeant Raymond Rolon told Moldea, "One of the investigators pointed to a hole in the doorframe and said, 'We just pulled a bullet out of there.'" Deputy Sheriff Thomas Beringer recalled a man in a tuxedo "trying to take a bullet out of the door frame with a silver knife, for a souvenir." SID Officer David Butler told Moldea he saw Wolfer take two .22-caliber bullets out of the center divider. They tore out the wood facing and laid it down on the steam table, and Wolfer disassembled it to get the bullets out. These bullets were never booked as evidence.

When the shooting victims were taken to the hospital, police at the crime scene had no way of knowing how many bullets had been fired. Word was that Kennedy had been shot twice, so finding bullets in the door frame was a good opportunity to build an airtight case against Sirhan. Even later, when it was found that Kennedy had been shot three times and a fourth bullet had gone through his shoulder pad, none of the officers at the scene realized the significance of the extra bullets in the door frame, except DeWayne Wolfer.[80]

In 1994, Sirhan's researcher Rose Lynn Mangan reentered the case after a long hiatus and conducted a thorough examination of the ballistics evidence and records at the new home of the police files, the California State Archives in Sacramento. She made two extremely important discoveries.

The first was that the inventory done by the firearms panel in 1975 suggested that the ID markings on the base of the Kennedy neck bullet and the Goldstein bullet had changed since 1968, breaking the chain of custody of two key bullets in the case.

Of the three bullets that hit Kennedy's body, one was lost in the ceiling, and one was so fragmented that Dr. Noguchi could not even confirm what caliber it was, so the bullet removed from Kennedy's neck was the only bullet that could link Sirhan's gun to the murder.

Dr. Noguchi's autopsy report describes the recovery of the Kennedy neck bullet at 8:40 a.m. on June 6: "The initials TN, and the numbers 31 are placed on the base of the bullet for future identification." But no bullet markings were noted when the bullet was booked into evidence and there is no further record of the ID marking "TN 31" in reference to this bullet. When Pat Garland made his inventory in 1975, he recorded the markings on the base of the Kennedy neck bullet as "TN DW." The "31" marked on the base by Dr. Noguchi had disappeared.

Similarly, the base of the Goldstein bullet was marked with an "X" by Dr. Finkel on extraction on June 5, 1968. By 1975, the "X" had been replaced by a "6," a new panel ID number added by Garland.

Identification markings on the base of a .22-caliber bullet are engraved with an electric needle and are so small, they would be extremely difficult to erase or write over. In 1974, Dr. Noguchi authenticated these bullets for Baxter Ward by visual observation, but we have no record to indicate that he checked the ID markings. While it's possible that the ID marks eroded over time or due to poor maintenance, the integrity of these bullets must be seriously questioned.

Mangan's second important discovery came in the form of a second test-shot envelope. The envelope for Exhibit 55 entered as evidence at the trial contained three test bullets and was dated June 6, with the name "Sirhan B. Sirhan," the crime "187 P.C." (murder), and the serial number of the Jake Williams gun, H-18602.

Wolfer had dismissed this wrong number as a "clerical error," but in 1994, Mangan discovered the test-shot envelope Wolfer submitted to the grand jury on June 7 as Exhibit 5-B. This contained Wolfer's four other test bullets, but the envelope was dated June 5, with the name "John Doe," the crime "217 P.C." (attempted murder—Kennedy was still alive), and the serial number of the Sirhan gun, H-53725.[81]

This strongly suggests that Wolfer conducted one test-firing on June 5, while Kennedy was still alive and before Sirhan's identity was known; and another on June 6, after Kennedy died. We also know that Dave Butler fired "a bootful" of shots from the Sirhan gun before it was sealed by the grand jury on June 7; that Wolfer had the Jake Williams gun on June 8 and possibly earlier; and that the Sirhan gun was not providing test bullets with sufficient striations for identification.

The permutations of which gun Wolfer used for these test-firings and which of the resulting test bullets he entered as evidence—none of which he marked for identification—is mind-boggling.

While the ballistics evidence to date was complex and inconclusive, there was one more hand to be played involving the acoustic evidence.

FIFTEEN

THE MANCHURIAN CANDIDATE

In 1959, Richard Condon published his second novel, *The Manchurian Candidate*, a heady psychodrama of assassination, conspiracy, and paranoia. It pushed all the hot buttons of the time—the Communist witch hunts of McCarthyism and the threat of Communist brainwashing evoked by American POWs returning from the Korean War with accounts of mind manipulation.

Protagonist Raymond Shaw is a hypnotically programmed assassin, a U.S. soldier brainwashed by the North Koreans whose father is running for vice president in a campaign orchestrated by his mother, Eleanor Iselin. The Iselins pose as McCarthyites but are actually Communist agents. Raymond's mission is to assassinate the presidential nominee so that his father and the Communists can rise to power. Every time Raymond hears the phrase "Why don't you pass the time by playing a little solitaire?" it triggers a hypnotic trance in which he kills, with no memory of having done so.

In 1962, with Frank Sinatra playing Major Bennett Marco, Shaw's former comrade (and Laurence Harvey as Shaw), John Frankenheimer directed the film of the book, which became a cult classic. Frankenheimer reflected on the film before his death in 2002:

> *I became good friends with Bobby, who loved the movie. I made all the films for Bobby's 1968 campaign, he stayed at my house, and I drove him to the Ambassador Hotel on the night he died. Did I think that the political assassination in The Manchurian Candidate prompted Sirhan Sirhan to kill Bobby? No way. But the incident affected my perspective on life because, with Bobby, I felt I was part of something that could change the world: he turned me into an idealist. Then, suddenly, it was gone and nothing mattered. My career was defused. It took a long time to reinvest my life with some kind of meaning. I finished the sixties with a bad case of burn-out . . . his death was the defining moment of my life.[1]*

By 1968, the idea of a "Manchurian candidate" was still dismissed as a Hollywood fantasy, and Dr. Diamond referred to the idea that Sirhan could have been programmed by someone else as a "crackpot theory." But unknown to the public or Sirhan's small army of psychiatrists, the CIA had in fact been working on their own "Manchurian candidate" since the early 1950s.

Dr. Diamond did, at least, agree that Sirhan was in a hypnotic trance at the time of the shooting, and there are a number of clues that suggest this. Between nine thirty and eleven that night, Sirhan stood staring, mesmerized by the Teletype machine in the Colonial Room, as described by Western Union operator Mary Grohs: "Well, he came over to my machine and started staring at it. Just staring. I'll never forget his eyes."[2]

Vincent Di Pierro's strongest impression of Sirhan was "that sick smile on his face" while he was shooting. Several other witnesses remarked on this strange smile; one also described how Sirhan's brow was furrowed in "tremendous concentration" as he fired.

In the struggle on the steam table, Earl Williman described Sirhan's "superhuman strength" as half a dozen burly Kennedy aides tried to prize the gun from his grasp. Frank Burns and Karl Uecker were also surprised at the strength of Sirhan's grip as Uecker smashed his hand on the steam table to try and shake the gun free. Despite the furious activity swirling around him, writer George Plimpton described Sirhan's eyes as "dark brown and enormously peaceful." Joe LaHive thought Sirhan looked "very tranquil" as he was being kicked and punched in the pantry. In a hypnotic session with Dr. Diamond, Sirhan remembered "resting" on the steam table, and these witness descriptions seem to fit his hypnotic mood.[3]

An urgent Teletype sent from the FBI office in Charlotte, North Carolina to Los Angeles at 12:55 p.m. on June 5 reported a call from a member of the Psychiatry Department at Duke University Medical Center in Durham. He had seen the suspect on live television and suspected he had "some physical symptoms of being on amphetamines or other type drug. If urine analysis not performed today or tomorrow, would probably not be medically possible to tell if suspect using some kind of drug." No analysis was made. Amphetamines increase concentration and energy, and could have deepened the hypnotic state and strengthened Sirhan's grip on the gun.[4]

How also to explain Sirhan's jovial banter in custody? According to Bill Jordan, "He was happy to talk about anything other than the Kennedy case. . . . I was impressed by Sirhan's composure and relaxation. He appeared less upset to me than individuals arrested for a traffic violation." Was Sirhan a callous, cold-blooded murderer, smugly dusting himself off after a job well done, or in a dissociated state, completely unaware of the shooting? At three thirty in the morning, he asked Deputy DA John Howard if he'd been arraigned yet. Sirhan seemed so disoriented, Howard had to remind him he was in Los Angeles.[5]

Later that morning, when examined by Dr. Crahan in his cell, Sirhan shivered, appearing to have a chill. Months later, every time Dr. Diamond brought Sirhan out of a trance, he had a habit of shivering as he readjusted to full consciousness.

Was he slowly emerging from a trance as Dr. Crahan examined him nine hours after the shooting?[6]

The combination of these factors, his interviews with Sirhan, and what he saw in the psychiatric sessions with Diamond and Pollack certainly convinced Bob Kaiser: "I hold it now, maybe ninety-five percent certainty . . . that he really didn't remember shooting Robert Kennedy, that he probably killed Kennedy in a trance and was programmed to forget that he'd done it, and programmed to forget the names and identities of others who might have helped him do it."[7]

Dr. Diamond told researcher Betsy Langman in 1974: "Let me immediately state that it was immediately apparent that Sirhan had been programmed. . . . His response to hypnosis was very different . . . strange, in many respects. And he showed this phenomenon of automatic writing, which is something that can be done only when one is pretty well trained."

Diamond was also surprised at how easy it was to hypnotize Sirhan: "Most people may take an hour or more to go under hypnosis the first time. A schizophrenic usually takes much longer, if he goes under at all. But it took less than ten minutes for Sirhan to go into a deep authentic sleep." He got the feeling Sirhan had been hypnotized before.[8]

The LAPD confirmed that Sirhan had indeed been hypnotized before. He'd gone to see stage hypnotist Richard St. Charles in late 1966 at a Pasadena night club within walking distance of his home. He volunteered to be hypnotized on stage and joined the performer's mailing list. St. Charles then wrote notes on his potential clients. "The notes that I had were that he was a very good subject." St. Charles felt Sirhan had "very definitely" been hypnotized before.[9]

Diamond believed Sirhan "programmed himself exactly as a computer is programmed by its magnetic tape [through a] correspondence course in self-hypnosis. . . . This seems the most logical explanation of all the things that happened."

But Kaiser was convinced Sirhan had been programmed by somebody else. Was it the Rosicrucians? Was it stable hand Tom Rathke or someone more sinister? He didn't know. The American public were still in their own twilight state, dissociated from what the CIA was doing in their name—assassinations, experimental testing, and mind control.[10]

In late May 1969, at the end of the trial, Sirhan was transferred to death row in the old tower at San Quentin. Over the summer, he received twenty weekly visits from the prison's senior psychologist, Dr. Eduard Simson. Simson had been a practicing clinical psychologist for thirteen years, with a BA from Stanford, an MA from New York University, and a PhD in psychology from Heidelberg University. He had worked at San Quentin for six years, studying thousands of prisoners, and was in charge of the prison's psychological testing program.

Simson was so disturbed by what he found in these sessions that he later wrote a twenty-three page affidavit outlining his findings. His key discovery was that "nowhere in Sirhan's test response was I able to find evidence that he is a 'paranoid schizophrenic' or 'psychotic,' as testified by the doctors at the trial. My findings were substantiated by the observations of the chief psychiatrist at San Quentin, Dr. Schmidt, who also did not see Sirhan as psychotic or paranoid schizophrenic.

"The fact that Sirhan was easy to hypnotize, as testified by Dr. Diamond, proves he was not a paranoid schizophrenic," wrote Simson. "Paranoid schizophrenics are almost impossible to hypnotize. They are too suspicious and do not trust anybody, including friends and relatives, not to speak of a hypnotist from, for him, the most hated race (Jewish). . . . Sirhan, however, was an unusually good hypnotic subject. . . . He had manufactured a hypno-disk, and was practicing self-hypnosis in his cell, an activity requiring considerable self-control, which no psychotic has."

Sirhan's decidedly average IQ of 89 presented at the trial was also much lower than the superior IQ of 127 that Simson later calculated using the same test procedure. Simson blamed the wide disparity on the stress of the trial and Sirhan not wanting to cooperate "with a Jewish doctor [doctors] he deeply distrusted. . . . This deep distrust, NORMAL [under the circumstances] was interpreted by his doctors as 'paranoia,' 'schizophrenia,' or 'psychosis.' None of these labels could describe Sirhan's behavior on Death Row where I found his behavior fell well within the normal range."

An Estonian émigré, used to regional political conflicts and neutral on the Middle East, Simson quickly gained Sirhan's trust. Sirhan told Simson the same story he had told the police, his attorneys, and the DA about the night of the shooting: he remembered pouring coffee for the girl, then the choking, but nothing in between. Simson felt that Sirhan spoke about the crime as if "reciting from a book" and was baffled by the lack of details. "A psychologist always looks for details," he said. "If a person is involved in a real situation, there are details." Simson thought the girl might have triggered the trance. "You can be programmed that if you meet a certain person or see something specific, then you go into a trance."

By now, Sirhan was coming around to the idea that he might have been hypnotized. "Sometimes, I go in a very deep trance so I can't even speak," he told Simson. "I don't remember what I do under hypnosis. I had to be in a trance when I shot Kennedy, as I don't remember having shot him. I had to be hypnotized! Christ!"

Sirhan asked Simson to use hypnosis to help him remember what happened, and they built up a strong rapport. "He was extremely eager to talk to me," Simson recalled. "He himself wanted to find out. If I had been allowed to spend as much time with him as necessary, I would have found out something." But before they could have their first hypnotic session, Simson's visits were abruptly terminated by Associate Warden James Park in September 1969. Park was concerned that Simson "appears to be making a career out of Sirhan." Simson was incensed. "A psychologist spends as much time with a patient as the disease demands," he said. He had never been cut off like that before, and immediately resigned.

After Simson's visits were terminated, Sirhan, through his family, asked Simson to review the psychiatric testimony at the trial. Several years later, after talking to William Harper about the ballistics issues in the case, Simson read the trial transcript and "was appalled at the conduct of the mental health professionals involved." He found "errors, distortions, even probable falsification of facts," largely because everybody assumed Sirhan alone had killed Kennedy.

"There is a dominant impression that the psychiatric-psychological team, largely made up of Jewish doctors, pooled their efforts to prove that Sirhan, the hated Arab, was guilty and insane, a paranoid schizophrenic. The evidence suggests Dr. Diamond was not objective enough and was not an impartial searcher for truth as a psychiatrist in such a grave situation involving a man's life and death should be. . . . Sirhan told me he did not trust Dr. Diamond, that he was making up stories for him to please and confuse him. . . . They were not in a position to unlock Sirhan's mind. This could only be done by a doctor Sirhan fully trusted."

Simson also felt that Sirhan's handwriting at San Quentin differed, "often drastically," from the writing he observed in the notebooks. "Whether someone else wrote the notebooks or whether they were written under some special influence, such as hypnosis, is entirely unsolved. If someone hypnotized him when the notebooks were written, who was it?"

Simson concluded that "Sirhan was the center of a drama that unfolded slowly, discrediting and embarrassing psychology and psychiatry as a profession. The drama's true center still lies very much concealed and unknown to the general public. Was Sirhan merely a double, a stand-in, sent there to attract attention? Was he at the scene to replace someone else? Did he actually kill Robert Kennedy? Whatever the full truth of the . . . assassination, it still remains locked in Sirhan's other, still anonymous minds. . . . A close study of the trial testimony and my own extensive study of Sirhan leads to one irrevocable and obvious conclusion: Sirhan's trial was, and will be remembered as, the psychiatric blunder of the century."

To Simson, Sirhan was the ideal "Manchurian candidate": "He was easily influenced, had no real roots, and was looking for a cause. The Arab-Israeli conflict could easily have been used to motivate him."[11]

Simson's thoughts are echoed by Dr. Herbert Spiegel, a world authority on hypnosis and professor of psychiatry at Columbia University since the early fifties, a man who devised two of the most widely used tests for measuring a subject's susceptibility to hypnosis.

When I visited Dr. Spiegel, he explained his chance introduction to the field while completing his residency in psychiatry in Washington, DC, during World War II. A visiting German professor agreed to teach him hypnosis in exchange for English lessons, and after Pearl Harbor, Spiegel was called up by the army, not as a psychiatrist but as a battalion surgeon for a thousand men with the First Infantry Division in the invasion of North Africa.

"I was in combat for about six months, and during that time, I treated hundreds of casualties and had a great opportunity to use hypnosis to deal with pain and anxiety and phobias of various kinds."

Dr. Spiegel defines hypnosis as a state of "attentive, receptive concentration" characterized by what he terms the "compulsive triad": (1) "a spontaneous amnesia to the post-hypnotic signal"; (2) "a compulsive need to comply with the signal"; and (3) a rationalization of why he's doing it. "He doesn't say, 'I'm doing it because the hypnotist told me to do it.' He comes up with his own rationalization to explain what he's doing."

Spiegel estimates that between 80 and 85 percent of the population have the capacity for hypnosis, and how hypnotizable a person is seems to be genetically determined. One of the standard testing procedures he devised to identify and grade this natural hypnotizability is called the Hypnotic Induction Profile: "On a zero-to-five scale, about fifteen to twenty percent of the population are zeros. That includes mentally ill people like schizophrenics, severely depressed people, and some with severe psychopathic personalities or severe obsessive compulsives; [they] are not hypnotizable—they don't have the biological capacity for it. Then, on the high side, about five to ten percent of the population are extremely hypnotizable, and then most people are in between." The higher on the scale a person is, the more can be achieved through hypnosis in psychotherapy.

If Sirhan was low on the scale, he could not have been programmed to shoot Robert Kennedy. "But, on the basis of what Dr. Diamond described, he seemed to be a very hypnotizable person. He had Sirhan act like a monkey or do all kinds of bizarre things which only a high [on the scale] could do. Now, if he were a one or a two, it'd be impossible for [Diamond] to get him to do that."

Dr. Spiegel felt that Sirhan "was on the high side, but I wanted to test him to establish his hypnotizability, to see he wasn't faking it." But when Sirhan's attorney Lawrence Teeter tried to arrange this, "the judge would not permit me to examine him at all."

Until Spiegel is allowed access to Sirhan by the courts, on the basis of Dr. Diamond's reports, "I just am assuming that he was what we call a grade five. And knowing what grade fives can do, I was able to postulate that if we have him in a trance state, he could possibly reveal a lot of information about how he was programmed and where he was going and what he was going to do about it; but we weren't allowed to do it."[12]

* * *

One of the perennial questions regarding hypnosis relates to its use in crime—can an individual be programmed to do something against his or her moral values? While there is some disagreement about this in the field, many of the naysayers seem more intent on protecting the reputation of hypnosis than on reporting the limits of what's possible. These include the late hypnotherapist Dr. William J.

Bryan, a technical adviser on the filming of *The Manchurian Candidate* and often cited as the man who programmed Sirhan. In his book *Legal Aspects of Hypnosis*, Bryan declared, "It is impossible by means of hypnosis to force a subject to commit an act which violates his basic moral code."[13]

But leaders in the field such as George Estabrooks and F.L. Marcuse refute this claim. They both argue that a person's "moral code" is not rigid and adapts to circumstances. Very few people "so abhor violence that they would not engage in it . . . to save their own lives," wrote Estabrooks. While a subject may resist a direct suggestion to do something he or she perceives as antisocial, Estabrooks reported no failures in experiments "of a more subtle type, where the hypnotist takes great care to alter his subject's perception of the situation to create in him the conviction that the required act is . . . actually desirable."

Estabrooks tells of an experiment by J.G. Watkins during World War II, in which a private in the U.S. Army was put into a deep trance and told, "'In a minute you will slowly open your eyes. In front of you, you will see a dirty Jap soldier. He has a bayonet, and is going to kill you unless you kill him first. You will have to strangle him with your bare hands.' A lieutenant colonel, the head psychiatrist . . . was placed directly in front of the subject and about ten feet away." He was soon attacked by the private.[14]

The moral code can also be sidestepped by appealing to a sense of higher moral purpose. Of several landmark cases in criminal history, the most famous is probably the Hardrup case in Denmark in 1952.

Palle Hardrup and Bjorn Nielsen befriended each other in prison, and after their release, Nielsen continued to develop Hardrup as a hypnotic foil for his criminal schemes. He conditioned Hardrup to go into a trance at the sight or sound of the letter "X"—his hypnotic cue or "key word." "X" represented a guardian spirit (Nielsen), who would appear to Hardrup in trance and give him orders.

First, Hardrup was forced to arrange for his girlfriend to have sex with Nielsen. Then, Hardrup was directed to rob banks to raise money for a new political party that would unify Scandinavia. The first robbery went well but during the second one, he shot dead two bank staff in Copenhagen and was captured by the police. The moral purpose of unifying Scandinavia had been sufficient justification for Hardrup's willingness to kill.

Once back in prison, Hardrup was examined by psychiatrist Dr. Paul J. Reiter, and his amnesia symptoms led Reiter to suspect hypnotic conditioning and programming. After nineteen months, Reiter finally "unlocked" Hardrup's mind, and the court freed him and sent Nielsen to prison for life for robbery and murder "planned and instigated by influence of various kinds, including suggestions of a hypnotic nature."

In 1967, Dr. Spiegel was asked to make a film with NBC newscaster Frank McGee. Titled *Fact or Fiction—An Experiment in Post-Hypnotic Compliance*, it provides an early illustration of how a grade five (highly hypnotizable person) could be hypnotically programmed and their moral values altered.

Dr. Spiegel's unrehearsed experiment was filmed at NBC on May 31, 1967, in the presence of McGee and the forty-year-old subject, Mr. Snyder, a New York businessman whose politics were "somewhat left of center" and whom Spiegel had determined to be a grade five.

After hypnotizing Snyder, Dr. Spiegel told him about "a Communist plot developing that is aimed to control all the major radio and TV networks in this country. . . . Later on, when you're questioned about this, no matter who doubts you and no matter how stringently others question you about this, you will hold firmly to this conviction, and furthermore, you will urge them to alert themselves to it. At some time you may be shown a sheet of paper with three names on it, and if you're pressed hard enough, you'll even reveal what you know about those three named persons."

Spiegel then brought him out of the formal trance, Snyder opened his eyes, and the posthypnotic phase began. Snyder couldn't remember what happened while he was in trance but did know he was at NBC studios. "As a matter of fact," he said, scratching the side of his face, "I wonder if NBC knows what's going on. . . . The front pages are covered with all kinds of news, but the Communist infiltration, my God, they don't know about the mass media. The radio and television stations of this country are important means of reaching the people and here we are unaware of it. . . . The people in charge of the programming could be the dupes of the Communist party, my God, we could brainwash the whole population."

Snyder said an unnamed friend gave him this information—he didn't want to betray him, "but I think friendship should stop at a certain point where the whole country could be in peril. . . . I hate the Communists."

"Suppose I told you that I knew the friend?" said McGee. "Is it Jack Harris?" he asked, conjuring an invented name.

Snyder averted his eyes, shifted uncomfortably, and shook his head.

"No . . . no . . . this man was a draft dodger and he was caught because he believed in the Communist party . . . I don't really think I should betray him." Under questioning, Snyder described hearing his friend discuss the plan "in a room over a little off-Broadway theater, right off Sheridan Square."

McGee pulled out a blank sheet of paper. "I asked you a while ago . . ." "About Richard Harris?"

"Yeah. Jack Harris. . . . Did you know him as Richard?"

"Yes."

"Uh-huh. I want to hand you a sheet of paper and ask you if the names on this paper were not present that night."

Responding to the hypnotic stimulus, Snyder hallucinated three names on the blank sheet of paper—"Richard Harris" and two others—providing detailed descriptions. On a count of three, Spiegel put him back in trance, and Snyder continued to comply with the program: "Slowly but surely, the networks . . . are going to be under the control of the Communist Party; that's already in full swing and . . . we better do something about it before people start believing the Communist way of life. . . . it makes me tremble to think what might happen in this country. . . . [Harris] is a demon. He should be tarred and feathered and got out of the country."

When Snyder was shown the completed film several days later, he had no recollection of the program. "I'm absolutely dumbfounded," he said. "I just can't conceive of having said the things I said. I don't think that way or believe that way. It worries me that I could be made to have these thoughts which are so foreign to my self-beliefs."

NBC never aired the experiment. "I suppose it was too graphic," Spiegel later told author and investigator William Turner. "It might have frightened a lot of people." After seeing the film, Turner asked, "If you had stuck a gun in the subject's hand and instructed him to shoot McGee, what would he have done?" "Ah," the doctor said, "the ultimate question. I'm afraid he might have shot him."[15]

Dr. Spiegel agreed that it's impossible to get most people to do something against their moral values "because eventually, they would have enough of their conscious awareness that . . . they would break off their hypnotic relationship, but with a high, they lose that connection with their everyday perspective . . . they're so compliant and uncritical, they adopt the new perspective 100 percent."[16]

"It can be described as brainwashing," Spiegel once said, "because the mind is cleared of its old values and emotions, which are replaced by implanting other suggestions. Highly hypnotizable persons, when under the control of unscrupulous persons, are the most vulnerable."[17]

The Spiegel film also illustrates how vulnerable hypnotized subjects are to deception. "Their desire to comply, both in and out of the formal trance, is such that they may convincingly invent information in an effort to give the hypnotist what he seems to want." So while careful and dispassionate regression can "uncover incredibly accurate and subtle factual and emotional experiences buried in the remote memory of the past," without independent corroboration, such memories may also be "stress-hallucinations" invented to please the hypnotist.[18]

Dr. Spiegel feels all of the above apply to Sirhan Sirhan:

The people who were programming him worked on the assumption that the Israeli-Arab War was an insult to him and I think they played on that and built up his first, skepticism, then his anger at the Israelis. . . . At first, he had no feelings about Kennedy but when they told him about how Kennedy was pro-Israeli, they built up his antagonism . . . to not so much focus on killing him but to focus on . . . getting rid of somebody who is such an enemy of the Arab culture. On the basis of that, they were able to program him to tell him that we're going to give you an occasion to sometime get in front of him and we're going to give you a gun and when the time comes, you're going to shoot him.

Spiegel believes the "automatic writing" in Sirhan's notebooks dates from the time he was being programmed—"writing it down was his way of reinforcing the direction of the programming that was going on."

Having established and reinforced Sirhan's antagonism toward Kennedy, the next step was to "control his environment and see to it he's present at the time, and tell him what he's going to do and even have a signal to tell him when to do it." How would you do that? "Well, there was this woman in the polka-dot dress and a man, whoever they are," said Dr. Spiegel. It was quite possible for the senior programmer to assign control of Sirhan to coconspirators, like the girl in the polka-dot dress. "You don't have to be a genius to program somebody. If somebody is highly hypnotizable and you can tap it, then almost anybody with a malevolent goal can program him to do it."

With the girl acting as a handler for Sirhan, Dr. Spiegel assumed that "up to the part [with] the coffee, he was not in a trance state . . . but probably after that, that's when they induced the hypnosis with him and from that time until it was all over, he was in a trance state, so he had a spontaneous amnesia for the whole event."

How much preparation time would be needed for something like this? "I would say within a few months is all that was necessary, because he was so highly hypnotizable, he could be very quickly programmed." How much every day would they need to see him to be able to program him? "If I were doing it, I think just one or two hours a day would be enough." And how would you mask that, so he wouldn't be able to remember going to a certain place? "Tell him, 'You won't tell anybody about it. This will be our secret.'"[19]

Contrary to previous books on this case, there is no evidence of a three-month gap where Sirhan went mysteriously missing in the months leading up to the shooting. Sirhan's family told that the FBI he slept at home every night in the year leading up to the assassination, so the idea that Sirhan was spirited away to a military installation in the desert for programming is simply not credible.[20]

Dr. Spiegel offered a much more plausible scenario. Sirhan was out of work for three months prior to the assassination and spent most of his time alone, with no regular friends to track his movements or report unusual acquaintances. Sirhan spent most days at the library or at the racetrack, "losing heavily," and frittering away the last of his insurance money. He therefore represented the perfect candidate—alienated, isolated, and highly hypnotizable, with deep feelings about the Arab-Israeli War that could be redirected toward Kennedy.

Sirhan was recruited and went to see the programmer every day for an hour or two at the "library" to further his "studies." At night, he went home and practiced the self-hypnosis in his room and wrote in his notebook, as a kind of homework to strengthen the programming. The programmer created an amnesia for his sessions with Sirhan and an amnesia for the notebook, so Sirhan couldn't remember writing in it.

By the time Kennedy hit California, plans were well advanced. If Sirhan wasn't aware of Kennedy's promise to send bombers to Israel, he could certainly be told by his programmers. On election night, Sirhan could be cued to shoot by a "keyword," or conditioned to respond to the program at the sight of Kennedy. If necessary, hypnotic control could be strengthened by amphetamines slipped into his coffee—to enhance concentration and conjure up the tremendous strength he would show during the struggle for the gun.

With all this in mind, the idea of a "Manchurian candidate" doesn't seem so outlandish after all.[21]

* * *

When it comes to clues that Sirhan was in a trance that night, Dr. Spiegel told me there are no physical symptoms that typify a trance state. The "sick smile" described by Vincent Di Pierro and the stomach cramps Sirhan complained of "could be somatic expressions of anxiety—he was under such pressure to comply with the hypnotic signal that, even though there was some resistance to it, he had to comply." Sirhan's shivering when he emerged from a trance with Dr. Diamond could also be "a somatic reflection of anxiety" due to the uncertainty of his reorientation to real life.

Contrary to previous writing on the subject, Dr. Spiegel also noted that as drugs and alcohol impair concentration, a hypnotic trance works best when the mind is clear. Back in the sixties, "they used to think hypnosis was a form of sleep and you exaggerate that by using drugs and alcohol. But since we now know that hypnosis is the opposite of sleep, today, if they were doing it, they would not use drugs or alcohol."

Dr. Spiegel also found Sirhan's bizarre behavior in custody entirely consistent with his having been programmed: "He does not have an emotional knowledge that he committed a crime, so in that sense, he's an honest liar. So he could easily feel at ease and sharp and alert because he doesn't feel guilty about anything. The last thing he knows, he was having coffee with this woman and to be in a police station—he has no knowledge of what happened, so why am I here? He had a total blank because he's totally dissociated from it."

Why didn't he ask, "Why am I being held? I want my rights," and so on. "Well, he's too compliant. He's with authority. As a compliant subject, 'If I'm here, I guess I'm supposed to here. What right do I have to question this?' That would be typical of the trance state, the automatic compliance to a situation and with no challenging at all of the circumstance."

According to Dr. Spiegel, Sirhan could well have stayed in the trance until he was arraigned later that morning. "If he fell asleep, then the odds are he would come out of the trance," but Sirhan didn't fall asleep during that time, and the shower he took would not have affected the trance.

Sirhan's subsequent rationalization that he must have killed Kennedy even though he couldn't remember the shooting, also fits this pattern of compliance: "One of the outstanding features of a grade five or highly hypnotizable subject is that they have this spontaneous amnesia and they don't critically appraise anything they're told . . . he confesses to doing it because his thinking was, 'Well, if you say I did it, I guess I did it. . . . I don't remember it but I have no reason to deny what you're telling me.'"

We finally turned to Dr. Diamond's diagnosis of Sirhan as a paranoid schizophrenic. "I think he was dead wrong!" exclaimed Dr. Spiegel. "All our research shows clearly that schizophrenia does not occur in hypnotizable people. I have never yet seen a schizophrenic that was hypnotizable."

Ultimately, Dr. Spiegel believes that a group of people programmed Sirhan— "one senior programmer and many accessories." The senior programmer could assign hypnotic control of Sirhan to colleagues like the girl in the polka-dot dress, and the whole project was "very carefully designed by people who were expert in brainwashing victims . . . finding him, training him, then having this man and a woman develop a comradeship with him so they got used to the idea of being together; and placing him there at the right spot, with a gun to use, as instructed."

Dr. Spiegel thinks it probable that these techniques are still used today but "the people who do it . . . don't go round advertising it. And if they do it, they can be very secretive, the way they were secretive with Sirhan. So I don't think we can say it's out of style now or it's not being used now; we don't know."[22]

The search for Sirhan's programmer inevitably leads to a discussion of the military uses of hypnosis. For centuries, "hypnotic couriers" have been used to convey messages, to lessen the chance these messages would fall into enemy hands. In 1500 B.C., the Egyptians used a hypnocourier system in which "programmed" virgins served the pharoah as royal "message-bearers from the gods." As Emery notes, these women were sent under military escort to distant dignitaries who knew the cue that would unlock the courier's lips and release the secret message locked in her unconscious." The courier had no conscious knowledge of the message, and no torture would release it without the right prompt.[23]

The use of hypnotic couriers in modern warfare was outlined by an early pioneer in the field, Dr. George E. Estabrooks, a Rhodes scholar with a doctorate from Harvard who formulated guidelines for the use of hypnosis in military intelligence in both world wars. Estabrooks described the "preparation" of Captain Smith, a "hypnotic courier" during World War II:

Captain Smith had undergone months of training. He was an excellent subject but did not realize it. I had removed from him, by post-hypnotic suggestion, all recollection of ever having been hypnotized. First I had the Service Corps call the captain to Washington [to deliver a report to Tokyo]. . . . Then I put him under deep hypnosis, and gave him—orally—a vital message to be delivered directly on his arrival in Japan to a [Colonel Brown] of military intelligence. Outside of myself, Colonel Brown was the only person who could hypnotize Captain Smith. This is "locking." I performed it by saying to the hypnotized Captain: "Until further orders from me, only Colonel Brown and I can hypnotize you. We will use a signal phrase 'the moon is clear.' Whenever you hear this phrase from Brown or myself you will pass instantly into deep hypnosis." When Captain Smith re-awakened, he had no conscious memory of what happened in trance. All that he was aware of was that he must head for Tokyo to pick up a division report.

On arrival there, Smith reported to Brown, who hypnotized him with the signal phrase. Under hypnosis, Smith delivered my message and received one to bring back. Awakened, he was given the division report and returned home by jet. There I hypnotized him once more with the signal phrase, and he spieled off Brown's answer that had been dutifully tucked away in his unconscious mind. The system is virtually foolproof. As exemplified by this case, the information was "locked" in Smith's unconscious for retrieval by the only two people who knew the combination. The subject had no conscious memory of what happened, so could not spill the beans. No one else could hypnotize him even if they might know the signal phrase."[24]

* * *

After investigating Soviet interrogation methods, the CIA began experimenting with hypnosis in April 1950, with the establishment of Project Bluebird. The project's initial objectives were defensive—discovering means of "conditioning personnel to prevent unauthorized extraction of information from them by unknown means" and "preventing hostile control of Agency personnel." Early CIA memos on the subject were preoccupied with "sealing" the programmed mind from attempts by other hypnotists to put their agent into a trance. The usual method of sealing was simply a hypnotic suggestion to prevent the subject from being hypnotized by any unauthorized person.

But the examination of possible offensive uses of hypnosis and drugs were soon added to the project's charter, and by December 1950, the Bluebird team had used drugs to induce a hypnotic-like trance. Between 1950 and 1952, Bluebird was redesignated Artichoke, and further goals were added, including the ability to induce amnesia.[25]

In 1951, CIA behavioral research coordinator Morse Allen became obsessed by hypnosis and took a four-day crash course from a leading stage hypnotist in New York. Allen learned enough to experiment on the secretaries back at CIA headquarters. As Melanson noted, he hypnoprogrammed them "to 'steal' secret files and pass them to strangers" and induced one secretary "to report to the bedroom of a complete stranger, where she fell into a preprogrammed trance."[26]

On April 13, 1953, CIA director Allen Dulles accepted a proposal from a senior official in clandestine operations, Richard Helms, to establish a research program "to develop a capability in the covert use of biological and chemical materials . . . enabling us to defend ourselves against a foe who might not be as restrained in the use of these techniques as we are." The detail didn't sound very restrained: "We intend to investigate the development of a chemical material which causes a reversible, nontoxic aberrant mental state, the specific nature of which can be reasonably well-predicted for each individual. This material could potentially aid in discrediting indi- viduals, eliciting information, and implanting suggestions and other forms of mental control."

The program was given an initial budget of three hundred thousand dollars and designated MKULTRA. It was to be run by thirty-six-year-old Sidney Gottlieb, head of the Chemical Division of the CIA's Technical Services Division (TSD)—a department tasked with devising bugs, disguised weapons, special cameras, and secret writing techniques.

Over the next ten years, the TSD would initiate 144 subprojects related to the control of human behavior in forty-four colleges and universities, fifteen research foundations, twelve hospitals, and three penal institutions.[27]

Subprojects included the implanting of electrodes in the brains of animals to enable experimenters to direct them by remote control, in the hope that they could be wired and used for eavesdropping. MKULTRA continued until 1963, when the CIA inspector general discovered the program during an inspection of TSD operations. His report noted that "present practice is to maintain no records of the planning and approval of test programs."[28]

By 1954, the CIA's pursuit of the possibility of a programmed assassin was proceeding in earnest. An agency memo dated January of that year discussed a "hypothetical problem": "Can an individual of ****** descent be made to perform an act of attempted assassination involuntarily under the influence of ARTICHOKE?"[29]

As the subject was identified as a heavy drinker, it was proposed that he "be surreptitiously drugged through the medium of an alcoholic cocktail at a social party, ARTICHOKE applied and the SUBJECT induced [involuntarily] to perform the act of attempted assassination at a later date . . . against a "prominent ****** politician or if necessary . . . an American official." The killing was described "as 'a trigger mechanism' for a bigger project." After the assassination, "it was assumed that the SUBJECT would be taken into custody by the *** Government and thereby 'disposed of.'"

Morse Allen provided a demonstration at CIA headquarters two months after the memo was written. He put one of his secretaries into a deep trance and hypnotized one of her colleagues—who was afraid of guns—telling her that if she could not awaken the first woman she would become so angry she would "kill" her while she slept. Allen's "assassin" obediently picked up a gun left by her boss and "shot" her sleeping colleague. When Allen brought her out of the trance, she had no memory of the "shooting."[30]

As these experiments developed, the doctors became more adventurous and learned how to split personalities into multiple parts. George Estabrooks was again one of the first to write about the military advances behind closed doors:

> *Suppose, for example, that we were to use hypnosis to create a multiple personality, which could be manipulated at will by the hypnotist who had produced it and was entirely resistant to hypnosis by anyone whom the hypnotist had not specifically designated. The job would take time, but it would be entirely possible to . . . split the subject's personality into completely dissociated parts.*
>
> *Before we begin to work on him, our subject is a completely loyal American . . . a man of democratic principles, to whom all the brutality and race-hatred of Nazism are repugnant beyond words. . . . After a few months of our kindly ministrations he emerges somewhat altered. Now he is anti-Semitic, antidemocratic . . . sadistic, warlike—perfect Storm Trooper material. And believing, as he now does, that the United States is decadent, that the Jews are subhuman, and that it is Hitler's historic mission to rule the world, he runs out and joins the local branch of the Nazi Bund and throws himself enthusiastically into all its activities. With his energy, vigor and conviction, he may even rise to a position of some importance in the organization. Now he is a dedicated Nazi, an enemy to everything his country stands for.*
>
> *How have we succeeded in producing this complete reversal? How can we make a monster out of a man? Unfortunately, it is quite simple. We tell the truth to the most important part of him—his unconscious.*
>
> *And if they got really clever and tried hypnosis? That would be a waste of time. Like all good little Nazis, our hero would be far too strong-minded and firm to be susceptible to it. Except, of course, by the American counterintelligence agent, a pleasant young man whom he met quite by accident in a restaurant one day shortly after his conversion to the Nazi ideal, with whom he struck up a casual friendship primarily on the basis of their mutual interest in checkers, and with whom he now plays that harmless game for a few hours every Thursday evening.*
>
> *Both checker players, of course, have ulterior motives in their friendship: the Nazi thinks the pleasant young man might ultimately be persuaded to the fascist way. And the pleasant young man knows that the Nazi has information for him. But how can the Nazi know this? How can he know that the meeting between the two men was planned . . . that every time the pleasant young man, puzzled over what move to make . . . pensively scratches the right*

*side of his nose, he, the good little Nazi, immediately falls into deep trance,
becomes a loyal American again, and reveals all the little Nazi plans he and
his playmates have made during the week? He cannot know. He has no more
reason to suspect the pleasant young man than his Nazi friends have to suspect
him. The trick is as close to foolproof as any human plan.[31]*

In a May 13, 1968, article in the *Providence Evening Bulletin*, Estabrooks was
more forthcoming. Described as a former consultant for the FBI and CIA, he was
quoted as saying that "the key to creating an effective spy or assassin rests in splitting a man's personality, or creating multipersonality, with the aid of hypnotism."
Estabrooks suggested that Lee Harvey Oswald and Jack Ruby could have been
controlled in this manner. "This is not science fiction. This has and is being done.
I have done it. It is child's play now to develop a multiple personality through hypnotism."[32]

On December 17, 1963, only weeks after the first Kennedy assassination, Richard Helms updated the CIA's deputy director on the program he'd created: "For
over a decade, the Clandestine Service has had the mission of maintaining a capability for influencing human behavior," he wrote, acknowledging that operational
targets were "unwitting," and detailing ongoing research into "chemical agents
which are effective in modifying the behavior and function of the central nervous
system." This included research into three key areas of interest: "Materials which
will render the induction of hypnosis easier or otherwise enhance its usefulness;
Materials and physical methods which will produce amnesia for events preceding
and during their use; Substances which alter personality structures in such a way
that the tendency of the recipient to become dependent upon another person is
enhanced."[33]

Partly in recognition of such pioneering work, Helms was made director of the
CIA in 1966 and was in charge at the time of the assassination of Robert Kennedy.
Before leaving office in 1973, Helms and Gottlieb ordered all records of these
mind-control programs destroyed as the first in a long series of scandals shook
the agency. But certain financial records were misplaced, and when they finally
surfaced in 1977, newly appointed CIA director Stansfield Turner and the Senate
Subcommittee on Health finally discovered the truth about MKULTRA.[34]

* * *

Within hours of the shooting at the Ambassador, and before Sirhan was identified,
hypnotherapist Dr. William J. Bryan told Ray Briem on Los Angeles radio station
KABC that the suspect probably acted under posthypnotic suggestion.

Bryan was the founder and executive director of the American Institute of
Hypnosis, a grand name concealing the fact that he had been refused membership in other, more traditional medical societies. He specialized in sex therapy
and criminology, and designed a switchboard of electronic instruments called the

Bryan Robot Hypnosis System, which allowed him to hypnotize and simultaneously monitor feedback from three different clients through the use of a control room, televisions, and multiple tape decks. In one room, someone was stopping smoking; in another someone was overcoming impotence; in another, someone was going through an age regression.[35]

Los Angeles Times sportswriter Jim Murray interviewed the 386-pound Bryan in 1963 and described him as looking more like a department store Santa Claus than a Svengali: "He is blond, round-faced (with a belly to match), he always talks as if a crowd had gathered. He has about as many self-doubts as Cassius Clay and can hypnotize himself at will, except he should do it more often when the mashed potatoes are coming."[36]

Bryan defined hypnosis as "increased concentration of the mind . . . increased relaxation of the body . . . and an increased susceptibility to suggestion." Sex and religion were his twin obsessions. He was an ordained priest in a fire-and-brimstone sect called the Old Roman Catholic Church and was a frequent guest preacher at fundamentalist churches in Southern California. He called prayer a form of hypnotism and the visions of prophets a form of autohypnosis—"in the Middle Ages, most of the prophets who heard the voice of God actually dissociated their own voices and heard themselves."[37]

The fundamentalist preacher also thought sex essential to his practice. He once told a *Playboy* interviewer: "I enjoy variety and I like to get to know people on a deep emotional level. One way of getting to know people is through intercourse." In 1969, the California Board of Medical Examiners gave Bryan five years' probation for sexually molesting women patients he had hypnotized to cure their "sexual disorders."[38]

In an interview on KNX radio in 1972, Bryan claimed to be the "chief of all medical survival training for the United States Air Force during the Korean War . . . which meant the brainwashing section." He detailed the brainwashing process in a later interview: "You have to have the person locked up physically, to have control over them; you have to use a certain amount of physical torture . . . and there is also the use of long-term hypnotic suggestion . . . probably drugs . . . whatever and so on. Under these situations, where you have all this going for you, like in a prison camp and so on, yes, you can brainwash a person to do just about anything. What I'm speaking about are the innumerable instances we ran into when I was running the country's brainwashing and anti-brainwashing programs."[39]

* * *

Authors Turner and Christian first noticed a link between Bryan and Sirhan's notebook in 1976, after a tip from Dr. Spiegel that anything mentioned to a subject under hypnosis was automatically etched in their subconscious. In one of Bryan's most famous cases, he had hypnotized Albert DeSalvo, the Boston Strangler, for attorney F. Lee Bailey. DeSalvo was the sexual psychopath who murdered thirteen women between 1962 and 1964.

Sirhan's notebook contains the reference "AMORC AMORC Salvo Salvo Di Di Salvo Die S Salvo," but it was clear from a conversation Sirhan had with Frank Foster in Central Jail in the hours after the shooting that he had no idea who DeSalvo was. This led Turner and Christian to ask: If Sirhan didn't know who De-Salvo was, why does the name appear in his notebook? As Bryan was prone to brag about his work with DeSalvo, did he imprint the name in Sirhan's mind?[40]

In 1974, researcher Betsy Langman interviewed Bryan at the American Institute of Hypnosis on Sunset Strip for a "general article on hypnosis." Bryan called himself "probably the leading expert in the world" on the use of hypnosis in criminal law—"I can hypnotize everybody in this office in five minutes."

Toward the end of the interview, Langman asked, "Do you feel Sirhan Sirhan could have been self-hypnotized?"

Bryan's mood changed abruptly. "I'm not going to comment on that case because I didn't hypnotize him."

"I was just asking your opinion," said Langman.

Bryan exploded. "You are going around trying to find some more ammunition to put out that same old crap—that people can be hypnotized into doing all these weird things. This interview's over!" he barked, charging out of his office.

A sympathetic secretary took the shaken Langman across the street for coffee, and recalled Arthur Bremer's assassination attempt in Laurel, Maryland, on George Wallace during the 1972 presidential campaign. Bryan had received an emergency call from Laurel minutes after Wallace was shot, and the call seemed to be connected with the shooting.

It's also worth noting that David Ferrie, a key suspect in Jim Garrison's 1967 probe into the JFK assassination, was also an ordained priest in the Old Roman Catholic Church; and James Earl Ray, the convicted assassin of Martin Luther King, Jr., consulted a hypnotist named Xavier von Koss in Los Angeles four months before the King assassination.

William Bryan was found dead in 1977 in his room at the Riviera Hotel, Las Vegas, apparently from natural causes. Hollywood reporter Greg Roberts had queried Bryan about the Sirhan case just before his death, but Bryan had strongly denied any involvement.

Two Beverly Hills call girls subsequently told Jonn Christian that they had been "servicing" Bryan twice a week for four years. Bryan regaled them with talk of his famous cases—how he had deprogrammed Albert DeSalvo and hypnotized Sirhan Sirhan. He said he had worked with the LAPD on a lot of murder cases, so they didn't think his work with Sirhan anything unusual. Bryan also told them he worked on "top secret projects" for the CIA.[41]

A close colleague of Bryan's later told Philip Melanson that Bryan flatly announced to him that he worked for the CIA and said the authorities had summoned him to hypnotize Sirhan. "It was actually, I believe, conducted in a prison cell. That's what I got [from Bryan]."[42]

The executor of Bryan's estate was John Miner, a deputy DA during the Sirhan trial, specializing in the "medical evidence." Miner later accompanied Enrique Hernandez to Wisconsin to interview Henry Peters, the priest who gave Sirhan Bible lessons—perhaps thinking that Peters might have "influenced" Sirhan—but Bryan himself was never interviewed.[43]

Bryan is by no means the only suspect in the search for Sirhan's programmer. When the police searched Sirhan's car, they found a copy of *Healing: The Divine Art,* by Manly Palmer Hall, on the backseat. Hall was the highly theatrical founder of the Philosophical Research Society. He was a master hypnotist with a practice in hypnotherapy.

Sirhan confirmed to Turner and Christian that he paid several visits to the headquarters of the Philosophical Research Society, an alabaster temple near Griffith Park. The police never interviewed Hall, and he was protected by strong links to Mayor Yorty, who had considered Hall his guru for the past twenty years.[44]

Candy Jones was a famous pinup model during World War II who later claimed to be a victim of CIA mind control during the sixties. She developed the alter ego "Arlene Grant," she said, and was used as a hypnocourier by the CIA in the manner described by Estabrooks.

In *The Control of Candy Jones,* author Donald Bain gave Jones's programmers the pseudonyms "Gilbert Jensen" and "Dr. Marshall Burger." Jensen, a disciple of Burger, was Candy's recruiter and primary programmer. He programmed himself into the role of her lover and was an associate of Dr. Bryan's. During deprogramming by her husband, John Nebel, in the early seventies, Jones recalled that under hypnosis, Burger talked about a racetrack in California and "bragged" about hypnotizing Sirhan. Jones also reenacted a visit to Dr. Burger's institute in Los Angeles on June 3, 1968. "Was he with the CIA?" she was asked. "He is the CIA," she said.

Dr. Spiegel worked closely with Candy Jones and John Nebel and wrote the foreword to Bain's book, believing Jones's claims to be authentic. When "Dr. Burger" died, his true identity was revealed as Dr. William Kroger.

By his own account, Dr. Kroger worked as a consultant to the FBI during the seventies, using hypnosis to assist memory recall through age regression, time compression, and automatic writing. Kroger also worked closely with Dr. Martin Reiser, who had run the behavioral science investigation program for the LAPD since 1968.[45]

In his book *Clinical and Experimental Hypnosis,* Kroger devoted a chapter to specialized hypnotic techniques, many of which touch on areas familiar to the Sirhan case. "After engrafting an amnesia for his own identity," he wrote, "the skillful therapist assumes the role of the sibling, a friend, a teacher, an employer, a lover or a mate" to encourage the patient to "reveal the way he felt toward significant persons in his life at different age levels."

Kroger traced the origin and development of the personality structure through age regression and handwriting samples by the same person at their current age and when regressed. The similarity between the variations in this writing in Kroger's illustrations and the variations in Sirhan's notebooks is striking. Could the different writing styles in Sirhan's notebooks—the writing he calls too "scribblish"—be attributed to the age regression or role-playing Kroger described?

Kroger went on to discuss how "dissociated or automatic handwriting" can be used to ascertain the reasons for a conflict. "After the arm and the hand are dissociated, the patient, upon direct questioning, may give one answer while his hand is writing something else. This is because his hand is released from cortical control (the normal motor functions controlled by the brain).

"Automatic writing, too, occurs at nonhypnotic levels. . . . Specifically, the subject is told that the dissociated hand holding the pencil will write even while he is engaged in conversation. It will do so without any attempt on his part to control its movements. He is also instructed that he will have no knowledge of what is being written, that after being dehypnotized, he will understand that the significance of the material appears nonsensical or cryptic, and that it can be interpreted by the subject in a subsequent session."[46]

Again, the parallels to Sirhan's lack of recognition of the writing in his notebooks is striking.

Kroger later worked at the Neuropsychiatric Institute at UCLA, run by Dr. Louis Jolyon West, an MKULTRA veteran. There, he wrote *Hypnosis and Behavior Modification*, with a preface by Martin Orne and H. J. Eysenck, two other MKULTRA veterans. The final chapters describe the chilling possibilities offered by combining hypnosis with electrical stimulation of the brain, brain implants, and conditioning.

While Dr. Spiegel indicated that hypnosis would be sufficient to program Sirhan, some odd notations in Sirhan's notebook suggest the use of drugs and electroshock techniques. One of the most bizarre pages is a mess of looping doodles, through which the repetition of several words is visible—"Danger Danger 8 8 8 8 8 fuck you fuck you Fuck you drugs drugs Drugs Drugs." On another page, "Electronic equipment this seems to be the right amount of pre-ponderance" is written upside down.

Sirhan described himself as a "square"—he hardly drank, he didn't take drugs, and he wasn't aware of any electroshock treatment. These references appear suddenly amid Sirhan's normal doodling on horses, girls, politics, and Robert Kennedy, and again suggest unconscious exposure to drugs and electroshock during his conditioning in the lead-up to the assassination. While Dr. Spiegel felt that most drugs impair the hypnotic effect, he admitted that amphetamines would help intensify concentration and provide the energy and strength Sirhan displayed in the struggle for the gun.[47]

Phillip Melanson interviewed Dr. Kroger in 1987 (giving him the pseudonym Jonathan Reisner in his book, *The Robert F. Kennedy Assassination*). Kroger said he knew Bryan "very well" but denied working with him. "He was brilliant but a discredit to his profession—too flamboyant, a genius but a grandstander."

Two of Melanson's sources who knew both men claimed they jointly conducted workshops on sex and hypnosis and shared an interest in the supposed links between mystical orders and hypnosis, as well as in the use of autohypnosis.

Bryan and Kroger believed that the mesmerization of an audience by a political speaker was a form of hypnosis and that Hitler was the greatest mass-hypnotist in history. They once made a joint television appearance to discuss the Sharon Tate murder case. At one point, Kroger was discussing Hitler and said "Sieg Heil!" seven times.

Both men also claimed to have been technical consultants on the film version of *The Manchurian Candidate*. Kroger told Melanson that the idea of a programmed robot assassin was "preposterous . . . it can't be done . . . you can't force people to do things against their will." He also denied any connection to CIA research.

Kroger did boast, however, that he could write himself out of the patient's memory by adopting the role of a lover, relative, or close friend and make the patient forget the hypnotist.

Near the end of their interview, Melanson brought up the subject of Candy Jones. Kroger dismissed the whole story as fictitious, but said he had threatened to sue the publishers: "There was a real problem with that book . . . except that [the doctor] was supposed to be in northern California, people could have thought it was me. I told the publishers that; I threatened to sue. You see, the problem was that I dated Candy a couple of times way back . . . when she was a model."[48]

While the doctor who programmed Sirhan is most likely dead, his lock remains on Sirhan's mind, and it will take a psychiatrist of great skill to recover Sirhan's memory and trace the guiding hand behind the assassination.

SIXTEEN

INTELLIGENCE CONNECTIONS

It's tempting to write off the LAPD's bullying, incompetence, omission, and destruction and manipulation of evidence as simply the cover-up of a botched investigation—the avoidance of another Dallas, by any means necessary—until you see the connections fanning out from the department to other government agencies, specifically the CIA.

By late 1967, LBJ was besieged by the antiwar movement. From his bunker at the White House, he looked out at the student dissent and disgust with government and could not believe it was the work of true Americans. Foreign influence must be at play, corrupting American youth, and he encouraged the CIA to root it out with the launch of Operation Chaos, a domestic surveillance operation on the protest movement and the Black Panthers. Through a network of informants and agent provocateurs, Chaos would determine if foreign powers were funding and fomenting this domestic unrest.

The program was tightly held, known only to director Richard Helms and his top lieutenants, Richard Ober and Cord Meyer, who helped establish and run it. One of the main cities targeted was Los Angeles, and links were established with the intelligence division of the LAPD, which was also responsible for the security of VIPs visiting Los Angeles. In sync with this effort, the CIA provided training to police departments in guerrilla techniques and tools of urban warfare. Former CIA officer Victor Marchetti told researcher Betsy Langman that while he was with the agency in 1967, the Chicago and Los Angeles police departments received several days of "training" from the Clandestine Services Division. When Marchetti asked why a dozen or so LAPD officers were at CIA headquarters, he was told it was a "special," "sensitive" activity that had been directly approved by the CIA director.[1]

In 1982, author Philip Melanson obtained a three-hundred-page "Domestic Police Training" file from the CIA through the Freedom of Information Act. These documents confirmed that during the sixties and seventies, the CIA had secret ties to police departments across the country, providing training and equipment in exchange for surveillance, break-ins, and the provision of police credentials to CIA operatives. Los Angeles was one of the cities that received this special training.[2]

The two men who had effective day-to-day control of the RFK investigation also had CIA connections. As day watch supervisor, Lieutenant Manuel Pena had to sign off and approve every report and decide who to reinterview and who to dismiss as the case was prepared for trial. This was the same Manny Pena who scrawled across several blank interview summaries relating to Sandra Serrano, "Polka-dot story of Serrano phony," "Polka dot story Serrano N.G."

Sergeant Enrique "Hank" Hernandez was Pena's chief interrogator, called on to administer polygraph tests to troublesome witnesses to determine if they were telling the truth. Without fail, whenever claims of conspiracy were sent to Hernandez, he bullied witnesses into retractions. Luckily, many of these tapes survive, so we can still hear the mockery Hernandez's bullying tactics make of this supposedly objective discipline. Hernandez also led the investigation probing possible conspiracy and oversaw the background checks on Sirhan and his family.[3]

Manuel Pena joined the LAPD in 1941 and served in the Pacific with the Naval Air Corps during World War II. He spent two years in Verdun, France, as a criminal investigator for the U.S. Army during the Korean War, and spoke fluent French and Spanish. He went on to spend sixteen years of his police career working in Robbery-Homicide, reaching the rank of lieutenant. Robert Kaiser recalls his nickname at LAPD was "Shoot 'em up Manny Pena"—"he killed several people in the line of duty, which wasn't very normal."

In November 1967, Pena retired from the department with a surprise testimonial dinner at the Sportsman's Club attended by Chief Reddin and top department brass. He was to accept a position with the Agency for International Development (AID), a State Department aid agency that among other roles served as a regular cover identity for CIA operatives abroad. He would serve as a "public safety adviser" and train the police forces of friendly dictatorships in sophisticated interrogation techniques to use on leftist insurgents and political dissidents.

FBI agent Roger LaJeunesse had known Pena for years and was the FBI liaison to the LAPD during the RFK case. LaJeunesse said Pena left the LAPD for a "special training unit" at CIA's Camp Peary base in Virginia. After nine weeks' training, he would be posted to Latin America, where he could use his Spanish. Pena had been doing special assignments for the CIA for a decade, mostly under AID cover. On some of these, he worked with CIA operative Dan Mitrione, a "US police adviser" who taught interrogation and torture techniques to the ruling junta in Uruguay and was killed by the Tupamaro guerrillas in 1970 as a result.

Pena's new career didn't last long. Robert Kennedy announced that he would run for president on March 16, 1968 and Pena was back in Los Angeles by April. Investigative reporter Fernando Faura was walking along a corridor in Parker Center one day when he noticed a familiar figure behind heavy horn-rim glasses and a black handlebar mustache.

"Hey, Manny, I damn near didn't recognize you with that disguise!"

Pena stopped and explained the AID job wasn't what he expected, so he quit and came back to Los Angeles.

When the LAPD subsequently unveiled Special Unit Senator (SUS), a special task force to investigate the assassination, the man put in charge of preparing the case for trial and supervising the day watch investigators was Manny Pena.[4]

In his 1970 book on the case, SUS Chief Robert Houghton wrote that Pena had "connections with intelligence agencies in several countries." In 1975, Pena's brother, a school principal, was interviewed for a local television show by host Stan Bohrman. During the commercial break, he mentioned how proud he was of his brother's service with the CIA. "Nobody's supposed to know about that. It's supposed to be secret."[5]

In 1977, researcher Betsy Langman interviewed Pena—then retired from the LAPD, presumably for good—and asked about his intelligence ties.

"I worked with the AID program out of the Office of Public Safety," said Pena. (The AID program had been unmasked in the mid-1970s as one of the CIA's main covers for clandestine activity abroad.)

"Is AID not CIA?" asked Langman.

"Ah, not to my knowledge," said Pena.

"Was your work away from LAPD in 1967 going to be for AID?"

"Yeah."

"What type of work was it?"

"Ah, that I can't ah . . . I don't think that's anybody's business."[6]

* * *

In 1992, while attorney Marilyn Barrett was working with Paul Schrade on a new petition to reopen the Sirhan case, she discovered that the uncle of a good friend of hers was none other than Manny Pena. Barrett kindly sent me CD copies of a four-hour interview she subsequently conducted with Pena, in which he attempted to correct misconceptions in what he calls "these novels" about the assassination.

Pena was, by that time, seventy-three years old and comes across as a disarming figure, a charming uncle seemingly open about all aspects of his career, and a world away from his sinister-looking LAPD ID photo taken in the late sixties.

Pena was happy to discuss his "intelligence background" outside the LAPD. During his two years in France, he worked closely with the army's Counter-Intelligence Corps and made lots of friends in the intelligence community. He also built up strong connections with Interpol: a senior official in the Mexican government was his "number one connection into Latin America," and he'd make frequent trips down there.

"Our own Internal Revenue used to use me to trace assets in Latin America when they wanted to keep away from diplomatic problems with the State Department. I could get information out of Latin America better than the government through personal friends . . . and [LAPD] Chief Parker allowed them to use me providing I never [talked about it]. . . . If you want to call that an intelligence background, there's nothing mysterious about it.

"In 1967, I decided to retire and go in the Aid for International Development part of the State Department; we call it AID. I was sent to Washington, DC, for orientation at the Foreign Service Institute. I went through their orientation and I was told I was going to be sent to Latin America. "Some of the instructors that talk to you there are from CIA, and I was made privy to how to read secret materials and stuff like that, which I can't discuss with you for obvious reasons."

At the time, Pena was recently divorced and had left his car and furniture in Los Angeles. "After I finished the orientation school, the chief of the AID Program, Byron Engle, told me they couldn't send me to Latin America; they wanted to keep me in Washington, DC, at their International Police Academy," where they trained a lot of Latin American officials.

Engle told him it was a permanent assignment, so he got his car sent to Washington by government transportation. "When the car arrived, they told me I owed them $965. I said, well, that couldn't be—the State Department said they were paying." But he was told his posting didn't qualify as a permanent change of station, so the government couldn't pay for it. Engle refused to pay, so Pena called Chief Reddin, who was a close friend, and Reddin said, "Tell them to go to hell and come home."

When he'd left the LAPD, Pena still had four months time-in-lieu on the books, so there were still a couple of weeks left before his official retirement date. So he got his car back and drove back to Los Angeles, "and this is what has caused this confusion that these writers write about . . . that I was retired with a great deal of fanfare, . . . and then all of a sudden, in two months, I'm back on the job over here and mysteriously returned."

The night of the shooting, Pena was home alone in an apartment in Van Nuys, and a friend called and said, "Switch on the TV; they just shot Kennedy." Two or three days later, Chief Houghton handpicked Pena as lead supervisor for the investigation. They picked "just about the forty sharpest guys in the department in every category" and set up SUS:

I was assigned to supervise the case preparation for trial, the conspiracy allegation investigation, [and] I arranged to have the backgrounds of the entire Sirhan family investigated in Jordan because the main defense attorney Grant Cooper was pushing diminished capacity—that Sirhan had suffered so much as a child and had gone through all kinds of horrible bombings in his home town in Jordan. . . . Well, I contacted the very same guy I fought with in the State Department, Byron Engle in Washington, DC, and I told him I need his help and I wanted the agents to conduct this portion of the investigation for me, and he says, "Good to hear from you," and he had agents—some of them from the CIA and some of them from the State Department—look into it, and they did a beautiful job.

And they established that Sirhan was never within 130 miles of any bombing in his youth . . . this was a fairy tale that Grant Cooper made up, and we busted him real wide with that in the trial. He was flabbergasted and a little angry that we had gotten the government to do that. But they did it for me, at my request. So we still had a friendship going there, even though I quit them.

It's ludicrous to state that Jerusalem, where Sirhan grew up, was never within 130 miles of bombing during the 1948 Arab-Israeli War. This illustrates how deluded Pena was during the original investigation, and how far the prosecution went to distort Sirhan's upbringing. The interview was yielding intriguing information on Pena's CIA links, and Barrett kept him talking.

"And these are the same people that I went to Latin America for later on."

"What was that trip about?" asked Barrett.

In late 1969 or early 1970, the State Department sent a three-man team to Colombia—the assistant attorney general of California, Howard Jewel, one of the counsels for a Supreme Court justice, and Pena as their investigative consultant.

"We were asked to make a survey of their criminal justice system," recalled Pena, "because there were complaints that people were disappearing in the justice system. They'd go in, be arrested, be arraigned, and go to court, and nobody'd ever hear of them again." The State Department asked him to stay on in Latin America for three-year stints in three different countries, to help reorganize their investigative systems, but, with the drug lords and corruption, Pena thought, "I don't want to stay down here, this is too damn dangerous."

When Pena got the check for the job, "it was paid from the International Legal Center, based in New York. I said, 'This isn't from the State Department,' and I had a detective friend in New York PD check out who it was. International Legal Center was a mail drop; it never existed and yet I got paid and the IRS accepted my tax report, so I had a suspicion it was probably a CIA operation down there. But I've never been told. That's just the policy in government work. If you don't need to know, they don't tell you. . . . I have never told . . . or admitted to anybody that I have been or am a CIA agent because no one has ever told me, 'Manny, you're actually a CIA agent."

"Do you think AID is a front for the CIA?" asked Barrett.

"It's been rumored very highly." Pena laughed.

Barrett also asked Pena about Hernandez's intelligence background.

"I'd rather let Hank explain for himself. He's never been with the CI . . . AID, that I know of . . . he was on the Sirhan case with us; he was a darned good polygraph man—the best—we used him a lot; he did a lot of the background investigation, too, on the conspiracy things. But I've never worked an intelligence assignment with him, so I don't know." Pena said he had never worked with Hernandez outside of the LAPD.

"The main thing I wanted to get straight," concluded Pena, "and I'm surprised that this latest novel didn't cover it correctly, was how I happened to retire twice, you know. The way they've written it, it sounds like I was brought back and put into the case as a plant by the CIA, so that I could steer something around and . . . guide the investigation to a point where no-one would ever discover a conspiracy or something . . . that's not so. Sirhan himself will tell you that nobody operated with him; he operated by himself. And, quite frankly—I say this kind of jokingly—but I wouldn't recognize somebody that was programmed hypnotically to commit an assassination if I was talking to one, you know? I don't know enough about it."

After her four-hour interview, Marilyn Barrett believed that Pena was not directly involved in any nefarious activity but had been given orders from the top to "shut this case down" to give the public closure, and to convey a sense that the police got their man, that the case had been solved quickly and definitively.

She thinks the LAPD did a very bad job, but doesn't think they were actively involved in any wrongdoing. When she brought her petition in 1992, somebody in the DA's office told her the case would never be reopened; they'd had orders from the top to shut it down. She also found memos by DA staff, saying they needed to shut this petition down.

Barrett tried to arrange a short telephone interview for me with Pena, but he was reported to be too old and ill to take my call.[7]

Like Pena, Enrique Hernandez had served with the army in Korea and spoke fluent Spanish. He was thirty-seven years old and had been with the LAPD for fifteen years at the time of Bobby Kennedy's assassination. He was the sole polygraph examiner for SUS, and he talked up his credentials to Sandra Serrano before her test began: "I have been called to South America, to Vietnam and Europe and I have administered tests. The last test that I administered was to the dictator in Caracas, Venezuela. He was a big man, a dictator. Pérez Jiménez was the last name. And this is when there was a transition in the government of Venezuela and President Betancourt came in . . . there was a great thing involved over there and I tested the gentleman."[8]

So what had an LAPD polygraph officer been doing in South America? Hernandez himself provided the answer for *Now It Can Be Told* in 1992, when reporter Alexander Johnson confronted him and Hernandez granted his only television interview:

"I conducted an interrogation of Sandra Serrano and my objective was to determine the truth and I think I accomplished that."

"And what was the truth at that point?" asked a determined Johnson.

Hernandez smiled awkwardly and paused, searching for the right words. "That the statements she made to the police investigators soon after the shooting were made up, and not true."

Hernandez did admit training Venezuelan police officers in the early sixties.

"I was loaned from the Los Angeles Police Department to the Department of State for a mission in Caracas, Venezuela."

"Did you work in any capacity for the CIA?"

"No, sir."

As a contract agent?"

"In any capacity whatsoever, no . . . I know people who have been and are with the CIA, but I've never worked with them."[9]

Venezuelan dictator Marcos Pérez Jiménez was overthrown in a military coup in January 1958 and fled via the Dominican Republic to Miami Beach, where he lived comfortably from February 1958 to 1963, when he was extradited by the Venezuelan government to stand trial, accused of having embezzled two hundred million dollars. He was tried and convicted by the Venezuelan Supreme Court and placed under house arrest until 1968, when he was released and fled to Spain. From this timeline, it seems most likely that Hernandez was training Venezuela police in 1963 when he was called in to help with the trial. Johnson did not ask when and why Hernandez went to Europe or Vietnam.

During the interview with Serrano, Hernandez also stated: "I know the layout of the hotel, and *after I arrived in Los Angeles* it's the first place they took me." This suggests that Hernandez was out of Los Angeles at the time of the assassination, perhaps on another foreign assignment.[10]

Shortly after the assassination, Hernandez was rumored to have swapped his solid middle-class neighborhood for a new home in upscale San Marino. But it wasn't until Hernandez died of cancer on December 18, 2005, at the age of seventy-four, that obituaries sourced by his son Enrique Junior would throw light on his extraordinary career.

Hernandez was born in Jerome, Arizona, in 1931 and moved to Los Angeles with his parents and eight siblings in 1941. After dropping out of high school, he joined the army at seventeen, initially stationed in Japan. He returned to Los Angeles after the Korean War and joined the LAPD in 1953, rising to lieutenant in the detective bureau and ending up in the department's "exclusive Scientific Investigation Department."

"In the early sixties," read the notice, "the Justice Department developed an initiative to send bilingual U.S. law enforcement experts to Latin American nations to offer training on policing techniques. Hernandez was part of the program."

After twenty years with the LAPD, Hernandez retired in 1973.

"From the kitchen table at his Monterey Park home, Hernandez and his wife developed a plan to go into the private security business. . . . His son said the firm's first major contract was with NASA at Edwards Air Force Base. Other NASA installations quickly followed. The firm now has wholly owned subsidiaries in nineteen countries and employs more than 30,000 people. Although its earnings are not public, some estimates put them at more than $1 billion annually."

There may be some truth in the romantic tale of a billion-dollar company hatched at the Hernandez family kitchen table, but it's a little hard to swallow. It would be a lucky start-up, indeed, that lands its first major contract with NASA. Hernandez's son Enrique Junior is now CEO of Inter-Con and sits on the board of McDonald's, Wells Fargo, and the Tribune Company (owners of the *Los Angeles Times*).[11]

In interviews, Pena and Hernandez both referred to the Office of Public Safety (OPS), a police assistance program set up during the Kennedy administration in November 1962. Until its demise in 1975, the program trained seventy-five hundred senior officers in U.S. facilities, and more than half a million foreign police overseas.[12]

The program was an aggressive Cold War effort to enhance domestic security among third world allies, and CIA Deputy Director Robert Amory sat on a White House Special Group with Robert Kennedy overseeing its creation. He described OPS as a joint project of the CIA and AID; it was decided AID would be its home, "but the brains are in CIA, so we'll move those brains over to AID. . . . So we just took the CIA men . . . and gave them the mission of training [foreign] police forces using American police forces occasionally as sort of sponsors . . . which is dangerous ground because you can get into Gestapo-type tactics and so on . . . but essentially bringing to bear good police methods, good filing systems, good fingerprinting systems, good systems of riot control."

The public safety program was expanded within U.S. AID and placed under the control of CIA veteran Byron Engle, who reported directly to the director and deputy director of the CIA. (Engle later personally recruited Pena from the LAPD.)

During his decade as OPS chief, Engle took advantage of early police retirements and started hiring ex-chiefs and technical specialists from police forces across America, attracted by good salaries and exotic climes. He also recruited CIA personnel and supplied cover for agency officers operating abroad.[13]

According to McClintock, OPS "became best known as a conduit for CIA training, assistance, and operational advice to foreign political police, and for linking the United States to the jailers, torturers, and murderers of the most repressive of 'free world' regimes [through] instruction in torture . . . the fabrication and use of terrorist devices and assassination weapons . . . as well as its key role in the best-known assassination program of them all, Vietnam's Operation PHOENIX," in which at least twenty thousand Vietnamese were killed.[14]

In 1962, President Romulo Betancourt's police force in Venezuela was struggling to control a militant group of Castro-inspired leftists, who had bombed a luxury hotel and attacked the U.S. embassy. According to A. J. Langguth, "under pressure from the Kennedys, Engle borrowed four Spanish-speaking officers from the LAPD and quietly sent them to Caracas to give intensive classes in police work." I think it highly likely Hernandez was one of these four LAPD officers; he later boasted to Sandy Serrano that he had received a personal commendation from Robert Kennedy, presumably after this secret mission.

In 1963, Kennedy helped set up the principal training establishment for the OPS, the International Police Academy (IPA). The basic course ran fifteen weeks and included modules on VIP protection and "Criminal Violence Control," dealing with airline security, bomb threats, kidnapping, extortion, and assassination.[15]

By 1968, its peak year, OPS fielded 458 advisers in thirty-four countries, with a budget of $55.1 million. By 1971, the program had trained more than a million policemen in forty-seven nations, including eighty-five thousand in South Vietnam and a hundred thousand in Brazil.[16]

But the program was by then highly controversial, and had become synonymous with human rights abuse and torture. CIA field operatives had used OPS as an ideal cover to train police forces in the agency's interrogation techniques.

The agency coached military and police interrogators throughout Latin America, promoting methods of torture that became the hallmark of the continent's military dictatorships. AID police advisers tortured political dissidents, and through its field offices in Panama and Buenos Aires, the agency's Technical Services Division shipped polygraph and electroshock machines in diplomatic pouches to public safety offices across Latin America. When embassy staff complained about these abuses, they were reminded that U.S. policy precluded interference in the internal affairs of other countries.

Ironically, it took the murder of an American—Dan Mitrione, a police adviser in Uruguay—to expose this involvement in torture and hasten the program's demise.[17]

In 1969, Mitrione, the former police chief of Richmond, Indiana, was appointed head of the OPS mission in Montevideo. His deputy, William Cantrell, was a CIA operations officer. The country was beset by strikes, student demonstrations, and a band of urban revolutionaries calling themselves Tupamaros, who captured the public's imagination with outrageous actions and a Robin Hood philosophy. They kidnapped and tried prominent figures before "people's courts" and ransacked an exclusive nightclub, scrawling their slogan on the walls: "Either everyone dances or no one dances."

Mitrione intensified the use of torture as the government fought back. He built a soundproofed room in the cellar of his house and demonstrated torture techniques to selected Uruguayan police officers, using beggars taken off the streets, some of whom died during the sessions.

On July 31, 1970, Mitrione was kidnapped by the Tupamaros, who demanded the release of 150 prisoners in exchange for his return. Nixon dug his heels in, and the Uruguayan government refused. Ten days later, Mitrione's dead body was found on the backseat of a stolen car. "Mr. Mitrione's devoted service to the cause of peaceful progress in an orderly world will remain as an example for free men everywhere," said the White House, as Frank Sinatra and Jerry Lewis visited Richmond, Indiana, to stage a benefit show for the family.[18]

Days later, the real story began to emerge. Alejandro Otero, the former Uruguayan chief of police intelligence, confirmed that Mitrione had used "violent techniques of torture . . . and a psychology to create despair, such as playing a tape in the next room of women and children screaming and telling the prisoner that it was his family being tortured."[19]

Otero was a CIA agent and had been trained at the IPA in Washington. What finally drove him to speak out was the torture of a female friend of his who was a Tupamaro sympathizer. When Otero complained, he was demoted.

In Uruguay and elsewhere in Latin America, OPS continued to train and serve as cover for death squads composed primarily of police officers, who bombed the homes of suspected Tupamaro sympathizers with material supplied by the Technical Services Division and engaged in assassination and kidnapping.[20]

In July 1975, finally aroused by persistent allegations of torture and police brutality, Congress cut all funds for "training or advice to police, prisons, or other law enforcement"—in effect, abolishing OPS.

While the foreign service of Pena and Hernandez may have been innocuous, the Office of Public Safety to which they were attached was implicated in human rights abuses and assassination from the late sixties through the early seventies. As we will see, a legendary CIA operative named David Morales took his own murderous revenge on the Tupamaros while working under OPS cover.[21]

* * *

Bill Jordan, the Rampart sergeant who interviewed Sirhan in custody, also had an intriguing CV. He joined the U.S. Marines at the age of fifteen in 1941 and served three years in combat in the Pacific. He graduated from the police academy in 1954 and, while with the Intelligence Division, provided security for Senator John Kennedy during the 1960 Democratic Convention in Los Angeles and was later assigned to protect Presidents Kennedy and Johnson and Martin Luther King, Jr., when they were in town.

According to his resume, Jordan also attended "special schools" in anti-terrorist techniques, special weapons, and riot control "conducted by the Federal Government and the military."[22]

After he retired from the LAPD, Jordan put some of this knowledge to work in 1978 when Costa Gratsos, a close associate of the recently deceased Aristotle Onassis, resurrected a plan to stage a coup d'état against "Papa Doc" Duvalier in Haiti, with the help of exiled Haitian banker Clemard Charles. Jordan told author Peter Evans that his security company had been hired to handle the policing of the island after the takeover.

But the closer Jordan looked at the plan, the less he liked it. "Clemard Charles was the problem. First, he gave me this short list. These are very bad people, they must be eliminated," he said. "Every time I saw him, he'd hand me another list. It was beginning to look like the Haitian phone book. Once a guy like Clemard

Charles got in you might be looking back and thinking what a wonderful guy Baby Doc was compared with this butcher."[23]

The invasion never happened, but Jordan's involvement in this world of coups and assassinations must be noted. Jordan died in September 2005, at age eighty-two.[24]

* * *

There are also a number of intelligence connections to Sirhan's defense investigators, Michael McCowan and Robert Kaiser. During the trial, Kaiser discovered he was under surveillance:

> *In the middle of the trial, more or less, I was living in a rented house in Hollywood and I had practically nightly conversations with Dr. Diamond about the progress of the trial. Anybody who was eavesdropping on those conversations would have been able to tip off the prosecutors on the strategy of the defense.*
>
> *So my suspicions were aroused when one day, I realized there was a lot of interference on the line, and I called the phone company and they said they'd send someone out to check the line. And a man came out wearing the denim clothes of a telephone repairman. He spent a bunch of time, maybe a half an hour there, and he said, "Well, things should be okay now," and then he left. Several weeks later, I was in the offices of the prosecuting attorneys, and I saw the same man coming out of one of the offices, and all of a sudden, a light went on over my head. I thought, "Wow, this guy is probably working for the DA's office and if he's tapping my phone, then the DA's office is privy to everything the defense is trying to do." I did not tell Cooper about it. I didn't tell anybody about it, I didn't know what to do.*
>
> *In retrospect, I probably have to blame myself for at least not telling Cooper about it. It could have led to a mistrial if we'd been able to prove that, but then what? A mistrial, so then we retry him, you know? Cooper, at that point, didn't want to hear it; that's probably why I didn't tell Cooper. . . . He was tired of this trial. . . . I could just see him throwing up his hands.[25]*

* * *

In 1999, while preparing an updated edition of his book, Kaiser tried to find out who the telephone repairman may have been. He remembered the fifteen-man investigative unit in the DA's office under the direction of George Stoner and interviewed Clay Anderson, who was part of that team. Anderson said the likeliest candidate for the repairman was their sound technician, Fred East, now deceased. "If East was doing anything illegal, I couldn't admit it [but] I never heard a whisper about [East] doing a wire tap [of anyone working on the Sirhan defense team]. I literally cannot imagine anyone having done that."[26]

"Fred East, Los Angeles County district attorney's investigator," was quoted in a 1964 *Time* magazine article on bugging devices, and it seems East was, indeed, the wire-tapping specialist at the DA's Bureau of Investigation and quite possibly the man who came to "fix" Kaiser's phone. East was also present when investigators from the DA's office asked Sandra Serrano to reconstruct her story at the Ambassador. He presumably recorded the interview and advised on the impossibility of Serrano having heard gunshots.[27]

Kaiser later gave Sirhan's attorney Larry Teeter a written declaration, professing his belief that the prosecution had had him wiretapped.[28]

* * *

Michael McCowan was still working on the Sirhan case in September 1970, when Sirhan's release was allegedly one of the conditions—later denied—for freeing the "Black September" hostages held by Palestinian guerrillas on two hijacked airliners in the Jordanian desert.

Sirhan's mother, Mary, accompanied by her son's new attorney Luke McKissack and "his investigator Michael McCowan," tried to travel to Jordan to discuss the guerrilla demands, but at Kennedy airport in New York, the State Department revoked the passports of the two men and denied Mary Sirhan permission to travel, as the trip "would be prejudicial to the foreign policy of the United States government."

McKissack was preparing Sirhan's appeal at the time, but why was McCowan still working as a pro bono investigator more than a year after the trial? McCowan's partner, Ronald Allen, put it simply: "Mike had been involved all along. You get into something and you don't want to let it down." But others accused McCowan of babysitting Sirhan for the CIA.[29]

By September 1974, McCowan was president of the guard and patrol division of American Protection Industries, supplying the Century Plaza and LA Hilton (and good friends with Frank Hendrix of Ace Guard Services). But he was in trouble again, convicted of giving a federal receiver eleven thousand dollars in return for the security guard service contract for a federally financed housing project. He was placed on five years' probation.[30]

In 1977, McCowan was characterized as "a private eye who specializes in tough insurance claims" in Desmond Wilcox's book, *Americans*. McCowan recounted a recent mission to Switzerland to retrieve stolen diamonds for an insurance company. "The wrong kind of people" knew about the cache, so he traveled back and forth disguised as a man with a broken neck, hiding the diamonds in his surgical collar and neck brace. He collected twenty-five thousand dollars for less than a week's work.

McCowan's name didn't surface again publicly until 1995, when author Dan Moldea published his book on the case, *The Killing of Robert Kennedy*.

The book climaxes with three interviews with Sirhan in California's Corcoran prison. In the penultimate chapter, after building a compelling case for conspiracy,

Moldea made an abrupt U-turn and declared Sirhan the lone assassin. On the last page of the book, Moldea described a prison visit by McCowan, in which he tried to reconstruct the murder with Sirhan: "Suddenly, in the midst of their conversation, Sirhan started to explain the moment when his eyes met Kennedy's just before he shot him. Shocked by what Sirhan had just admitted, McCowan asked, 'Then why, Sirhan, didn't you shoot him between the eyes?' With no hesitation and no apparent remorse, Sirhan replied, 'Because that son of a bitch turned his head at the last second.'"[31]

Robert Kaiser told Moldea of McCowan's allegations in late May 1994, and Moldea later claimed he asked Sirhan about them during their final meeting the following week. But Moldea was never allowed to see Sirhan alone, and Sirhan and his brother Adel—who was at all three meetings—insisted the subject was never raised. Moldea's own notes of the meeting, given to Sirhan to confirm their accuracy, also omit any mention of such a conversation.

Eight months later, Moldea finally located and interviewed McCowan by telephone. McCowan confirmed Kaiser's quote, and signed a statement verifying the story and approving its accuracy. Moldea put it in the book. In a letter to his long-time legal researcher Lynn Mangan dated June 24, 1995, Sirhan wrote the following about the matter: "I flatly deny making the statement Moldea ascribes to me in his book via Kaiser via McCowan. This quote was never mentioned by Moldea during any of his visits with me."[32]

On McCowan, Sirhan wrote: "Whenever he came with the others (he seldom came alone) I told him all I could remember of the shooting night—the same stuff that I told whoever asked me including the psychiatrists. McCowan was much more interested in my background than in the shooting scene. He always had that smooth chatty 'I am your best friend' attitude—an insincere chumminess, and he made statements that included the answer or inference that he wanted to establish. . . . McCowan has very, very seldom come to mind over the years because I realized when I was on Death Row that he did not give a damn about me from the outset, and that he was out for all the glory he could get at my expense, like Parsons and Cooper."

McCowan told Kaiser about Sirhan's alleged comments, but only after the trial.

"McCowan did report Sirhan saying that," Kaiser told me. "And I didn't know whether to believe McCowan or not. McCowan was a puzzle to me. He had his own agenda. There's been some suggestion that Mike McCowan was, in fact, a plant in the defense investigation team for another agency."

Kaiser remembered talking to the FBI's Roger LaJeunesse in 1999, a year before the former agent died, about the curious visit from the man who came to fix his phone. When Kaiser asked him about possible FBI liaisons with the CIA, "I have a vague recollection that he said he thought Michael McCowan was working with the CIA."

It wouldn't have surprised Kaiser. "McCowan was kicked off the LAPD when he got a federal conviction for mail tampering, and he had every reason to cooperate with the CIA/FBI during the case."[33]

Kaiser put me in touch with Pete Noyes, a veteran investigative journalist in Los Angeles, now seventy-five years old and still working in the investigative unit at the local Fox affiliate, Channel 11. Noyes was working for KNXT in Los Angeles on the night of the assassination, the same channel as Don Schulman.

Noyes confirmed that another investigator from the Treasury Department (now deceased) told him that McCowan was planted on the defense team by the CIA to find out anything he could about Sirhan. In return, after the Sirhan trial, his civil rights would be restored after his earlier mail-fraud conviction. Noyes added, "I can't understand how Kaiser didn't know McCowan was CIA, because everybody else seemed to."

Mention of the Treasury brought to mind the only Arabic page in Sirhan's notebook—a letter written to his mother. One sentence is translated as: "I am also waiting for a check from the American Treasury Department which you are to send (P P Peggy)."[34]

* * *

When I first tracked Michael McCowan down, he confirmed the telephone interview with Dan Moldea and stood by the alleged Sirhan confession—"Sirhan said that to me." He said he'd be happy to meet up for an interview when I came to the States, and I asked a few final questions.

"Who were your main contacts at the LAPD?"

"Nobody. I was on the defense team. People have said I was FBI or CIA, but that's all nonsense."

"Have you ever had any indication the CIA were involved?"

"Let's talk about that when you get here."

* * *

During our interview a few months later, McCowan constantly circled back to three issues that were key to his understanding of the case—the "many more will come" reference in Sirhan's school textbook; the disputed sighting of Sirhan following Hubert Humphrey down to San Diego; and Sirhan's disputed confession.

He reenacted Sirhan's statement three or four times but broke eye contact with me after each telling. It was the most important point in the interview and, for me, the least convincing.

Toward the end of our conversation, I brought up the accusations of Noyes, Kaiser, LaJeunesse, and others that McCowan had been a plant on the defense team for another agency.

"Roger LaJeunesse was a really good friend of mine," said McCowan. "I always liked him . . . and I think he was liaison for the FBI at the Sirhan case, and he would have never said that about me. I don't believe." He seemed genuinely hurt by the idea and sure his friend would never have betrayed him like that.

"Not blow my cover!" he said, followed by a big, hearty laugh.

"And the Treasury guy saying you were CIA—where would that come from?" I asked.

"That's interesting. Why the Treasury guy? What would it have to do with the Treasury Department?"

I offered, "Apparently, they were one of the agencies doing their own investigation for whatever reason.

"On me or on Kennedy?"

"No, no, on Sirhan. . . . The Bureau of Alcohol, Tobacco and Firearms—would that be part of their jurisdiction?"

"Oh, yeah, with the gun thing and all, probably. I don't know. I don't recall ever talking to the Treasury people. Ever."

Pete Noyes later told me his source was in IRS intelligence.

"Just to clarify it," I asked McCowan, "did you ever work in any way with the FBI or CIA as an informant or agent?"

"Never," said McCowan. "Didn't work with the CIA. Was never a CIA operative. Never was an FBI operative. I dealt with some FBI guys and I knew some CIA guys and I could see why somebody would think, 'Okay, I'm planted in there because I've done some strange things in my life . . . My present wife thinks I'm a CIA guy. . . . but I'm not getting a pension! If I was getting a pension from the FBI or the CIA, my wife would know about it! And I'm not. . . .

"But I don't find it unreasonable for people to think that . . . but I don't think they'll ever find or there is any concrete evidence that I've ever been involved with either of those agencies."

"You weren't getting compensated," I asked, "so why did you work for Sirhan from June 1968 through to possibly going out to Jordan (for free) if you weren't a CIA babysitter?"

"Okay, well here's the real simple explanation to that. When I had the opportunity to do this, being an investigator and a lawyer, it's a great opportunity to see how good you are. It was a wonderful experience for me. I didn't expect the money and I didn't write a book about it or I didn't try to promote it. I never have given an interview, really. It just was something that was exciting for me to do and I did it."

Although he seemed wary recalling the details of the case, McCowan was at his most relaxed and jovial discussing these accusations, and I found his answers pretty convincing. As he conceded, he'd done a lot of strange things in his life and seemed to have a tendency to schmooze various agencies for information, blurring the boundaries of his relationship with the prosecution, LAPD, FBI, and Secret Service; but I found nothing concrete to tie Michael McCowan to the CIA.[35]

* * *

In the mid-nineties, Jean Scherrer, the LAPD's "man who wasn't there," also reappeared. When author C. David Heymann interviewed former LAPD officer Daniel Stewart for his book on Robert Kennedy, the former head of VIP security tagged along.

Stewart had been assigned to Good Samaritan Hospital on the night of the shooting and was present with Sergeant Bill Jordan at the autopsy. Scherrer claimed to be the LAPD official assigned to work with Kennedy, went along to the hotel because he had "a premonition," and later was Rafer Johnson's chaperone when he delivered the gun to the LAPD. As noted previously, Scherrer told Heymann that for five thousand dollars, he would go into more detail about the assassination.[36]

In 1996, the paths of Scherrer and Michael McCowan crossed in an apparent attempt to compromise Sirhan's attorney Larry Teeter and legal researcher Rose Lynn Mangan.

Photographer Scott Enyart was suing the city of Los Angeles over pictures he had taken on the night of the shooting that the LAPD confiscated and never returned. Enyart claimed he was in the pantry, standing on a steam table at the time of the shooting, taking pictures of the senator. When the police finally returned his photographs, the images of those key moments in the pantry were missing.

Two weeks before the case began, Sirhan's researcher Rose Lynn Mangan was approached by a neighbor in Carson City, Nevada, by the name of Jerry Vaccaro. Vaccaro told Mangan he'd been interviewed during the investigation into the JFK assassination and, it turned out, he was a friend of Mike McCowan's dating back to the mail fraud charges in 1966.

Vaccaro set up a lunch meeting in Burbank with Mangan, Adel Sirhan, and Larry Teeter, and he brought along Jean Scherrer. According to Vaccaro, Mike McCowan had applied for a presidential pardon in the mid-seventies to clear the mail-fraud case from his record. The pardon was denied, but McCowan's petition included confidential FBI documents showing that McCowan had been an FBI plant on the Sirhan defense team. In return for these embarrassing documents, Scherrer and Vaccaro wanted the movie rights to Sirhan's life story.

Mangan and Teeter immediately smelled a rat and flatly turned the offer down. Teeter wrote to Police Chief Willie Williams and the DA's office documenting the offer. The timing was worrying—it seemed an obvious "sting operation" to compromise Mangan before she testified at the Enyart trial. The only response they ever got from the authorities was a postcard of acknowledgment.[37]

When I asked Mike McCowan about the offer, he said he'd never heard of Larry Teeter and knew nothing about it. I spoke briefly to Danny Stewart, but he didn't want to discuss the case—"most of the LAPD guys prefer not to." He'd lost touch with Jean Scherrer, and I haven't been able to find him.[38]

* * *

When I discussed a possible assassination plot with seasoned operatives, they invariably pointed to a man on the inside as an essential element of such an operation. He could have been an insider working for Kennedy or the hotel who knew what was going on and could have, perhaps unwittingly, passed information to the plotters or been manipulated into directing the senator into the "killing zone."

While I don't suspect Pierre Salinger of any conscious connection to the shooting, some of his business relationships are worth examining with this in mind.[39]

In Salinger's 1995 autobiography, *P.S. A Memoir,* he writes of his friendship with Bob Six, the founder of Continental Airlines. In the summer of 1965, Six was setting up a subsidiary in Southeast Asia called Continental Air Services (CAS). It would provide air services to the CIA as an alternative to the agency's own carrier, Air America, which was in danger of being banned from certain countries due to regional tensions over Vietnam. CAS would have no direct links to the agency; all contracts would go through the usual cover organization, AID.

Six had meetings at the CIA with William Colby, then director of covert operations and later head of the CIA. Colby told Six he needed someone with top secret government clearance to work at a high level in the new company. Salinger had such clearance during his career in the Kennedy White House and was perfect for the job.

Salinger accepted the offer "because it sounded like an exciting job" and flew out with Six to start work at the new headquarters of CAS—a converted motel in Vientiane, Laos. CAS would take over from Air America in supplying the U.S.-funded Meo army to the north, who were repelling North Vietnamese incursions along the Ho Chi Minh trail.

Each morning, CAS DC-3s took off with sacks of "hard rice," full of military equipment to be parachuted to the Meo. According to Salinger, half the staff had CIA links. CAS also made daily reconnaissance flights, to report on North Vietnamese troop movements along the Ho Chi Minh trail, information that was used by the U.S. Air Force for their covert and illegal bombing raids in Laos.

Salinger worked for Continental Air Services for the next two years, bringing him into the same orbit as CIA operatives Tom Clines and David Morales, whom we'll discuss in the next chapter.[40]

Another odd Salinger connection was Robert Maheu, right-hand man to Howard Hughes and the liaison connecting the CIA, John Rosselli, and the Chicago Mob during earlier attempts to assassinate Castro. During the California campaign, Kennedy staff decided to approach Hughes for a campaign contribution.

Salinger thought Hughes was approachable and got the assignment—"I knew Hughes' right-hand man, Robert Maheu, quite well, so I called and made an appointment with him." The morning after their meeting, Maheu called to say that Hughes had agreed to give Kennedy twenty-five thousand dollars.[41]

By 1968, the Hughes organization, through Maheu, was working hand in glove with the CIA. John Meier was Hughes's third in command and an arch-nemesis of Maheu's. In an interview with researcher Lisa Pease, Meier claimed that Maheu had connections to Thane Eugene Cesar and the upper ranks of the LAPD. According to Pease, "Meier saw enough dealings [within the Hughes organization] before and after the assassination to cause him to approach J. Edgar Hoover with what he knew . . . Hoover expressed his frustration, saying words to the effect of "Yes, we know this was a Maheu operation. People think I'm so powerful, but when it comes to the CIA, there's nothing I can do."[42]

I subsequently met Meier in person, and while he claims to know who financed, organized, and carried out the assassination of Robert Kennedy, I have yet to see any evidence of this.[43]

* * *

When they retired, two legendary figures of American intelligence also held photographs of Robert Kennedy's autopsy in their personal safes—FBI chief J. Edgar Hoover and CIA counterintelligence chief James Angleton. As author Anthony Summers noted, of all the famous deaths in Hoover's long career, the gruesome color pictures of the RFK autopsy are the only death pictures preserved in his official and confidential files, segregated from the main FBI filing system.[44]

Angleton's colleagues were astonished by their bizarre find in his personal safe when he retired. They had no idea why Angleton had the pictures or "why it was appropriate for CIA staff files to contain them. They were accordingly destroyed."[45]

SEVENTEEN

THE CIA AT THE HOTEL

Four years ago, the story you've just read inspired me to write a screenplay on the case. It would be a challenge to distill the complexities and conundrums into a two-hour film, but the biggest problem was that I still didn't know "who did it." I didn't believe the official version of events. I didn't believe Sirhan acted alone, so I went in search of an ending and became, to use a very seventies term, an "assassinologist."

I read all the books on the case and was particularly affected by Robert Blair Kaiser's sublime portrayal of the struggles to unlock Sirhan's mind. The more I listened to Sirhan speak, in custody, with Kaiser, or under hypnosis, the more credible I found his memory block and the possibility that he was a "Manchurian candidate."

In subsequent books on the case, author Phillip Melanson presented the most convincing scenario to me: Sirhan as a hypnotically controlled "patsy" with a programmed memory block; two guns—the second wielded by Cesar or someone else; Pena and Hernandez covering up within the LAPD; and unnamed doctors and CIA operatives filling out the conspiracy.[1]

But this last part, about the CIA operatives, seemed undeveloped. Pena and Hernandez, with their CIA connections, could supervise the cover-up, but there was no evidence of a CIA presence at the hotel on the night of the shooting.

If you're researching one Kennedy assassination, you've got to research the other. If there was a conspiracy in Los Angeles and the CIA was involved, I reasoned, the same team was probably involved in Dallas as well. Yet the existing books on the Robert Kennedy case were very light on connections between the two assassinations.

So, this was my starting point—to look at CIA operatives suspected of involvement in Dallas in 1963 who might also have been in Los Angeles five years later. One of the first people I looked at was David Sanchez Morales.[2]

* * *

Morales was a legendary CIA operative, about whom little was known until the late eighties, when Bradley Ayers began to investigate the man he had worked with at the CIA's secret Miami base, JMWAVE, in 1963. Morales was chief of operations and went by the nickname "El Indio"—the "Big Indian." Close friends called him "Didi." He was half Mexican and half Yaqui-Pima Indian, known as big more for his weight (250 pounds) and oversized reputation than his height (a modest five-ten). The first known photograph of Morales, taken in Havana in 1959, was initially released in the Cuban press in 1978, the year he died.[3]

Ayers located two close friends of Morales in his hometown of Phoenix—Morales's best friend since childhood, Ruben Carbajal, and his former lawyer, Robert Walton—and they were interviewed in 1992 by author Gaeton Fonzi for his book *The Last Investigation*.

Fonzi spent several days with both men before a final joint interview. The friends recalled a drinking session with Morales and Walton's wife, Florene, at the Dupont Plaza hotel in Washington in the spring of 1973. At one point, Walton let slip that he had done some volunteer work for Kennedy.

"[Morales] flew off the bed on that one," said Walton. "I remember he was lying down and he jumped up screaming, 'That no good son of a bitch motherfucker!' He started yelling about what a wimp Kennedy was, and talking about how he had worked on the Bay of Pigs and how he had to watch all the men he had recruited and trained get wiped out because of Kennedy.

"Suddenly, Morales stopped, sat down on the bed and added, 'Well, we took care of that son of a bitch, didn't we?'"

Fonzi looked over at Ruben Carbajal, who had been listening silently. Carbajal looked at Fonzi and nodded. "Yes, he was there, it was true," Fonzi wrote. "But, in all the long hours we had spent together and all the candid revelations he had provided, it was a remembrance he couldn't bring himself to tell me about his friend Didi."[4]

Author Noel Twyman interviewed Walton and Carbajal separately three years later for his rare, self-published book, *Bloody Treason*. Neither man had any doubt that Morales had been involved in the JFK assassination and again recalled the hotel drinking session.

"He said, 'We got that son of a bitch, and I was in Los Angeles also when we got Bobby,'" recalled Walton.

"When 'we' got Bobby?"

"'When we got Bobby.' And when he said 'also' I linked that back to Dallas. I'm not sure he ever said 'I was in Dallas' but he did say 'I was in Los Angeles when we got Bobby.'"

Ruben was now more open about the Dallas comment. "By 'we took care of that son of a bitch,' does 'we' mean the CIA?" asked Twyman.

"Goddamn right, that's what it means," replied Carbajal.

Twyman asked Ruben about Walton's quote, essentially, "and I was in Los Angeles when we got Bobby."

"I don't remember that part right now," said Ruben carefully. "I don't remember that part. . . . Because he could have been there. He was there many times. Two sisters, you know, lived there and one of his daughters."

Ruben had gotten used to Morales's involvement in Dallas, but he wasn't ready to finger him for another Kennedy assassination.

* * *

As Twyman's huge and impressive tome focused on the JFK assassination, he never pursued the Los Angeles angle. Morales's SOB line regarding Dallas became widely known through Fonzi's book, but the Los Angeles addendum was overlooked, remaining buried on page 471 of Twyman's book until 2004.

Twyman told me the main source of his information on Morales was Bradley Ayers, who, last he'd heard, was living in the woods in Minnesota. I did a search and found that Ayers had moved to Frederic, Wisconsin. I couldn't find a phone number, so I e-mailed Gary King, the editor of the local paper. Brad popped in occasionally, so Gary would call and ask if he'd be willing to talk to me. A few days later, word came back that Brad Ayers was willing to cooperate, and my introduction to the world of David Morales began.[5]

* * *

Brad was understandably cagey in our initial discussions, but very willing to help any investigation into the Kennedy assassinations. He suggested I get a copy of his book, *The War That Never Was*, a whistle-blowing account of his time at JM-WAVE, first published in 1976. His publisher had insisted on pseudonyms to protect operatives' identities, but Brad faxed me a key to the true cast of characters.[6]

He also told me he had a witness in a "Southwest city" who had matched the 1959 photo of Morales to a man seen at the Ambassador Hotel the night of the RFK assassination. He would go into details when we talked a bit more but, approaching seventy years old, he was eager to get things "on the record."[7] He later summarized his background:

> *I was a regular army captain in 1963, with a specialty in covert and paramilitary intelligence operations. Suddenly, I was beckoned to Washington, DC, asked to report to the Office of Special Warfare at the Pentagon, and subsequently offered an opportunity to serve with the CIA in its secret war against Cuba. I transferred to South Florida, to JMWAVE, the only CIA station that was ever established on U.S. soil.*
>
> *I arrived in April 1963, and Ted Shackley, as chief of station, welcomed me. I met the assistant chief of station, a fellow by the name of Gordon Campbell, who later became my case officer on a particular mission shortly before the Kennedy assassination. I also worked under a fellow by the name of David Morales, who was the chief of operations. The concept was to conduct*

covert paramilitary operations involving infiltration and commando raids in an effort to destabilize Castro's Cuba. We also embarked on efforts to assassinate Fidel Castro.[8]

Kennedy had been handed the CIA's plan for the invasion of Cuba on assuming office in January 1961. Brigade 2506, a small military contingent of commandos—approximately fifteen hundred CIA-trained Cuban exiles—would be landed on the south shore of the island at the Bay of Pigs, and then penetrate inland and take over the country, in the belief that the Cuban population would rise up against Castro. From a military planning standpoint, it was an ill-conceived operation and really stood no chance of succeeding without air support.

But CIA director Allen Dulles assured the young Kennedy it would be another quick, bloodless coup in the manner of the CIA overthrow of Arbenz in Guatemala in 1954. Kennedy pressed ahead but made it clear it must be a Cuban operation, with no U.S. hand visible. Aging American warplanes, repainted with Cuban markings, attempted to bomb Castro's air force in advance of the landing but failed miserably. The Kennedys refused to authorize further air support, and Castro's planes picked off the fifteen hundred invaders with ease, killing many and capturing the rest.[9]

It was a spectacular embarrassment for the Kennedy brothers three months into JFK's presidency, and the CIA would never be trusted again. Dulles was fired, and the president threatened to "shatter the CIA into a thousand pieces, and scatter it to the winds."

He chose his brother, Attorney General Robert Kennedy, to personally oversee a new secret effort to overthrow Castro and reclaim the Kennedy honor. Bobby chaired the same "Special Group, Counterinsurgency" that would oversee the creation of the Office of Public Safety, the police advisory body headed by Byron Engle that would later provide operational cover for Pena, Hernandez, and David Morales. And so, Robert Kennedy, chairing the special group, proceeded to micromanage the secret war on Castro.[10]

* * *

The special group soon identified a need for paramilitary training for Cuban exiles willing to go on infiltration raids into Cuba, and Bradley Ayers got the call. He went by the cover name "Daniel B. Williams" and was initially assigned to the operations branch:

"Dave, the big New Mexican Indian who ran it, was the only branch chief who treated us less than respectfully. He ran all the station's activities with a heavy hand and was famous for his temper." Morales resented Ayers's intruding on his turf and repeatedly tried to block his path to station chief Ted Shackley, raising objections to his proposals to train the Cubans properly in response to failed missions.

In *The War That Never Was*, Ayers refers to Assistant Chief of Station Gordon Campbell by the pseudonym "Keith Randall." He judged Campbell to be around forty years old, "in robust physical condition . . . dressed as if he had just come off the golf course, tanned, clean shaven, with a trim build, balding blond hair, and penetrating blue eyes." Campbell also ran the Maritime branch and lived with his wife on a yacht berthed at Dinner Key Marina in Miami.

* * *

Ayers would sit in on briefings with Shackley, Campbell, Morales, other branch chiefs from JMWAVE, and visiting personnel from Washington, DC, such as Des Fitzgerald and William Harvey. Bobby Kennedy was demanding quick results and was on top of everything.

"Robert Kennedy, chairing the special group, had to pass on each and every mission," Brad recalled, "and you had these suits sitting there in Washington under Robert Kennedy's control—and all well-meaning of course—but they weren't in the field. The majority of them had no military background. It created a huge amount of resentment on the part of the operational people at JMWAVE. Particularly, I know for a fact, Morales would go absolutely berserk when the word came down that an operation had to be changed or possibly even canceled because the risk of attribution and unintended consequences was too great."[11]

* * *

In the summer of 1963, Ayers was taken by airboat to a covert meeting at the Waloos Glades Hunting Camp in the Everglades. At dusk, some men were standing around a campfire in the middle of a clearing, with lights burning in two Quonset huts and two helicopters parked in the shadows.

The door to a Quonset hut swung open and four men emerged. One was Gordon Campbell, and "I caught my breath at the appearance of the second man. It was the attorney general, Robert Kennedy. The four men talked in low voices for a few minutes, and then the attorney general came over and shook hands with each of us, wishing us good luck and God's speed on our mission."

Toward the end of November, as Ayers trained Cuban exile commandos on a tiny island in the Florida Keys, he recognized a plane passing overhead "as the single-engine Cessna based at the CIA headquarters in Miami. . . . A white object was released directly over the old house. It was a roll of toilet tissue, streaming as it fell. It landed only a few feet away. . . . The center tube of the tissue roll had been closed with masking tape. . . . Hastily, I opened up the tube and pulled out the paper inside. It was Campbell's printing:

NOVEMBER 22 1963
PRESIDENT KENNEDY HAS BEEN SHOT BY AN ASSASSIN. SUSPEND ALL ACTIVITY. KEEP MEN ON ISLAND. COME ASHORE WITHOUT DELAY. GORDON[12]

* * *

Ayers saw very little of Campbell after that, and more than a month after the assassination, Campbell told him to ease off on the training and then pretty much disappeared.

"The word around the station," Brad told me later, "was that Castro had killed Kennedy, and that Oswald was a pro-Castro operative. I don't know why, but deep in my guts, I had some feeling that what we had been doing down there was in some way connected. I had a gnawing suspicion about some of the things I had heard at the station. The anti-Kennedy comments. The sentiments that were expressed about the Bay of Pigs. The resentment that I couldn't help but overhear—just disgust with the Kennedy administration. From that point forward, I had growing suspicions about the agency's role in John Kennedy's assassination."[13]

* * *

As I read Brad's book, I sought out film footage of the night of Robert Kennedy's assassination. If Morales said he was there, perhaps his highly distinctive features would appear in the material shot that night. I ordered tapes of network news footage of Kennedy's victory speech and the shooting aftermath.

A week later, at the end of September 2004, the tapes arrived. The first one was a raw video feed recorded by a CBS camera at the Ambassador, minutes before Kennedy took the stage. About fifteen minutes into the tape, less than a minute after Kennedy left the stage and headed toward the pantry, the camera panned across the ballroom. Standing at the back in a white shirt was a "dead ringer" for the Morales in the 1959 photo. I couldn't believe it. It was a wide shot, so "Morales" was quite small in the frame and the lack of detail was frustrating, but as the camera held on him for a few seconds, my gut feeling said this was Morales.

I played the tape on. Twenty-eight minutes later, I saw him again, floating around the darkened ballroom with a shorter colleague with a pencil mustache. They loitered behind CBS reporter Terry Drinkwater as he prepared a piece for the camera. I got a closer look at the bronzed complexion and strikingly distinctive features. His belly protruded from his gray suit, and his colleague scribbled notes as the pair surveyed the room. Not only did it look like Morales; they were acting like spooks.

* * *

I had also ordered a copy of the LAPD's "composite of motion picture films" from the California State Archives, the repository of the LAPD investigation files since the late eighties. SUS had assembled a twenty-minute film of footage shot at the hotel before, during, and after Kennedy's speech, capturing some of the shooting aftermath. The picture quality is admittedly very poor—ungraded 16-millimeter prints, crudely spliced together into a rough chronology—but the film contains a key scene that promised to unlock the secrets of the assassination.

Within moments of the shooting, NBC producer Chris Michon ran from the pantry doorway out into the ballroom, climbed up on a viewing platform, pointed an imaginary gun to his head, and mouthed the words "bang, bang, bang" to alert his camera team on risers at the back of the room to start rolling. Next to NBC on the risers, Walter Dombrow's CBS camera picked up Michon's panicked reaction as ripples of hysteria began to sweep the room.

Dombrow zoomed out to pick up the commotion, then reframed on a balding man in a blue jacket walking calmly through the crowd toward the back of the room. He seemed to be coming from the direction of the pantry, and he held his right arm across his chest, with what seemed to be a small container in his hand. A shorter Latin man with a mustache, alongside him to his right, had both arms raised, motioning him toward an exit. The bald man glanced at the Latin man, who waved toward the exit again, and the bald man left in that direction. As panic swirled around these men, they seemed composed and alert and moved through the room with a sense of purpose.[14]

* * *

I was intrigued. Repeated viewings of this clip suggested that the bald man may have been leaving the pantry with a disguised weapon in his hand, as a Latin accomplice (who fit a Cuban profile) waved him toward an exit.

I sent frame-grabs of my discoveries by e-mail to Brad's local paper. Gary King printed them out, and Brad reviewed the images of "Morales" and the second suspicious character who seemed to be leaving with a package in his hand. Brad's response was immediate. Allowing for the quality of the images, he gave a strong indication that this was, indeed, Morales. But the real surprise was the other suspicious character. "Less a little hair," Brad saw him as a "dead ringer" for Gordon Campbell, suggesting that two JMWAVE veterans were at the hotel, with two unidentified associates, on the night Bobby Kennedy was murdered. I had a potentially incredible story on my hands.

I now came to a fork in the road. Thoughts of a screenplay were being rapidly overtaken by plans for a documentary. Why fictionalize a story whose every twist and turn was this strange and unpredictable? The facts of the case were all-important and could not be muddied by dramatic license. A documentary it would be.

To finance it, I would need to shoot some footage to give potential backers a sense of the story—key interviews with Brad and others who knew Morales and Campbell and could identify them on camera.

In January 2005, surfing my credit card, I flew to snowbound Minneapolis to finally meet Brad and show him these clips in person.

In response to the first clip, of the bronzed figure at the back of the ballroom, he said, "Yeah, that's the figure that I had previously identified as Morales to a very high degree, I would say 90 percent. I'm a little bit troubled by the configuration of the nose . . . but the general facial impression except for the nose, is an individual that I would identify as Morales to a practically hundred percent degree."

The second clip, in which the same man is seen surveying the room with a colleague, seemed to strengthen his ID: "This, definitely from the profile, is hugely similar. The body language is very, very much characteristic of Morales. See how he moves back and forth very casually, so as not to attract attention to himself. That is [him], no question. The second clip reduces any significant question I have about the first clip. And, to me, it reinforces my opinion that that's Morales."

Why was Morales there? The CIA had no domestic jurisdiction, and wouldn't normally be there protecting Bobby Kennedy. Given Morales's frequently expressed hatred of the Kennedys, Brad concluded that his presence at the hotel could mean only one thing—he was involved in the assassination.

* * *

With the Morales ID confirmed in Brad's mind, we moved to a possible identification of Gordon Campbell, and I showed the clip of the balding man as he moved through the room: "Yeah, that's excellent. I could certainly verify 90 percent ID of Gordon Campbell. Less a little hair, as I remembered him. The facial features are certainly his. Absolutely. And, you know, I'm looking beyond the face, I'm looking at the body, the carriage."[15]

There were no photos of these men publicly available in 1968, so the likelihood of them being identified by any of Kennedy's staff was minimal: "It does not surprise me at all that these folks would be so audacious as to believe that they could pull this off; in fact they did."[16]

* * *

I had also found an amateur photograph of the same man standing in the Embassy Ballroom earlier in the night with a swarthy, Mediterranean-looking colleague. Brad confirmed that this was the same Gordon Campbell as in the video clip. The swarthy figure next to him looked familiar, but he couldn't identify him. So, at this point, there were five possible conspirators: An initial ID on Morales and Campbell, and three other men pictured with them at various times in the hotel.

I couldn't find anyone else who knew Gordon Campbell, so on this first trip, the focus was on David Morales. I flew to Phoenix, his hometown, where Ayers had first come in the late eighties as a private investigator, to explore the shadow world of "El Indio."

Much of what we now know about Morales was dug up by Ayers on this initial investigation. He was mugged, had his briefcase stolen, and was continually under surveillance. But he located Walton, Carbajal and a possible witness to Morales at the Ambassador Hotel. True to his word, Brad now put me in touch with David Rabern.

* * *

David was now CEO of a million-dollar security firm, the most prominent in the Southwest. He was a highly respected figure in his industry, coauthoring a textbook for the certification of security professionals. We grabbed a discreet corner in a local restaurant and David sketched in how he came to be at the Ambassador Hotel that night.

In 1968, Rabern was an undercover operative in Los Angeles, freelancing for a number of different agencies, and specializing in concealed-alarm installation, sweeping buildings for bugging devices, and planting some of his own, often in a variety of disguises. He lived close to the Ambassador and had just worked on a short project in alarm systems with "a group of people . . . that had worked for Central Intelligence":

> *And they had mentioned that, at the Ambassador Hotel—they says, "They're going to have a big to-do there, you gonna be there?" and I said, "Yeah, I could be there." . . . That's not an unusual thing for any of the agencies. Even police departments will give free tickets to functions and such as that, just to have their people in the audience.*
>
> *I was walking across [the lobby] going towards the front doors when I heard the gunshots and . . . it was just like a little pop-pop-pop-popping sound that you could barely hear. Could [Sirhan] have done it alone? I don't think so. I don't think the man's makeup would have allowed him to do that in the first place. I think there was probably a lot of people involved. Why that never came out is a mystery still.*

When Brad Ayers visited Rabern in the late eighties, he took the 1959 photo of Morales from his briefcase and got an instant reaction. "I told him I'd seen the guy on the premises. I didn't see him in the ballroom. I saw him out in the lobby area. In fact, I probably saw him several times. He was in and out."

When I played David the video clips, he instantly recognized "Morales" as the same man.

"Yes. I'll be darned. . . . Oh, that's him, yeah. . . . That's him. . . . They were certainly observing and collecting information," he said as "Morales" surveyed the room with a colleague.

I asked David if he recognized anyone in the photograph of "Campbell" and his swarthy colleague in the ballroom. "This man here, the bald one . . . I think he was talking to Morales at one time. . . . "

"So you'd be sure then, that the man on the left in the photograph was talking to Morales at one point?" I asked.

"I'm almost certain, yeah. . . . You've got the military stance, arms behind their back; that's a dead giveaway." He laughed.

The video of Campbell confirmed the identification. While Rabern didn't know Morales and Campbell by name, he remembered seeing them at the hotel that night and connected them, seeing them talking together at one point.

But he also sounded a word of caution at this stage: "Because they're Central Intelligence doesn't make them bad guys automatically. They're out there protecting our country like everyone. By the same token, it doesn't mean they can't have turned bad."

We began to analyze how such an operation might have been put together. "Sirhan Sirhan was probably one of several that were armed and ready to take him. Sirhan Sirhan was, in my opinion also, a throwaway. He's what we call the shooter in the public's eye but who the real shooter was? This level here, you get a professional. And a professional, you'll never see . . . you'll never know anything except they were there, that's about it."

A second gun could be disguised: "We camouflaged firearms in all different kinds of configurations. Sometimes, they'd look like a day-timer . . . purse-like situation. It'd show a zipper on the outside but it had Velcro and you could pop it open."

Would the assassin have used a silencer, so witnesses wouldn't hear the extra shots? "Strongly possible, yes. Silencers can be made out of all kinds of things, too. Maybe a book or something like that, could be inside that and could be muffled. . . . That would have been the proper way to do it, and just disappear. Not get out there like Sirhan Sirhan did, and start shooting his gun. . . . I mean that could have been to draw that away from the real shooter."

Overall, David thought it was an impressive presentation.

"Suspicion? High, high suspicion. . . . I can't deny that. Why they were doing the things that they were doing . . . I'm surprised that that was never investigated. After all of these years, you'd think that someone would have noticed these things and done something about them."[17]

* * *

While in Phoenix, I also interviewed Robert Walton, a good friend of Morales's who had also acted as his lawyer during the seventies. Now sixty-nine, Walton was struggling with the onset of Alzheimer's.

It was true, he told me, that Morales hated the Kennedys after the Bay of Pigs and saw them as rich, spoiled brats. David also hated Communists. When he went on a parachute jump one time, he found out some of his co-fliers were playing for the other side and he proceeded to cut the straps on their parachutes.

We discussed the drinking session at the Dupont Plaza in 1973, when Morales gave his "five-minute self-indictment" in the presence of Walton, his wife, Florene, and Ruben Carbajal. The tirade was sparked by an admission that Walton had worked for Kennedy as a volunteer.

"You did work for Kennedy?" asked Morales.

"Yeah, I did," said Walton. "Well, that motherfucker . . .," raged Morales as he launched into a tirade.

"He didn't hit anybody," recalled Walton, "but he was striding around the room and . . . he was just out of control. I don't ever recall seeing him lose it like that before."

"And what was his actual comment then, that finished that?" I asked.

"Well, it was something like . . . 'I was in Dallas when we got that mother-fucker and I was in Los Angeles when we got the little bastard.' . . . Just right out of the blue. . . . I mean, boom, and then, everybody was kind of stunned. I don't remember anything being said after that. Everybody was in my room and everybody else left.

"What it said to me was that he was in some way implicated with the death of John Kennedy and, let's go one step further, and also Bobby . . . but there were no details."

"Did you ever talk to him about that subject again?" I asked.

"I never had the opportunity to risk having my nose broken." Robert laughed. He looked at the footage but couldn't say if it was Morales one way or the other. It had been a long time, and the quality of the images and his waning eyesight proved inconclusive.[18]

* * *

The next day, I drove down to Nogales on the Mexican border to meet Morales's best friend since childhood, Ruben "Rocky" Carbajal. Now in his late seventies, Ruben was a pugnacious character, with a neat mustache and a silver tongue. We talked in the private bar of his home, bought from the police chief, on a hill overlooking the town. Ruben chain-smoked throughout, a bourbon lined up on the counter.

"They called him a man of a thousand faces," he began. "He was one of the most interesting men you ever want to meet." Ruben knew Morales by his nickname, "Didi." They grew up together in the barrios of Phoenix. David's father abandoned the family when he was five years old, "so he grew up with us, you know, in and out of our house all the time. We went through high school together. My parents wanted him to be with me to make sure nobody messed around with me, 'cause everybody's brother wanted to kick the shit out of me."

According to Ruben, David rose to the rank of brigadier general in the CIA and was fiercely patriotic: "He's what you call a hundred percent American all the way through—you don't mess with him—and he'll blow your ass apart."[19]

Ruben talked me through Didi's exploits over the years: "Well, he's the one, him and Tony Sforza, that did up Che Guevara up there in Bolivia. Didi cut his head off; get that through your head."

After the death of Dan Mitrione, Morales was brought in to cleanse Uruguay of Tupamaros. "They went from door to door," said Ruben, knocking on the counter, "and as soon as they opened the door, they had to kill children, old men, children, old men, anybody that was there got killed, right down the line . . . and that's how they gave the government back to the people. . . ."

"So they just wiped out all the leaders of the Tupamaros?"

"They wiped out their families and everybody," said Ruben. "All these holy people that think by talking to people, you gonna get it done; you gotta kill 'em!"[20]

From there, David went on to Chile to "overthrow old Allende" in 1973, allegedly stealing ten million dollars from the Chilean treasury in the process. Earlier that year, Walton and Carbajal had joined Didi for a drinking session at the Dupont Plaza. Ruben had his own take on the incident.

"They were sort of wanting some information about what happened down there, you know, at Dallas. And we were drinking and finally Didi . . . let them know in a roundabout way, 'Well, we got the son of a bitch,' that's what he said. You don't have to be a brain to figure out what he meant, you know."

Ruben made it clear that Didi hated the Kennedys for going back on their word and withdrawing air support at the last moment at the Bay of Pigs, and he was sure Morales's comment was more than idle boasting—"You don't make comments like that, if you don't know what's going on."

"Did he ever tell you anything else about Dallas?"

"No, I didn't ask no more. The more you ask, the less chance you got of living."

Then Ruben launched into a tirade about Robert Kennedy, and it was easy to hear Morales echoed in his voice.

"And then I don't have no respect for that Robert, when he put down in the newspaper . . . 'The blacks, take anything you want, it belongs to you.' What kind of a goddamn asshole . . . all the ethnic groups we have in the United States, what about the rest of them, huh? I tell you, that man is crazy, he wants to start a civil war right here in the United States, with that stupid talk like that. And then he got knocked off in a hurry, didn't he?"

* * *

I asked Ruben about the Los Angeles part of David's confession. Bob Walton heard Morales say "I was in Los Angeles, when we got the little bastard," meaning Bobby.

"No. He was in Los Angeles but he didn't say 'We got him,' you know. That 'they got him.' Just a difference [in] the wording, you know."

Great, I thought. Back to Sandra Serrano country. "We shot him." "They got him." Did he think David was involved in the Bobby Kennedy shooting?

"No, he probably . . . might have known behind the scenes what was going on, but that has never been clear to me, you know, exactly what happened."

"He didn't say 'we got the little bastard'?"

"No, he didn't say that. That wasn't his words at all. Not to me. Robert Walton might have interpreted it that way, but I didn't interpret it that way. 'Cause the only reason he'd be in that area at that moment, 'cause his daughters were married and one of them was living over there, you know."[21]

* * *

But June of 1968 was too early for Morales' daughters to be married. His eldest, Rita (a pseudonym), was only sixteen, and the family was about to leave Boston to join Morales in Laos, where he'd been stationed for almost a year. If Morales was in Los Angeles, he wasn't visiting family, that's for sure.[22]

* * *

When I showed the video clips to Ruben, he was instantly dismissive.

"See the figure in the white shirt here?" I said, pointing out the figure at the back of the room.

"No way. No way; that's not him at all."

"Is there any resemblance at all?"

"No."

I showed him the second clip.

"Well, that's the same person there was before. No, those are security guards there for Kennedy. I guarantee you he was no security guard for him. That's not him. I guarantee you it's not him."

Ruben's reaction puzzled Brad Ayers.

"I really don't know why Ruben would respond that way. I guess probably when confronted with a photograph, which would be pretty hard evidence, putting him on the spot, he may be reluctant to condemn his lifelong friend. He can live with the thought that Morales may have been involved in some way, almost be proud of it. But to ID him, that may be just too far a reach for him. And it doesn't surprise me."

* * *

Bob Walton thought the interview "was a very difficult assignment" for Ruben. "He doesn't want to admit to dirty tricks or a murder committed by his friend and is still trying to protect his reputation. It's the legal problem of 'declaration against interest'—not wanting to be caught up in a murder-accident investigation and keeping quiet about it."

Walton held firm—David had definitely said "we" in relation to Bobby. He'd talked to his wife, Florene, about it a couple of times, and she had heard David say "we" for Dallas and Los Angeles as well. But photo identification was difficult— "plus David was a master of disguise, so it's not easy to identify him in the first place!"[23]

* * *

I pondered whether to believe Ruben or not. His denial of Morales in the video was immediate and convincing, but I found his shifting of "we got him" to "they got him" problematic. When Noel Twyman first asked Ruben about the Los Angeles part of the statement, he said "I don't remember that part right now." Ten years later, his memory seemed to have improved. The clincher for me was the suggestion that Morales was in Los Angeles to see family. I found this preposterous. Ayers's and Walton's thoughts on Ruben's dilemma were persuasive, and I concluded that he was still trying to protect his friend.[24]

* * *

I was out of Morales leads for now, so my attention turned to Gordon Campbell. While much had been written about the "Big Indian," the only other book to mention Campbell, *Deadly Secrets*, used Brad Ayers as its main source. The authors added some new details, describing Campbell as a tall man with close-cropped silvering hair and a military bearing. He oversaw the maritime branch of JMWAVE, taking charge of all CIA naval operations in the Caribbean.[25]

The Miami telephone book for 1962 and 1963 did list a Gordon S. Campbell at 10091 Sterling Drive, south Miami, but a public record search revealed that he died on September 19, 1962, age fifty-seven. Not our man.

It seemed the only way to discover the truth about Campbell at this late stage was to speak to others who knew him at JMWAVE. But that wasn't going to be easy. Very few seemed to know Campbell. Ted Shackley made no mention of him in his posthumously released autobiography, and I had no secondary confirmation that he was, in fact, deputy chief of station.[26]

* * *

The more David Rabern thought about that night at the Ambassador, the more came back to him and the more he seemed willing to share over the next few months. He remembered seeing "Morales" out in the parking lot before the shooting, with two of the guys he'd worked with on the alarm project. He also saw the bald head of "Campbell" within fifteen minutes of the shooting, walking briskly back through the lobby toward the kitchen area.

He remembered a briefing meeting at a bank building on Wilshire Boulevard. Operatives were given packets of instructions for a particular assignment and he recalled seeing "Campbell" leaving the meeting as he was just coming in. I got the sense these operations were targeted at the antiwar movement and compatible with something like Chaos, but David wouldn't elaborate.

Rabern remembered seeing "Campbell" probably half a dozen times in a two-year period before the assassination, usually in a downtown police station environment, in the company of two men and a woman, all of whom he assumed to be LAPD officers.

The woman was in uniform and had a nice body and a vivacious personality; she wasn't beautiful, but she caught his attention. One of the guys was Mexican, in his early to mid-thirties, six-one, 200 pounds, and he talked to "Campbell." The other guy was Caucasian, six-two or six-three, 220 pounds. The two men associating with "Campbell" weren't wearing uniforms but were law enforcement and had a certain gait that showed they were carrying guns. He remembered "Campbell" wearing a light blue sweater and carrying a sidearm, which means he would have to have been with the police or in some official capacity.[27]

* * *

Meanwhile, I was still trying to identify the other man standing with "Campbell" in the ballroom. To me, he had an undeniably Mediterranean look. As I researched possible colleagues of Campbell who bore these features, two figures from the Greek mafia within the CIA caught my attention—deputy director Thomas Karamessines and George Joannides.

Karamessines's obituary photograph in the *Washington Post* quickly told me it wasn't him, but Joannides's notice from 1990 didn't carry a picture, and it seemed that no photograph of Joannides had ever been made public. Joannides had become something of a cause célèbre in assassination circles, as outlined in a series of articles by *Washington Post* reporter Jefferson Morley.[28]

In 1976, after numerous scandals exposed unauthorized and illegal CIA covert operations, Congress appointed a House Select Committee on Assassinations (HSCA) to reinvestigate the JFK assassination. In 1978, as the committee's aggressive young investigators probed through layers of CIA records, the man the agency called out of retirement to act as their liaison to the committee was George Joannides. To the young investigators examining possible links between Lee Harvey Oswald and the CIA, Joannides was a smart and highly efficient lawyer, but at no time did they suspect he had played a key role in the story of Lee Harvey Oswald fifteen years before.

* * *

Joannides was born in Athens in 1922 and grew up in New York City, graduating with a law degree from St. John's University in Queens. Joannides joined the CIA in 1951 and spent eleven years in Greece and Libya before a posting to JMWAVE in Miami as deputy to the chief of psychological warfare operations, David Atlee Phillips.

Joannides was a cosmopolitan man, fluent in French and Greek and competent in Spanish. His brother-in-law was George Kalaris, who would later succeed James Angleton as CIA director of counterintelligence.

In November 1962, CIA deputy director of plans Richard Helms handpicked Joannides to be the case officer for the most popular group of militant anti-Castro exiles in Miami, the DRE (Directorio Revolucionario Estudantil or Revolutionary Student Directorate).

David Phillips had been funding the DRE's anti-Castro propaganda campaign to the tune of twenty-five thousand dollars a month and Joannides's job over the next year or so involved trying to dampen the group's military ambitions while encouraging their propaganda campaigns and intelligence collection. The DRE knew their case officer as "Howard."

On July 31, 1963, Joannides was promoted to chief of psychological warfare operations at JMWAVE, and the following week, Carlos Bringuier, the DRE delegate in New Orleans, began to report a man actively promoting Castro in New Orleans. His name was Lee Harvey Oswald. On August 5, Oswald walked into the DRE's local office and offered to train commandos to fight Castro. Four days later, a DRE supporter spotted Oswald on a street corner handing out pamphlets for the Fair Play for Cuba Committee, the most prominent pro-Castro group in the country at the time. Bringuier and his friends went to confront this Castro double agent. As they angrily denounced him, a crowd gathered and police broke up the altercation.

Twelve days later, Bringuier and Oswald debated the Cuban revolution on Bill Stuckey's weekly radio show on WDSU, and Oswald revealed he had lived in Russia and advertised his Marxist credentials. All of this was fed back to "Howard."

As the DRE unveiled an ambitious new invasion plan, Ted Shackley recommended that all funds to the directorate's military section be cut off. Helms agreed, and on November 19, 1963, Joannides told the DRE that the agency was cutting off its support. Three days later, Kennedy was assassinated.

After Oswald's arrest, the DRE went public with details of Oswald's pro-Castro activism in New Orleans, setting the tone for early press coverage of John Kennedy's assassin. Did Joannides and the DRE conspire to create a Communist legend for Oswald? We still don't know.

* * *

In April 1964, Joannides left Miami and was transferred to Athens with a job evaluation that praised his performance as "exemplary." Joannides stayed in Athens until 1968 and was posted to Vietnam in 1970 to once again work for Ted Shackley, by now Saigon station chief. He returned to Washington in 1972 to work in the general counsel's office at CIA headquarters until he retired in 1976 to set up a practice in immigration law.

After his stint liaising with the HSCA, Joannides retired in January, 1979. He once told one of his children that he was skeptical of JFK conspiracy theories, but he did not explain why. His heart problems worsened in later years, and he died on March 9, 1990, at the age of sixty-seven. His obituary in the *Washington Post* made no mention of his twenty-eight years of CIA service, stating only that he had been a lawyer at the Defense Department whose assignments included service in Vietnam and Greece.[29]

* * *

I was intrigued and called Jefferson Morley in search of a photograph of Joannides. There were none in the public domain, he said, and the Joannides family refused to give him one. I told him I thought I might have a photograph of Joannides at the Ambassador Hotel. These guys were master spies, he said. They wouldn't let themselves be photographed. He wasn't interested.[30]

Undeterred, I began to e-mail the photograph to as many of those who knew Joannides as I could. Outside the CIA, the most objective place to start seemed to be the HSCA investigators who worked with Joannides in 1978. Former chief counsel G. Robert Blakey told me he had only limited contact with Joannides, but the two investigators who saw him most were two Cornell law students he had assigned to investigate Oswald and Mexico City—Dan Hardway and Ed Lopez. "They had almost daily contact with Joannides."

Both men are still practicing lawyers—Hardway in North Carolina, Lopez in Rochester, New York. I e-mailed them the photo, and the results were encouraging. Hardway's initial response was: "This could be him. Much younger in the picture than in the seventies, and it's been a long time." He suggested I talk to Ed Lopez, and I was stunned by his response—Lopez was "ninety-nine percent sure" it was Joannides.[31]

* * *

Next up was the DRE. Cofounder Juan-Manuel Salvat told me Dr. Luis Fernandez-Rocha was the main contact for Joannides. Dr. Fernandez-Rocha confirmed this in a telephone interview. He remembered meeting "Howard" once a month, and he liked him very much—"he was very cordial and charming, a very well-educated man with excellent manners." His last contact with Joannides was at the end of 1963 or early 1964.

After my call, I e-mailed him the photograph, and when we spoke four days later, he came right to the point: "Regarding the photograph—this is important. I cannot confirm or deny that this is him. The photograph is a little fuzzy and he looks much thinner than I remember. He has a different haircut and different glasses, but these things can easily change. Number two: I didn't know he had any involvement with Robert Kennedy. I didn't meet Robert Kennedy, and I have no idea of any connection between him and Robert Kennedy." He stressed that it was important I quote him this way, and at the time, the tension in his voice and choice of words gave the impression of a man with something to protect.[32]

I also spoke to Robert Keeley, who had served as a political officer at the Athens embassy from 1966 to 1970 and later returned as ambassador. He recalled Joannides working downtown as a CIA officer. It was common for Greek Americans to come over with their language skills, often under joint U.S. military–AID cover, and Joannides was one of the more senior people there.

Keeley would meet Joannides once in a while at social gatherings, and their wives were good friends. But his response to the photo was inconclusive: "The photo is a bit fuzzy. I can't help you one way or the other. I cannot say that it is his image, and I can't say it isn't."[33]

* * *

On the left, two men, allegedly Gordon Campbell and George Joannides, stand in the Embassy Ballroom. On the right, "Campbell," "Joannides," and an unidentified third man.

When I was finally commissioned to make the BBC story, I headed straight to Rochester to show the photograph to Ed Lopez in person.[34]

Today, Lopez is a distinguished lawyer at Cornell University. He grew up a Puerto Rican in New York, and back in 1978, he was a twenty-two-year-old hippie law student, described by fellow investigator Gaeton Fonzi as "a brilliant free spirit with an infectious smile, long, curly locks, baggy jeans and flip-flops."

"I was a bit of a rebel," remembered Lopez. "Dan and I would dress up in cut-off shorts just below our crotch area and cut-off shirts and show up at the CIA in these outfits." The CIA was understandably suspicious of "these two little hippies coming in to look at the files to make a decision about whether they might have been involved in the assassination." They put the young law students under surveillance, and there was a white van parked regularly outside their apartment.

Blakey assigned Lopez and Hardway to examine Oswald's activities in Mexico City prior to the John F. Kennedy assassination, when he allegedly visited the Cuban and Russian embassies and made contacts in a city that was a hotbed of espionage at the time. Ultimately, "the Lopez report basically concluded that there was some type of a relationship between the CIA and Lee Harvey Oswald. Exactly what that relationship was we could never tell." What was his personal view? "I have no doubt in my mind that he was being run by someone at the CIA . . . Was there a connection to the point where they were running the assassination? . . . That we could not confirm."

* * *

Lopez first met George Joannides in the early summer of 1978, when Joannides was assigned as the new CIA liaison to the HSCA investigators. "Joannides was our point person, the guy who controlled what we could see and what we couldn't see at the CIA. He was probably in his mid-fifties. . . . He was a dapper guy, funny and affable . . . five-eleven or so, in shape, with graying hair, slightly receding."

The HSCA knew practically nothing about Morales or Campbell at the time, and to Lopez, Joannides was nothing more than an extremely competent clerk providing access to the files. Joannides never disclosed his history with the DRE at JMWAVE, even though this was one of the areas the committee was investigating.

After Joannides died, Lopez finally found out about his past. "At first, I was shocked; then I was angry because I felt like we had been taken. And then, being a lawyer, I said, 'My God, this is obstruction of justice.' But the guy himself, he did his job perfectly."

Joannides never blanched as Lopez and Hardway discussed his past colleagues, and Lopez was very clear on Joannides's mission: "The CIA wanted someone who knew what had been going on back then to control what was made available to us. . . . How could we trust anything the CIA was giving us if the guy that was our point of contact, who controlled what we saw or didn't see, happened to have been a person who we would have investigated back then had we known who he was?"

* * *

When I showed Lopez the ballroom photograph in person, he seemed extremely confident of his identification: "When I look at this picture, to me it's a younger George Joannides. I couldn't say one hundred percent that it's him . . . but I'm ninety-nine percent sure that it's George Joannides."

I had also found two additional photographs of "Campbell" and "Joannides" standing in the same position in the ballroom. These were taken from behind, and showed a third man beside them, with blond hair and horn-rim glasses. These new images also brought an immediate smile of recognition. "I don't mean to be funny, but I often saw the back of Joannides because he would come down to get us at Langley and we'd be following him. Again, it looks to me just the way George looked. Same posture, hair . . . like I said, I'm ninety-nine percent sure that it's him."

Ed reflected on the photographs: "George Joannides is an enigma to me. After he died, when I heard that he'd been involved with JMWAVE, that he'd been involved with the DRE, and now looking at this photo . . . it doesn't surprise me for a minute to find him at the Ambassador Hotel on the day that Bobby Kennedy was shot. If he was the level operative that he appears to have been through DRE and JMWAVE, if another operation was going on that was key, he would have been there."

Was there a benign reason why he might be at the hotel? "Can I give an alternative explanation for George Joannides being there other than to, like, run an assassination? God help us. The agency hated the Kennedy brothers. Every CIA operative I met from the early sixties hated John Kennedy because of the Bay of Pigs. These are people who'll do anything for the good of their country . . . and if it meant assassinating a second Kennedy to make sure that he didn't rise to power because he would be dangerous for the country, they'd do it."

* * *

Lopez was clear on what was needed now. "I think the key people at the CIA need to go back to anybody who might have been around back then, bring them in, and interview them. Ask: 'Is this Gordon Campbell? Is this George Joannides? Did you know about any operation going on? If you didn't, then why the hell were they there?'

"Do I expect that to happen? No. I expect a very short, pat answer. 'We don't know why he was there. It's a rogue element.' That's the way the CIA worked. Everybody was a rogue element because no one can know what everybody else is doing."

As we wrapped up, Ed said I should go visit his fellow investigator Dan Hardway and talk to him face-to-face; he had a phenomenal memory.[35]

* * *

After interviewing Ed Lopez, I traveled to Washington, DC, to meet a still skeptical Jefferson Morley. Having invested ten years in the Joannides story, he was literally shaking as we sat at his kitchen table and I showed him the photographs in the ballroom and the alleged video of Morales and Campbell.

My own attempts to contact the Joannides family had met a wall of silence, but Morley planned to visit one of Joannides's daughters that weekend. For years, Morley has been involved in a laudable and protracted struggle to get the CIA to comply with the JFK Records Act and release Joannides's operational records from JMWAVE. He has been supported by a who's who of respected authors on the Kennedy assassination, a bipartisan group mixing Oliver Stone and Gerald Posner, the most famous proponent of Oswald as lone gunman. Although Joannides's wife is dead, Morley has courted the Joannides children during this period, believing that their cooperation would ultimately help lead to the records' release.

When he visited one of the daughters that weekend and showed her the main photograph in the ballroom, the response was a terse "No comment." Weeks later, a second daughter, now a superior court judge in Alaska, would give the same response. You had to wonder: If it wasn't their father in the photograph, why were they being so defensive?

* * *

While in Washington, I also visited Wayne Smith, who during twenty-five years with the State Department (1957–1982) served as executive secretary of President Kennedy's Latin American Task Force and came to know Morales well.

The moment Smith saw the bronzed figure at the back of the ballroom, he exclaimed, "That's him. That's Dave Morales."

"Really?" I said, surprised at the speed of recognition.

Smith gave a deep, visceral sigh, as if taken aback by the implications. "Yes, I'm virtually certain; is there anything [more]?"

I played the second, longer clip, and he watched intently. "Yeah, that's . . . yeah, when he turns sideways, that's Morales. That's Morales."

Smith was intrigued and recounted his connection to Morales. "He worked in the CIA station in Havana when I was third secretary of the Political Section [from] fifty-nine until we broke relations in sixty-one." He saw him again a number of times after that, passing each other in corridors at the State Department and they had dinner together when Morales visited Buenos Aires in 1975.

"When I saw him in Argentina," Smith recalled, "we got into an argument about Kennedy, the Bay of Pigs and all that . . . and what he said was that 'Kennedy got what was coming to him.'"

Did he give any indication that he might have been involved in some way? "He didn't," said Smith. "He said 'Kennedy got what was coming to him,' and he said it in a very determined way, as if he took great satisfaction in it, but no, he didn't."

I asked Smith if there was a benign explanation for Morales's presence at the hotel? "Well, I don't see any . . . if the CIA or the Security Division of the Department of State ordered him to be there to protect Bobby Kennedy, that'd be one thing, but I don't think that's the case. And if they didn't, then there is no benign explanation I can think of."

Was Morales a suitable figure to protect Bobby Kennedy? "No!" Smith laughed. "No, I mean, in my wildest imagination, I couldn't imagine assigning David Morales to protect any of the Kennedys. . . . Bobby Kennedy is assassinated [and] David Morales is there? The two things have to be related."[36]

* * *

Smith's ID of Morales was hugely significant, validating Brad's identification and supporting Brad's credibility in his ID of Gordon Campbell.

David Rabern had placed "Morales" and "Campbell" together. "Campbell" and "Joannides" were photographed together. It seemed three senior figures from JM-WAVE who worked under Bobby Kennedy in the war on Castro were at the Ambassador Hotel the night he died, and they certainly weren't there to protect Kennedy.

I continued to seek further corroboration from four former CIA colleagues. Felix Rodriguez canceled, and Grayston Lynch was ill, but I did meet Tom Clines and Ed Wilson, Morales's closest associates in the agency, next to the late Tony Sforza, according to Ruben.[37]

I met Clines at the Marriott in Tysons Corner, Virginia, a stone's throw from CIA headquarters. He didn't want to appear on camera, but we talked for an hour or so about his time at JMWAVE. He had started off training a select band of twenty-nine guys for the Bay of Pigs and went on to be the case officer for Cuban exile leaders such as Manuel Artime and Rafael Quintero. He worked in covert operations in Miami. Morales was his boss, and later in his career, he was Morales's boss. He said Gordon Campbell wasn't deputy chief—that was a guy by the name of R.B. Moore, "a pretty ineffectual guy not worth talking about."

He described Chief of Station Ted Shackley as "a one-man brigade." He went to Clines, Morales, and Sforza for difficult missions. They'd attempt crazy operations that often ended disastrously, but a good few were successful.

Bobby Kennedy was seen as an irritant by the covert ops people because he had a back channel to the Cubans, who would skirt around the bureaucracy to get boats quickly by calling Bobby from a pay phone. Clines never met Kennedy personally but described him as overanxious to get results, complaining that the agency was slow and sidestepping them with the Cubans. He smiled when I asked if mobster Johnny Rosselli worked at the station but wouldn't answer directly.

When I first spoke to Clines, he brought up the "assassination of Kennedy Senior" at the end of the call. When I asked his opinion, he said he wouldn't discuss it on the phone, but in person, he didn't want to touch it either, dismissing Morales's hotel-room rant as "just bullshit."

As talk turned to the matter at hand, Clines fondly remembered Brad Ayers as a wild character who would bring snakes up from the swamps to show the women in the office. Then I showed him the video of Morales, twice. He said it looked like Dave but it wasn't him. "Dave was fatter and walked with more of a slouch," he said. "He would have had his tie down." It seemed an odd comment. To me, the "Morales" in the video did walk with a slouch and his tie down. Was this a coded way of saying it was him?

I also showed Clines the alleged photograph of Campbell and Joannides. He said he knew both men, and that it wasn't them, either. "Campbell was good to know," he added, "because he came from a rich family, but he wasn't a memorable guy—if you gave him a gun for an operation like that, he was likely to shoot himself. That's why we sent him up to Canada, as the CIA liaison up there."

Clines discounted Brad's ID because he wasn't at JMWAVE very long, but he was surprised by Wayne Smith's. "Smith knew Dave, and he would know, but I don't think it's him."

By 1968, Morales was again working for Ted Shackley in Laos. Could Shackley have masterminded such an operation? "But he was in Southeast Asia," protested Clines. Supposedly, so was Morales. "Why don't you ask his wife, Hazel?" Clines said. "She knew everything."[38]

It was a strange meeting. Clines's comments on Morales seemed ambivalent to me—"It looks like him but it's not him." What does that mean? When I spoke to David Rabern later, he was sure Clines would have been briefed by the agency before the interview and suggested I take what Clines said with a pinch of salt.[39]

* * *

A few days later, I met Ed Wilson in the boardroom of his attorney's office in Seattle. Wilson is currently suing the CIA for falsely imprisoning him for twenty-two years for selling explosives to Libya. Wilson has always insisted that the deal was an agency operation and that the CIA hung him out to dry. An appeals court in Houston freed him in 2004, and he is now suing for compensation.

Wilson appeared tall, as sharp as a tack, and very distinguished in a tweed jacket and neatly trimmed moustache. He was in his late seventies, worked out every morning, and was an engaging raconteur. Every Morales anecdote was accompanied by a disbelieving guffaw. He was clearly very fond of Dave.

They knew each other mainly in Washington from 1971 to 1976. When Dave was in town to go to language school with Clines, he would stay at one of Wilson's apartments. "He and Clines couldn't go a night without drinking. And Morales couldn't go to bed at night without getting laid."

Morales was fiercely loyal to Ted Shackley: "Shackley liked guys like Morales that would just do anything. If the operation was military, it would probably be Clines and Morales. In the Dominican Republic deal, the opposition had a radio station across the river. So Dave got his bag and rowed across and said, 'Hi, I'm Doctor Mendes, I want to visit my patient,' and pretty soon, the radio station just blew up." Wilson guffawed. "I tell you these stories because that's Dave, you know, he's a nutcase. He was a helluva character, a dedicated, loyal American; he really was. I don't know about the Allende thing, but I'm sure if Shackley was involved; he was involved 'cause they were, like, connected at the hip, you know."

But work always came above family. "Dave, one time, was working on an operation in a Miami safe house, and they were all around a table working on it, and Dave got a phone call, and he said, 'Is there anything I can do?' and listened—'No, nothing you can do.' He went on with the meeting. Come to find out that his kid had [fallen] in the swimming pool and was close to death and they pulled him back. When I think of Dave, I think of that story. What a cold-blooded bastard. I would have got in my car and gone there, but not Dave. If there was nothing he could do, he continued with the meeting."

When it came to Dave's outburst at the Dupont Plaza, Wilson was as dismissive as Clines: "I think that comment was just Dave being a big shot. That's bullshit, you know."

Would he be capable of something like that? "He'd be capable, but what would be his purpose unless somebody [ordered] him . . . which is probably what you're after, but I don't believe it. . . . He's too smart. . . . Why would anybody risk their whole career to do something off the record or illegal? . . . You know damn well you're gonna get caught."

Finally, I showed Ed the video clips of "Morales" in the ballroom: "That's not Dave. No. He has negroid features; Dave didn't. Indian Dave had dark features, but he had Indian features. . . . The complexion's not that far off, but that's not Dave. That's not his mouth; that's not his eyes. That's not his nose. I'm pretty good on faces. I'd bet my life on it, that's not him."

* * *

It was a very definite "no" from a man with no agenda; but the strange thing was that Wilson didn't recognize Morales in the 1959 photo, either. His response to the photo of the two men standing in the ballroom was also interesting.

"I seen that guy with the glasses somewhere, but God, I can't tell you where for the moment. . . . The other guy with the bald head looks familiar too. . . . He looks a little like Helms, in a way. The other guy looks like a normal CIA spook. Doesn't have his cloak and dagger with him, but . . ."

He guffawed again, the laugh of a man wrongfully imprisoned by the CIA for twenty-two years, freed of bitterness but with a well-honed sense of the absurd.[40]

* * *

Wilson was free with his opinions and very persuasive, but he didn't know Morales in 1968 and he didn't recognize him in the earlier 1959 photo. Who could I trust? Two independent witnesses outside the agency, or close confidants of Morales, some still consulting for the CIA?

With the Morales ID, the scales were now finely balanced, but with the identifications of Campbell and Joannides at the hotel on the same night, a Morales look-alike talking to Campbell out in the lobby seemed too freakish a coincidence. I had to give Ayers and Smith the benefit of the doubt.

On balance, I still felt I was on the right track with my three suspects, so I aired the story in a segment on the BBC on November 20, 2006—Robert Kennedy's eighty-first birthday, had he lived.[41]

EIGHTEEN

CHASING SHADOWS

Brad hoped my BBC film would be a "smoke-out," and in the months following its broadcast, much new information came to light on all three operatives allegedly at the Ambassador Hotel on the night Bobby Kennedy was murdered.

While blogs quickly picked up on the story—and the Cuban government newspaper, *Granma Internacional*, gave it a ringing endorsement, splashed across the front page—not a single U.S. media outlet followed it up.[1]

First out of the gate with a critique online was Jefferson Morley. Within hours of the broadcast, perhaps to placate the Joannides family, he publicly declared the piece "unfounded and unfair . . . to make such serious allegations on such flimsy evidence is irresponsible." This was the same guy who, the week before, told me he'd found the "no comment" of the Joannides family "telling."

The following day, we had a robust discussion and Morley amended his comments: "thinly-sourced can be true if the source is good . . . [and Lopez's] near-certainty that Joannides appears in the photo . . . has to be taken seriously. If Joannides was there, the implications are profound. The CIA must be compelled to abandon its JFK stonewalling and disclose fully about George Joannides' actions and whereabouts in 1963 and 1968."[2]

* * *

As I worked on my BBC film, I was contacted by Brad Johnson, a senior news writer with a global television network based in the United States. Over the years, Brad had amassed, without doubt, the most comprehensive archive in existence of news coverage of the assassination. Two days after my BBC story aired, Brad contacted me with further sightings of my three CIA suspects.

Together, we reviewed every frame of film or video recorded at the hotel that night by the national networks, local television stations, and independent filmmakers—almost a hundred hours' worth of material.

Thanks to his ingenuity and much dogged research, we found many more clips of the people we believed might be Morales and Campbell at the Ambassador Hotel that night. We were able to trace the movements of "Gordon Campbell" throughout the evening, with the help of his distinctive blue sports coat and receding hairline, and could also sketch in a rough chronology for "David Morales."

At 12:16 a.m., in the space of five seconds, Robert Kennedy and five others were shot in the pantry. Twenty-one seconds later, "Morales" is first spotted in the footage, not in the Embassy Ballroom, where I first thought, but at the back of the Ambassador Ballroom, one floor below. This makes sense. Kennedy was due to go downstairs for another speech. If he wasn't diverted into the pantry and Plan B had to be activated, "Morales" was ready and waiting.

At 12:47, "Morales" emerged from the pantry and walked into the ballroom among a group of police officers. Moments earlier, a Kennedy volunteer is seen blocking this doorway to the public. The sequence strongly implies that "Morales" is one of the investigators at the crime scene.

At 1:03, "Morales" is clocked comparing notes with the shorter man with the pencil mustache in the darkened ballroom. If this wasn't Morales, who was he? His behavior across all these clips was consistent with a plainclothes operative or undercover cop monitoring the situation, yet there was supposedly no police presence at the hotel at the time of the shooting.[3]

* * *

British author and former school deputy principal Mel Ayton has devoted his retirement to shooting down conspiracy theories. He was soon taking poor-quality video-grabs of my BBC film and e-mailing them across the pond. JMWAVE veteran Grayston Lynch had been ill when I tried to interview him a few weeks earlier, but after the BBC broadcast, he recovered to tell Ayton that the men in his bootlegged images were not Morales and Campbell.[4]

Lynch subsequently refused to speak to me. His wife, Karen, said Gray was furious at "conspiracy theorists," and in no mood to look at the new material. Her e-mails were friendly, funny but blunt:

> *If you believe ANYTHING Bradley Ayers has to say on any subject concerning the CIA, I have some ocean front property in Kansas City I would like to try and interest you in. It always amazes me how these weasels ingratiate themselves with the media and have their disinformation spread so unwittingly. Ayers was drummed out of the Agency and has a real bone to pick with them. Sorry, you hit a nerve.*
>
> *Happy Christmas, Karen.*[5]

* * *

The Lynches' comments netted out to very little: an agency veteran unlikely to admit it was Morales, whatever the circumstances, and scorn for Bradley Ayers, a man I had come to trust implicitly, for all the vagaries of photo identification. And for the record, Ayers was not "drummed out" of the agency. He resigned his commission when he saw a close colleague thrown out of a helicopter, and his credibility cannot be questioned. Ted Shackley corroborated many key details in Brad's book, and Tom Clines fondly remembered him. Brad had been seconded to the CIA from the army but was not a contract employee, so he was not bound by the secrecy oath, as Clines and Lynch were. His whistle-blowing could not be so easily brushed off.[6]

* * *

At this point, I thought I had run out of Morales's associates, but Ayton found two more through author Don Bohning, former Latin American editor for the *Miami Herald*. Manuel Chavez and Luis Fernandez were both in their late seventies and had worked out of the CIA's public office in Miami in the early sixties. For a few months, they worked alongside Dave Morales before he moved to JMWAVE.

Ayton had e-mailed "six sets of very grainy and dark photos" to Chavez, who tried to enhance two of the better ones in Photoshop and sent them on to Fernandez. This did not sound ideal for comparison purposes, so I contacted the extremely receptive Chavez and sent him a DVD of best-quality images to review instead.

Manny Chavez first met Morales in Caracas, Venezuela in February 1957. Chavez was the assistant U.S. air attaché and Morales was assigned to the CIA office in the embassy. The families were close until Morales left in the wake of the coup in January, 1958.

Chavez saw Morales again in Miami in late 1961 when he was working out of the CIA's public office downtown for a few months before he moved to JMWAVE. Manny said the 1959 photo "looks almost exactly as I remember Dave Morales," but some of the later photos of Morales in the seventies were foreign to both him and Luis—"Could there have been another Dave Morales?"

* * *

Once my DVD arrived, Manny got to work immediately: "After reviewing it alone twice, I then called Bernice, my Managing Director of 63 years, and ran it for her, also twice. We then carefully looked at it together and concluded it probably is not the David Morales that we knew in Miami and Caracas.

"Yes, there is some resemblance—tall, dark complexion, but we both agreed that there are two essential differences. The David Morales we knew during 1957/58 and again in 1961/62 had a much rounder and darker face and a full set of black hair. The person in the photo has a receding hairline that I do not recall David Morales having."

On further analysis, Manny thought that the Morales he knew was also shorter and fatter than the man in the video. Manny then sent the DVD on to Luis Fernandez.

"I reviewed the DVD that you sent three times," he wrote, "and conclude that the person who is shown walking around in the crowd and then sticking his head around the corner of a partition is not David Morales with whom I worked in Miami."

Manny asked Luis if he had any doubts. "Definitely, he is not Dave Morales," said Luis. "This person seems taller, more slender and lighter color. Dave was fat, round faced and darker complexion, like a true Mexican Indian, whereas those of the man in the DVD are of an African-American."

"Shane, this is our honest opinion," wrote Manny. "We have no reason to withhold or cover-up any information on the identity of David Morales. Had Bernice and I had any doubts, we would have said so, and I am sure that Luis Rodriguez feels the same way. Rest assured I will try to help you get the truth to the best of my ability, even if I later learn that I may have been wrong."

Manny continued to help me get to the bottom of things, and the candid, guileless generosity of both him and Luis made me seriously reconsider the ID of Morales for the first time.[7]

* * *

I also followed up with Felix Rodriguez, who had worked with Morales for several months in Vietnam. "Last time I saw Dave Morales was in early 1972 [when] I visited him in Na Trang. I saw the clip and definitely that is not Dave Morales. I scanned the picture you sent me and I sent it to my former supervisor in Vietnam. He also agrees with me that the man in the picture is not Dave Morales."

Clines's former supervisor was Rudy Enders, a colleague of Morales at JM-WAVE. "I mentioned to him the name of Gordon Campbell and he knew him well since Gordon was his boss in Miami, but for your information, Gordon Campbell died in 1962 at the CIA facility in Miami from a massive heart attack and my friend was there when it did happen. You better check your sources on that. This will be easy to verify by you with Gordon's family or the agency."

Well, the agency refused to verify the identities of previous employees, so they weren't going to be any help. But I wondered how Gordon Campbell could have died in 1962 if Bradley Ayers met him in 1963? Tom Clines never mentioned him dying; he said they'd sent him up to Canada.

"I just talked to Rudy," Felix replied, "and he assured me that Gordon Campbell died in front of him; he was one of the people who tried to revive him. He said Bradley Ayers was in training and did not work with Gordon Campbell and if Tom Clines said that, he was probably thinking of someone else, since Gordon Campbell died right in front of him. Just for your info, another retired agency officer under Rudy at the time told him that he can attest that Brad Ayers arrived in Miami long after Gordon Campbell died. He read Brad's book and said he thought it was . . . all lies and fabrication. I guess your source is not very reliable. Felix."

Clearly, these old agency hands had no liking for Brad, but this account of Campbell's death didn't make sense.

Did Brad just make up all those details about Campbell in his whistle-blowing book in 1976? Any kind of fabrication would have made it easy for agency veterans to instantly destroy his credibility and defeat the purpose of the book. That didn't make sense. It was curious that former colleagues had waited thirty years to start attacking a work Shackley and Clines had previously corroborated. I seemed to have touched a nerve.[8]

* * *

But as I began to edit my feature documentary, I was out of time and money to do any more research in the States. Then, just before Christmas, I received a very excit-ed call from journalist David Talbot, who was completing his first book, *Brothers*, on Robert Kennedy's response to his brother's death. Talbot was intrigued by this new evidence and had secured funding from the *New Yorker* magazine to follow up my investigation. His coauthor would be Jefferson Morley, who admitted "I spoke too soon in November."

* * *

It was a risk to share my research with other journalists, but if I didn't have the resources to carry the investigation further, I was glad they did. I sent David what video and photographs I had so they could verify and perhaps build on my findings with the best materials available. Talbot and Morley hit the road to investigate my story over the next six weeks, and David called with updates along the way. Their initial focus was on Joannides.

They started off knocking on doors in Washington, brandishing the ballroom photograph to aging associates in doorways to a chorus of denials. But the Joan-nides family themselves remained tight-lipped, sticking to a frosty "no comment."

* * *

Next stop was North Carolina. Talbot and Morley took HSCA investigator Dan Hardway out to lunch and had the face-to-face meeting Ed Lopez had recom-mended. While at first Hardway hadn't wanted to get involved, now he opened up and said, yes, the man in the photo was Joannides.[9]

I called Hardway several weeks later, and he still clearly remembered his days at the HSCA with Lopez. "We were arrogant young kids, trying to intimidate CIA clerks into giving us records." Joannides was brought in to get them under control and slow the process down. He totally changed the access program. Hardway re-membered him as "imperious, with a contemptuous look." He saw Joannides only two or three times at most.

"When I first looked at that photograph," he said, "I thought, 'That's not him.' But then I thought, 'I'm fifty-four now and Joannides was fifty-four when I knew him.' I realized how quickly your appearance changes at that point in your life, added to the fact that Joannides had heart trouble."

So while he couldn't be positive, he told me his exact words to Talbot and Morley, from the look of the man at the Ambassador and the way he was standing, was that "he could very well be the guy that I remember—I'd be surprised if it wasn't him."[10]

* * *

Ed Lopez reconfirmed his identification to Morley and Talbot, so as they traveled down to Florida, the congressional investigators said it was Joannides, while Washington friends said it wasn't. In Miami, they quickly found another member of the DRE who recognized Joannides. Isidro "Chilo" Borja was the military director of the DRE and now runs an air-conditioning business in Miami. As he later confirmed to me, he met Joannides only a couple of times, forty years earlier, but yes, the man in the photograph looked like Joannides.[11]

The last leg of Talbot and Morley's journey took them to see Joannides's former station chief in Saigon, Tom Polgar. Word came back that before Talbot and Morley mentioned his name, Polgar identified Joannides in the photograph. Polgar also identified the blond man in horn-rimmed glasses in the other ballroom photographs as James Critchfield, the CIA's chief in the Middle East at the time.

This was extraordinary. But a couple of weeks later, according to Talbot, Polgar realized the import of what he'd said and backtracked. He no longer thought it was Joannides.

I called Thomas Polgar to clarify all of this. He was now eighty-five years old, a very friendly, lucid, open man with a strong Hungarian accent. He had looked up my story on the Internet after Talbot and Morley's visit and recalled their meeting. They had briefed him on what they wanted to talk about—namely, George Joannides, James Critchfield, and David Morales.

Polgar didn't know Morales, but Joannides had worked for him as a branch chief in Saigon for most of 1972. When he was shown the ballroom photographs, Polgar told Talbot and Morley—and later confirmed to me—that the man at the Ambassador was "not incompatible" with the Joannides he knew in Saigon, but he couldn't positively identify him.

Polgar identified the third man as "not incompatible with James Critchfield." He first met Critchfield in 1949 and would have seen him again in 1968 at one of the group meetings of senior CIA staff. Polgar left Washington for South America around that time, while Critchfield was in charge of the Middle East and Germany.

Even if it was Joannides in the photograph, Polgar didn't see any great significance. "Politically interested people were always attracted by free drinks at a party for a big primary. There was no Internet then; it was a big social occasion. A lot of agency people traveled commercially through Los Angeles en route overseas, and the place to stay was the Ambassador. Joannides could have been on home leave." He advised me to check the registered guests at the hotel. "A senior officer like Critchfield wouldn't travel on a false passport and would have registered under his real name."

I asked if Joannides's presence could suggest something darker. "If it was a planned assassination, they wouldn't have been within a thousand miles of there," Polgar said, adamant that senior officers would not have been involved in something like this.[12]

* * *

In the early seventies, Critchfield married his third wife, Lois, herself a CIA officer. When he got back to Washington, Jeff Morley showed her the photograph, but she denied it was her late husband. He also contacted Timothy Kalaris, son of the former CIA counterintelligence chief and nephew of Joannides. "That is not my uncle; I can tell you that," said Kalaris. "I don't know how anybody who ever knew him could say that's him."

George Joannides, Saigon, 1973.

* * *

While Talbot and Morley were on the road, the death of legendary CIA operative E. Howard Hunt was announced, and a few weeks later, his memoir, *American Spy*, was published. Hunt called Morales a "cold-blooded killer . . . possibly completely amoral" and on March 21, *Rolling Stone* magazine ran an interview with Hunt's eldest son, St. John, titled "The Last Confessions of E. Howard Hunt."

In 2003, Hunt thought he had months to live. He was bedridden with lupus, pneumonia, and cancer of the jaw and prostate, and gangrene had forced the amputation of his left leg. As he faced death, he spoke to his son about the planners of the JFK assassination. He scribbled a crude diagram connecting LBJ at the top to senior agency figures Cord Meyer and Bill Harvey (who first brought Morales to JMWAVE). The arrows continued down to the names "David Morales" and

"David Phillips." A line was drawn from Morales to the framed words "French Gunman Grassy Knoll."[13]

Hunt had worked with Morales and Phillips on the Arbenz coup in Guatemala in 1954. Phillips recruited Joannides as his deputy in the psychological warfare branch at JMWAVE and worked closely with Morales throughout his career. Morales admitted to Ruben Carbajal and Robert Walton that he was in Dallas, and before he died, so, famously, did Phillips. He called his estranged brother, trying to make his peace, and his brother asked, "Were you in Dallas on that day?" "Yes," said Phillips, and his brother hung up.[14]

* * *

As the Hunt circus played out in the media, the last leg of David Talbot's trip took him to meet the two eldest daughters of Morales, Rita and Sandra (a pseudonym). A few months later, I spoke to them myself in ninety-minute conversations, during which they talked openly about the legends that have grown around their father.

Morales joined the army at twenty, in April 1946, and was sent to Germany three years later, to be based at the European Command in Munich. Within a year, the CIA's intelligence chief in Germany, Richard Helms, requested clearance for Morales to "be enrolled for basic cryptographic training." Helms would rise to CIA director by the time Robert Kennedy was assassinated.

Joan Kerrigan was half Irish and half Scottish and grew up in Boston. After college, Catherine Gibbs Secretarial sent her to work for the CIA in Germany, and there she met and married Morales in March 1951. Their first daughter, Rita, was born the following year, and Joan's boss became Rita's godfather and recruited Morales as a contract agent for the CIA.

A second daughter, Sandra, was born fifteen months later, but when the family came back from Germany in October 1953, her maternal grandfather, a first-generation Kerrigan, didn't meet them at the airport because he didn't approve of the mixed-race marriage.

According to Rita, Morales joined the army "because he was dirt-poor, everyone else was joining and it seemed a way out" of the barrios in Phoenix. "If he hadn't met our mother and joined the CIA, he would have left the army at the end of his tour and gone back to Arizona. He felt he got lucky and owed his good fortune to the company and would never have gone rogue or jeopardized his status."

After returning to the States, Morales spent the next ten months on PB Success, planning the Arbenz coup in Guatemala, and soon became a permanent CIA employee. After a posting in Venezuela, he was transferred to Batista's Cuba in May 1958, as an attaché at the U.S. embassy. On Sundays, Morales would take his kids into the office, and they'd play on the typewriters.

There were eight kids in the family—seven of whom are still alive—and they lived with Morales during all his postings except Vietnam (his family was part of his cover). Growing up, Morales's daughters remembered their father as a stern disciplinarian with a hot temper. "It wasn't a democracy. It was a monarchy and he was in charge." He was a distant workaholic. "He didn't strive to know us," remembered Rita. "I never took any money for college because I would be tied down by him. . . . He had a chip that he had to work harder being Hispanic, but when he wasn't drinking, he was a good guy."

Morales never discussed politics, and they found out only late in his life that he voted Republican. But Sandra clearly remembered her Bostonian mother going to vote in 1960, wanting Kennedy to win.

In October 1960, the family moved to Miami, where they stayed for the next five years. Morales grew very close to the Cuban exiles as he was put to work on JMARC, a Cuban invasion plan that would end so disastrously at the Bay of Pigs.

* * *

Rita was in sixth grade when President Kennedy was shot in Dallas. She remembered her father being home that evening and showing no reaction to what had happened. He never spoke about the Kennedys. Sandra thought he was home that evening but was less certain. She couldn't see him as a shooter in Dallas, though: "He was a wingtip-and-white-shirt guy. I always saw him in a suit. . . . I never saw him with weapons or target shooting."

If he wasn't a shooter, could he have masterminded the operation? "Who knows?" said Sandra. "I've no knowledge of that. Just he worked for the CIA, and they probably did a lot of stuff."

The family had heard about the recent Hunt revelations through a brother-in-law. Could Morales have been at a planning meeting for the assassination? "He might have been there," said Rita, "but who were the others? He didn't organize it. Who was above him? If my father got a direct order to do it, I'm sure he did it. He knew the type of people who could get the job done."

* * *

In June 1965, Morales was posted to Peru. His own cover history statement reads: "I was detailed to the Agency of International Development (AID) as a Public Safety Advisor. After attending the International Police Academy, I was assigned as one of two senior public safety advisors to the Peruvian National Police (Guardia Nacional) as a counter-insurgency advisor." This was the same program used by Pena and Hernandez.

CIA records indicate that Morales stayed in Peru until February 1967 and shipped out to Laos in late 1967, where he would be reunited with Ted Shackley as a "community development officer," again under AID cover. The gap in his CV between these postings fits the timeframe of the search for Che Guevara perfectly. The hunt formally began in late April, when sixteen Green Berets were sent over to train the Bolivian search team. Guevara was captured and shot on October 9.

Morales's daughters said he was in Laos for about a year before the family followed. He would come home for a month at a time and be gone for five. He built them a house, and Rita remembered arriving in Vientiane on July 4, 1968. It took them two weeks to get there, traveling through Japan and Hong Kong with their father. Sandra confirmed these dates. She was going to school in Massachusetts at the time of the RFK assassination. School got out around June 20; then they left for Laos. Morales met them in Japan, and they spent a week there before traveling through Hong Kong and Thailand to Pakse.

Morales never left Laos afterward, so Rita didn't think he could have been in Los Angeles, but these dates place the beginning of their trip East two weeks after the assassination. Sandra thought that Morales would have been in Laos on June 5, and he was the boss, so it wasn't like he could disappear for long periods without it being noticed. But the family was not with their father until at least two weeks after the shooting of Robert Kennedy.

The family stayed in Laos for a year and then moved back to the States. Morales went on a two-year tour to Vietnam in October 1969, and when he came back, he'd go on three-month temporary assignments to places such as Uruguay, Paraguay, and Argentina—supporting Ruben's tales of the Tupamaros.

Morales officially retired on July 31, 1975, but he continued to consult for the company. He bought a place in Flagstaff but his doctors said he couldn't handle the altitude, so they moved out to Wilcox, Arizona, and lived in a mobile home while building a new house on 186 acres of land seventeen miles outside of town. Sandra debunked stories that the house was alarmed like a fortress—there were no alarms, and they never locked the doors.

* * *

In January 1978, Rita had her first son, Morales's first grandchild. They went to Wilcox to see him in March, and after the trip, Rita told her sisters he wouldn't live much longer. He was coughing badly, smoked a couple of packs a day, "drank horribly" (he was an alcoholic), and "ate terribly."

Morales finally died in May 1978 of a massive heart attack brought on by his alcoholism and an existing heart condition. His daughters emphatically stated that his death was not suspicious. An autopsy requested by Sandra showed that one of his ventricles was enlarged.

* * *

"The company" contacted the family in the "eighties or nineties" to ask if they could publicly release Morales's personnel file, but the family had a meeting and said no, because all their names were in the file. Many of Morales's records were finally released in the late nineties under the JFK Records Act.

* * *

When it came to the man at the Ambassador, both daughters were clear. They did not think it was their father.

Rita thought her father was more broad-shouldered than the guy in the video and had a very dark complexion, with stronger Indian features. The man at the Ambassador looked African American to her, with a "café au lait complexion" and a higher hairline. "My father always had a full head of hair; it never even thinned before he died. It was gray when he came back from Vietnam but black before then, and he always wore a heavy mustache."

Sandra also pointed out noticeable differences: "The way he turned his head doesn't look like my father. He has a pointier nose, he's younger, and the bottom of his face is different. My father had broad, full lips; a broad nose, almost flat, and was very dark skinned, darker than the guy in the video." She thought the man at the Ambassador looked like a light-skinned black man. Her father was five-eleven but this guy was taller, and by 1968, her father had salt-and-pepper hair and a heavy "walrus" mustache.

I had expected Morales's daughters to be defensive, but they weren't that way at all. Rita had done a lot of research on her father, and both daughters were familiar with Gaeton Fonzi's book *The Last Investigation*. "He may have done a lot of stuff I don't want to know about, but those were the times," Rita said. But she was annoyed at the legends that have grown up around her father. She said Ruben Carbajal was "full of shit and delusional—he and my father were so drunk, they could have been saying anything." Her mother was now in her eighties—"she has good days and bad days but generally she doesn't want to talk about it. I don't think she'd talk to you."

When we spoke, Rita's son—the grandson Morales saw before his death—was now grown up and preparing to ship out to Iraq. He'd inherited his grandfather's intelligence and personality, she said. He'd watched my BBC story on the Internet and said it didn't look like his grandfather.

* * *

When Sandra first met David Talbot, she showed him a family photo taken in Laos during the year after the RFK assassination. It convinced Talbot and his assistant that "the Morales in the picture (who looks very similar to other published photos of Morales) is not the Ambassador man." But Sandra didn't want to release a family photo to the media or get involved, so I had to take David's word for it.[15]

The mixed evidence he found on his trip led the *New Yorker* to pass on the story. Talbot concluded, "I still wouldn't be surprised if it turns out there was an intelligence operation at the Ambassador that night. It just needs a lot more reporting to pin it down. And unfortunately, as is often the case on Kennedy investigations, Jeff and I ran out our thread. I do believe that Morales probably played some role in the RFK killing (and certainly did in the JFK plot). But the Ambassador photo story, to me, is a blind alley."[16]

David Morales in Havana, 1959, and in Vietnam, 1969–1971.

* * *

A couple of months later, after my discussion with Sandra, she realized the importance of photographs of her father in laying the story to rest. She didn't want to release the family photo but found three others from the same time period and sent them to me and David. One was a tourist snapshot taken in Cuzco, Peru, in 1966 or 1967, Sandra thought. It shows an overweight Morales with a mustache, salt-and-pepper hair, and a high hairline.

The two other photographs were from Morales's tour in Vietnam (1969–1971), three or four years later. Morales wears a bolo and has radically slimmed down.

The flat, distinctive nose and high hairline are the consistent features across these photographs, but if you weren't looking for a match, the Morales in Peru and the Morales in Vietnam seem like two different people. It's quite bizarre how Morales seems to have changed so much from one year to the next.

When I compared these photographs to the video of the man at the Ambassador, my gut reaction was the same as Talbot's. It didn't seem to be the same person.

But when I sent these new photographs to Bradley Ayers and Wayne Smith, it merely reinforced their previous identifications. They accepted that these were authentic pictures of Morales yet were equally sure he was the man at the Ambassador.[17]

* * *

I was subsequently contacted by Morales's son, Frank (a pseudonym) who had seen my film on YouTube: "My initial impression is the person you identify as my father is not him, the gentleman seems to have a lighter skin complexion, his hair does not seem to match nor his facial features. His build is also not heavy enough to match my father's during that time period . . . I would like to assist you in your quest for the facts, to include providing you photos of my father during that time period."

When I sent Frank a DVD of the video clips of his father, it confirmed his initial impression: "It is not my father. I believe the person shown is of African-American heritage, he seems to have short curly hair, my father's hair was wavy. Also the depicted individual has a smaller chin and a lighter complexion than my father. He seems taller than my father, who was 5ft 11 1/2 inches, and that person has a smaller build than my father."[18]

* * *

Photo identification is notoriously difficult, and obviously I never met David Morales. These images are of insufficient quality for biometric testing, so it comes down to a judgment call. While I have great respect for the identifications of Ayers and Smith, when I look at the photographs objectively, the man in the photo at the Ambassador seems to me a different person from the man in the photos provided by the Morales family. It can be argued that his family and former colleagues have a vested interest in protecting his name, but my sense from the family, Manny Chavez, Luis Rodriguez, Ed Wilson, and, even now, perhaps Ruben Carbajal, is that they were giving me their honest opinion.

But while I may have misidentified David Morales in the video, that does not mean he wasn't at the Ambassador Hotel. I simply identified a different person. While I greatly appreciate the openness and wealth of biographical detail shared by the Morales family, they couldn't account for their father's whereabouts on June 4–5, 1968, and the CIA has declined to provide Morales's travel records.

The fact remains: Morales said he was in Los Angeles the night Bobby Kennedy was shot. Bob and Florene Walton heard him implicate himself in the shooting, and Ruben Carbajal's suggestion that he was visiting his daughter was clearly not correct. But where do you go with that?

* * *

When Sandra changed her mind and released the photos, she asked that they not be attributed to the family because "that would start other stories." Unfortunately, when Talbot and Morley published them online in July 2007 in an article detailing their investigation, they credited Morales's daughters.

The same article also saw the release of the first alleged photos of Joannides. Two prints showed him at a CIA party in Saigon in June 1973, five years after the assassination and before he met Lopez and Hardway.

Morley noted, "Joannides wears glasses as did the man in the BBC report, but he has a more pointed jaw, larger ears, a different hairline, and a more olive complexion. The CIA declined to release Joannides' travel records. Most likely, he was in Athens in June 1968."[19]

But when I showed the new photos to Dan Hardway, his view remained unchanged. He found the two sets of photos compatible with each other and the man he knew in 1978. He'd still be surprised if the man at the Ambassador wasn't Joannides. Ed Lopez didn't know what to think as he tried to reconcile two images of a man he knew thirty years before.[20]

* * *

While the Morales ID was in grave doubt and the Joannides ID was under question, very little had emerged regarding Gordon Campbell. Rudy Enders had told me he died of a massive heart attack in 1962, and now another JMWAVE officer, Mickey Kappes, told David Talbot the same story. I knew that Kappes and Enders were neighbors in Florida—was this a "red herring"?

No, it seemed legitimate. Jeff Morley dug up a *Miami Herald* obituary from September 21, 1962, for a Colonel Gordon S. Campbell, a World War II veteran who moved to Miami from Washington twenty years earlier and was a maritime consultant. He was to be buried in Arlington National Cemetery. This was the same man I'd previously found listed in the Miami phone book.

Enders said Campbell was "a yachtsman and army colonel who served as a contract agent helping the agency ferry anti-Castro guerrillas across the straits of Florida. . . . I was right there when he died," he told Morley. "He was getting a drink at the drinking fountain [at JMWAVE]. . . . He stood up and started shaking, and he collapsed and we tried to revive him. We gave him mouth to mouth resuscitation and it just didn't work. It was a real bad heart attack."

Campbell's death certificate, which identified him as a "maritime adviser," states that he passed away on September 19, 1962. Morley and Talbot concluded, "He could not have been at the scene of Bobby's Kennedy's assassination on June 5, 1968, because he died in 1962."[21]

* * *

But this was an extraordinarily pat statement. Consider the facts: Colonel Gordon S. Campbell died in September 1962 at JMWAVE in Miami at the age of fifty-seven. In the summer and fall of 1963, Bradley Ayers worked closely with a man who introduced himself as "Gordon Campbell," as meticulously detailed in his book. This man was forty years old and could not have been fifty-seven, according to Brad. He was known around the station as "Gordon Campbell" and was the man Ayers later recognized at the Ambassador.

What's so strange about this is that while Campbell supposedly died before Bradley Ayers arrived in Miami and was much older than the man Ayers knew, the profile in the obituary—a maritime consultant—fits the man Ayers knew precisely.

Why had Tom Clines told me that after JMWAVE, Campbell was sent to Canada to act as the CIA liaison there? Neither he nor Grayston Lynch mentioned anything about Campbell dying of a massive heart attack in 1962—something you might expect regulars at the station to remember.

Had Bradley Ayers fabricated his entire association with Campbell, as first published in 1976, predating my investigation by thirty years? If he was going to invent a case officer for his book, why choose a guy who had died of a massive heart attack the year before he arrived?

It didn't make sense. The possibility that Ayers had invented his "Gordon Campbell" seemed highly unlikely, since so much of his book had been authenticated over the years. Ted Shackley, Tom Clines, and official CIA records all confirmed his service at JMWAVE.

Perhaps there were two Gordon Campbells. Or perhaps the dead man's name was used as a cover identity by the man Ayers knew, as was common at the agency. Either way, I needed to find out if the man Brad knew at JMWAVE was really the man at the Ambassador.

* * *

I went back to the new sightings of "Campbell" in the footage located by Brad Johnson.

At 11:29 p.m., a burly man in a mustard-colored coat called out "Mike," and "Campbell" joined a group at the back of the ballroom, shaking hands, laughing, and apparently gesturing at the TV cameras behind him. At 11:52, Campbell walked toward the exit with a colleague, but he was back among the same group at the back of the ballroom as Kennedy made his speech.

As Kennedy left the stage, the crowd began to disperse, and a minute or so later, Kennedy was shot. As cries from the pantry ignited panic in the Embassy Ballroom, we see "Campbell" walk forward from the back of the room toward the commotion. It's clear he was not coming from the pantry but had been watching the speech from the back of the ballroom. The Latin man with the mustache had also been watching the speech, a little closer to the stage. When I obtained a new, clean transfer of the original "Campbell" footage, it was also clear that he was holding his right hand across his chest as he walked through the room but his hands were empty. There was no container and no disguised weapon. Why he held his hand across his chest and why the Latin man was waving toward an exit remain a mystery.

At 12:52 a.m., "Campbell" was still in the Embassy Ballroom, listening to interviews with witnesses Booker Griffin, Kristi Witker, and Cap Hardy.[22]

* * *

When I showed Bradley Ayers this footage, it reinforced his identification of Campbell. The stance, bearing, behavior, and facial expressions all called to mind the man he knew at JMWAVE. While to me Campbell seemed jovial and at ease, Brad read him as nervous, in anticipation of something.

But who was the group with Campbell? Why the seemingly jovial mood? I had seen this group before in a photograph taken just before Kennedy's speech and included in the police investigation files. The LAPD had circled a number of these men and written their names on the back of the photograph.

A man similar to "Campbell" was shown in profile, but his hairline seemed a little different, and at first I disregarded him. Seeing "Campbell" in this new footage, I realized this was also him in the police photograph.[23]

The LAPD identified him as Michael Roman, and the burly companion who called out "Mike" was his brother Charles. The group were salesmen for the Bulova Watch Company, attending a regional sales conference at the hotel from Monday, June 3, to Thursday, June 6. Twenty-three Bulova guests were registered at the hotel, the largest corporate group in residence. Michael D. Roman, it turned out, was vice president and national sales manager of Bulova.[24]

* * *

Roman was finally interviewed by the FBI on November 26 while attending a seminar at Harvard: "He stated that he was in the Embassy Room at the hotel around midnight [during the speech and] remained in the room when Kennedy and a group departed and went through the kitchen area. Roman stated he heard the shooting and was subsequently advised Kennedy had been shot. Roman had never seen Sirhan previously, and had no reason to believe anyone else was involved in the shooting."[25]

The weekend after the assassination, Roman was in Chicago for a divisional meeting, giving sales tips to the *Chicago Times*. According to an article in the Business section, he commanded an ad budget set to rise to seven million dollars. [26]

Was Roman a legitimate businessman, crisscrossing the country to regional sales meetings and by chance winding up at the Ambassador? Or were Roman and Campbell the same person? Sales manager at Bulova was an ideal cover identity— the sales convention gave him every reason to be at the hotel in the days leading up to the shooting.

* * *

I started to research Michael D. Roman, immediately coming across his obituary. He shared a birthday with Robert Kennedy—born on November 20, 1918, and died suddenly on December 22, 2002.

The *New York Times* turned up several articles on Roman, the most interesting dated August 3, 1964. Under the headline "Vice President Named by Bulova Watch Co." appeared a photograph of Michael D. Roman, instantly recognizable as the man at the Ambassador: "The election of Michael D. Roman as a vice president of the Bulova Watch Company was announced over the weekend by Gen. Omar N. Bradley, chairman of the watch manufacturer."[27]

* * *

Roman's promotion was announced by General Omar Bradley? Dwight Eisenhower and Omar Bradley were the only surviving five-star generals in the army. Campbell was working for Bradley, for a watch company that was having its sales conference at the hotel where Kennedy would be assassinated? It boggled the mind.

* * *

In Bradley's autobiography, *A General's Life*, he told how his connection to Bulova started. For two years after the war, Bradley was head of the Veterans Administration and took a special interest in the highly successful Joseph Bulova School of Watchmaking, which provided free training for disabled veterans, and guaranteed work placements at American jewelry stores.

Bradley visited the school often and became close friends with founder Ardé Bulova and his brother-in-law, Harry D. Henshel, who was vice chairman of the company and had received a Bronze Star for organizing the airlift of supplies for Bradley during the Battle of the Bulge.

In 1949, Bradley became the first chairman of the Joint Chiefs of Staff, stepping down in August 1953 to become chairman of Bulova Research and Development Laboratories, a subsidiary of the Bulova Watch Company devoted to the development of precision defense items.

Bulova had just built a state-of-the-art ten-million-dollar factory in Jackson Heights, Queens, focused on secret defense research. Bradley would advise Bulova scientists on military needs, and while Bulova continued to make jeweled watches, clocks, and radios, defense work accounted for 40 percent of sales. When Ardé Bulova died in 1958, Bradley was named chairman of the Bulova Watch Company, and in fiscal 1959 the company delivered "more than twenty million dollars in defense items to the armed forces on sales of fifty-eight million dollars."

* * *

Over the next eight years, Bradley helped the company double annual sales, lobbying the Senate Armed Services Committee to maintain tariffs on watch imports so that the United States would not become "the only major power without a watch manufacturing industry." He argued that the watch industry was essential to national security and made significant contributions to national defense and space technology.[28]

In the summer of 1967, Bradley went to Vietnam on assignment for *Look* magazine to report on the war. After a two-week tour of the battlefront, Bradley was convinced that Vietnam was "a war at the right place, at the right time and with the right enemy—the Communists."

After a winter at the races in Southern California, he bought a new custom-designed home on a hilltop in Beverly Hills and was one of the "Wise Men" advising Johnson on his war strategy through the spring of 1968. Bradley's diaries at West

Point show that he traveled to the Bulova offices in New York on May 31, 1968 and returned to California on the evening of June 6.[29]

I don't associate a much-loved war hero with a political assassination lightly, but if Campbell was operating undercover as Michael D. Roman, Bradley was a powerful connection.

* * *

The problem was that Michael D. Roman seems to have been too busy selling watches to take on extra work for the CIA. He'd worked his way up through the jewelry industry since his days carrying sample bags for the Gruen Watch Company in Chicago in 1936, at age seventeen. After military service in World War II, he became Midwest sales manager for the company before joining Bulova in the early sixties.

In 1976, Roman became chairman and executive director of the Retail Jewelers of America, the national trade association for the industry. On his retirement in 1995, he was hailed as "a giant in our industry" and, shortly before his death, was honored by the American Gem Society with a Lifetime Achievement Award, one of the industry's highest honors.[30]

* * *

Michael Roman's son was quite surprised to receive my call but extremely open and cooperative. I was making a film on Robert Kennedy, I said, and had been told his father may have worked for U.S. intelligence. At first, he thought I had the wrong person. Michael D. Roman of Bulova? Oh, yes, that was his father all right, but working for the CIA? "That's a new one on me."

His father had told him he was at the Ambassador Hotel the night Kennedy was shot and that the CIA interviewed him afterward (actually, it was the FBI). But he had no knowledge that his father had ever done intelligence work.

"Although it is exciting to think my father had a double identity," he wrote later in an e-mail, "in checking with my mother and sisters, no one had any suspicions that my father was something else besides a businessman. Both my mother and I recall the circumstances of him being in the same hotel as Robert Kennedy—that being a sales meeting for the Bulova Watch Company. . . . I can only assume, with our family's association with his co-workers over the years and his awards from the industry, that he did work at his vocation full-time. Thus, I suggest that Mr. Ayers is mistaken in his identification."

Roman's son graciously allowed me to e-mail him the ballroom photographs and he shared them with the family. At first, Roman wasn't sure the bald man was his father. One sister said he looked gaunt, but another said it was definitely him, and the rest of the family soon agreed. One sister had worked alongside her father for some time and dismissed the idea that he could have been a high-ranking executive while also a spy as ludicrous.

The Roman family also recognized the figure of "Joannides" in the photographs: "Both my sister and mother confirm the darker-haired man (looks a bit like Henry Kissinger) is Frank Owens. He died a number of years ago and his wife may also have passed away or is at a care facility. . . ."

* * *

Owens was a regional sales manager for Michael Roman, and seems to match a "Frank S. Owen" from New York interviewed by the FBI on October 21. Owen registered at the Ambassador on June 4, listened to Kennedy's speech in the Embassy Ballroom, and remained there during the shooting.

I made a follow-up call to Roman a few weeks later. He had searched for "Gordon Campbell" on the Internet and was curious about the controversies in the case. I ran him through the history and significance of these new characters—Bradley Ayers, his relationship with Campbell, and Brad's belief that Michael D. Roman was a "dead ringer" for Campbell.

The key point I took from our conversation was that Roman's son was in high school in 1963 and didn't remember his father being away for any length of time. His father was working in New York and living with the family in Connecticut, so the idea that he was living on a houseboat in Miami, conducting a secret war on Castro, seemed impossible.[31]

* * *

Did Roman and Owens lead double lives as CIA operatives Gordon Campbell and George Joannides? It seems highly unlikely. The identification of the "Joannides" figure in the photograph as Roman's colleague Frank Owens seems to drain away any remaining possibility that the two men standing in the ballroom were once colleagues at JMWAVE.

I now believe the Campbell and Joannides identifications are, most likely, a case of mistaken identity. Of course, it bothers me that of all companies to have a sales convention at the Ambassador Hotel that day, it would be Bulova, headed by the most senior army general in the nation. But coincidence does not always mean conspiracy, and once more, the search for possible accomplices left me chasing shadows.

NINETEEN

WHAT REALLY HAPPENED?

Sirhan is guilty. Sirhan said he was guilty.
If he isn't guilty, it's the sweetest frame in the world.
—John Howard, Sirhan prosecutor[1]

As evidence of CIA suspects at the hotel began to unravel, something extraordinary happened, and, again, American journalist Brad Johnson was behind it.

In spring 2004, as I was still writing my screenplay, Brad was listening to a little-known audiotape of the shooting that had been largely overlooked for nearly forty years. The audiotape ran about thirty minutes and the quality of the recording was poor, but in the crucial five seconds of gunfire, Brad was sure he heard more than eight shots.

The audiotape had been recorded on a hot new item in the summer of 1968—a battery-operated portable cassette recorder. Its proud owner was Stanislaw "Stas" Pruszynski, a Polish reporter living in Canada who had taken a sabbatical from the *Montreal Gazette* to cover the presidential race for a book on U.S. politics. Attaching a microphone to his recorder, Pruszynski taped Kennedy's speech, gathering quotes he could transcribe later for his book.

In September 2004, Brad traced Pruszynski to Warsaw, where he was now a well-known café owner, and got some background on Pruszynski's whereabouts at the time of the shooting and how the recording was made. In spring 2005, Brad contacted Phil Van Praag, an electrical engineer with thirty-five years' experience in the audio industry and the author of a seminal textbook on sound recorders.[2]

"The very first time I heard it," recalled Van Praag, "I was not impressed at all, but I thought, 'I'll take this back with me and just put it on my instruments and just see what's there.' And when I did that, the spark was ignited."[3]

* * *

On June 6, 2007, the Discovery Times Channel aired the one-hour special *Conspiracy Test: The RFK Assassination*, the centerpiece of which was an examination

425

of the never-before-broadcast Pruszynski recording by Van Praag and several other audio experts, which provided startling new evidence of a second gun.

The producers visited Pruszynski in Warsaw to authenticate the recording, and he identified himself in footage at the hotel. He described how after the Kennedy party left the stage, he stooped down to pick up his recorder from the west side of the podium, gathered up his microphone, and walked across the stage toward the pantry. As he walked down three steps on the east side of the stage, the first two shots were fired.

At this moment, Pruszynski was about forty feet southwest of where Kennedy was standing, and unaware that his tape recorder was still recording. His mic was pointed upward in his direction of travel, toward the pantry. Two sets of open doors allowed the sounds of shots to carry to his microphone, and the sounds of these shots got louder as Pruszynski moved through the door at the east end of the stage and into the backstage corridor that led into the pantry.

The resulting tape is the only known audio recording of the shooting of Robert Kennedy—not that Pruszynski realized this at the time. There were so many radio and TV reporters there that night, he never thought the shots on his tape were anything special. But it turned out everybody else had stopped recording after the speech. Reporter Andy West and Don Schulman's interviewer Jeff Brent switched on their recorders again only after the shots were fired. Pruszynski never followed the controversies in the case and eventually left journalism and returned to Poland after the fall of the Soviet bloc.[4]

* * *

The LAPD didn't ask Pruszynski for his tape on the night of the shooting, and he went back to Canada. Later, however, American friends who'd been with him at the hotel told authorities about the recording. In early 1969, the FBI asked the Royal Canadian Mounted Police to interview Pruszynski in Montreal. A reel-to-reel dub of the recording was sent to the FBI, and they forwarded it to their lab in Washington for analysis. Pruszynski kept the original.

With the limited technology available back then, the FBI concluded there was nothing of investigative value on the tape but did send copies to their Los Angeles office and the LAPD. The police never examined the recording but, unlike other evidence, managed not to destroy it, and it was among materials transferred to the California State Archives in 1988. It sat there, relatively unnoticed, for another sixteen years until Brad's discovery.[5]

* * *

In September 2005, with Brad's assistance, Van Praag convinced the director of the California State Archives to let him make high-quality copies of the CSA's open-reel dub of the Pruszynski recording. Van Praag played back the tape once, making five simultaneous recordings of the tape on five different recorders, both analog and digital, to gain as many perspectives on the audio as possible.

Van Praag believes the California State Archives dub is a fourth- or fifth-generation copy. The original is missing, believed lost by Pruszynski.

Van Praag then spent months analyzing his recordings with different types of decks, electronic recording equipment, and computer programs back at his laboratory in Tucson, Arizona. He knew that Sirhan's gun held eight bullets and he didn't reload, so more than eight shots would mean a second gun was fired in the pantry.

Through careful and meticulous analysis of the five second sequence of shots, Van Praag made two sets of startling discoveries: "I have located approximately thirteen shot sounds," he said. "Now, I cannot absolutely guarantee that thirteen is the correct number. However, it's greater than eight; I can certainly say that."

Logically, a second weapon would not fire in perfect synchronization with the first, so Van Praag next looked at the detailed intervals between the shot sounds.

"Within the thirteen captured shot sounds, there are a couple of instances of what I call 'double-shots'—two shots that occur so closely together . . . they couldn't really have come from a single weapon. It simply isn't possible to fire a weapon that fast." Sirhan didn't have two guns, so this again clearly pointed to a second gunman.

Van Praag located these "double-shot sound intervals" between shots three and four and shots seven and eight. One second comprises 1,000 milliseconds, and Van Praag measured one of these "double-shot" intervals as 120 milliseconds, just over a tenth of a second.

The Discovery Times producers then hired firearms expert Phil Spangenburger to do a test with the same .22-caliber Iver Johnson Cadet model revolver Sirhan had used. Firing off eight shots as fast as he could, Spangenburger's best time was 2.93 seconds, averaging 366 milliseconds between shots. When he tried to fire two shots as fast as he could, the interval was 550 milliseconds.

* * *

The producers then sought a second opinion from forensic audio specialists Audio Engineering Associates in Pasadena, just two miles from the Sirhan family home. Van Praag brought along his master recordings and the machines on which they were recorded, "to present as accurate a reproduction of those recordings as possible."

Company owner Wes Dooley, a member of the American College of Forensic Examiners, examined the recording for a couple of days with his associate Paul Pegas. They independently concluded that there were at least ten "shot sounds" on the recording, including one "double shot."

Dooley sent a digital dub of the Pruszynski recording to Eddie Brixson, a forensic audio and ballistics expert in Denmark. He also confirmed at least ten gunshots, including a "double shot" interval between shots six and seven.

Van Praag had previously explored whether the second shot sound in the "double shots" could be an echo or a ricochet, pinging off a door frame or the ceiling.

He ruled both out and Dooley agreed, reasoning that a .22-caliber bullet travels at a thousand feet per second, similar to the speed of sound, "so if it's twenty feet from one side of the room to the other, that's only twenty milliseconds, so I'd say this is not a ricochet; this seems to be another shot."

* * *

The shots also had an interesting pattern. There were two shots, then a second-and-a-half pause, then the rest of the shots in a fairly brisk cadence at intervals of a third of a second or half a second, except for the double shots. This seemed to fit witness descriptions of two shots, then a pause, then a barrage. It also echoed Karl Uecker's claim that he grabbed Sirhan's hand after the first two shots and had pushed him away, when the shooting started again.

What this seemed to indicate was that Sirhan started firing, his gun arm was diverted by Uecker after the second shot, and then the "double shots" and "extra shots" started as a second gun began firing from behind and to the right of Kennedy.[6]

There was a dissenting opinion from Phillip Harrison, an English forensic audio expert who had examined the recording for author Mel Ayton, unaware of the other tests and before the Discovery Times program aired. Harrison found only seven shots on the Pruszynski recording, with possible locations for an eighth shot that weren't clear. The problem was that once again, Ayton had not researched the recording properly.

Ayton had provided Harrison with a copy of one of Van Praag's new master dubs, without giving him the necessary context in which the recording was made. He wasn't told the location of Pruszynski's microphone and how it was moving closer to the pantry as the shots were fired, information that is critical to an accurate analysis of the recording.[7]

* * *

Van Praag continues to examine the recording for further layers of insight into what happened in the pantry during those crucial five seconds, and he was to present his findings to the sixtieth-anniversary scientific meeting of the American Academy of Forensic Sciences in Washington, DC, in late February 2008.

But thanks to his pioneering work, and Brad's relentless journalism, we have, for the first time, independent, stand-alone forensic evidence to establish a second shooter in the pantry.

"There's a lot of conjecture, and there always will be, as to how many shots were fired," said Van Praag. "However, there had to have been more than one weapon involved."[8]

* * *

We no longer need to rely on extra bullet holes in the pantry door frames and ceiling panels—evidence the LAPD destroyed before Sirhan's appeal. We no longer need to visualize Sirhan's gymnastics as he somehow managed to fire into Kennedy's suit coat at an upward angle of eighty degrees.

We have a new paradigm, based on a high degree of scientific probability, that two guns were fired that night. We can now go back to the two firing positions William Harper first described in 1970: Firing Position A, several feet in front of Kennedy, from where Sirhan missed the senator but hit the rest of the shooting victims; and Firing Position B, behind and to the right of the senator, from where a second gunman fired the shots that hit Kennedy.

An analysis of the sequence of shots suggests the second-and-a-half pause after the first two shots gave Uecker reaction time to lunge at Sirhan and grab his gun hand. Eddie Minasian saw Paul Schrade fall first, and Kennedy asked, "Is Paul okay?" suggesting that Schrade was hit with Sirhan's first shot and that his second hit Kennedy. Sirhan's arm was then diverted away, and between shots three and four, Van Praag found the first "double shot interval." From this we can infer that Sirhan got off another shot before or just after Uecker grabbed his hand; then the second gunman started firing.[9]

In October 1993, Dan Moldea interviewed coroner Thomas Noguchi about the sequence of Kennedy's wounds. "The injury to the back of the right ear . . . would render him helpless. Kennedy could not be standing if he had such an injury. He would collapse to the floor. . . . The bullet from the .22 had a great deal of power. Striking the hard bone and the bone shattering would have taken him off his feet. . . . That means the other shots must have been prior to the senator collapsing."

How did Noguchi explain Kennedy's raised arm at the time of the other three shots? "Kennedy could have been waving his arm to guard off from an oncoming assailant . . . or he could have just heard the gunfire and then raised his right arm, whereby his shoulder pad was raised and the bullet went through, not striking his body." Either he saw the gun, raised his arm, and ducked, or heard the first shot hit Paul Schrade behind him.

Noguchi concluded that the sequence was as follows: "The shoulder pad shot as he was raising his arm, the two shots to his right armpit . . . and, lastly, the shot to the mastoid. . . . In other words, the nonfatal wounds first and then the fatal wound."

Noguchi thus described the fifth shot as the one that killed Kennedy. If Uecker was correct in saying that he grabbed Sirhan's hand after the second shot, how could the fatal shot have been fired by Sirhan?[10]

* * *

This new audio evidence seems to vindicate key eyewitnesses like Kennedy aides Paul Schrade and Frank Burns, TV producer Richard Lubic, and photographer

Evan Freed. For forty years, they have all insisted that Sirhan never got close enough to fire the fatal shot described in the autopsy. Yet they were never asked about this at trial. Even witness Vincent Di Pierro, who thinks Sirhan acted alone, provided further evidence of extra bullet holes with the orange turtleneck suppressed by prosecutor John Howard.

But there are still other questions to be resolved. Sirhan fired eight shots and Kennedy was hit three times, with a fourth bullet passing clean through his shoulder pad. If Van Praag's thirteen shots are correct, Harper's firing positions make sense. The second gunman fired five times, accounting for Kennedy's three wounds and the shot through his shoulder pad.[11]

But if there are only ten "shot sounds," as two of the audio experts say, the second shooter fired only twice, so Sirhan must be responsible for two of the shots fired within an inch of Kennedy. Which two? The two armpit shots were fired at almost contact distance an inch apart, so these must have been fired by the same shooter. The shot through the shoulder pad was from a similar firing position and even steeper trajectory, but the fatal shot came from a much shallower angle.[12]

It's possible, then, that Sirhan hit Kennedy under the armpit while a second gunman fired the fifth and fatal shot that killed the senator. But if any of Sirhan's bullets hit Kennedy, it would prove he had come within an inch of the senator, contrary to what the witnesses saw.

We must also remember that the firearms panel examiners in 1975 concluded that the Kennedy neck bullet, the Goldstein bullet, and the Weisel bullet all came from the same gun. Goldstein and Weisel were clearly in Sirhan's line of fire, so Sirhan may well have hit Kennedy under the armpit before a second gunman applied the fatal shot just behind Kennedy's right ear. But how two gunmen could get so close to the senator without anybody seeing them is a mystery. While this new forensic evidence is extremely exciting, there is still much work to be done.

* * *

Two guns would further implicate the LAPD's Scientific Investigation Division in a cover-up. If at least ten shots were fired, it's likely the two extra bullets were, indeed, those reportedly retrieved from the center divider between the swinging doors of the pantry. Where did these bullets go? Two spent slugs with wood tracings were discovered under a newspaper on the front seat of Sirhan's car almost twenty-four hours after the shooting. Were they planted there, or did Wolfer just get rid of them? DeWayne Wolfer and his colleague, William Lee, both now retired, should be called to testify.

* * *

If, as now seems likely, there were coconspirators, who were they? I thought my CIA suspects provided the answer, but while my original confidence in their identifications has slipped away, the "Morales" figure in the video still troubles me. If he's not Morales, who is he? He seems to be there in some sort of law enforcement capacity, yet we're told there were no police or other agencies present at the hotel at the time of the shooting. Who is his companion with the pencil mustache? What agency were they working for? And why does "Morales" emerge from the pantry with police investigators forty minutes after the shooting?

Serious questions also remain regarding the recruitment of Pena and Hernandez to marshal case preparation, conspiracy allegations, and the background of the Sirhan family—the three crucial areas that backstopped conspiracy. The connections to the Office of Public Safety here are alarming. Given Morales's high profile in Latin American operations at the time, it's quite possible he came into contact with the Hispanic LAPD officers, either on assignment in South America or at the International Police Academy in Washington.

The main suspect for a second gun over the years has been security guard Thane Cesar. He currently lives in the Philippines and has never been called to testify under oath. A new inquiry could also seek testimony from Sergeant Paul Sharaga and Sandra Serrano, who are still around to testify to the girl in the polka-dot dress.

* * *

If there were two guns, where does this leave Sirhan? Dan Moldea once asked him if he was part of a conspiracy.

"Do you think I would conceal anything about someone else's involvement and face the gas chamber in the most literal sense?" replied Sirhan. "I have no knowledge of a conspiracy. . . . I wish there had been a conspiracy. It would have unraveled before now."

"Why don't you just accept responsibility for this crime?" Moldea asked.

"It would be a hell of a burden to live with—having taken a human life without knowing it. . . . It's not in my mind, but I'm not denying it. I must have been there, but I can't reconstruct it mentally."[13]

Sirhan clearly was not aware of any conspiracy. There is also nothing to indicate he was paid to kill Kennedy, and he has consistently stated he acted alone. The *"Please pay to the order of"* in his notebook is probably Sirhan daydreaming of the belated insurance check he would receive for his injuries after the fall from the horse. It's curious that Sirhan's choice of the crowded pantry also gave him very little hope of getting away.

* * *

So the choice to the reader seems a simple one: either Sirhan consciously premeditated the murder of Bobby Kennedy in cold blood and has lied about it ever since, fooling highly experienced psychiatrists and his defense team with a seamless, unerring performance over forty years; or he honestly does not remember shooting Kennedy due to spontaneous amnesia, caused either by the trauma of the shooting or a memory block initiated by an unknown programmer.

Our view of the case boils down to whether we believe Sirhan when he says he doesn't remember the shooting or the writing in his notebooks. If we don't believe him, we simply accept the cold-blooded murderer portrayed by the prosecution and discount the near unanimity of the psychiatrists who said he was a paranoid schizophrenic with diminished capacity. But we must also ask why an assassin who sacrificed his freedom for his country chose to remain anonymous while in custody and didn't proclaim his cause until the middle of the trial eight months later.

* * *

I have tried to quote Sirhan himself at great length in this book—his interviews in custody, the psychiatric sessions, both in and out of hypnosis, his volatile court testimony, and his interviews with Jack Perkins, William Klaber, and Dan Moldea—because listening to Sirhan speak about this case, both in and out of hypnosis, is the most persuasive evidence to me that he had no conscious awareness of committing the assassination.[14]

This view is shared by the two men closest to Sirhan as he struggled to recover his memory of the shooting—Dr. Diamond and Robert Blair Kaiser. Diamond believed Sirhan was in a dissociated trance state induced by the mirrors at the hotel, and programmed himself to shoot Robert Kennedy. He was extremely brave in calling it as he saw it and risking his professional reputation with a theory so "preposterous, unlikely and incredible."

While Dr. Spiegel contested his diagnosis of paranoid schizophrenia, Diamond's sense that Sirhan had been programmed proved prescient in light of later revelations about the CIA's "preposterous, unlikely and incredible" MKULTRA program. If Diamond had known of such CIA testing in 1969, he might have placed more stock in the idea of an outside programmer.

While some of Sirhan's evasions give him pause, Bob Kaiser still holds it "a 95 percent certainty" that Sirhan was a programmed assassin. "Not completely, because of certain things that Sirhan told me that implied that he knew more than he was telling us, but the fact that so many years have passed and he's stuck to that story lead me to think that he really didn't remember shooting Robert Kennedy, that he probably killed Kennedy in a trance and was programmed to forget that he'd done it and programmed to forget the names and identities of others who might have helped him do it."[15]

* * *

Kaiser's position is similar to my own. I also can't say with one hundred percent certainty that I believe Sirhan. I still have qualms about the notebook; I find it hard to believe that Sirhan did not read back through it at some point in a conscious state unless his writing was controlled completely by programmers. He has also been evasive regarding his movements on June 3, and occasionally a voice in the back of my head tells me Sirhan acted alone and has been tricking us all along (the seed of doubt that grew and eventually swayed Dan Moldea).

But what made Moldea's attempted ambush so unconvincing was the unblinking response of Sirhan, so consistent in his story over forty years. For all the outbursts during his trial, no evidence has emerged to indicate that he does remember the shooting.

I don't believe Sirhan made the incriminating comment to McCowan and, even if he did, it could just as easily be dismissed as braggadocio. Kaiser, Diamond, and Simson are more reliable witnesses, and they all believe Sirhan regarding his memory block. Diamond and Spiegel described Sirhan's behavior in custody as typical of a dissociated state and felt his postrationalization regarding the bombers had a "canned" feel, providing a heroic rationale for actions Sirhan clearly couldn't understand.

* * *

Now that the fortieth anniversary of the RFK assassination is upon us, the overriding question we're left with is: Is Sirhan's conviction just? Is he guilty of first-degree murder beyond a reasonable doubt? To me, the answer is a resounding "no," and, in light of the new audio evidence, this case should be reopened. This is not ancient history. Sirhan is still in prison and will stay there until he dies, unless changes in public opinion alter political perceptions of this case. I hope the evidence presented here gives you everything you need to make up your own mind.

* * *

We must also ask if Sirhan got a fair trial. I don't believe he did. Grant Cooper did a terrible job as his defense attorney, while reminding Sirhan throughout the trial how much his time was worth on the open market. "I had the best criminal lawyer in California," Sirhan later told author William Klaber. "He knew all the tricks of the trade. Unfortunately, he used them all on me."[16]

While Sirhan's late attorney Larry Teeter connected Cooper to a convoluted plot involving the FBI, Johnny Rosselli, the CIA, and U.S. Attorney Matt Byrne, I would charge negligence of a more mundane nature—utterly inadequate preparation; misguided arrogance in his power to sway the jury; a near-criminal neglect of the ballistics evidence; worrying complicity with the prosecution and a naive trust in the LAPD; and a betrayal of his own esteemed psychiatrists in a long-winded and confused closing statement. Cooper's strategy failed miserably.[17]

"Grant Cooper conned me to say that I killed Robert Kennedy," recalled Sirhan. "I went along with him because he had my life in his hands. I was duped into believing he had my best interests in mind. It was a futile defense. Cooper sold me out. . . . When I got to death row, I started reading the law about diminished capacity and the requirements for premeditation. There was no way that I could have summoned the prerequisite for first-degree murder. That was no part of me.

They said that I didn't understand the magnitude of what I had done. They're right. I don't truly appreciate it, because I have no awareness of having aimed the gun at Bobby Kennedy."[18]

It's clear that Sirhan did himself no favors during the trial with his outbursts and odd behavior. The jury didn't like him and didn't buy his memory blocks. The prosecution and jury also had no time for the psychiatrists, in large part because Cooper tortured them with ridiculously long-winded and laborious testimony. Diamond testified for three and a half days; then Cooper disavowed him.

But how would a jury react today, given what we know now about the CIA's MKULTRA program? If they knew there were at least ten shots fired in the pantry; that the two men in day-to-day charge of the police investigation were heavily linked to the CIA; and that, forty years after the shooting, Sirhan has never changed his story?

The bottom line is that even if there were no conspirators, the psychiatrists concluded Sirhan suffered from diminished capacity and was entitled to a charge of second-degree murder. In typical cases, he would have been freed after seven years. Forty years later, Sirhan is still inside.

* * *

When I visited Sirhan's brother Munir at the family home in Pasadena in December 2006, he was nervous before his first television interview and had a last cigarette on the balcony, recalling "little Sirhan" with great fondness. He is the last remaining family member in a house Sirhan may never see again. Later, he showed me Sirhan's room at the back of the house, where he had written in his notebooks thirty-eight years earlier.

* * *

Munir was the closest brother to Sirhan growing up. "He liked to play pool. He liked music. He liked to read a lot. . . . He and mother would sit and study the Bible. Just a typical, good ole Christian American boy."

He recalled the time after the assassination: "When we first saw him in jail, I think Mother and I went up [to him] first. . . . He says, 'Mother, I don't remember, I don't know what happened.' And he says that to this day when you ask him about the particulars of that night. He doesn't recall. One thing that has not changed is the fact that he does not remember."

Munir rejected the idea that Sirhan was the first Arab terrorist, launching into an impassioned defense of his brother. "You know, sitting here, you're in Sirhan's home. If we were sitting here and a fly happened to venture in, you know, your reaction or mine would be, grab the flyswatter, you know, grab something, kill that fly, get it out of here. Sirhan would open the door and try to make it go out the door again. Life meant something to him, especially through the things he went through, we all went through—the upheavals in the Middle East and what have you. It's just not conceivable to me that he would take a gun and actually use it against a person."

* * *

I was unable to interview Sirhan for this book. He lives in a climate of fear, and Munir has not been able to visit him since before 9/11. His last interviews took place in the early nineties, when authors William Klaber and Dan Moldea accompanied Adel Sirhan and Rose Lynn Mangan to see him. They met Sirhan twice in 1993, and Moldea returned in June 1994 to taunt Sirhan about his mother and engineer the anticlimax to his book.[19]

Then, as now, Sirhan was living in the Protective Housing Unit, a high-security wing reserved for high-risk and high-profile prisoners in danger from other inmates. Sirhan was the only prisoner in the unit to prefer a radio in his cell to a television. He listened to the evening news program *All Things Considered* on the local NPR affiliate and liked to jog and lift weights in his spare time. When Klaber and Moldea first visited Sirhan in September 1993, he had filled out with age, now weighing 140 pounds, but he looked well as he approached fifty, and savored a Mounds bar during the conversation, regarding it as a "delicacy."[20]

* * *

Sirhan had no memory of getting his gun from the car on the night of the shooting. "At that point, I blacked out. . . . I only know that my goal was to get some coffee." He remembered a girl with brown hair by the coffee urn—"she was very pretty, with brown hair [but] forget about polka dots. I don't remember what she was wearing."

"I don't remember being in the kitchen pantry. I don't remember seeing Robert Kennedy, and I don't remember shooting him. All I remember is being choked and getting my ass kicked."

"You don't remember the shooting at all?" asked Moldea.

"No, nothing. It just isn't in my mind. . . . I don't remember aiming the gun and saying to myself I'm going to kill Robert Kennedy. I don't remember any adrenaline rush. . . . I just remember being choked."

Sirhan couldn't remember the notebooks either. "I believe the notebook is mine. I just don't remember writing those things. I must have known about the jets," he said, but his words lacked conviction.

Moldea asked if he thought Dr. Simson, his psychiatrist at San Quentin, was right. Had he been programmed? Perhaps, said Sirhan, but your guess is as good as mine. Simson may have been dismissed because "he might have been getting too close to what really happened."

Discussing the ballistics evidence, Sirhan suddenly stopped. "You must understand, you know much more about this than I do. I don't spend my time thinking about these things. If I did, I would surely go crazy."

After twenty-five years, there was a resignation to his answers.

"Whether I was drunk, programmed or outmaneuvered, what has happened has happened."[21]

* * *

Sirhan still couldn't understand his random fate. "If the horses were running that night, I would have been down at the track. . . . I wish I had just gone up and shaken his hand. If I could bring him back to life, of course, I would do it. If I could go back and trade my life for his, I would do that too—he was the father of eleven children. But none of us have that power."

Klaber asked what he would do if he was released.

"Live a quiet life somewhere. Help people if I could. . . . I'd like to walk down a street, say hello to someone, go into a store, buy a quart of milk."[22]

* * *

That seems unlikely to happen. Fifteen years after that interview, Sirhan is still in prison, with no imminent prospect of parole.

"He's been turned down thirteen times, and always on the same grounds," recalled Larry Teeter before he died—"he lacks remorse. But it's circular, because how can you lack remorse if the basis for that finding of lack of remorse is that you don't remember and, if, in fact, you're telling the truth when you say you don't remember? Of course, he's telling the truth, that's why he's requested hypnosis in order for him to be able to recall."[23]

* * *

Sirhan finally came up for parole in 1985. Prison psychiatrist Phillip Hicks gave him a glowing review in a psychiatric report he presented to the three-member Parole Board: "Sirhan is an exemplary inmate . . . a man who is in good contact with reality . . . a pleasant, cooperative person who demonstrates maturity and good judgement concerning his situation. He is of average intelligence, intellectually curious with a remarkably good memory for detail. There appears to be no psychiatric contra-indication to parole consideration. He has no demonstrable predilection toward violence at this time."

Sirhan's attorney Luke McKissack argued that Sirhan had paid his debt to society and was no longer a threat to the public.

"A message must be sent that political assassination will not be tolerated in California," countered Deputy DA Lawrence Trapp. Parole was denied.[24]

* * *

For his first parole hearing at Corcoran in 1992, an escort officer told Sirhan he would have to be led into the hearing room in manacles and chains. Sirhan refused and was led away, to wait another two years for his next hearing. "What board," he asked, "is going to believe that I'm ready for the outside if I'm brought in tied up like an animal?"

Sirhan told Klaber about the hoops he was asked to jump through at the parole hearings. "I come before the board. I have done well in school, my record is good, but they say I need more psychological tests. Two years later, I have the tests, the tests say I'm fine, but then the board wants me to go through the AA program. I haven't had a drink in twenty-six years, but I go through the AA program and I come back two years later, but now they say they want to see my job offers. Job offers? Just what's supposed to be on my resume?"[25]

* * *

Unlike his fellow prisoners, Sirhan prefers a radio in his cell to a television. On death row in San Quentin, he used to play the great Arabic alto Umm Kulthum on his record player—rich, slow, two-hour laments of religious fervor and unrequited love.

In the late seventies, a departing prisoner at Soledad gave him a portable black-and-white TV, and he watched a lot of public television—especially English dramas such as *I, Claudius, Upstairs, Downstairs,* and *The Forsyte Saga*—until it broke eight months later.[26]

In 2001, a couple of days before 9/11 a departing prisoner again gave him his television. Munir picked up the story.

"Right after 9/11, he had just gotten out of the shower; a day or two prior, he had gotten a haircut and because the air-conditioning was a little high in his immediate area and due to the fact that he had just gotten a haircut, he had wrapped a towel around his head and he was watching TV; and one of the guards came, saw him sitting there with a towel around his head, watching TV, and said . . . something to the effect that he had prior knowledge to 9/11 . . . which is hideous. The poor guy's been up there for thirty-five years. Every letter goes through their hands. Every visitor is scrutinized and searched when they see him. There's no way any of us would have known 9/11 is coming."

But the guard saw a towel on his head, saw him watching the round-the-clock news coverage of 9/11, and jumped to this absurd conclusion. A month later, prison authorities leaked the story to the *Washington Post*:

The Post's Petula Dvorak reports that prison authorities in California wonder why Robert F. Kennedy assassin Sirhan Sirhan shaved his head and requested a television on Sunday, Sept. 9, two days before the terrorist attacks. "These are unusual requests for him; he is usually pretty much isolated and reclusive," prison spokesman Lt. Johnny Castro told Dvorak. The 57-year-old Palestinian immigrant . . . frequently mails letters to outsiders, and the FBI is probing whether Sirhan's letters were not monitored because they were written in Arabic. But Sirhan lawyer Lawrence Teeter said his client "was outraged at the terrorist attacks and remarked spontaneously in a letter to his brother he hopes that the people who did this are burning in Hell."27

Prison spokesperson Sabrina Johnson later confirmed they had "documentation" to show that Sirhan was a threat, and he was disciplined accordingly. According to Munir, this meant "he was thrown into solitary confinement for the next year until we were finally able to prove he was innocent of their claims and get him out. He was allowed out of his cell, I think it was seven minutes twice a week to shower, and he was shackled, hands and legs."

This outrageous treatment was founded solely on the crass assumption that wearing a towel on your head makes you a Muslim terrorist.

"Sirhan is a Christian," said Munir. "The whole family's Christian. . . . In every letter he tells me, at the end of it, 'If God is with us, who is against us?'—Mom always used to say that—and I understand they believe he's a Moslem."

After his year in solitary, Sirhan reverted to his previous status, but according to Munir, "now the guards have poisoned the thoughts of other prisoners against him, and they still think he is a Moslem and he's afraid they'll try to kill him. He's afraid to leave for anything except a shower twice a week, because he believes the guards either won't protect him or will be out for him themselves for filing complaints about this situation. He wants to transfer to another prison, but they won't let him."

Munir hasn't seen Sirhan since, partly because Sirhan is afraid to make the walk from his cell to the visiting room. "Where he's at is very dangerous. There are killings that go on there quite frequently. In fact, a couple of months ago, he wrote to me and said there was some sort of a stabbing that occurred [on the trip] from his particular housing cell to the visiting area. And he was fearful of making that trek. Something might happen to him. He's more fearful of the guards than the inmates."28

In the years since 9/11, Sirhan's mother and two of his brothers have passed away, as well as his extremely dedicated lawyer for eleven years, Larry Teeter.

In March 2006, Sirhan was again denied parole. He was given just three days' notice of his hearing, was awaiting a new attorney, and was unprepared, so he didn't attend. The board's denial came as no surprise. His next hearing is scheduled for 2011.29

* * *

When I wrote to Sirhan in prison, he responded through Munir, expressing support for my investigation and comparing himself to a character in a Kafka novel, a man locked away for forty years for a crime he doesn't remember committing, as confused by the mystery as everyone else.

The good news is that he has a new lawyer. Highly respected civil rights attorney Dr. William Pepper has recently filed papers to represent Sirhan. Pepper famously represented James Earl Ray—convicted assassin of Martin Luther King, Jr.—for ten years until Ray's death in 1998. The following year, Pepper prosecuted a wrongful death civil suit brought by the King family against Lloyd Jowers and other unknown coconspirators. At the end of the thirty-day trial, the jury took an hour and a half to conclude that a conspiracy existed in the murder of Dr. King that included agents of the city of Memphis, the state of Tennessee, and the government of the United States.

The King family spoke publicly of their relief "that the truth about this terrible event has finally been revealed. . . . The overwhelming weight of evidence also indicated that James Earl Ray was not the triggerman and, in fact, was an unknowing patsy."

* * *

Larry Teeter filed two petitions for writ of habeas corpus (unlawful detention), the second of which is still pending in the Central District of California. Pepper will continue to pursue this petition, but "the ultimate goal is to have a new trial . . . and to bring before the court evidence that has begun to surface that was not available before."

Pepper is particularly fond of a quote of Dr. King's—"Truth crushed to earth will rise again." I hope this book and my accompanying documentary will help provide a platform for that, leading to a reopening of the investigation into the death of Robert Kennedy, and acting as a "smoke-out" to generate new leads and witnesses and further corroborate material presented here.[30]

The Ambassador Hotel closed in 1989 and was demolished in 2006, and the Kennedy family is supporting the building of a new school project on the site as a "living memorial" to Bobby Kennedy. The contents of the pantry sit in a container on a lot somewhere in Los Angeles, but forty years after the assassination, the mystery around this case still remains. Paul Schrade leads the planning for the new school while renewing calls for a new investigation: "I was standing with Robert Kennedy that night and was wounded, but I will never give up trying to solve this case."[31]

The most likely breakthrough seems to lie with Sirhan himself and efforts to get past his memory block and uncover what happened that night. Los Angeles County Supervisor Baxter Ward tried unsuccessfully to bring Sirhan back to the Ambassador in 1977 to jog his memory, but the courts wouldn't allow it, and more recent attempts by Larry Teeter and Dr. Herbert Spiegel to deprogram Sirhan have also run into legal obstacles.

"With a proper, well-designed regression technique, it's possible to uncover that memory," said Dr. Spiegel. "With his permission, it's possible to regress him and take him back in time to his childhood and come up, year by year, to the time this happened; and it's quite possible when we bring him up to the time he was being programmed by whoever did this, we could uncover his memory of what was going on. He could possibly reveal how he was programmed and where he was going and what he was going to do about it, but the Court would not give me permission to do it."[32]

At the time of this writing, William Pepper is set to begin new psychological evaluations of Sirhan with a psychiatrist recommended by Dr. Spiegel who is a leading specialist in regression therapy. Prison authorities seem receptive, so it may still be possible to recover Sirhan's memory of what happened that night. But time is running out. Regression is possible only while Sirhan's brain is still healthy and active. As he ages, it will become more difficult.[33]

Bob Kaiser, who sat in on Dr. Diamond's sessions with Sirhan and first outlined the "Manchurian candidate" theory of the assassination in his book, is accustomed to the many twists and turns of the case over the last forty years. "See, this is not an Agatha Christie mystery story," he told me, "where everything is neatly tied up in a bow in Chapter 23 at the end of the book. It's one of our most enduring murder mysteries and it will probably continue to be such. That's the way life is. Nothing is ever quite resolved, is it?"[34]

* * *

"What can be done with the case now?" I asked Munir.

"To find the truth; to find the truth. As I've grown up with this case, there are just things that boggle the mind that should be looked into, for the love of humanity. If all of this leads to where we suspect it's gonna lead, we don't want it to ever happen again."[35]

EPILOGUE, 2017

Since the publication of the first edition of this book in 2008, there has been a tremendous amount of activity in this case through the dogged persistence of Sirhan's legal team, Paul Schrade, Brad Johnson, Phil Van Praag and Sirhan himself, who made his first public appearance for fourteen years at his parole hearing in 2011, after appearing to give up hope following an acrimonious hearing in the late nineties. In the last ten years, he has reengaged with the legal process, and efforts to recover his memory of the shooting and the events that led up to it.

Central to this effort has been Dr. Daniel Brown, an Associate Clinical Professor in Psychology at Harvard Medical School. Dr. Brown is an expert witness on "psychological assessment, memory, memory for trauma, and the effects of suggestive influence . . . and hypnosis." His expert testimony at The International War Crimes Tribunal in the Netherlands "was adopted as the standard of evidence by the tribunal regarding the reliability of memory in extremely traumatized witnesses" and he "wrote the current guidelines on forensic interviewing with hypnosis."[1]

As noted in the previous chapter, Bill Pepper took over as Sirhan's attorney in 2007 and was soon joined by co-attorney Laurie Dusek, who grew up with Kennedy posters on her walls and always felt Robert Kennedy was "the last great American statesman." Dusek once thought Sirhan was guilty but after learning more about the case, she became convinced of his innocence and was very impressed by Sirhan when they first met. "He was bright, articulate, with plenty of insight–except into what he couldn't remember about that night. He told me, 'If anything happens to me, I didn't do it.' His faith in God is so strong and that's how he's survived this."[2]

Dusek has been Sirhan's most frequent visitor over the last decade and most of her trips have been alongside Dr. Brown. Since May 2008, he has spent over 100 hours directly interviewing and testing Sirhan, in nine two-day sessions, with Dusek always present. No electronic recording is allowed, so they take separate notes, for independent corroboration.[3]

The first four two-day sessions took place at Corcoran State Prison, where Sirhan was confined to the protective housing unit with other high-risk prisoners like Charles Manson. During visits, Brown and Dusek had to speak to him by phone, separated by a Plexiglas screen, and guards kept walking in and out, giving them no privacy. In the first meeting, they were given an interview room where the phone didn't work.[4]

In 2009, Sirhan requested a transfer from Corcoran, where, according to his brother Munir, he felt unsafe "after he was singled out after the Sept. 11 attacks by guards who thought he was a Muslim, even though he is a Christian." Without notifying his lawyers, prison authorities moved him to Pleasant Valley State Prison in Coalinga that October, where he was housed among the general prison population. He could now mix more and speak to visitors, face-to-face, at a table.[5]

In late 2010, Sirhan's new attorneys reactivated Larry Teeter's dormant habeas corpus petition, ten years after it was filed in the US Central District Court of California. Over the next year, they made four substantial filings to update and expand on the original petition. At the heart of their case were detailed declarations concerning two major new pieces of evidence developed over the last ten years that crystallize the second gun and "Manchurian candidate" theories that first emerged in the early seventies. Declarations from Dr. Brown and Alan Scheflin addressed the hypnotic programming of Sirhan; while Phil Van Praag detailed further discoveries he had made concerning the Pruszynski recording, which will be discussed later in the chapter.[6]

Dr. Brown submitted a further declaration to the Board of Parole Hearings in California in 2016, when they barred him from presenting an independent evaluation at Sirhan's parole hearing. Subsequent interviews conducted with Brown and Dusek for this chapter provide further detail on their sessions with Sirhan for the first time.[7]

* * *

According to Dr. Brown's most recent declaration, the aim of these sessions was threefold: to "conduct a detailed forensic psychological assessment" of Sirhan's mental status; to allow Sirhan "to develop a more complete memory, in a non-suggestive context, for the events leading up to and of the night of the assassination"; and to determine whether Sirhan was the "subject of coercive suggestive influence" at the time of the shooting and if this accounted for his amnesia.[8]

As discussed in chapter 10, during Sirhan's trial, Dr. Diamond and six of the other eight defense and prosecution experts diagnosed him as a paranoid schizophrenic, based in part on their subjective interpretations of his response to the Rorschach Inkblot Test. Using a more sophisticated and "scientifically reliable" scoring system (the Thought Disorder Index) developed since the trial, Dr. Brown did not find "any evidence of disordered thinking either on the original Rorschach test . . . nor on the Rorschach I re-administered to [Sirhan] in 2008." He sent both tests out "blind" to an expert in the field, who agreed. Brown concluded, "the diagnosis of paranoid schizophrenia admitted at trial is completely inaccurate and based on junk science."[9]

In Brown's expert opinion, after many hours of psychological testing, Sirhan is normal, does not have a psychiatric condition or personality disorder and shows no evidence of any "violence risk" if released (the primary consideration for any parole panel). In a submission to Sirhan's 2011 parole hearing, Dr. Carrera, the staff psychologist at Pleasant Valley Prison, independently assessed Sirhan, and using many of the same tests, agreed with these conclusions.[10]

While Sirhan was not psychologically disturbed, Dr. Brown found that he does exhibit an "unusual combination of personality factors" which leave him "extremely vulnerable to coercive social influence . . . [and making] an internalized false confession."[11]

The first factor is "extremely high hypnotizability"—Brown calls Sirhan "one of the most hypnotizable individuals I have ever met and the magnitude of his amnesia for actions not under his voluntary [control] in hypnosis is extreme." Sirhan also demonstrates "high social compliance"–"an eagerness to please . . . [to] avoid conflict with authority . . . [that would] go along with a defense strategy at trial in ways that did not best represent his interests . . . [and leave him] most vulnerable to suggestive influence."[12]

On three occasions during his work with Dr. Brown, Sirhan switched into a "hypnotically-induced altered personality state that responds in a robot-like fashion upon cue and adopts the behavior of firing a gun at a firing range"—a state Brown describes as "range mode":

> This altered personality state only occurs while Mr. Sirhan is in an hypnotic or self-hypnotic state, and only in response to certain cues. This state never spontaneously manifests. While in this altered personality state Mr. Sirhan shows both a loss of executive control and complete amnesia . . . This distinctive alter personality state is cue-specific and state-dependent . . . [and] likely the product of coercive suggestive influence and hypnosis.

Brown also assessed Sirhan as having an "extreme dissociative coping style." After being "induced to engage in uncharacteristic actions" while in an altered state, Sirhan would "be 'out of it' and . . . confused and amnesic" for his behavior.

* * *

After listening to audio recordings of Dr. Diamond's interviews and hypnosis sessions with Sirhan before the trial, "as an expert in suggestive influence and hypnosis," Dr. Brown felt Diamond's approach was "unduly suggestive":

> Dr. Diamond systematically supplied specific suggestions to Mr. Sirhan to fill in the gaps of [his] memory for the day and evening of the assassination . . . Mr. Sirhan is likely to have given a coerced-compliant, involuntary false confession.[13]

In working with Sirhan "to develop a more complete memory" of the events leading up to the assassination, Brown used "non-suggestive interview techniques" to allow Sirhan to freely recall what he remembered about "the target event"; context reinstatement (also known as the "cognitive interview") to bring him back to the date in question and yield new information; and free recall under hypnosis.

Dr. Brown traces the seeds of this "coercive suggestive influence" back to Sirhan's experience of his younger sister dying of leukemia in 1965. Sirhan became fascinated with the question of whether there was life after death, and was introduced to theosophy and the occult by Tom Rathke. He became a "corresponding member" of the Rosicrucians and began to study mysticism and self-hypnosis. When asked about Sirhan's fall from a horse in 1966, his best friend Terry Welch told the FBI Sirhan "was admitted to the hospital at Corona, where he remained in critical condition for several weeks . . . Sirhan underwent a complete personality change after the accident." In late August 1968, a clearly concerned Lt. Enrique Hernandez visited Welch's home with Deputy DA John Miner and persuaded Welch to retract his story. He now said, "It could have been one but more probably two days . . . in the hospital . . . [and] no, Sirhan was the same person [after the accident]–always very polite and considerate of other people's feelings."[14]

Brown asked Sirhan about the hospital stay under free recall and then under hypnosis. Sirhan remembered staying for two weeks in "a prison-like hospital unit, where he drifted in and out of consciousness." There were bars on the windows and they kept taking blood and urine samples. He recognized other local ranch workers there too, all with head injuries. Brown believes he was "likely under the influence of hallucinogenic or psychiatric drugs and hypnotic suggestions . . . " and that "the horse fall was drug-induced and staged . . . and whatever was done to him [at the hospital] caused a fundamental change in his personality," as later described by family and friends. Sirhan only remembered the hospital stay under hypnosis, not during free recall.[15]

For the next fifteen months, Sirhan had a series of follow-up appointments with eye doctors. After taking eye drops at one of these appointments, Sirhan became disoriented and didn't want to drive home, so he went to a nearby coffee shop and met the "radio man"–a character he talked about in his first session with Brown and Dusek but who it took them a long time to figure out. From day one, Sirhan also talked about his love of shortwave radio—he listened to it for hours in his bedroom at night after buying a set from a neighbor. This was later confirmed by his brother Munir.[16]

The man in the coffee shop had a new shortwave radio on the table in front of him and that's what attracted Sirhan's attention. They started talking and the "radio man" showed him his thesis about overthrowing the government–which Sirhan thought was poorly written—and "told him that government officials needed to be killed."

He was a right-wing militia-type guy, with "a foreign or Cajun accent" and a turned down handle-bar moustache. He knew Sirhan had a shortwave radio, too. In those days, you would keep an antenna on the roof of your house to improve radio reception and Munir confirmed they had this, too. Sirhan met the "radio man" twice at the coffee shop after eye appointments but didn't recall meeting him again. As Dr. Brown notes, Sirhan's "passionate hobby as a short wave radio [enthusiast] was never explored at trial."[17]

* * *

As discussed in chapter 4, the prosecution handwriting expert at trial confirmed Sirhan signed the Corona police range log book on Saturday, June 1, but range master William Marks' description of him was at least eight inches too tall, double Sirhan's weight and the wrong hair color. Marks said "Sirhan" was accompanied by another man in his twenties who didn't shoot–he had brown hair, a pencil moustache, horn-rim glasses and a foreign accent. While Marks' descriptions are confused, Brown believes there may be a connection between the "radio man" and the man seen with Sirhan at the police range who has a similar description.[18]

At trial, Sirhan remembered the range master asking him to sign in at the range that day and seeing "a policeman there instructing a new policeman on this silhouette [target] . . . He had a little class there, some kids, some boys; and he was teaching them how to fire correctly . . . I agree with what he taught them . . . [about] firing the guns, because that's the way I was taught too." As Turner and Christian note, neither prosecution or defense "asked the who and why behind this curious answer" but it remains intriguing.[19]

In the sessions with Dr. Brown, Sirhan remembered "learning to shoot at vital organs and human targets with a 'range master' at Corona Police Firing Range." He mentioned K5, which is the head and chest area on a police silhouette target of the human body, where you score points by aiming to kill (K) or disable (D) a "human target." These details would become critical when Dr. Brown later found the hypnotic cue to induce Sirhan to enter "range mode." But first, he asked Sirhan to freely recall what he remembered about the night of the shooting.

* * *

Sirhan returned to the hotel from his car on election night, too drunk to drive home, and retraced his steps to the bar in search of coffee. He found the bartender who had served him the Tom Collins earlier, chatting to an attractive woman sitting at the bar:

> She over-heard Mr. Sirhan asking for coffee and she said that she knew where the coffee was . . . [She] then took Mr. Sirhan by the hand and led him to the ante-room behind the stage where Senator Kennedy was speaking. There they discovered a large silver coffee urn and cups.[20]

After pouring her a cup of coffee, Sirhan started "getting very sexual ideas with the girl . . . I made up my mind I'm going to make it with this girl tonight . . . she didn't lead me on . . . it was my job to woo her . . . "[21]

While Sirhan was flirting with the girl, "an official with a suit and clip board" told them they would have to move for security reasons and instructed the girl to take Sirhan into the pantry. Sirhan followed the girl into the dark, deserted kitchen "like a puppy" and she sat up on the steam table. There was a security guard sitting in a chair by the doorway talking to someone but in that part of the kitchen, they were alone:

> I'm thinking what if I go after this girl and the girl cries out with the cop there? . . . I'm still sleepy . . . very sleepy . . . I was flirting with her . . . the place was darkish . . . we were the only ones in that area . . . I don't know where the hell it was . . . a deep place to get romantic with that girl . . . Then she sat up on the table facing with her back to the wall . . . her thighs and legs are right here . . . I am just looking at her trying to take her beauty in . . . I am trying to figure out how to hit on her . . . That's all that I can think about. . . . She sat on the steam table. I was leaning. I was fascinated with her looks . . . She was sitting. I was standing. I was engrossed . . . She was busty, looked like Natalie Wood. She never said much. It was very erotic. I was consumed by her. She was a seductress with an unspoken unavailability.

As Sirhan was planning his next move, suddenly the girl became distracted and started looking over his head, toward the far doorway Senator Kennedy and his party were about to walk through:

> Then she taps me or pinches me . . . It is startling . . . It was like a wake up . . . the contact with my body . . . This is too abnormal for people to pinch like that for no given reason . . . It was like when you're stuck with a pin or pinched . . . a very sharp pinch . . . I thought she did it with her fingernails . . . like a wake-up . . . it snapped me out of my doldrums . . . yet I'm still sleepy . . . She points back over my head . . . She says, "Look, look, look." I turn around . . . I don't know what happened after that . . . She spun me around or turned my body around . . . She was directing my attention to the rear . . . way back . . . There are people coming back through the doors . . . I am still puzzled about what she is directing me to . . . It didn't seem relevant to me . . . Some people started streaming in . . . She kept motioning toward the back . . . Then all of a sudden she gets more animated . . .

After the girl tapped him on the elbow, Sirhan remembered taking his firing stance and "seeing circular targets in his field of vision . . . at a local firing range":[22]

> Then I was at the target range . . . I didn't know that I had a gun . . . there was this target, like a flashback to the target range . . . I could be

fantasizing or dreaming that I was at the gun range . . . I thought that I was at the range more than I was actually shooting at any person, let alone Bobby Kennedy . . . I loaded and reloaded quite a few times and the target was 100 feet away . . . I was trying to get dead certain . . . a lot of X' s . . . . [What did the target look like?] Circles . . . Circles . . . I think I shot one or two shots . . .

Sirhan described his mental state as "drunk and sleepy" until they started choking him on the steam table. Then, he "snapped out of it" and thought, "I am not at a firing range, I just shot somebody . . . Then everything gets blurry . . . I didn't know what was going on." In a later session, he added:

When she turned me around, the Kennedy group kept coming in and she was trying to get my attention. When I spun around, that was the last time I saw her. I don't remember shooting. I don't remember aiming at Bobby Kennedy. I don't remember seeing him as a target . . . It was like a continuation of being at the target range . . . Like an indoor target range . . . They say I called Bobby Kennedy a son-of-a-bitch. I don't remember doing that . . . I wasn't aware of a lot of people . . . mostly me and her . . . the girl. She pointed to the entry . . . That's where I thought I fired.

In summarizing Sirhan's recall, Dr. Brown notes that:

The bartender, the girl in the polka dot dress, and an unknown official all play a central role in leading Mr. Sirhan to the scene of the crime, whereupon the girl taps him on the shoulder and Mr. Sirhan responds upon cue with automatic and compulsive behaviour–what Mr. Sirhan eventually described as "range mode"–wherein Mr. Sirhan takes his firing stance and experiences a "flashback" that he is firing at a circle target at a firing range, in a way that has been well practiced.[23]

Mr. Sirhan did not go with the intent to shoot Senator Kennedy, but did respond to a specific hypnotic cue given to him by that woman to enter "range mode," during which Mr. Sirhan automatically and involuntarily responded with a "flashback" that he was shooting at a firing range at circle targets. At the time, Mr. Sirhan did not know that he was shooting at people nor did he know that he was shooting at Senator Kennedy.[24]

The girl in the polka dress seemed to lead Mr. Sirhan into the pantry, was waiting for RFK to come through, and was clearly distracted looking for Kennedy to arrive.[25]

Almost all Sirhan's "free recall" of the event was gleaned without the use of hypnosis, but under hypnosis, Sirhan did remember the girl disappearing when he entered "range mode" and he also recalled seeing a "gun flash" in front of his eyes in the pantry—"very bright spots . . . then, everything went blank." When asked if the flash came from his own gun, he said, "my gun does not flash," suggesting to Dr. Brown that he "saw the flash from another gun at the time of the assassination."

Given the new evidence of a second gunman found on the Pruszynski recording, it is Dr. Brown's expert opinion that Sirhan "was trained through a variety of coercive persuasion techniques to serve as a distractor on the night of the assassination, so that a second professional shooter could render the fatal shot . . ." Sirhan fired his gun on cue, carrying out an involuntary post-hypnotic suggestion and his "strong dissociative coping style . . . would cause him to be 'out of it' and be confused and amnesic for such actions."

* * *

After hearing Sirhan describe the post-hypnotic cue to enter "range mode" on the night of the shooting, Brown and Dusek witnessed "at least three automatic demonstrations of 'range mode' behavior in hypnosis" over forty years later.

Dr. Brown accidentally triggered Sirhan's alter personality state during a hypnotic session by asking him "Did anyone ever tell you to shoot on command?" Sirhan immediately stood up and took his firing stance. Giving Sirhan the verbal cue to "shoot on command" and a non-verbal cue by touching his right elbow induced Sirhan to shift personality states and enter "range mode"—"upon hypnotic cue, Mr. Sirhan takes his firing stance, hypnotically hallucinates that he is shooting at circle targets at a firing range, automatically starts shooting and subsequently is completely amnesic for the hypnotically induced behavior." During the brief re-enactment, Sirhan described "shooting at vital human organs . . . in an uncharacteristic robot-like voice."

In 2011, British mentalist and broadcaster Derren Brown used the "range mode" methodology described in Dr. Brown's first court declaration to construct a one-hour episode of *The Experiments* called "The Assassin" around Sirhan's case. I consulted on the program, which explored whether "it was possible to program somebody to kill . . . without them realizing it." The episode showed it was possible to induce a highly-hypnotizable subject to "shoot" the British celebrity Stephen Fry from a theatre balcony and have complete amnesia for his actions when subsequently brought out of trance.[26]

* * *

The self-incriminating writing in Sirhan's notebooks has always been cited as primary evidence of premeditated murder. The most famous page begins with the line: "May 18 9.45 AM—68 My determination to eliminate R.F.K. is becoming more the more of an unshakable obsession." Underneath this is a series of concentric circles that Sirhan compared "in an open-eye hypnotic trance . . . [to] targets at a target range":

In other words, Mr. Sirhan had drawn firing range targets on the same page on his notebook as he wrote the RFK assassination entries, as if firing at target range targets and firing at a human target like RFK are somehow intertwined in his mind.[27]

After exploring Sirhan's "responsiveness to automatic writing in hypnosis," Dr. Brown concluded that the automatic writing in his notebooks was "a product of coercive persuasion by a third party":

> Mr. Sirhan was an avid enthusiast of short wave radios. He had a short wave radio in his bedroom, and spent most nights before the assassination communicating on his short wave radio to third parties. Mr. Sirhan frequently entered a hypnotic state while [doing this] . . . While in trance, Mr. Sirhan would automatically write down what was communicated to him, and subsequently was amnesic for the content of his automatic writing in the spiral notebooks.[28]

In other words, incriminating phrases in Sirhan's notebooks were dictated to him by "third parties" over the shortwave radio. Dr. Brown "compares the notebooks to "a coerced internalized false confession" and claims they should have been ruled inadmissible at trial.[29]

Who programmed Sirhan? Dr. Brown suspects CIA-funded psychiatrist Louis Jolyon West, who examined Jack Ruby in his cell and was an expert in coercion and "brainwashing." Declassified government documents show "experiments" to create "unconscious assassins" were conducted in the early sixties using a combination of hallucinogenic drugs, hypnotic suggestion and sensory deprivation. Brown showed Sirhan a photo spread including Jolyon West and six "dummies" and he picked him out as "familiar" but could give no further details. According to Dr. Brown, West had a special lab in Santa Anita, near the race track Sirhan frequented.[30]

* * *

Dan Brown has pursued this case, effectively pro bono, at great personal cost. His tax records were audited four times under the Bush administration. His accountant was told by an IRS agent that there was a tag on his US Treasury account by a top Treasury Department official to "harass this guy for the rest of his life." Bill Pepper has also been harassed by the IRS with tax audits but this intimidation stopped when Obama came to power.

In 2008, five days after visiting Sirhan in Corcoran prison, Brown flew into St. Louis, where two friends were picking him up. They all witnessed an airport worker take his bags off the carousel. When Brown challenged him, and threatened to make a scene, the worker told him his orders were that "all bags for the Kennedy party were to be taken to a military base in San Diego." During his frequent travels over the next two years, his bags regularly went "missing" for two or three days. When returned, they had obviously been searched.[31]

* * *

The California Board of Parole Hearings is a highly political office. Its twelve commissioners are appointed by the State Governor and, as a firm of criminal defense lawyers notes, "the governor's political agenda will likely dictate who will be released and who will remain incarcerated," with the governor retaining the right to veto parole board decisions in murder cases.[32]

According to California law, "a life prisoner shall be found unsuitable for and denied parole if in the judgment of the panel the prisoner will pose an unreasonable risk of danger to society if released from prison." In considering whether the prisoner is ready "to re-enter society," the panel considers the crime itself, the prisoner's "social history; past and present mental state; past criminal history . . . past and present attitude toward the crime; and any other information which bears on the prisoner's suitability for release."[33]

Through a Public Records Act request to the California Department of Corrections and Rehabilitation (CDCR), I recently secured the release of the transcripts of all but one of Sirhan's parole hearings dating back to 1985 and put them online with the support of the Mary Ferrell Foundation. They make fascinating reading and really filled in the gaps in my knowledge about how the parole system works, Sirhan's life in prison over the last thirty years and what passes for "due process" in this case in California.[34]

In form, the hearings are very similar: A statement of facts outlining Sirhan's original conviction; a review of his social and criminal history before the life crime, which amounts to two traffic violations; a review of the crime itself, including questions to Sirhan, if he chooses to answer them; a review of the inmate's prison file– counseling reports and psychological evaluations since the last hearing; his work history and behavior in prison; vocational and educational accomplishments; and involvement in self-help therapy programs; a review of his parole plans, if released– where he would live and how he would support himself; letters from the District Attorney and LAPD, who always oppose his release and letters from members of the public received ten days before the trial; closing statements by Sirhan and the deputy District Attorney; and after a recess for deliberation, the decision of the panel.

In 1975, Sirhan was granted a parole date in 1986. Prisoners convicted of first-degree murder had been freed, on average, after eleven years and given Sirhan's record of good behavior, they couldn't justify giving him more time because of who he killed. The chairman of the panel told the press he was "proud as hell that [they] didn't search for some bogus reason to deny him . . . This should prove we don't have any political prisoners."[35]

It's striking that when Sirhan feels he has some hope of parole, he makes a concerted attempt at rehabilitation. Transcripts of his progress review hearings in the late seventies show he was a straight A student, going on to obtain an A.A. degree from Hartnell College. He received laudatory commendations from the prison staff and psychologists and the parole panel seemed to be behind him, gradually bringing his parole date forward two years for good behavior.[36]

After intense political pressure from L.A. County District Attorney John Van de Kamp–who was running for state Attorney General–a ten-day hearing was called in 1982 to review Sirhan's parole date. The panel resurrected isolated outbursts from Sirhan years earlier—like the "Hey Punk" letter threatening Robert Blair Kaiser in 1971 (discussed in Chapter 14) that even Kaiser dismissed as a man on death row venting steam. In his closing statement, Sirhan said:

> No person can feel better or richer in spirit for taking another person's life. I sincerely believe that if Robert Kennedy were alive today, he would not countenance singling me out for this kind of treatment. I think he would be amongst the first to say that however horrible a deed I committed fourteen years ago, it should not be the cause for denying me equal treatment under the laws of this country.

The panel rescinded Sirhan's parole date, noting, "he views himself as a political prisoner, not a political assassin." Deputy District Attorney Lawrence Trapp was the guiding hand behind the rescission hearings and an ever-present at Sirhan's parole hearings in the eighties and nineties. Trapp told the press after the 1983 hearing, "Political assassination in America must never be rewarded by freedom." But as William Klaber notes, Trapp made schoolboy errors in his statements to the panel, repeatedly claiming Sirhan began to plot Kennedy's death on January 31, 1968, based on automatic writing Sirhan produced under hypnosis eight months after the shooting, in preparation for trial.[37]

The long shadow of the infamous 1985 hearing–when the assembled press accidentally listened in to a jokey three-minute deliberation and heard a member of the parole board discuss transferring Sirhan to another prison and say, "we'll send his ass down there for as long as possible"–still hangs over the subsequent hearings in the late eighties. The legal counsel and one of the commissioners involved in 1985 returned to hear Sirhan's case four years later. Sirhan's attorney Luke McKissack was incredulous but his objections were overruled.

After losing his parole date, Sirhan lost hope in the American justice system and later told David Frost:

> The system proceeded admirably well after the death sentence . . . was abolished and when my release date was established. And nothing really would have stopped my release except the political ambitions of a political upstart in Los Angeles named John Van de Kamp, who was district attorney

at the time and who wanted to achieve a higher political office, sir . . . You must distinguish between politics and the rule of law. If you want to say, we want to make a political decision never to let you go, at least, have the courage and tell me that . . . [38]

Larry Teeter took over as Sirhan's attorney in the mid-nineties and his habeas corpus petition was filed two days after the 1997 hearing. The hearing itself marked the first time Sirhan claimed innocence of the shooting, based on the new exculpatory evidence in Teeter's petition. The Commissioner almost threw Teeter out of the hearing when he skillfully tried to apply some of this new evidence to Sirhan's parole criteria. Sirhan was left fuming that his attorney had been repeatedly told to shut up and subsequently refused to cooperate with the parole board or attend his next three hearings. According to psychological reports, he became increasingly withdrawn and disappeared from public view for fourteen years.

* * *

Since Sirhan's interview with Frost for *Inside Edition* in 1989, recorded interviews with inmates have been banned in California, so parole hearings are Sirhan's only chance to publicly state his case for release. Video coverage of Sirhan's 2011 parole hearing shows him clearly struggling for breath, having contracted Valley fever at Pleasant Valley Prison.

In determining suitability for parole, Commissioner Prizmich said they would be exploring his "insight into the crime"—his remorse and the responsibility he took for his actions—but the panel were "compelled to go along with what the court found was true and accurate, so . . . we're not retrying the case."

Sirhan went back over his memory of election night at the hotel and described what he was accused of doing as "the most horrible thing that any human being can do to another . . . You don't kill human beings, period." They discussed the girl he met while searching for coffee:

"Nobody knows who the hell she was . . . she just disappeared."
"Well you remember quite a bit about that."
"Well, I talked with Dr. Brown about it."

This was the first of several "tells" from Prizmich, foreshadowing his predetermined conclusions. In video coverage of the hearing, he comes across as brusque and impatient, trying to catch Sirhan out with his questions and repeatedly interrupting his answers. Sirhan agreed that his notebooks were "incriminating" and "damning" but he couldn't remember writing them. Bill Pepper described three years of psychological testing Sirhan had undergone with Dr. Brown and how, even under deep hypnosis, there were still gaps in his recall.

Sirhan has not broken any prison rules since 1972 and was generally described as a model prisoner, working unpaid, raking leaves and mowing the lawn. But the panel raised a couple of angry episodes from 2010, when Sirhan's radio was taken away from him when he moved prison and one of the new guards challenged him to a fight. When Sirhan reported the provocation to his counselor, she ridiculed him and when the guard called him a motherfucker, he returned the compliment, so the guard wouldn't think him a "pushover." The panel seized on these innocuous episodes where Sirhan lost his temper, when provoked, as evidence he still had anger management issues. Sirhan contended he was merely a prisoner "raising hell about my rights" in a pressure-cooker environment.

Perhaps the most ridiculous aspect of the proceeding came when Prizmich asked Sirhan how he'd reacted to guards accusing him of foreknowledge of 9–11. Sirhan told the guards "they were crazy"–a departing prisoner had given him his TV and when the guards saw him watching it with a towel on his head after a shower, they concluded he was an Arab terrorist and told the press. Instead of apologizing to Sirhan for defamatory remarks and press leaks, Prizmich scolded him for making an "immature comment" about 9–11 and probed his possession of a Koran. Sirhan said he used the Koran to "keep up" his Arabic but reiterated that he's been a practicing Christian all his life, attends church every week and the Bible was his favorite book, with one passage in Luke holding special meaning for him:

> The spirit of the Lord is upon me, He has sent me to heal the brokenhearted, to proclaim liberty to the captives . . . to set at liberty those who are oppressed . . . (Luke 4:18)

"It renews my hope I will be found suitable for parole and get out because Christ promised that to all the believers," he said, before adding in his closing statement:

> Every day of my life, I have great remorse and deeply regret the fact that I participated in [this] horrible event . . . As the panel knows, I was granted a parole date in 1975 . . . The District Attorney took away this parole date . . . and this . . . really changed my mind and heart towards the system. I lost faith and confidence in this very system because I realized that . . . your word is not as good as it should be, in all candor.

After a forty-five-minute deliberation, the panel decided the prisoner "was not yet suitable for parole and would pose an unreasonable risk of threat or danger to public safety if released from prison" despite a long history of psychiatric reports stating the opposite. As they were "compelled to go with" the appellate decision, "it was undisputed that the defendant fired the shot that killed Senator Kennedy":[39]

So there were multiple victims, the evidence is quite clear that the offence was carried out in a calculated manner . . . and it seems quite clear, in your planning, that you focused on Mr. Kennedy and your focus was bore out by him being killed . . .

The panel commended Sirhan for his demeanor but said there were still "deep-seated issues" where he had "failed in several areas." As Prizmich explained them, his cordial relationship with Sirhan began to unravel.

Firstly, Prizmich told Sirhan he had not taken "adequate responsibility" for "the magnitude of this crime" and "your lack of understanding of the impact of this crime was of great concern to us." The assassination had transformed the way politicians interact with the public and Prizmich didn't feel Sirhan appreciated that.

On the subject of remorse, the panel noted "with some degree of . . . distrust, quite frankly, you remembering parts of this and not remembering others" and made no attempt to engage with Dr. Brown's work to recover Sirhan's memory of the shooting:

The gaps in your memory . . . leave us with an uneasy feeling . . . that you are minimizing your conduct in this matter. You have vaguely made reference to any number of conspiracies, not only in the crime, but also a conspiracy that law enforcement somehow set you up, the CIA somehow set you up on this, the DA was a party to this. It seemed as though, in your mind, everything that occurred in a negative way to you . . . was really someone else's fault . . .

While the prison authorities are to be lauded for allowing Dr. Brown repeated access to Sirhan, it was perverse of the panel to gloss over his validation of Sirhan's amnesia.

Throughout the hearing, Sirhan expressed remorse to the public, the Kennedy family and the other shooting victims–including William Weisel, who was present–saying the news of their injuries "broke my heart." He described how painful it was to dwell on the details of such a "horrible nightmare" and Prizmich later seized on this and Sirhan's description of the other victim wounds as "flesh injuries" for an extended rant:

Your description of their injuries was a very off-handed 'They were flesh wounds.' They were much more serious than that . . . if one has insight, if one has remorse, as you expressed you do, you'd have some level of understanding as to what damage you caused these people. Now, I know it's been a long time ago but you had none. Flesh wounds were not what these people suffered, so that gave me concern.

The Oxford English Dictionary defines a flesh wound as "a wound that breaks the skin but does not damage bones or vital organs," which is an accurate description of what the victim injuries were.

Finally, the panel told Sirhan more self-help programming and anger management was needed to give him an "ability to articulate in a deep-seated, meaningful way to the panel your understanding of the magnitude of the loss of this man."

Self-help options are limited in Sirhan's high-security unit, so he recently joined the Alcoholics Anonymous (AA) group, even though he barely touched alcohol before the four Tom Collins cocktails he consumed on the night of the shooting. In the early nineties, Sirhan served as chairman of the AA group in his unit for three years but stopped when meetings conflicted with his work roster and he openly questioned why he should jump through hoops for the parole board when they showed no sign of ever granting him parole. The panel commended him for joining AA again but criticized him for not being able to cite "any of the twelve steps nor what their purpose was . . . " Again, they overlooked the insight Sirhan gained from three years "looking into himself" with Dr. Brown.

The three criteria outlined above are clearly difficult to surmount for Sirhan. He cannot change the nature and impact of the crime until the case is re-adjudicated and legal attempts to reopen it have so far failed. How can you express full remorse if you don't remember committing the crime and if you're still contesting the case? How do you perform remorse in these circumstances before a parole board that you feel has already made up its mind?

* * *

In November 2011, forensic audio expert Phil Van Praag submitted an eighteen-page declaration to federal court, expanding on the two initial discoveries made during his analysis of the Pruszynski recording, and discussed in the previous chapter. As well as finding thirteen "shot sounds" over a five-second interval on the recording and two instances of "double shots," Van Praag made another remarkable discovery. He found that five of the thirteen "shot sounds" had a unique audio resonance characteristic that was also present in "one, and only one, of each double shot pair."[40]

He conducted independent firing range tests of two 22-caliber revolvers—the Iver Johnson Cadet 55SA model used by Sirhan; and a Harrington and Richardson (H&R) 922, the gun type owned by Thane Eugene Cesar, the security guard behind Kennedy at the time of the shooting. Van Praag positioned two microphones "forty feet from the guns, to mimic the average distance between Pruszynski's microphone and the guns" he suspected in the pantry. One microphone was placed "in front and slightly to the side of the guns" (Sirhan's position), the other "behind and slightly to the side" (Cesar's position).[41]

The results of these tests showed the same frequency anomaly found in the Pruszynski recording was also present on audio of the H&R 922, recorded from forty feet behind (Pruszynski's microphone in relation to Cesar). Van Praag concluded that five of the thirteen shots on the recording were "fired from a west-to-east direction." It's important to note that witnesses observed Sirhan firing east-to-west; said Robert Kennedy was facing east when the shooting began; and the autopsy report concluded all bullets striking the Senator and his clothing were fired from behind Kennedy. As Van Praag told me in a short film I made about his work: "This provided very, very strong evidence then, that the source of the second gun was, in fact, an H&R 922."

As discussed in Chapters 13 and 14, while the bullet found in Kennedy's neck and two other key victim bullets have never been matched to Sirhan's gun, the 1975 firearms panel concluded they were fired from a gun with the same rifling characteristics as Sirhan's revolver. The H&R 922 is the only other known model with the same rifling characteristics. Van Praag concluded that, of the thirteen shots found in the Pruszynski recording, Sirhan fired the first, second, fourth, sixth, seventh, ninth, eleventh and thirteenth shots while the second gunman fired the third, fifth, eighth, tenth and twelfth. Shots three and four, and seven and eight, were "double shots," shots fired so close together they couldn't have come from the same weapon.

As discussed in the previous chapter, this seems to indicate that Sirhan fired the first two shots before his gun arm was diverted by Karl Uecker and there was a short pause. One of these shots hit Paul Schrade in the head. Then, both guns started firing simultaneously but Sirhan's gun arm had been directed away from the Senator.

In 2008, Brad Johnson obtained further copies of the Pruszynski recording from the FBI through a Freedom of Information Act request—one was an FBI-created digital copy of the as-received reel-to-reel dub the Bureau had obtained from the Canadian police in 1969. Van Praag also presented his findings to the sixtieth-anniversary scientific meeting of the American Academy of Forensic Sciences in Washington, DC.

Van Praag's discoveries eventually got the attention of Robert F. Kennedy Jr. who, on September 25, 2012, privately wrote to U.S. Attorney General Eric Holder supporting a request by Paul Schrade for a new investigation of his father's murder, including a 21st century FBI analysis of the Pruszynski recording:

Paul was a close friend and advisor to my father. He was standing beside my father when Daddy was killed and Paul was himself wounded by a bullet. With boundless energy and clear mind, Paul continues to pursue my father's ideas, an endeavor to which he has devoted his life. He organized with the support of my mother and my family the building of the new Robert F. Kennedy Community Schools on the former Ambassador Hotel site. Paul and his team . . . strongly believe this new evidence is conclusive and requires a new investigation. I agree and support his request for a new investigation.

At Holder's direction, the FBI Laboratory conducted a very limited and deeply flawed examination of the Pruszynski recording and reportedly "could not confirm the number of shots or determine the identification of specific weapons." The FBI refused to accept the papers Van Praag had written detailing his methodologies and discoveries, and refused to communicate with him in any way.[42]

The FBI's examination report, obtained through another Freedom of Information Act request by Johnson, shows the Bureau used outdated methodologies and failed to provide their own analyst with critical background materials about the shooting scene. These included witness statements, the autopsy report and movements of key people, including Stanislaw Pruszynski himself, at the time of the shooting.

The FBI analyst describes searching for videos of Van Praag's work on YouTube and working from low-resolution screen grabs of my own 2008 film on Van Praag's discoveries to find out precisely where to look, how to look, and what to look for. Accurate, detailed information, sufficient for an in-depth FBI analysis, could have been discovered through a simple phone call to Van Praag, or inviting him to the FBI's Quantico laboratory for a briefing.

Phil Van Praag would like more research to be done on the Pruszynski recording. In recent years, he helped draft a plan for "a world-renowned security firm" to independently verify his findings while developing new software tools for law enforcement to use in "the identification of guns based on the recorded acoustic signature of gunshots." So far, the projected cost of $70,000 has not been raised but there are hopes it might be funded through a broadcast documentary. Unless a new audio recording of the shooting is discovered, further independent verification of his findings would be the best way to strengthen his case.[43]

* * *

California State Archives received the Sirhan case file from the Los Angeles County Sheriff's Department in January 1996 and opened it to researchers on ten rolls of microfilm in August 2011, forty-two years after the file was closed. I was pleased to see the release of the last major collection on the case and ordered digital scans of the microfilm, totaling over 19,000 pages. The belated release of the files yielded an important new discovery, throwing light on LAPD efforts to get another agency to independently verify DeWayne Wolfer's ballistics work before Sirhan's trial.[44]

As noted in chapter 3, the FBI refused to re-examine the firearms evidence, partly because newspaper reports quoted Grant Cooper "as stating in open court, 'There will be no denial of the fact that Sirhan B. Sirhan fired the shot or shots that killed Robert F. Kennedy.'"[45] On January 30, 1969, ten days after the FBI refusal, the Sheriff's files reveal that LAPD chief Thomas Reddin wrote to Sherriff Pitchess with the same request:

Desiring to maintain the highest level of integrity in every phase of the investigation, the Chief of Police and the District Attorney agree that a back-up analysis by personnel of your agency would obviously strengthen this phase of the investigation. A separate and independent analysis would be of value in later refuting any claims attacking the validity of the examination by a single department and should preclude disputes or frivolous complaints.[46]

Two weeks later, Ray Noble, the head of the Sheriff's crime laboratory, Head Criminalist Harry McKeehan and a colleague from the Homicide Bureau were briefed on the evidence by DeWayne Wolfer and his colleagues at LAPD headquarters. Wolfer summarized "his expert findings" in case "back-up testimony" was deemed "necessary or desirable." All three visitors "formed the opinion that our presence was very much resented on the part of Officer Wolfer, the Ballistics Expert." Noble concluded that if a court order was obtained to examine the evidence, Sheriff's Department experts would probably be called to "testify as to our independent findings . . . [and even] slightly different opinions . . . could possibly weaken the case against the defendant" and "cast doubt" on Wolfer's opinion. He suggested it might be better to await the outcome of the Kirschke appeal, in which Wolfer's credibility was then embroiled.[47]

On February 14, the day after Noble's memo, Pitchess wrote to Reddin, as the defense team made their opening statement in the trial:

If the District Attorney will obtain the court order making the evidence available, we are prepared to give immediate and full attention to performing the necessary analyses . . . in our own facility.

On March 5, having discussed the matter again with the District Attorney's office, Reddin replied:

It was their considered opinion that the comprehensive examinations conducted to date are conclusive from a legal standpoint.[48]

In the interim, on February 24, Wolfer had testified and Grant Cooper had stipulated to the physical evidence, giving Wolfer a "free pass." A golden opportunity to catch Wolfer's mistakes was lost until the firearms re-testing in 1975, by which time the bullets had degraded.

* * *

The Sheriff's Department Records also included some fascinating material detailing Sirhan's first year in custody. The late Robert Blair Kaiser worked as a defense investigator for Sirhan and was granted access to these records after the trial for his mesmerizing insider account of the case, *R.F.K. Must Die!* (1970). As the inventory of the records notes, Sirhan was under constant surveillance:

The jail logs document Sirhan's behavior, meals, visitors, and movements on a 24-hour basis, recorded by deputies at least every fifteen minutes and often more frequently, from June 5, 1968 to May 22, 1969. Log entries include titles of books requested and received by Sirhan during his imprisonment. The jail logs also record Sirhan's sleeping and eating patterns and exercise activities . . .

Four thousand pages of personal deputies' statements, handwritten on index cards, describe in detail conversations between Sirhan and his jailers during this period. On the orders of Dr. Crahan, he was rationed to two candy bars and ten cigars a day, bought with money placed on deposit for him by his family and attorneys. His most frequent questions are: "What time is it? How about some candy bars? How about some cigars? What are you thinking? What are the papers saying about me?"

Over the course of Sirhan's first year in custody, they build into a fascinating record of Sirhan's confinement, and humanize a man demonized for a crime he can't remember committing, as he struggles to keep his sanity under the constant gaze of sheriff's deputies under strict orders "to give very brief answers and not to engage Sirhan in conversation."

The sheriff's deputies spy on Sirhan's privileged meetings with his attorneys, conversations with his family and hypnotic sessions with defense psychiatrist Dr. Diamond. Sirhan regularly talks to himself in the mirror, perhaps under self-hypnosis. He tells his guards he can't remember the shooting and wonders if he's as crazy as the doctors say he is. He's a Christian but believes in the Rosicrucian theory of rebirth and orders books on Mid-East politics and mysticism. For days, sometimes weeks at a time, Sirhan has no communication with anybody. Day by day, these diaries bring you into a crazy, mixed-up case in all its depth and mystery.

In January 2016, I published an edited collection of 450 of these entries as an eBook titled, *In Jail with Sirhan Sirhan*. They provide insights into the case, and Sirhan's fragile state of mind, as his situation grows increasingly desperate and he is finally condemned to death and moved out of sheriff's custody to San Quentin.[49]

* * *

After interviewing Sandra Serrano for my film, I have continued to pursue leads in the search for the identity of the girl in the polka-dot dress and this led in two interesting directions. In 2012, a woman I will simply call Elaine died in Texas and her family members compared notes about the strange life she had led. A few days later, her nephew contacted me to say he believed his Aunt Elaine was the woman in the polka-dot dress. At the request of the family, I have changed the names below to protect their privacy.[50]

Elaine was born in California in 1948. She attended high school in Los Angeles and married her high-school sweetheart Antonio in 1966. Their daughter Anne was born that summer. In June 1968, Elaine was nineteen years old and living in Long Beach. She separated from Antonio in early 1968 and they divorced four months after the assassination.

Antonio told me Elaine was very flighty. She would take off with her young daughter and he would lose track of where she was. Sometimes, he would see her around Long Beach but he didn't think she was working at the time and couldn't think of any connection to the RFK story. He thinks she lived in a commune in the early 1970s and other family members remember her living in a cult and a nudist colony.

According to her family, Elaine's ancestry was a mix of Irish, Greek and Cherokee/Native American. She had wide cheekbones, was 5'8" tall, carried herself "regally" and was very attractive. She was a natural brunette with a tinge of red and had long flowing hair she would sometimes tie up in a bun. She had nine siblings and her family were conservative Christians and Republican, and lived in the Chino area.

After another short-lived marriage in the early seventies, Elaine married Jack, a well-known musician in the summer of 1973. He was twenty years her senior and they had met at Chino Airport in the early seventies, where Jack was a partner in Chino Aircraft Service, an aviation repair and leasing business. They were introduced by "a very shady character" Jack's age who was friends with Elaine and may have been dating her at the time. According to Jack's sister Miriam, this mutual friend took Elaine up flying once "and the tail fell off and they barely made it down, and she was terrified of flying after that."[51]

The family moved back to Jack's home state of Missouri before Christmas that year and they had two sons shortly thereafter. Jack was still involved in the music business while also marketing a board game on numerology. They were both Christian fundamentalists and he was big into guns. According to his sister Miriam, Jack introduced Elaine to movie stars and led her to believe he had money but reality hit when he moved back to his parents' old house in Los Angeles in the mid-seventies and Miriam and Elaine finally met:

> She had him figured out pretty well by then. He was supposedly going to law school, but years later, it came out he had just taken some correspondence courses. Elaine said the only thing he learned was how to cheat people. He took the Bar exam many times but was never able to pass it. He was a "floor-flusher"—either flush with money or flat broke.

At some point in the early seventies, Elaine and Jack were "on the run" from the FBI and hid out at Miriam's place in Arizona. In the late seventies, Elaine and Jack had a heated argument when Elaine decided to wear a white dress with black polka dots to church. According to her children, she kept it in a box on top of a cabinet and even got her daughter to try it on. Anne remembers it was a chiffon dress, with a collar or bow, in a contemporary style and "very form-fitting."

Jack knew a lot of people in law enforcement and was close to the local sher-iff–her children believe he had their mother's phone tapped. He would be abusive to Elaine and they soon split up and she took Anne to Missouri, leaving the two boys with Jack. Soon after that, Jack visited Miriam with the boys and told her and her husband that Elaine had told him she was the woman in the polka dot dress.

Elaine could never stay in one place. Just when things were stable, she would disappear and Anne lived her life on the run. She was never at the same school for more than a year growing up until high school. Jack went from Hollywood parties and money and success in the music industry to living completely off the grid in the eighties. The boys grew up on a farm with no running water or electricity and a paranoid father. They felt they were "on the run until we were about ten years old, both scared shitless."

According to his sister Miriam, Jack spent four years in the air force and claimed he was a fighter pilot during the Korean conflict but he never saw action. He was a trainer pilot, stationed in Texas, and only went to Korea after the fighting stopped for a year. He said he knew Jack Ruby and had dinner with him the week before JFK was killed. He was an expert on the Kennedy assassinations but also a "blowhard," Miriam says, so it was hard to know "what he was messed up in."

Jack told her and his children he worked for the CIA in the sixties and was involved in mind control experiments, using LSD. He talked about "Manchurian Candidates" and said he could "pick your mind" using mind control and "paper bracelets" with a chemical in them that made you "do what they told you to do." He claimed he had a security clearance and that the CIA wanted him to come back and fly planes for them, to do courier work and "black operations." Jack died in the late nineties and his sister Miriam thinks he was evil:

> Jack was capable of anything. He got the boys away from Elaine by threatening to kill her, just like he told me he would kill me if I showed up at Mother's funeral. I know that even now a lot of people don't believe me, but Jack was a very evil person. Elaine told me when they lived in Missouri that he would buy wine and force her to drink it, then told everyone she was an alcoholic. Anne told me how he made her walk to school alone when they lived in Los Angeles. she was five or six years old and afraid. At seventy-five years old, I still have scars from third degree burns he inflicted on me as a baby, not once but three times. I have said all this to say one thing: HE WAS CAPABLE OF ANYTHING.

Elaine's son Tom had little contact with his mother after she moved to Mis-souri. In her later years, Elaine was a critical care nurse for twenty-five years, caring for terminal patients. She was an alcoholic and is believed to have died of cirrhosis of the liver. She had moved to Texas with a Tent Revival movement in the early eighties and had books on Christian fundamentalism and the 12-step program. In the words of one relative, "she was always on the run and never in her children's lives. She was never around to see her grandkids born, didn't know her grandkids and never could find peace . . . " A few months before she died, Tom contacted her and they started talking again and shortly before her death, Elaine told him Jack had been involved with the CIA during the sixties, up to 1971.

If Elaine was at the Ambassador Hotel in 1968, Miriam thinks she was probably hired to be somebody's escort or "arm candy." She could get any man she wanted and there was a family rumor she may have been a "call girl" around that time. Miriam didn't think she would deliberately get involved in anything like that but she could have been there without knowing what was planned. Jack kept a sailboat in a Long Beach marina in the mid-sixties and was living in the Long Beach area in February 1968, when his first wife Judy died of lupus, but there's no evidence he met Elaine prior to the assassination.

It's very difficult to assess this story. Elaine is dead and the dress was not found in the belongings she left behind. I can't find anyone who was close to Elaine in June 1968, except her daughter Anne—who was two at the time. Elaine had already split up and lost touch with Antonio. Jack is dead and I can't find any evidence to verify his claims. He does not seem to have met Elaine until the 1971–2 period but it's possible they met in the Long Beach area before then. I visited Elaine's children and I know they feel haunted by this and really want to find out the truth about their mother, so I'm putting this information out here, in the hope that a further lead may add to what we know about Elaine's story.

* * *

In late 2015, award-winning journalist Fernando Faura contacted me and I helped him follow up on an important lead concerning Gilderdine Oppenheimer, the strange young woman John Fahey met in the coffee shop of the Ambassador Hotel on the morning of the California Democratic primary. As discussed in Chapter 5, she invited Fahey to "Kennedy's winning reception" that night, where "they were going to take care of Mr. Kennedy."

After Senator Kennedy was taken care of, she planned to leave the country via San Francisco, using the Flying Tiger Line. She said she had just come from New York three days earlier, where she met Mrs. Chennault, the Vice President of the Flying Tiger Line and the influential socialite and lobbyist who is alleged to have brokered Nixon's election victory by keeping the South Vietnamese away from the Paris Peace Talks. Faura was now finishing a book chronicling his reporting on the case titled *The Polka Dot File on the Robert F. Kennedy Killing: The Paris Peace Talks Connection* (Trine Day, 2016). A week after the assassination, as Fahey retraced his steps with Faura on a trip to Ventura, he recalled Gilderdine saying she had met with Mrs. Chennault in New York three days earlier. Now, Faura was picking up the lead almost fifty years later. Did the "girl in the polka dot dress" meet with Anna Chennault three days before the assassination?

Six months later, we visited Madame Chennault in the Watergate penthouse she's lived in since the late sixties. By then ninety years old, she was very gracious and thought Bobby Kennedy had stood a good chance of defeating Nixon in 1968. But she didn't remember anyone by the name of Gilderdine Oppenheimer and she didn't recognize the girl in the artist sketches Faura had made based on Fahey's description. According to her calendar, she was in Colorado at a US Air Force Academy award ceremony on June 1 and returned to Washington, D.C. the following day. Anna Chennault remains an intriguing figure and a character I'll explore in more depth in my forthcoming book *Dirty Tricks*.[52]

* * *

In the days before Sirhan's parole hearing in February 2016, the harassment of his legal team continued. The Board of Parole Hearings wouldn't allow Dr. Brown to appear to report on his work with Sirhan, and the day before the hearing, Bill Pepper was also blocked, when it was falsely claimed there were issues with his law license. Moments before the parole hearing, Pepper and Dusek were threatened with criminal charges for not being cleared to represent Sirhan from out of state until Dusek produced proof to the contrary. Laurie Dusek describes this as a pattern of "deliberate harassment," not just bureaucratic incompetence.[53]

According to his attorneys, Sirhan was physically sick after the last hearing in 2011, when he felt he had been "abused" by the commissioners. After a protracted bout of Valley fever, Sirhan moved to his current facility, the Richard J. Donovan Correctional Facility in San Diego, in November 2013, on the fiftieth anniversary of the JFK assassination. He wasn't planning to attend the 2016 hearing but changed his mind when shooting victim Paul Schrade asserted his "victim rights" and decided to make a lengthy statement to the parole commissioners.

Only one Associated Press reporter and one AP photographer were allowed into the hearing room and the parole board recently banned audio and video recording of parole hearings, censoring Sirhan's voice from the continuing debate about his case. At this rate, the public may never see or hear from him again.[54]

The hearing was hotly contested. David Dahle, a retired prosecutor representing the district attorney's office, opposed Sirhan's release, called him a "terrorist," guilty of "an attack on the American political process . . . [who] has still not come to grips with what he has done." Bill Pepper and Paul Schrade called Sirhan "a political prisoner" and Schrade chastised Dahle for his "venomous" attack on Sirhan: "It's not just a political crime, Mr. Dahle, but also a political crime keeping him in prison."[55]

Pepper and Schrade were both close to Bobby Kennedy and invoked his name in calling for Sirhan's release. Pepper was Citizens' Chairman for Kennedy's senate run in 1964 and said: "If Bob Kennedy were alive and were viewing [the available evidence, he] would urge this Panel to finally grant this man parole."

* * *

Sirhan was surprised and thankful that he was treated more respectfully this time and the panel commended him for being "very cooperative and very restrained". They also praised his clean disciplinary record and history of consistently positive work evaluations in prison jobs ranging from clerk to yard crew, tram worker, part cleaner, tailor, laundry worker, porter, and his most recent position of cook.[56]

Sirhan again stuck to his story that he didn't remember shooting Robert Kennedy. He felt remorse for the victims but couldn't take full responsibility for the crime: "If you want a confession, I can't make it now . . . I just wish this whole thing had never taken place."[57]

When it came to recalling the crime itself, Sirhan seemed a little weary of repeating himself, forty-seven years after the event. When the panel resurrected long-discredited claims from convicted con man Carmen Falzone and trash collector Alvin Clark, Sirhan denied ever telling anybody he had deliberately shot Robert Kennedy. Falzone had sold a story to *Playboy* in 1977 in which Sirhan confessed his guilt about the Kennedy murder and conspired with fellow inmate Falzone to smuggle plutonium to Gaddafi in Libya. This ludicrous plot was used as evidence by the state in its successful attempt to rescind Sirhan's parole date in 1982.[58]

When the panel asked Sirhan why he pleaded guilty at trial, Sirhan repeatedly answered, "I was told I had shot him . . . I was told . . . " He had no memory of the shooting but his trial attorney Grant Cooper told him "there was no defense against it."[59]

"So, what do you take responsibility for, sir?" asked Commissioner Roberts.

"Whatever I'm guilty of in this case . . . [but] not murder," replied Sirhan, adding it was for prosecutors to determine what he was guilty of.

"If you don't believe you're responsible for shooting somebody . . . tell me what you think you're responsible for?"

"It's a good question. Legally speaking, I'm not guilty of anything . . . I'm responsible for being there . . . "

"Anything else that you're responsible for other than being there?"

"Knowing what I know now about the case, no."

"What do you mean by that?"

"That I did not commit the crime."[60]

Sirhan said he had remorse "as far as I am criminally responsible" but seemed to imply that, as he was in a dissociated state at the time, he wasn't criminally responsible for anything. He expressed "extreme remorse" for the death of Robert Kennedy and "for his family's loss and for the country's loss." In the past, before he knew of evidence exonerating him, he "did take full responsibility." Even though he couldn't remember the crime, "I thought I was guilty, you know, and it bothered me":

> And it still bothers me now because I'm still a part of this scene, of this situation. But I don't really know how to prove [my remorse] to you. It's

too abstract. It's an internal thing . . . How do you manifest the illustration of it?[61]

Later, he added, "This is such a traumatic . . . horrendous experience, that . . . to keep dwelling on it is harmful to me . . . For my own mental health, I try to avoid . . . thinking about it."[62]

Sirhan's attorney William Pepper tried to make sense of the fragmented testimony by summing up his client's dilemma:

> The problem that he faces is, he legitimately does not recall what happened. And if he doesn't recall what happened, he cannot say that he was accountable and legally responsible and therefore he is remorseful. He's remorseful about what happened to Robert Kennedy.[63]

Pepper quoted Dr. Brown's report, which notes Sirhan was in a dissociated state "at the time of the assassination, [so] it should not be assumed at the parole hearing that he should manifest either knowledge or remorse for, or a clear memory for, an event wherein his behavior was likely compulsively induced involuntarily and for which he still has little memory."[64] In his submission to the parole board, Dr. Brown concluded:

> Mr. Sirhan has been incarcerated for over four decades for a crime he is unlikely to have committed. Extensive psychological testing by me and others shows no evidence for any clinically significant psychiatric condition and low evidence for violence risk, combined with the new evidence that raises reasonable doubt that Mr. Sirhan was the assassin of Robert F. Kennedy, and also reasonable doubt about his previous written and verbal self-incriminating statements being voluntary and reliable, there is, in my opinion, no justifiable reason to deny his parole. Since he has spent all of his adult life in prison for a crime that he may not have committed, nor has volition about, knowledge of, nor memory for, the compassionate response would be to let Mr. Sirhan live the remainder of his life free. There is little risk here.[65]

Later, Deputy Commissioner Stanton asked Sirhan to confirm that he felt "not legally responsible for anything," given what he had learned since the trial:

> I would say that I'm not guilty of murder . . . I feel that if I had a proper defense at the time that the results would have been quite different than what happened. My trial attorney did not conduct a crime scene investigation. He never really examined any of the witnesses. He conceded everything before even examining the bullets . . . there was hardly anything that he did other

than concede my guilt. And he said that numerous times. And he convinced me of it. He made me guilty without even knowing that I am guilty.[66]

There were a few odd notes in Sirhan's testimony. He didn't remember visiting the Ambassador Hotel two nights before the California primary, something he did recall at trial and in an NBC interview thereafter. He also said he went down to the Ambassador Hotel on election night "with another guy who was at the Kuchel headquarters," which I don't recall hearing before. But after forty-seven years, such quirks of memory are to be expected.[67]

If paroled, Sirhan hoped he would be deported to Jordan or could stay with his brother in Pasadena, "to live out my life peacefully and in harmony with my fellow man . . . I would daresay, with respect, that you guys are the obstacle to [those] aspirations."[68]

Asked for a final comment, he said: "I think I'm way overdue for parole." And his closing statement at the end of the hearing was brief and to the point: "Please let me go home. Thank you."[69]

* * *

Victims of a crime have the right to make a statement at the end of a parole hearing. They can say what they want and have as much time as they want, so Paul Schrade's appearance "provided much of the drama," according to the Associated Press reporter, and his voice "cracked with emotion during an hour of testimony."[70]

The parole panel normally bar any attempt to retry the case but Schrade's victim rights gave him carte blanche to put the key evidence of a second gun on the record—arguing that the witness testimony, the autopsy report and the only audio recording of the shooting prove that thirteen shots were fired and an unidentified second shooter killed Kennedy. While Schrade stopped short of saying Sirhan was hypnotized, he does feel Sirhan didn't know what he was doing and should not be held fully accountable for shooting him and other bystanders, or attempting to shoot Robert Kennedy.

Meeting Sirhan for the first time since the 1969 trial, Schrade apologized for not attending his previous parole hearings or doing more to win his release: "I should have been here long ago and that's why I feel guilty for not being here to help you and to help me understand what happened":[71]

[Bob] Kennedy was a man of justice. So far, justice has not been served in this case. And I feel obliged as both a shooting victim and as an American to speak out about this—and to honor the memory of the greatest American I've ever known, Robert Francis Kennedy . . . There are no conspiracy theories needed here. I'm referring only to official documents and scientific results. And the way I've been saying this to my friends these days is that my job is prosecuting the prosecutors in this case, because they're the guilty ones in putting Sirhan in prison, knowing that he didn't and couldn't do it.[72]

When Schrade turned to address Sirhan, he "angrily ignored" the commissioner's instructions not to speak or make eye contact with the prisoner:

> Sirhan, I want to forgive you. You've been charged with shooting me, Robert Kennedy and four others. I don't believe the charges against you for shooting Robert Kennedy are true. And I don't hold it against you because I don't think you knew what you were doing . . . The fatal bullet struck Bob in the back of the head. And as the autopsy shows . . . you were never in the position to do that . . . There is clear evidence of a second gunman in that kitchen pantry who shot Robert Kennedy.[73]

Sirhan nodded politely and seemed appreciative as Schrade told him he wasn't guilty and that Robert Kennedy would be appalled, not only by the parole board's unjust treatment of Sirhan, but by the fact that he was not being given parole based on his rights under law. Schrade then directed the panel's attention to documents submitted in advance of the hearing, which proved that Sirhan "could not and did not shoot Robert Kennedy:" [74]

> Sirhan only had full control of his gun at the beginning, when he fired his first two shots, one of which hit me. Sirhan had no opportunity to fire four precisely placed, point-blank bullets into the back of Bob Kennedy's head or body while he was pinned against that steam table and while he and Bob were facing each other.
>
> What I am saying to you is that Sirhan himself was a victim. Obviously, there was someone else there in that pantry also firing a gun. While Sirhan was standing in front of Bob Kennedy and the shots were creating a distraction . . . the other shooter secretly fired at the senator from behind and fatally wounded him. Bob died 25 hours later . . . I believe you should grant Sirhan Sirhan parole and I ask you to do that today.[75]

As federal authorities have no criminal jurisdiction over the case, towards the end of the hearing, Schrade asked Dahle to inform Los Angeles County District Attorney Jackie Lacey that he was formally requesting her to order a new investigation. He plans to make the same request to Los Angeles Police Chief Charlie Beck and noted a previous request to Lacey three years earlier never got a reply.[76]

After an hour, commissioner Brian Roberts asked Schrade to wrap up. "Quite frankly, you're losing us," he said. "I think you've been lost for a long time," Schrade replied, before concluding:[77]

Let me finally say that I wouldn't be here today saying what I'm saying if it wasn't for my love of Robert Kennedy and what he meant to me and what he meant to the country and to the world. He was a fantastic person . . . [and] I am bearing witness for him because I know that he would not want . . . what's happening to Sirhan to happen to him at all. He was a very forgiving person. And I want to honor his memory by talking about justice for Sirhan and justice for Robert Kennedy. Because we still don't know who that second gunman is even though the prosecution had plenty of evidence that there was a second gunman but proceeded against Sirhan anyway.[78]

* * *

In their decision, the panel acknowledged there were positive factors showing Sirhan's suitability for parole. He had no criminal record prior to the murder of Robert Kennedy in 1968, and has maintained a very good disciplinary record in prison. Following a traumatic childhood in war-torn Jerusalem, the panel felt Sirhan had "a stable social history" after settling in Pasadena with his family as Palestinian refugees in 1957.

Sirhan's age "reduces the probability of recidivism" and he had "made realistic plans for release" and "developed marketable skills" to gain employment and support himself. There is an immigration hold on Sirhan, so, if paroled, he would probably be deported to Jordan, where he has family and is a citizen.

However, the panel felt these positives were "far outweighed by other circumstances that tend to show unsuitability for parole and suggest that if released that you would pose a potential threat to public safety. Chief among these were the "particularly heinous and atrocious and offensive manner" of the murder and the "magnitude of the crime":

> Insight is specifically critical in cases such as this where an individual has no prior propensity towards violence . . . It is critical to have a significant understanding as to why he would resort to violence in this case. While anger appears to be at the core of it, [Sirhan] has yet to make the necessary connections between his anger and his violence . . . Absent sufficient insight, he cannot develop the necessary or requisite coping mechanisms or skillsets that would assist him in abating this very specific mindset [in the future].[79]

Once more, these present several Catch 22 scenarios for Sirhan: How can you show remorse and insight into the crime when you can't remember what happened? And how can you accept full responsibility for the crime when you're still contesting the case, and the state's version of events has been superseded by new exculpatory evidence the courts refuse to hear?

The panel acknowledged that the evidence submitted did raise "provocative questions regarding what exactly transpired" on the night of the shooting but they are bound to accept the facts of Sirhan's conviction. They did not find Sirhan's "claim of memory loss to be credible, given his other testimony, his other recall and the testimony of others":

> We feel that you failed to [show] adequate signs of remorse and to accept full responsibility for your criminal actions. Perhaps you did better at the last hearing. I read in the last hearing you at least accepted responsibility for the shooting of the other victims. And today you didn't even do that. Today you indicated you were not responsible for anything. And we know those who don't take full responsibility for their criminal acts and those who do not show adequate signs of remorse, these people are likely to recidivate. And that makes you a current danger to the public safety.[80]

The panel recommended that he stay disciplinary-free and engage in self-help programs in anger management and alcohol use, as requested by the previous panel. Sirhan's claim that he didn't need anger management classes because he had learned to walk away in provocative situations, and his pledge to simply avoid alcohol in the future were not enough:

> You were unable to identify skillsets and coping mechanisms . . . that you could or would use should you find yourself in similar circumstances such as anger and being in a place where alcohol is being used . . . And absent those skillsets and coping mechanisms we feel you are a current risk of danger to public safety because you are likely to react as you have in the past.[81]

Sirhan was again denied for five years but can request an earlier hearing within three years if "there's been a change of circumstance or new information that establishes a reasonable likelihood that you don't require additional incarceration."[82]

* * *

As Sirhan got up to leave, Schrade reportedly shouted, "Sirhan, I'm so sorry this is happening to you. It's my fault." Sirhan tried to shake hands with Schrade but a guard blocked him. Schrade refused to shake hands with Commissioner Roberts, telling him, "What you've done to this man is appalling and Robert Kennedy would find what you did appalling" before turning away.[83]

Schrade found the hearing "very abusive" and upsetting. He later told reporters waiting outside that "Sirhan was being tortured in there." In a radio interview, he said the parole board was "cold and ruthless about keeping this guy in jail, knowing there's evidence [of his innocence] in the files". He found the panel's treatment of Sirhan "despicable," destroying his dignity with petty questions that made the commissioners "look like amateur psychiatrists."[84]

Robert Kennedy Jr. permitted Schrade to include his 2012 letter to Attorney General Holder in the documents submitted to the parole board, signalling publicly, for the first time, his support for a new investigation of his father's murder. "You're doing the right thing," he told Schrade, days before the Sirhan hearing.

Kennedy's book, *Framed*, challenging the murder conviction of his cousin Michael Skakel, was published five months after Sirhan's parole hearing. RFK Jr. reflects on his family's "plea to the judge" to spare his father's "alleged killer, Sirhan Sirhan . . . the death penalty," and the dangers of seeking vengeance, given the recent Van Praag audio discoveries:

> And what if, God forbid, the object of our revenge turns out to be innocent? For several decades, my father's close friend Paul Schrade, who took one of Sirhan's bullets, has argued that Sirhan Sirhan did not fire the shot that killed my father. Recent forensic evidence supports him. How would we have felt now, if our family had demanded his execution?[85]

While "pleased and honored" to meet Paul Schrade, Sirhan returned to his cell to find it "ransacked" and his belongings moved around. His next parole hearing is scheduled for February 2021.

* * *

Three months after the parole hearing, Dan Brown and Laurie Dusek paid their most recent visit to Sirhan. This time, they brought an MP3 player, following up a lead from the previous meeting. When they had asked Sirhan what he did in the evenings on the weekend before the assassination, Sirhan said he was on his shortwave radio:

> We reconstructed that Sirhan sat at his desk as home, and used a dangling crystal to hypnotize himself. This was verified by [Sirhan's brother] Munir. So, I simply told him to imagine the crystal and go into trance. While in trance, he spoke of "getting a strong signal" that was distinctive from someone on the radio, and while he said this, he started tapping out Morse code. Upon awakening, he claimed that he didn't know Morse code and was unaware of any tapping.[86]

Brown recorded ten general statements and ten inculpatory statements from Sirhan's notebook in Morse code. He played them back to Sirhan under hypnosis and watched as Sirhan recognized inculpatory statements such as "The time has come to take action . . . " and wrote them out in the same "automatic writing" style seen in his infamous notebooks. In his normal waking state, Sirhan couldn't remember doing the "automatic writing" and insisted he didn't know Morse code. Munir confirmed to Dr. Brown that he would hear Morse code coming from

Sirhan's short wave radio in the evenings. Sirhan would have a notebook and take notes.[87]

This, along with the discovery of the "range mode" alter personality, are major advances in what the Attorney General of California calls "Petitioner's fantastic hypnotic automaton theory." As Dr. Brown argues, given the documented history of mind control programming, "the fact that it may be 'fantastic' . . . does not mean that it is not true . . . Petitioner's theory is 'fantastic' only because [the AG] does not appear to be familiar with that history."[88]

According to Dr. Brown, one of the research projects conducted by US intelligence agencies in the early 1960s was to see if it was possible to create "unconscious couriers," where individuals would carry and disclose sensitive information to a target source without knowing they were doing so. Morse code was used in this research.[89]

* * *

2018 will mark the fiftieth anniversary of Robert Kennedy's death and fifty years of Sirhan's confinement. Next March, he will turn seventy-four years old. I tried to visit him recently but he doesn't want to see anyone except his brother and legal team. Laurie Dusek has never seen him so urgently seeking his release. "He doesn't want to wait another year for all the media around the anniversary to happen. He wants out now."

Aside from his job in prison, Sirhan listens to the radio, reads a lot and exercises. He told his brother Munir he does 500 sit-ups a day. He writes to Munir two or three times a week and Munir calls him occasionally, but the brothers haven't met for several years. His attorneys write him in prison but Sirhan is wary of visitors or giving interviews, having been used by reporters before, and fearing potential repercussions from prison officials or fellow inmates.[90]

In January 2015, Sirhan's habeas corpus petition was dismissed, without even an evidentiary hearing to assess the merits of the new evidence from Brown and Van Praag. Leave to appeal was denied by the federal court in the Central District of California, the US Court of Appeals for the Ninth Circuit and the Supreme Court, effectively ending Sirhan's hopes of a new trial in criminal court. The only domestic option remaining is a civil trial in California but this would cost several hundred thousand dollars. Even with Sirhan's attorneys continuing to work pro bono, they would have to pay for the judge, a venue, and travel and lodging for witnesses.[91]

Laurie Dusek sees Sirhan as a political prisoner whose rights are being denied and who cannot get a fair hearing in the US. Bill Pepper recently filed a petition with the Inter-American Commission on Human Rights, in the hope that Sirhan's case can be heard before the Inter-American Court, to at least get the facts on the record. The court has no jurisdiction in the US but could issue a judgment or opinion on the case for referral to US legal authorities.[92]

The District Attorney's Office never replied to Paul Schrade but D.A. Lacey recently created a Conviction Review Unit to examine wrongful convictions and claims of innocence based on new credible evidence that may exonerate them. But the decision not to review claims from those who previously confessed has drawn criticism from legal experts who say this "could eliminate the opportunity to exonerate someone who was coerced to falsely admit guilt." Sirhan's absurd "confession" in court–"I killed Robert Kennedy willfully, premeditatedly with 20 years of malice aforethought"—was dredged up again at his 2016 hearing and continues to hang over his case, taken out of context and tracing the planning for the assassination back to a four-year-old Sirhan in war-torn Jerusalem.[93]

The best hope for a new investigation–and justice for Sirhan and Bobby Kennedy–is media exposure and Kennedy family intervention. A major new documentary series on the case is currently in production, backed by Showtime, Netflix and Robert Redford's Sundance Productions, and directed by award-winning filmmaker Dawn Porter. It will feature Dan Brown's work as well as interviews with Paul Schrade and Munir Sirhan, and is scheduled to air on the fiftieth anniversary. Paul Schrade tells me Robert Kennedy Jr. is also ready to go public and give media interviews expressing his support for reopening the case. His direct intervention, combined with the documentary series, may finally stir California authorities into action.

Meanwhile, Sirhan will continue to work with Dr. Brown and his attorneys to solve the mystery of what happened to him almost fifty years ago. It's been a heroic effort to keep his case going, pro bono, for so long and his team have incurred significant personal expenses, as no-one has stepped forward to financially support Sirhan's defense. The release of the remaining JFK assassination records this year and the anniversary year coverage of the RFK case in 2018 may finally lead to public acceptance that the Kennedy assassinations were more complex than they seemed, and that one of the victims is still being held in prison in San Diego. Whether there's the political will to do anything about that remains to be seen. I would argue that even if you believe Sirhan is guilty as charged, he has now served his time. If released, he would be deported to Jordan and would be a danger to nobody.

BIBLIOGRAPHY

ARCHIVE COLLECTIONS

California State Archives (CSA), Sacramento, CA
Burns, Frank. Written statement. June 12, 1968.

Firearms panel. Firearms examiner worksheets, panel evidence inventory, photographs, and special exhibits; individual examiner reports (October 4, 1975) and Initial and Comprehensive Joint Reports of the Firearms Examiners (October 3–4, 1975).

Firearms panel. Order for Retesting of Exhibits, *People v. Sirhan*. September 18, 1975.

Firearms panel. Order for Retesting of Exhibits (Order No. 5), September 26, 1975.

LAPD. Records relating to reinvestigations of the assassination. Microfilm roll 22, including unpublished "Reply to Questions Submitted by Allard K. Lowenstein" (December 20, 1974). LAPD. Records of the Wolfer Board of Inquiry. Microfilm rolls 23–24.

Sirhan, Sirhan B. Notebooks. Photocopies.

Sirhan, Sirhan B. Writing on legal pad in psychiatric sessions. Photocopies.

Special Unit Senator (SUS), Detective Bureau, Los Angeles Police Department (LAPD). Investigation Files. Microfilm rolls 4–11, 15–20.

Special Unit Senator (SUS), Detective Bureau, Los Angeles Police Department (LAPD). *An Investigation Summary of the Robert F. Kennedy Assassination, The Final Report*. February 1969. Microfilm roll 12.

Timanson, Uno. Written statement. June 6, 1968.

Federal Bureau of Investigation, Washington, DC
Records of the FBI Investigation into the Assassination of Senator Robert F. Kennedy, Code Name KENSALT. FBI files 56–156 and 62–587. CD-ROM. 1968–1969.

The Report of Thomas F. Kranz on the Assassination of Senator Robert F. Kennedy. March 1977.

John F. Kennedy Presidential Library and Museum, Boston, MA (JFK Library)
Amory, Robert. Oral history interview.

Los Angeles County Superior Court Archives

Los Angeles County Clerk records relating to the Sirhan B. Sirhan case, 1969–1976.

Wenke, Robert (superior court judge). Hearing testimony. *People v. Sirhan.*

Wolfer testimony at Wenke hearings. *People v. Sirhan.* September 16–18, 1975.

National Archives, College Park, MD

Freedom of Information Act releases under the President John F. Kennedy Assassination Records Collection Act of 1992 (JFK Records Act) regarding David Sanchez Morales, George Joannides, Bradley Ayers, and the Directorio Revolucionario Estudantil (or Revolutionary Student Directorate, DRE).

Robert F. Kennedy Assassination Archives, University of Massachusetts, Dartmouth (RFKAA)

Crahan, Dr. Marcus. Report to District Attorney Evelle Younger regarding Sirhan B. Sirhan. February 20, 1969. With transcript of sessions.

Criminal case no. 14026. *The People of Los Angeles County v. Sirhan Bishara Sirhan.* Convened January 6, 1969, and concluded with a conviction on April 17, 1969.

Harper, William. Statement to American Academy of Forensic Sciences. February 19, 1975.

Langman, Betsy. Research notes.

Los Angeles County Superior Court. Proceedings of *The People of Los Angeles County v. Sirhan Bishara Sirhan.* February 5–April 17, 1969. Clerk's Transcript of the Court Trial.

Lubic, Richard. Written statement to American Academy of Forensic Sciences. February 1975.

Melanson, Phillip. Research notes.

Moldea, Dan. Research notes.

Proceedings of the Los Angeles County Grand Jury, June 7, 1968. Transcript.

Sharaga, Paul. Interview with Art Kevin, KMPC, Los Angeles, December 20, 1974. Transcript.

Uecker, Karl. Written statement to Allard Lowenstein. February 20, 1975.

Urso, Lisa. Statement to DA's office investigator William Burnett. August 10, 1977.

Rose Lynn Mangan Collection, www.sirhansresearcher.com

Mangan, Rose Lynn. Robert F. Kennedy/Sirhan Evidence Report. 1996.

Simson, Dr. Eduard. Affidavit.

Other rare documents regarding the assassination of RFK.

Other Documents

Bradley, Omar N. Bulova Trip Diaries. May–June 1968. United States Military Academy Library, West Point, NY.

Harper, William. Affidavit, December 28, 1970. Printed in Turner and Christian, *Assassination of Robert F. Kennedy*, appendix.

Harper, William. "Notes on *People vs Sirhan*." January 1, 1971. Published in *Los Angeles Free Press*, January 21, 1971.

Hecker, Dr. Michael. Written statement. Witnessed by Robert Joling. December 15, 1982.

Rockefeller Commission. Report of the Rockefeller Commission on CIA Activities Within the United States. June 1975.

Sirhan, Sirhan B. Legal pad writings recalling his movements at the Ambassador Hotel and striking a deal with President Johnson, nd. Courtesy of Michael McCowan.

Sharaga, Paul (sergeant, LAPD). Copy of original report for Captain Phillips. June 5, 1968. Sharaga, Paul. Notarized written declaration. July 25, 1991.

Sharaga, Paul. Written statement. November 17, 1992.

Teeter, Lawrence. (2nd) Petition for Writ of Habeas Corpus. Filed with the Supreme Court of California. July 19, 2002.

Witness statements. Obtained by Vincent T. Bugliosi. Printed in the appendix of Turner and Christian, *Assassination of Robert F. Kennedy*, and comprising statements from William Bailey (November 14, 1976), Angelo Di Pierro (December 1, 1975), Thomas Noguchi (December 1, 1975), Martin Patrusky (December 12, 1975), and Robert Rozzi (November 15, 1975).

PICTURE AND SOUND ARCHIVE COLLECTIONS

While making my film and writing this book, I was helped immensely by senior news writer and journalist Brad Johnson, who has amassed the most comprehensive sound and image archive in existence regarding the assassination of Robert Kennedy. Thanks also go to Dave Hawkins at the Collector's Archives, Quebec, Canada.

Selected Audio

Barrett, Marilyn. Interview with Manuel Pena. September 12, 1992.

Black Op Radio. Interviews with Phil Van Praag (August 9, 2007) and William Pepper (October 11, 2007). www.blackopradio.com/archives2007.html

Brent, Jeff. Recordings made at the Ambassador Hotel. June 5, 1968.

Burnett, William. Interview with William Bailey. 1977. RFKAA.

Frank, Barbara. Recordings made at the Ambassador Hotel. June 5, 1968.

Langman, Betsy. Interviews with Grant Cooper, Frank Hendrix, Roger La Jeunesse, Russell Parsons, Don Schulman, Paul Sharaga, Dr. Herbert Spiegel. Various dates, 1971–1976. RFKAA.

LAPD. Interviews of Sirhan in custody. June 5, 1968. CSA.

LAPD. Logging tapes. June 4–5, 1968. Courtesy CSA/Phil Van Praag.

LAPD. Witness interviews. Various dates. CSA.

LAPD. Reinterview with Jack Merritt. July 26, 1971.

Los Angeles County District Attorney's Office. Reinterview with Thane Cesar. July 14, 1971.

Los Angeles County District Attorney's Office. Reinterview with Don Schulman. July 23, 1971. Marshall, John. Recordings made at the Ambassador Hotel. June 5, 1968.

Pruzynski, Stas. Recordings made at the Ambassador Hotel. June 5, 1968.

Rather, Dan. Interviews with Frank Burns and Boris Yaro for the CBS documentary *The American Assassins*. January 1976.

Schulman, Don. Interview with Special Counsel Thomas Kranz. October 24, 1975.

Simson, Dr. Eduard. Interview with Mae Brussell. June 13, 1977.

Sirhan, Sirhan B. Psychiatric sessions with Dr. Diamond, Dr. Pollack, and Robert Blair Kaiser. Various dates, January–February 1969. CSA and RFKAA.

West, Andrew. Recordings made at the Ambassador Hotel. June 5, 1968.

Selected Video

The Assassination of Robert Kennedy, Tim Tate for Channel 4 and A&E. 1992.

Conspiracy Test: The RFK Assassination. Discovery Times Channel. June 6, 2007.

Dr. Robert Joling Lecture on RFK case at Arizona University. Featuring Dr. Thomas Noguchi and Dr. Herbert McDonell. 1975.

Frost, David. Interview with Sirhan B. Sirhan. Broadcast on *Inside Edition*. 1989.

LAPD. Witness reconstructions. 1968 and 1977. CSA and RFKAA.

The Life and Death of RFK. Channel 4 Eye-Witness News. San Francisco. 1988.

Perkins, Jack (NBC reporter). Interview with Sirhan. Recorded May 22, 1969. Broadcast as *First Tuesday: The Mind of an Assassin*. June 3, 1969.

"The RFK Assassination: Shadows of Doubt." *A Current Affair*. 1992.

R.F.K. Must Die: The Assassination of Bobby Kennedy. Shane O'Sullivan. Dokument Films. 2007.

RFK segment. *BBC Newsnight*. November 20, 2006.

The R.F.K. Story. Fox. 1988.

The Robert Kennedy Assassination. Tim Tate for Channel 4. 1992.

Spiegel, Herbert. *Fact or Fiction*. Columbia University Film Series. 1967.

Special Unit Senator. Appendix C: List of Motion Picture Films, including SUS composite film. CSA.

The Second Gun. Alcan/Charach. 1973.

Television coverage of the California Democratic primary, RFK's speech, and the shooting aftermath: ABC, BBC, CBS, KCRA, KNXT, KTLA, KTTV, NBC.

Unsolved History: The RFK Assassination. Discovery Channel. 2005.

Unsolved Mysteries: A Second Gun in the RFK Assassination. NBC. 1990.

Vanocur, Sander. NBC interviews with Robert Kennedy (June 4, 1968) and Sandra Serrano (June 5, 1968).

"Who Really Killed Robert Kennedy?" *Now It Can Be Told*. 1992.

NEWSPAPERS AND JOURNALS

Boston Herald American
Chicago Tribune
Granma Internacional
The Guardian
Jewelers Circular
Keystone Life
Long Beach Press Telegram
Los Angeles Herald Examiner
Los Angeles Sentinel
Los Angeles Times
Miami Herald
Miami New Times
The Nation
New York Times
Pasadena Independent Star-News
Pasadena Star-News
Pasadena Weekly
Playboy
Riverside Press-Enterprise
Salon.com
San Fernando Valley Times
Santa Monica Evening Outlook
Science Digest
Washington Post
USA Today

BOOKS AND ARTICLES

Ayers, Bradley Earl. *The War That Never Was.* Indianapolis: Bobbs Merrill, 1976.

Ayers, Bradley E. *The Zenith Secret.* New York: Vox Pop, 2006.

Ayton, Mel. "Did the CIA Kill Bobby Kennedy? The BBC's Blunder." History News Network. www.hnn.us

Ayton, Mel. *The Forgotten Terrorist.* Dulles, VA: Potomac Books, 2007.

Bain, Donald. *The CIA's Control of Candy Jones.* Fort Lee, NJ: Barricade Books, 2002.

Blum, William. "Killing Hope: US Military and CIA Interventions Since World War II." www.killinghope.org

Bohning, Don. *The Castro Obsession.* Dulles, VA: Potomac Books, 2005.

Bowart, Walter. *Operation Mind Control.* Glasgow: Fontana/Collins, 1978.

Bradley, Omar N. *A General's Life.* New York: Simon and Schuster, 1983.

Calder, Michael. *JFK vs. CIA.* Los Angeles: West LA Publishers, 1998.

Cannon, Martin. "The Controllers." www.whale.to/b/cannon.html

Charach, Theodore. "Why Sirhan Could Not Have Killed Robert Kennedy." *Knave*, March and April, 1976.

Christian, Jonn. "California Assassination Archives—Robert F. Kennedy: A Special Report." *Easy Reader*, November 17, 1988.

Christian, Jonn. "Fatal Connections." Book proposal. 1992.

Connery, Donald S. *The Inner Source: Exploring Hypnosis with Dr. Herbert Spiegel.* New York: Holt Rinehart Winston, 1984.

Corn, David. *Blond Ghost.* New York: Simon and Schuster, 1994.

DiEugenio, James, and Lisa Pease. *The Assassinations.* Los Angeles: Feral House, 2003.

Divale, William Tulio. *I Lived Inside the Campus Revolution.* New York: Cowles Book Company, 1970.

Emery, Carla. *Secret, Don't Tell.* www.hypnotism.org

Eppridge, Bill, and Hays Gorey. *The Last Campaign.* New York: Harcourt Brace, 1993.

Estabrooks, G.H. *The Future of the Human Mind.* London: Museum Press, 1961.

Estabrooks, G.H. *Hypnotism.* New York: E.P. Dutton, 1957.

Evans, Peter. *Nemesis.* New York: Regan Books, 2004.

Frank, Gerold. *The Boston Strangler.* London: Pan Books, 1983.

Fonzi, Gaeton. *The Last Investigation.* New York: Thunder's Mouth Press, 1993.

Garland, Patrick, ed. *AFTE Journal: Special Edition on RFK Firearms Panel* 8, 3 (October 1976).

Griffin, Booker. "Fatalism, Destiny: Fear Now Real." *L.A. Sentinel*, June 5.

"Guarding the Dream." *Time*, June 8, 1988.

Hancock, Larry. *Someone Would Have Talked.* Southlake, TX: JFK Lancer, 2003.

Hedegaard, Erik. "The Last Confessions of E. Howard Hunt." *Rolling Stone*, March 23, 2007.

Heymann, David C. *RFK.* New York: Dutton, 1998.

Hinckle, Warren, and William Turner. *Deadly Secrets.* New York: Thunder's Mouth Press, 1992.

Houghton, Robert A. *Special Unit Senator.* New York: Random House, 1970.

Isaac, Godfrey. *I'll See You in Court.* Chicago: Contemporary Books, 1979.

Jansen, Godfrey. *Why Robert Kennedy Was Killed.* New York: Third Press, 1970.

Johnson, Haynes. *The Bay of Pigs.* New York: W.W. Norton, 1964.

Kaiser, Robert Blair. *"R.F.K. Must Die!"* New York: E. P. Dutton, 1970.

Kaiser, Robert B. "Sirhan in Jail." *Life*, January 17, 1969.

Klaber, William, and Philip Melanson. *Shadow Play.* New York: St. Martin's Press, 1998.

Kroger, William S. *Clinical and Experimental Hypnosis in Medicine, Dentistry and Psychology.* Philadelphia: J. B. Lippincott, 1977.

Lane, Mark. *Plausible Denial.* New York: Thunder's Mouth Press, 1991.

Langguth, A. J. *Hidden Terrors.* New York: Pantheon Books, 1978.

Langman, Betsy, and Alexander Cockburn. "Sirhan's Gun." *Harper's*, January 1975.

Maheu, Robert. *Next to Hughes.* New York: Harper Paperbacks, 1992.

Mangold, Tom. *Cold Warrior.* London: Simon and Schuster, 1993.

Marcuse. F. L. *Hypnosis: Fact and Fiction.* London: Penguin Books, 1976.

Matte, James Allan. *Forensic Psychophysiology Using the Polygraph: Scientific Truth Verification—Lie Detection.* Williamsville, NY: J.A.M. Publications, 1996.

McClintock, Michael. *Instruments of Statecraft.* www.statecraft.org/

McQuen, J. M. *The Psychiatrist in the Courtroom: Selected Papers of Bernard L. Diamond, M.D.* Hillsdale, NJ: Analytic Press, 1994.

Melanson, Philip H. "The CIA's Secret Ties to Local Police." *Nation*, March 26, 1983.

Melanson, Philip H. *The Robert F. Kennedy Assassination.* New York: Shapolsky, 1991.

"The Men Who Didn't Talk." *Playboy*, December 2007.

Milstein, Uri. *History of Israel's War of Independence.* Vol. 2. Lanham, MD: University Press of America, 1997.

Moldea, Dan E. *The Killing of Robert Kennedy.* New York: W. W. Norton, 1995.

Moldea, Dan E. "Who Really Killed Bobby Kennedy?" *Regardie's*, June 1987.

Morley, Jefferson. "Celebrated Authors Demand That the CIA Come Clean on JFK Assassination." Salon.com. December 17, 2003.

Morley, Jefferson. "Revelation 19.62." *Miami New Times*, April 12, 2001.

Morley, Jefferson, and David Talbot. "The BBC's Flawed RFK Story." Mary Ferrell Foundation. www.maryferrell.org

Morrow, Robert D. *The Senator Must Die.* Santa Monica, CA: Roundtable Publishing, 1988.

Noguchi, Thomas A. *Coroner.* New York: Simon and Schuster, 1993.

Noyes. Peter. *Legacy of Doubt.* New York: Pinnacle Books, 1973.

O'Sullivan, Shane. "Did These Men Kill Bobby Kennedy?" *Guardian.* November 20, 2006.

Pena, Manuel S. *Practical Criminal Investigation.* 4th ed. Incline Village, NV: Copperhouse Publishing, 1997.

Pepper, William F. *An Act of State.* London: Verso, 2003.

Plimpton, George, and Jean Stein. *American Journey: The Times of Robert Kennedy.* New York:

Harcourt Brace Jovanovich, 1970.

Powers, Thomas. *The Man Who Kept the Secrets.* New York: Alfred A. Knopf, 1979.

Rappleye, Charles, and Ed Becker. *All American Mafioso: The Johnny Rosselli Story.* New York: Doubleday, 1991.

Richelsen, Jeffrey T. *Wizards of Langley.* Boulder, CO: Westview, 2001.

Rogers, Warren. *When I Think of Bobby.* New York: Harper Collins, 1993.

Ross, Colin A. *Bluebird.* Richardson, TX: Manitou Communications, 2000.

Russo, Gus. *Live by the Sword*. Baltimore: Bancroft Press, 1998.

Salinger, Pierre. *P.S. A Memoir*. New York: St. Martin's Press, 1995.

Schlesinger, Arthur M., Jr. *Robert Kennedy and His Times*. London: Futura Publications, 1979.

Seigenthaler, John. *A Search for Justice*. Nashville: Aurora Publishers, 1971.

Shackley, Ted. *Spymaster: My Life in the CIA*. Dulles, VA: Potomac Books, 2005.

Stone, Gregory. *Selected Corrections of the Report of Special Counsel Krantz*. July 27, 1977. Collector's Archives.

Summers, Anthony. *Official and Confidential: The Secret Life of J. Edgar Hoover*. London: Corgi Books, 1994.

Talbot, David. *Brothers: The Hidden History of the Kennedy Years*. New York: Free Press, 2007.

Turner, William, and Jonn Christian. *The Assassination of Robert F. Kennedy*. New York: Random House, 1978.

Twyman, Noel. *Bloody Treason*. Rancho Santa Fe, CA: Laurel Publishing, 1997.

Wilcox, Desmond. *Americans*. New York: Delacorte Press, 1978.

Witcover, Jules. *85 Days*. New York: Ace Publishing, 1969.

ACKNOWLEDGMENTS
TO THE 2008 EDITION

Revisiting the hope and turmoil of America in 1968 with the many contributors to this book has been a deeply rewarding experience. My accidental foray into criminal investigation has brought lasting and cherished friendships born of shared values and a desire and need for justice after all these years.

I've had two "godfathers" since the start, sending support and encouragement from the hills above Los Angeles and the woods of Wisconsin. Paul Schrade and Bradley Ayers were left physically and emotionally scarred by their experiences in the Ambassador pantry and at JMWAVE, respectively. But for most of my lifetime, they have fought deeply felt crusades to find answers to the mysteries behind the deaths of John and Robert Kennedy. I have tremendous admiration for them both.

I have also been blessed by my friendship with David Rabern, who's been an invaluable sounding board through the twists and turns of my investigation.

My thanks, too, to Robert Blair Kaiser, through whose captivating book *"R.F.K. Must Die!"* the mysteries of this case first took hold. Kaiser has encouraged me throughout, first during the making of my film, then in this book, by sharing key materials. Kaiser was personally present at the defense psychiatrist's recorded interviews with Sirhan and reported on them extensively in his book. Kaiser has graciously given me broad leeway to use the transcripts of those interviews here.

I am grateful to *BBC Newsnight* editor Peter Barron for his courage in commissioning my initial story, producer Simon Enright for helping bring it to the screen, and George Dougherty, my cameraman, for his support and second opinion as we crisscrossed America.

Thanks to Phil Daoust at the *Guardian* for commissioning a feature on the BBC story that set the blogs chatting about the case again, and to Greg Newman at MPI for helping my feature documentary *R.F.K. Must Die* get to the finish line.

I'm very grateful to witnesses such as Sandra Serrano, Frank Burns, Vincent Di Pierro, and Evan Freed, who agreed to relive their experiences at the Ambassador Hotel again, however painful; and I respect Michael McCowan for not dodging the difficult questions.

Warm regards to Genevieve Troka and the extremely dedicated staff at the California State Archives, whose willingness to explore even the most arcane detail was much appreciated. Thanks, too, to Pat Sikora for being such a wonderful host on my visit to the RFK Assassination Archives at UMass Dartmouth, and to Judy Farrar for allowing me to scan the Sirhan trial transcript to PDF instead of camping out for weeks in New Bedford.

My sincere thanks to journalist Brad Johnson, whose huge video and audio archive helped unlock the mystery of Gordon Campbell, et al. *Abrazos* to Manuel Chavez for his determined efforts to find the truth on my behalf and to Don Bohning for putting us together. I also salute Patrick Garland and Stanton Berg for talking me through the workings of the 1975 firearms panel.

Thanks to Michael Calder for his digging at the Superior Court Archives and to Rose Lynn Mangan for sharing her vast archive and insights on the history of the case and the history of the evidence. I'm sorry I could not include more of this material here.

As each year passes, more heroes of the struggle to tell this story slip away. I salute the work of Larry Teeter, Jonn Christian, Philip Melanson, and William Bailey, all of whom passed away while I was working on this project.

I'm grateful to the families of David Morales and Michael Roman for candidly addressing serious allegations about loved ones with a refreshing openness. I also thank Phil Van Praag, Malcolm Blunt, John Simkin, James Richards, Betsy Langman, Wayne Smith, Ed Wilson, Dr. Herbert Spiegel, Dan Hardway, Leslie Brittain, Larry Hancock, Ed Lopez, Tom Clines, Ruben Carbajal, Robert Walton, Mark Sobel, Marilyn Barrett, Robert Joling, Summer Reese, and William Pepper for their help along the way.

I'm grateful to Munir Sirhan for agreeing to speak about a case that has haunted him every day for forty years. I hope the new psychiatric evaluations with Sirhan are the first step toward clarity for us all.

Finally, huge thanks to the team at Union Square Press who shepherded me through the writing of my first book with great skill and understanding. I first met editorial director Philip Turner over breakfast in New York at the end of my first research trip and intuitively sensed he "got it." Two years later, Philip had the vision to see the resonance this story has for a contemporary audience. I thank him for his patience and advice. Also, kudos to John F. Baker for his judicious and sensitive cutting as we worked together to edit the manuscript; Eileen Chetti for her meticulous project management; Iris Blasi for keeping everything on track; Chrissy Kwasnik for her design and layout; and Becky Maines for coordinating all their efforts.

I am very grateful to Tony Lyons and the team at Skyhorse for publishing the second edition of this book as we approach the fiftieth anniversary of the assassination and reassess the true nature of this tragic event and its cost to the country. Special thanks to Caroline Russomanno and her team for supervising the reformatting of the manuscript and adding the new epilogue and images.

INDEX

ABOUT THE AUTHOR

Shane O'Sullivan is an Irish author and filmmaker based in London. His work includes the acclaimed documentaries *RFK Must Die* (2007), *Children of the Revolution* (2010) and *Killing Oswald* (2013), and the forthcoming book *Dirty Tricks* (2018). He holds a PhD in Film from Roehampton University and is a Senior Lecturer in Filmmaking at Kingston School of Art, London. He blogs about the case at *whokilledbobby.net*.

ENDNOTES

Chapter 1

1. Photocopy of page from Sirhan's notebook, CSA. Sirhan practiced self-hypnosis by candlelight in front of a mirror in his room. Defense psychiatrist Dr. Diamond concluded that he wrote this page during one such hypnotic session.

2. Kennedy had entered the presidential race on March 16, four days after McCarthy's strong showing against incumbent President Johnson in New Hampshire. Johnson announced that he wouldn't run for a second term on March 31. By June, Vice President Hubert Humphrey led in the delegate count, but Kennedy and McCarthy marshaled the support of the burgeoning antiwar movement. If Kennedy could beat McCarthy and win his support ahead of the Chicago convention, he stood a strong chance of gaining the Democratic nomination.

3. "Kennedy Hints at Withdrawal If He Loses in California Test," *Los Angeles Times*, May 30.

4. Witcover, *85 Days*, 250–51.

5. Salinger, *P.S. A Memoir*, 185–87; Schlesinger, *Robert Kennedy*, 968.

6. The LAPD final report lists Sirhan as five-two, 115 pounds. His LAPD booking form states his height as five-three, and several hours later, Dr. Crahan recorded his height as five-two-and-a-half. Sirhan claimed he was five-four-and-a-half during the trial (Sirhan trial testimony, 4881). On timings: Sirhan testified that he got up around nine or ten (Sirhan trial testimony, 5145), but his brother Munir saw him buying a newspaper around eight thirty (Munir Sirhan, FBI interview, June 5), and the LAPD activity chart for Sirhan (LAPD, 618) quotes his mother, Mary Sirhan, as saying he drove off for a paper around eight o'clock. According to the LAPD activity chart, Sirhan answered the phone at home at eleven o'clock. At trial, Sirhan said he then bought some ammunition, stopped off for coffee, and arrived at the gun range around noon. The police have him going straight to the gun range and arriving between eleven and eleven thirty (LAPD, 602). Richard Grijalva signed in below Sirhan and arrived at noon. As soon as Grijalva arrived, he saw a man closely resembling Sirhan shooting rapid-fire on the pistol range (Richard Grijalva LAPD interview, July 2). Based on the above data, I estimate Sirhan's arrival as "about eleven thirty."

7. Witcover, *85 Days*, 253; LAPD, 121. Dutton, a veteran of the JFK administration, made decisions on the road, while Kennedy's brother-in-law Steve Smith was his campaign manager.

8. Witcover, *85 Days*, 254. 7

9. LAPD, 619.

10. Kaiser, *"R.F.K. Must Die!"* 15; LAPD, 121–22; Witcover, *85 Days*, 255. According to the police, Kennedy arrived at the hotel at eight fifteen (LAPD, 137). Frankenheimer timed it as 8:05 (John Frankenheimer LAPD interview, July 18).

11. Dutton-Kennedy chat before TV interview. The vote count was delayed because the new IBM computers weren't scanning the punch cards correctly. Los Angeles County was home to 38 percent of voter registrations (Witcover, *85 Days*, 255).

12. Witcover, *85 Days*, 257.

13. LAPD, 136.

14. LAPD, 138, 620. I doubt the police timing for Bidstrup's encounter with Sirhan and discuss it further in Chapter 9. On "sneaking in the back way," see Albert Soifer LAPD interview, July 15.

15. Mary Grohs LAPD interviews (July 22, 1968, and February 25, 1969); Kaiser, *"R.F.K. Must Die!"* 531–32. In her first police interview, Grohs stated that she spoke to Sirhan between nine thirty and eleven. During the trial, she was reinterviewed and apparently narrowed the time frame to between

nine thirty and ten. Robert Houghton, who led the police investigation, later stuck with the wider time frame in his book (Houghton, *Special Unit Senator*, 224). So do I.

16. Kaiser, *"R.F.K. Must Die!"* 16.

17. NBC footage of Kennedy-Vanocur off-air conversation, June 4.

18. CBS and NBC network coverage of the California primary. Around 11:10, CBS projected a Kennedy victory by 50 percent to McCarthy's 38 percent. Around 11:50, NBC had Kennedy ahead by 49 percent to 40 percent.

19. Kennedy aide David Hackett calculated that after the double victory that night, "Humphrey [had] 944 delegates; Kennedy 524.5; McCarthy, 204; 872 undecided. The objective by convention time was 1432.5 for Kennedy, 1152.5 for Humphrey. . . . The key was McCarthy . . . 'his people must know after tonight that I'm the only candidate against the war that can beat Humphrey,'" said Kennedy (Schlesinger, *Robert Kennedy*, 981).

20. Sandra Serrano interviews with NBC and LAPD, June 5, and FBI, June 7.

21. Jesus Perez LAPD interview, June 5; Perez grand jury testimony, June 7; Martin Patrusky written statement to Vincent Bugliosi, December 12, 1975, in which he recalled first seeing Sirhan twenty minutes before the shooting.

22. Sharaga written statement, November 17, 1992.

23. Timanson written statement, June 6; LAPD, 143.

24. Videotape of ABC live video feed.

25. TV footage. The LAPD used CBS television coverage to confirm the time Kennedy entered the ballroom as 12:02:10 a.m. He began his speech thirty seconds later and turned to leave the stage at 12:14:47 a.m. (Cecil Lynch LAPD interview, June 18). According to the LAPD, the shooting began at 12:16 a.m.

26. Patrusky FBI statement, June 7.

27. Network footage of the Kennedy speech.

28. Network footage of Kennedy leaving the stage; LAPD, 146–47.

29. Frank Burns written statement, June 12; Karl Uecker grand jury testimony; Thane Eugene Cesar LAPD interview transcript, June 5.

30. Patrusky LAPD interview transcript, June 5; Vincent Di Pierro FBI interview, June 7; Robin Casden LAPD interview, July 1.

31. Perez LAPD interview transcript, June 5; For Romero, see "Guarding the Dream," *Time*, June 8, 1988.

32. Uecker trial testimony, 3091–97.

33. Lisa Urso LAPD interview, June 27; Melanson, *Robert F. Kennedy Assassination*, 18–19, 122–28.

34. Richard Lubic "observed an arm with a gun, come up and point at the Senator's head" (Lubic LAPD interview, July 17); Pete Hamill saw Sirhan's "arm fully extended and his face in tremendous concentration" (Hamill FBI interview, August 5). Martin Patrusky, Juan Romero, and Vincent Di Pierro also said Sirhan "looked like he was smiling." (Patrusky LAPD interview transcript, June 5; Juan Romero FBI interview, June 6; Di Pierro grand jury testimony, July 7).

35. Richard Lubic FBI interview, June 25. Lubic heard a voice say, "Kennedy, you son of a bitch," and heard two shots that sounded like a starter pistol at a track meet. For Urso, see Kaiser, *"R.F.K. Must Die!"* 26.

36. Jimmy Breslin FBI interview, June 20; Bob Funk FBI interview, June 21; Paul Schrade FBI interview, June 7.

37. Freddy Plimpton FBI interview, July 1.

38. Schrade FBI interview, June 7. Casden LAPD interview; Di Pierro FBI interview; Patrusky LAPD interview. Casden told police "the man who fell beside me [Schrade] was either hit by the first or second shot, because there were two definite shots and someone fell." Schrade was heavily sedated on June 7 after the shooting and surprised at the detail in his FBI summary. He later told author Dan Moldea that he was "four or five feet" behind Kennedy (Moldea, *Killing of Robert Kennedy*, 34; Schrade, interview with the author).

39. Cesar LAPD interview transcript, June 5.

40. LAPD, 155; Uecker grand jury testimony, June 7; Burns written statement, June 12; Eddie Minasian FBI statement, June 7.

41. Burns LAPD interview, June 19; Romero LAPD interview transcript, June 5; Perez LAPD interview transcript, June 5.

42. Ira Goldstein FBI interview, June 6; William Weisel FBI interview, June 7; Evans FBI interview, June 6; LAPD, 179–83.

43. Jesse Unruh FBI interview, June 13; Kaiser, *"R.F.K. Must Die!"* 27; LAPD, 156; Jack Gallivan FBI interview, June 14; George Plimpton FBI interview, June 27. 15 "Get a rope": Burns written statement, June 12; George Plimpton LAPD interview, June 5; Cesar FBI interview, June 10; LAPD, 155. 15 "Paul Schrade lay on the floor": LAPD, 177.

44. John William Lewis FBI interview, June 28; James Wilson LAPD statement, June 21; CBS footage of the pantry in the aftermath of the shooting. On "Fuck America" comment, see Jack Newfield interview in "The RFK Assassination: Shadows of Doubt."

45. West recordings, June 5; network footage and photographs of the chaos in the pantry collected by SUS.

46. Romero FBI interview, June 6; "'I Want to Be Dreaming, Busboy Says,'" *Los Angeles Times*, June 6; Romero LAPD interview, June 17.

47. Paul Grieco LAPD interview, July 30.

48. "Shocked Aide Clutched Shoes and Wouldn't Give Them Up," *Boston Globe*, June 6; Hugh McDonald LAPD statement, June 21; Fred Dutton LAPD interview, June 5.

49. Bill Barry LAPD interview, June 5, and FBI interview, June 19; Rosey Grier FBI interview, June 11; Rafer Johnson FBI interview, June 13.

50. Gallivan FBI interview, June 14; Earl Williman summary in LAPD, 1214–15.

51. Goldstein LAPD interview transcript, June 5; LAPD, 182–83; Kaiser, *"R.F.K. Must Die!"* 29.

52. Kaiser, *"R.F.K. Must Die!"* 30. Dr. Stanley Abo LAPD interview, July 24.

53. "Bobby's Last, Longest Day," *Newsweek*, June 17; West recordings; Johnson FBI interview.

54. George Plimpton LAPD interview; Jimmy Breslin LAPD interview, June 20.

55. Booker Griffin, "Fatalism, Destiny: Fear Now Real," *L.A. Sentinel*, June 5; Gabor Kadar LAPD interview, July 30.

56. Unruh FBI interview, June 13.

57. Johnson FBI interview.

58. Michael Wayne LAPD interview, July 25; LAPD, 432, 910, 1028; Juan Anguiano FBI interview, June 11; Fontanini LAPD interview, June 28. Ace security guard August Mallard in an LAPD interview (July 8) said that there was no gun hidden in the rolled-up posters.

59. Serrano interviews with NBC and LAPD, June 5; and FBI, June 7

60. LAPD, 186. Schiller recalled "answering several telephone calls from unknown persons wishing to speak to the watch commander . . . minutes prior to hearing the radio call of the shooting at the Ambassador" at 12:20 (Schiller LAPD interview, November 13).

61. LAPD, 197, 201; LAPD audiotape of emergency call from the Ambassador, CSA.

62. Transcript of Sharaga interview with Kevin, RFKAA; Sharaga written statement, November 17, 1992; Moldea, *Killing of Robert Kennedy*, 40; audiotape of LAPD radio dispatches, June 5, CSA; LAPD, 198.

63. Timanson written statement, June 6; Kaiser, *"R.F.K. Must Die!"* 34.

64. Placencia and White trial testimony, February 18–20, 1969.

65. Max Behrman LAPD interview, July 5; ambulance driver Robert Hulsman LAPD interview, July 15; Witcover, *85 Days*, 273.

66. Transcript of Sharaga interview with Kevin, RFKAA; Sharaga written statement, November 17, 1992; Moldea, *Killing of Robert Kennedy*, 40; audiotape of LAPD radio dispatches, June 5, CSA.

67. White and Placencia trial and grand jury testimony; Unruh FBI interview, June 13.

68. Behrman LAPD interview, July 5; Hulsman LAPD interview, July 15; LAPD, 165–66.

69. Witcover, *85 Days*, 276.

70. West recordings.

Chapter 2

1. Audio recording of Don Schulman interview with Jeff Brent (Brent recordings), June 5; Klaber and Melanson, *Shadow Play*, 118. According to journalist Brad Johnson, the Brent-Schulman interview began at 12:40 a.m.

2. Johnson noted that KLA reporter Phil Cogan read out a UPI wire report on air at 12:52 a.m., quoting Schulman as saying that Kennedy "was shot three times by a gunman who stepped out of the crowd" and that the gunman himself was then shot by Kennedy bodyguards and taken into custody. *France Soir*, July 5, as cited by Gerard Alcan in *The Second Gun*; Moldea, *Killing of Robert F. Kennedy*, 146.

3. Audio recording of Cesar interview with John Marshall (Marshall recordings), June 5. Johnson times this at 12:30 a.m.

4. LAPD, 307; Kaiser, *"R.F.K. Must Die!"* 41. Chief Houghton later regretted this omission at an interagency meeting with Bill Nolan (FBI), U.S. Attorney Matt Byrne, Deputy DAs Howard and Fitts, and others on September 5. Notes of the meeting have him state, "Re our critique of the entire transaction . . . Suspect (and possibly others) should have been given a blood-alcohol." In a later interview, Sergeant Jordan stated that "he did not give Sirhan a Breathalyzer test because in his opinion Sirhan did not show any symptoms of being under the influence of any drug or alcohol." (Jordan LAPD interview, February 6, 1969).

5. Melanson, research notes, RFKAA.

6. David Lawrence, "Paradoxical Bob," *Pasadena Independent Star- News*, May 26.

7. Officer 3909 was Officer Placencia.

8. LAPD audiotape 28925, June 5, 12:45 a.m., and tape transcript.

9. Frank Mankiewicz LAPD interview transcript, June 21, 17.

10. LAPD 166–69. "Ethel Kennedy Found Sound of Heart Reassuring," *Los Angeles Times*, June 6.

11. Serrano interview with Vanocur, NBC; Vanocur LAPD interview, September 20.

12. LAPD log of radio dispatches, June 5, quoted in DiEugenio and Pease, *The Assassinations*, 547–48.

13. LAPD audiotape 28925 (continued) and tape transcript.

14. Jordan report to Lt. M.S. Pena, October 9, 2–3; Sirhan medical treatment record in LAPD final report, 734. Lanz examined Sirhan at 2:01 a.m. One photograph of Sirhan being led out of the pantry shows his pants zipper half open, possibly explaining these remarks.

15. LAPD audiotape 28916, June 5, 2:05–2:20 a.m., and tape transcript.

16. Jordan report to Pena, 3; Sirhan booking and identification record in LAPD final report, 735; Kaiser, *"R.F.K. Must Die!"* 58.

17. Kaiser, *"R.F.K. Must Die!"* 56. At trial, Patchett said he asked, "Ashamed of what you did tonight?" But within days of the shooting, Patchett told the FBI he asked "Ashamed of your name?" an important difference.

18. Jordan report to Pena, 3. Officer De La Garza made the comments about his shower. LAPD audiotape 28918, June 5, 3:15 a.m., and tape transcript.

19. LAPD audiotape 28976, June 5, 3:45 a.m., and tape transcript.

20. LAPD audiotape 28917, June 5, 4 a.m., and tape transcript.

21. At one point, Jordan thought Sirhan's name might be Jesse. This can be traced to a 12:32 a.m. entry in the LAPD Emergency Control Center Journal: "Possible suspect Jesse GREER, male, Cauc. Enroute Rampart Station (info. Received from Jesse Unruh)."

22. When asked if he was being treated all right, Sirhan told the investigators he had been "most wonderfully entertained" by their conversations while in custody.

23. LAPD audiotape 28917 (continued).

24. "Your eyes are clear" contrasts to the dilated eyes observed by Officer Placencia in the patrol car after Sirhan's arrest.

25. LAPD, 312; Jordan report to Pena, 4.

26. LAPD log of Captain Carroll Kirby, Commander, Communications Division, June 5.

27. LAPD audiotape 28976, June 5, 6 a.m., and tape transcript; Kaiser, *"R.F.K. Must Die!"* 79–80.

28. Kaiser, *"R.F.K. Must Die!"* 83; "Suspect Arraigned," *New York Times*, June 6.

29. Kaiser, *"R.F.K. Must Die!"* 85. Jordan report to Pena, 4–5. Jordan stated that Sirhan was arraigned at 7:25 a.m.

30. Kaiser, *"R.F.K. Must Die!"* 259.

31. Report of Sergeant William E. Brandt, LAPD files, CSA.

32. Kaiser, *"R.F.K. Must Die!"* 87–88. Munir Sirhan, interview with the author.

33. Kranz Report, quoting Dr. Attalla.

34. Crahan report to Younger, RFKAA.

35. Kaiser, *"R.F.K. Must Die!"* 92–93; Klaber and Melanson, *Shadow Play*, 25.
36. Brandt report, LAPD files, CSA.
37. Television coverage of Yorty's news conference.
38. Kaiser, *"R.F.K. Must Die!"* 97; Brandt report, LAPD files, CSA.
39. Brandt report, LAPD files, CSA.
40. Kaiser, *"R.F.K. Must Die!"* 97; "Suspect, Arab Immigrant, Arraigned," *New York Times*, June 6.
41. "Arabs Link Death to Policy of US," *New York Times*, June 7.
42. "Woman Is Sought in Kennedy Death," June 7; "Despite Rebuke, Yorty Again Discusses Sirhan," *Los Angeles Times*, June 7.
43. Kaiser, *"R.F.K. Must Die!"* 97–98.
44. "Kennedy Is Dead, Victim of Assassin," *Los Angeles Times*, June 6.
45. "Yorty Reveals Suspect's Memo Set Death Date," *Los Angeles Times*, June 6; "Family Remains Silent," *New York Times*, June 7; "A Life on the Way to Death," *Time*, June 14.
46. LAPD, 330–33.
47. "Kennedy Is Dead, Victim of Assassin," *New York Times*, June 6.
48. "People in Nations Around the World Voice Grief and Sympathy," *New York Times*, June 7; "Despair Grips Youth in Wake of Shooting," *Los Angeles Times*, June 6.
49. "Woman Is Sought in Kennedy Death," and "Suspect Requests Theosophic Works and Newspapers," *New York Times*, June 7.
50. Crahan report transcript, RFKAA.
51. Kaiser, *"R.F.K. Must Die!"* 108.
52. Crahan report transcript, RFKAA.
53. "Aboard Kennedy Plane," *New York Times*, June 8; "A Life on the Way to Death," *Time*, June 14.
54. Audio recording of Edward Kennedy eulogy, JFK Library.

Chapter 3

1. Rafer Johnson FBI interview, June 13. 51 "Two plainclothes detectives": LAPD, 233.
2. Heymann, *RFK*, 493, 500.
3. LAPD Intelligence Division Log, LAPD files, CSA; LAPD, 235; Heymann, interview with the author.
4. Johnson LAPD interview, June 5. When Valerie Schulte first saw the gun, she thought it was a toy (Schulte FBI interview, August 13). She told the police "it looked like a cap gun" (Schulte LAPD interview, July 9).
5. Wolfer's log, June 26, LAPD files, CSA; LAPD, 211; transcript of Charles Collier interview with Dan Moldea, December 16, 1989; LAPD, 800, 820.
6. LAPD, 169, 170, 766–67. At Good Samaritan, doctors initially diagnosed two gunshot wounds behind the right ear and in the right shoulder, with no exit wounds. Later, X-rays revealed a third entry wound in the right armpit and an exit wound "in front of the right shoulder." Despite this new information, the police and press continued to report two Kennedy wounds. The Emergency Control Center summary to Chief Reddin covering the period up to 2:30 p.m. on June 6 reported "two shots hit the Senator . . . in the head and the shoulder." Based on this, Wolfer may not have been initially aware of the third bullet that hit Kennedy.
7. Wolfer's log, June 26, LAPD files, CSA; LAPD, 628, 649–50.
8. Dr. Noguchi autopsy report, LAPD, 732; Noguchi grand jury testimony, June 7.
9. Wolfer's log, June 26, LAPD files, CSA; Wolfer trial testimony, 4153–65.
10. Wolfer's log, June 26, LAPD files, CSA; LAPD, 650. The Evans fragments were booked in the early afternoon of June 5 (LAPD, 180–81, 274, 778), and the Weisel bullet and Schrade fragments were booked at six p.m. on June 6 and transferred to the crime lab "for comparison with gun of arrestee" (LAPD, 782). The fragments from the fatal bullet were released to the FBI on June 5 at three p.m. From Wolfer's log, it seems he first received them on June 13 at nine thirty a.m. (LAPD, 777; Wolfer's log, June 26, LAPD files, CSA).
11. Wolfer grand jury testimony, June 7; Klaber and Melanson, *Shadow Play*, 104.
12. LAPD, 650; LAPD progress report, June 18, CSA.
13. Comprehensive Joint Report of the Firearms Examiners, October 4, 1975, CSA.

14. Reddin/Houghton letter to Lieutenant Hewitt, July 1, LAPD Correspondence Files, CSA.
15. Dr. Noguchi grand jury testimony, June 7.
16. Moldea, *Killing of Robert F. Kennedy*, 159.
17. Karl Uecker, Eddie Minasian, and Vincent Di Pierro grand jury testimony, June 7.
18. Dr. Noguchi autopsy report, 38–40 (LAPD, 732); Wolfer's log, June 26, LAPD files, CSA; LAPD, 822.
19. LAPD, 594.
20. Romero FBI interview, June 6.
21. Uecker written statement to Allard Lowenstein, February 20, 1975.
22. Burns, interview with Dan Rather for the 1976 documentary *The American Assassins*.
23. Patrusky written statement to Vincent Bugliosi, December 12, 1975.
24. Perez LAPD interview, June 5.
25. Thane Eugene Cesar FBI interview, June 10; Pete Hamill LAPD interview, October 9; Valerie Schulte trial testimony, 3426.
26. Lubic, quoted in Klaber and Melanson, *Shadow Play*, 96; Freed, interview with the author.
27. Lisa Urso LAPD interview, June 27; Melanson, *Robert F. Kennedy Assassination*, 122–28; VHS tape of Urso 1977 reenactment, RFKAA; Urso statement to DA's office investigator William Burnett, August 10, 1977.
28. Bill Barry LAPD interview, June 5.
29. Boris Yaro FBI interview, June 7; Yaro, interview with Dan Rather for *The American Assassins*, 1976.
30. Di Pierro grand jury testimony, June 7; "Expert Discounts RFK 2d-Gun Theory," *Washington Post*, December 19, 1974. In the *Post* story, Di Pierro "said it was true that Sirhan was standing about three feet from Kennedy [but] when he fired the shots, Sirhan lunged forward, bringing the muzzle of his Ivor-Johnson revolver within several inches of Kennedy's head." Di Pierro had Kennedy turned to his left shaking hands and "noted that Sirhan's gun was pitched slightly upward." In a recent interview, Di Pierro gave me a very similar account, contradicting his grand jury testimony, two days after the shooting.
31. Sirhan letter to Mangan, September 1972, Rose Lynn Mangan Collection. His reach to his longest stretched finger was twenty-eight inches. If he extended his arm in a normal standing position, it was raised fifty-three inches from the floor. On tiptoe, as some witnesses described, it measured fifty-eight inches. See discussion of height in Chapter 1 notes, page 6.
32. Wolfer's log, June 26, LAPD files, CSA; Wolfer Analyzed Evidence Report, June 7 (LAPD, 823).
33. Wolfer's log, June 26, LAPD files, CSA; LAPD photos (Coroner's enactment of shooting, Trial Exhibit 81–2).
34. Burns written statement, June 12; Yaro LAPD interview, June 24; Yaro quoted in "Robert Kennedy Case Still Stirs Questions," *Los Angeles Times*, July 13, 1975; Yaro, interview with Dan Rather for *The American Assassins*, 1976.
35. Wolfer's log, June 20, LAPD files, CSA; LAPD, 812, 818.
36. Wolfer's log, June 26, LAPD files, CSA; Wolfer's trajectory report, July 8. The SUS Daily Summary of Activity for July 10 reads: "Had conference with . . . Case Prep Team—(Deputy DA) Fitts. Established that case is in satisfactory shape with exception of firearms ID lab work (pending)." Two days after Wolfer's trajectory study, the rest of his ID work was still pending.
37. LAPD, 650–52.
38. Paul Schrade FBI interview, June 7; Moldea, *Killing of Robert Kennedy*, 87.
39. LAPD, 742; Elizabeth Evans FBI interview, June 6; Melanson, *Robert F. Kennedy Assassination*, 40.
40. Melanson, *Robert F. Kennedy Assassination*, 40–41; Vincent Di Pierro, interview with the author.
41. Paul Grieco LAPD interview, July 30; Minasian LAPD interview, June 5; Schrade LAPD interview, June 24.
42. Lubic FBI interview, June 25; Burns written statement, June 12; Burns interview with the author.
43. Romero, quoted in *Los Angeles Herald Examiner*, June 5; FBI interview, June 6; LAPD interview, June 17.
44. Uecker LAPD interview, June 5; FBI interview, June 7; grand jury testimony, June 7.
45. Uecker interview with DA's office, July 15, 1971; written statement to Allard Lowenstein, February 20, 1975.

46. Minasian FBI interview, June 7; LAPD interview, June 5.
47. Patrusky FBI statement, June 7; written statement to Vincent Bugliosi, December 12, 1975.
48. Pete Hamill FBI interview, August 6.
49. Schrade FBI interview, June 7.
50. Di Pierro LAPD interview, June 5; FBI interview, June 7; grand jury testimony, June 7.
51. Cesar FBI interview, June 7.
52. Schulte LAPD interview, July 9; FBI interview, August 13; trial testimony, 3417–38.
53. Freddy Plimpton FBI interview, June 27.
54. Urso LAPD interview, June 27; Melanson, *Robert F. Kennedy Assassination*, 35.
55. Lubic LAPD interview, July 17; FBI interview, June 25.
56. Yaro LAPD interviews, June 24 and July 8; "Gunman Fired at Point Blank Range," *Los Angeles Times*, June 6; "Robert Kennedy Case Still Stirs Questions," *Los Angeles Times*, July 13, 1975; Yaro FBI interview, June 6.
57. LAPD, 591–94.
58. Color and black-and-white footage of these reenactments, CSA, RFKAA.
59. Dr. Vincent Guinn testimony, Baxter Ward hearings, May 13, 1974, 73–75, Rose Lynn Mangan Collection; Wolfer testimony at Wenke hearing, September 16, 1975, 82–83, LA County Superior Court Archives.
60. FBI memo, Special Agent in Charge (SAC), LA to Director, October 22, FBI files; Guinn testimony, 76, Rose Lynn Mangan Collection.
61. FBI memo from Wesley Grapp, SAC, LA to Hoover, 56-15-2665, January 9, 1969; FBI memo, Hoover to SAC, LA 56-156-2676, January 16, 1969. "Kensalt" was the codename given to the FBI investigation.
62. Younger letter to SUS Chief Houghton, May 6, 1969, referencing letter from Pitchess, February 14, 1969, FBI files.
63. Noguchi, *Coroner, 108*.

Chapter 4

1. LAPD 338; "Yorty Reveals Suspect's Memo Set Death Date," *Los Angeles Times*, June 6.
2. Jansen, *Why Robert Kennedy Was Killed*, 43–46.
3. LAPD, 339.
4. Jansen, *Why Robert Kennedy Was Killed*, 54–55.
5. On Damascus Gate, see Milstein, *Israel's War of Independence*, 51. On Deir Yassin, see Jansen, *Why Robert Kennedy Was Killed*, 56–57. The *New York Times* at first estimated the number slain as 254 in its report on April 13, but a 1987 study by Birzeit University found that "the numbers of those killed does not exceed 120."
6. LAPD, 340–41.
7. LAPD, 344–45.
8. LAPD, 345–46; Mary Sirhan LAPD interview, June 19.
9. LAPD, 389.
10. LAPD, 353–58.
11. Hornbeck, quoted in LAPD, 353–54, 1003.
12. Sirhan's English and social studies teacher, Samuel Soghomonian, quoted in LAPD, 354–55. Soghomonian was Armenian and "understood Sirhan's problem as a foreigner."
13. LAPD, 355.
14. LAPD, 346–47, 355, 357, 372.
15. Darwin R. Russell, quoted in LAPD, 358.
16. LAPD, 379.
17. LAPD, 359, 361–63, 368, 370. On "sixty to eighty dollars," see Mohan Goel, quoted in LAPD, 370.
18. LAPD, 383.
19. LAPD, 349, 359–60, 363, 368, 381–84.
20. LAPD, 363–64, 398.

21. LAPD 364, 371, 386–87; Mary Sirhan LAPD interview, June 19; Genevieve Taylor LAPD interview, December 18. Van Antwerp inexplicably disappeared on the afternoon of June 4 and turned up in Eureka two weeks later.
22. The Rosicrucians received Sirhan's membership application on June 23, 1966; LAPD, 393–94.
23. Terry Welch FBI interview, June 6; LAPD, 385–86.
24. Sirhan talked to Kaiser about Osterkamp in Kaiser, *"R.F.K. Must Die!"* 282; on Osterkamp, see LAPD, 386.
25. Sirhan trial testimony, 4886–93; LAPD, 365; Lawrence Heinemann LAPD interview, July 24.
26. LAPD, 375–77; Burt Altfillisch LAPD interview, July 16.
27. LAPD, 365, 377, 1210.
28. "Sirhan Threatened Doctor in Disability Check Quest," *Los Angeles Herald Examiner*, June 8.
29. FBI memo to SAC, Los Angeles, June 14; FBI Chronology of Sirhan's Life, December 16; LAPD, 369.
30. Mary Sirhan quoted in *Riverside Press-Enterprise*, June 8; Welch FBI interview, June 6.
31. Rathke LAPD interview, quoted in Melanson, *Robert F. Kennedy Assassination,* 180.
32. Sharif Sirhan LAPD interview, quoted in Melanson, *Robert F. Kennedy Assassination,* 180, 200; Kaiser, *"R.F.K. Must Die!"* 132–34.
33. Sirhan trial testimony, 4896–4902
34. John and Patricia Strathman trial testimony, 5381–5415; Kaiser, *"R.F.K. Must Die!"* 212–13.
35. Sirhan trial testimony, 4916–22; LAPD, 393, 399.
36. Photocopy of pages from Sirhan's notebook, CSA.
37. LAPD, 464, 471.
38. Photocopy of page from Sirhan's notebook, CSA.
39. Sirhan trial testimony, 4986–93.
40. LAPD, 371, 375–78; "Sirhan Threatened Doctor in Disability Check Quest," *Los Angeles Herald Examiner*, June 8. This article states that in a settlement filed on March 15, "a referee calculated Sirhan was 5.5 percent disabled for 22 weeks and deserved $1155 plus the $95 in doctors' bills." A doctor reviewing the settlement finally settled on $2,000 as "adequate," to include the doctors' bills and $200 for Sirhan's attorney. Therefore, Sirhan could not have known the figure was $2,000 until March 15—the day before Robert Kennedy announced he would run for president.
41. LAPD, 366, 371.
42. "Yorty Reveals Suspect's Memo Set Death Date," *Los Angeles Times*, June 6.
43. Boyko FBI interview, June 13.
44. Sirhan trial testimony, 5120–22, 5279–82, 5287; Erhard trial testimony, 3749–55; Price trial testimony, 3756–61; Munir Sirhan, interview with the author.
45. LAPD, 346, 348–50; "Deportation for Sirhan's Brother?" *Los Angeles Herald Examiner*, June 24, 1969.
46. Sirhan trial testimony, 5277–78 (cross-examination by prosecutor Lynn Compton).
47. Sirhan trial testimony, 5121–23 (questioning by Cooper).
48. Munir Sirhan, interview with the author; LAPD, 393.
49. LAPD, 366–67, 380; Boyko FBI interview, June 13.
50. LAPD, 367.
51. Family friend Linda Damakian, quoted in LAPD, 388.
52. Mary, Adel, and Munir Sirhan FBI interviews, June 5.
53. Sirhan trial testimony, 4923–24.
54. Sirhan trial testimony, 5120–26.
55. LAPD, 371–72; Mary Sirhan FBI interview, June 5; Clark FBI interview, September 11.
56. LAPD, 4670–74; Kaiser, *"R.F.K. Must Die!"* 227–28.
57. Sirhan trial testimony, 5102–8.
58. Sirhan trial testimony, 4972–74.
59. Jansen, *Why Robert Kennedy Was Killed*, 193.
60. Kaiser, *"R.F.K. Must Die!"* 420–21. Authors Godfrey Jansen and Mel Ayton incorrectly date the first broadcast as May 15. *Los Angeles Times* TV listings confirm May 20 as the first screening in the Los Angeles area.
61. Sirhan trial testimony, 4970–74.

62. Jansen, *Why Robert Kennedy Was Killed*, 189; David Lawrence, "Paradoxical Bob," *Pasadena Independent Star-News*, May 26.

63. Jansen, *Why Robert Kennedy Was Killed*, 189–90; Kaiser, *"R.F.K. Must Die!"* 126, 420–21. On June 10, Sirhan received the first of several letters from John Lawrence, a pro-Arab, anti-Zionist campaigner in New York, informing him of Kennedy's promise to send the bombers in his May 26 speech. Kaiser argued that this was the first Sirhan heard about the bombers and that he postrationalized the shooting in the light of Kennedy's pledge. But, at trial, Sirhan insisted he saw the documentary and heard the radio broadcast before the shooting.

64. This photograph is reprinted in Godfrey Jansen's *Why Robert Kennedy Was Killed*.

65. Sirhan trial testimony, 4976–78. Sirhan is mixing up the two speeches here. A hot news report about sending the bombers would have referred to the speech in Portland rather than the Jewish Club in Beverly Hills.

66. LAPD, 387; Houghton, *Special Unit Senator*, 248; "Family Remains Silent," *New York Times*, June 7.

67. Sirhan trial testimony, 5126–30; LAPD, 394–96.

68. LAPD, 372.

69. LAPD, 605–7; William Marks LAPD interview, December 13; Harry Starr LAPD interview, December 13; SUS Daily Summary of Activities (Lieutenant Keene), December 19.

70. Starr trial testimony, 4261–67.

71. Sirhan trial testimony, 5153–54; Larry Arnot FBI interview, June 16; LAPD, 497–501, 605.

72. Ben and Donna Herrick FBI interviews, June 16; Adel Sirhan FBI interview, June 17; LAPD, 601, 998.

73. Jansen, *Why Robert Kennedy Was Killed*, 191–92.

74. Sirhan trial testimony, 5130–35.

75. Sirhan trial testimony, 5136–45.

76. Sirhan interview with NBC reporter Jack Perkins, recorded May 22, 1969, broadcast as *First Tuesday: The Mind of an Assassin*, June 3, 1969.

77. Sirhan trial testimony, 5145–46.

Chapter 5

1. Audio recording of Dr. Bernard L. Diamond's psychiatric session with Sirhan, January 26, 1969; Diamond trial testimony, 6935–44; Kaiser, *"R.F.K. Must Die!"* 304–5, 349–51.

2. William Schneid FBI interview, June 19; Carl Jackson FBI interview, June 20.

3. Albert LeBeau FBI interview, June 7; LeBeau summary in LAPD, 1038.

4. Joseph and Margaret Sheehan FBI interviews, June 26; Houghton, *Special Unit Senator*, 246.

5. Laverne Botting FBI interview, July 19; Botting summary in LAPD, 887; Melanson, *Robert F. Kennedy Assassination*, 222–23.

6. Ethel Crehan LAPD interviews, June 7 and August 7; Crehan FBI interview, July 19.

7. Botting LAPD interview, cited in Melanson, *Robert F. Kennedy Assassination*, 222.

8. Turner and Christian, *Assassination of Robert F. Kennedy*, 222; Dean Pack summary in LAPD, 1098.

9. John Henry Fahey FBI interviews, June 6, 7, and 20; transcript of Fernando Faura interview with Fahey, June 12; Kaiser, *"R.F.K. Must Die!"* 116–17.

10. Serrano interview with Vanocur, broadcast at approximately 1:30 a.m. on June 5 by NBC; audiotapes and tape transcripts of Serrano LAPD interviews, June 5 (2:35 a.m. and 4:00 a.m.); Serrano FBI interview, June 6–7.

11. Serrano quoted the girl as saying "We've shot him" in her NBC and first LAPD interviews and "We shot him" at times thereafter; John Ambrose FBI interview, June 10.

12. Di Pierro FBI interview, June 10.

13. Di Pierro LAPD interview, June 5; grand jury testimony, June 7.

14. Serrano FBI interview, June 6–7. 125 "Early descriptions of Sirhan": Serrano, interview with the author.

15. LAPD, 767. SUS Chief Houghton claimed in his book that this APB "was put out around 3 a.m." (Houghton, *Special Unit Senator*, 31). There is no paperwork to support this, and the APB in the

LAPD final report timed it as 11:50 a.m. Houghton also stated, "Her companion was also sought: 'Male, Mexican-American, 23, wearing a gold sweater.'" This is not true. By 3 a.m., Sharaga's APB had been canceled, and no further call went out for the girl's male companion.

16. Similar notations were scrawled across six other interview summaries relating to the polka-dot dress investigation, dated June 6 or 7. The writing is apparently Pena's, but as Melanson notes, these dates are before SUS was set up and Pena had even started work on the case (Melanson, *Robert F. Kennedy Assassination*, 240; DiEugenio and Pease, *The Assassinations*, 586).

17. FBI Teletype from Oklahoma City office to Director, June 5.

18. FBI Teletype to Director from SAC, Los Angeles, June 8, quoting Lieutenant Charles Hughes, LAPD Rampart Division.

19. "Dancer Tells Sheriff She May Be 'Girl in Polka-Dot Dress,'" *Los Angeles Times*, June 8; FBI report on Fulmer, June 11.

20. "Witness Eliminates Dancer as 'Girl in Polka-Dot Dress,'" *Los Angeles Times*, June 9; LAPD, 418.

21. FBI report on Serrano, June 12; LAPD, 410–11; Irene Chavez summary in LAPD, 907; David Haines FBI interview, June 11.

22. LAPD, 412–13.

23. Serrano LAPD interviews, June 5, 2:35 a.m. and 4 a.m.

24. Serrano confirmed to the author that the police did not show her Sirhan's picture on the morning of the shooting. The first time she saw it was in the *Los Angeles Times* the following day, June 6.

25. FBI "urgent" Teletype summary to Director on Serrano, dated June 11, 12–13.

26. Ibid., 12; LAPD audiotape of interview on stairway, June 10.

27. Rose Haimes summary in LAPD, 984 (Haimes was Serrano's supervisor at the United Insurance Company of America).

28. FBI report on Serrano phone call, dated June 12.

29. LAPD, 413–14.

30. LAPD, 413, titled "Elements of the Investigation Conflict."

31. Sharaga's Command Post Log, June 5, LAPD files, CSA; LAPD log of radio dispatches, June 5, quoted in DiEugenio and Pease, *The Assassinations*, 547–48; Sharaga's copy of his original report for Captain Phillips, June 5; Houghton, *Special Unit Senator*, 14; Transcript of Sharaga interview with Kevin, RFKAA; Turner and Christian, *Assassination of Robert F. Kennedy*, 73–77; Notarized written declaration of Sharaga, July 25, 1991; written statement of Sharaga, November 17, 1992; Moldea, *Killing of Robert Kennedy*, 40, 60, 71–72.

32. Irene Gizzi LAPD interview, June 6.

33. Jeanette Prudhomme LAPD interview, June 5.

34. Katie Keir LAPD interviews, June 5 and August 7.

35. Mary Ann Wiegers FBI interview, October 9. While Wiegers's account quotes the girl as saying "a black dress with white polka dots," Keir clearly described a white dress with black polka dots in her LAPD interviews.

36. Richard Houston LAPD interview, September 22.

37. Merritt FBI interview, June 9; Merritt LAPD interview, June 21.

38. Green FBI interviews, June 6 and July 15. In a later LAPD interview (August 1), Green supposedly put Sirhan's height at five foot and described a "dark dress [with] . . . some kind of white dots," so the LAPD dismissed him (Green summary, LAPD, 975–76). But as Melanson notes, there are no tapes of this interview, so we can't be sure this interview summary wasn't just another LAPD tactic to smear another witness to a girl in a polka-dot dress fleeing the kitchen (Melanson, *Robert F. Kennedy Assassination*, 277).

39. Kaiser, *"R.F.K. Must Die!"* 174–75; Turner and Christian, *Assassination of Robert F. Kennedy*, 83; Fahey LAPD interview summary, September 13. Gugas, a past president of the American Polygraph Association, worked for the CIA in Greece and Turkey in the fifties and became one of America's foremost polygraph experts, twice giving polygraph tests to James Earl Ray and concluding that Ray was lying when he claimed innocence in the King murder. Gugas tested Fahey on August 24 and told the LAPD that he felt Fahey had been truthful during the examination and that "no one could tell such a convincing story" unless he was telling the truth (Gugas obituary, *Washington Post*, November 12, 2007, and *Los Angeles Times*, November 15, 2007; LAPD, 564–65).

Note: There were many more witnesses to a girl in a polka-dot dress at the hotel, but I have chosen to include only those I feel are the most credible and consistent with other descriptions. There were many women wearing polka-dot dresses at the hotel that night (head of security William Gardner estimated as many as thirty), but the witness descriptions of the girl's behavior and appearance outlined here bear great similarities to one another.

Chapter 6

1. Houghton, *Special Unit Senator*, 120.
2. Manuel Pena's four-hour interview with attorney Marilyn Barrett, September 12, 1992. Barrett kindly sent me an audio recording of this interview and forwarded my request to Pena's family for an interview. Unfortunately, Pena was eighty-nine at the time and too ill to be interviewed, even by phone. Nonetheless, much of the Barrett interview has been previously overlooked by researchers, and helps illuminate Pena's career in Chapter 16.
3. see discussion of "backfires/gunshots" in previous chapter.
4. Pena, *Practical Criminal Investigation*, 127.
5. Matte, *Forensic Psychophysiology*, 20.
6. *U.S. v. Scheffer*, 523 U.S. 303, 1998.
7. "Telling the Truth About Lie Detectors," *USA Today*, September 9, 2002.
8. Sergeant Enrique Hernandez SUS profile, LAPD files, CSA.
9. Pena interview with Barrett; Pena, *Practical Criminal Investigation*, 130.
10. LAPD audiotapes of Hernandez's pre-polygraph interviews with Sandra Serrano (June 20) and Vincent Di Pierro (July 1).
11. According to the LAPD transcript, Serrano's post-polygraph interview with Hernandez began at 10:15 p.m. They had changed rooms, and he had gone off to find a stenographer and a tape recorder. Working back from this point, I agree with Melanson and estimate that the polygraph test was conducted between nine and ten (Melanson, *Robert F. Kennedy Assassination*, 248). On Pena comment, see Pena interview with Barrett.
12. Serrano, interview with the author.
13. LAPD audiotapes of Serrano's pre-polygraph and polygraph interviews with Hernandez, June 20.
14. LAPD audiotape and tape transcript of Serrano's post-polygraph interview with Hernandez, June 20.
15. Di Pierro FBI interview, June 10.
16. Hernandez report to Captain Brown, December 16; LAPD, 415–16.
17. "Police Halt Hunt for Mystery Girl in Kennedy Case," *Los Angeles Times*, June 22; Canceled APB, LAPD, 768.
18. Rose Haimes summary in LAPD, 984; Turner and Christian, *Assassination of Robert F. Kennedy*, 82; Gregory Abbott LAPD interview, July 17.
19. Melanson, *Robert F. Kennedy Assassination*, 256.
20. Pena interview with Barrett.
21. Serrano, interview with the author.
22. LAPD audiotapes of Di Pierro's interview with Hernandez, July 1.
23. Ibid.; LAPD transcript of Di Pierro statement taken on July 1, 12:52 p.m.
24. Di Pierro, interview with the author.
25. Di Pierro LAPD interview, July 1; Di Pierro grand jury testimony, June 7; Di Pierro trial testimony, 3205–21 (February 14), 3231–59 (February 17). Di Pierro was on the stand for less than an hour total, either side of the weekend. He was cross-examined by Cooper for less than twenty minutes.
26. Houghton, *Special Unit Senator*, 212.
27. Gizzi LAPD interview, June 6. Gizzi's original interview report (June 6) starts with the line "Re-interview all persons named in this interview." The report seems to have been revised after the Hernandez interview with Serrano.
28. LAPD progress report on "Students for Kennedy" investigation by Lieutenant Higbie, August 16; Gizzi LAPD interview, August 6; Keir LAPD interview, August 7; Prudhomme LAPD interview, August 8.
29. Hernandez summary of LAPD interviews with Fahey, September 13. This report covers Fahey's previous accounts, the polygraph conducted on September 5, and the reinterview four days later. LAPD tape transcript of Fahey interview, September 9; Kaiser, *"R.F.K. Must Die!"* 224–25.

30. LAPD, 567. Fahey died in 1996. He was never interviewed again about Gilda Dean, aka Gilderdene Oppenheimer. Oppenheimer has never been found.
31. LAPD, 421–22; LAPD photographs of Schulte (three black and white, one color), CSA.
32. Schulte LAPD interview, July 9, 1969; FBI interview, August 13.
33. LAPD audiotape and transcript of Di Pierro interview, June 5; Di Pierro FBI interview, June 7.
34. Di Pierro trial testimony.
35. Di Pierro trial testimony; Di Pierro, interview with the author.
36. Sharaga's Command Post Log, June 5, LAPD files, CSA; LAPD log of radio dispatches, June 5, quoted in DiEugenio and Pease, *The Assassinations*, 547–48; Sharaga's copy of his original report for Captain Phillips, June 5; Sharaga's alleged LAPD interview, September 26; Houghton, *Special Unit Senator*, 14; transcript of Sharaga interview with Kevin, RFKAA; Turner and Christian, *Assassination of Robert F. Kennedy*, 73–77, 83; Sharaga letter to Christian, June 22, 1988; Special Report by Christian, *Easy Reader*, November 17, 1988, RFKAA; notarized written declaration of Sharaga, July 25, 1991; written statement of Sharaga, November 17, 1992; Moldea, *Killing of Robert Kennedy*, 40, 60, 71–72.
37. Sharaga, telephone interview with the author.
38. Pena interview with Barrett.

Chapter 7

1. Rogers, *When I Think of Bobby*, 53.
2. Heymann, *RFK*, 492; Schlesinger, *Robert Kennedy*, 722; Plimpton and Stein, *American Journey*, 182.
3. Witcover, *85 Days*, 113–14.
4. Ibid., 149.
5. Ibid., 203.
6. Ibid., 91.
7. Ibid., 246; Schlesinger, *Robert Kennedy*, 968.
8. Kennedy most famously used this quote during a statement on the assassination of Martin Luther King, Jr., in Indianapolis, Indiana, April 4: "Aeschylus wrote: In our sleep, pain which cannot forget falls drop by drop upon the heart until, in our despair, against our will, comes wisdom through the awful grace of God. What we need in the United States is not division; what we need in the United States is not hatred; what we need in the United States is not violence or lawlessness; but love and wisdom, and compassion toward one another, and a feeling of justice toward those who still suffer within our country, whether they be white or they be black. . . . Let us dedicate ourselves to what the Greeks wrote so many years ago: to tame the savageness of man and make gentle the life of the world" (RFK, "Statement on the Assassination of Martin Luther King," April 4, JFK Library).
9. Plimpton and Stein, *American Journey*, 291; Witcover, *85 Days*, 147; Heymann, *RFK*, 492.
10. Schlesinger, *Robert Kennedy*, 969.
11. Schlesinger, *Robert Kennedy*, 969; Plimpton and Stein, *American Journey*, 292–93.
12. Plimpton and Stein, *American Journey*.
13. Witcover, *85 Days*, 207; Plimpton and Stein, *American Journey*, 299–300.
14. LAPD, 578.
15. LAPD, 127–30; "Police Charge 100 Traffic Violations to Kennedy Caravan," *Los Angeles Times*, May 30.
16. Dutton obituary, *Los Angeles Times*, June 27, 2005.
17. LAPD, 1–2, 124–26, 131–32.
18. "Personal Bodyguards at Hotel Were Only Security Measure," *Los Angeles Times*, June 6.
19. Did RFK's Order Seal His Death?" *Los Angeles Herald Examiner*, August 29, 1976; article on Marion Hoover, *National Enquirer*, October 26, 1976; Turner and Christian, *Assassination of Robert F. Kennedy*, 318–19.
20. *The R.F.K. Story* in 1988 broadcast claim and counterclaim. Mayor Sam Yorty said, "When they came to Los Angeles, he wouldn't let us give him any police protection." "That is wrong," countered Salinger. "We asked for it and were refused protection at that time by Mayor Yorty."
21. Juan Romero FBI interview, June 6; Frances Bailey FBI interview, June 14.

22. Mark Armbruster LAPD interview, August 19.
23. Bill Barry quoted in LAPD, 131.
24. Richard Kline FBI interview, June 12.
25. LAPD, 131–33. Jack Gallivan FBI interview, June 14; Eddie Minasian LAPD interview transcript, June 5; Rosey Grier LAPD interview, June 19.
26. Uno Timanson written statement, June 6.
27. Karl Uecker trial testimony, 3081, 3086, 3118–19; network footage of Kennedy leaving the stage.
28. By the end of July, Sergeant Varney "had developed a list of 53 names, all reported to be in the Colonial Room at the time of the shooting . . . of these, 28 have (so far) been interviewed" (Colonial Room Progress Report, July 30, LAPD files, CSA).
29. Fred Dutton LAPD interviews, June 5 and September 6 (from LAPD audiotapes and interview summaries).
30. Colonial Room Progress Report.
31. Barry LAPD interviews, June 5 and 21.
32. Thadis Heath LAPD interview, July 23.
33. Timanson FBI interview, June 7; Witcover, *85 Days*, 265.
34. Gallivan FBI interview, June 14.
35. Stanley Kawalec FBI interview, June 7.
36. James Marooney FBI interview, September 25.
37. *Life* photographer Bill Eppridge recalled, "We had a procedure where a couple of photographers and the television crew would form a wedge to get him through a crowd. Behind the point of the wedge was his bodyguard, Bill Barry. The Senator could shake hands . . . could move around behind us as we walked backwards through the crowd, photographing him. It worked well for everybody" ("The Last Campaign," Nikon *Legends Behind the Lens* series, 2004).
38. Kaiser, *"R.F.K. Must Die!"* 24; Witcover, *85 Days*, 265; Nina Rhodes FBI interview, July 9.
39. Network footage of Kennedy leaving the stage; audio recording of Barbara Frank.
40. In footage of Kennedy leaving the stage, he either ignores or doesn't see Bill Barry. CBS electrician John Lewis, onstage with Wilson, heard Barry say, "'Bobby, we're supposed to go this way' . . . through the crowd. The Senator answered 'no' and headed down the steps toward the rear" (Lewis FBI interview, June 20). *Life* photographer Bill Eppridge heard Barry twice beckon Kennedy offstage the same way he came on, but the senator didn't reply (Eppridge FBI interview, June 17).
41. LAPD audiotape of Barry interview, June 5; Barry trial transcript, 3446–47.
42. Dutton LAPD interview transcript, September 6.
43. Rosey Grier LAPD interview, June 19; Barry FBI interview, June 18.
44. Uecker trial testimony, 3119–20. Before the grand jury on June 7, Uecker said, "Their minds were changed at the last minute. When I came out [into the back hallway], I just remember that somebody told me, 'Turn to your right. Bring towards the Colonial Room. . . . I think it was Mr. Uno Timanson.'" Minasian also heard the new directions but in the dark couldn't say who gave them (Uecker and Minasian grand jury testimony).
45. Rick Rosen LAPD interview, June 27; FBI interview, July 12; Gallivan FBI interview, June 14; Gallivan trial testimony, 3444–47; Timanson written statement, June 6; Barry LAPD interview, June 5. Rosen said he and Gallivan were "ten or fifteen feet ahead." Gallivan told the FBI he was twenty to twenty-five feet ahead of Kennedy.
46. Bob Funk FBI interview, June 21.
47. Grier and Rafer Johnson LAPD interviews, June 19; Dutton LAPD interview, June 5.
48. Confidential background check on Dutton, LAPD files, CSA; Timanson, phone conversation with the author; Barry, phone conversation with the author.
49. LAPD, 142–44.
50. Dick Drayne undated FBI interview; Jimmy Breslin FBI interview, June 20; Richard Kline trial testimony, 4108–17; Judy Royer trial testimony, 3906–7. Kline was told of the change "about fifteen to twenty minutes before the Senator spoke." He then asked Royer to go brief the press in the Colonial Room.
51. Robert Thomas LAPD interview, August 15.
52. James B. Jones LAPD interview, July 18; Captain Kenneth Held LAPD interview, July 19.
53. Breslin LAPD interview, July 30.

54. For Sirhan's encounter with Perez and Patrusky, see Chapter 1, page 10.

55. Bradley Ayers, interview with the author; David Rabern, interview with the author.

56. In 1975, Uecker told attorney Vincent Bugliosi: "There is no way the shots described in the autopsy could have come from Sirhan's gun. . . . Sirhan never got close enough for a point blank shot, never."

57. William Gardner LAPD interview, June 14; FBI interview, June 8; Murphy LAPD interview, June 17; for "looked ridiculous," see audiotape of Lloyd Curtis LAPD interview, June 17.

58. LAPD, 122, 133–35; Moldea, *Killing of Robert Kennedy*, 24; Jack Merritt LAPD interview, July 26, 1971.

59. Merritt LAPD interview, June 21; Albert Stowers LAPD interview, June 20; LAPD, 134, 137.

60. The guards were Lloyd Curtis and Willie Bell.

61. LAPD, 134; Marcus McBroom LAPD interview, July 5; Valerie Schulte LAPD interview, July 9; Royer LAPD interview, July 23.

62. Audiotape of Thane Eugene Cesar LAPD interview, July 24; Moldea, *Killing of Robert Kennedy*, 208.

63. Audiotape of Murphy LAPD interview, June 17.

64. Gardner LAPD interview, June 14; Jesus Perez FBI interview, June 8; Cesar LAPD interviews, June 5 and 24; Murphy LAPD interview, June 17.

65. Gardner FBI interview, June 8.

66. Audiotape of Lloyd Curtis LAPD interview, June 17.

67. Bell FBI interview, June 9.

68. Gardner FBI interview, June 12; Kawalec FBI interview, June 7; Gardner LAPD interview, June 14.

69. Gardner FBI interview, August 12; Frank Hendrix interview with Betsy Langman, RFKAA.

70. Merritt FBI interview, June 9; LAPD interview, June 21.

71. Merritt was interviewed by LAPD sergeants Varney and O'Steen. O'Steen reinterviewed Cesar alone three days later. His initial interview was on the morning of the shooting, and audiotapes of both interviews suggest that his gun was never checked.

72. LAPD audiotape of Merritt interview, July 26, 1971, CSA; Merritt death certificate, June 8, 1975.

73. In his second police interview, Cesar said Murphy told him "to go out through the main kitchen openings, where the swinging doors are, and to get the other security guard to keep the crowd out." He identified this guard to researcher Ted Charach as Jack Merritt (audiotape of Cesar interview with Charach, 1969) and later told Dan Moldea he summoned both Merritt and Stowers into the pantry (Moldea, *Killing of Robert Kennedy*, 212).

74. The suspects Merritt saw fled north through the kitchen. Serrano was sitting on the stairs leading down from the southwest corner of the Embassy Ballroom.

75. Stowers LAPD interview, June 20.

76. LAPD audiotape of Merritt interview, July 26, 1971.

77. Merritt death certificate; Moldea, *Killing of Robert Kennedy*, 201. A 1974 CIA memo quoted in DiEugenio and Pease states that the "DCD [Domestic Contacts Division] has had a close and continuing relationship with . . . Hughes Aircraft Company since 1948 . . . [and] has contacted over 250 individuals in the company since the start of our association" (DiEugenio and Pease, *The Assassinations*, 604).

Chapter 8

1. LAPD, 42, 106. The LAPD final report lists both 7:08 and 7:25 a.m. as the time of Sirhan's arraignment. Sergeant Jordan, who was present, timed it at 7:25 a.m. (Jordan report to Lt. M.S. Pena, October 9).

2. Kaiser, *"R.F.K. Must Die!"* 293, 428.

3. LAPD audiotapes of Sirhan in custody; Sirhan NBC interview with Perkins.

4. Kaiser, *"R.F.K. Must Die!"* 92; Kaiser e-mail to author; Rose Lynn Mangan, interview with the author.

5. Lane, *Plausible Denial*, 52, quoted in DiEugenio and Pease, *The Assassinations*, 573–74.

6. LAPD, 106; "Jail Chapel Used as Court to Bar 'Another Dallas,'" *New York Times*, June 8.

7. Kaiser, interview with the author.
8. Russell Parsons, interview with Langman, 1974, RFKAA; Kaiser, *"R.F.K. Must Die!"* 123.
9. Klaber and Melanson, *Shadow Play*, 26.
10. "Priceless Defenders," *Time*, January 17, 1969.
11. Kaiser, interview with the author; Kaiser, *"R.F.K. Must Die!"* 122–24.
12. "Five Found Guilty in Friars Cheating Case" and "U.S. Probes Alleged Transcript Bribe in Friars Club Trial," *Los Angeles Times*, December 3.
13. Russo, *Live by the Sword*, 395, from presidential recording released by the Lyndon Baines Johnson Library and Museum, Austin, TX.
14. Russo, *Live by the Sword*, 417, citing "LBJ diary page discovered by researcher G.R. Dodge in the handwriting file at the LBJ Library in Austin, TX."
15. Ayers, *The War That Never Was*, 38, and *The Zenith Secret*, 57.
16. Klaber and Melanson, *Shadow Play*, 27.
17. Kaiser, *"R.F.K. Must Die!"* 127–29.
18. "Sirhan Hires New Defence Attorney," *Los Angeles Times*, June 20.
19. Kaiser, *"R.F.K. Must Die!"* 245; LAPD, 1430.
20. Parsons, interview with Langman.
21. Klaber and Melanson, *Shadow Play*, 32.
22. Kaiser, *"R.F.K. Must Die!"* 152, 202.
23. Teeter, Petition for Writ of Habeas Corpus, July 19, 2002, 31–33.
24. Parsons, interview with Langman, RFKAA; Allen, interview with Langman, 1973, RFKAA.
25. McCowan, interview with the author.
26. Teeter petition, 32–33.
27. "U.S. Probes Alleged Transcript Bribe in Friars Club Trial," *Los Angeles Times*, December 3; "Lawyer Admits He Lied About Friars Transcript," *Los Angeles Times*, January 4, 1969; "Cooper Ordered to Answer Friars Transcript Quiz," January 8, 1969; "Grant Cooper, 10 Others Indicted," *Los Angeles Times*, August 7, 1969; Klaber and Melanson, *Shadow Play*, 44–49.
28. LAPD, 107; McCowan, interview with the author. For "forty- member," see SUS roster prepared by Sergeant Michael Nielsen, November 5, LAPD files, CSA. The roster lists forty investigators and two secretaries. In his interview with Barrett, Manuel Pena described setting up "a forty-man task force to handle the case." With Chief Houghton and Captain Brown, he picked "just about the fortiest sharpest guys on the Department in every category . . . and started the unit."
29. Parsons, interview with Langman; Allen, interview with Langman.
30. "Three Months to See Why?" *Los Angeles Herald Examiner*, August 3.
31. Kaiser, interview with the author.
32. Kaiser, *"R.F.K. Must Die!"* 175–78.
33. Unpublished preface to planned second edition of Kaiser, *"R.F.K. Must Die!"* 1999.
34. Parsons, interview with Langman; McCowan, interview with Langman, RFKAA. No date is given for the McCowan interview, but it was probably conducted in 1973, when Langman interviewed McCowan's partner, Ron Allen.
35. Kaiser, *"R.F.K. Must Die!"* quoted in Klaber and Melanson, *Shadow Play*, 28–29.
36. McCowan, interview with the author; Kaiser interview with the author.
37. McCowan, interview with the author.
38. Muzzey, *History of the American People* (Boston: Ginn, 1929), 527.
39. *The Transformation of Modern Europe*, 576. Photocopies of the pages from both books supplied by McCowan.
40. Kaiser, *"R.F.K. Must Die!"* 170–71; McCowan, interview with the author.
41. Eric Marcus trial testimony, 6791, 6796–97; Bernard Diamond trial testimony, 6896; both cited in Teeter petition, 36–37.
42. Teeter petition, 34–39.
43. McCowan, interview with the author.
44. Kaiser, interview with the author.
45. Sirhan undated notes on yellow legal pad, supplied by McCowan. I read these notes onto tape during my visit with McCowan, so I could later make a transcript.
46. Kaiser, *"R.F.K. Must Die!"* 235.

47. Kaiser, interview with the author. For Kaiser agreement, see Kaiser, *"R.F.K. Must Die!"* 221–23.
48. Kaiser, *"R.F.K. Must Die!"* 238–39.
49. "Completion Dates for S.U.S. Personnel," September 11, LAPD files, CSA. After September 20, fourteen men would stay on to wrap up the case.
50. Marcus trial testimony, 6811–14; Kaiser, *"R.F.K. Must Die!"* 229–31.
51. Kaiser, *"R.F.K. Must Die!"* 237–38.
52. LAPD, 678.
53. Klaber and Melanson, *Shadow Play*, 36, 151–53; "Both Sides Agree Sirhan Was Alone," *Los Angeles Times*, October 15.
54. Kaiser, interview with the author.
55. Cooper later told Betsy Langman: "I came into the case with a pre-conceived notion that Sirhan had done the shooting . . . I never dreamed that anybody else fired a shot . . . that thought never entered my head" (Cooper, interview with Langman, 1971, RFKAA).
56. McCowan, interview with the author; Kaiser, interview with the author.
57. McCowan, interview with the author; McCowan summaries on Di Pierro and Cesar, RFKAA.
58. Cesar FBI interview, June 10; Cooper, interview with Langman; Parsons, interview with Langman.
59. Kaiser, interview with the author; McCowan, interview with the author; Kaiser, *"R.F.K. Must Die!"* 59.
60. SUS Daily Summary of Activities (DSA), November 1 and 4, cited in Teeter petition, 97.
61. Kaiser, *"R.F.K. Must Die!"* 240.
62. Ibid., 242.
63. Klaber and Melanson, *Shadow Play*, 39, 42; Kaiser, *"R.F.K. Must Die!"* 244.
64. Kaiser, interview with the author.
65. Kaiser, *"R.F.K. Must Die!"* 244–45. 209 "From this point on": Ibid., 258.
66. Ibid., 247–48.
67. Ibid., 249–54.
68. FBI memo to Director, December 13, 1969.
69. LAPD, 681; Kaiser, *"R.F.K. Must Die!"* 259–61.
70. Kaiser, "Sirhan in Jail."

Chapter 9

1. LAPD activity chart for Sirhan (LAPD, 616–21), quoting Mary Sirhan and Sidney McDaniel.
2. FBI memorandum from SA Richards to SAC, Los Angeles, November 18.
3. The LAPD activity chart quotes Mary Sirhan as saying that Sirhan was home from twelve thirty p.m. to one p.m. and from four thirty p.m. on. His whereabouts in between are "unknown."
4. Kaiser, *"R.F.K. Must Die!"* 534.
5. Sirhan trial testimony, 5145. Cooper goes straight from a discussion of June 2 to June 4.
6. LAPD, 350. FBI report of Amedee O. Richards, June 9, 923–24, and August 1, 1969, 27–28; "Deportation for Sirhan's Brother?" *Los Angeles Herald Examiner*, June 24, 1969. Munir was arrested on June 10, 1966, for possession of and offering to sell marijuana to a state narcotics officer. He was found guilty of possession four months later and sentenced to a year in jail and five years' probation. As Munir was nineteen at the time of the incident, Munir's attorney later persuaded the court to vacate the sentence and transfer it to juvenile court. On July 11, 1967, Munir was ordered deported to Jordan due to his felony conviction but subsequently appealed the deportation order in light of his vacated sentence. A decision was pending at the time of the shooting.
7. Vernon Most LAPD interview, June 6.
8. Elizabeth Raaegep LAPD interview, June 6; LAPD summary, 1119. It's not clear from LAPD reports how the conversation about guns started. Raaegep told officers her sons owned rifles "and I was telling Joe about hand gun laws that I had heard about." Her LAPD summary states, "Mr. Most was discussing guns and gun laws with Munir."
9. Most LAPD interview, June 6.
10. LAPD, 493–96; Darrel K. Gumm LAPD interviews, June 11 and 18. The first interview notes that "Gumm spoke with Munir on 6-10-68 pm and Munir denied buying the gun. Gumm met Sirhan

several times but only in connection with his visits to the home to talk to Munir." Gumm was not related to Gwendalee Gum, the girl Sirhan had a crush on at PCC.

11. Munir Sirhan FBI interview, June 10.

12. "Deportation for Sirhan's Brother?" *Los Angeles Herald Examiner*, June 24, 1969.

13. LAPD activity chart for Sirhan, quoting Mary Sirhan; Munir Sirhan FBI interview, June 5. Sirhan testified he got up around nine or ten (Sirhan trial testimony, 5145), but Munir saw him buying a newspaper around eight thirty. On Sirhan's plans for the day, see Sirhan trial testimony, 5147–48, 5150–51.

14. Sirhan trial testimony, 5152–55. Strangely, I can find no record of Sirhan's visit to the East Pasadena Firearms Co. in LAPD files. On the timing of Sirhan's arrival at the gun range, see note for Chapter 1, page 6. LAPD Officer Harry Lee appears on the sign-in sheet seven names above Sirhan. He was shooting on the rifle range, five hundred yards away, between ten thirty a.m. and one p.m. but did not see Sirhan (Lee LAPD interview, July 10).

15. Sirhan trial testimony, 5156. 215 "Sirhan's gun had a fixed sight": Ibid., 5157–58.

16. Ibid., 5156, 5159.

17. Michael Soccoman LAPD interview, June 5, quoted in Kaiser, *"R.F.K. Must Die!"* 117–18; Soccoman summary in LAPD, 1141–42; Sirhan trial testimony, 5159–61, in which Cooper mistakenly refers to another witness at the range, David Montellano, instead of Soccoman.

18. Sirhan trial testimony, 5161.

19. Claudia and Ronald Williams FBI interviews, June 20; Sirhan trial testimony, 5162–64.

20. Williams call to Officer Goodman, six p.m., June 6, LAPD phone log.

21. Sirhan trial testimony, 5164–65.

22. Analyzed evidence reports, included in LAPD, 842–43.

23. Gaymoard Mistri LAPD interview, July 11; Sirhan trial testimony, 5168–72. While Sirhan timed this meeting with Mistri as occurring at five fifteen, he didn't have a watch with him and spent only about forty-five minutes with Mistri. As the Arab friends left for a seven o'clock class, here I follow the timings Mistri gave the LAPD on July 11.

24. Sirhan trial testimony, 5172–86.

25. Audiotape of Sirhan interview with Dr. Pollack, January 28, 1969.

26. Sirhan trial testimony, 5187–89, 5198–5205.

27. Cordero and Rabago FBI statements, June 6; Sirhan trial testimony, 5205–7.

28. At trial, Sirhan described leaving normal tips, and the police couldn't find a waiter who'd gotten a twenty-dollar tip. I think this twenty-dollar comment was an exaggeration.

29. Gonzalo Cetina-Carrillo FBI interview, June 12. Cetina trial testimony, 5509, 5514–16.

30. Lonny Worthey FBI interview, June 7.

31. "I was mesmerized" from Moldea, *Killing of Robert Kennedy,* 29; "The keys" from Sirhan trial testimony, 5212.

32. Mary Grohs LAPD interviews, July 22, 1968, and February 25, 1969. On timing of Grohs talking to Sirhan, see note for Chapter 1, page 8.

33. Kaiser, *"R.F.K. Must Die!"* 531–32.

34. Moldea, *Killing of Robert Kennedy,* 29.

35. Hans Bidstrup FBI interview, June 10; LAPD interview, July 23. Bidstrup said at trial that it was around ten. When Sirhan wrote out his memories of the night on a yellow legal pad for Michael McCowan soon after the shooting, he placed his chat with Bidstrup directly after his encounter with Cetina (after ten o'clock). But in Bidstrup's second LAPD interview (September 24), he timed his meeting with Sirhan as between eight forty five and nine fifteen. This is the timing the LAPD used in their activity chart, but on balance, between ten and eleven seems more likely.

36. Bidstrup trial testimony, 5481.

37. Moldea, *Killing of Robert Kennedy,* 28; Sirhan trial testimony, 5208–16.

38. Judy Royer FBI interview, June 13; Royer trial testimony, 3912–16.

39. Robert Klase FBI interview, July 30.

40. Jesus Perez LAPD interview transcript, June 5; Perez trial testimony, 3373–76; Martin Patrusky trial testimony, 3383–89.

41. Sirhan trial testimony, 5208.

42. Barbara Rubin LAPD interview, September 10.

43. Sirhan trial testimony, 5216–22.
44. Ibid., 5229–32.

Chapter 10

1. Diamond trial testimony, 6845.
2. Ibid., 6876–77, 6881–83.
3. Ibid., 6847; Kaiser, *"R.F.K. Must Die!"* 261–67.
4. Diamond trial testimony, 6883–86.
5. Kaiser, *"R.F.K. Must Die!"* 293–94.
6. Diamond trial testimony, 6916–17.
7. Ibid., 6921–24.
8. Kaiser, *"R.F.K. Must Die!"* 295–97.
9. Diamond trial testimony, 6922.
10. Ibid., 6925–27.
11. Kaiser, *"R.F.K. Must Die!"* 290–97.
12. Diamond noted that as part of Sirhan's wake-up routine after hypnotic experiments, "He would visibly shiver and complain of being cold" (Diamond trial testimony, 6976).
13. Ibid., 6928.
14. Ibid., 6931–34; Kaiser, *"R.F.K. Must Die!"* 302–5.
15. In his testimony, Dr. Diamond times these pauses as "four seconds" and "a second or two," respectively. As the audiotape of this session is no longer available, I favor Kaiser's description for accuracy. Kaiser was also present and had access to this tape while writing his book. Kaiser and subsequent psychiatrists who studied the case saw great significance in these pauses, while Dr. Diamond glossed over them briefly in the trial.
16. Kaiser, *"R.F.K. Must Die!"* 305–7.
17. Diamond trial testimony, 6887–99.
18. Kaiser, *"R.F.K. Must Die!"* 323–27.
19. Ibid., 333–45.
20. Ibid., 151, 254.
21. Ibid., 345–48.
22. Audiotape of Diamond and Pollack's psychiatric session with Sirhan, January 26, 1969; Diamond trial testimony, 6935–44; Kaiser, *"R.F.K. Must Die!"* 348–56.
23. Audiotape of Pollack's psychiatric interviews with Sirhan, January 27, 28, and 31, 1969; Kaiser, *"R.F.K. Must Die!"* 357–64.
24. Audiotape of Diamond and Pollack's psychiatric session with Sirhan, February 1, 1969; Sirhan's writing on the yellow legal pad from this session, CSA; Diamond trial testimony, 6947–77; Kaiser, *"R.F.K. Must Die!"* 365–69.
25. Diamond trial testimony, 6851.
26. Ibid., 6879–80.
27. Ibid., 6928, 6981–83; Kaiser, *"R.F.K. Must Die!"* 373–75.
28. Diamond trial testimony, 6989–90.
29. Ibid., 6992.
30. Ibid., 6877.
31. Ibid., 6881.

Chapter 11

1. Klaber and Melanson, *Shadow Play*, 88; Cooper, interview with Betsy Langman; Russell Parsons, interview with Betsy Langman.
2. Klaber and Melanson, *Shadow Play*, 92.
3. Kaiser, interview with the author.
4. "Lawyer Admits He Lied About Friars Transcript," *Los Angeles Times*, January 4, 1969.
5. FBI Teletype to Director, January 3, 1969.
6. Teeter, Petition for Writ of Habeas Corpus, July 19, 2002, 14–15; Kaiser, *"R.F.K. Must Die!"* 300.

7. McCowan, interview with the author.
8. LAPD, 1397–1409.
9. Trial transcript, 2651–62.
10. Ibid., 2725–29.
11. LAPD, 1400.
12. McCowan, interview with the author.
13. Kaiser, interview with the author.
14. Emile Zola Berman trial testimony, 3049–59; Kaiser, *"R.F.K. Must Die!"* 384–85.
15. La Vallee trial testimony, 3073–74.
16. Karl Uecker trial testimony, 3114–33.
17. Juan Romero trial testimony, 3199–3201.
18. Vincent Di Pierro trial testimony, 3212–21, 3231–59; Di Pierro LAPD interviews, June 5 and July 1.
19. Valerie Schulte trial testimony, 3417–38.
20. LAPD, 1403.
21. Royer trial testimony, 3903–24; Kaiser, 388.
22. Clark trial testimony, 4010–17; Clark FBI interview, September 11; LAPD progress report on Clark.
23. Placencia trial testimony, 3482–3566.
24. Travis White trial testimony, 3810–68.
25. James Pineda trial testimony, February 18–19, 1969; George Erhard trial testimony, February 18–19, 1969; Robert Calkins trial testimony, February 18–19, 1969; Rafer Johnson trial testimony, February 18–19, 1969.
26. DeWayne Wolfer trial testimony, 4128–4229. 274 "In the absence of Sirhan": Teeter petition, 18.
27. Wolfer trial testimony, 4140–55.
28. Wolfer trial testimony, 4184–85.
29. Ibid., 4200–4226.
30. William Brandt trial testimony, 4268–86; 4299–4316.
31. Trial transcript, 4294–98; Kaiser, *"R.F.K. Must Die!"* 390–92.
32. Trial transcript, 4382; Kaiser, *"R.F.K. Must Die!"* 392–94.
33. Trial transcript, 4474–80.
34. Noguchi trial testimony, 4504–36.
35. There were two sets of autopsy measurements for the trajectories of Wounds 2 and 3, one viewing Kennedy from the front, the other viewing Kennedy from behind and to the right. In his trial testimony, Dr. Noguchi gave the frontal measurements. See Robert Joling diagrams in Chapter 3 for an illustration of both frontal and lateral measurements.
36. LAPD, 1401–2.

Chapter 12

1. Trial testimony, 4644–54; Kaiser, *"R.F.K. Must Die!"* 406–7.
2. Kaiser, *"R.F.K. Must Die!"* 415–16.
3. Sirhan trial testimony, 5233–39.
4. Ibid., 5243–54.
5. Ibid., 5257–61, 5272–75.
6. Ibid., 5317–19, 5326–27.
7. Ibid., 5339–57.
8. LAPD, 1406–7.
9. Richard Lubic trial testimony, 5523–25.
10. Lubic written statement to American Academy of Forensic Sciences, February 1975; Lubic quoted in *Los Angeles Times*, July 13, 1975; LAPD, 1405.
11. LAPD, 1407–8.
12. Kaiser, interview with the author.
13. Diamond trial testimony, 6994–99.
14. Diamond trial testimony, 7094–97.

15. Ibid., 7185–90.
16. Kaiser, interview with the author.
17. LAPD, 1408.
18. "Cooper Admits Defendant" *Los Angeles Times*, April 11, 1969; "Final Argument in Sirhan Trial Begun by State," *Los Angeles Times*, April 12, 1969; Russell Parsons trial testimony, 8478–8549; Emile Zola Berman trial testimony, 8478–8549.
19. Cooper trial testimony, 8550–8707; "Juror Shift Shakes Up Sirhan Trial," *Los Angeles Herald Examiner*, April 14, 1969.
20. Compton trial testimony, 8711–14.
21. Ibid., 8773.
22. Ibid., 8754–55.
23. Ibid., 8779.
24. LAPD, 1408–9; "Sirhan May Receive Second-Degree Verdict," *Los Angeles Herald Examiner*, April 17, 1969. On McCowan, see Kaiser, *"R.F.K. Must Die!"* 494.
25. "Sirhan: A Long Wait for Death," *Los Angeles Herald Examiner*, April 24, 1969; Kaiser, *"R.F.K. Must Die!"* 509–10.
26. "Most Jurors in Favor of Death Penalty from Start, One Says," *Los Angeles Times*, April 24, 1969.
27. Kaiser, interview with the author; McCowan, interview with the author.
28. Kaiser, *"R.F.K. Must Die!"* 514–18.
29. "Sirhan Gets Death Despite Kennedy Plea," *Los Angeles Times*, May 22, 1969.
30. "Sirhan Retains 3 New Lawyers in Life Fight," *Los Angeles Times*, July 3, 1969.
31. *First Tuesday: The Mind of an Assassin*, NBC, broadcast June 3, 1969; "Sirhan Voices Regret at Having Killed Kennedy," *New York Times*, June 3, 1969.

Chapter 13

1. Moldea, *Killing of Robert Kennedy*, 30–31, 199–202, 206; Ace owner Frank Hendrix interview with Betsy Langman, 1973.
2. Audiotape of Cesar LAPD interview, June 24.
3. Moldea, *Killing of Robert Kennedy*, 207–8.
4. Audiotape of Cesar LAPD interview, June 5.
5. Cesar LAPD interview, June 24.
6. Cesar FBI interview, June 10.
7. Audiotape of Cesar interview with John Marshall, June 5.
8. Paul Hope LAPD interview, August 14; DiEugenio and Pease, *The Assassinations*, 602.
9. Boris Yaro was a photographer for the *Los Angeles Times*.
10. Jack Merritt LAPD interview, June 21; Albert Stowers LAPD interview, June 21; CBS television coverage of the shooting aftermath.
11. Cesar, interview with Special Counsel Thomas Kranz, November 1975, cited in Kranz Report, Sec. 2, 6; audiotapes of Cesar LAPD interviews and transcripts, June 5 and 24.
12. LAPD, 406. The report continues, "No one considered Sirhan to be suspicious, although he was observed loitering in the pantry."
13. Audiotape of Don Schulman, interview with Deputy DA Richard Hecht and others, for Wolfer Board of Inquiry, July 23, 1971; Schulman, interview with Ted Charach in *The Second Gun*, 1971; audiotape of Schulman, interview with Kranz and others, October 24, 1975.
14. Audiotape of Brent recording, June 5 (author's transcript of the tape, referring to a previous transcript in Melanson, *Robert F. Kennedy Assassination*, 66. Although Schulman recalled meeting Brent within ten minutes of the shooting, journalist Brad Johnson has timed the start of the Brent Schulman interview as 12:40 a.m.
15. Schulman, interview with Hecht; Schulman, interview with Kranz; Dunphy aircheck in *The Second Gun*; LAPD logs of Cogan broadcast and KNXT news release, echoing Dunphy's report; Brad Johnson, e-mail to author.
16. Schulman, interview with Hecht; Schulman, interview with Kranz; CBS footage of the Schulman interview with Ruth Ashton-Taylor.
17. Schulman, interview with Hecht.

18. Schulman, interview with Kranz.
19. Kranz Report, Sec. 2, 7; *The Second Gun.*
20. LAPD log of media reports, appended to Schulman file. 320 "I said, . . . 'The Senator'": Schulman, interview with Kranz.
21. *The Second Gun*; Schulman, interview with Baxter Ward, July 6, 1971.
22. Schulman LAPD interview summary, August 9.
23. Cesar LAPD interview, June 24; Schulman, interview with Hecht.
24. Cooper interview with Langman; Mike McCowan, interview with the author; McCowan summary on Cesar, RFKAA.
25. Charach NBC interview with Sander Vanocur, June 5; LAPD, 664; LAPD intelligence files on Charach, CSA; *The Second Gun.*
26. Schulman, interview with Hecht; Schulman, interview with Kranz.
27. Moldea, *Killing of Robert Kennedy*, 201, 203–4, 212; Charach, "Why Sirhan Could Not," part 2; *The Second Gun.*
28. Moldea, *Killing of Robert Kennedy*, 283, citing an audiotape of the Cesar pretest interview with polygraph examiner Edward Gelb.
29. "Who Really Killed RFK?" *Los Angeles Free Press*, June 12, 1970; Isaac, *I'll See You in Court*, 1 9, 23–31.
30. Carl George editorial and Dunphy aircheck in *The Second Gun*; CBS, ABC, NBC, and KTLA footage of Kennedy entering the ballroom, showing Schulman's position; later NBC footage showing Viazenko filming the crowd from the podium, with his back turned to Schulman; Schulman, interview with Kranz; Kaiser, "Journey Through the Killing Ground" *Los Angeles Times*, January 30, 1972.
31. Schulman, interview with Hecht; Schulman, interview with Kranz; *The Second Gun.*
32. Intelligence report by the DA's Bureau of Investigation on Charach screening on May 21, 1971, CSA microfilm roll 23; *The Second Gun.*
33. DA's Bureau of Investigation files, CSA microfilm roll 23; Cesar, interview with Deputy DA Sidney Trapp, DA investigators William Burnett and DeWitt Lightner, and LAPD sergeants Charles Collins and Phil Sartuche, July 14, 1971; Melanson, *Robert F. Kennedy Assassination*, 80–81; Cesar, LAPD interview with Collins and Sartuche, December 24, 1974.
34. Moldea, *Killing of Robert Kennedy*, 214–15.
35. LAPD unpublished "Reply to Questions Submitted by Allard K. Lowenstein," December 20, 1974, IV-2b.
36. *The Second Gun*
37. Audiotape of Schulman, interview with Hecht.
38. Moldea, *Killing of Robert Kennedy*, 201; for Hughes-CIA links, see DiEugenio and Pease, *The Assassinations*, 604.
39. Audiotape of Hendrix, interview with Langman, 1973; Moldea, *Killing of Robert Kennedy*, 206; DiEugenio and Pease, *The Assassinations*, 606; McCowan, interview with Langman, 1973.
40. *The Second Gun* promotional material supplied by Charach; for Lowenstein and Schrade, see Chapter 14.
41. Kaiser, *"R.F.K. Must Die!"* 29; Charach "Why Sirhan Could Not," part 2; Lubic written statement to American Academy of Forensic Sciences Convention, February 19, 1975, Chicago; Lubic interview, "The RFK Assassination: Shadows of Doubt," 1992.
42. Audiotape of Schulman, interview with Kranz.
43. Kranz report, Sec. 2, 3–10.
44. Audiotapes of Cesar LAPD interviews, June 5 and 24.
45. Kranz membership biography for the Pacific Council on International Policy. His term in the Bush administration ended in March 2004, and he is currently an attorney with the Inman Law Firm in Beverly Hills.
46. Moldea, *Killing of Robert Kennedy*, 199–216.
47. Moldea, "Who Really Killed Bobby Kennedy?"
48. Eara Marchman LAPD interview, June 25.
49. Melanson, *Robert F. Kennedy Assassination*, 65, 124.

50. Klaber and Melanson, *Shadow Play*, 141–42; Rhodes FBI interview, July 9; LAPD interview, August 22.
51. LaHive radio interview replayed in *The Second Gun*.
52. Moldea, *Killing of Robert Kennedy*, 201, 281; Moldea, interview with the author.
53. Moldea, *Killing of Robert Kennedy*, 281–90.
54. "Investigating the Murder of Robert Kennedy (IV): When Wisdom Comes Late," June 2, 2000, www.moldea.com
55. Moldea, interview with the author, August 2005, and follow-up conversation, November 2006.
56. Thane E. and Eleanor Cesar bankruptcy filing and list of creditors, June 6, 1994, Case no. 94–12390, U.S. Bankruptcy Court records; *Thane E. Cesar v. Anheuser-Busch, Inc, et al.*, Los Angeles County Superior Court case no. LC036786, filed May 24, 1996.
57. *Unsolved History: The RFK Assassination*; Michael Yardley, interview with the author; Charach "Why Sirhan Could Not," part 2; *The Second Gun*.

Chapter 14

1. Rose Lynn Mangan, interview with the author; Robert Joling, interview with the author; Mangan, "Sirhan Evidence Report," 21; the Wolfer photomicrograph was later labeled Special Exhibit 10 during the Wenke hearings that led to the refiring of the Sirhan gun in 1975.
2. "Coroner Faces Threat of Ouster Proceedings," *Los Angeles Times*, February 22, 1969; Noguchi, *Coroner*, 139–40; "Noguchi Charged with Kennedy 'Death Dance,'" *Los Angeles Times*, May 13, 1969.
3. "Coroner Noguchi Quits in Feud with Hollinger," *Los Angeles Times*, February 26, 1969; "Board Fires Coroner Noguchi," *Los Angeles Times*, March 19, 1969.
4. "Noguchi's 'Joy' over Influenza Autopsies Told," *Los Angeles Times*, May 17, 1969; "Pathologists Defend Noguchi in Dispute," *Los Angeles Times*, February 23, 1969.
5. "Noguchi Cleared and Reinstated to Coroner Post," *Los Angeles Times*, August 1, 1969.
6. "Deputy Coroner Arrested as Impostor with Fake Degree," *Los Angeles Times*, February 3, 1972; "Noguchi Lawyer Accuses Four Witnesses of False Testimony," *Los Angeles Times*, June 25, 1969.
7. "Former Deputy Coroner Fined," *Los Angeles Times*, April 14, 1972; "Deputy Coroner Pleads Guilty to False Claim," *Los Angeles Times*, March 2, 1972; Turner and Christian, *Assassination of Robert F. Kennedy*, 164–65.
8. "Grant Cooper, 10 Others Indicted," *Los Angeles Times*, August 7, 1969; "Grant Cooper Pleads Guilty to Using Secret Friars Transcript," *Los Angeles Times*, August 26, 1969.
9. "Lawyers Cooper, Morgan Get $1000 Contempt of Court Fine," *Los Angeles Times*, September 24, 1969; "Cooper's Action Was Turpitude, State Bar Says," *Los Angeles Times*, November 29, 1970; "Grant Cooper Reprimanded by High Court Over Friars Case," *Los Angeles Times*, July 2, 1971.
10. "No Evidence of Plot Found in Kennedy Slaying," *Los Angeles Times*, May 29, 1969.
11. Moldea, *Killing of Robert Kennedy*, 130–32.
12. LAPD, 642, 800.
13. Wolfer's log, LAPD files, CSA.
14. LAPD, 818–20.
15. Rose Lynn Mangan, interview with the author; "Sirhan Files Suit to Block Book on Life and Trial," *Los Angeles Herald Examiner*, March 24, 1970; "Judge Rejects Sirhan Biography Injunction," *Los Angeles Times*, April 18, 1970.
16. Copy of Sirhan letter, www.moldea.com
17. Kaiser, interview with the author. Kaiser added, "Well, he's a human being and he has emotions and sometimes, they burst forth. I can only imagine what it must be like to be in prison for forty years, knowing you're never going to get out. I would build up a tremendous head of steam inside myself if somebody gave me any reason to write him an angry note. So, he's a human being. Very sad."
18. Turner and Christian, *Assassination of Robert F. Kennedy*, 157–59; Harper biographical details from Harper affidavit, December 28, 1970; Los Angeles County Clerk's records regarding access to exhibits, 1969–1976.
19. Harper, statement to American Academy of Forensic Sciences (AAFS) Convention, February 19, 1975, Chicago.

20. Harper affidavit and Harper's accompanying "Notes on the *People vs. Sirhan*," January 1, 1971.

21. Evidence envelopes for People's 47 and People's 55; Harper, interview with Deputy DA Richard Hecht, June 10, 1971.

22. Special Exhibit 5—LAPD records of the Jake Williams gun, CSA. 357 "Wolfer had custody": Wolfer's log, LAPD files, CSA.

23. Wolfer testimony, Wenke hearings, September 17, 1975, 104–40; Wolfer's log, LAPD files, CSA.

24. Special Exhibit 5—LAPD records of Jake Williams gun, CSA.

25. Turner and Christian, *Assassination of Robert F. Kennedy*, 160–61; Klaber and Melanson, *Shadow Play*, 114.

26. Schulman, interview with Hecht, July 23, 1971; Klaber and Melanson, *Shadow Play*, 109.

27. Turner and Christian, *Assassination of Robert F. Kennedy*, 168. 359 "As Harper was the only researcher": Ibid., 157–58.

28. Moldea, *Killing of Robert Kennedy*, 142–43.

29. Klaber and Melanson, *Shadow Play*, 114.

30. "Sirhan Case—Was There a 2nd Gunman?" *Los Angeles Times*, Aug 16, 1971; Turner and Christian, *Assassination of Robert F. Kennedy*, 161.

31. Turner and Christian, *Assassination of Robert F. Kennedy*, 215.

32. Klaber and Melanson, *Shadow Play*, 317–18.

33. Charach, "Why Sirhan Could Not," part 1.

34. *Hampton v. City of Chicago, et al*, in the United States Court of Appeals, January 4, 1978; MacDonell five-page affidavit, November 28, 1973.

35. Moldea, *Killing of Robert Kennedy*, 158–61; "A Strange and Ghoulish Inquiry," *Los Angeles Times*, May 16, 1974.

36. "Sirhan Case Bid Rejected," *Los Angeles Times*, December 17, 1974; "DA Says Sirhan Acted Alone," *Los Angeles Herald Examiner*, December 17, 1974; "Action to Reopen Sirhan Case Slated," *Santa Monica Evening Outlook*, December 25, 1974.

37. *Santa Monica Evening Outlook*, December 23, 1974.

38. "High Court Rejects Sirhan's Plea," *Los Angeles Times*, February 14, 1975; "Second Gun Theory May Reopen Sirhan Case," *Los Angeles Herald Examiner*, January 19, 1975.

39. Harper statement to AAFS Convention, February 19, 1975; "New Probe in Slaying of Sen. Kennedy Demanded," *Los Angeles Times*, May 10, 1975. 363 "At the end of May": "Sirhan Receives 1986 Parole Date from State Board," *Los Angeles Times*, May 21, 1975.

40. "Unruh Calls Sirhan Parole Ruling Asinine," *Los Angeles Herald Examiner*, May 22, 1975; "Unruh Calls Sirhan a Traitor," *Los Angeles Times*, June 6, 1975.

41. "Robert Kennedy Case Still Stirs Questions," *Los Angeles Times*, July 13, 1975.

42. "Experts Seek New Probe of Assassination," *Los Angeles Times*, July 14, 1975.

43. "Release of Files on Sen. Kennedy Slaying Urged," *Los Angeles Times*, July 25, 1975.

44. "Counsel for RFK Probe Sworn In," *Los Angeles Herald Examiner*, August 14, 1975.

45. "Some Material on Kennedy Destroyed," *Los Angeles Times*, August 22, 1975; Morrow quoted in the *Sacramento Daily Journal*, August 21, 1975.

46. "Final OK Due in Sirhan Probe," *Los Angeles Herald Examiner*, September 11, 1975; "Court Here Orders New Sirhan Probe," *Los Angeles Herald Examiner*, September 12, 1975.

47. Wolfer testimony, Wenke hearings, September 17, 1975; Dr. Noguchi autopsy report, 24 (LAPD, 732); for Finkel, see LAPD, 183; firearms panel evidence inventory, September 24, 1975, reprinted in Garland, ed., *AFTE Journal: Special Edition*.

48. Wolfer testimony, Wenke hearings, September 17, 1975; Bradford individual report, firearms panel, October 4, 1975, CSA; Garland, *AFTE Journal: Special Edition*; Klaber and Melanson, *Shadow Play*, 117–19.

49. Wolfer colleague letter to Rose Lynn Mangan, November 21, 2001.

50. Order for Retesting of Exhibits, *People v. Sirhan*, September 18, 1975.

51. Garland, *AFTE Journal: Special Edition*.

52. Bradford, Berg, and Cunningham individual reports, firearms panel, October 4, 1975, CSA.

53. Garland, *AFTE Journal: Special Edition*; Order for Retesting of Exhibits (Order No. 5), September 26, 1975, firearms panel, CSA.

54. Cunningham individual report; Garland, *AFTE Journal: Special Edition*.

55. Initial and Comprehensive Joint Reports of the Firearms Examiners, October 3–4, 1975; Bradford individual report, October 4, 1976. 368 "Garland later noted": Garland, *AFTE Journal: Special Edition*.

56. Herbert MacDonell, interview with the author.

57. Comprehensive Joint Report of the Firearms Examiners, October 4, 1975.

58. Bradford individual report, October 4, 1975.

59. "Shot Said Probably Sirhan's," *Santa Monica Evening Outlook*, November 18, 1975.

60. "No 2nd Gun, Kennedy Case Panel Reports," *Los Angeles Times*, October 7, 1975.

61. "2nd Gun Question Not Settled, Probe Critics Say," *Los Angeles Times*, October 9, 1975.

62. "Sirhan's Gun Probably Fired Shots, Expert Says," *Los Angeles Times*, December 17, 1975.

63. Moldea, *Killing of Robert Kennedy*, 319–21.

64. Rozzi affidavit to Bugliosi, November 15, 1975.

65. Moldea, *Killing of Robert Kennedy*, 240.

66. "Question of 2nd Kennedy Case Gun Raised Again," *Los Angeles Times*, November 19, 1975.

67. Noguchi affidavit to Bugliosi, December 1, 1975.

68. Di Pierro affidavit to Bugliosi, December 1, 1975.

69. Patrusky affidavit to Bugliosi, December 12, 1975.

70. Melanson, *Robert F. Kennedy Assassination*, 44–45.

71. "New Panel in Kennedy Death Probe Urged," *Los Angeles Times*, December 5, 1975.

72. Bailey affidavit, November 14, 1976.

73. Audiotape of Bailey interview with Burnett, RFKAA.

74. Bailey interview for "The RFK Assassination."

75. Bailey interview for *Unsolved Mysteries*. I could not interview William Bailey due to continuing ill health. Sadly, Bailey died in August 2007 of lung cancer.

76. Kranz Report, March 1977; Stone, *Selected Corrections*.

77. Melanson, *Robert F. Kennedy Assassination*, 92–93, 102. While Melanson notes that 3,470 interviews were conducted during the original police investigation, the LAPD final report puts the figure at 4,818.

78. Moldea, *Killing of Robert Kennedy*, 249.

79. Ibid., 255.

80. Ibid., 235–38.

81. Mangan, telephone interviews with the author; Mangan, Special Exhibit 10 Report; Noguchi autopsy report, 24 (LAPD, 732); for Finkel, see LAPD, 183; firearms panel evidence inventory, reprinted in Garland, *AFTE Journal: Special Edition*; handwritten log by Noguchi of his visits to the county clerk's office to examine and photograph exhibits in April 1974, CSA; evidence envelopes for Exhibit 55 and Grand Jury Exhibit 5B.

Chapter 15

1. "My Not So Brilliant Career," *Guardian*, November 20, 1998.

2. Kaiser, *"R.F.K. Must Die!"* 374, 531; Mary Grohs LAPD interview, July 22.

3. Di Pierro, LAPD interview, June 5. Juan Romero and Martin Patrusky also saw Sirhan smiling (see note in Chapter 1, page 14) 381 "In the struggle": Earl Williman summary in LAPD, 1214–15; Frank Burns, interview with the author; Karl Uecker trial testimony, 3123–24; George Plimpton LAPD interview, June 5; for Joe LaHive, see Turner and Christian, *Assassination of Robert F. Kennedy*, 197.

4. Teletype from FBI Charlotte to FBI Los Angeles, June 5.

5. Jordan report to Lt. M.S. Pena, October 9; LAPD audiotape 28918, June 5, 3:15 a.m., and tape transcript.

6. Transcript of Sirhan interview with Dr. Crahan, June 5; Kaiser, *"R.F.K. Must Die!"* 296–97.

7. Kaiser, interview with the author.

8. Diamond, interview with Betsy Langman.

9. Turner and Christian, *Assassination of Robert F. Kennedy*, 202–3.

10. Diamond trial testimony, 6996.

11. Simson affidavit, March 9, 1973; Turner and Christian, *Assassination of Robert F. Kennedy*, 199 202.

12. Herbert Spiegel, interview with the author.

13. Turner and Christian, *Assassination of Robert F. Kennedy*, 207.
14. Estabrooks, *Future of the Human Mind*, 218–19.
15. Turner and Christian, *Assassination of Robert F. Kennedy*, 207–8. 387 "In 1967": Spiegel, interview with the author; Spiegel, *Fact or Fiction*; Turner and Christian, *Assassination of Robert F. Kennedy*, 204–6.
16. Spiegel, interview with the author.
17. Turner and Christian, *Assassination of Robert F. Kennedy*, 208.
18. Spiegel foreword to Bain, *CIA's Control of Candy Jones*.
19. Spiegel, interview with the author.
20. Mary, Adel, and Munir Sirhan FBI interviews, June 5.
21. Spiegel, interview with the author.
22. Dr. Crahan reported that in the days after the shooting, Sirhan "lacked appetite, had some gastric upset but no vomiting or nausea" (Crahan report to Younger, February 20, 1969, RFKAA).
23. Emery, *Secret, Don't Tell*, 108.
24. Estabrooks, "Hypnosis Comes of Age," *Science Digest*, April 1971, 44–50.
25. CIA memo quoted in Emery, *Secret, Don't Tell*, 107–9.
26. Melanson, *Robert F. Kennedy Assassination*, 173.
27. Calder, *JFK vs. CIA*, 258–60, citing the United States Senate Joint Hearings before the Select Committee on Intelligence and the Subcommittee on Health and Scientific Research of the Committee on Human Resources: Project MKULTRA, the CIA's Program of Research in Behavioral Modification.
28. Richelsen, *Wizards of Langley*, 9–11.
29. CIA memo re Artichoke, January 1954, in Melanson, *Robert F. Kennedy Assassination*.
30. Melanson, *Robert F. Kennedy Assassination*, 174.
31. Estabrooks, *Future of the Human Mind*, 221–24.
32. *Providence Evening Bulletin* article cited in Ross, *Bluebird*, 162.
33. Calder, *JFK vs. CIA*, 260, citing MKULTRA Hearings, 123.
34. Ibid., 2–3.
35. Turner and Christian, *Assassination of Robert F. Kennedy*, 226.
36. "Look into My Eyes", Jim Murray, *Los Angeles Times*, June 27, 1963.
37. Melanson, *Robert F. Kennedy Assassination*, 209.
38. Ibid., 203.
39. Bryan KNX radio interview cited in Turner and Christian, *Assassination of Robert F. Kennedy*, 226. Later interview broadcast in Tim Tate documentary *The Robert Kennedy Assassination*.
40. Turner and Christian, *Assassination of Robert F. Kennedy*, 225.
41. Ibid., 226–29.
42. Melanson, *Robert F. Kennedy Assassination*, 206–7.
43. Turner and Christian, *Assassination of Robert F. Kennedy*, 229. John Miner confirmed to the author that he was Bryan's executor and that Bryan was also a preacher. Miner would not comment on Bryan's alleged ties to government agencies.
44. Turner and Christian, *Assassination of Robert F. Kennedy*, 224–25.
45. Bain, *CIA's Control of Candy Jones*; Bain e-mails with the author; Cannon, "The Controllers," chap. 4, citing the files of author John Marks (*The Search for the Manchurian Candidate*).
46. Kroger, *Clinical and Experimental Hypnosis*, 16, 21, 115–16, 361, 372–74.
47. Cannon, "The Controllers," chap. 4.
48. Melanson, *Robert F. Kennedy Assassination*, 208–14.

Chapter 16

1. Report of the Rockefeller Commission on CIA Activities Within the United States, June 1975, chap. 11, www.history-matters.com; for Marchetti-Langman, see Melanson, *Robert F. Kennedy Assassination*, 290.
2. Melanson, "CIA's Secret Ties."
3. LAPD rosters outlining Pena and Hernandez responsibilities, CSA.

4. Pena interview with Marilyn Barrett; Kaiser, interview with the author; Turner and Christian, *Assassination of Robert F. Kennedy*, 64–66.
5. Turner and Christian, *Assassination of Robert F. Kennedy*, 272–75.
6. Pena interview with Betsy Langman, 1977.
7. Barrett, interview with the author; audio recordings of Pena interview with Barrett.
8. Enrique Hernandez resume, LAPD files, CSA; audiotape of Serrano interview with Hernandez, June 20.
9. Hernandez interview, *Now It Can Be Told*, 1992.
10. Manuel Chavez, U.S. assistant air attaché to Venezuela, 1957–59, e-mails to the author.
11. Hernandez obituary, *Los Angeles Times*, December 20, 2005, and *Pasadena Star-News*, December 21, 2005.
12. National Security Action Memorandum 177, cited in McClintock, *Instruments of Statecraft*, chap. 7, "The CIA and OPS."
13. Robert Amory oral history interview, 25, JFK Library.
14. McClintock, *Instruments of Statecraft*, chap. 7.
15. Langguth, *Hidden Terrors*, 125–27, based on an interview with Byron Engle.
16. McClintock, *Instruments of Statecraft*, chap. 7.
17. Langguth, *Hidden Terrors*, 125–28, 138–40, 251–52.
18. Blum, *Killing Hope*, chap. 33, "Uruguay 1964–70."
19. Langguth, *Hidden Terrors*, 285–87; *New York Times*, August 15, 1970.
20. Langguth, *Hidden Terrors*, 232–33, 253–54. 414 "In Uruguay and elsewhere": Ibid., 245–46, 253.
21. Ibid., 299–301.
22. Jordan CV on WCJ, Inc., Web site, www.wcj-inc.com
23. Evans, *Nemesis*, 257.
24. William C. Jordan obituary, *Long Beach Press Telegram*, September 28, 2005.
25. Kaiser, interview with the author.
26. Preface to an updated edition of Kaiser, *"R.F.K. Must Die!"* accessed on a previous Web site of his (which is no longer available) and confirmed by e-mail with Kaiser; Clayton Anderson confirmed information in telephone interview with the author.
27. "Bug Thy Neighbor," *Time*, March 6, 1964.
28. Teeter, Petition for Writ of Habeas Corpus, 102–4.
29. "U.S. Halts Sirhan's Mother on Trip to Appeal for Hostages," *Los Angeles Times*, September 9, 1970; Ronald Allen, interview with Langman.
30. McCowan, interview with Langman; Hendrix interview with Langman; "Man Accused of Death Threats in Kickback Scheme," *Los Angeles Times*, November 8, 1974; "3 Get Probation in Housing Project Kickback Scheme," *Los Angeles Times*, February 11, 1975.
31. Moldea, *Killing of Robert Kennedy*, chap. 29 and p. 326.
32. DiEugenio and Pease, *The Assassinations*, 630–31; "Re: DiEugenio's 'The Curious Case of Dan Moldea,'" www.moldea.com; Mangan, letter to Moldea's publisher, August 13, 1995; Adel Sirhan statement, August 17, 1995; Sirhan, letter to Mangan, June 24, 1995; these three documents can be found at www.sirhansresearcher.com/j.pdf
33. Sirhan letter to Rose Lynn Mangan, June 24, 1995. 418 "McCowan told Kaiser": Kaiser, interview with the author; Rose Lynn Mangan subsequently checked the Confidential Investigative Report McCowan gave Grant Cooper before the trial. There is no mention of Sirhan making such a comment in McCowan's report.
34. Pete Noyes, interview with the author. Noyes published a book, *Legacy of Doubt*, on both Kennedy assassinations in 1973.
35. McCowan, interview with the author.
36. Heymann, interview with the author; Heymann, *RFK*, 493.
37. Teeter, interview with the author; Mangan, interview with the author.
38. McCowan, interview with the author; Stewart, interview with the author.
39. Bradley Ayers, interview with the author; David Rabern, interview with the author.

40. Salinger, *P.S. A Memoir*, 180–82; Salinger, interview transcript, Booknotes, C-SPAN, November 12, 1995, www.booknotes.org; "Arms and the Men at Continental," *Time*, July 1, 1966; "Six at 61," *Time*, July 5.
41. Salinger, *P.S. A Memoir*, 195, 198.
42. DiEugenio and Pease, *The Assassinations*, 607–8.
43. Meier, interview with the author.
44. J.E.H. Official and Confidential Files 97, cited in Summers, *Official and Confidential*, 456.
45. CIA document, "Extracts from CI History," DDO/CI files 104-1031-10011, cited in Talbot, *Brothers*, 370.

Chapter 17

1. An updated edition of Kaiser's 1970 book, *"R.F.K. Must Die!"* will be published this year. I refer to Philip Melanson's landmark 1991 book on the case, *The Robert F. Kennedy Assassination*, here. Much of this material was later absorbed into another excellent book, *Shadow Play*. Melanson shared the writing credit for his original material, while primary author William Klaber took the trial of Sirhan as his main focus, providing new insights into a failure of American justice.
2. Another early figure to fit the criteria was a soldier of fortune called Gerry Hemming, a hulk of a man at six feet eight and 260 pounds. Hemming was never a CIA operative but fought a lot of the same wars as a freelancer with his group of soldiers for hire, Interpen. Hemming and his two closest associates, Roy Hargraves and "Fat Larry" Howard, are regularly mentioned as possible shooters in Dallas, and all three were in Los Angeles in June 1968. Hemming told me that Hargraves was working for the CIA's MH Chaos program "on a tight leash," smuggling drugs and guns to the Black Panthers and Brown Berets to foment a race war and connect the Black Panthers to North Vietnam. Hargraves worked as a bodyguard for Eldridge Cleaver, who, Hemming alleged, was working for the CIA. Hemming told me he was in Los Angeles, a couple of blocks from the Ambassador, on the night of the shooting and that the next morning, he pulled up to Sirhan's house in a black-and-white (patrol car) and went inside. On November 5, 2005, he described this visit on John Simkin's online Education Forum: "I was working full time for the City of Los Angeles . . . from 1967 thru 1970. My brother and I worked part time as Special Agents for the "Special Problems Unit" . . . . an Intel Unit working out of Mayor Sam Yorty's office. . . . Early next morn, drove my B & W to Sirhan Sirhan's mother's house— parked in front and walked towards the open front door (in my best suit, and packing a .357 Magnum "Python"). . . . Upon entering, I discovered that some family members were sitting there almost in a catatonic state. But no other LAPD officer in sight . . . Politely mumbled a few 'Salaams' and 'Inshallahs' and got the hell out of there."

   Hemming has never revealed why he supposedly went to Sirhan's house, and his credibility has been attacked on numerous occasions. As the Sirhan house was empty until the police arrived with the Sirhan brothers after questioning, Hemming's story makes little sense. At one point, Hemming's Interpen colleague Roy Hargraves suggested to Noel Twyman that he may have "pulled that operation," but the offhand remark got lost in cross-talk during their interview, Twyman didn't probe further, and now Hargraves and Hemming are dead (Transcript of Twyman interview with Hargraves, Hancock, *Someone Would Have Talked*, Appendix A, 276).

   Bradley Ayers, interview with the author. Morales put his height at five-ten on documents in his CIA personnel file. His son put his height at five-eleven-and-a-half, and Bradley Ayers felt that he was at least six foot. While Ayers recalled his nickname as "El Indio," this moniker was not familiar to the Morales family. His daughters told me he was called "Didi" or "Poncho."
3. Fonzi, *Last Investigation*, 380–90.
4. Twyman, *Bloody Treason*, 447–76.
5. The publisher's insistence on pseudonyms can be traced to the fact that, unknown to Ayers, retired CIA officer William Harvey was an editor at publisher Bobbs-Merill at the time (Ayers, *Zenith Secret*, 7).
6. I later discovered that Brad had first given this information to Christopher Barger of the congressionally appointed Assassination Records Review Board (ARRB) on May 12, 1995. The lead was never followed up (ARRB memo from Barger to Jeremy Gunn, May 18, 1998, National Archives.

7. Ayers, interview with the author, January 2005.
8. Ayers, interview with the author; Haynes Johnson, interview with the author.
9. Talbot, *Brothers*, 51.
10. Ayers, interview with the author; Ayers, *Zenith Secret*, 46.
11. Ayers, *War That Never Was*, 147, 179.
12. Ayers, interview with the author.
13. My attention was first drawn to the balding man by researcher Peter Fokes, whose newsgroup posting suggested that there was a man resembling CIA director Richard Helms in the Ambassador footage on the SUS film.
14. Ayers, interview with the author.
15. According to Fonzi, the first photograph of Morales was printed in a Cuban government newspaper in 1978. It identified him as "an officer of the CIA Station in Havana, 1959." I have not been able to find a photograph of Gordon Campbell.
16. David Rabern, interview with the author.
17. Robert Walton, interview with the author.
18. Ruben Carbajal, interview with the author.
19. It's widely acknowledged that Felix Rodriguez was the only CIA agent present during the capture and shooting of Che Guevara in 1967 and that Guevara's hands were cut off by the Bolivian army. While I take Ruben's story with a pinch of salt, CIA photos of the dead Guevara do suggest stitching around the neck, and there is an eight-month gap in Morales's CIA records that would fit the hunt for Che Guevara perfectly (see discussion on page 463).
20. Walton alleges that shortly after the Chilean coup, Morales asked him to act as his nominee to buy land in Tombstone, Arizona, with his share of the bounty—two million dollars. The Morales family claims no knowledge of this hidden wealth, and Walton has not provided legal records to corroborate the story.
21. Author interviews with Morales's two eldest daughters, Rita and Sandra, and son Frank. The family asked me to respect their privacy, so these are all pseudonyms.
22. Walton, follow-up telephone conversation with the author, after Carbajal interview.
23. Twyman, *Bloody Treason*, 463.
24. Hinckle and Turner, *Deadly Secrets*, 126, 152, 218, 250. According to *Deadly Secrets*, Campbell worked under the cover of Marine Engineering and Training Corporation of Homestead, Florida; the 1962 incorporation papers list its business as "offshore surveys" but, unsurprisingly, make no mention of Campbell.
25. Telephone directory search with the kind assistance of the Miami-Dade Public Library. Public records identified Gordon S. Campbell, aka Gordon Sutherland, born July 5, 1905. His wife, Gertrude H. Campbell, was six years his junior and died in 1995.
26. Rabern, follow-up telephone conversations with the author.
27. "T.H. Karamessines, Ex-Chief of CIA Covert Work, Dies," *Washington Post*, September 8, 1978; Joannides obituary, *Washington Post*, March 14, 1990.
28. Most of what we know about George Joannides has come from the reporting of Jefferson Morley. The background of Joannides is sourced from Freedom of Information Act releases on Joannides from the National Archives and the following articles by Morley: "Revelation 19.62," *Miami New Times*, April 12, 2001; "Celebrated Authors Demand That the CIA Come Clean on JFK Assassination," Salon.com, December 17, 2003; "The Men Who Didn't Talk," *Playboy*, December 2007.
29. Morley, telephone conversation with the author.
30. G. Robert Blakey, telephone conversation with the author; Dan Hardway, e-mails and follow-up calls with the author; Ed Lopez, e-mails and follow-up calls with the author.
31. Juan-Manuel Salvat, telephone conversation with the author; Luis Fernandez-Rocha, telephone interview and follow-up call with the author.
32. Robert Keeley, telephone interview and e-mail exchange with the author.
33. I showed a nine-minute trailer of the alleged CIA men at the Ambassador and corroborating interviews to *BBC Newsnight* editor Peter Barron on October 25, 2006. Five days later, he commissioned a twelve-minute segment, for broadcast on November 20.
34. Edwin Lopez-Soto, interview with the author.

35. Jefferson Morley, meeting with the author; Morley, letters to the *New York Review of Books*, December 18, 2003; August 11, 2005; March 15, 2007; Morley, follow-up call with the author after Morley's meeting with the daughter of Joannides. 447 "While in Washington": Wayne Smith, interview with the author.

36. Felix Rodriguez canceled an interview in Miami due to a scheduling clash but later watched a DVD of the Ambassador footage and was very helpful with the identifications. For his opinions and Grayston Lynch, see Chapter 18.

37. Tom Clines, interview with the author. A week before my BBC story aired, a mild paranoia about possible last-minute CIA intervention was fueled by the appearance of Derek, a "friend and business partner" of Clines. During the interview, he described planting eighteen men in a hotel lobby, undetected, for a surveillance operation. I wondered who was listening to our meeting.

38. Rabern, follow-up call with the author.

39. Ed Wilson, interview with the author. Another story tends to corroborate Morales's involvement on the Guevara operation: "One time, he was down in South America somewhere, I think on the Che Guevara thing . . . and flew up to see the director of CIA, and he got into town in the late afternoon, and Dave and Tom and that whole crew went out and got drunk as skunks. And about two in the morning, they rolled a paddywagon up on Fourteenth Street and took 'em all down to jail. Well, by about seven o'clock in the morning, Morales had some documents that convinced them he was an ambassador of somewhere and they turned them loose. He went home, took a shower, and eight o'clock, he's in briefing the director."

40. Twelve-minute segment, *BBC Newsnight*; Jeremy Paxman (presenter, *BBC Newsnight*), follow-up interview with the author, November 20, 2006. *Newsnight* producer Simon Enright asked the CIA to confirm the employment of Morales, Campbell, and Joannides and to respond to issues raised by the broadcast. He got the following response: "It is CIA policy—we do not confirm or deny employment of an individual . . . so I could not possibly comment on the status of these individuals. Please also keep in mind that the CIA does not operate on domestic soil—our mission is focused abroad only. The FBI works on US soil."

Chapter 18

1. "Robert Kennedy, Also Victim of a Conspiracy?" *Granma Internacional*, December 22, 2006.

2. Morley postings to *BBC Newsnight* Web site; Morley, telephone conversation with the author.

3. Brad Johnson, e-mail exchange with the author; CBS, NBC, ABC, BBC, KNXT, KTLA, KCRA, and KTTV coverage of the California Democratic primary, Kennedy's speech, and the shooting aftermath.

4. Ayton, "Did the CIA."

5. Karen Lynch, e-mail exchange with the author. One "researcher" had mailed Lynch a twenty-dollar bill, asking him to identify close colleague Rip Robertson in a photo taken in Dealey Plaza the day JFK was assassinated. I cringed. "Rip was with Gray in Key West when Kennedy was killed," wrote Karen. "He says tell them the CIA didn't have anything to do with any of this and for them to get a life."

6. Ayers, *Zenith Secret*, 133–34; Clines, interview with the author; CIA records on Ayers released under the JFK Records Act, National Archives. Don Bohning asked Shackley about Ayers during an interview for his book, *The Castro Obsession* (131–32), and Shackley corroborated Brad's account in *The War That Never Was*.

7. "Did the CIA"; Don Bohning, interview and e-mail exchange with the author; and Manuel Chavez, interview and e-mail exchange with the author; Luis Fernandez, written statement to the author, forwarded by Chavez.

8. Felix Rodriguez, e-mail exchange with the author; Rodriguez also passed on feedback on Goron Campbell from Rudy Enders. When I e-mailed the CIA in an attempt to confirm Campbell's death, I received this e-mail response: "It is our policy—we do not confirm or deny employment of an individual. So you see how your request is difficult for me to help you with."

9. David Talbot, e-mail exchange and telephone conversations with the author; Morley, e-mail to the author. Morley and Talbot later wrote up their trip in "The BBC's Flawed RFK Story." I give my account of the trip as I heard it, week by week, from Talbot here. Talbot also wrote of the trip in *Brothers*, 397–401.

10. Hardway, telephone interview with the author.
11. Isidro Borja, telephone interview with the author.
12. Polgar, telephone interview with the author.
13. Hedegaard, "The Last Confessions."
14. Shawn Phillips (son of James) e-mail, quoted in full at www.jfkmurdersolved.com/phillips.htm
15. Rita Morales, telephone interview with the author; Sandra Morales, telephone interview with the author; Morales's cover history statement and CIA personnel file, listing posting dates, released under the JFK Records Act and sourced from the National Archives; these and additional Morales documents kindly supplied by National Archives and Records Administration master researcher Malcolm Blunt. It was Ted Shackley that Rita remembered the most: "He was Mr. Geek, a computer geek who wore a white shirt and black suit in the heat of Laos with a protector in his pocket for his pens. He and my father were extremely close. He would come to the house and my father was very loyal to him and would never have gone over him. My father was not a 'Lone Ranger.' The company gave him his education."
16. There was a big family funeral in Wilcox after Morales died but, contrary to Gaeton Fonzi's book, Rita said there were no agency people there at all. "Two strangers turned up from Mexico City the day after, but that was it."
17. Talbot, e-mail to author.
18. Bradley Ayers, telephone interview with the author; Wayne Smith, e-mail exchange with the author.
19. Frank Morales, e-mail exchange and telephone conversation with the author.
20. The Morales and Joannides photos were published online on July 20, 2007, to accompany the Morley-Talbot article "The BBC's Flawed RFK Story."
21. Hardway, telephone interview with the author; Lopez, telephone interview with the author.
22. Campbell obituary, *Miami Herald*, September 21, 1962; Morley and Talbot, "The BBC's Flawed Story."
23. Network coverage of the California primary, Kennedy's speech, and the shooting aftermath.
24. Ayers, telephone interview with the author; photographs collated by LAPD investigators, CSA microfilm rolls 16 and 17.
25. The names of the Roman brothers were written on the back of the circled photograph; LAPD and FBI interviews of various Bulova salesmen; LAPD, 136; Hotel guest rosters, LAPD files, CSA.
26. Roman FBI interview, November 26.
27. "Bulova Man Takes Time to Talk About Consumer Salesmen," *Chicago Tribune*, June 10.
28. "Former JA Chairman Roman Dies," *Jewelers Circular Keystone*, December 23, 2002; "Vice President Named by Bulova Watch Co., *New York Times*, August 3, 1964. The *Times* article continued, "Mr. Roman will continue as national sales manager. He joined the company in 1960 as regional sales manager. Before moving here last year, he served as police commissioner of Winfield, Ill., where he also raised ponies and collies."
29. Bradley, *A General's Life*, 461–62; Bulova company Web site, www.bulova.com; "Bradley Takes Over Tomorrow," *New York Times*, August 16, 1953; "Bradley Named Chairman of Bulova," *New York Times*, March 28, 1958; "Personality: General Maps Bulova Tactics," *New York Times*, October 11, 1959.
30. Bradley, *A General's Life*, 667–68; Bradley, Bulova Trip Diaries.
31. Roman's son, telephone interview with the author; "Saying Goodbye to an Industry Leader," *Jewelers Circular Keystone*, July 1, 1995; "Former JA Chairman Roman Dies."
32. Roman's son, e-mail exchange and telephone interviews with the author; Frank S. Owen FBI interview, October 21. To respect Mr. Roman's privacy, I refer to him only as "Michael Roman's son." I have not been able to authenticate the identification of Owens or his death. Roman's brother Charles died of heart trouble in 1974, and in response to my Freedom of Information Act request, the FBI informed me that records regarding Michael Roman "were destroyed on February 1, 1990; July 10, 1990; and October 1, 1992."

Chapter 19

1. Deputy DA John Howard statement in 1975, cited in DiEugenio and Pease, *The Assassinations*, 536.

2. Brad Johnson, e-mail exchange with the author. In late 1982, forensic acoustics expert Dr. Michael Hecker examined three recordings (by Andrew West, Jeff Brent, and ABC television) and concluded that "no fewer than ten gunshots are ascertainable" (Hecker written statement, witnessed by Robert Joling, December 15, 1982. In February 1992, author Jonn Christian became aware of the Pruszynski recording at CSA, and further auditory testing suggested that there were nine shots on the tape. He added these to the sounds on the previous three tapes to rather implausibly conclude that twenty-four shots were fired, "a minimum of three weapons at the crime scene . . . . eight of which were blanks." It was subsequently determined that the Pruszynski recording was the only recording of actual gunshots, and it lay dormant in CSA vaults until Johnson realized its significance in 2004.
3. Van Praag interview on Black Op Radio, August 9, 2007.
4. *Conspiracy Test.*
5. The LAPD never interviewed Pruszynski. A December 19 FBI memo sets out Pruszynski as a possible lead, with an unidentified friend advising "that Pruszynski had claimed that he had made a tape recording." Pruszynski was subsequently interviewed by the FBI, but after examining his tape, the FBI laboratory concluded, "it does not appear that anything pertinent to this investigation is contained on this recording. . . . The original recording was of extremely poor quality" (final report of FBI Special Agent Amadee O. Richards, August 1, 1969).
6. *Conspiracy Test*; Van Praag interview on Black Op Radio; Van Praag, interview with the author.
7. *Conspiracy Test*; Ayton, *Forgotten Terrorist*, 277–80.
8. Van Praag, interview with the author; Van Praag interview on Black Op Radio. Also present at the AAFS meeting, supporting Van Praag's work, were to be Robert Joling and Paul Schrade, reprising their 1975 campaign to reopen the case on the basis of the firearms evidence.
9. Minasian LAPD interview, June 5; grand jury testimony, June 7; Van Praag, interview with the author.
10. Moldea, *Killing of Robert Kennedy*, 311–12.
11. Harper affidavit, December 28, 1970.
12. This assumes that Sirhan fired eight times, based on the eight empty CCI shell casings found by Sergeant Calkins in the barrel of Sirhan's revolver at 1:45 a.m. on June 5, and subsequently booked as evidence.
13. Moldea, *Killing of Robert Kennedy*, 300–301.
14. Sirhan, interview with Jack Perkins, NBC. Sirhan was also interviewed by *Washington Post* reporter Cynthia Gorney in 1979 (see note to page 489) and David Frost in 1989. Dan Rather also had a lengthy meeting with Sirhan while researching the 1976 CBS documentary *The American Assassins.*
15. Bernard Diamond trial testimony; Robert Kaiser, interview with the author.
16. Sirhan, interviews with William Klaber, September 26 and October 10, 1993, as quoted in Klaber and Melanson, *Shadow Play*, 365. Dan Moldea, Adel Sirhan, and Rose Lynn Mangan were also present.
17. Teeter Petition for Writ of Habeas Corpus, 49–72.
18. Sirhan, third and final interview with Dan Moldea, June 5, 1994, as quoted in Moldea, *Killing of Robert Kennedy*, 301–2. Adel Sirhan was also present.
19. Munir Sirhan, interview with the author.
20. Klaber and Melanson, *Shadow Play*, 364–65.
21. These Sirhan quotes are taken from Klaber's accounts based on the first two interviews (Klaber and Melanson, *Shadow Play*, 367–69) and Moldea's account of his third interview (*Killing of Robert Kennedy*, 298–300).
22. Klaber and Melanson, *Shadow Play*, 366, 369–70.
23. Larry Teeter, interview with the author.
24. Sirhan was initially scheduled for parole in 1982, but this was rescinded after a petition from LA County DA John Van de Kamp. Sirhan's next parole hearing took place in 1985.
25. Klaber and Melanson, *Shadow Play*, 367–68.
26. Sirhan, interview with Cynthia Gorney, "Sirhan," *Washington Post*, August 20, 1977.
27. Munir Sirhan, interview with the author; "The Reliable Source," *Washington Post*, October 12, 2001.

28. "The Real Manchurian Candidate," *Pasadena Weekly*, November 16, 2006; Munir Sirhan, interview with the author.
29. "Sirhan Again Denied Parole," Reuters, March 15, 2006.
30. Sirhan, response to author through his brother Munir; William Pepper, interview with the author, January 2008; Pepper interview on Black Op Radio, October 11, 2007.
31. Paul Schrade, interviews and e-mail exchange with the author.
32. Moldea, *Killing of Robert Kennedy*, 300; "Sirhan Can't Remember," *Washington Post*, June 3, 1977; Herbert Spiegel, interview with the author.
33. Pepper, interview with the author.
34. Kaiser, interview with the author.
35. Munir Sirhan, interview with the author.

Epilogue, 2017

1. Brown declaration to Sirhan Parole Hearing (February 8, 2016), 1.
2. Dusek interview, 13 May 2017
3. Brown (2016), 2; Ibid.
4. Brown interview, February 21 2017; Dusek interview
5. "Sirhan Sirhan moved to new prison," Pasadena Star News, November 2, 2009; Ibid.
6. Sirhan v. Galaza, Warden, et al., Supplemental Brief on the Issues of Equitable Tolling and Actual Innocence, April 23, 2011; Sirhan v. Galaza, Warden, et al., Reply Brief on the Issue of Actual Innocence, November 20, 2011. These court filings are available online at Maryferrell.org
7. Brown interview
8. Brown (2016), 1; my discussion of Dr. Brown is drawn from an earlier article, "The Full Story of the Sirhan Sirhan Parole Hearing," Whowhatwhy.org, February 16, 2016
9. Ibid., 2
10. Ibid.
11. Brown declaration, April 23, 2011 (Sirhan v. Galaza, Warden, et al., Supplemental Brief, Exhibit I), 4; Brown declaration, November 19, 2011 (Sirhan v. Galaza, Warden, et al., Reply Brief, Exhibit H), 23–4
12. Brown (2011a), 5.
13. Brown (April 2011), 7–8
14. Brown interview; Welch FBI interview, June 11, 1968; Welch LAPD interview, August 29, 1968
15. Brown and Dusek interviews; Brown declarations
16. Ibid.; Munir Sirhan interview, May 18, 2017
17. Brown interview; Brown (November 2011), 22
18. Brown interview
19. Sirhan trial testimony, March 6, 1969, 5302–3; Turner and Christian, 222
20. Brown (April 2011), 10
21. Ibid.
22. Brown (2016), 4
23. Brown (April 2011), 12–3
24. Ibid., 8
25. Ibid., 12
26. "The Experiments—The Assassin," Channel 4 (UK), October 21, 2011
27. Brown (April 2011), 14
28. Brown (2016), 4
29. Ibid. Sirhan listened to the radio, he did not transmit.
30. Brown (April 2011), 13–4; Brown (November 2011), 17–20; Brown interview
31. Brown interview
32. "California Board of Parole (Lifer) Hearing Lawyers," Shouse Law Group; "Life without Parole," The Marshall Project, 10 July 2015. This section on the parole process and Sirhan's parole hearing draws on two previous essays—one written to preface the release of the Sirhan Parole Hearing Transcripts at maryferrell.org, January 2016; the other, "Enemy of the State: Framing the Political

Assassin," a chapter in Mark de Valk's edited collection, Screening the Tortured Body: The Cinema as Scaffold. London: Palgrave (2016), 303–8.

33. "California Code of Regulations, Determination of Suitability (15 CCR § 2281)," 2015
34. Available at www.maryferrell.org/pages/Featured_Sirhan_Parole_Hearing_Transcripts.html
35. "Straight A student," Sirhanbsirhan.com blog, January 25, 2016
36. Ibid.
37. Shadow Play (St. Martin's Press, 1997), 296–7
38. "Parole cancelled," Sirhanbsirhan.com blog, January 26, 2016
39. Klaber and Melanson (1997), 297–8
40. Philip Van Praag declaration, November 14, 2011 (Sirhan v. Galaza, Warden, et al., Reply Brief on the Issue of Actual Innocence, Exhibit C), 45; Van Praag also presented his findings in a book, "An Open & Shut Case" (2008), co-authored with Robert Joling. Thanks to Brad Johnson and Phil Van Praag for their input in this section.
41. Ibid., 46; "RFK Must Die—Epilogue," E2 Films (2008)
42. My discussion of the FBI tests draws on my article "The Full Story of the Sirhan Sirhan Parole Hearing," Whowhatwhy.org, February 16, 2016
43. Phil Van Praag email correspondence, February 14, 2017
44. Inventory of the Los Angeles County Sheriff's Department Records–Sirhan Sirhan Case File, California State Archives (LACSD)
45. FBI memo 62-587-1070, January 14, 1969
46. Letter from Reddin to Pitchess, January 30, 1969 (LACSD, Box 8–8)
47. Memo from Noble to Knox, February 13, 1969 (LACSD, Box 8–8)
48. Reddin to Pitchess, 5 March 1969
49. This section draws on my Introduction to *In Jail with Sirhan Sirhan*.
50. This section is based on interviews and email correspondence with family members and public records.
51. 51
52. Chennault interview, May 23, 2016; Chennault Papers, Schlesinger Library, Radcliffe Institute, Harvard University, MA.
53. Dusek interview
54. "Why New Ban on Televising Sirhan Parole Hearing?" Whowhatwhy.org, February 10, 2016
55. This section draws on two articles written for Whowhatwhy.org on the 2016 parole hearing: "The Full Story of the Sirhan Sirhan Parole Hearing," February 16, 2016; "The Tortured Logic Behind Sirhan's Parole Denial," March 14, 2016
56. Sirhan Sirhan Parole Hearing transcript, State of California Board of Parole Hearings, February 10, 2016, 210
57. Ibid., 75, 102.
58. Ibid., 84–6
59. Ibid., 66
60. Ibid., 68–70
61. Ibid., 72–5
62. Ibid., 106
63. Ibid., 80
64. Ibid., 81
65. Brown (2016), 5
66. Ibid., 102–3
67. Ibid., 41, 58–9
68. Ibid., 129–30
69. Ibid., 115–6, 159
70. "Panel denies parole to Sirhan, assassin of Robert F. Kennedy," Associated Press (AP), February 11, 2016
71. Ibid., 185
72. Ibid., 162–3
73. Ibid., 162–3
74. Ibid., 164

75. Ibid., 165
76. AP report, February 11, 2016; Ibid., 178
77. Ibid, 188–9
78. Ibid.
79. Ibid., 195–7, 205
80. Ibid., 197, 210
81. "The Tortured Logic behind Sirhan Sirhan's Parole Denial," Whowhatwhy.org, March 14, 2016; Ibid., 198
82. Ibid., 210
83. AP report, February 11, 2016
84. Schrade Black Op Radio interview, February 11, 2016
85. "Framed," Skyhorse Publishing, 271
86. Brown email correspondence, May 20, 2017
87. Brown interview and email correspondence, May 18, 2017
88. Brown (November 2011), 21; Sirhan v. Galaza, Warden et al., Supplemental Brief Regarding Actual Innocence; Memorandum of Points and Authorities, September 26, 2011, 11–14
89. Brown email correspondence, May 18, 2017
90. Munir Sirhan interview; Dusek interview
91. Dusek interview
92. "Petition and Case System," Inter-American Commission on Human Rights, Organization of American States, 2010
93. "Why a conviction review unit is needed," Los Angeles Daily News, June 25, 2015: "D.A. creates unit to review claims of innocence," Los Angeles Times, 29 June 2015: see Chapter 10 for the full context of Sirhan's statement